Mometrix TEST PREPARATION

TExES

Mathematics/Physical Science/Engineering 6-12 (274)

Secrets Study Guide

Part 1 of 3

DEAR FUTURE EXAM SUCCESS STORY

First of all, **THANK YOU** for purchasing Mometrix study materials!

Second, congratulations! You are one of the few determined test-takers who are committed to doing whatever it takes to excel on your exam. **You have come to the right place.** We developed these study materials with one goal in mind: to deliver you the information you need in a format that's concise and easy to use.

In addition to optimizing your guide for the content of the test, we've outlined our recommended steps for breaking down the preparation process into small, attainable goals so you can make sure you stay on track.

We've also analyzed the entire test-taking process, identifying the most common pitfalls and showing how you can overcome them and be ready for any curveball the test throws you.

Standardized testing is one of the biggest obstacles on your road to success, which only increases the importance of doing well in the high-pressure, high-stakes environment of test day. Your results on this test could have a significant impact on your future, and this guide provides the information and practical advice to help you achieve your full potential on test day.

Your success is our success

We would love to hear from you! If you would like to share the story of your exam success or if you have any questions or comments in regard to our products, please contact us at **800-673-8175** or **support@mometrix.com**.

Thanks again for your business and we wish you continued success!

Sincerely,
The Mometrix Test Preparation Team

Need more help? Check out our flashcards at:
http://mometrixflashcards.com/TExES

TABLE OF CONTENTS

Introduction

Thank you for purchasing this resource! You have made the choice to prepare yourself for a test that could have a huge impact on your future, and this guide is designed to help you be fully ready for test day. Obviously, it's important to have a solid understanding of the test material, but you also need to be prepared for the unique environment and stressors of the test, so that you can perform to the best of your abilities.

For this purpose, the first section that appears in this guide is the **Secret Keys**. We've devoted countless hours to meticulously researching what works and what doesn't, and we've boiled down our findings to the five most impactful steps you can take to improve your performance on the test. We start at the beginning with study planning and move through the preparation process, all the way to the testing strategies that will help you get the most out of what you know when you're finally sitting in front of the test.

We recommend that you start preparing for your test as far in advance as possible. However, if you've bought this guide as a last-minute study resource and only have a few days before your test, we recommend that you skip over the first two Secret Keys since they address a long-term study plan.

If you struggle with **test anxiety**, we strongly encourage you to check out our recommendations for how you can overcome it. Test anxiety is a formidable foe, but it can be beaten, and we want to make sure you have the tools you need to defeat it.

Secret Key #1 – Plan Big, Study Small

There's a lot riding on your performance. If you want to ace this test, you're going to need to keep your skills sharp and the material fresh in your mind. You need a plan that lets you review everything you need to know while still fitting in your schedule. We'll break this strategy down into three categories.

Information Organization

Start with the information you already have: the official test outline. From this, you can make a complete list of all the concepts you need to cover before the test. Organize these concepts into groups that can be studied together, and create a list of any related vocabulary you need to learn so you can brush up on any difficult terms. You'll want to keep this vocabulary list handy once you actually start studying since you may need to add to it along the way.

Time Management

Once you have your set of study concepts, decide how to spread them out over the time you have left before the test. Break your study plan into small, clear goals so you have a manageable task for each day and know exactly what you're doing. Then just focus on one small step at a time. When you manage your time this way, you don't need to spend hours at a time studying. Studying a small block of content for a short period each day helps you retain information better and avoid stressing over how much you have left to do. You can relax knowing that you have a plan to cover everything in time. In order for this strategy to be effective though, you have to start studying early and stick to your schedule. Avoid the exhaustion and futility that comes from last-minute cramming!

Study Environment

The environment you study in has a big impact on your learning. Studying in a coffee shop, while probably more enjoyable, is not likely to be as fruitful as studying in a quiet room. It's important to keep distractions to a minimum. You're only planning to study for a short block of time, so make the most of it. Don't pause to check your phone or get up to find a snack. It's also important to **avoid multitasking**. Research has consistently shown that multitasking will make your studying dramatically less effective. Your study area should also be comfortable and well-lit so you don't have the distraction of straining your eyes or sitting on an uncomfortable chair.

The time of day you study is also important. You want to be rested and alert. Don't wait until just before bedtime. Study when you'll be most likely to comprehend and remember. Even better, if you know what time of day your test will be, set that time aside for study. That way your brain will be used to working on that subject at that specific time and you'll have a better chance of recalling information.

Finally, it can be helpful to team up with others who are studying for the same test. Your actual studying should be done in as isolated an environment as possible, but the work of organizing the information and setting up the study plan can be divided up. In between study sessions, you can discuss with your teammates the concepts that you're all studying and quiz each other on the details. Just be sure that your teammates are as serious about the test as you are. If you find that your study time is being replaced with social time, you might need to find a new team.

Secret Key #2 – Make Your Studying Count

You're devoting a lot of time and effort to preparing for this test, so you want to be absolutely certain it will pay off. This means doing more than just reading the content and hoping you can remember it on test day. It's important to make every minute of study count. There are two main areas you can focus on to make your studying count.

Retention

It doesn't matter how much time you study if you can't remember the material. You need to make sure you are retaining the concepts. To check your retention of the information you're learning, try recalling it at later times with minimal prompting. Try carrying around flashcards and glance at one or two from time to time or ask a friend who's also studying for the test to quiz you.

To enhance your retention, look for ways to put the information into practice so that you can apply it rather than simply recalling it. If you're using the information in practical ways, it will be much easier to remember. Similarly, it helps to solidify a concept in your mind if you're not only reading it to yourself but also explaining it to someone else. Ask a friend to let you teach them about a concept you're a little shaky on (or speak aloud to an imaginary audience if necessary). As you try to summarize, define, give examples, and answer your friend's questions, you'll understand the concepts better and they will stay with you longer. Finally, step back for a big picture view and ask yourself how each piece of information fits with the whole subject. When you link the different concepts together and see them working together as a whole, it's easier to remember the individual components.

Finally, practice showing your work on any multi-step problems, even if you're just studying. Writing out each step you take to solve a problem will help solidify the process in your mind, and you'll be more likely to remember it during the test.

Modality

Modality simply refers to the means or method by which you study. Choosing a study modality that fits your own individual learning style is crucial. No two people learn best in exactly the same way, so it's important to know your strengths and use them to your advantage.

For example, if you learn best by visualization, focus on visualizing a concept in your mind and draw an image or a diagram. Try color-coding your notes, illustrating them, or creating symbols that will trigger your mind to recall a learned concept. If you learn best by hearing or discussing information, find a study partner who learns the same way or read aloud to yourself. Think about how to put the information in your own words. Imagine that you are giving a lecture on the topic and record yourself so you can listen to it later.

For any learning style, flashcards can be helpful. Organize the information so you can take advantage of spare moments to review. Underline key words or phrases. Use different colors for different categories. Mnemonic devices (such as creating a short list in which every item starts with the same letter) can also help with retention. Find what works best for you and use it to store the information in your mind most effectively and easily.

Secret Key #3 – Practice the Right Way

Your success on test day depends not only on how many hours you put into preparing, but also on whether you prepared the right way. It's good to check along the way to see if your studying is paying off. One of the most effective ways to do this is by taking practice tests to evaluate your progress. Practice tests are useful because they show exactly where you need to improve. Every time you take a practice test, pay special attention to these three groups of questions:

- The questions you got wrong
- The questions you had to guess on, even if you guessed right
- The questions you found difficult or slow to work through

This will show you exactly what your weak areas are, and where you need to devote more study time. Ask yourself why each of these questions gave you trouble. Was it because you didn't understand the material? Was it because you didn't remember the vocabulary? Do you need more repetitions on this type of question to build speed and confidence? Dig into those questions and figure out how you can strengthen your weak areas as you go back to review the material.

Additionally, many practice tests have a section explaining the answer choices. It can be tempting to read the explanation and think that you now have a good understanding of the concept. However, an explanation likely only covers part of the question's broader context. Even if the explanation makes perfect sense, **go back and investigate** every concept related to the question until you're positive you have a thorough understanding.

As you go along, keep in mind that the practice test is just that: practice. Memorizing these questions and answers will not be very helpful on the actual test because it is unlikely to have any of the same exact questions. If you only know the right answers to the sample questions, you won't be prepared for the real thing. **Study the concepts** until you understand them fully, and then you'll be able to answer any question that shows up on the test.

It's important to wait on the practice tests until you're ready. If you take a test on your first day of study, you may be overwhelmed by the amount of material covered and how much you need to learn. Work up to it gradually.

On test day, you'll need to be prepared for answering questions, managing your time, and using the test-taking strategies you've learned. It's a lot to balance, like a mental marathon that will have a big impact on your future. Like training for a marathon, you'll need to start slowly and work your way up. When test day arrives, you'll be ready.

Start with the strategies you've read in the first two Secret Keys—plan your course and study in the way that works best for you. If you have time, consider using multiple study resources to get different approaches to the same concepts. It can be helpful to see difficult concepts from more than one angle. Then find a good source for practice tests. Many times, the test website will suggest potential study resources or provide sample tests.

Practice Test Strategy

If you're able to find at least three practice tests, we recommend this strategy:

Untimed and Open-Book Practice

Take the first test with no time constraints and with your notes and study guide handy. Take your time and focus on applying the strategies you've learned.

Timed and Open-Book Practice

Take the second practice test open-book as well, but set a timer and practice pacing yourself to finish in time.

Timed and Closed-Book Practice

Take any other practice tests as if it were test day. Set a timer and put away your study materials. Sit at a table or desk in a quiet room, imagine yourself at the testing center, and answer questions as quickly and accurately as possible.

Keep repeating timed and closed-book tests on a regular basis until you run out of practice tests or it's time for the actual test. Your mind will be ready for the schedule and stress of test day, and you'll be able to focus on recalling the material you've learned.

Secret Key #4 – Pace Yourself

Once you're fully prepared for the material on the test, your biggest challenge on test day will be managing your time. Just knowing that the clock is ticking can make you panic even if you have plenty of time left. Work on pacing yourself so you can build confidence against the time constraints of the exam. Pacing is a difficult skill to master, especially in a high-pressure environment, so **practice is vital**.

Set time expectations for your pace based on how much time is available. For example, if a section has 60 questions and the time limit is 30 minutes, you know you have to average 30 seconds or less per question in order to answer them all. Although 30 seconds is the hard limit, set 25 seconds per question as your goal, so you reserve extra time to spend on harder questions. When you budget extra time for the harder questions, you no longer have any reason to stress when those questions take longer to answer.

Don't let this time expectation distract you from working through the test at a calm, steady pace, but keep it in mind so you don't spend too much time on any one question. Recognize that taking extra time on one question you don't understand may keep you from answering two that you do understand later in the test. If your time limit for a question is up and you're still not sure of the answer, mark it and move on, and come back to it later if the time and the test format allow. If the testing format doesn't allow you to return to earlier questions, just make an educated guess; then put it out of your mind and move on.

On the easier questions, be careful not to rush. It may seem wise to hurry through them so you have more time for the challenging ones, but it's not worth missing one if you know the concept and just didn't take the time to read the question fully. Work efficiently but make sure you understand the question and have looked at all of the answer choices, since more than one may seem right at first.

Even if you're paying attention to the time, you may find yourself a little behind at some point. You should speed up to get back on track, but do so wisely. Don't panic; just take a few seconds less on each question until you're caught up. Don't guess without thinking, but do look through the answer choices and eliminate any you know are wrong. If you can get down to two choices, it is often worthwhile to guess from those. Once you've chosen an answer, move on and don't dwell on any that you skipped or had to hurry through. If a question was taking too long, chances are it was one of the harder ones, so you weren't as likely to get it right anyway.

On the other hand, if you find yourself getting ahead of schedule, it may be beneficial to slow down a little. The more quickly you work, the more likely you are to make a careless mistake that will affect your score. You've budgeted time for each question, so don't be afraid to spend that time. Practice an efficient but careful pace to get the most out of the time you have.

Secret Key #5 – Have a Plan for Guessing

When you're taking the test, you may find yourself stuck on a question. Some of the answer choices seem better than others, but you don't see the one answer choice that is obviously correct. What do you do?

The scenario described above is very common, yet most test takers have not effectively prepared for it. Developing and practicing a plan for guessing may be one of the single most effective uses of your time as you get ready for the exam.

In developing your plan for guessing, there are three questions to address:

- When should you start the guessing process?
- How should you narrow down the choices?
- Which answer should you choose?

When to Start the Guessing Process

Unless your plan for guessing is to select C every time (which, despite its merits, is not what we recommend), you need to leave yourself enough time to apply your answer elimination strategies. Since you have a limited amount of time for each question, that means that if you're going to give yourself the best shot at guessing correctly, you have to decide quickly whether or not you will guess.

Of course, the best-case scenario is that you don't have to guess at all, so first, see if you can answer the question based on your knowledge of the subject and basic reasoning skills. Focus on the key words in the question and try to jog your memory of related topics. Give yourself a chance to bring the knowledge to mind, but once you realize that you don't have (or you can't access) the knowledge you need to answer the question, it's time to start the guessing process.

It's almost always better to start the guessing process too early than too late. It only takes a few seconds to remember something and answer the question from knowledge. Carefully eliminating wrong answer choices takes longer. Plus, going through the process of eliminating answer choices can actually help jog your memory.

Summary: Start the guessing process as soon as you decide that you can't answer the question based on your knowledge.

How to Narrow Down the Choices

The next chapter in this book (**Test-Taking Strategies**) includes a wide range of strategies for how to approach questions and how to look for answer choices to eliminate. You will definitely want to read those carefully, practice them, and figure out which ones work best for you. Here though, we're going to address a mindset rather than a particular strategy.

Your odds of guessing an answer correctly depend on how many options you are choosing from.

Number of options left	5	4	3	2	1
Odds of guessing correctly	20%	25%	33%	50%	100%

You can see from this chart just how valuable it is to be able to eliminate incorrect answers and make an educated guess, but there are two things that many test takers do that cause them to miss out on the benefits of guessing:

- Accidentally eliminating the correct answer
- Selecting an answer based on an impression

We'll look at the first one here, and the second one in the next section.

To avoid accidentally eliminating the correct answer, we recommend a thought exercise called **the $5 challenge**. In this challenge, you only eliminate an answer choice from contention if you are willing to bet $5 on it being wrong. Why $5? Five dollars is a small but not insignificant amount of money. It's an amount you could afford to lose but wouldn't want to throw away. And while losing $5 once might not hurt too much, doing it twenty times will set you back $100. In the same way, each small decision you make—eliminating a choice here, guessing on a question there—won't by itself impact your score very much, but when you put them all together, they can make a big difference. By holding each answer choice elimination decision to a higher standard, you can reduce the risk of accidentally eliminating the correct answer.

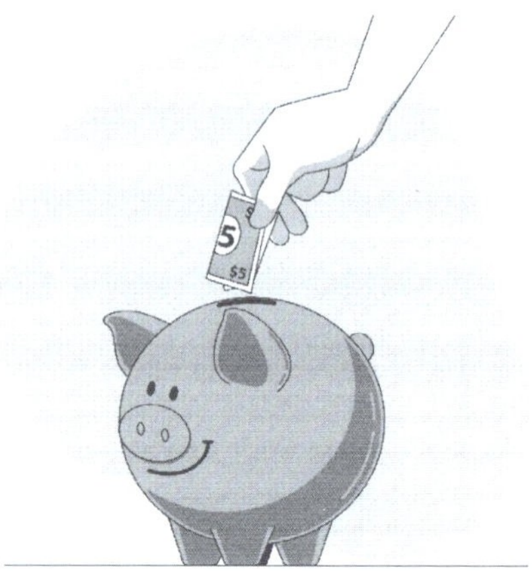

The $5 challenge can also be applied in a positive sense: If you are willing to bet $5 that an answer choice *is* correct, go ahead and mark it as correct.

Summary: Only eliminate an answer choice if you are willing to bet $5 that it is wrong.

Which Answer to Choose

You're taking the test. You've run into a hard question and decided you'll have to guess. You've eliminated all the answer choices you're willing to bet $5 on. Now you have to pick an answer. Why do we even need to talk about this? Why can't you just pick whichever one you feel like when the time comes?

The answer to these questions is that if you don't come into the test with a plan, you'll rely on your impression to select an answer choice, and if you do that, you risk falling into a trap. The test writers know that everyone who takes their test will be guessing on some of the questions, so they intentionally write wrong answer choices to seem plausible. You still have to pick an answer though, and if the wrong answer choices are designed to look right, how can you ever be sure that you're not falling for their trap? The best solution we've found to this dilemma is to take the decision out of your hands entirely. Here is the process we recommend:

Once you've eliminated any choices that you are confident (willing to bet $5) are wrong, select the first remaining choice as your answer.

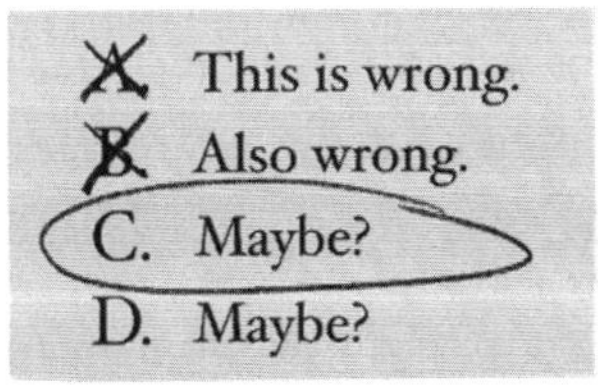

Whether you choose to select the first remaining choice, the second, or the last, the important thing is that you use some preselected standard. Using this approach guarantees that you will not be enticed into selecting an answer choice that looks right, because you are not basing your decision on how the answer choices look.

This is not meant to make you question your knowledge. Instead, it is to help you recognize the difference between your knowledge and your impressions. There's a huge difference between thinking an answer is right because of what you know, and thinking an answer is right because it looks or sounds like it should be right.

Summary: To ensure that your selection is appropriately random, make a predetermined selection from among all answer choices you have not eliminated.

Test-Taking Strategies

This section contains a list of test-taking strategies that you may find helpful as you work through the test. By taking what you know and applying logical thought, you can maximize your chances of answering any question correctly!

It is very important to realize that every question is different and every person is different: no single strategy will work on every question, and no single strategy will work for every person. That's why we've included all of them here, so you can try them out and determine which ones work best for different types of questions and which ones work best for you.

Question Strategies

☑ Read Carefully

Read the question and the answer choices carefully. Don't miss the question because you misread the terms. You have plenty of time to read each question thoroughly and make sure you understand what is being asked. Yet a happy medium must be attained, so don't waste too much time. You must read carefully and efficiently.

☑ Contextual Clues

Look for contextual clues. If the question includes a word you are not familiar with, look at the immediate context for some indication of what the word might mean. Contextual clues can often give you all the information you need to decipher the meaning of an unfamiliar word. Even if you can't determine the meaning, you may be able to narrow down the possibilities enough to make a solid guess at the answer to the question.

☑ Prefixes

If you're having trouble with a word in the question or answer choices, try dissecting it. Take advantage of every clue that the word might include. Prefixes can be a huge help. Usually, they allow you to determine a basic meaning. *Pre-* means before, *post-* means after, *pro-* is positive, *de-* is negative. From prefixes, you can get an idea of the general meaning of the word and try to put it into context.

☑ Hedge Words

Watch out for critical hedge words, such as *likely, may, can, often, almost, mostly, usually, generally, rarely,* and *sometimes.* Question writers insert these hedge phrases to cover every possibility. Often an answer choice will be wrong simply because it leaves no room for exception. Be on guard for answer choices that have definitive words such as *exactly* and *always.*

☑ Switchback Words

Stay alert for *switchbacks.* These are the words and phrases frequently used to alert you to shifts in thought. The most common switchback words are *but, although,* and *however.* Others include *nevertheless, on the other hand, even though, while, in spite of, despite,* and *regardless of.* Switchback words are important to catch because they can change the direction of the question or an answer choice.

⊘ Face Value

When in doubt, use common sense. Accept the situation in the problem at face value. Don't read too much into it. These problems will not require you to make wild assumptions. If you have to go beyond creativity and warp time or space in order to have an answer choice fit the question, then you should move on and consider the other answer choices. These are normal problems rooted in reality. The applicable relationship or explanation may not be readily apparent, but it is there for you to figure out. Use your common sense to interpret anything that isn't clear.

Answer Choice Strategies

⊘ Answer Selection

The most thorough way to pick an answer choice is to identify and eliminate wrong answers until only one is left, then confirm it is the correct answer. Sometimes an answer choice may immediately seem right, but be careful. The test writers will usually put more than one reasonable answer choice on each question, so take a second to read all of them and make sure that the other choices are not equally obvious. As long as you have time left, it is better to read every answer choice than to pick the first one that looks right without checking the others.

⊘ Answer Choice Families

An answer choice family consists of two (in rare cases, three) answer choices that are very similar in construction and cannot all be true at the same time. If you see two answer choices that are direct opposites or parallels, one of them is usually the correct answer. For instance, if one answer choice says that quantity x increases and another either says that quantity x decreases (opposite) or says that quantity y increases (parallel), then those answer choices would fall into the same family. An answer choice that doesn't match the construction of the answer choice family is more likely to be incorrect. Most questions will not have answer choice families, but when they do appear, you should be prepared to recognize them.

⊘ Eliminate Answers

Eliminate answer choices as soon as you realize they are wrong, but make sure you consider all possibilities. If you are eliminating answer choices and realize that the last one you are left with is also wrong, don't panic. Start over and consider each choice again. There may be something you missed the first time that you will realize on the second pass.

⊘ Avoid Fact Traps

Don't be distracted by an answer choice that is factually true but doesn't answer the question. You are looking for the choice that answers the question. Stay focused on what the question is asking for so you don't accidentally pick an answer that is true but incorrect. Always go back to the question and make sure the answer choice you've selected actually answers the question and is not merely a true statement.

⊘ Extreme Statements

In general, you should avoid answers that put forth extreme actions as standard practice or proclaim controversial ideas as established fact. An answer choice that states the "process should be used in certain situations, if..." is much more likely to be correct than one that states the "process should be discontinued completely." The first is a calm rational statement and doesn't even make a definitive, uncompromising stance, using a hedge word *if* to provide wiggle room, whereas the second choice is far more extreme.

✓ BENCHMARK

As you read through the answer choices and you come across one that seems to answer the question well, mentally select that answer choice. This is not your final answer, but it's the one that will help you evaluate the other answer choices. The one that you selected is your benchmark or standard for judging each of the other answer choices. Every other answer choice must be compared to your benchmark. That choice is correct until proven otherwise by another answer choice beating it. If you find a better answer, then that one becomes your new benchmark. Once you've decided that no other choice answers the question as well as your benchmark, you have your final answer.

✓ PREDICT THE ANSWER

Before you even start looking at the answer choices, it is often best to try to predict the answer. When you come up with the answer on your own, it is easier to avoid distractions and traps because you will know exactly what to look for. The right answer choice is unlikely to be word-for-word what you came up with, but it should be a close match. Even if you are confident that you have the right answer, you should still take the time to read each option before moving on.

General Strategies

✓ TOUGH QUESTIONS

If you are stumped on a problem or it appears too hard or too difficult, don't waste time. Move on! Remember though, if you can quickly check for obviously incorrect answer choices, your chances of guessing correctly are greatly improved. Before you completely give up, at least try to knock out a couple of possible answers. Eliminate what you can and then guess at the remaining answer choices before moving on.

✓ CHECK YOUR WORK

Since you will probably not know every term listed and the answer to every question, it is important that you get credit for the ones that you do know. Don't miss any questions through careless mistakes. If at all possible, try to take a second to look back over your answer selection and make sure you've selected the correct answer choice and haven't made a costly careless mistake (such as marking an answer choice that you didn't mean to mark). This quick double check should more than pay for itself in caught mistakes for the time it costs.

✓ PACE YOURSELF

It's easy to be overwhelmed when you're looking at a page full of questions; your mind is confused and full of random thoughts, and the clock is ticking down faster than you would like. Calm down and maintain the pace that you have set for yourself. Especially as you get down to the last few minutes of the test, don't let the small numbers on the clock make you panic. As long as you are on track by monitoring your pace, you are guaranteed to have time for each question.

✓ DON'T RUSH

It is very easy to make errors when you are in a hurry. Maintaining a fast pace in answering questions is pointless if it makes you miss questions that you would have gotten right otherwise. Test writers like to include distracting information and wrong answers that seem right. Taking a little extra time to avoid careless mistakes can make all the difference in your test score. Find a pace that allows you to be confident in the answers that you select.

⊘ KEEP MOVING

Panicking will not help you pass the test, so do your best to stay calm and keep moving. Taking deep breaths and going through the answer elimination steps you practiced can help to break through a stress barrier and keep your pace.

Final Notes

The combination of a solid foundation of content knowledge and the confidence that comes from practicing your plan for applying that knowledge is the key to maximizing your performance on test day. As your foundation of content knowledge is built up and strengthened, you'll find that the strategies included in this chapter become more and more effective in helping you quickly sift through the distractions and traps of the test to isolate the correct answer.

Now that you're preparing to move forward into the test content chapters of this book, be sure to keep your goal in mind. As you read, think about how you will be able to apply this information on the test. If you've already seen sample questions for the test and you have an idea of the question format and style, try to come up with questions of your own that you can answer based on what you're reading. This will give you valuable practice applying your knowledge in the same ways you can expect to on test day.

Good luck and good studying!

Number Concepts

Number Basics

Classifications of Numbers

Numbers are the basic building blocks of mathematics. Specific features of numbers are identified by the following terms:

Integer – any positive or negative whole number, including zero. Integers do not include fractions $\left(\frac{1}{3}\right)$, decimals (0.56), or mixed numbers $\left(7\frac{3}{4}\right)$.

Prime number – any whole number greater than 1 that has only two factors, itself and 1; that is, a number that can be divided evenly only by 1 and itself.

Composite number – any whole number greater than 1 that has more than two different factors; in other words, any whole number that is not a prime number. For example: The composite number 8 has the factors of 1, 2, 4, and 8.

Even number – any integer that can be divided by 2 without leaving a remainder. For example: 2, 4, 6, 8, and so on.

Odd number – any integer that cannot be divided evenly by 2. For example: 3, 5, 7, 9, and so on.

Decimal number – any number that uses a decimal point to show the part of the number that is less than one. Example: 1.234.

Decimal point – a symbol used to separate the ones place from the tenths place in decimals or dollars from cents in currency.

Decimal place – the position of a number to the right of the decimal point. In the decimal 0.123, the 1 is in the first place to the right of the decimal point, indicating tenths; the 2 is in the second place, indicating hundredths; and the 3 is in the third place, indicating thousandths.

The **decimal**, or base 10, system is a number system that uses ten different digits (0, 1, 2, 3, 4, 5, 6, 7, 8, 9). An example of a number system that uses something other than ten digits is the **binary**, or base 2, number system, used by computers, which uses only the numbers 0 and 1. It is thought that the decimal system originated because people had only their 10 fingers for counting.

Rational numbers include all integers, decimals, and fractions. Any terminating or repeating decimal number is a rational number.

Irrational numbers cannot be written as fractions or decimals because the number of decimal places is infinite and there is no recurring pattern of digits within the number. For example, pi (π) begins with 3.141592 and continues without terminating or repeating, so pi is an irrational number.

Real numbers are the set of all rational and irrational numbers.

Review Video: Classification of Numbers
Visit mometrix.com/academy and enter code: 461071

Review Video: Prime and Composite Numbers
Visit mometrix.com/academy and enter code: 565581

NUMBERS IN WORD FORM AND PLACE VALUE

When writing numbers out in word form or translating word form to numbers, it is essential to understand how a place value system works. In the decimal or base-10 system, each digit of a number represents how many of the corresponding place value—a specific factor of 10—are contained in the number being represented. To make reading numbers easier, every three digits to the left of the decimal place is preceded by a comma. The following table demonstrates some of the place values:

Power of 10	10^3	10^2	10^1	10^0	10^{-1}	10^{-2}	10^{-3}
Value	1,000	100	10	1	0.1	0.01	0.001
Place	thousands	hundreds	tens	ones	tenths	hundredths	thousandths

For example, consider the number 4,546.09, which can be separated into each place value like this:

4: thousands
5: hundreds
4: tens
6: ones
0: tenths
9: hundredths

This number in word form would be *four thousand five hundred forty-six and nine hundredths.*

Review Video: Place Value
Visit mometrix.com/academy and enter code: 205433

Number Lines

A number line is a graph to see the distance between numbers. Basically, this graph shows the relationship between numbers. So a number line may have a point for zero and may show negative numbers on the left side of the line. Any positive numbers are placed on the right side of the line. For example, consider the points labeled on the following number line:

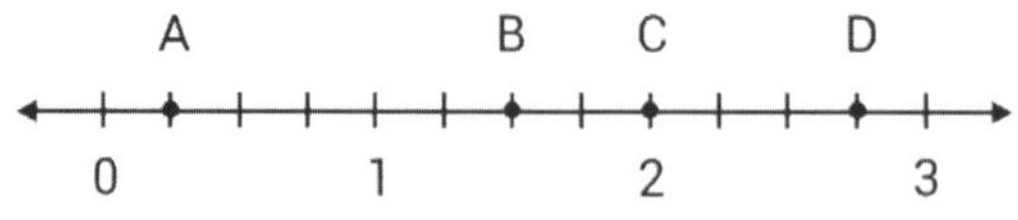

We can use the dashed lines on the number line to identify each point. Each dashed line between two whole numbers is $\frac{1}{4}$. The line halfway between two numbers is $\frac{1}{2}$.

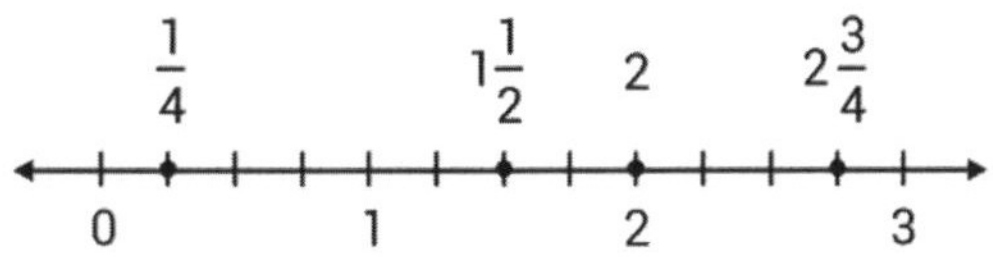

Review Video: The Number Line
Visit mometrix.com/academy and enter code: 816439

Comparing Numbers

Inequality Notation

The symbols $<$ and $>$ mean "is less than" and "is greater than," respectively. For instance, $3 < 5$ means "3 is less than 5," and $7 > 4$ means "7 is greater than 4." Statements like $3 < 5$ and $7 > 4$ are **inequalities**, and the symbols $<$ and $>$ are **inequality symbols**.

Whole Numbers and Decimal Numbers

To compare whole or decimal numbers, we look at the most significant place (the leftmost digit) at which they differ. The number with the larger digit in that place is larger. For instance, $0.3\underline{8}74$ and $0.3\underline{9}$ differ in the hundredths place (underlined). Since 8 is smaller than 9, we see $0.3874 < 0.39$. This is clearer if we make the decimals equal in length by writing extra zeroes: $0.3874 < 0.3900$. Similarly, $2\underline{3}.984 < 2\underline{5}.112$ because 3 is smaller than 5, or 23 is smaller than 25.

Fractions

If fractions have the same denominator, the fraction with the larger numerator is larger. For instance, $\frac{2}{7} < \frac{5}{7}$ since $2 < 5$. We compare fractions with different denominators by finding a common denominator. When comparing the fractions with a common denominator we only compare the numerator, so as a shortcut, we can multiply each numerator by the denominator of the other fraction. The numerator that produces the larger product belongs to the larger fraction. For example, to compare $\frac{7}{8}$ and $\frac{5}{6}$, we note that $7 \cdot 6 = 42$ is larger than $5 \cdot 8 = 40$. Since the numerator 7 produces the larger product, we see $\frac{7}{8} > \frac{5}{6}$. We can also compare fractions by converting them to decimals. For instance, since $\frac{3}{4} = 0.75$ and $\frac{4}{5} = 0.8$ and $0.75 < 0.8$, we conclude $\frac{3}{4} < \frac{4}{5}$.

Mixed Numbers

To compare mixed numbers we compare their whole number parts. If those are equal, then we compare their fractional parts. For instance, $5\frac{3}{8} > 4\frac{7}{8}$ because $5 > 4$, but $3\frac{5}{9} < 3\frac{8}{9}$ because $\frac{5}{9} < \frac{8}{9}$.

Square Roots

To compare square roots, we convert them to decimals, usually with a calculator. To compare two square roots, we compare their radicands. For instance, $\sqrt{11} < \sqrt{14}$ because $11 < 14$.

NEGATIVE NUMBERS

A negative number is always less than a positive number. Two negative numbers compare in the reverse order of their opposites. For instance, $-6 < -2$ (that is, -6 is smaller, more negative, than -2) because $6 > 2$.

Absolute Value

A precursor to working with negative numbers is understanding what **absolute values** are. A number's absolute value is simply the distance away from zero a number is on the number line. The absolute value of a number is always positive and is written $|x|$. For example, the absolute value of 3, written as $|3|$, is 3 because the distance between 0 and 3 on a number line is three units. Likewise, the absolute value of -3, written as $|-3|$, is 3 because the distance between 0 and -3 on a number line is three units. So $|3| = |-3|$.

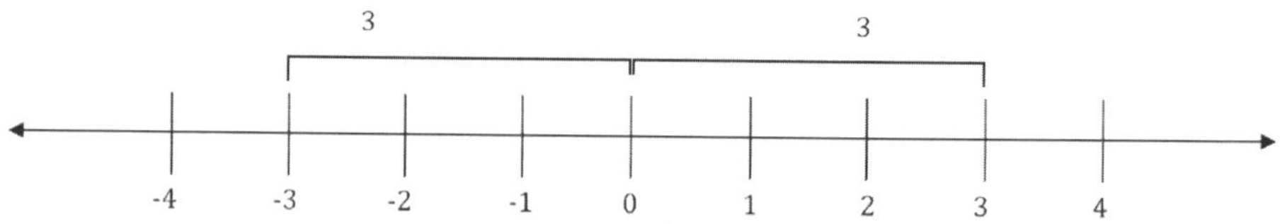

Review Video: Absolute Value
Visit mometrix.com/academy and enter code: 314669

Operations

An **operation** is simply a mathematical process that takes some value(s) as input(s) and produces an output. Elementary operations are often written in the following form: *value operation value*. For instance, in the expression $1 + 2$ the values are 1 and 2 and the operation is addition. Performing the operation gives the output of 3. In this way we can say that $1 + 2$ and 3 are equal, or $1 + 2 = 3$.

ADDITION

Addition increases the value of one quantity by the value of another quantity (both called **addends**). Example: $2 + 4 = 6$ or $8 + 9 = 17$. The result is called the **sum**. With addition, the order does not matter, $4 + 2 = 2 + 4$.

When adding signed numbers, if the signs are the same simply add the absolute values of the addends and apply the original sign to the sum. For example, $(+4) + (+8) = +12$ and $(-4) + (-8) = -12$. When the original signs are different, take the absolute values of the addends and subtract the smaller value from the larger value, then apply the original sign of the larger value to the difference. Example: $(+4) + (-8) = -4$ and $(-4) + (+8) = +4$.

SUBTRACTION

Subtraction is the opposite operation to addition; it decreases the value of one quantity (the **minuend**) by the value of another quantity (the **subtrahend**). For example, $6 - 4 = 2$ or $17 - 8 = 9$. The result is called the **difference**. Note that with subtraction, the order does matter, $6 - 4 \neq 4 - 6$.

For subtracting signed numbers, change the sign of the subtrahend and then follow the same rules used for addition. Example: $(+4) - (+8) = (+4) + (-8) = -4$

Multiplication

Multiplication can be thought of as repeated addition. One number (the **multiplier**) indicates how many times to add the other number (the **multiplicand**) to itself. Example: $3 \times 2 = 2 + 2 + 2 = 6$. With multiplication, the order does not matter, $2 \times 3 = 3 \times 2$ or $3 + 3 = 2 + 2 + 2$, either way the result (the **product**) is the same.

If the signs are the same, the product is positive when multiplying signed numbers. Example: $(+4) \times (+8) = +32$ and $(-4) \times (-8) = +32$. If the signs are opposite, the product is negative. Example: $(+4) \times (-8) = -32$ and $(-4) \times (+8) = -32$. When more than two factors are multiplied together, the sign of the product is determined by how many negative factors are present. If there are an odd number of negative factors then the product is negative, whereas an even number of negative factors indicates a positive product. Example: $(+4) \times (-8) \times (-2) = +64$ and $(-4) \times (-8) \times (-2) = -64$.

Division

Division is the opposite operation to multiplication; one number (the **divisor**) tells us how many parts to divide the other number (the **dividend**) into. The result of division is called the **quotient**. Example: $20 \div 4 = 5$. If 20 is split into 4 equal parts, each part is 5. With division, the order of the numbers does matter, $20 \div 4 \neq 4 \div 20$.

The rules for dividing signed numbers are similar to multiplying signed numbers. If the dividend and divisor have the same sign, the quotient is positive. If the dividend and divisor have opposite signs, the quotient is negative. Example: $(-4) \div (+8) = -0.5$.

> **Review Video: Mathematical Operations**
> Visit mometrix.com/academy and enter code: 208095

Parentheses

Parentheses are used to designate which operations should be done first when there are multiple operations. Example: $4 - (2 + 1) = 1$; the parentheses tell us that we must add 2 and 1, and then subtract the sum from 4, rather than subtracting 2 from 4 and then adding 1 (this would give us an answer of 3).

> **Review Video: Mathematical Parentheses**
> Visit mometrix.com/academy and enter code: 978600

Exponents

An **exponent** is a superscript number placed next to another number at the top right. It indicates how many times the base number is to be multiplied by itself. Exponents provide a shorthand way to write what would be a longer mathematical expression. Example: $2^4 = 2 \times 2 \times 2 \times 2$. A number with an exponent of 2 is said to be "squared," while a number with an exponent of 3 is said to be "cubed." The value of a number raised to an exponent is called its power. So 8^4 is read as "8 to the 4th power," or "8 raised to the power of 4."

Review Video: Exponents
Visit mometrix.com/academy and enter code: 600998

Roots

A **root**, such as a square root, is another way of writing a fractional exponent. Instead of using a superscript, roots use the radical symbol ($\sqrt{\ }$) to indicate the operation. A radical will have a number underneath the bar, and may sometimes have a number in the upper left: $\sqrt[n]{a}$, read as "the nth root of a." The relationship between radical notation and exponent notation can be described by this equation:

$$\sqrt[n]{a} = a^{\frac{1}{n}}$$

The two special cases of $n = 2$ and $n = 3$ are called square roots and cube roots. If there is no number to the upper left, the radical is understood to be a square root ($n = 2$). Nearly all of the roots you encounter will be square roots. A square root is the same as a number raised to the one-half power. When we say that a is the square root of b ($a = \sqrt{b}$), we mean that a multiplied by itself equals b: ($a \times a = b$).

A **perfect square** is a number that has an integer for its square root. There are 10 perfect squares from 1 to 100: 1, 4, 9, 16, 25, 36, 49, 64, 81, 100 (the squares of integers 1 through 10).

Review Video: Roots
Visit mometrix.com/academy and enter code: 795655

Review Video: Perfect Squares and Square Roots
Visit mometrix.com/academy and enter code: 648063

Word Problems and Mathematical Symbols

When working on word problems, you must be able to translate verbal expressions or "math words" into math symbols. This chart contains several "math words" and their appropriate symbols:

Phrase	Symbol
equal, is, was, will be, has, costs, gets to, is the same as, becomes	$=$
times, of, multiplied by, product of, twice, doubles, halves, triples	$\times$
divided by, per, ratio of/to, out of	$\div$
plus, added to, sum, combined, and, more than, totals of	$+$
subtracted from, less than, decreased by, minus, difference between	$-$
what, how much, original value, how many, a number, a variable	x, n, etc.

Review Video: Understanding Word Problems
Visit mometrix.com/academy and enter code: 499199

Examples of Translated Mathematical Phrases

- The phrase four more than twice a number can be written algebraically as $2x + 4$.
- The phrase half a number decreased by six can be written algebraically as $\frac{1}{2}x - 6$.
- The phrase the sum of a number and the product of five and that number can be written algebraically as $x + 5x$.

- You may see a test question that says, "Olivia is constructing a bookcase from seven boards. Two of them are for vertical supports and five are for shelves. The height of the bookcase is twice the width of the bookcase. If the seven boards total 36 feet in length, what will be the height of Olivia's bookcase?" You would need to make a sketch and then create the equation to determine the width of the shelves. The height can be represented as double the width. (If x represents the width of the shelves in feet, then the height of the bookcase is $2x$. Since the seven boards total 36 feet, $2x + 2x + x + x + x + x + x = 36$ or $9x = 36$; $x = 4$. The height is twice the width, or 8 feet.)

Subtraction with Regrouping

A great way to make use of some of the features built into the decimal system would be regrouping when attempting longform subtraction operations. When subtracting within a place value, sometimes the minuend is smaller than the subtrahend; **regrouping** enables you to 'borrow' a unit from a place value to the left in order to get a positive difference. For example, consider subtracting 189 from 525 with regrouping.

First, set up the subtraction problem in vertical form:

$$\begin{array}{r} 525 \\ -\ 189 \\ \hline \end{array}$$

Notice that the numbers in the ones and tens columns of 525 are smaller than the numbers in the ones and tens columns of 189. This means you will need to use regrouping to perform subtraction:

$$\begin{array}{rrrr} & 5 & 2 & 5 \\ - & 1 & 8 & 9 \\ \hline \end{array}$$

To subtract 9 from 5 in the ones column you will need to borrow from the 2 in the tens column:

$$\begin{array}{rrrr} & 5 & 1 & 15 \\ - & 1 & 8 & 9 \\ \hline & & & 6 \end{array}$$

Next, to subtract 8 from 1 in the tens column you will need to borrow from the 5 in the hundreds column:

$$\begin{array}{rrrr} & 4 & 11 & 15 \\ - & 1 & 8 & 9 \\ \hline & & 3 & 6 \end{array}$$

Last, subtract the 1 from the 4 in the hundreds column:

$$\begin{array}{rrrr} & 4 & 11 & 15 \\ - & 1 & 8 & 9 \\ \hline & 3 & 3 & 6 \end{array}$$

Review Video: Subtracting Large Numbers
Visit mometrix.com/academy and enter code: 603350

Order of Operations

The **order of operations** is a set of rules that dictates the order in which we must perform each operation in an expression so that we will evaluate it accurately. If we have an expression that includes multiple different operations, the order of operations tells us which operations to do first. The most common mnemonic for the order of operations is **PEMDAS**, or "Please Excuse My Dear Aunt Sally." PEMDAS stands for parentheses, exponents, multiplication, division, addition, and subtraction. It is important to understand that multiplication and division have equal precedence, as do addition and subtraction, so those pairs of operations are simply worked from left to right in order.

For example, evaluating the expression $5 + 20 \div 4 \times (2 + 3)^2 - 6$ using the correct order of operations would be done like this:

- **P:** Perform the operations inside the parentheses: $(2 + 3) = 5$
- **E:** Simplify the exponents: $(5)^2 = 5 \times 5 = 25$
  - The expression now looks like this: $5 + 20 \div 4 \times 25 - 6$
- **MD:** Perform multiplication and division from left to right: $20 \div 4 = 5$; then $5 \times 25 = 125$
  - The expression now looks like this: $5 + 125 - 6$
- **AS:** Perform addition and subtraction from left to right: $5 + 125 = 130$; then $130 - 6 = 124$

Review Video: Order of Operations
Visit mometrix.com/academy and enter code: 259675

Properties of Operations

The Commutative Property

The commutative property applies to addition and multiplication and states that these operations can be completed in any order. The **commutative property of addition** states that numbers and terms can be added together in any order to still get the same value. For example, $3 + 4 = 7$ and $4 + 3 = 7$. Also, we can use the commutative property of addition to show that $3x + 4 + 2^2$ is equivalent to $4 + 3x + 2^2$ and $2^2 + 4 + 3x$. When adding terms, you can add in any order and get the same value.

The **commutative property of multiplication** states that numbers and terms can be multiplied in any order to get the same value. For example, 12×3 is equivalent to 3×12. Additionally, we can use the commutative property of multiplication to assume that $(5 + 3) \times (36 - 6)$ is equivalent to $(36 - 6) \times (5 + 3)$. You can multiply terms in any order and still get the same value.

The Associative Property

The **associative property of addition** states that if three or more terms are being added together, the value is the same regardless of the groupings.

For example, given the expression $3 + 4 + 6$, these terms can be grouped and added in any form. $3 + 4 + 6$ is equivalent to $(3 + 4) + 6$ and is also equivalent to $3 + (4 + 6)$. This can be applied to write equivalent expressions in a variety of ways.

For example, suppose we are given the expression $5 + (y + 2) + 4$. We can generate equivalent expressions knowing the associative property. Knowing that when three or more terms are added, the grouping is irrelevant, we can say that this expression is equivalent to $5 + y + (2 + 4)$, and it is equivalent to $(5 + y) + (2 + 4)$. It is even equivalent to $5 + y + 2 + 4$.

The **associative property of multiplication** states that if three or more terms are being multiplied together, the value is the same regardless of the grouping. We can use this property to identify and generate equivalent expressions.

For example, given the expression $2 \times 7 \times 3$, these terms can be grouped in any way and still get the same value. $2 \times 7 \times 3$ is equivalent to $(2 \times 7) \times 3$ or $2 \times (7 \times 3)$.

The Identity Property

The **identity property of multiplication** states that when a number is multiplied by 1, you get the same number. That is, anything multiplied by 1 is itself. For example, $2 \times 1 = 2$, or $1 \times -36 = -36$. Using the identity property of multiplication, we can identify and generate equivalent expressions. Let's say that we are given the expression $15 - (3 \times 4)$. We can generate equivalent expressions using the identity property. One equivalent expression example would be $(15 \times 1) - (3 \times 4)$. Another example would be $15 - (1 \times 3 \times 4)$. We can say these expressions are equivalent because the identity property of multiplication states that we can multiply any portion of an expression by 1 to get the same value.

The **identity property of addition** states that when 0 is added to a number, you get the same number. For example, $2 + 0 = 2$, or $0 + -3 = -3$. We can also use this property to identify and generate equivalent expressions. For example, if we are given the expression $2 \times (1 + 2)$, we could write the equivalent expressions $2 \times (0 + 1 + 2)$ or $(2 + 0) \times (1 + 2)$.

The Inverse Property

The **inverse property of addition** states that the sum of a number and its opposite is always equal to 0. Remember, the opposite of a number is a number that is opposite on the number line from zero, or the same number with the opposite sign. For example, −4 is opposite to 4, and 1,726.9 is opposite to −1,726.9. So, the inverse property of addition states that if you add opposite numbers, their sum is zero. For example, $5 + (-5) = 0$ and $-5 + 5 = 0$.

The **inverse property of multiplication** states that a number multiplied by its reciprocal is always equal to 1. The **reciprocal** of a number is its "flipped" fraction. For example, the reciprocal of 5 is $\frac{1}{5}$, or the reciprocal of $\frac{2}{3}$ is $\frac{3}{2}$. The inverse property of multiplication can be applied for these values, $5 \times \frac{1}{5} = 1$ and $\frac{2}{3} \times \frac{3}{2} = 1$. This is because when you multiply across, you get a fraction that is equal to 1.

$$\frac{2}{3} \times \frac{3}{2} = \frac{6}{6} = 1$$

The Distributive Property

The **distributive property** explains how multiplication and addition interact. It says that when multiplying one number by the sum of two other numbers, the same result can also be obtained by multiplying the one number by each of the numbers individually and then adding the products. For example, to multiply 2 by the sum of 7 and 3, the direct approach says, "the sum of 7 and 3 is 10, and 2 times 10 is 20." This would be expressed as $2 \times (7 + 3) = 2 \times 10 = 20$. On the other hand, the distributive property states that the same answer can be achieved by multiplying each number inside the parentheses and adding the products. That is, "the product of 2 and 7 is 14, the product of

2 and 3 is 6, and the sum of 14 and 6 is 20." This would be expressed as $2 \times (7 + 3) = 2 \times 7 + 2 \times 3 = 14 + 6 = 20$, and it is demonstrated below.

$$2 \times (7 + 3) = 2 \times 7 + 2 \times 3$$

This same concept can be used when multiplying a number by the difference of two numbers. For example, $5 \times (10 - 4) = 5 \times 10 - 5 \times 4$. Since $5 \times 10 = 50$ and $5 \times 4 = 20$, the result is $50 - 20 = 30$. This answer can be checked by subtracting inside the parentheses first and then multiplying: $5 \times (10 - 4) = 5 \times 6 = 30$.

Review Video: Commutative, Associative, and Distributive Properties
Visit mometrix.com/academy and enter code: 483176

Properties of Exponents

The properties of exponents are as follows:

Property	Description
$a^1 = a$	Any number to the power of 1 is equal to itself
$1^n = 1$	The number 1 raised to any power is equal to 1
$a^0 = 1$	Any number raised to the power of 0 is equal to 1
$a^n \times a^m = a^{n+m}$	Add exponents to multiply powers of the same base number
$a^n \div a^m = a^{n-m}$	Subtract exponents to divide powers of the same base number
$(a^n)^m = a^{n \times m}$	When a power is raised to a power, the exponents are multiplied
$(a \times b)^n = a^n \times b^n$ $(a \div b)^n = a^n \div b^n$	Multiplication and division operations inside parentheses can be raised to a power. This is the same as each term being raised to that power.
$a^{-n} = \frac{1}{a^n}$	A negative exponent is the same as the reciprocal of a positive exponent

Note that exponents do not have to be integers. Fractional or decimal exponents follow all the rules above as well. Example: $5^{\frac{1}{4}} \times 5^{\frac{3}{4}} = 5^{\frac{1}{4}+\frac{3}{4}} = 5^1 = 5$.

Review Video: Properties of Exponents
Visit mometrix.com/academy and enter code: 532558

Factors and Multiples

Factors and Greatest Common Factor

A whole number a is a **factor** (or **divisor**) of a whole number b if a divides b evenly. In other words, a is a factor of b if the quotient $b \div a$ is a whole number with a remainder of 0. For instance, 3 is a factor of 12 because $12 \div 3 = 4$ with no remainder. Another way to say this is that a is a factor of b if we can multiply a by another whole number to get b. So, we can also show that 3 is a factor of 12 by noting that $3 \times 4 = 12$.

Every positive whole number has 1 and itself as factors. If a whole number greater than one has *only* 1 and itself as factors, we call it a **prime number**. For instance, 5 is a prime number because its only factors are 1 and 5. The first several prime numbers are 2, 3, 5, 7, 11, and 13.

If a whole number greater than 1 is not prime—that is, if it has factors besides 1 and itself—then it is a **composite number.** For instance, 10 is a composite number because it has factors 2 and 5 in addition to 1 and 10. The first several composite numbers are 4, 6, 8, 9, 10, 12, 14, and 15.

A **prime factor** of a whole number is a factor that is also a prime number. For example, the prime factors of 12 are 2 and 3. The prime factors of 15 are 3 and 5.

A **common factor** of two (or more) whole numbers is a number that is a factor of both (or all) of them. For example, the factors of 12 are $\underline{1}$, 2, $\underline{3}$, 4, 6, and 12, while the factors of 15 are $\underline{1}$, $\underline{3}$, 5, and 15. The common factors (underlined) of 12 and 15 are 1 and 3.

The **greatest common factor** (**GCF**) of two (or more) whole numbers is the largest number that is a factor of both (or all) of them. For example, the factors of 15 are $\underline{1}$, 3, $\underline{5}$, and 15; the factors of 35 are $\underline{1}$, $\underline{5}$, 7, and 35. Therefore, the greatest common factor of 15 and 35 is 5.

Review Video: Factors
Visit mometrix.com/academy and enter code: 920086

Review Video: Prime Numbers and Factorization
Visit mometrix.com/academy and enter code: 760669

Multiples and Least Common Multiple

A whole number b is a **multiple** of a whole number a when a is a factor of b. This means that b is the product of a and another whole number. For example, the multiples of 7 are $0 \times 7 = 0, 1 \times 7 = 7, 2 \times 7 = 14, 3 \times 7 = 21, 4 \times 7 = 28, 5 \times 7 = 35$, ... Dividing 0, 7, 14, 21, 28, and 35 by 7 results in the whole numbers 0, 1, 2, 3, 4, and 5, respectively, showing that 7 is a factor of these numbers.

The least common multiple (**LCM**) of two (or more) whole numbers is the smallest number that is a multiple of both (or all) of them. For example, the multiples of 3 are 3, 6, 9, 12, $\underline{15}$, ...; the multiples of 5 are 5, 10, $\underline{15}$, 20, ... The smallest number that appears in both lists is 15, so the least common multiple of 3 and 5 is 15.

Review Video: Multiples
Visit mometrix.com/academy and enter code: 626738

Review Video: Greatest Common Factor and Least Common Multiple
Visit mometrix.com/academy and enter code: 838699

Fractions

A **fraction** is a number that is expressed as one integer written above another integer, with a dividing line between them $\left(\frac{x}{y}\right)$. It represents the **quotient** of the two numbers "x divided by y." It can also be thought of as x out of y equal parts.

The top number of a fraction is called the **numerator**, and it represents the number of parts under consideration. The 1 in $\frac{1}{4}$ means that 1 part out of the whole is being considered in the calculation.

The bottom number of a fraction is called the **denominator**, and it represents the total number of equal parts. The 4 in $\frac{1}{4}$ means that the whole consists of 4 equal parts. A fraction cannot have a denominator of zero; this is referred to as "*undefined*."

Fractions can be manipulated, without changing the value of the fraction, by multiplying or dividing (but not adding or subtracting) both the numerator and denominator by the same number. If you divide both numbers by a common factor, you are **reducing** or simplifying the fraction. Two fractions that have the same value but are expressed differently are known as **equivalent fractions**. For example, $\frac{2}{10}, \frac{3}{15}, \frac{4}{20}$, and $\frac{5}{25}$ are all equivalent fractions. They can also all be reduced or simplified to $\frac{1}{5}$.

When two fractions are manipulated so that they have the same denominator, this is known as finding a **common denominator**. The number chosen to be that common denominator should be the least common multiple of the two original denominators. Example: $\frac{3}{4}$ and $\frac{5}{6}$; the least common multiple of 4 and 6 is 12. Manipulating to achieve the common denominator: $\frac{3}{4} = \frac{9}{12}; \frac{5}{6} = \frac{10}{12}$.

Review Video: Overview of Fractions
Visit mometrix.com/academy and enter code: 262335

Proper Fractions and Mixed Numbers

A fraction whose denominator is greater than its numerator is known as a **proper fraction**, while a fraction whose numerator is greater than its denominator is known as an **improper fraction**. Proper fractions have values *less than one* and improper fractions have values *greater than one*.

A **mixed number** is a number that contains both an integer and a fraction. Any improper fraction can be rewritten as a mixed number. Example: $\frac{8}{3} = \frac{6}{3} + \frac{2}{3} = 2 + \frac{2}{3} = 2\frac{2}{3}$. Similarly, any mixed number can be rewritten as an improper fraction. Example: $1\frac{3}{5} = 1 + \frac{3}{5} = \frac{5}{5} + \frac{3}{5} = \frac{8}{5}$.

Review Video: Proper and Improper Fractions and Mixed Numbers
Visit mometrix.com/academy and enter code: 211077

Adding and Subtracting Fractions

If two fractions have a common denominator, they can be added or subtracted simply by adding or subtracting the two numerators and retaining the same denominator. If the two fractions do not already have the same denominator, one or both of them must be manipulated to achieve a common denominator before they can be added or subtracted. Example: $\frac{1}{2} + \frac{1}{4} = \frac{2}{4} + \frac{1}{4} = \frac{3}{4}$.

Review Video: Adding and Subtracting Fractions
Visit mometrix.com/academy and enter code: 378080

Multiplying Fractions

Two fractions can be multiplied by multiplying the two numerators to find the new numerator and the two denominators to find the new denominator. Example: $\frac{1}{3} \times \frac{2}{3} = \frac{1 \times 2}{3 \times 3} = \frac{2}{9}$.

Dividing Fractions

Two fractions can be divided by flipping the numerator and denominator of the second fraction and then proceeding as though it were a multiplication problem. Example: $\frac{2}{3} \div \frac{3}{4} = \frac{2}{3} \times \frac{4}{3} = \frac{8}{9}$.

Review Video: Multiplying and Dividing Fractions
Visit mometrix.com/academy and enter code: 473632

Multiplying a Mixed Number by a Whole Number or a Decimal

When multiplying a mixed number by something, it is usually best to convert it to an improper fraction first. Additionally, if the multiplicand is a decimal, it is most often simplest to convert it to a fraction. For instance, to multiply $4\frac{3}{8}$ by 3.5, begin by rewriting each quantity as a whole number plus a proper fraction. Remember, a mixed number is a fraction added to a whole number and a decimal is a representation of the sum of fractions, specifically tenths, hundredths, thousandths, and so on:

$$4\frac{3}{8} \times 3.5 = \left(4 + \frac{3}{8}\right) \times \left(3 + \frac{1}{2}\right)$$

Next, the quantities being added need to be expressed with the same denominator. This is achieved by multiplying and dividing the whole number by the denominator of the fraction. Recall that a whole number is equivalent to that number divided by 1:

$$= \left(\frac{4}{1} \times \frac{8}{8} + \frac{3}{8}\right) \times \left(\frac{3}{1} \times \frac{2}{2} + \frac{1}{2}\right)$$

When multiplying fractions, remember to multiply the numerators and denominators separately:

$$= \left(\frac{4 \times 8}{1 \times 8} + \frac{3}{8}\right) \times \left(\frac{3 \times 2}{1 \times 2} + \frac{1}{2}\right)$$
$$= \left(\frac{32}{8} + \frac{3}{8}\right) \times \left(\frac{6}{2} + \frac{1}{2}\right)$$

Now that the fractions have the same denominators, they can be added:

$$= \frac{35}{8} \times \frac{7}{2}$$

Finally, perform the last multiplication and then simplify:

$$= \frac{35 \times 7}{8 \times 2} = \frac{245}{16} = \frac{240}{16} + \frac{5}{16} = 15\frac{5}{16}$$

Comparing Fractions

It is important to master the ability to compare and order fractions. This skill is relevant to many real-world scenarios. For example, carpenters often compare fractional construction nail lengths when preparing for a project, and bakers often compare fractional measurements to have the correct ratio of ingredients. There are three commonly used strategies when comparing fractions. These strategies are referred to as the common denominator approach, the decimal approach, and the cross-multiplication approach.

Using a Common Denominator to Compare Fractions

The fractions $\frac{2}{3}$ and $\frac{4}{7}$ have different denominators. $\frac{2}{3}$ has a denominator of 3, and $\frac{4}{7}$ has a denominator of 7. In order to precisely compare these two fractions, it is necessary to use a common denominator. A common denominator is a common multiple that is shared by both denominators. In this case, the denominators 3 and 7 share a multiple of 21. In general, it is most efficient to select the least common multiple for the two denominators.

Rewrite each fraction with the common denominator of 21. Then, calculate the new numerators as illustrated below.

$$\frac{2}{3} \overset{\times 7}{=} \frac{\mathbf{14}}{21} \qquad \frac{4}{7} \overset{\times 3}{=} \frac{\mathbf{12}}{21}$$

For $\frac{2}{3}$, multiply the numerator and denominator by 7. The result is $\frac{14}{21}$.

For $\frac{4}{7}$, multiply the numerator and denominator by 3. The result is $\frac{12}{21}$.

Now that both fractions have a denominator of 21, the fractions can accurately be compared by comparing the numerators. Since 14 is greater than 12, the fraction $\frac{14}{21}$ is greater than $\frac{12}{21}$. This means that $\frac{2}{3}$ is greater than $\frac{4}{7}$.

Using Decimals to Compare Fractions

Sometimes decimal values are easier to compare than fraction values. For example, $\frac{5}{8}$ is equivalent to 0.625 and $\frac{3}{5}$ is equivalent to 0.6. This means that the comparison of $\frac{5}{8}$ and $\frac{3}{5}$ can be determined by comparing the decimals 0.625 and 0.6. When both decimal values are extended to the thousandths place, they become 0.625 and 0.600, respectively. It becomes clear that 0.625 is greater than 0.600 because 625 thousandths is greater than 600 thousandths. In other words, $\frac{5}{8}$ is greater than $\frac{3}{5}$ because 0.625 is greater than 0.6.

Using Cross-Multiplication to Compare Fractions

Cross-multiplication is an efficient strategy for comparing fractions. This is a shortcut for the common denominator strategy. Start by writing each fraction next to one another. Multiply the numerator of the fraction on the left by the denominator of the fraction on the right. Write down the result next to the fraction on the left. Now multiply the numerator of the fraction on the right by the denominator of the fraction on the left. Write down the result next to the fraction on the right. Compare both products. The fraction with the larger result is the larger fraction.

Consider the fractions $\frac{4}{7}$ and $\frac{5}{9}$.

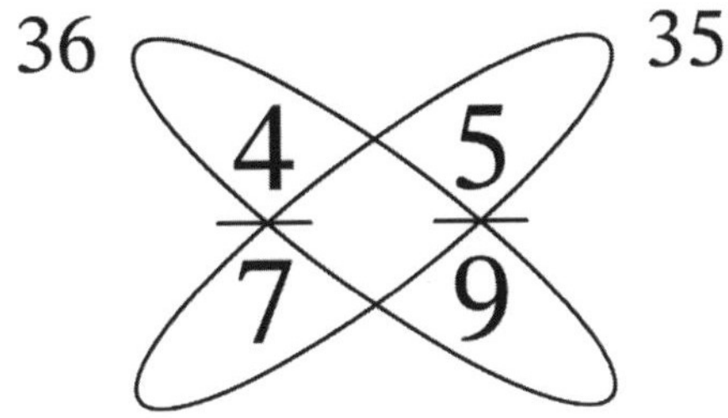

36 is greater than 35. Therefore, $\frac{4}{7}$ is greater than $\frac{5}{9}$.

Decimals

Decimals are one way to represent parts of a whole. Using the place value system, each digit to the right of a decimal point denotes the number of units of a corresponding *negative* power of ten. For example, consider the decimal 0.24. We can use a model to represent the decimal. Since a dime is worth one-tenth of a dollar and a penny is worth one-hundredth of a dollar, one possible model to represent this fraction is to have 2 dimes representing the 2 in the tenths place and 4 pennies representing the 4 in the hundredths place:

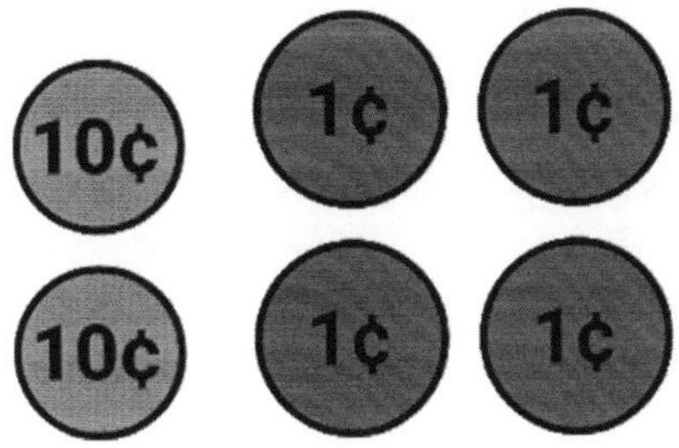

To write the decimal as a fraction, put the decimal in the numerator with 1 in the denominator. Multiply the numerator and denominator by tens until there are no more decimal places. Then simplify the fraction to lowest terms. For example, converting 0.24 to a fraction:

$$0.24 = \frac{0.24}{1} = \frac{0.24 \times 100}{1 \times 100} = \frac{24}{100} = \frac{6}{25}$$

Review Video: Decimals
Visit mometrix.com/academy and enter code: 837268

Operations with Decimals

Adding and Subtracting Decimals

When adding and subtracting decimals, the decimal points must always be aligned. Adding decimals is just like adding regular whole numbers. Example: $4.5 + 2.0 = 6.5$.

If the problem-solver does not properly align the decimal points, an incorrect answer of 4.7 may result. An easy way to add decimals is to align all of the decimal points in a vertical column visually. This will allow you to see exactly where the decimal should be placed in the final answer. Begin adding from right to left. Add each column in turn, making sure to carry the number to the left if a column adds up to more than 9. The same rules apply to the subtraction of decimals.

Review Video: Adding and Subtracting Decimals
Visit mometrix.com/academy and enter code: 381101

MULTIPLYING DECIMALS

A simple multiplication problem has two components: a **multiplicand** and a **multiplier**. When multiplying decimals, work as though the numbers were whole rather than decimals. Once the final product is calculated, count the number of places to the right of the decimal in both the multiplicand and the multiplier. Then, count that number of places from the right of the product and place the decimal in that position.

For example, 12.3×2.56 has a total of three places to the right of the respective decimals. Multiply 123×256 to get 31,488. Now, beginning on the right, count three places to the left and insert the decimal. The final product will be 31.488.

Review Video: How to Multiply Decimals
Visit mometrix.com/academy and enter code: 731574

DIVIDING DECIMALS

Every division problem has a **divisor** and a **dividend**. The dividend is the number that is being divided. In the problem $14 \div 7$, 14 is the dividend and 7 is the divisor. In a division problem with decimals, the divisor must be converted into a whole number. Begin by moving the decimal in the divisor to the right until a whole number is created. Next, move the decimal in the dividend the same number of spaces to the right. For example, 4.9 into 24.5 would become 49 into 245. The decimal was moved one space to the right to create a whole number in the divisor, and then the same was done for the dividend. Once the whole numbers are created, the problem is carried out normally: $245 \div 49 = 5$.

Review Video: Dividing Decimals
Visit mometrix.com/academy and enter code: 560690

Review Video: Dividing Decimals by Whole Numbers
Visit mometrix.com/academy and enter code: 535669

Percentages

Percentages can be thought of as fractions that are based on a whole of 100; that is, one whole is equal to 100%. The word **percent** means "per hundred." Percentage problems are often presented in three main ways:

- Find what percentage of some number another number is.
  - Example: What percentage of 40 is 8?
- Find what number is some percentage of a given number.
  - Example: What number is 20% of 40?
- Find what number another number is a given percentage of.
  - Example: What number is 8 20% of?

There are three components in each of these cases: a **whole** (W), a **part** (P), and a **percentage** (%). These are related by the equation: $P = W \times \%$. This can easily be rearranged into other forms that may suit different questions better: $\% = \frac{P}{W}$ and $W = \frac{P}{\%}$. Percentage problems are often also word problems. As such, a large part of solving them is figuring out which quantities are what. For example, consider the following word problem:

In a school cafeteria, 7 students choose pizza, 9 choose hamburgers, and 4 choose tacos. What percentage of students choose tacos?

To find the whole, you must first add all of the parts: $7 + 9 + 4 = 20$. The percentage can then be found by dividing the part by the whole $\left(\% = \frac{P}{W}\right)$: $\frac{4}{20} = \frac{20}{100} = 20\%$.

Review Video: Computation with Percentages
Visit mometrix.com/academy and enter code: 693099

Calculating Percent Change

Suppose a quantity has a particular value (the *old value*) and then we add something (the *change*) to it to get another value (the *new value*). We can describe this process by the simple equation (old value) + change = (new value). If we know the old and new values, we can rearrange this equation to find the change, getting change = (new value) − (old value). For instance, if a store's price for a box of computer paper goes from \$20 last week to \$25 this week, this is a change of (new value) − (old value) = \$25 − \$20 = \$5. Or, if the size of the freshman class at a college goes from 500 students one year to 440 students the next year, this is a change of (new value) − (old value) = 440 − 500 = −60 students. So, we see that change can be positive or negative.

Instead of the word *change*, we sometimes use the words *increase* or *decrease* to specify whether the value goes up or down, respectively. In the examples above, the price of computer paper increases by \$5 and the freshman class decreases by 60 students. Note that the decrease is 60 students and not -60 because the word *decrease* already means that the value goes down. So, *increase* is the same as positive change and *decrease* is the opposite or negative change.

If the changing quantity represents an amount (how much of something there is), we can also calculate the **percent change**. This is the change expressed as a percentage of the old amount. To calculate this, we divide the change by the old amount and express the quotient as a percent. That is, we use the formula percent change $= \frac{\text{change}}{\text{old value}}$, converting the resulting decimal answer to a percent. In the examples above, the price of a box of computer paper has a percent change of $\frac{\text{change in price}}{\text{old price}} = \frac{\$5}{\$20} = 0.25 = 25\%$, and the size of the freshman class at the college has a percent change of $\frac{\text{change in enrollment}}{\text{old enrollment}} = \frac{-60}{500} = -0.12 = -12\%$. We can also use the terms *percent increase* and *percent decrease*, saying that the price of computer paper increases by 25% and the size of the freshman class decreases by 12%. Note that the denominator is always the old amount, never the new amount.

Example: Your landlord raises your rent from \$1,500 to \$1,700 per month. To find the percent change in your rent (rounded to the nearest tenth of a percent), you calculate as follows.

$$\text{percent change in rent} = \frac{\text{change in rent}}{\text{old rent}} = \frac{(\text{new rent}) - (\text{old rent})}{\text{old rent}}$$
$$= \frac{\$1{,}700 - \$1{,}500}{\$1{,}500} = \frac{\$200}{\$1{,}500} = 0.1333\ldots \approx 13.3\%$$

Therefore, the percent change in your rent is approximately 13.3%.

Review Video: Percent Change
Visit mometrix.com/academy and enter code: 907890

Converting Between Percentages, Fractions, and Decimals

Converting decimals to percentages and percentages to decimals is as simple as moving the decimal point. To *convert from a decimal to a percentage*, move the decimal point **two places to the right**. To *convert from a percentage to a decimal*, move it **two places to the left**. It may be helpful to remember that the percentage number will always be larger than the equivalent decimal number. Example:

$$0.23 = 23\% \qquad 5.34 = 534\% \qquad 0.007 = 0.7\%$$
$$700\% = 7.00 \qquad 86\% = 0.86 \qquad 0.15\% = 0.0015$$

To convert a fraction to a decimal, simply divide the numerator by the denominator in the fraction. To convert a decimal to a fraction, put the decimal in the numerator with 1 in the denominator. Multiply the numerator and denominator by tens until there are no more decimal places. Then simplify the fraction to lowest terms. For example, converting 0.24 to a fraction:

$$0.24 = \frac{0.24}{1} = \frac{0.24 \times 100}{1 \times 100} = \frac{24}{100} = \frac{6}{25}$$

Fractions can be converted to a percentage by finding equivalent fractions with a denominator of 100. Example:

$$\frac{7}{10} = \frac{70}{100} = 70\% \quad \frac{1}{4} = \frac{25}{100} = 25\%$$

To convert a percentage to a fraction, divide the percentage number by 100 and reduce the fraction to its simplest possible terms. Example:

$$60\% = \frac{60}{100} = \frac{3}{5} \quad 96\% = \frac{96}{100} = \frac{24}{25}$$

Review Video: Converting Fractions to Percentages and Decimals
Visit mometrix.com/academy and enter code: 306233

Review Video: Converting Percentages to Decimals and Fractions
Visit mometrix.com/academy and enter code: 287297

Review Video: Converting Decimals to Fractions and Percentages
Visit mometrix.com/academy and enter code: 986765

Review Video: Converting Decimals, Improper Fractions, and Mixed Numbers
Visit mometrix.com/academy and enter code: 696924

Rational and Irrational Numbers

The term **rational** means that the number can be expressed as a ratio or fraction. That is, a number, r, is rational if and only if it can be represented by a fraction $\frac{a}{b}$ where a and b are integers and b does not equal 0. The set of rational numbers includes integers and decimals. If there is no finite way to represent a value with a fraction of integers, then the number is **irrational**. Common irrational numbers are π and the square roots of whole numbers that are not perfect squares (e.g., $\sqrt{5}$ or $\sqrt{21}$). The sum or product of an integer and an irrational number is always irrational (e.g., 3π or $7 + \sqrt{6}$).

Review Video: Rational and Irrational Numbers
Visit mometrix.com/academy and enter code: 280645

Review Video: Ordering Rational Numbers
Visit mometrix.com/academy and enter code: 419578

Review Video: Irrational Numbers on a Number Line
Visit mometrix.com/academy and enter code: 433866

Chapter Quiz

Ready to see how well you retained what you just read? Scan the QR code to go directly to the chapter quiz interface for this study guide. If you're using a computer, simply visit the online resources page at **mometrix.com/resources719/texesmathpse** and click the Chapter Quizzes link.

Patterns and Algebra

Proportionality

Proportions and Ratios

Proportions

There is a **proportion** between two variable quantities if there is a constant relationship between their products or quotients, a relationship that does not change as the quantities themselves change.

Given variable quantities x and y, we say that they are **directly proportional** (or that y **varies directly with** x) if their quotient or *ratio* is constant—that is, if there is a constant k such that $\frac{y}{x} = k$ is always true. Another way of saying this is that y is a constant multiple of x, so that $y = kx$ is always true. We call the number k the **constant of proportionality**. For example, if you drive at a constant 50 miles per hour, then the distance, y, that you travel in miles is 50 times the number of hours, x, that you drive. In symbols, $y = 50x$ miles (or $\frac{y}{x} = 50$ mph). So, the distance you travel, y, is directly proportional to (or varies directly with) the time you travel, x, with constant of proportionality $k = 50$ mph.

The quantities x and y are **inversely proportional** (or y varies inversely with x) if their product is constant—that is, if there is a constant k such that $xy = k$ is always true. Another way of saying this is to say that y is a constant multiple of the reciprocal of x so that $y = \frac{k}{x}$ is always true. For instance, suppose you drive at speed (rate) y mph for x hours, going a total of 120 miles. Since rate $\times$ time $=$ distance, we get $xy = 120$ miles (or $y = \frac{120}{x}$ miles per hour). Thus, your driving speed, y, is inversely proportional to (or varies inversely with) your drive time, x, with constant of proportionality $k = 120$ miles.

Review Video: Proportions
Visit mometrix.com/academy and enter code: 505355

Ratios

A **ratio** expresses the sizes of two quantities relative to each other. For instance, suppose we have 3 copies of sheet music to share among 6 singers. We can divide the singers into groups of 2 and give each group 1 copy of the music. Thus, there is 1 copy of the music for every 2 singers, and we say that the **ratio** of sheet music to singers is 1 to 2, which we write either as a fraction $\frac{1}{2}$ or using a colon $1 : 2$. Of course, it is also true there are 3 copies for every 6 singers so that the ratio of sheet music to singers is also 3 to 6, which we write as $\frac{3}{6}$ or $3 : 6$. So, the ratios $\frac{1}{2}$ and $\frac{3}{6}$ express the same relative quantities of music and singers. We say that these ratios are equal or **equivalent**, and we note that ratios are equal precisely when their fractions are equal (so, in this case, $\frac{1}{2} = \frac{3}{6}$ as fractions). We can also express the quantities in the other order and say that the ratio of singers to music is $\frac{2}{1}$ or $2 : 1$ (or $\frac{6}{3}$ or $6 : 3$).

Review Video: Ratios
Visit mometrix.com/academy and enter code: 996914

Constant of Proportionality

If variable quantities x and y are proportional and we know a pair of corresponding values for them, then we can find their constant of proportionality. If they are directly proportional, we use the formula $\frac{y}{x} = k$. If they are inversely proportional, we use the formula $xy = k$.

Example: The cost in dollars, y, of buying fence posts is directly proportional to the number, x, that you buy. If it costs $51 to buy 17 fence posts, what is the constant of proportionality? Because of direct proportionality, we know that $\frac{y}{x} = k$. Since this works for every pair of corresponding x- and y-values, it also works for $x = 17$ and $y = 51$. This gives us $\frac{51}{17} = k$, which simplifies to $k = 3$. Note also that this is the unit price, namely $3 per fence post.

Work/Unit Rate

Unit rate expresses a quantity of one thing in terms of one unit of another. For example, if you travel 30 miles every two hours, a unit rate expresses this comparison in terms of one hour: in one hour you travel 15 miles, so your unit rate is 15 miles per hour. Other examples are how much one ounce of food costs (price per ounce) or figuring out how much one egg costs out of the dozen (price per 1 egg, instead of price per 12 eggs). The denominator of a unit rate is always 1. Unit rates are used to compare different situations to solve problems. For example, to make sure you get the best deal when deciding which kind of soda to buy, you can find the unit rate of each. If soda #1 costs $1.50 for a 1-liter bottle, and soda #2 costs $2.75 for a 2-liter bottle, it would be a better deal to buy soda #2, because its unit rate is only $1.375 per liter, which is cheaper than soda #1. Unit rates can also help determine the length of time a given event will take. For example, if you can paint 2 rooms in 4.5 hours, you can determine how long it will take you to paint 5 rooms by solving for the unit rate per room and then multiplying that by 5.

Review Video: Rates and Unit Rates
Visit mometrix.com/academy and enter code: 185363

Linear Expressions and Equations

Cross Multiplication

Finding an Unknown in Equivalent Expressions

It is often necessary to apply information given about a rate or proportion to a new scenario. For example, if you know that Jedha can run a marathon (26.2 miles) in 3 hours, how long would it take her to run 10 miles at the same pace? Start by setting up equivalent expressions:

$$\frac{26.2 \text{ mi}}{3 \text{ hr}} = \frac{10 \text{ mi}}{x \text{ hr}}$$

Now, cross multiply and solve for x:

$$\begin{aligned} 26.2x &= 30 \\ x &= \frac{30}{26.2} = \frac{15}{13.1} \\ x &\approx 1.15 \text{ hrs } or \text{ } 1 \text{ hr } 9 \text{ min} \end{aligned}$$

So, at this pace, Jedha could run 10 miles in about 1.15 hours or about 1 hour and 9 minutes.

Review Video: Cross Multiplying Fractions
Visit mometrix.com/academy and enter code: 893904

Linear Expressions

Terms and Coefficients

Mathematical expressions consist of a combination of one or more values arranged in terms that are added together. As such, an expression could be just a single number, including zero. A **variable term** is the product of a real number, also called a **coefficient**, and one or more variables, each of which may be raised to an exponent. Expressions may also include numbers without a variable, called **constants** or **constant terms**. The expression $6s^2$, for example, is a single term where the coefficient is the real number 6 and the variable term is s^2. Note that if a term is written as simply a variable to some exponent, like t^2, then the coefficient is 1, because $t^2 = 1t^2$.

Linear Expressions

A **single variable linear expression** is the sum of a single variable term, where the variable has no exponent, and a constant, which may be zero. For instance, the expression $2w + 7$ has $2w$ as the variable term and 7 as the constant term. It is important to realize that terms are separated by addition or subtraction. Since an expression is a sum of terms, expressions such as $5x - 3$ can be written as $5x + (-3)$ to emphasize that the constant term is negative. A real-world example of a single variable linear expression is the perimeter of a square, four times the side length, often expressed: $4s$.

In general, a **linear expression** is the sum of any number of variable terms so long as none of the variables have an exponent and none of the terms have two variables multiplied together. For example, $3m + 8n - \frac{1}{4}p + 5.5q - 1$ is a linear expression, but $3y^3$ and $5xy$ are not. In the same way, the expression for the perimeter of a general triangle $(a + b + c)$ is linear, but the expression for the area of a square (s^2) is not.

Slope

Finding Slope Given Graph or Table

On a graph with two points, (x_1, y_1) and (x_2, y_2), the **slope** is found with the formula $m = \frac{y_2 - y_1}{x_2 - x_1}$; where $x_1 \neq x_2$ and m stands for slope. If the value of the slope is **positive**, the line has an *upward direction* from left to right. If the value of the slope is **negative**, the line has a *downward direction* from left to right. Consider the following example:

A new book goes on sale in bookstores and online stores. In the first month, 5,000 copies of the book are sold. Over time, the book continues to grow in popularity. The data for the number of copies sold is in the table below.

# of Months on Sale	1	2	3	4	5
# of Copies Sold (In Thousands)	5	10	15	20	25

So, the number of copies that are sold and the time that the book is on sale is a proportional relationship. In this example, an equation can be used to show the data: $y = 5x$, where x is the number of months that the book is on sale. Also, y is the number of copies sold. So, the slope of the corresponding line is $\frac{\text{rise}}{\text{run}} = \frac{5}{1} = 5$.

Finding Slope Given an Equation

When given an equation of a line, it is necessary to solve for y to determine the slope of the line. Given the equation $6x + 2y = 8$, find the slope. First, subtract $6x$ from both sides of the equation, resulting in $2y = -6x + 8$. Then divide both sides of the equation by 2, resulting in $y = -3x + 4$. This then allows us to conclude that the slope of the line is $m = -3$, the coefficient of x. Once an equation is in the form $y = mx + b$, the slope and y-intercept can easily be determined. For this reason, we refer to the equation $y = mx + b$ as "slope-intercept form" of the equation of a line.

Review Video: Finding the Slope of a Line
Visit mometrix.com/academy and enter code: 766664

Linear Equations

Equations like $5x = 100$ and $8x - 120 = 200$ and $6x + 4y = 240$ are **linear equations**. Linear equations are named based off the number of distinct variables they include. For example, the equation $3x + 30 = 8x$ is a **one-variable linear equation** because it involves only the single variable x. It does not matter that x appears more than once. Any equations that can be written as $ax + b = 0$, where $a \neq 0$, falls into this category. Furthermore, the equation $3x - 5y = 14 + 9y$ is a **two-variable linear equation** because it involves the two variables x and y. The equation $7x + 8y - 12z + 14w = 56$ is a linear equation in four variables.

Satisfying the Equation

When given a one-variable linear equation, the goal is typically to solve it. This means that we want to find the number that makes the equation true if we substitute it for the variable. That number is the **solution,** or root, of the equation. For instance, the equation $5x = 10$ has the solution $x = 2$. This is true because when 2 is substituted for x, the result is $5 \cdot 2 = 10$, which is true. On the other hand, $x = 6$ can not be a solution because $5 \cdot 6 \neq 10$, so it is false. Two equations with the same solution are **equivalent equations**. For example, the equations $5x = 10$ and $5x + 3 = 13$ are equivalent because both have the same solution of $x = 2$.

Determining a Solution Set

The **solution set** is the set of all solutions of an equation. In the previous example, the solution set would be 2. Solutions to a linear equation in two variables consist of pairs of numbers. For instance, the equation $6x + 4y = 240$ has the solution $x = 20$ and $y = 30$ since $6 \cdot 20 + 4 \cdot 30 = 240$ is true. We can write this solution as the ordered pair (20,30) and plot it as a point on the coordinate plane. Such equations usually have infinitely many solutions; and if we plot the points for all these solutions we get a line, which is a picture of all the solutions. We call this **graphing the equation**. When an equation has no true solutions, it is referred to as an **empty set**.

Linear Equation Forms

Linear equations can be written many ways. Below is a list of some forms linear equations can take:

- **Standard Form**: $Ax + By = C$; the slope is $\frac{-A}{B}$ and the y-intercept is $\frac{C}{B}$
- **Slope Intercept Form**: $y = mx + b$, where m is the slope and b is the y-intercept
- **Point-Slope Form**: $y - y_1 = m(x - x_1)$, where m is the slope and (x_1, y_1) is a point on the line

- **Two-Point Form**: $\frac{y-y_1}{x-x_1} = \frac{y_2-y_1}{x_2-x_1}$, where (x_1, y_1) and (x_2, y_2) are two points on the given line
- **Intercept Form**: $\frac{x}{x_1} + \frac{y}{y_1} = 1$, where $(x_1, 0)$ is the point at which a line intersects the x-axis, and $(0, y_1)$ is the point at which the same line intersects the y-axis

Review Video: Slope-Intercept and Point-Slope Forms
Visit mometrix.com/academy and enter code: 113216

Review Video: Converting Between Standard and Slope-Intercept Forms
Visit mometrix.com/academy and enter code: 982828

Review Video: Linear Equations Basics
Visit mometrix.com/academy and enter code: 793005

SOLVING EQUATIONS

MANIPULATING EQUATIONS

LIKE TERMS

Like terms are terms in an equation that have the same variable, regardless of whether they also have the same coefficient. This includes terms that *lack* a variable; all constants (i.e., numbers without variables) are considered like terms. If the equation involves terms with a variable raised to different powers, the like terms are those that have the variable raised to the same power.

For example, consider the equation $x^2 + 3x + 2 = 2x^2 + x - 7 + 2x$. In this equation, 2 and -7 are like terms; they are both constants. The terms $3x$, x, and $2x$ are like terms, they all include the variable x raised to the first power. The terms x^2 and $2x^2$ are like terms, they both include the variable x, raised to the second power. The terms $2x$ and $2x^2$ are not like terms; although they both involve the variable x, the variable is not raised to the same power in both terms. The fact that they have the same coefficient, 2, is not relevant.

Review Video: Rules for Manipulating Equations
Visit mometrix.com/academy and enter code: 838871

CARRYING OUT THE SAME OPERATION ON BOTH SIDES OF AN EQUATION

When solving an equation, the general procedure is to carry out a series of operations on both sides of an equation, choosing operations that simplify the equation when doing so. The reason why the same operation must be carried out on both sides of the equation is because that leaves the meaning of the equation unchanged, and yields a result that is equivalent to the original equation. This would not be the case if we carried out an operation on one side of an equation and not the other. Consider what an equation means: it is a statement that two values or expressions are equal. If we carry out the same operation on both sides of the equation—add 3 to both sides, for example—then the two sides of the equation are changed in the same way, and so remain equal. If we do that to only one side of the equation—add 3 to one side but not the other—then that wouldn't be true; if we change one side of the equation but not the other then the two sides are no longer equal.

COMBINING LIKE TERMS

Combining like terms refers to adding or subtracting like terms—terms with the same variable—and therefore reducing sets of like terms to a single term. The main advantage of doing this is that it simplifies the equation. Often, combining like terms can be done as the first step in solving an equation, though it can also be done later, such as after distributing terms in a product.

For example, consider the equation $2(x+3)+3(2+\ x+3)=-4$. The 2 and the 3 in the second set of parentheses are like terms, and we can combine them, yielding $2(x+3)+3(x+5)=-4$. Now we can carry out the multiplications implied by the parentheses, distributing the outer 2 and 3 accordingly: $2x+6+3x+15=-4$. The $2x$ and the $3x$ are like terms, and we can add them together: $5x+6+15=-4$. Now, the constants 6, 15, and -4 are also like terms, and we can combine them as well: subtracting 6 and 15 from both sides of the equation, we get $5x=-4-6-15$, or $5x=-25$, which simplifies further to $x=-5$.

Review Video: Solving Equations by Combining Like Terms
Visit mometrix.com/academy and enter code: 668506

Canceling Terms on Opposite Sides of an Equation

Two terms on opposite sides of an equation can be canceled if and only if they *exactly* match each other. They must have the same variable raised to the same power and the same coefficient. For example, in the equation $3x+2x^2+6=2x^2-6$, $2x^2$ appears on both sides of the equation and can be canceled, leaving $3x+6=-6$. The 6 on each side of the equation *cannot* be canceled, because it is added on one side of the equation and subtracted on the other. While they cannot be canceled, however, the 6 and -6 are like terms and can be combined, yielding $3x=-12$, which simplifies further to $x=-4$.

It's also important to note that the terms to be canceled must be independent terms and cannot be part of a larger term. For example, consider the equation $2(x+6)=3(x+4)+1$. We cannot cancel the x's, because even though they match each other they are part of the larger terms $2(x+6)$ and $3(x+4)$. We must first distribute the 2 and 3, yielding $2x+12=3x+12+1$. Now we see that the terms with the x's do not match, but the 12s do, and can be canceled, leaving $2x=3x+1$, which simplifies to $x=-1$.

Isolating Variables

To isolate a variable means to manipulate the equation so that the variable appears by itself on one side of the equation, and does not appear at all on the other side. Generally, an equation or inequality is considered to be solved once the variable is isolated and the other side of the equation or inequality is simplified as much as possible. In the case of a two-variable equation or inequality, only one variable needs to be isolated; it will not usually be possible to simultaneously isolate both variables.

For a linear equation—an equation in which the variable only appears raised to the first power—isolating a variable can be done by first moving all the terms with the variable to one side of the equation and all other terms to the other side. (*Moving* a term really means adding the inverse of the term to both sides; when a term is *moved* to the other side of the equation its sign is flipped.) Then combine like terms on each side. Finally, divide both sides by the coefficient of the variable, if applicable. The steps need not necessarily be done in this order, but this order will always work.

Review Video: Solving Equations for Specific Variables
Visit mometrix.com/academy and enter code: 130695

Review Video: Solving Equations Involving Algebraic Fractions
Visit mometrix.com/academy and enter code: 237770

Review Video: Solving One-Step Equations
Visit mometrix.com/academy and enter code: 777004

Solving One-Variable Linear Equations

Equations with One Solution (the Usual Case)

To solve a one-variable linear equation, we use the techniques above to isolate the variable.

1. If any coefficients or constants are fractions, it is often helpful first to multiply both sides of the equation by the least common denominator (of all fractions) to clear the fractions.
2. Simplify both sides of the equation by combining any like terms.
3. Put all terms with the variable on one side of the equation and all constant terms on the other side, by adding or subtracting the same terms on both sides of the equation.
4. Divide both sides by the coefficient of the variable (or multiply both sides by its reciprocal).
5. When we have a value for the variable, we can check it by substituting the value into the original equation to make sure it produces a true result.

Consider the following example for solving the equation $\frac{2}{3}x + 8 = 14$:

$3 \cdot \left(\frac{2}{3}x + 8\right) = 3 \cdot 14$	Clear fractions by multiplying both sides by 3.
$2x + 24 = 42$	Simplify, remembering to apply the distributive property.
$2x + 24 - 24 = 42 - 24$	Subtract 24 from both sides to isolate $2x$.
$2x = 18$	Simplify by combining like terms.
$\frac{2x}{2} = \frac{18}{2}$	Divide both sides by 2 to isolate x.
$x = 9$	Simplify

Finally, we check this answer by substituting $x = 9$ into the original equation to make sure we get a true result.

$$\frac{2}{3}x + 8 = \frac{2}{3}(9) + 8 = 6 + 8 = 14$$

This is correct, so the value of x is 9.

> **Review Video: Solving Equations Using the Distributive Property**
> Visit mometrix.com/academy and enter code: 765499

Equations with More Than One Solution

Some types of non-linear equations, such as equations involving squares of variables, may have more than one solution. For example, the equation $x^2 = 4$ has two solutions: 2 and -2. Equations with absolute values can also have multiple solutions: $|x| = 1$ has the solutions $x = 1$ and $x = -1$.

It is possible for a linear equation to have more than one solution but only if the equation is true regardless of the value of the variable. We call such an equation an **identity**. In this case, the equation has infinitely many solutions, because every possible value of the variable is a solution. We discover that a linear equation is an identity when our attempts to isolate the variable cause the variable to disappear, leaving a *true* equation involving only constants. For example, consider the equation $2(3x + 5) = x + 5(x + 2)$. Distributing, we get $6x + 10 = x + 5x + 10$; combining like terms gives $6x + 10 = 6x + 10$, and the $6x$-terms cancel to leave $10 = 10$. This is clearly true, so the original equation is an identity. We could also cancel the 10's leaving $0 = 0$, which is also is clearly true—in general if both sides of the equation can be reduced to match one another exactly, the original equation is an identity.

Equations with No Solution

Some types of non-linear equations, such as equations involving squares of variables, may have no solution. For example, the equation $x^2 = -2$ has no solutions in the real numbers because the square of a real number must be positive. Similarly, $|x| = -1$ has no solution because the absolute value of a number is always positive.

It is also possible for a linear equation to have no solution. We call such an equation a **contradiction**. We discover that a linear equation is a contradiction when our attempts to isolate the variable cause the variable to disappear, leaving a *false* equation involving only constants. For example, the equation $2(x + 3) + x = 3x$ has no solution. We can see this by trying to solve it: first we distribute, leaving $2x + 6 + x = 3x$. Combining like terms gives us $3x + 6 = 3x$, and cancelling the term $3x$ on both sides leaves us with $6 = 0$. This is clearly false, so the original equation is a contradiction, having no solutions.

Features of Equations That Require Special Treatment

A linear equation is an equation in which variables only appear by themselves: not multiplied together, not with exponents other than one, and not inside absolute value signs or any other functions. For example, the equation $x + 1 - 3x = 5 - x$ is a linear equation; while x appears multiple times, it never appears with an exponent other than one, or inside any function. The two-variable equation $2x - 3y = 5 + 2x$ is also a linear equation. In contrast, the equation $x^2 - 5 = 3x$ is *not* a linear equation, because it involves the term x^2. The equation $\sqrt{x} = 5$ is not linear, because it involves a square root. The equation $(x - 1)^2 = 4$ is not linear because even though there's no exponent on the x directly, it appears as part of an expression that is squared. The two-variable equation $x + xy - y = 5$ is not linear because it includes the term xy, where two variables are multiplied together.

As we see above, linear equations can always be solved (or shown to have no solution) by combining like terms and performing simple operations on both sides of the equation. Some non-linear equations can be solved by similar methods, but others may require more advanced methods of solution, if they can be solved analytically at all.

Solving Equations Involving Roots

In an equation involving roots, the first step is to isolate the term with the root, if possible, and then raise both sides of the equation to the appropriate power to eliminate it. Consider an example equation, $2\sqrt{x+1} - 1 = 3$. In this case, begin by adding 1 to both sides, yielding $2\sqrt{x+1} = 4$, and then dividing both sides by 2, yielding $\sqrt{x+1} = 2$. Now square both sides, yielding $x + 1 = 4$. Finally, subtracting 1 from both sides yields $x = 3$.

Squaring both sides of an equation (or raising both sides to any *even* power) may, however, yield a spurious solution—a solution to the squared equation that is *not* a solution of the original equation. It's therefore necessary to plug the solution back into the original equation to make sure it works. In this case, it does: $2\sqrt{3+1} - 1 = 2\sqrt{4} - 1 = 2(2) - 1 = 4 - 1 = 3$.

The same procedure applies for other roots as well. For example, given the equation $3 + \sqrt[3]{2x} = 5$, we can first subtract 3 from both sides, yielding $\sqrt[3]{2x} = 2$ and isolating the root. Raising both sides to the third power yields $2x = 2^3$; i.e., $2x = 8$. We can now divide both sides by 2 to get $x = 4$.

Review Video: Solving Equations Involving Roots
Visit mometrix.com/academy and enter code: 297670

Solving Equations with Exponents

In solving an equation with powers of a variable, sometimes it is possible to eliminate all but one term involving the variable. In that case, we can isolate the power of the variable and then take the appropriate root of both sides to eliminate the exponent. For instance, for the equation $2x^3 + 17 = 5x^3 - 7$, we can subtract $5x^3$ from both sides to get $-3x^3 + 17 = -7$, and then subtract 17 from both sides to get $-3x^3 = -24$. Finally, we can divide both sides by –3 to get $x^3 = 8$. Since this isolates the cube of the variable, we can take the cube root of both sides to get $x = \sqrt[3]{8} = 2$.

One important but often overlooked point is that equations with an exponent greater than 1 may have more than one answer. The solution to $x^2 = 9$ isn't simply $x = 3$; it's $x = \pm 3$ (that is, $x = 3$ or $x = -3$). For a slightly more complicated example, consider the equation $(x - 1)^2 - 1 = 3$. Adding 1 to both sides yields $(x - 1)^2 = 4$; taking the square root of both sides yields $x - 1 = 2$. We can then add 1 to both sides to get $x = 3$. However, there's a second solution. We also have the possibility that $x - 1 = -2$, in which case $x = -1$. Both $x = 3$ and $x = -1$ are valid solutions, as can be verified by substituting them both into the original equation.

Review Video: Solving Equations with Exponents
Visit mometrix.com/academy and enter code: 514557

Review Video: Adding and Subtracting with Exponents
Visit mometrix.com/academy and enter code: 875756

Solving Equations with Absolute Values

When solving an equation with an absolute value, the first step is to isolate the absolute value term. We then consider two possibilities: when the expression inside the absolute value is positive or when it is negative. In the former case, the expression in the absolute value equals the expression on the other side of the equation; in the latter, it equals the additive inverse of that expression—the expression times negative one. We consider each case separately and finally check for spurious solutions.

For instance, consider solving $|2x - 1| + x = 5$ for x. We can first isolate the absolute value by moving the x to the other side: $|2x - 1| = -x + 5$. Now, we have two possibilities. First, that $2x - 1$ is positive, and hence $2x - 1 = -x + 5$. Rearranging and combining like terms yields $3x = 6$, and hence $x = 2$. The other possibility is that $2x - 1$ is negative, and hence $2x - 1 = -(-x + 5) = x - 5$. In this case, rearranging and combining like terms yields $x = -4$. Substituting $x = 2$ and $x = -4$ back into the original equation, we see that they are both valid solutions.

Note that the absolute value of a sum or difference applies to the sum or difference as a whole, not to the individual terms; in general, $|2x - 1|$ is not equal to $|2x + 1|$ or to $|2x| - 1$.

Review Video: Solving Absolute Value Equations
Visit mometrix.com/academy and enter code: 501208

Extraneous Solutions

An **extraneous solution** may arise when we square both sides of an equation (or raise both sides to an even power) as a step in solving it or under certain other operations on the equation. It is a solution to the squared or otherwise modified equation that is *not* a solution of the original equation. To identify an extraneous solution, it's useful when you solve an equation involving roots or absolute values to plug the solution back into the original equation to make sure it's valid.

Two-Variable Equations

Similar to methods for a one-variable equation, solving a two-variable equation involves isolating a variable: manipulating the equation so that a variable appears by itself on one side of the equation, and not at all on the other side. However, in a two-variable equation, you will usually only be able to isolate one of the variables; the other variable may appear on the other side along with constant terms, or with exponents or other functions. If an equation has multiple variables, the problem should tell you which variable to isolate.

Review Video: Solving Equations with Variables on Both Sides
Visit mometrix.com/academy and enter code: 402497

Graphing Equations

Graphical Solutions to Equations

When equations are shown graphically, they are usually shown on a **Cartesian coordinate plane.** The Cartesian coordinate plane consists of two number lines placed perpendicular to each other and intersecting at the zero point, also known as the origin. The horizontal number line is known as the x-axis, with positive values to the right of the origin, and negative values to the left of the origin. The vertical number line is known as the y-axis, with positive values above the origin, and negative values below the origin. Any point on the plane can be identified by an ordered pair in the form (x, y), called coordinates. The x-value of the coordinate is called the abscissa, and the y-value of the coordinate is called the ordinate. The two number lines divide the plane into **four quadrants**: I, II, III, and IV.

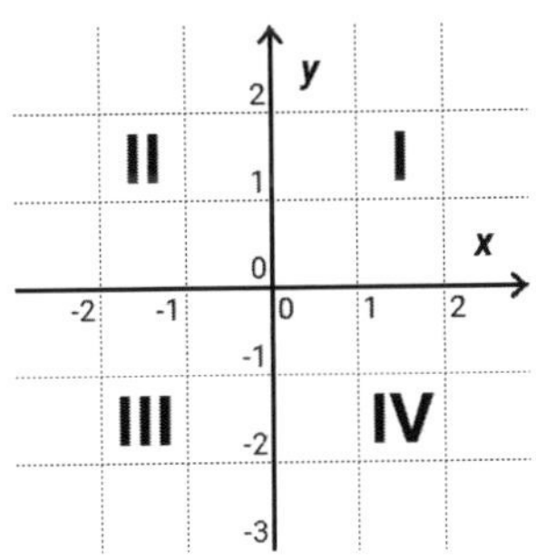

Note that in quadrant I $x > 0$ and $y > 0$, in quadrant II $x < 0$ and $y > 0$, in quadrant III $x < 0$ and $y < 0$, and in quadrant IV $x > 0$ and $y < 0$.

Recall that if the value of the slope of a line is positive, the line slopes upward from left to right. If the value of the slope is negative, the line slopes downward from left to right. If the y-coordinates are the same for two points on a line, the slope is 0 and the line is a **horizontal line**. If the x-coordinates are the same for two points on a line, there is no slope and the line is a **vertical line**.

Two or more lines that have equivalent slopes are **parallel lines**. **Perpendicular lines** have slopes that are negative reciprocals of each other, such as $\frac{a}{b}$ and $\frac{-b}{a}$.

Review Video: Cartesian Coordinate Plane and Graphing
Visit mometrix.com/academy and enter code: 115173

GRAPHING EQUATIONS IN TWO VARIABLES

One way of graphing an equation in two variables is to plot enough points to get an idea for its shape and then draw the appropriate curve through those points. A point can be plotted by substituting in a value for one variable and solving for the other. If the equation is linear, we only need two points and can then draw a straight line between them.

For example, consider the equation $y = 2x - 1$. This is a linear equation—both variables only appear raised to the first power—so we only need two points. When $x = 0, y = 2(0) - 1 = -1$. When $x = 2, y = 2(2) - 1 = 3$. We can therefore choose the points $(0, -1)$ and $(2, 3)$, and draw a line between them:

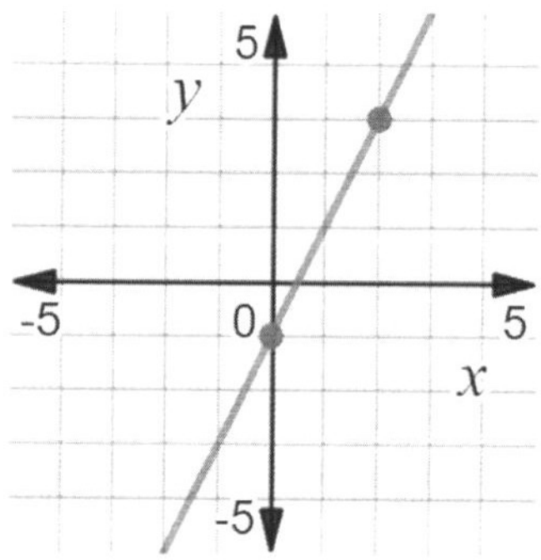

Inequalities

INEQUALITIES

Commonly in algebra and other upper-level fields of math you find yourself working with mathematical expressions that do not equal each other. The statement comparing such expressions with symbols such as $<$ (less than) or $>$ (greater than) is called an *inequality*. An example of an inequality is $7x > 5$. To solve for x, simply divide both sides by 7 and the solution is shown to be $x > \frac{5}{7}$. Graphs of the solution set of inequalities are represented on a number line. Open circles are used to show that an expression approaches a number but is never quite equal to that number.

Review Video: Solving One-Step Inequalities
Visit mometrix.com/academy and enter code: 229684

Review Video: Solving Multi-Step Inequalities
Visit mometrix.com/academy and enter code: 347842

Review Video: Solving Inequalities Using All 4 Basic Operations
Visit mometrix.com/academy and enter code: 401111

TYPES OF INEQUALITIES

Conditional inequalities are those with certain values for the variable that will make the condition true and other values for the variable where the condition will be false. **Absolute inequalities** can have any real number as the value for the variable to make the condition true, while there is no real number value for the variable that will make the condition false. Solving inequalities is done by following the same rules for solving equations with the exception that when multiplying or dividing by a negative number the direction of the inequality sign must be flipped or reversed. **Double inequalities** are situations where two inequality statements apply to the same variable expression. Example: $-c < ax + b < c$.

> **Review Video: Conditional and Absolute Inequalities**
> Visit mometrix.com/academy and enter code: 980164

SOLVING INEQUALITIES

DETERMINING SOLUTIONS TO INEQUALITIES

To determine whether a coordinate is a solution of an inequality, you can substitute the values of the coordinate into the inequality, simplify, and check whether the resulting statement holds true. For instance, to determine whether $(-2,4)$ is a solution of the inequality $y \geq -2x + 3$, substitute the values into the inequality, $4 \geq -2(-2) + 3$. Simplify the right side of the inequality and the result is $4 \geq 7$, which is a false statement. Therefore, the coordinate is not a solution of the inequality. You can also use this method to determine which part of the graph of an inequality is shaded. The graph of $y \geq -2x + 3$ includes the solid line $y = -2x + 3$ and, since it excludes the point $(-2,4)$ to the left of the line, it is shaded to the right of the line.

> **Review Video: Graphing Linear Inequalities**
> Visit mometrix.com/academy and enter code: 439421
>
> **Review Video: Graphing Solutions to Inequalities**
> Visit mometrix.com/academy and enter code: 391281

FLIPPING INEQUALITY SIGNS

When given an inequality, we can always turn the entire inequality around, swapping the two sides of the inequality and changing the inequality sign. For instance, $x + 2 > 2x - 3$ is equivalent to $2x - 3 < x + 2$. Aside from that, normally the inequality does not change if we carry out the same operation on both sides of the inequality. There is, however, one principal exception: if we *multiply* or *divide* both sides of the inequality by a *negative number*, the inequality is flipped. For example, if we take the inequality $-2x < 6$ and divide both sides by -2, the inequality flips and we are left with $x > -3$. This *only* applies to multiplication and division, and only with negative numbers. Multiplying or dividing both sides by a positive number, or adding or subtracting any number regardless of sign, does not flip the inequality. Another special case that flips the inequality sign is when reciprocals are used. For instance, $3 > 2$ but the relation of the reciprocals is $\frac{1}{3} < \frac{1}{2}$.

COMPOUND INEQUALITIES

A **compound inequality** is an equality that consists of two inequalities combined with *and* or *or*. The two components of a proper compound inequality must be of opposite type: that is, one must be greater than (or greater than or equal to), the other less than (or less than or equal to). For instance, "$x + 1 < 2$ or $x + 1 > 3$" is a compound inequality, as is "$2x \geq 4$ and $2x \leq 6$." An *and* inequality can be written more compactly by having one inequality on each side of the common part: "$2x \geq 1$ and $2x \leq 6$," can also be written as $1 \leq 2x \leq 6$.

In order for the compound inequality to be meaningful, the two parts of an *and* inequality must overlap; otherwise, no numbers satisfy the inequality. On the other hand, if the two parts of an *or* inequality overlap, then *all* numbers satisfy the inequality and as such the inequality is usually not meaningful.

Solving a compound inequality requires solving each part separately. For example, given the compound inequality "$x + 1 < 2$ or $x + 1 > 3$," the first inequality, $x + 1 < 2$, reduces to $x < 1$, and the second part, $x + 1 > 3$, reduces to $x > 2$, so the whole compound inequality can be written as "$x < 1$ or $x > 2$." Similarly, $1 \leq 2x \leq 6$ can be solved by dividing each term by 2, yielding $\frac{1}{2} \leq x \leq 3$.

Review Video: Compound Inequalities
Visit mometrix.com/academy and enter code: 786318

Solving Inequalities Involving Absolute Values

To solve an inequality involving an absolute value, first isolate the term with the absolute value. Then proceed to treat the two cases separately as with an absolute value equation, but flipping the inequality in the case where the expression in the absolute value is negative (since that essentially involves multiplying both sides by −1.) The two cases are then combined into a compound inequality; if the absolute value is on the greater side of the inequality, then it is an *or* compound inequality, if on the lesser side, then it's an *and.*

Consider the inequality $2 + |x - 1| \geq 3$. We can isolate the absolute value term by subtracting 2 from both sides: $|x - 1| \geq 1$. Now, we're left with the two cases $x - 1 \geq 1$ or $x - 1 \leq -1$: note that in the latter, negative case, the inequality is flipped. $x - 1 \geq 1$ reduces to $x \geq 2$, and $x - 1 \leq -1$ reduces to $x \leq 0$. Since in the inequality $|x - 1| \geq 1$ the absolute value is on the greater side, the two cases combine into an *or* compound inequality, so the final, solved inequality is "$x \leq 0$ or $x \geq 2$."

Review Video: Solving Absolute Value Inequalities
Visit mometrix.com/academy and enter code: 997008

Solving Inequalities Involving Square Roots

Solving an inequality with a square root involves two parts. First, we solve the inequality as if it were an equation, isolating the square root and then squaring both sides of the equation. Second, we restrict the solution to the set of values of x for which the value inside the square root sign is non-negative.

For example, in the inequality, $\sqrt{x - 2} + 1 < 5$, we can isolate the square root by subtracting 1 from both sides, yielding $\sqrt{x - 2} < 4$. Squaring both sides of the inequality yields $x - 2 < 16$, so $x < 18$. Since we can't take the square root of a negative number, we also require the part inside the square root to be non-negative. In this case, that means $x - 2 \geq 0$. Adding 2 to both sides of the inequality yields $x \geq 2$. Our final answer is a compound inequality combining the two simple inequalities: $x \geq 2$ and $x < 18$, or $2 \leq x < 18$.

Note that we only get a compound inequality if the two simple inequalities are in opposite directions; otherwise, we take the one that is more restrictive.

The same technique can be used for other even roots, such as fourth roots. It is *not*, however, used for cube roots or other odd roots—negative numbers *do* have cube roots, so the condition that the quantity inside the root sign cannot be negative does not apply.

Review Video: Solving Inequalities Involving Square Roots
Visit mometrix.com/academy and enter code: 800288

SPECIAL CIRCUMSTANCES

Sometimes an inequality involving an absolute value or an even exponent is true for all values of x, and we don't need to do any further work to solve it. This is true if the inequality, once the absolute value or exponent term is isolated, says that term is greater than a negative number (or greater than or equal to zero). Since an absolute value or a number raised to an even exponent is *always* non-negative, this inequality is always true.

GRAPHING INEQUALITIES

GRAPHING SIMPLE INEQUALITIES

To graph a simple inequality, we first mark on the number line the value that signifies the end point of the inequality. If the inequality is strict (involves a less than or greater than), we use a hollow circle; if it is not strict (less than or equal to or greater than or equal to), we use a solid circle. We then fill in the part of the number line that satisfies the inequality: to the left of the marked point for less than (or less than or equal to), to the right for greater than (or greater than or equal to).

For example, we would graph the inequality $x < 5$ by putting a hollow circle at 5 and filling in the part of the line to the left:

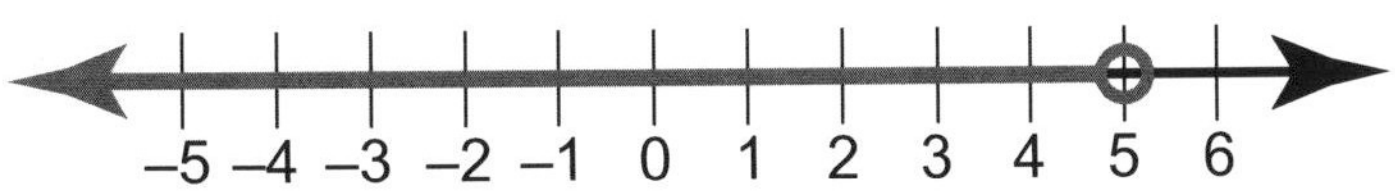

GRAPHING COMPOUND INEQUALITIES

To graph a compound inequality, we fill in both parts of the inequality for an *or* inequality, or the overlap between them for an *and* inequality. More specifically, we start by plotting the endpoints of each inequality on the number line. For an *or* inequality, we then fill in the appropriate side of the line for each inequality. Typically, the two component inequalities do not overlap, which means the shaded part is *outside* the two points. For an *and* inequality, we instead fill in the part of the line that meets both inequalities.

For the inequality "$x \leq -3$ or $x > 4$," we first put a solid circle at –3 and a hollow circle at 4. We then fill the parts of the line *outside* these circles:

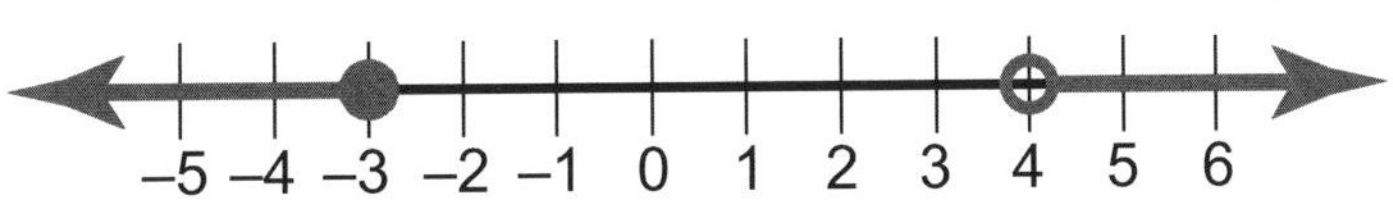

GRAPHING INEQUALITIES INCLUDING ABSOLUTE VALUES

An inequality with an absolute value can be converted to a compound inequality. To graph the inequality, first convert it to a compound inequality, and then graph that normally. If the absolute value is on the greater side of the inequality, we end up with an *or* inequality; we plot the endpoints of the inequality on the number line and fill in the part of the line *outside* those points. If the absolute value is on the smaller side of the inequality, we end up with an *and* inequality; we plot the endpoints of the inequality on the number line and fill in the part of the line *between* those points.

For example, the inequality $|x + 1| \geq 4$ can be rewritten as $x \geq 3$ or $x \leq -5$. We place solid circles at the points 3 and -5 and fill in the part of the line *outside* them:

GRAPHING INEQUALITIES IN TWO VARIABLES

To graph an inequality in two variables, we first graph the border of the inequality. This means graphing the equation that we get if we replace the inequality sign with an equals sign. If the inequality is strict ($>$ or $<$), we graph the border with a dashed or dotted line; if it is not strict ($\geq$ or $\leq$), we use a solid line. We can then test any point not on the border to see if it satisfies the inequality. If it does, we shade in that side of the border; if not, we shade in the other side. As an example, consider $y > 2x + 2$. To graph this inequality, we first graph the border, $y = 2x + 2$. Since it is a strict inequality, we use a dashed line. Then, we choose a test point. This can be any point not on the border; in this case, we will choose the origin, (0,0). (This makes the calculation easy and is generally a good choice unless the border passes through the origin.) Putting this into the original inequality, we get $0 > 2(0) + 2$, i.e., $0 > 2$. This is *not* true, so we shade in the side of the border that does *not* include the point (0,0):

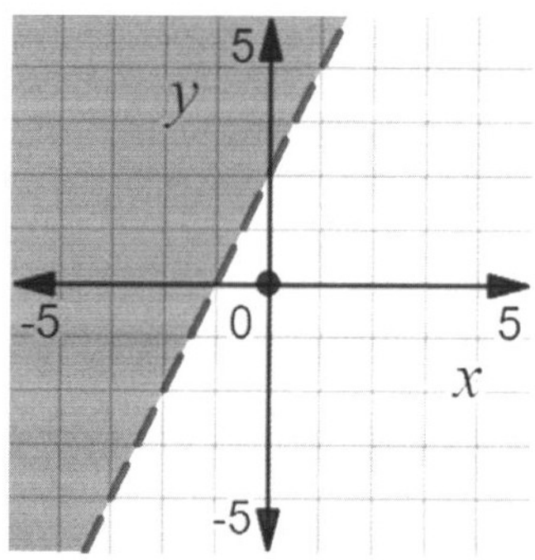

GRAPHING COMPOUND INEQUALITIES IN TWO VARIABLES

One way to graph a compound inequality in two variables is to first graph each of the component inequalities. For an *and* inequality, we then shade in only the parts where the two graphs overlap; for an *or* inequality, we shade in any region that pertains to either of the individual inequalities.

Consider the graph of "$y \geq x - 1$ and $y \leq -x$":

We first shade in the individual inequalities:

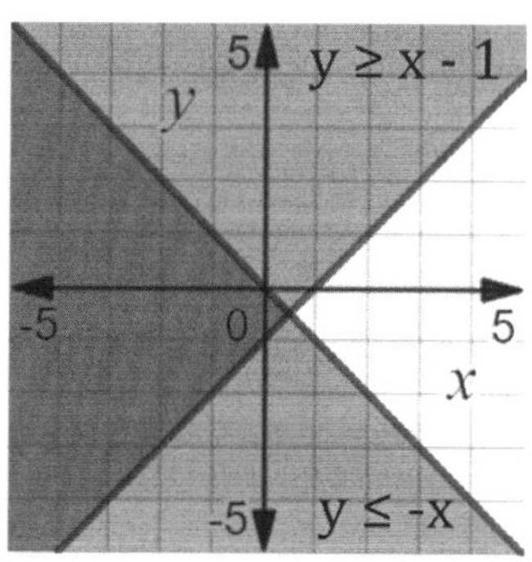

Now, since the compound inequality has an *and*, we only leave shaded the overlap—the part that pertains to *both* inequalities:

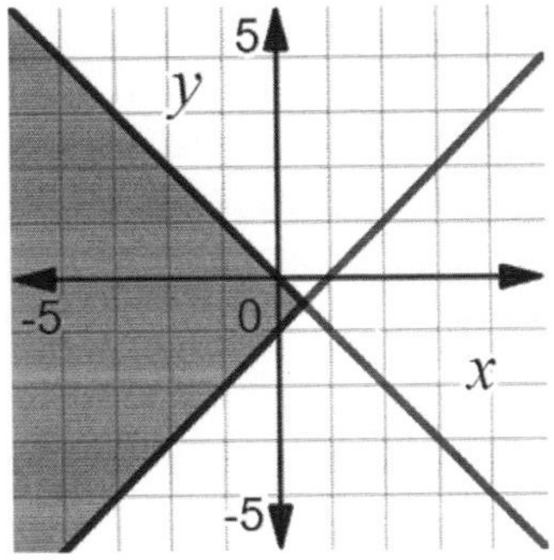

If instead the inequality had been "$y \geq x - 1$ or $y \leq -x$," our final graph would involve the *total* shaded area:

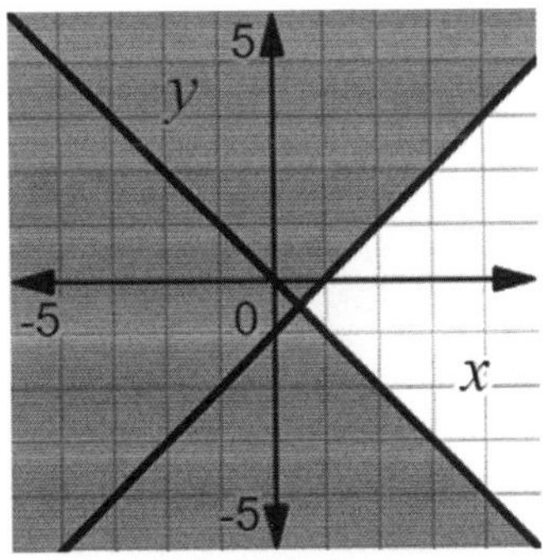

Review Video: Graphing Solutions to Inequalities
Visit mometrix.com/academy and enter code: 391281

Advanced Expressions and Equations

Systems of Equations

Solving Systems of Equations

A **system of equations** is a set of simultaneous equations that all use the same variables. A solution to a system of equations must be true for each equation in the system. **Consistent systems** are those with at least one solution. **Inconsistent systems** are systems of equations that have no solution.

Review Video: Solving Systems of Linear Equations
Visit mometrix.com/academy and enter code: 746745

Substitution

To solve a system of linear equations by **substitution**, start with the easier equation and solve for one of the variables. Express this variable in terms of the other variable. Substitute this expression in the other equation and solve for the other variable. The solution should be expressed in the form

(x, y). Substitute the values into both of the original equations to check your answer. Consider the following system of equations:

$$x + 6y = 15$$
$$3x - 12y = 18$$

Solving the first equation for x: $x = 15 - 6y$

Substitute this value in place of x in the second equation, and solve for y:

$$\begin{aligned} 3(15 - 6y) - 12y &= 18 \\ 45 - 18y - 12y &= 18 \\ 30y &= 27 \\ y &= \frac{27}{30} = \frac{9}{10} = 0.9 \end{aligned}$$

Plug this value for y back into the first equation to solve for x:

$$x = 15 - 6(0.9) = 15 - 5.4 = 9.6$$

Check both equations if you have time:

$$\begin{aligned} 9.6 + 6(0.9) &= 15 \\ 9.6 + 5.4 &= 15 \\ 15 &= 15 \end{aligned} \qquad \begin{aligned} 3(9.6) - 12(0.9) &= 18 \\ 28.8 - 10.8 &= 18 \\ 18 &= 18 \end{aligned}$$

Therefore, the solution is (9.6,0.9).

Review Video: The Substitution Method
Visit mometrix.com/academy and enter code: 565151

Review Video: Substitution and Elimination
Visit mometrix.com/academy and enter code: 958611

ELIMINATION

To solve a system of equations using **elimination**, begin by rewriting both equations in standard form $Ax + By = C$. Check to see if the coefficients of one pair of like variables add to zero. If not, multiply one or both of the equations by a non-zero number to make one set of like variables add to zero. Add the two equations to solve for one of the variables. Substitute this value into one of the original equations to solve for the other variable. Check your work by substituting into the other equation. Now, let's look at solving the following system using the elimination method:

$$5x + 6y = 4$$
$$x + 2y = 4$$

If we multiply the second equation by -3, we can eliminate the y-terms:

$$5x + 6y = 4$$
$$-3x - 6y = -12$$

Add the equations together and solve for x:

$$2x = -8$$
$$x = \frac{-8}{2} = -4$$

Plug the value for x back in to either of the original equations and solve for y:

$$-4 + 2y = 4$$
$$y = \frac{4+4}{2} = 4$$

Check both equations if you have time:

$$5(-4) + 6(4) = 4$$
$$-20 + 24 = 4$$
$$4 = 4$$

$$-4 + 2(4) = 4$$
$$-4 + 8 = 4$$
$$4 = 4$$

Therefore, the solution is $(-4,4)$.

Review Video: The Elimination Method
Visit mometrix.com/academy and enter code: 449121

GRAPHICALLY

To solve a system of linear equations **graphically**, plot both equations on the same graph. The solution of the equations is the point where both lines cross. If the lines do not cross (are parallel), then there is **no solution**.

For example, consider the following system of equations:

$$y = 2x + 7$$
$$y = -x + 1$$

Since these equations are given in slope-intercept form, they are easy to graph; the y-intercepts of the lines are (0,7) and (0,1). The respective slopes are 2 and –1, thus the graphs look like this:

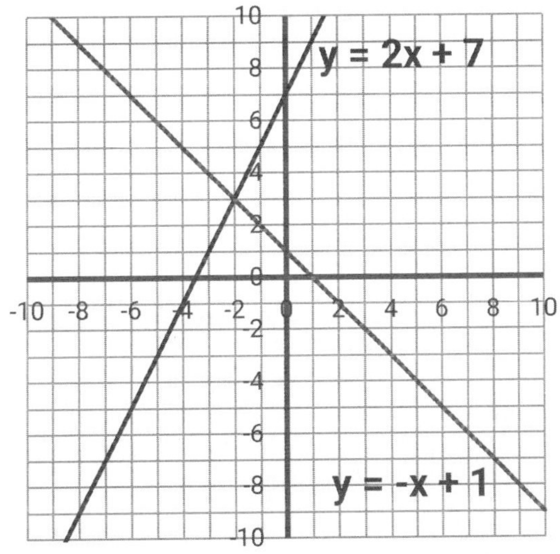

The two lines intersect at the point $(-2,3)$, thus this is the solution to the system of equations.

Solving a system graphically is generally only practical if both coordinates of the solution are integers; otherwise the intersection will lie between gridlines on the graph and the coordinates will be difficult or impossible to determine exactly. It also helps if, as in this example, the equations are in slope-intercept form or some other form that makes them easy to graph. Otherwise, another method of solution (by substitution or elimination) is likely to be more useful.

Review Video: Solving Systems by Graphing
Visit mometrix.com/academy and enter code: 634812

Solving Systems of Equations Using the Trace Feature

Using the trace feature on a calculator requires that you rewrite each equation, isolating the y-variable on one side of the equal sign. Enter both equations in the graphing calculator and plot the graphs simultaneously. Use the trace cursor to find where the two lines cross. Use the zoom feature if necessary to obtain more accurate results. Always check your answer by substituting into the original equations. The trace method is likely to be less accurate than other methods due to the resolution of graphing calculators but is a useful tool to provide an approximate answer.

Advanced Systems of Equations

Solving a System of Equations with a Linear Equation and a Quadratic Equation

Algebraically

Generally, the simplest way to solve a system of equations consisting of a linear equation and a quadratic equation algebraically is through the method of substitution. One possible strategy is to solve the linear equation for y and then substitute that expression into the quadratic equation. After expansion and combining like terms, this will result in a new quadratic equation for x, which, like all quadratic equations, may have zero, one, or two solutions. Plugging each solution for x back into one of the original equations will then produce the corresponding value of y.

For example, consider the following system of equations:

$$x + y = 1$$
$$y = (x+3)^2 - 2$$

We can solve the linear equation for y to yield $y = -x + 1$. Substituting this expression into the quadratic equation produces $-x + 1 = (x+3)^2 - 2$. We can simplify this equation:

$$\begin{aligned} -x + 1 &= (x+3)^2 - 2 \\ -x + 1 &= x^2 + 6x + 9 - 2 \\ -x + 1 &= x^2 + 6x + 7 \\ 0 &= x^2 + 7x + 6 \end{aligned}$$

This quadratic equation can be factored as $(x+1)(x+6) = 0$. It therefore has two solutions: $x_1 = -1$ and $x_2 = -6$. Plugging each of these back into the original linear equation yields $y_1 = -x_1 + 1 = -(-1) + 1 = 2$ and $y_2 = -x_2 + 1 = -(-6) + 1 = 7$. Thus, this system of equations has two solutions, $(-1,2)$ and $(-6,7)$.

It may help to check your work by putting each x- and y-value back into the original equations and verifying that they do provide a solution.

GRAPHICALLY

To solve a system of equations consisting of a linear equation and a quadratic equation graphically, plot both equations on the same graph. The linear equation will, of course, produce a straight line, while the quadratic equation will produce a parabola. These two graphs will intersect at zero, one, or two points; each point of intersection is a solution of the system.

For example, consider the following system of equations:

$$y = -2x + 2$$
$$y = -2x^2 + 4x + 2$$

The linear equation describes a line with a y-intercept of $(0,2)$ and a slope of -2.

To graph the quadratic equation, we can first find the vertex of the parabola: the x-coordinate of the vertex is $h = -\frac{b}{2a} = -\frac{4}{2(-2)} = 1$, and the y-coordinate is $k = -2(1)^2 + 4(1) + 2 = 4$. Thus, the vertex lies at $(1,4)$. To get a feel for the rest of the parabola, we can plug in a few more values of x to find more points; by putting in $x = 2$ and $x = 3$ in the quadratic equation, we find that the points $(2,2)$ and $(3,-4)$ lie on the parabola; by symmetry, so must $(0,2)$ and $(-1,-4)$. We can now plot both equations:

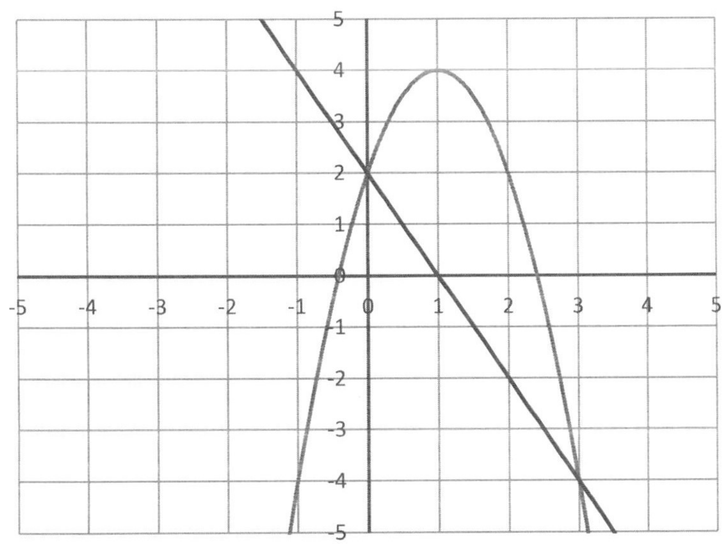

These two curves intersect at the points $(0,2)$ and $(3,-4)$, thus these are the solutions of the equation.

> **Review Video: Parabolas**
> Visit mometrix.com/academy and enter code: 129187
>
> **Review Video: Vertex of a Parabola**
> Visit mometrix.com/academy and enter code: 272300
>
> **Review Video: Solving a System of Linear and Quadratic Equations**
> Visit mometrix.com/academy and enter code: 194870

MIDPOINT AND DISTANCE FORMULAS

If you know the coordinates of the endpoints of a line segment, you can calculate the midpoint and length of the line segment. Conveniently, the length of the line segment is also the distance between the two endpoints.

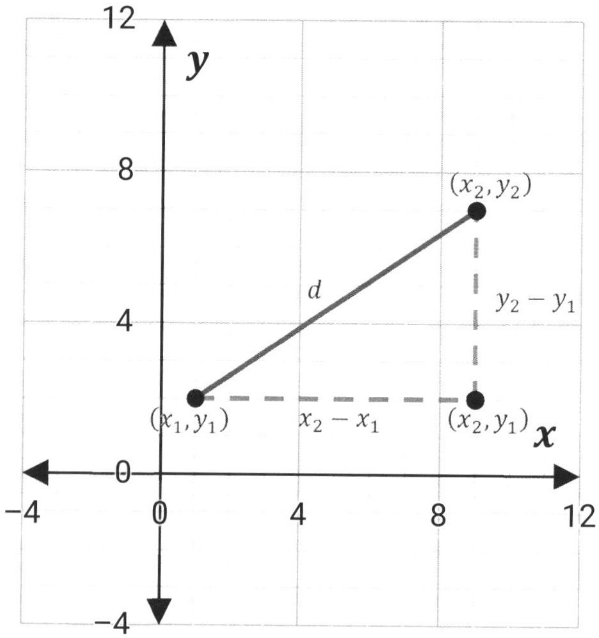

To find the **midpoint** of the line segment with endpoints (x_1, y_1) and (x_2, y_2), average the x-coordinates to get the x-coordinate of the midpoint, and average the y-coordinates to get the y-coordinate of the midpoint. Thus, the **midpoint formula** is:

$$\left(\frac{x_1 + x_2}{2}, \frac{y_1 + y_2}{2}\right)$$

The **distance** between points (x_1, y_1) and (x_2, y_2) is the same as the length of the hypotenuse of a right triangle with the two given points as endpoints, and the two sides of the right triangle parallel to the x-axis and y-axis, respectively. The length of the segment parallel to the x-axis is the difference between the x-coordinates of the two points. The length of the segment parallel to the y-axis is the difference between the y-coordinates of the two points. Use the Pythagorean theorem $a^2 + b^2 = c^2$ or $c = \sqrt{a^2 + b^2}$ to find the distance. Thus, the **distance formula** is:

$$d = \sqrt{(x_2 - x_1)^2 + (y_2 - y_1)^2}$$

Review Video: Calculations Using Points on a Graph
Visit mometrix.com/academy and enter code: 883228

Polynomials

Monomials and Polynomials

A **monomial** is a single constant, variable, or product of constants and variables, such as 7, x, $2x$, or x^3y. There will never be addition or subtraction symbols in a monomial. Like monomials have like variables, but they may have different coefficients. A **polynomial** is a monomial or the result of combining two or more monomials by sums or differences. In a polynomial we call each monomial a **term**. Two terms make a **binomial** (e.g., $2x + 3y$), three terms make a **trinomial** (e.g., $5x^2 - 4x + 9$). The **degree of a monomial** is the sum of the exponents of the variables. The **degree of a polynomial** is the highest degree of any individual term.

> **Review Video: Polynomials**
> Visit mometrix.com/academy and enter code: 305005

Simplifying Polynomials

Simplifying polynomials requires combining like terms. The like terms in a polynomial expression are those that have the same variables raised to the same powers. It is often helpful to connect the like terms with arrows or lines in order to separate them from the other monomials. Once you have determined the like terms, you can rearrange the polynomial by placing them together. Remember to include the sign that is in front of each term. Once the like terms are placed together, you can apply each operation and simplify. When adding and subtracting polynomials, only add and subtract the **coefficients**, or the number part; the variable and exponent stay the same.

Adding Polynomials

To add polynomials, you need to add like terms. These terms have the same variable part. For example, the terms $4x^2$ and $3x^2$ both include x^2 terms. To find the sum of like terms, find the sum of the coefficients. Then, keep the same variable part. You can use the distributive property to distribute the plus sign to each term of the polynomial. For example:

$$(4x^2 - 5x + 7) + (3x^2 + 2x + 1) =$$
$$(4x^2 - 5x + 7) + 3x^2 + 2x + 1 =$$
$$(4x^2 + 3x^2) + (-5x + 2x) + (7 + 1) =$$
$$7x^2 - 3x + 8$$

Subtracting Polynomials

To subtract polynomials, you need to subtract like terms. To find the difference of like terms, find the difference of the coefficients. Then, keep the same variable part. You can use the distributive property to distribute the minus sign to each term of the polynomial. For example:

$$(-2x^2 - x + 5) - (3x^2 - 4x + 1) =$$
$$(-2x^2 - x + 5) - 3x^2 + 4x - 1 =$$
$$(-2x^2 - 3x^2) + (-x + 4x) + (5 - 1) =$$
$$-5x^2 + 3x + 4$$

> **Review Video: Adding and Subtracting Polynomials**
> Visit mometrix.com/academy and enter code: 124088

Multiplying Polynomials

In general, multiplying polynomials is done by multiplying each term in one polynomial by each term in the other and adding the results. In the specific case for multiplying binomials, there is a useful acronym, FOIL, that can help you make sure to cover each combination of terms. The **FOIL method** for $(Ax + By)(Cx + Dy)$ would be:

F	Multiply the *first* terms of each binomial	$(\overbrace{Ax}^{first} + By)(\overbrace{Cx}^{first} + Dy)$	ACx^2
O	Multiply the *outer* terms	$(\overbrace{Ax}^{outer} + By)(Cx + \overbrace{Dy}^{outer})$	$ADxy$
I	Multiply the *inner* terms	$(Ax + \overbrace{By}^{inner})(\overbrace{Cx}^{inner} + Dy)$	$BCxy$
L	Multiply the *last* terms of each binomial	$(Ax + \overbrace{By}^{last})(Cx + \overbrace{Dy}^{last})$	BDy^2

Then, add up the result of each and combine like terms: $ACx^2 + (AD + BC)xy + BDy^2$.

For example, using the FOIL method on binomials $(x + 2)$ and $(x - 3)$:

$$\begin{aligned}
&\text{First: } (\boxed{x} + 2)(\boxed{x} + (-3)) \rightarrow (x)(x) = x^2 \\
&\text{Outer: } (\boxed{x} + 2)(x + \boxed{(-3)}) \rightarrow (x)(-3) = -3x \\
&\text{Inner: } (x + \boxed{2})(\boxed{x} + (-3)) \rightarrow (2)(x) = 2x \\
&\text{Last: } (x + \boxed{2})(x + \boxed{(-3)}) \rightarrow (2)(-3) = -6
\end{aligned}$$

This results in: $(x^2) + (-3x) + (2x) + (-6)$

Combine like terms: $x^2 + (-3 + 2)x + (-6) = x^2 - x - 6$

> **Review Video: Multiplying Polynomials**
> Visit mometrix.com/academy and enter code: 598293
>
> **Review Video: Multiplying Terms Using the FOIL Method**
> Visit mometrix.com/academy and enter code: 854792

DIVIDING POLYNOMIALS

Use long division to divide a polynomial by either a monomial or another polynomial of equal or lesser degree.

When **dividing by a monomial**, divide each term of the polynomial by the monomial.

> **Review Video: Dividing Monomials**
> Visit mometrix.com/academy and enter code: 584409

When **dividing by a polynomial**, begin by arranging the terms of each polynomial in order of one variable. You may arrange in ascending or descending order, but be consistent with both polynomials. To get the first term of the quotient, divide the first term of the dividend by the first term of the divisor. Multiply the first term of the quotient by the entire divisor and subtract that product from the dividend. Repeat for the second and successive terms until you either get a remainder of zero or a remainder whose degree is less than the degree of the divisor. If the quotient has a remainder, write the answer as a mixed expression in the form:

$$\text{quotient} + \frac{\text{remainder}}{\text{divisor}}$$

For example, we can evaluate the following expression in the same way as long division:

$$\frac{x^3 - 3x^2 - 2x + 5}{x - 5}$$

$$\begin{array}{r}
x^2 \quad + 2x \quad + 8 \\
x - 5 \overline{) \; x^3 - 3x^2 \quad - 2x \quad + 5} \\
\underline{-(x^3 - 5x^2)} \qquad\qquad\quad \\
2x^2 \quad - 2x \qquad\quad \\
\underline{-(2x^2 - 10x)} \qquad\quad \\
8x \quad + 5 \\
\underline{-(8x - 40)} \\
45
\end{array}$$

$$\frac{x^3 - 3x^2 - 2x + 5}{x - 5} = x^2 + 2x + 8 + \frac{45}{x - 5}$$

Review Video: Dividing Polynomials by Monomials
Visit mometrix.com/academy and enter code: 253551

Review Video: Dividing Trinomials by Binomials
Visit mometrix.com/academy and enter code: 651465

When **factoring** a polynomial, first see whether you can factor out a nontrivial greatest common factor (GCF). For example, the trinomial $3x^5 - 18x^4 + 15x^3$ has a GCF of $3x^3$ since the GCF of 3, 18, and 15 is 3 and the GCF of x^5, x^4, and x^3 is x^3. Factoring out the GCF simplifies the expression to $3x^3(x^2 - 6x + 5)$.

To factor a quadratic trinomial (this comes up frequently), first check whether it is a perfect square trinomial (see bulleted list below). If not, see if you can factor it by trial and error by making clever choices of values for a and b (or a, b, c, and d) in the formulas below (this amounts to trying to use the FOIL mnemonic backwards):

$$x^2 + (a + b)x + ab = (x + a)(x + b)$$
$$(ac)x^2 + (ad + bc)x + bd = (ax + b)(cx + d)$$

For instance, you would try to factor the trinomial $x^2 - 6x + 5$ using the equation $x^2 + (a + b)x + ab = (x + a)(x + b)$. This means that you need to find integers a and b such that $a + b = -6$ and $ab = 5$. Starting with $ab = 5$, you can see that the only ways to write 5 as a product of integers are $(1)(5) = 5$ and $(-1)(-5) = 5$. So, it is easy to see that you want $a = -1$ and $b = -5$ since $a + b = -1 + (-5) = -6$ and $ab = (-1)(-5) = 5$. This tells you that $x^2 - 6x + 5 = (x - 1)(x - 5)$.

For polynomials with four terms (usually a cubic polynomial), sometimes factoring by grouping works: You group the two higher-power terms and the two lower-power terms, factor the GCF out of each group, and then factor out the resulting common binomial factor, if there is one. For example, $x^3 + 5x^2 + 3x + 15 = (x^3 + 5x^2) + (3x + 15) = x^2(x + 5) + 3(x + 5) = (x^2 + 3)(x + 5)$.

Once you have found the factors, write the original polynomial as the product of all the factors. Make sure all of the factors are either monomials, or else linear or irreducible quadratic polynomials (*irreducible* means they have no real zeros, which is easy to check with the quadratic formula). Check your work by multiplying the factors to make sure you get the original polynomial.

Review Video: Factoring Out Common Monomial Factors
Visit mometrix.com/academy and enter code: 398578

Review Video: Factoring Trinomials of the Form x^2+bx+c
Visit mometrix.com/academy and enter code: 270556

Below are patterns of some special products to remember to help make factoring easier:

- Perfect square trinomials: $x^2 + 2xy + y^2 = (x + y)^2$ or $x^2 - 2xy + y^2 = (x - y)^2$. For example, $x^2 + 10x + 25 = (x + 5)^2$.
- Difference between two squares: $x^2 - y^2 = (x + y)(x - y)$. For example, $x^2 - 9 = (x + 3)(x - 3)$.
- Sum of two cubes: $x^3 + y^3 = (x + y)(x^2 - xy + y^2)$. For example, $x^3 + 27 = (x + 3)(x^2 - 3x + 9)$.
    - Note: the second factor is *not* the same as a perfect square trinomial, so do not try to factor it further.
- Difference between two cubes: $x^3 - y^3 = (x - y)(x^2 + xy + y^2)$. For example, $x^3 - 1000 = (x - 10)(x^2 + 10x + 100)$.
    - Again, the second factor is *not* the same as a perfect square trinomial.
- Perfect cubes: $x^3 + 3x^2y + 3xy^2 + y^3 = (x + y)^3$ and $x^3 - 3x^2y + 3xy^2 - y^3 = (x - y)^3$

Review Video: Factoring the Difference of Two Squares
Visit mometrix.com/academy and enter code: 128954

Rational and Irrational Expressions

Rational Expressions

Rational expressions are fractions with polynomials in both the numerator and the denominator; the value of the polynomial in the denominator cannot be equal to zero. Be sure to keep track of values that make the denominator of the original expression zero as the final result inherits the same restrictions. For example, a denominator of $x - 3$ indicates that the expression is not defined when $x = 3$ and, as such, regardless of any operations done to the expression, it remains undefined there.

To **add or subtract** rational expressions, first find the common denominator, then rewrite each fraction as an equivalent fraction with the common denominator. Finally, add or subtract the numerators to get the numerator of the answer, and keep the common denominator as the denominator of the answer.

When **multiplying** rational expressions, factor each polynomial and cancel like factors (a factor which appears in both the numerator and the denominator). Then, multiply all remaining factors in the numerator to get the numerator of the product, and multiply the remaining factors in the denominator to get the denominator of the product. Remember: cancel entire factors, not individual terms.

To **divide** rational expressions, take the reciprocal of the divisor (the rational expression you are dividing by) and multiply by the dividend.

Review Video: Rational Expressions
Visit mometrix.com/academy and enter code: 415183

Simplifying Rational Expressions

To simplify a rational expression, factor the numerator and denominator completely. Factors that are the same and appear in the numerator and denominator have a ratio of 1. For example, look at the following expression:

$$\frac{x-1}{1-x^2}$$

The denominator, $(1-x^2)$, is a difference of squares. It can be factored as $(1-x)(1+x)$. The factor $1-x$ and the numerator $x-1$ are opposites and have a ratio of -1. Rewrite the numerator as $-1(1-x)$. So, the rational expression can be simplified as follows:

$$\frac{x-1}{1-x^2}=\frac{-1(1-x)}{(1-x)(1+x)}=\frac{-1}{1+x}$$

Note that since the original expression is only defined for $x \neq \{-1, 1\}$, the simplified expression has the same restrictions.

Review Video: Reducing Rational Expressions
Visit mometrix.com/academy and enter code: 788868

Review Video: Simplifying Algebraic Expressions with Parentheses
Visit mometrix.com/academy and enter code: 850843

Irrational Expressions

Irrational expressions are mathematical expressions that contain an irrational number and cannot be simplified into a rational form. Usually, this includes expressions that contain radicals or constants such as π. Most commonly, you will encounter these in the forms of expressions containing roots of non-perfect squares.

Basic Operations on Radical Expressions

To add or subtract radical numbers, the numbers within the radicals must match, similar to finding a common denominator in fractions:

$$a\sqrt{x}+b\sqrt{x}=(a+b)\sqrt{x}$$

$$a\sqrt{x}-b\sqrt{x}=(a-b)\sqrt{x}$$

To multiply radicals, the numbers outside the radical are multiplied together and the numbers inside the radical are multiplied together:

$$a\sqrt{x}\times b\sqrt{y}=ab\sqrt{xy}$$

To divide radicals, the radical must be eliminated from the denominator by multiplying both numerator and denominator by a value that will make the denominator a rational number:

$$\frac{a\sqrt{x}}{b\sqrt{y}} = \frac{a\sqrt{x}\sqrt{y}}{b\sqrt{y}\sqrt{y}} = \frac{a\sqrt{xy}}{by}$$

Review Video: Adding and Subtracting Radical Expressions
Visit mometrix.com/academy and enter code: 752176

EXAMPLE

To solve $\frac{(3\sqrt{6})(2\sqrt{3})}{4\sqrt{5}}$, we first multiply the numerator, inside the radical and out: $3 \times 2\sqrt{6 \times 3} = 6\sqrt{18} = 18\sqrt{2}$. To divide, we multiply both numerator and denominator by a value that will eliminate the radical:

$$\frac{18\sqrt{2} \times \sqrt{5}}{4\sqrt{5} \times \sqrt{5}} = \frac{18\sqrt{10}}{4 \times 5} = \frac{18\sqrt{10}}{20} = \frac{9\sqrt{10}}{10}$$

ALGEBRAIC THEOREMS

According to the **fundamental theorem of algebra**, every non-constant, single-variable polynomial has exactly as many roots as the polynomial's highest exponent. For example, if x^4 is the largest exponent of a term, the polynomial will have exactly 4 roots. However, some of these roots may have multiplicity or be complex numbers. For instance, in the polynomial function $f(x) = x^4 - 4x + 3$, the only real root is 1, though it has multiplicity of 2 – that is, it occurs twice. The other two roots, $(-1 - i\sqrt{2})$ and $(-1 + i\sqrt{2})$, are complex, consisting of both real and non-real components.

The **remainder theorem** is useful for determining the remainder when a polynomial is divided by a binomial. The remainder theorem states that if a polynomial function $f(x)$ is divided by a binomial $x - a$, where a is a real number, the remainder of the division will be the value of $f(a)$. If $f(a) = 0$, then a is a root of the polynomial.

The **factor theorem** is related to the remainder theorem and states that if $f(a) = 0$ then $(x - a)$ is a factor of the function.

According to the **rational root theorem,** any rational root of a polynomial function $f(x) = a_nx^n + a_{n-1}x^{n-1} + \cdots + a_1x + a_0$ with integer coefficients will, when reduced to its lowest terms, be a positive or negative fraction such that the numerator is a factor of a_0 and the denominator is a factor of a_n. For instance, if the polynomial function $f(x) = x^3 + 3x^2 - 4$ has any rational roots, the numerators of those roots can only be factors of 4 (1, 2, 4), and the denominators can only be factors of 1 (1). The function in this example has roots of 1 (or $\frac{1}{1}$) and -2 (or $\frac{-2}{1}$).

QUADRATICS

SOLVING QUADRATIC EQUATIONS

A quadratic equation is an equation that can be written (possibly after simplification) in the form $ax^2 + bx + c = 0$. Thus, the **solutions** of this equation are precisely the **zeros** of the quadratic polynomial $P(x) = ax^2 + bx + c$. On the graph of this polynomial the zeros, if any, appear as

x-intercepts. There are several ways to find these solutions including the quadratic formula, factoring, completing the square, and graphing the function.

Review Video: Quadratic Equations Overview
Visit mometrix.com/academy and enter code: 476276

Review Video: Solutions of a Quadratic Equation on a Graph
Visit mometrix.com/academy and enter code: 328231

Quadratic Formula

The **quadratic formula** gives the zeros of a quadratic polynomial. It always works, but it is sometimes a little harder to use than other methods. To use it to solve a quadratic equation, rewrite the equation in the form $ax^2 + bx + c = 0$, where a, b, and c are coefficients. Now, as explained above, the solutions of the equation are the zeros of the quadratic polynomial $P(x) = ax^2 + bx + c$. To find them, substitute the values of a, b, and c into the Quadratic Formula:

$$x = \frac{-b \pm \sqrt{b^2 - 4ac}}{2a}$$

After simplification this formula produces two, one, or zero real solutions, depending on whether the **discriminant** (the number $b^2 - 4ac$ under the radical) is positive, zero, or negative. It is a good practice to check each solution by substituting it into the original equation. Incidentally, if the discriminant is negative, then the equation does have two complex solutions, but you often ignore these as meaningless in real-world settings.

Review Video: Using the Quadratic Formula
Visit mometrix.com/academy and enter code: 163102

Factoring

To solve a quadratic equation by factoring, begin by rewriting the equation in the standard form, $ax^2 + bx + c = 0$. In the important special case that $a = 1$, the goal of factoring is to find numbers f and g such that $x^2 + bx + c = (x + f)(x + g) = x^2 + (f + g)x + fg$. In other words, you want to choose f and g to make $fg = c$ and $f + g = b$. To do this, find pairs of numbers (factors) whose product is c and look for a pair whose sum is b.

For example, suppose you want to find the solutions of the equation $x^2 + 6x - 16 = 0$ by factoring. Here $b = 6$ and $c = -16$. First, you find the pairs of numbers whose product is -16. These are -4 and 4, -8 and 2, -2 and 8, -1 and 16, and 1 and -16. The pair -2 and 8 has a sum of 6. This means $f = -2$ and $g = 8$. So, the factorization is $x^2 + 6x - 16 = (x + f)(x + g) = (x - 2)(x + 8)$, allowing you to rewrite the original equation as $(x - 2)(x + 8) = 0$. The only way for a product to equal zero is for one of the factors to equal zero; so, either $x - 2 = 0$ (in which case $x = 2$) or $x + 8 = 0$ (in which case $x = -8$). Thus, the equation has the solution $x = 2$ or $x = -8$.

In the case that $a \neq 1$, you can attempt to factor the quadratic polynomial $ax^2 + bx + c$ in the form $(mx + f)(nx + g)$ by a similar trial-and-error procedure, but the work tends to be much harder.

Review Video: Factoring Quadratic Equations
Visit mometrix.com/academy and enter code: 336566

COMPLETING THE SQUARE

The technique of completing the square comes from a simple observation: Suppose you have the expression $x^2 + bx$. If you take half the linear coefficient, b, square it, and add the result to the expression, the result is always a perfect square trinomial:

$$x^2 + bx + \left(\frac{b}{2}\right)^2 = \left(x + \frac{b}{2}\right)^2$$

For example, if you begin with $x^2 + 6x$ and add the square of half of 6 (half of 6 is 3, and $3^2 = 9$), then you get a perfect square trinomial:

$$x^2 + 6x + 9 = (x + 3)^2$$

This also works if b is negative. For instance, if you begin with the expression $x^2 - 10x$ and complete the square by adding 25 (half of -10 is -5, and $(-5)^2 = 25$), then you get another perfect square trinomial:

$$x^2 - 10x + 25 = (x - 5)^2$$

Now, suppose you want to solve the equation $x^2 + bx + c = 0$. Subtract c from both sides, to get the equation $x^2 + bx = -c$. Complete the square on the left side by adding $(b/2)^2$, but also add this same term to the right side so that the new equation is equivalent to the old one:

$$x^2 + bx + \left(\frac{b}{2}\right)^2 = -c + \left(\frac{b}{2}\right)^2$$
$$\left(x + \frac{b}{2}\right)^2 = -c + \left(\frac{b}{2}\right)^2$$

Take square roots of both sides:

$$x + \frac{b}{2} = \pm\sqrt{-c + \left(\frac{b}{2}\right)^2}$$

Remember to include $\pm$ since every positive number has both a positive and a negative square root. Subtract $b/2$ from both sides to isolate the variable x to finish the problem:

$$x = -\frac{b}{2} \pm \sqrt{-c + \left(\frac{b}{2}\right)^2}$$

This may sound complicated, but in practice it is not hard. For example, suppose you want to solve the equation $x^2 + 6x - 16 = 0$ by completing the square. First, add 16 to both sides:

$$x^2 + 6x = 16$$

Half of 6 is 3 and $3^2 = 9$, so complete the square by adding 9 to both sides of the equation:

$$x^2 + 6x + 9 = 16 + 9$$
$$(x + 3)^2 = 25$$

Now take square root of both sides, remembering to include the $\pm$:

$$\sqrt{(x+3)^2} = \pm\sqrt{25}$$
$$x + 3 = \pm 5$$
$$x = -3 \pm 5$$

So we see that the two solutions to the equation are $x = 2$ and $x = -8$.

Review Video: Completing the Square
Visit mometrix.com/academy and enter code: 982479

Using Given Solutions to Find a Quadratic Equation

To find a quadratic equation with given numbers as solutions, simply find a quadratic polynomial that has those numbers as zeros and set that polynomial equal to zero. This is easy because a polynomial has the number p as a zero precisely when it has the binomial $x - p$ as a factor. Thus, for instance, to find a quadratic polynomial with zeros at $x = 3$ and $x = -5$, construct the polynomial $P(x) = (x - 3)\big(x - (-5)\big) = (x - 3)(x + 5) = x^2 + 2x - 15$. Setting this equal to zero produces an equation, $x^2 + 2x - 15 = 0$, whose solutions are $x = 3$ and $x = -5$.

Of course, any constant multiple $P(x) = a(x - 3)(x + 5)$ will also have the same zeros. For instance, if you choose $a = 4$, then you get the polynomial $P(x) = 4(x - 3)(x + 5) = 4x^2 + 8x - 60$, which also has zeros at $x = 3$ and $x = -5$. From this you can get another equation, $4x^2 + 8x - 60 = 0$, with solutions $x = 3$ and $x = -5$.

Functions

Basics of Functions

Definition of a Function

A function is a rule that assigns to every number in a given set (called the **domain**) exactly one corresponding value. For example, if our domain is the set $\{-2,1,2,3\}$, we can define a function by assigning to each number its square. This function assigns to -2 the value 4, to 1 the value 1, to 2 the value 4, and to 3 the value 9 (since $(-2)^2 = 4$, $1^2 = 1$, $2^2 = 4$, and $3^2 = 9$). The set of all the values assigned by a function is the **range** of the function. The range of the function in our example is the set $\{1, 4, 9\}$. We may think of a function as a kind of machine: we give it a number as an input, and it uses its rule to produce a number as an output. In the squaring function above, the input 3 produces the output 9.

Review Video: What is a Function?
Visit mometrix.com/academy and enter code: 784611

Function Notation

We usually name a function by a letter, often the letter f (for *function*—if we need to talk about more than one function, we name the second one g, the third one h, etc.). To specify the value (the output) corresponding to a particular number in the domain (the input), we write the function letter followed by the input number in parentheses. For instance, in the example above the notation $f(3)$ means the value that the function assigns to the number 3, namely 9—that is, $f(3) = 9$. We read the symbols $f(3)$ as, "f of 3," and we call 3 the **argument** of the function and 9 the **value** of the function (so *argument* means *input* and *value* means *output*).

Using function notation we can define the squaring function above by listing the values the function assigns to each argument in the domain: $f(-2) = 4$. $f(1) = 1$, $f(2) = 4$, and $f(3) = 9$. More efficiently, we can define the function by the single equation $f(x) = x^2$, which says that if x is a number from the domain, then we calculate the value assigned to it by substituting the number x in the formula x^2. For instance, we calculate $f(5) = 5^2 = 25$. Similarly, if we define a function g by the equation $g(x) = x^2 - 4x + 7$, then we calculate the value $g(3)$ by substituting 3 for each x in the formula: $g(3) = 3^2 - 4 \cdot 3 + 7 = 9 - 12 + 7 = 4$.

OTHER WAYS TO DEFINE FUNCTIONS

Instead of denoting the value of the function by $f(x)$, sometimes we simply use another letter, usually y. For instance, instead of defining the squaring function by the equation $f(x) = x^2$, we might use the equation $y = x^2$. In this case, we refer to x (the input) as the **independent variable** and y (the output) as the **dependent variable** because the value, y, depends on the number we choose for x.

A formula (with y or $f(x)$) is the most common way to define a function; but sometimes, if the domain is small enough, we prefer to list explicitly the possible inputs and their corresponding outputs. Some ways of doing this appear above, but a more common approach is to put the input-output pairs in a table. For instance, we can define the squaring function above by the table

x	−2	1	2	3
y	4	1	4	9

We see that the domain of this function is the set of all numbers in the x-row and the range is the set of all numbers in the y-row. We note that numbers cannot repeat in the x-row (because a function assigns exactly one value to each argument in the domain) but they can repeat in the y-row (because the function can assign the same value to multiple arguments—for instance, the number 4 appears twice in the y-row).

We can also define a function by writing the inputs and corresponding outputs as ordered pairs of x- and y-values. For instance, we can write the squaring function above as the set of ordered pairs $\{(-2,4), (1,1), (2,4), (3,9)\}$. Further, by treating these ordered pairs as coordinates and plotting the corresponding points on the coordinate plane, we get the **graph** of the function:

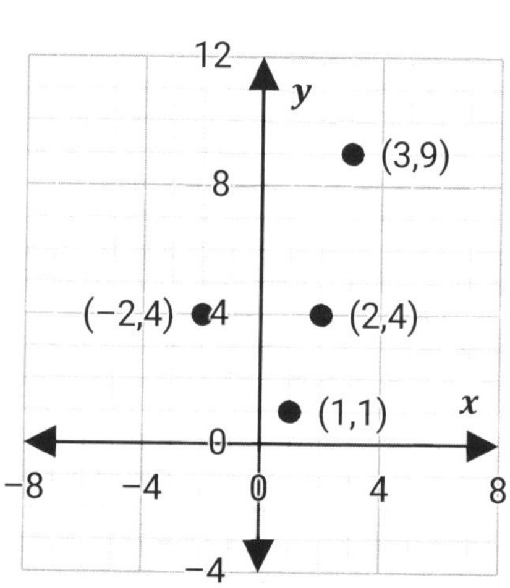

Turning this around, we can potentially use a graph to define a function, namely the function consisting of the coordinate pairs of all the points in the graph. This always works unless the graph

has two points with the same x-coordinate (because then the function would assign two different y-values to the same x). It is easy to detect such points: because they have the same x-coordinate, a vertical line passes through both of them. Thus, a graph always defines a function unless it is possible to draw a vertical line that intersects the graph in two or more points. We call this condition the **vertical line test**. For example, if our graph is a circle, then by the Vertical Line Test the graph does not define a function because there are vertical lines that will intersect the circle in two different points.

MORE ON DOMAINS AND RANGES

When we define a function by a formula and do not specify the domain, then by default the domain consists of all real numbers for which the formula produces an answer. For instance, suppose we define a function f by the formula $f(x) = 1/x$. If $x = 0$, then $1/x = 1/0$, which is undefined. But if x is any other real number, then we can calculate the value of $1/x$. So, the default domain of this function is all real numbers except zero. Because of this domain convention, the graph of a function defined by a formula usually consists of infinitely many points that "connect to" each other in a way that produces a line or curve (see examples below) rather than the isolated points we see in the squaring function above.

If we have the graph of a function, its domain consists of all numbers on the x-axis with corresponding points on the graph and its range consists of all numbers on the y-axis with corresponding points on the graph. For example, consider the function $f(x) = x^2 + 3$:

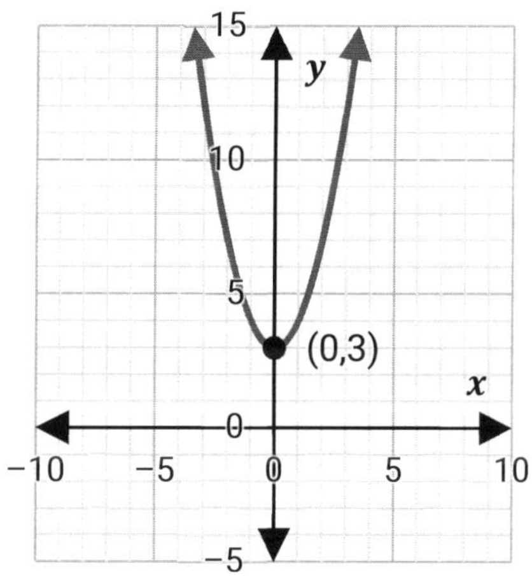

Since the graph continues infinitely to the left and right beyond what we can see, every point on the x-axis has a corresponding point on the graph; so, the domain of this function is all real numbers. On the other hand, the lowest point on this graph has a y-value of 3, and the graph passes through all higher y-values. So, the range of this function is all real numbers greater than or equal to 3, which we can denote algebraically by $y \geq 3$ or, using interval notation, by $[3, \infty)$.

Review Video: How to Find Domain and Range
Visit mometrix.com/academy and enter code: 778133

Review Video: Domain and Range of Quadratic Functions
Visit mometrix.com/academy and enter code: 331768

MONOTONIC AND EVEN/ODD FUNCTIONS

A function, f, is **increasing** if it always assigns larger values to larger arguments. It is **decreasing** if it always assigns smaller values to larger arguments. That is, f is increasing if $a < b$ always guarantees $f(a) < f(b)$, and it is decreasing if $a < b$ always guarantees $f(a) > f(b)$. The graph of an increasing function consistently rises from left to right, and the graph of a decreasing function consistently falls from left to right. For example, the function $f(x) = 2x$ is an increasing function because doubling a larger number always gives us a larger result than doubling a smaller number. The graph of $f(x) = 2x$ is a line with slope $m = 2$, which, as we expect, rises from left to right. We call a function **monotonic** if it is either increasing or decreasing.

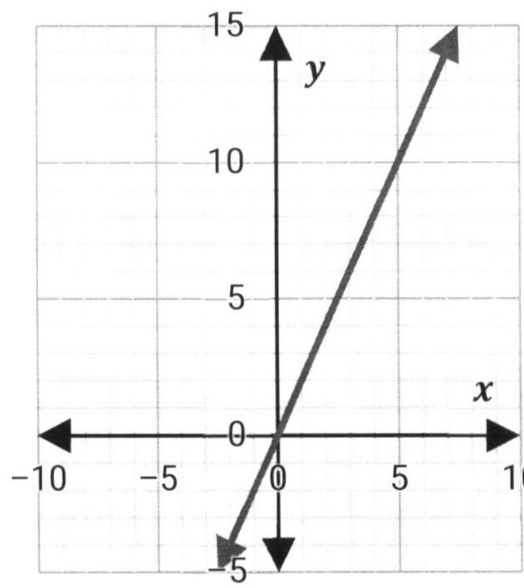

A function, f, is **even** if changing the sign of its argument produces the same value. It is **odd** if changing the sign of its argument produces the same value except with the opposite sign. That is, f is even if $f(-x) = f(x)$ and odd if $f(-x) = -f(x)$ for every argument x. The function $f(x) = x^2 + 3$ is even because substituting opposite arguments always produces the same value. For instance, $f(5) = 28$ and $f(-5) = 28$ because $5^2 + 3 = 25 + 3 = 28$ and $(-5)^2 + 3 = 25 + 3 = 28$. The function $f(x) = 2x$ is odd because substituting opposite arguments always produces opposite values. For instance, $f(10) = 20$ and $f(-10) = -20$ because $2(10) = 20$ and $2(-10) = -20$. The graph of an even function is always symmetric with respect to the y-axis, making the left and right halves of the graph mirror images of each other, as in the graph of the even function $f(x) = x^2 + 3$ above. The graph of an odd function is always symmetric with respect to the origin. This means that if we rotate the graph 180° around the origin (think of sticking a pin through the origin on a sheet of graph paper and rotating the paper halfway around) the graph looks the same, as in the graph of the odd function $f(x) = 2x$ above.

It is worth noting that most functions are neither increasing nor decreasing (that is, they are not monotonic) and most functions are neither even nor odd. For example, the function $f(x) = x^2 -$

x is neither increasing nor decreasing and neither even nor odd: its graph neither rises nor falls consistently, and it is symmetric with respect to neither the y-axis nor the origin.

Review Video: Even and Odd Functions
Visit mometrix.com/academy and enter code: 278985

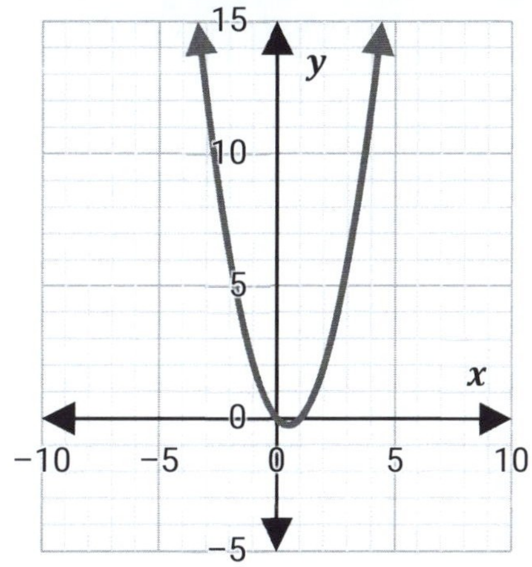

Invertible (One-to-One) Functions

A function, f, is one-to-one if it never assigns the same value to different arguments—that is, if $f(a)$ and $f(b)$ are different whenever a and b are different. The graph of a one-to-one function never has two points that lie on the same horizontal line because such points would have different x-values but the same y-value. Thus, a function is one-to-one if it is impossible to draw a horizontal line that intersects its graph in more than one point. We call this condition the **horizonal line test**. For example, the graph of the function $f(x) = 2x$ above is a line that rises from left to right. Every horizontal line intersects this line in exactly one point, so the function $f(x) = 2x$ is one-to-one. This is also clear without the graph because it is impossible to double two different numbers and get the same answer.

When a function, f, is one-to-one, it is possible to define its inverse function, f^{-1}, that "undoes" what f does, assigning to each output from f the input that produced it. That is, for each x in the domain of f, if $y = f(x)$, then $f^{-1}(y) = x$. For example, the inverse of the function $f(x) = 2x$ above is $f^{-1}(y) = y/2$. So, for instance, $f(5) = 2 \cdot 5 = 10$, and $f^{-1}(10) = 10/2 = 5$ (and similarly for every other value of x). Thus, the domain of f^{-1} is the range of f and vice versa. If a function, f, has an inverse, we say that f is **invertible**. Since a function has an inverse precisely when it is one-to-one, the terms *invertible* and *one-to-one* are synonyms.

If f is an invertible function defined by a formula, then to find its inverse we simply write the equation $y = f(x)$ and solve it for x (that is, we isolate the x). The result will be the equation $f^{-1}(y) = x$. For instance, starting with the function $f(x) = 2x$, we write $y = 2x$ and isolate the x by dividing both sides of the equation by 2. This gives us $y/2 = x$, so we know that $f^{-1}(y) = y/2$. Although this procedure is theoretically simple, in practice the algebra can be difficult.

Common Functions

Certain functions and certain kinds of functions are particularly useful, coming up frequently in mathematics and its applications. Once we know some basic function terminology and concepts, it is useful to begin developing a mental library of the most common and useful functions.

Review Video: Common Functions
Visit mometrix.com/academy and enter code: 629798

Constant Functions

A function of the form $f(x) = a$, where a is a real number, is a **constant function**. This function assigns the same value, a, to every real argument x. For instance, given the constant function $f(x) = 5$, we have $f(2) = 5$, $f(100) = 5$, and $f(-7.1) = 5$.

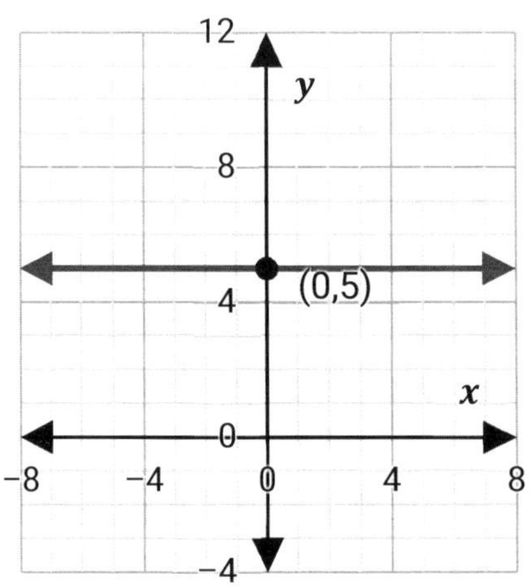

The domain of a constant function is the set of all real numbers, and the range is the set containing the single number a. Its graph is a horizontal line passing through the number $y = a$ on the y-axis (we call the number at which a function's graph intersects the y-axis the ***y*-intercept** of the function).

The Identity Function

The function $f(x) = x$ is the **identity function**. Its value always equals its argument. Thus, for instance, $f(2) = 2$, $f(100) = 100$, and $f(-7.1) = -7.1$.

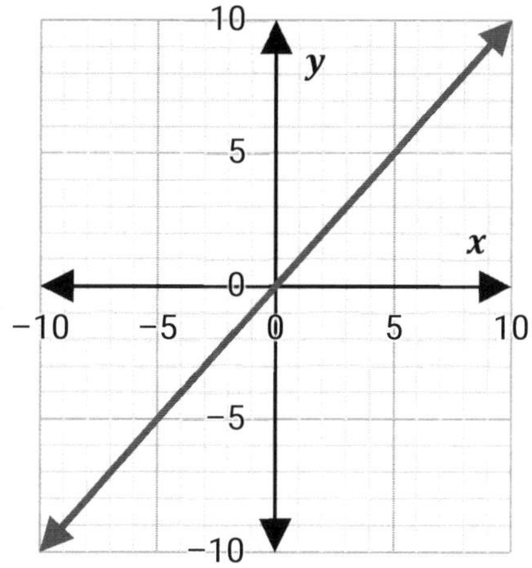

Its domain and range are the set of all real numbers. It is both an increasing function and an odd function. Its graph is a line that passes through the origin and rises from left to right at a 45° angle to the horizontal. Since it passes through the origin, its y intercept is $y = 0$ and it also has an ***x*-intercept** (a number at which the function's graph intersects the x-axis) of $x = 0$.

Linear Functions

A function of the form $f(x) = ax + b$, where a and b are real numbers (with $a \neq 0$), is a **linear function** (the identity function is a linear function with $a = 1$ and $b = 0$). Its domain and range are the set of all real numbers. Its graph is a line (the word *linear* contains the root word *line*) with one x-intercept (at $x = -b/a$), with a y-intercept at $y = b$, and with a direction and steepness that depend on the coefficient a, which we call the **slope**. Specifically, the slope a is the amount the y-value increases for each increase of 1 in the x-value. Thus, for $a > 0$, the line rises from left to right (making f an increasing function), and larger values of a produce steeper ascents. Similarly, for $a < 0$, the line falls from left to right (making f a decreasing function), and smaller (more negative) values of a produce steeper descents. For instance, the graph of the linear function

$f(x) = (1/2)x + 3$ is a line that passes through the point $y = 3$ on the y-axis and that rises by $1/2$ unit for every unit that x increases.

Review Video: Linear Functions
Visit mometrix.com/academy and enter code: 200735

Review Video: Graphing Linear Functions
Visit mometrix.com/academy and enter code: 699478

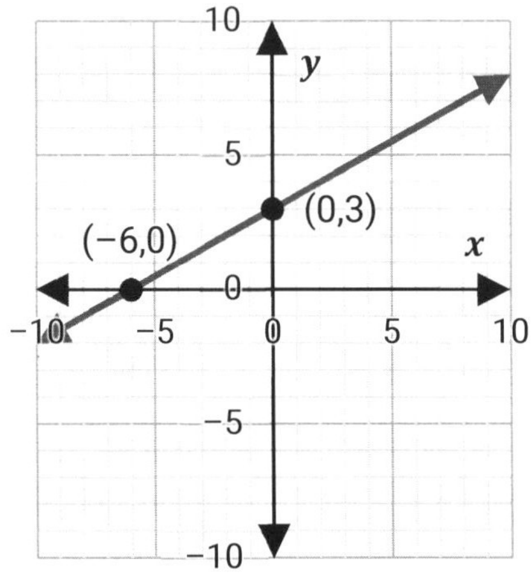

In many contexts it is standard to use the letter m for slope and thus to write the general form of a linear function as $f(x) = mx + b$, known as **slope-intercept form**.

The Squaring Function

The function $f(x) = x^2$ is the **squaring function**.

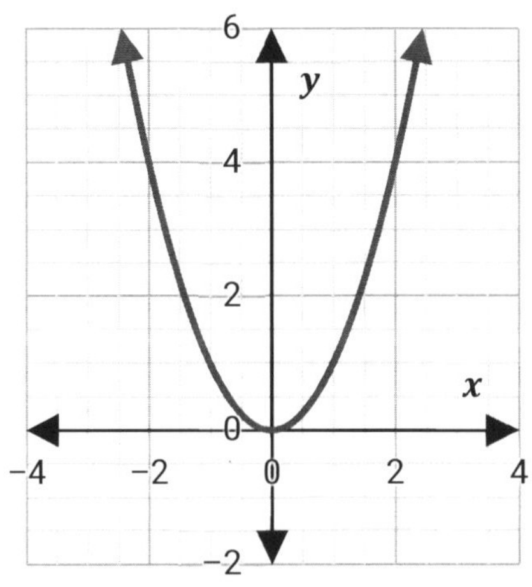

Its graph is U-shaped, opening upward as shown, a shape known as a **parabola**. It has a lowest point, its **vertex**, at the origin, which is also the location of its single x-intercept and single y-intercept. Thus, its **minimum** is $y = 0$, its domain is the set of all real numbers, and its range is the set of nonnegative real numbers (that is, $y \geq 0$). It is an even function and thus symmetric with respect to the y-axis (which we call the **axis of symmetry**), meaning that the left half of the graph is the mirror image of the right half, with the mirror standing on the y-axis.

Quadratic Functions

A function of the form $f(x) = ax^2 + bx + c$, where a, b, and c are real numbers (with $a \neq 0$), is a **quadratic function** (the squaring function is a quadratic function with $a = 1, b = 0$, and $c = 0$). Its domain is the set of all real numbers, and its graph is a parabola. It is symmetric with respect to its axis of symmetry, the vertical line $x = -b/(2a)$. If $a > 0$, the parabola opens upward, so that its vertex is at its lowest point (its minimum) and its range consists of all real numbers greater than or equal to this minimum y-value. If $a < 0$, the parabola opens downward, so that its vertex is at its highest point (its maximum) and its range consists of all real numbers less than or equal to this maximum y-value. Its y-intercept is $y = c$ since $f(0) = c$, and it may have zero, one, or two x-intercepts. For example, the function $f(x) = x^2 - 6x + 5$ has $a = 1, b = -6$, and $c = 5$.

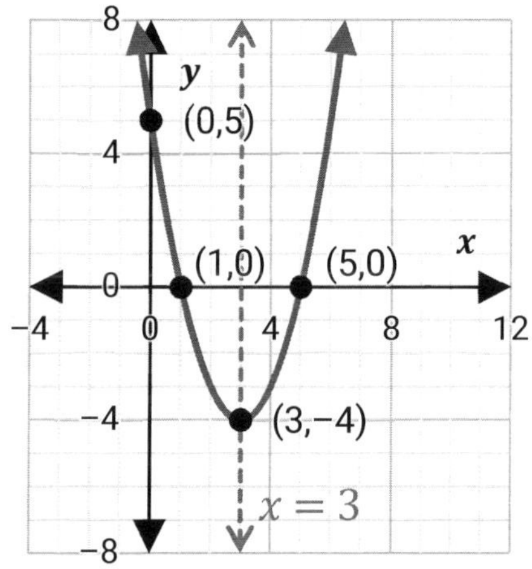

Its graph opens upward (because $a > 0$) and its axis of symmetry is the vertical line $x = 3$ (since $-b/(2a) = -(-6)/(2 \cdot 1) = 3$). Its y-intercept is at $y = 5$. It turns out to have its vertex at the point $(3, -4)$, making its minimum value $y = -4$. So, its domain is the set of all real numbers, and its range is $y \geq -4$. It also turns out to have two x-intercepts, at $x = 1$ and at $x = 5$ (since $f(1) = 0$ and $f(5) = 0$).

Polynomial Functions

A function of the form $f(x) = a^n x^n + a^{n-1} x^{n-1} + \cdots + a_2 x^2 + a_1 x + a_0$, where n is a whole number and $a_0, a_1, a_2, \ldots a_{n-1}, a_n$ are real numbers, is a **polynomial function of degree *n***. Its domain is the set of all real numbers (it is complicated to describe its range in general), and its y-intercept is $y = a_0$ (since $f(0) = a_0$). Constant functions, linear functions, and quadratic functions are polynomial functions of degrees 0, 1, and 2, respectively. In general, a polynomial function of degree n has up to n zeros (x-intercepts) and up to $n - 1$ "bends." For example, the fourth degree polynomial function $f(x) = x^4 - 11x^3 + 41x^2 - 61x + 30$, whose graph appears here, has four x-intercepts (at $x = 1, x = 2, x = 3$, and $x = 5$) and three "bends," and its y-intercept (not visible on the graph) is at $y = 30$.

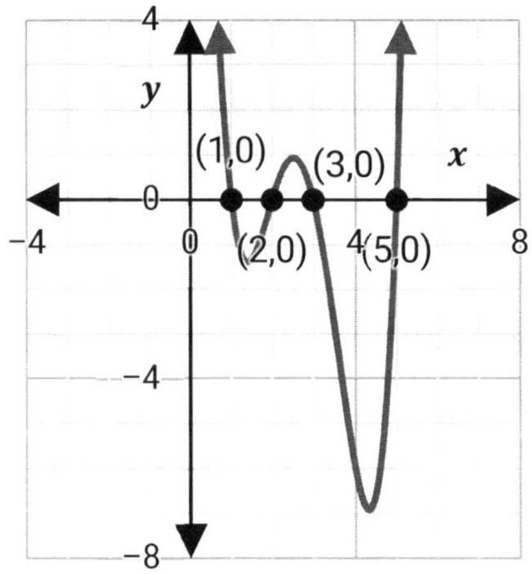

RATIONAL FUNCTIONS

A function of the form $f(x) = P(x)/Q(x)$, where P and Q are polynomials, is a rational function (we note that the word *rational* includes the root word *ratio*, indicating that a rational function is a ratio of polynomial functions). The domain of a rational function is all real numbers except the zeros of $Q(x)$ since division by zero is undefined (the range can be difficult to describe in general). Its y-intercept is $f(0)$, if this is defined; and its x-intercepts are the zeros of $P(x)$ that are in the domain of f, if there are any. A rational function may also have vertical asymptotes (vertical lines that the graph approaches without crossing) and a horizontal asymptote (a horizontal line that the curve approaches as x becomes very small or very large (toward the left and right edges of the graph). For example, the rational function $f(x) = (2x^2 + x - 1)/(x^2 + x - 2)$ has as its domain the set of all real numbers except $x = -2$ and $x = 1$ (since those numbers make the denominator zero).

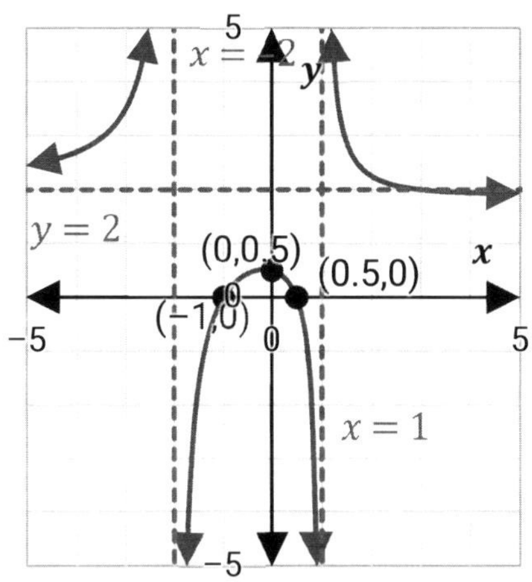

It has a y-intercept of $y = 1/2$ since $f(0) = (-1)/(-2) = 1/2$, and it has x-intercepts at $x = -1$ and at $x = 1/2$ since those numbers make the numerator zero. It has vertical asymptotes at $x = -2$ and $x = 1$ (not coincidentally, these are the numbers omitted from the domain) and a horizontal asymptote at $y = 2$. It is important to note that vertical asymptotes cannot be crossed in rational functions, but horizontal asymptotes can be crossed if the function tends near the asymptote at infinity and does not go past all possible turning points.

> **Review Video:** Simplifying Rational Polynomial Functions
> Visit mometrix.com/academy and enter code: 351038
>
> **Review Video:** Horizontal Asymptotes
> Visit mometrix.com/academy and enter code: 747796

The Square Root Function

The function $f(x) = \sqrt{x}$ is the square root function.

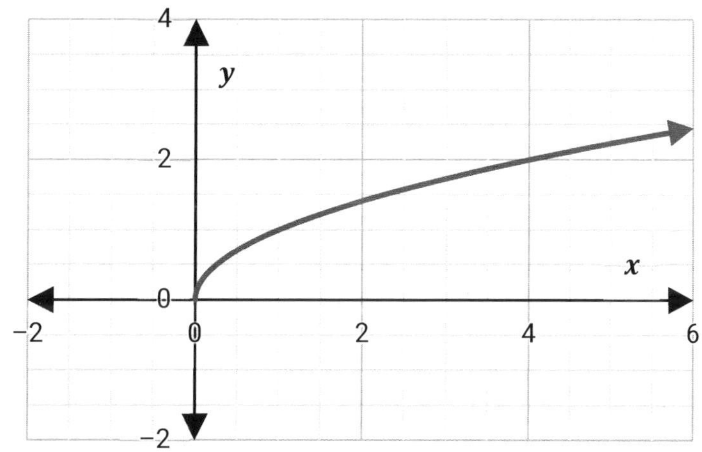

It is an increasing function, and its domain and range are both the set of all nonnegative real numbers. It has one x-intercept and one y-intercept, both appearing at the origin. Its graph is the upper half of a parabola opening to the right. The square root function is the inverse of the squaring function with domain restricted to the nonnegative real numbers (that is, $f(x) = x^2$ for $x \geq 0$).

Piecewise-Defined Functions

As the name suggests, a **piecewise-defined function** (or, simply, a **piecewise function**) is a function defined by different rules on different pieces of the domain. We define such a function using the following form:

Function Name	Rule to Apply	Piece of the Domain on Which the Rule Applies
$f(x) =$	Rule 1,	First Piece of the Domain
	Rule 2,	Second Piece of the Domain
	Rule 3,	Third Piece of the Domain
	etc.,	etc.

The pieces of the domain should not overlap, and together they should cover the whole domain. For example, we might craft a piecewise-defined function by

$$f(x) = \begin{cases} x^2, & \text{if } x < 2 \\ 3x - 5, & \text{if } x \geq 2 \end{cases}$$

The two pieces of the domain—namely, $x < 2$ and $x \geq 2$—do not overlap, and together they include all real numbers. To evaluate the function for a particular argument x, we determine which piece of the domain includes x and then apply the corresponding rule. For instance, to find $f(4)$, we note that $4 \geq 2$; so, we apply the rule $3x - 5$ to get the value $f(4) = 3 \cdot 4 - 5 = 7$. Similarly, to find $f(-6)$, we note that $-6 < 2$; so, we apply the rule x^2 to get the value $f(-6) = (-6)^2 = 36$.

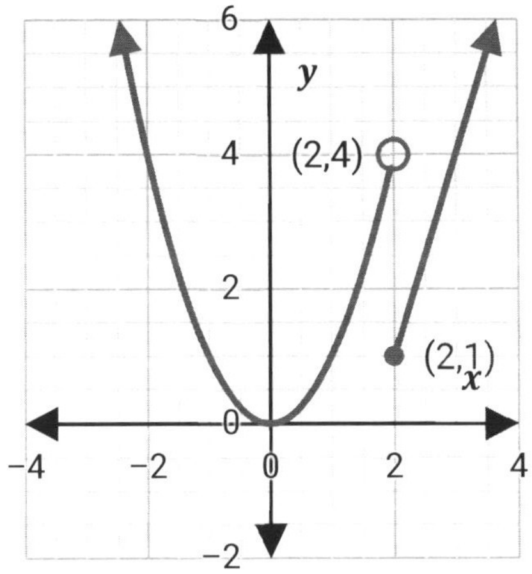

To graph this function, we sketch the graph of the parabola $y = x^2$ on the part of the plane where $x < 2$ and we sketch the line $y = 3x - 5$ on the part of the plane where $x \geq 2$. This produces a graph with a jump at $x = 2$ (a discontinuity—piecewise-defined functions are useful for producing graphs with discontinuities). We plot an open circle at the point (2,4), the end of the left part of the graph, to show that this point is not part of the graph. And we plot a solid dot at the point (2,1), the start of the right part of the graph, to show that this point *is* part of the graph.

Review Video: Piecewise Functions
Visit mometrix.com/academy and enter code: 707921

THE ABSOLUTE VALUE FUNCTION

A particularly useful piecewise-defined function is the absolute value function. It is so important that instead of naming it $f(x)$ or $g(x)$, we denote it using the special notation $|x|$. Its definition is

$$|x| = \begin{cases} -x, & \text{if } x < 0 \\ x, & \text{if } x \geq 0 \end{cases}$$

For instance, $|8| = 8$ (since $8 \geq 0$) and $|-5| = -(-5) = 5$, since $-5 < 0$. So, the absolute value function acts like the identity function for nonnegative numbers (it leaves them unchanged), and it gives the opposite of negative numbers (it effectively strips off the minus sign). Thus, we can think of the absolute value of a real number as its distance from zero on the number line, without taking into consideration whether the number is larger than or smaller than zero. For instance, $|-3| = 3$ and $|3| = 3$, showing that both -3 and 3 are three units away from zero. The absolute value function is an even function with a V-shaped graph that looks like the line $y = x$ (the identity function) on the right "half" of the plane (for $x \geq 0$) and the line $y = -x$ on the left "half" of the plane (for $x < 0$).

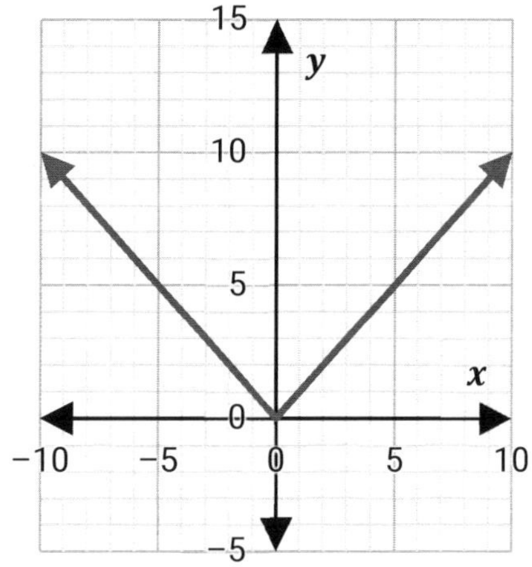

TRIGONOMETRIC FUNCTIONS

The basic trigonometric functions are sine (abbreviated 'sin'), cosine (abbreviated 'cos'), and tangent (abbreviated 'tan'). The simplest way to think of them is as describing the ratio of the side lengths of a right triangle in relation to the angles of the triangle.

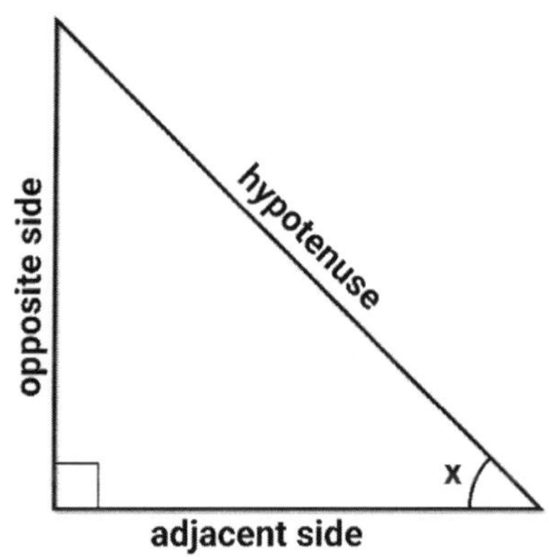

$$\sin x = \frac{\text{opposite side}}{\text{hypotenuse}}$$
$$\cos x = \frac{\text{adjacent side}}{\text{hypotenuse}}$$
$$\tan x = \frac{\text{opposite side}}{\text{adjacent side}}$$

APPLYING TRIGONOMETRIC FUNCTIONS

Suppose we have a point (x, y) at distance r from the origin such that the line segment between this point and the origin forms an angle of measure θ with the positive x-axis (We allow θ to be any real number, with the angle measured counterclockwise from the x-axis if $\theta > 0$ and clockwise if $\theta < 0$). Then we can define the trigonometric functions sine, cosine, and tangent by the formulas $\sin\theta = y/r$, $\cos\theta = x/r$, and $\tan\theta = y/x$ (and their reciprocal functions cosecant, secant, and cotangent accordingly). These functions are periodic because increasing the angle θ by 2π radians (that is,

360°) turns the line segment all the way around the origin so that it ends at the same point (x, y) again.

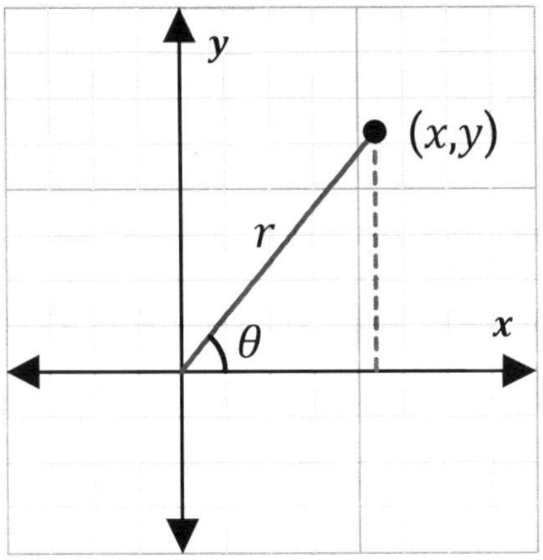

If the angle in the above diagram is acute, we can think of the line segment as the hypotenuse of a right triangle so that we get the familiar formulas $\sin\theta = (\text{opposite leg})/\text{hypotenuse}$, $\cos\theta = (\text{adjacent leg})/\text{hypotenuse}$, and $\tan\theta = (\text{opposite leg})/(\text{adjacent leg})$. In this form, the trigonometric functions are useful for finding missing sides of triangles. For example, suppose that standing 30 feet from the base of a tree, we have to look up at a 58° angle to see the top of the tree (see diagram). If we let x be the height of the tree, then we get the equation $\tan 58° = x/(30\text{ feet})$. Multiplying both sides of the equation by 30 gives us the height of the tree, namely, $x = 30\tan 58° \approx 48$ feet.

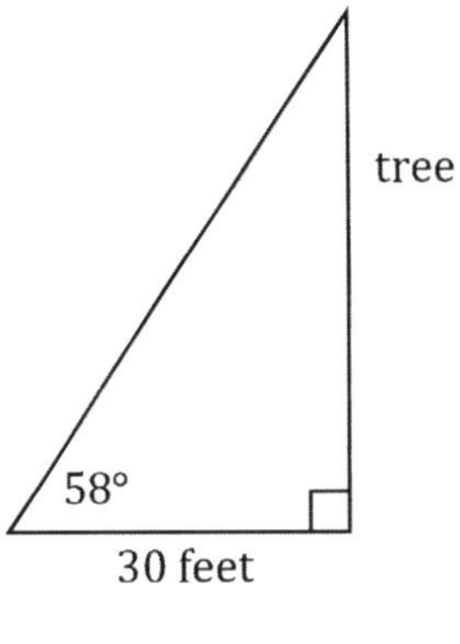

Graphing Trigonometric Functions

Sine

To graph the sine function, we let x (rather than θ) be the angle measure (usually in radians) and y be the value of the sine. That is, we graph the equation $y = \sin x$. From the definition of sine above we can show that $\sin 0 = 0$, $\sin(\pi/2) = 1$, $\sin\pi = 0$, $\sin(3\pi/2) = -1$, and $\sin 2\pi = 0$. Thus, the graph of the sine function begins at the origin, peaks at the point $(\pi/2, 1)$, crosses the x-axis at $(\pi, 0)$, has its lowest point at $(3\pi/2, -1)$, and returns to the x-axis at $(2\pi, 0)$. Because the sine function is periodic with period 2π radians (or 360°), this curve represents one complete cycle of the graph. The remainder of the graph of $y = \sin x$ consists of infinitely many repetitions of this cycle, producing the familiar "sine wave."

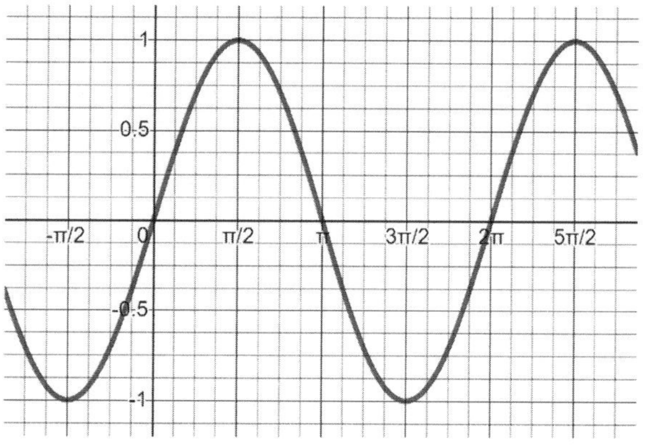

Review Video: Sine
Visit mometrix.com/academy and enter code: 193339

By suitable choice of the parameters A, B, C, and D, we can construct a "custom" sine function $y = A\sin(Bx + C) + D$ with any desired amplitude (the vertical distance the curve extends above and below its midline), period (distance between successive peaks), phase shift (horizontal shift), and midline (the horizontal line halfway between the peaks and troughs).

COSINE

Similarly, the graph of the cosine function is the graph of the equation $y = \cos x$. Proceeding as above, we get a graph with the same shape as that of the sine function but shifted by $\pi/2$ to the left.

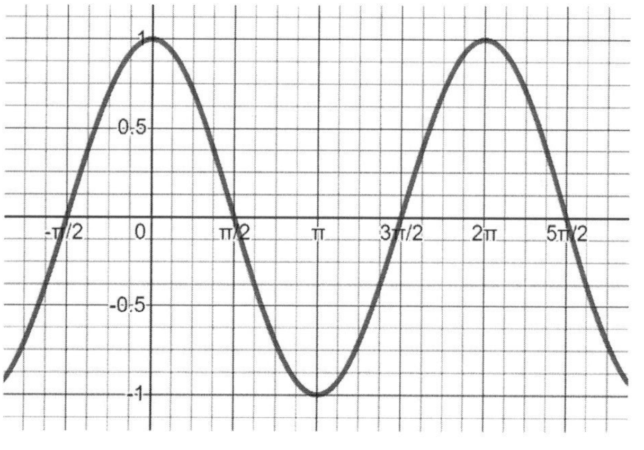

Review Video: Cosine
Visit mometrix.com/academy and enter code: 361120

As for the sine function, we can construct custom cosine graphs with desired amplitude, period, phase shift, and midline by choosing suitable values of the parameters in the equation $y = A\cos(Bx + C) + D$.

TANGENT

The graph of the tangent function (that is, the graph of the equation $y = \tan x$) turns out to be periodic with period π radians (or 180°). It consists of an infinite sequence of smooth curves crossing the x-axis at every multiple of π radians (180°) and having as asymptotes the vertical lines $x = \frac{k\pi}{2}$ radians ($x = k \times 90°$), for every odd integer k (which also means that the domain of the tangent function excludes these x-values).

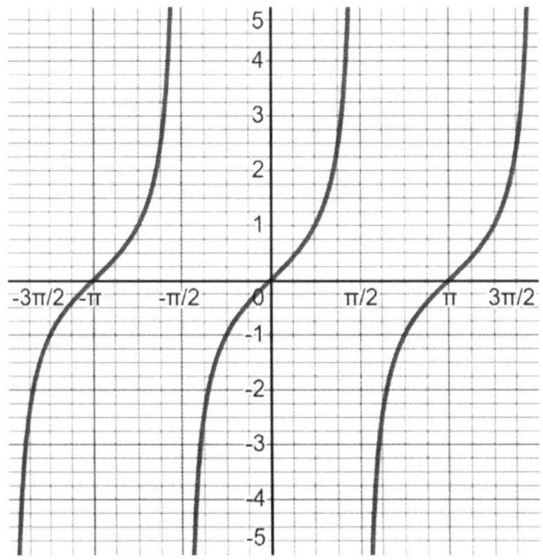

Review Video: Tangent
Visit mometrix.com/academy and enter code: 947639

WORKING WITH FUNCTIONS

MANIPULATION OF FUNCTIONS

Translation occurs when values are added to or subtracted from the x- or y-values. If a constant is added to the y-portion of each point, the graph shifts up. If a constant is subtracted from the y-portion of each point, the graph shifts down. This is represented by the expression $f(x) \pm k$, where k is a constant. If a constant is added to the x-portion of each point, the graph shifts left. If a constant is subtracted from the x-portion of each point, the graph shifts right. This is represented by the expression $f(x \pm k)$, where k is a constant.

Stretching, compression, and reflection occur when different parts of a function are multiplied by different groups of constants. If the function as a whole is multiplied by a real number constant greater than 1, $(k \times f(x))$, the graph is stretched vertically. If k in the previous equation is greater than zero but less than 1, the graph is compressed vertically. If k is less than zero, the graph is reflected about the x-axis, in addition to being either stretched or compressed vertically if k is less than or greater than −1, respectively. If instead, just the x-term is multiplied by a constant greater than 1 $(f(k \times x))$, the graph is compressed horizontally. If k in the previous equation is greater than zero but less than 1, the graph is stretched horizontally. If k is less than zero, the graph is reflected about the y-axis, in addition to being either stretched or compressed horizontally if k is greater than or less than −1, respectively.

Review Video: Manipulation of Functions
Visit mometrix.com/academy and enter code: 669117

Applying the Basic Operations to Functions

For each of the basic operations, we will use these functions as examples: $f(x) = x^2$ and $g(x) = x$.

To find the sum of two functions f and g, assuming the domains are compatible, simply add the two functions together: $(f + g)(x) = f(x) + g(x) = x^2 + x$.

To find the difference of two functions f and g, assuming the domains are compatible, simply subtract the second function from the first: $(f - g)(x) = f(x) - g(x) = x^2 - x$.

To find the product of two functions f and g, assuming the domains are compatible, multiply the two functions together: $(f \times g)(x) = f(x) \times g(x) = x^2 \times x = x^3$.

To find the quotient of two functions f and g, assuming the domains are compatible, divide the first function by the second: $\left(\frac{f}{g}\right)(x) = \frac{f(x)}{g(x)} = \frac{x^2}{x} = x\,; x \neq 0$.

The example given in each case is fairly simple, but on a given problem, if you are looking only for the value of the sum, difference, product, or quotient of two functions at a particular x-value, it may be simpler to solve the functions individually and then perform the given operation using those values.

The composite of two functions f and g, written as $(f \circ g)(x)$ simply means that the output of the second function is used as the input of the first. This can also be written as $f\big(g(x)\big)$. In general, this can be solved by substituting $g(x)$ for all instances of x in $f(x)$ and simplifying. Using the example functions $f(x) = x^2 - x + 2$ and $g(x) = x + 1$, we can find that $(f \circ g)(x)$ or $f\big(g(x)\big)$ is equal to $f(x + 1) = (x + 1)^2 - (x + 1) + 2$, which simplifies to $x^2 + x + 2$.

It is important to note that $(f \circ g)(x)$ is not necessarily the same as $(g \circ f)(x)$. The process is not always commutative like addition or multiplication expressions. It *can* be commutative, but most often this is not the case.

Evaluating Linear Functions

A **function** can be expressed as an equation that relates an input to an output where each input corresponds to exactly one output. The input of a function is defined by the x-variable, and the output is defined by the y-variable. For example, consider the function $y = 2x + 6$. The value of y, the output, is determined by the value of the x, the input. If the value of x is 3, the value of y is $y = 2(3) + 6 = 6 + 6 = 12$. This means that when $x = 3$, $y = 12$. This can be expressed as the ordered pair $(3,12)$.

It is common for function equations to use the form $f(x) =$ instead of $y =$. However, $f(x)$ and y represent the same thing. We read $f(x)$ as "f of x." The expression "f of x" implies that the value of f depends on the value of x. The function used in the example above could be expressed as $y = 2x + 6$ or $f(x) = 2x + 6$. Both functions represent the same line when graphed.

Functions that are expressed in the form $f(x) =$ are evaluated in the same way the equations are evaluated in the form $y =$. For example, when evaluating the function $f(x) = 3x - 2$ for $f(6)$, substitute 6 in for x, and simplify. In this case, $f(x) = 3x - 2$ becomes $f(6) = 3(6) - 2 = 18 - 2 = 16$. When x is 6, $f(x)$ is 16.

Example: To find the value of $f(8)$, calculate as follows:

$$f(x) = 3x - 2$$
$$f(8) = 3(8) - 2$$
$$f(8) = 22$$

Review Video: Evaluating Functions
Visit mometrix.com/academy and enter code: 588515

Advanced Functions

Step Functions

The double brackets indicate a step function. For a step function, the value inside the double brackets is rounded down to the nearest integer. The graph of the function $f_0(x) = [\![x]\!]$ appears on the left graph. In comparison $f(x) = 2\left[\!\left[\frac{1}{3}(x-1)\right]\!\right]$ is on the right graph. The coefficient of 2 shows that it's stretched vertically by a factor of 2 (so there's a vertical distance of 2 units between successive "steps"). The coefficient of $\frac{1}{3}$ in front of the x shows that it's stretched horizontally by a factor of 3 (so each "step" is three units long), and the $x - 1$ shows that it's displaced one unit to the right.

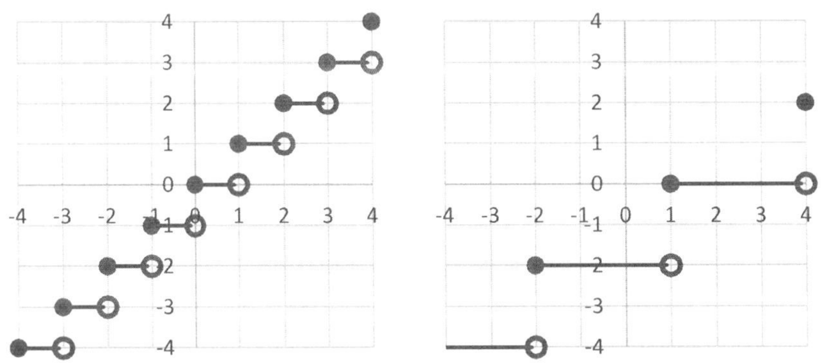

Transcendental Functions

Roughly speaking, algebraic functions are functions defined by formulas involving numbers and variables combined by addition, subtraction, multiplication, division, powers (but not variable powers), and roots. **Transcendental functions** are functions that are not algebraic. A function that includes logarithms, trigonometric functions, or variables as exponents, is transcendental, not algebraic, even if the function also includes polynomials or roots.

EXPONENTIAL FUNCTIONS

Exponential functions are functions that have the form $y = b^x$, where base $b > 0$ and $b \neq 1$. The exponential function can also be written $f(x) = b^x$. The following properties apply to exponential expressions:

Property	Description
$a^x a^y = a^{x+y}$	The product of exponentials with the same base equals the base raised to the sum of the powers
$a^x / a^y = a^{x-y}$	The quotient of exponentials with the same base equals the base raised to the difference of the powers
$(a^x)^y = a^{xy}$	An exponential raised to a power equals the base raised to the product of the powers
$(ab)^x = a^x b^x$	Exponentiation distributes over multiplication
$(a/b)^x = a^x / b^x$	Exponentiation distributes over division

The graph of an example exponential function, $f(x) = 2^x$, is below:

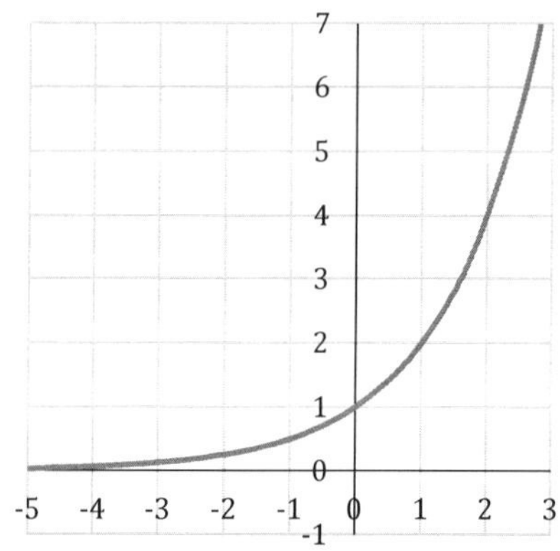

Note in the graph that the y-value approaches zero to the left and infinity to the right. One of the key features of an exponential function is that there will be one end that goes off to infinity and another that asymptotically approaches a lower bound. Common forms of exponential functions include the following:

Geometric sequences: The terms of a geometric sequence have the form $a_n = a_1 \times r^{n-1}$, where a_n is the value of the nth term, a_1 is the initial term, and r is the common ratio between succesive terms. Note that $a_1 \times r^{1-1} = a_1 \times r^0 = a_1 \times 1 = a_1$

Review Video: Geometric Sequences
Visit mometrix.com/academy and enter code: 140779

General exponential growth or decay: The general exponential growth or decay function is $f(t) = a(1 + r)^t$, where the value of $f(t)$ is the amount (of whatever quantity we are measuring) at time t, the constant a is the initial amount (the amount at time $t = 0$), and the constant r is the fixed rate of increase (if $r > 0$) or decrease (if $r < 0$) per unit time. For example, if we invest \$1000 at an interest rate of 6% interest compounded annually and we measure time in years, then our investment will grow according to an exponential model with $a = \$1000$ and $r = 6\% = 0.06$. Thus, after t years the value of our investment will be $f(t) = \$1000(1 + 0.06)^t$. After 5 years, for instance, the investment will grow to $f(5) = \$1000(1 + 0.06)^5 \approx \$1338.23$.

Compound interest: We can modify the general exponential growth function above slightly to get a formula for interest compounded n times per year. Replacing the constant a with P (for principal, the initial amount we invest), the total value of our investment after t years is $f(t) = P\left(1 + \frac{r}{n}\right)^{nt}$, where r is the nominal annual interest rate. Thus, if we change our \$1000 investment above by having the interest rate be 6% compounded *semiannually* (two times per year—so $n = 2$), the value of our investment after t years is $f(t) = \$1000\left(1 + \frac{0.06}{2}\right)^{2t} = \$1000(1 + 0.03)^{2t}$. After 5 years, for instance, the investment will grow to $f(5) = \$1000(1 + 0.03)^{10} \approx \$1343.92$. This is slightly higher than the previous investment because the interest compounds twice as often.

Review Video: Compound Interest Formula
Visit mometrix.com/academy and enter code: 100366

Review Video: Interest Functions
Visit mometrix.com/academy and enter code: 559176

Population growth and continuously compounded interest: When a quantity grows (or decays) continuously at a rate that stays constant relative to the size the quantity has already attained, then we can model its size at time t with the function $f(t) = ae^{rt}$, where a is the initial amount, r is the relative growth rate (which we often call simply the **growth rate**), and e is the irrational constant known as Euler's number (approximately 2.718; scientific calculators have a button for finding e^x, which is known as the **natural exponential function**). For instance, under some circumstances, if an initial population (of people, plants, or animals, for example) of size a grows at constant relative rate r, then the size of the population at time t is $f(t) = ae^{rt}$. Similarly, if we invest principal P (instead of a) for t years at nominal annual interest rate r compounded *continuously*, then after t years the value of the investment is $f(t) = Pe^{rt}$.

For example, suppose the initial population of a town is $a = 1{,}200$ people and the relative annual growth rate is $r = 5\% = 0.05$. Then the population of the town after t years is $f(t) = ae^{rt} = 1200e^{0.05t}$. After 10 years, for instance, the town population is $f(10) = 1200e^{0.05 \cdot 10} = 1200e^{0.5} \approx 1978$ people.

Review Video: Population Growth
Visit mometrix.com/academy and enter code: 109278

Logarithmic Functions

The **logarithmic function base b** is the function $y = \log_b x$ or $f(x) = \log_b x$, where the base b may be any positive number except one. The most common bases for logarithms are base 10 (the **common logarithm**) and base e (the **natural logarithm**). We usually write the common logarithm as $y = \log x$ (that is, $\log x$, with no base listed, means $\log_{10} x$) and the natural logarithm as $y = \ln x$ (that is, $\ln x$ means $\log_e x$).

Exponential functions and logarithmic functions with the same base are inverse functions. That is, if $f(x) = b^x$, then $f^{-1}(x) = \log_b x$. This means that the two equations $y = b^x$ (exponential form) and $x = \log_b y$ (logarithmic form) express the same relationship between the quantities x and y. We often solve problems involving logarithms by rewriting them in exponential form, and vice versa. Also, because of this inverse relationship, logarithms and exponentials cancel each other. That is, $\log_b b^x = x$ and $b^{\log_b x} = x$.

The following properties apply to logarithmic expressions:

Property	Description
$\log_b 1 = 0$	The log of 1 is equal to 0 for any base
$\log_b b = 1$	The log of the base is equal to 1
$\log_b b^p = p$	The log of the base raised to a power is equal to that power
$\log_b MN = \log_b M + \log_b N$	The log of a product is the sum of the log of each factor
$\log_b \frac{M}{N} = \log_b M - \log_b N$	The log of a quotient is equal to the log of the dividend minus the log of the divisor
$\log_b M^p = p \log_b M$	The log of a value raised to a power is equal to the power times the log of the value

Logarithms are helpful in solving equations in which the variable appears in an exponent. For instance, consider the example above in which we model the population of a town by the function $f(t) = 1200e^{0.05t}$. Suppose we want to know how long it will take the population of the town to double to 2400 people from its original value of 1200. We find this by solving the equation $1200e^{0.05t} = 2400$. First, we divide both sides of the equation by 1200 to get $e^{0.05t} = 2$. Then we take natural logarithms of both sides to get $\ln e^{0.05t} = \ln 2$, which simplifies (because natural logarithms and natural exponentials are inverse functions) to $0.05t = \ln 2$. Finally, we divide both sides by 0.05 to get $t = (\ln 2)/0.05$, which we evaluate with a calculator to get $t \approx 13.9$ years.

The graph of an example logarithmic function, $f(x) = \log_2(x + 2)$, is below:

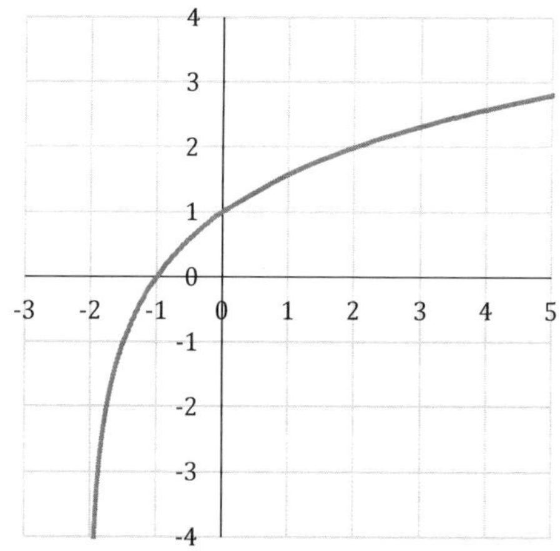

Review Video: Logarithmic Function
Visit mometrix.com/academy and enter code: 658985

Sequences and Series

Sequences

A **sequence** is an ordered set of numbers that continues in a defined pattern. The function that defines a sequence has a domain composed of the set of positive integers. Each member of the sequence is an element, or individual term. Each element is identified by the notation a_n, where a is the term of the sequence, and n is the integer identifying which term in the sequence a is.

There are two different ways to represent a sequence that contains the element a_n. The first is the simple notation $\{a_n\}$. The second is the expanded notation of a sequence: $a_1, a_2, a_3, \ldots a_n, \ldots$. Notice that the expanded form does not end with the nth term. There is no indication that the nth term is the last term in the sequence, only that the nth term is an element of the sequence.

Arithmetic Sequences

An **arithmetic sequence**, or arithmetic progression, is a special kind of sequence in which a specific quantity, called the common difference, is added to each term to make the next term. The common difference may be positive or negative. The general form of an arithmetic sequence containing n terms is $a_1, a_1 + d, a_1 + 2d, \dots, a_1 + (n-1)d$, where d is the common difference. The general formula for any term of an arithmetic sequence is $a_n = a_1 + (n-1)d$, where a_n is the term you are looking for and d is the common difference. To find the sum of the first n terms of an arithmetic sequence, use the formula $s_n = \frac{n}{2}(a_1 + a_n)$.

Review Video: Arithmetic Sequence
Visit mometrix.com/academy and enter code: 676885

Monotonic Sequences

A **monotonic sequence** is a sequence that is either nonincreasing or nondecreasing. A **nonincreasing** sequence is one whose terms either get progressively smaller in value or remain the same. Such a sequence is always bounded above, that is, all elements of the sequence must be less than some real number. A **nondecreasing** sequence is one whose terms either get progressively larger in value or remain the same. Such a sequence is always bounded below, that is, all elements of the sequence must be greater than some real number.

Recursive Sequences

When one element of a sequence is defined in terms of a previous element or elements of the sequence, the sequence is a **recursive sequence**. For example, given the recursive definition $a_1 = 1; a_2 = 1; a_n = a_{n-1} + a_{n-2}$ for all $n > 2$, you get the sequence 1,1,2,3,5,8, … . This is known as the Fibonacci sequence: a continuing sequence of numbers in which each number (after a_2) is the sum of the two previous numbers. The Fibonacci sequence can be defined as starting with either 1,1 or 0,1. Both definitions are considered correct in mathematics. Make sure you know which definition you are working with when dealing with Fibonacci numbers.

Sometimes in a recursive sequence, the terms can be found using a general formula that does not involve the previous terms of the sequence. Such a formula is called a **closed-form** expression for a recursive definition—an alternate formula that will generate the same sequence of numbers. However, not all sequences based on recursive definitions will have a closed-form expression. Some sequences will require the use of the recursive definition.

The Golden Ratio and the Fibonacci Sequence

The golden ratio is approximately 1.6180339887 and is often represented by the Greek letter phi, Φ. The exact value of Φ is $\frac{(1+\sqrt{5})}{2}$ and it is one of the solutions to $x - \frac{1}{x} = 1$. The golden ratio can be found using the Fibonacci sequence, since the ratio of a term to the previous term approaches Φ as the sequence approaches infinity:

n	a_n	a_{n-1}	$\frac{a_n}{a_{n-1}}$
3	2	1	2
4	3	2	1.5
5	5	3	$1.\overline{6}$
6	8	5	1.6
7	13	8	1.625
8	21	13	$1.\overline{615384}$
9	34	21	$1.\overline{619047}$
⋮	⋮	⋮	⋮
20	6,765	4,181	1.618033963 ...

Geometric Sequences

A geometric sequence is a sequence in which each term is multiplied by a constant number (called the common ratio) to get the next term. Essentially, it's the same concept as an arithmetic sequence, but with multiplication instead of addition.

Consider the following example of a geometric sequence: Andy opens a savings account with $10. During each subsequent week, he plans to double the amount from the previous week.

Sequence: $10, 20, 40, 80, 160, \ldots$

Function: $a_n = 10 \times 2^{n-1}$

This is a geometric sequence with a common ratio of 2. All geometric sequences represent exponential functions. The nth term in any geometric sequence is $a_n = a_1 \times r^{n-1}$, where a_n represents the value of the nth term, a_1 is the initial term, r is the common ratio, and n is the number of terms. Thus, substituting the initial value of 10 and common ratio of 2 gives the function $a_n = 10 \times 2^{n-1}$.

Review Video: Geometric Sequences
Visit mometrix.com/academy and enter code: 140779

Advanced Sequences and Series

Limit of a Sequence

Some sequences will have a **limit**—a value the sequence approaches, or sometimes even reaches, but never passes. A sequence with a limit is called a **convergent** sequence because all the values of the sequence seemingly converge at that point. Sequences that do not converge at a particular limit are **divergent** sequences. The easiest way to determine whether a sequence converges or diverges is to find the limit of the sequence. If the limit is a real number, the sequence is convergent. If the limit is infinity, the sequence is divergent.

Remember the following rules for finding limits:

- $\lim_{n \to \infty} k = k$, for all real numbers k
- $\lim_{n \to \infty} \frac{1}{n} = 0$

- $\lim_{n\to\infty} n = \infty$
- $\lim_{n\to\infty} \frac{k}{n^p} = 0$, for all real numbers k and positive rational numbers p
- The limit of the sum of two sequences is equal to the sum of the limits of the two sequences: $\lim_{n\to\infty}(a_n + b_n) = \lim_{n\to\infty} a_n + \lim_{n\to\infty} b_n$
- The limit of the difference between two sequences is equal to the difference between the limits of the two sequences: $\lim_{n\to\infty}(a_n - b_n) = \lim_{n\to\infty} a_n - \lim_{n\to\infty} b_n$
- The limit of the product of two sequences is equal to the product of the limits of the two sequences: $\lim_{n\to\infty}(a_n \times b_n) = \lim_{n\to\infty} a_n \times \lim_{n\to\infty} b_n$
- The limit of the quotient of two sequences is equal to the quotient of the limits of the two sequences, with some exceptions: $\lim_{n\to\infty}\left(\frac{a_n}{b_n}\right) = \frac{\lim_{n\to\infty} a_n}{\lim_{n\to\infty} b_n}$. In the quotient formula, it is important that $b_n \neq 0$ and that $\lim_{n\to\infty} b_n \neq 0$.
- The limit of a sequence multiplied by a scalar is equal to the scalar multiplied by the limit of the sequence: $\lim_{n\to\infty} ka_n = k \lim_{n\to\infty} a_n$, where k is any real number

Review Video: Limit of a Sequence
Visit mometrix.com/academy and enter code: 847732

Infinite Series

Both arithmetic and geometric sequences have formulas to find the sum of the first n terms in the sequence, assuming you know what the first term is. The sum of all the terms in a sequence is called a series. An **infinite series** is an infinite sum. In other words, it is what you get by adding up all the terms in an infinite sequence: $\sum_{n=1}^{\infty} a_n = a_1 + a_2 + a_3 + \cdots + a_n + \cdots$. This notation can be shortened to $\sum_{n=1}^{\infty} a_n$ or $\sum a_n$.

While we can't add up an infinite list of numbers one at a time, we can still determine the infinite sum. As we add the terms in a series, we can imagine an infinite sequence of partial sums, where the first partial sum is the first element of the series, the second partial sum is the sum of the first two elements of the series, and the nth partial sum is the sum of the first n elements of the series.

Every infinite sequence of partial sums (infinite series) either converges or diverges. As with the test for convergence in a sequence, finding the limit of the sequence of partial sums will indicate whether it is a converging series or a diverging series. If there exists a real number S such that $\lim_{n\to\infty} S_n = S$, where S_n is the sequence of partial sums, then the series converges. If the limit equals infinity, then the series diverges. If $\lim_{n\to\infty} S_n = S$ and S is a real number, then S is also the convergence value of the series.

To find the sum as n approaches infinity for the sum of two convergent series, find the sum as n approaches infinity for each individual series and add the results.

$$\sum_{n=1}^{\infty}(a_n + b_n) = \sum_{n=1}^{\infty} a_n + \sum_{n=1}^{\infty} b_n$$

The same idea works for subtraction.

$$\sum_{n=1}^{\infty}(a_n - b_n) = \sum_{n=1}^{\infty} a_n - \sum_{n=1}^{\infty} b_n$$

To find the sum as n approaches infinity for the product of a constant (also called a scalar) and a convergent series, find the sum as n approaches infinity for the series and multiply the result by the scalar.

$$\sum_{n=1}^{\infty} ka_n = k\sum_{n=1}^{\infty} a_n$$

Review Video: Infinite Series
Visit mometrix.com/academy and enter code: 271404

The $\boldsymbol{n}^{\text{th}}$ **term test for divergence** means taking the limit of a sequence a_n as n goes to infinity $\left(\lim_{n\to\infty} a_n\right)$ and checking whether the limit is zero. If the limit is not zero, then the series $\sum a_n$ is a diverging series. This test only works to prove divergence, however. If the limit is zero, the test is inconclusive, meaning the series could be either convergent or divergent.

Review Video: Nth Term Test for Divergence
Visit mometrix.com/academy and enter code: 346400

Matrices

Matrix Basics

A **matrix** (plural: matrices) is a rectangular array of numbers or variables, often called **elements**, which are arranged in columns and rows. A matrix is generally represented by a capital letter, with its elements represented by the corresponding lowercase letter with two subscripts indicating the row and column of the element. For example, n_{ab} represents the element in row a column b of matrix N.

$$N = \begin{bmatrix} n_{11} & n_{12} & n_{13} \\ n_{21} & n_{22} & n_{23} \end{bmatrix}$$

A matrix can be described in terms of the number of rows and columns it contains in the format $a \times b$, where a is the number of rows and b is the number of columns. The matrix shown above is a 2×3 matrix. Any $a \times b$ matrix where $a = b$ is a square matrix. A **vector** is a matrix that has exactly one column (**column vector**) or exactly one row (**row vector**).

The **main diagonal** of a matrix is the set of elements on the diagonal from the top left to the bottom right of a matrix. Because of the way it is defined, only square matrices will have a main diagonal. For the matrix shown below, the main diagonal consists of the elements $n_{11}, n_{22}, n_{33}, n_{44}$.

$$\begin{bmatrix} n_{11} & n_{12} & n_{13} & n_{14} \\ n_{21} & n_{22} & n_{23} & n_{24} \\ n_{31} & n_{32} & n_{33} & n_{34} \\ n_{41} & n_{42} & n_{43} & n_{44} \end{bmatrix}$$

A 3×4 matrix such as the one shown below would not have a main diagonal because there is no straight line of elements between the top left corner and the bottom right corner that joins the elements.

$$\begin{bmatrix} n_{11} & n_{12} & n_{13} & n_{14} \\ n_{21} & n_{22} & n_{23} & n_{24} \\ n_{31} & n_{32} & n_{33} & n_{34} \end{bmatrix}$$

A **diagonal matrix** is a square matrix that has a zero for every element in the matrix except the elements on the main diagonal. All the elements on the main diagonal must be nonzero numbers.

$$\begin{bmatrix} n_{11} & 0 & 0 & 0 \\ 0 & n_{22} & 0 & 0 \\ 0 & 0 & n_{33} & 0 \\ 0 & 0 & 0 & n_{44} \end{bmatrix}$$

If every element on the main diagonal of a diagonal matrix is equal to one, the matrix is called an **identity matrix**. The identity matrix is often represented by the letter I.

$$I = \begin{bmatrix} 1 & 0 & 0 & 0 \\ 0 & 1 & 0 & 0 \\ 0 & 0 & 1 & 0 \\ 0 & 0 & 0 & 1 \end{bmatrix}$$

A **zero matrix** is a matrix that has zero as the value for every element in the matrix.

$$\begin{bmatrix} 0 & 0 & 0 & 0 \\ 0 & 0 & 0 & 0 \\ 0 & 0 & 0 & 0 \\ 0 & 0 & 0 & 0 \end{bmatrix}$$

The zero matrix is the *identity for matrix addition*. Do not confuse the zero matrix with the identity matrix.

The **negative of a matrix** is also known as the additive inverse of a matrix. If matrix N is the given matrix, then matrix $-N$ is its negative. This means that every element n_{ab} is equal to $-n_{ab}$ in the negative. To find the negative of a given matrix, change the sign of every element in the matrix and keep all elements in their original corresponding positions in the matrix.

If two matrices have the same order and all corresponding elements in the two matrices are the same, then the two matrices are **equal matrices**.

A matrix N may be **transposed** to matrix N^T by changing all rows into columns and changing all columns into rows. The easiest way to accomplish this is to swap the positions of the row and column notations for each element. For example, suppose the element in the second row of the third column of matrix N is $n_{23} = 6$. In the transposed matrix N^T, the transposed element would be $n_{32} = 6$, and it would be placed in the third row of the second column.

$$N = \begin{bmatrix} 1 & 2 & 3 \\ 4 & 5 & 6 \end{bmatrix}; \; N^T = \begin{bmatrix} 1 & 4 \\ 2 & 5 \\ 3 & 6 \end{bmatrix}$$

To quickly transpose a matrix by hand, begin with the first column and rewrite a new matrix with those same elements in the same order in the first row. Write the elements from the second column of the original matrix in the second row of the transposed matrix. Continue this process until all columns have been completed. If the original matrix is identical to the transposed matrix, the matrices are symmetric.

Basic Operations with Matrices

There are two categories of basic operations with regard to matrices: operations between a matrix and a scalar, and operations between two matrices.

Scalar Operations

A scalar being added to a matrix is treated as though it were being added to each element of the matrix. The same is true for subtraction, multiplication and division:

$$M + \mathrm{k} = \begin{bmatrix} m_{11} + k & m_{12} + k \\ m_{21} + k & m_{22} + k \end{bmatrix}$$

$$M - k = \begin{bmatrix} m_{11} - k & m_{12} - k \\ m_{21} - k & m_{22} - k \end{bmatrix}$$

$$M \times k = \begin{bmatrix} m_{11} \times k & m_{12} \times k \\ m_{21} \times k & m_{22} \times k \end{bmatrix}$$

$$M \div k = \begin{bmatrix} m_{11} \div k & m_{12} \div k \\ m_{21} \div k & m_{22} \div k \end{bmatrix}$$

Matrix Addition and Subtraction

All four of the basic operations can be used with operations between matrices (although division is usually discarded in favor of multiplication by the inverse), but there are restrictions on the situations in which they can be used. Matrices that meet all the qualifications for a given operation are called **conformable matrices**. However, conformability is specific to the operation; two matrices that are conformable for addition are not necessarily conformable for multiplication.

For two matrices to be conformable for addition or subtraction, they must be of the same dimension; otherwise, the operation is not defined. If matrix M is a 3×2 matrix and matrix N is a 2×3 matrix, the operations $M + N$ and $M - N$ are meaningless. If matrices M and N are the same size, the operation is as simple as adding or subtracting all of the corresponding elements:

$$\begin{bmatrix} m_{11} & m_{12} \\ m_{21} & m_{22} \end{bmatrix} + \begin{bmatrix} n_{11} & n_{12} \\ n_{21} & n_{22} \end{bmatrix} = \begin{bmatrix} m_{11} + n_{11} & m_{12} + n_{12} \\ m_{21} + n_{21} & m_{22} + n_{22} \end{bmatrix}$$

$$\begin{bmatrix} m_{11} & m_{12} \\ m_{21} & m_{22} \end{bmatrix} - \begin{bmatrix} n_{11} & n_{12} \\ n_{21} & n_{22} \end{bmatrix} = \begin{bmatrix} m_{11} - n_{11} & m_{12} - n_{12} \\ m_{21} - n_{21} & m_{22} - n_{22} \end{bmatrix}$$

The result of addition or subtraction is a matrix of the same dimension as the two original matrices involved in the operation.

MATRIX MULTIPLICATION

The first thing it is necessary to understand about matrix multiplication is that it is not commutative. In scalar multiplication, the operation is commutative, meaning that $a \times b = b \times a$. For matrix multiplication, this is not the case: $A \times B \neq B \times A$. The terminology must be specific when describing matrix multiplication. The operation $A \times B$ can be described as A multiplied (or **post-multiplied**) by B, or B **pre-multiplied** by A.

For two matrices to be conformable for multiplication, they need not be of the same dimension, but specific dimensions must correspond. Taking the example of two matrices M and N to be multiplied $M \times N$, matrix M must have the same number of columns as matrix N has rows. Put another way, if matrix M has the dimensions $a \times b$ and matrix N has the dimensions $c \times d$, b must equal c if the two matrices are to be conformable for this multiplication. The matrix that results from the multiplication will have the dimensions $a \times d$. If a and d are both equal to 1, the product is simply a scalar. Square matrices of the same dimensions are always conformable for multiplication, and their product is always a matrix of the same size.

The simplest type of matrix multiplication is a 1×2 matrix (a row vector) times a 2×1 matrix (a column vector). These will multiply in the following way:

$$\begin{bmatrix} m_{11} & m_{12} \end{bmatrix} \times \begin{bmatrix} n_{11} \\ n_{21} \end{bmatrix} = m_{11}n_{11} + m_{12}n_{21}$$

The two matrices are conformable for multiplication because matrix M has the same number of columns as matrix N has rows. Because the other dimensions are both 1, the result is a scalar. Expanding our matrices to 1×3 and 3×1, the process is the same:

$$\begin{bmatrix} m_{11} & m_{12} & m_{13} \end{bmatrix} \times \begin{bmatrix} n_{11} \\ n_{21} \\ n_{31} \end{bmatrix} = m_{11}n_{11} + m_{12}n_{21} + m_{13}n_{31}$$

Once again, the result is a scalar. This type of basic matrix multiplication is the building block for the multiplication of larger matrices.

To multiply larger matrices, treat each **row from the first matrix** and each **column from the second matrix** as individual vectors and follow the pattern for multiplying vectors. The scalar value found from multiplying the first-row vector by the first column vector is placed in the first row, first column of the new matrix. The scalar value found from multiplying the second-row vector by the first column vector is placed in the second row, first column of the new matrix. Continue this pattern until each row of the first matrix has been multiplied by each column of the second matrix.

Below is an example of the multiplication of a 3×2 matrix and a 2×3 matrix.

$$\begin{bmatrix} m_{11} & m_{12} \\ m_{21} & m_{22} \\ m_{31} & m_{32} \end{bmatrix} \times \begin{bmatrix} n_{11} & n_{12} & n_{13} \\ n_{21} & n_{22} & n_{23} \end{bmatrix} = \begin{bmatrix} m_{11}n_{11} + m_{12}n_{21} & m_{11}n_{12} + m_{12}n_{22} & m_{11}n_{13} + m_{12}n_{23} \\ m_{21}n_{11} + m_{22}n_{21} & m_{21}n_{12} + m_{22}n_{22} & m_{21}n_{13} + m_{22}n_{23} \\ m_{31}n_{11} + m_{32}n_{21} & m_{31}n_{12} + m_{32}n_{22} & m_{31}n_{13} + m_{32}n_{23} \end{bmatrix}$$

This process starts by taking the first column of the second matrix and running it through each row of the first matrix. Removing all but the first M row and first N column, we would see only the following:

$$[m_{11} \ m_{12}] \times \begin{bmatrix} n_{11} \\ n_{21} \end{bmatrix} = m_{11}n_{11} + m_{12}n_{21}$$

The first product would then be $m_{11}n_{11} + m_{12}n_{21}$. This process will be continued for each column of the N matrix to find the first full row of the product matrix, as shown below.

$$[m_{11}n_{11} + m_{12}n_{21} \quad m_{11}n_{12} + m_{12}n_{22} \quad m_{11}n_{13} + m_{12}n_{23}]$$

After completing the first row, the next step would be to simply move to the second row of the M matrix and repeat the process until all of the rows have been finished. The result is a 3×3 matrix.

$$\begin{bmatrix} m_{11} & m_{12} \\ m_{21} & m_{22} \\ m_{31} & m_{32} \end{bmatrix} \times \begin{bmatrix} n_{11} & n_{12} & n_{13} \\ n_{21} & n_{22} & n_{23} \end{bmatrix} = \begin{bmatrix} m_{11}n_{11} + m_{12}n_{21} & m_{11}n_{12} + m_{12}n_{22} & m_{11}n_{13} + m_{12}n_{23} \\ m_{21}n_{11} + m_{22}n_{21} & m_{21}n_{12} + m_{22}n_{22} & m_{21}n_{13} + m_{22}n_{23} \\ m_{31}n_{11} + m_{32}n_{21} & m_{31}n_{12} + m_{32}n_{22} & m_{31}n_{13} + m_{32}n_{23} \end{bmatrix}$$

If the operation were done in reverse ($N \times M$), the result would be a 2×2 matrix.

$$\begin{bmatrix} n_{11} & n_{12} & n_{13} \\ n_{21} & n_{22} & n_{23} \end{bmatrix} \times \begin{bmatrix} m_{11} & m_{12} \\ m_{21} & m_{22} \\ m_{31} & m_{32} \end{bmatrix} = \begin{bmatrix} m_{11}n_{11} + m_{21}n_{12} + m_{31}n_{13} & m_{12}n_{11} + m_{22}n_{12} + m_{32}n_{13} \\ m_{11}n_{21} + m_{21}n_{22} + m_{31}n_{23} & m_{12}n_{21} + m_{22}n_{22} + m_{32}n_{23} \end{bmatrix}$$

Review Video: Matrices: The Basics
Visit mometrix.com/academy and enter code: 516658

Advanced Matrices

Elementary Row Operations

Elementary row operations include multiplying a row by a non-zero scalar, adding scalar multiples of two rows, and switching rows. These operations can be done using matrix multiplication with specialized transformation matrices. Elementary row operations are left multiplied, $A' = MA$.To do the same type of operations on the columns, then the transformation matrix is right multiplied, $A' = AM$. **Row switching** is achieved by swapping the corresponding rows in the identity matrix. For example, consider switching row 2 and row 3 in a 3×3 matrix:

$$M_{R_2 \leftrightarrow R_3} = \begin{bmatrix} 1 & 0 & 0 \\ 0 & 0 & 1 \\ 0 & 1 & 0 \end{bmatrix}$$

The transformation matrix for **row multiplication** is also based on the identity matrix with the scalar multiplication factor in place of the 1 in the corresponding row. Multiplying row 1 by –4 in a 3×3 matrix:

$$M_{-4R_1 \to R_1} = \begin{bmatrix} -4 & 0 & 0 \\ 0 & 1 & 0 \\ 0 & 0 & 1 \end{bmatrix}$$

The transformation matrix for **row addition** consists of the identity matrix with a 1 in the element corresponding to the two rows being added in the column where you want the result to go. Adding row 2 to row 1 in a 3×3 matrix:

$$M_{R_1+R_2 \to R_1} = \begin{bmatrix} 1 & 1 & 0 \\ 0 & 1 & 0 \\ 0 & 0 & 1 \end{bmatrix}$$

Review Video: Matrices: Elementary Row Operations
Visit mometrix.com/academy and enter code: 493170

Determinants and Inverses of Matrices

The **determinant** of a matrix is a scalar value that is calculated by taking into account all the elements of a square matrix. A determinant only exists for square matrices. Finding the determinant of a 2×2 matrix is as simple as remembering a simple equation. For a 2×2 matrix $M = \begin{bmatrix} m_{11} & m_{12} \\ m_{21} & m_{22} \end{bmatrix}$, the determinant is obtained by the equation $|M| = m_{11}m_{22} - m_{12}m_{21}$. Anything larger than 2×2 requires multiple steps. Take matrix $N = \begin{bmatrix} a & b & c \\ d & e & f \\ g & h & j \end{bmatrix}$. The determinant of N is calculated as $|N| = a\begin{vmatrix} e & f \\ h & j \end{vmatrix} - b\begin{vmatrix} d & f \\ g & j \end{vmatrix} + c\begin{vmatrix} d & e \\ g & h \end{vmatrix}$ or $|N| = a(ej - fh) - b(dj - fg) + c(dh - eg)$.

There is a shortcut for 3×3 matrices: add the products of each unique set of elements diagonally left-to-right and subtract the products of each unique set of elements diagonally right-to-left. In matrix N, the left-to-right diagonal elements are (a, e, j), (b, f, g), and (c, d, h). The right-to-left diagonal elements are (a, f, h), (b, d, j), and (c, e, g). $\det(N) = aej + bfg + cdh - afh - bdj - ceg$.

Calculating the determinants of matrices larger than 3×3 is rarely, if ever, done by hand.

The **inverse** of a matrix M is the matrix that, when multiplied by matrix M, yields a product that is the identity matrix. Multiplication of matrices will be explained in greater detail shortly. Not all matrices have inverses. Only a square matrix whose determinant is not zero has an inverse. If a matrix has an inverse, that inverse is unique to that matrix. For any matrix M that has an inverse, the inverse is represented by the symbol M^{-1}. To calculate the inverse of a 2×2 square matrix, use the following pattern:

$$M = \begin{bmatrix} m_{11} & m_{12} \\ m_{21} & m_{22} \end{bmatrix};\ M^{-1} = \begin{bmatrix} \frac{m_{22}}{|M|} & \frac{-m_{12}}{|M|} \\ \frac{-m_{21}}{|M|} & \frac{m_{11}}{|M|} \end{bmatrix}$$

Another way to find the inverse of a matrix by hand is use an augmented matrix and elementary row operations. An **augmented matrix** is formed by appending the entries from one matrix onto the end of another. For example, given a 2×2 invertible matrix $N = \begin{bmatrix} a & b \\ c & d \end{bmatrix}$, you can find the inverse N^{-1} by creating an augmented matrix by appending a 2×2 identity matrix: $\left[\begin{array}{cc|cc} a & b & 1 & 0 \\ c & d & 0 & 1 \end{array}\right]$. To find the inverse of the original 2×2 matrix, perform elementary row operations to convert the original matrix on the left to an identity matrix: $\left[\begin{array}{cc|cc} 1 & 0 & e & f \\ 0 & 1 & g & h \end{array}\right]$. For instance, the first step might be to multiply the second row by $\frac{b}{d}$ and then subtract it from the first row to make its second column a zero. The end result is that the 2 × 2 section on the right will become the inverse of the original matrix: $N^{-1} = \begin{bmatrix} e & f \\ g & h \end{bmatrix}$.

Review Video: Transposition, Determinants, and Augmentation of Matrices
Visit mometrix.com/academy and enter code: 521365

Reduced Row-Echelon Forms

When a system of equations has a solution, finding the transformation of the augmented matrix will result in one of three reduced row-echelon forms. Only one of these forms will give a unique solution to the system of equations, however. The following examples show the solutions indicated by particular results:

$\begin{bmatrix} 1 & 0 & 0 & x_0 \\ 0 & 1 & 0 & y_0 \\ 0 & 0 & 1 & z_0 \end{bmatrix}$ gives the unique solution $x = x_0;\ y = y_0;\ z = z_0$

$\begin{bmatrix} 1 & 0 & k_1 & x_0 \\ 0 & 1 & k_2 & y_0 \\ 0 & 0 & 0 & 0 \end{bmatrix}$ gives a non-unique solution $x = x_0 - k_1 z;\ y = y_0 - k_2 z$

$\begin{bmatrix} 1 & j_1 & k_1 & x_0 \\ 0 & 0 & 0 & 0 \\ 0 & 0 & 0 & 0 \end{bmatrix}$ gives a non-unique solution $x = x_0 - j_1 y - k_1 z$

Geometric Transformations

The four *geometric transformations* are **translations**, **reflections**, **rotations**, and **dilations**. When geometric transformations are expressed as matrices, the process of performing the transformations is simplified. For calculations of the geometric transformations of a planar figure, make a $2 \times n$ matrix, where n is the number of vertices in the planar figure. Each column represents the rectangular coordinates of one vertex of the figure, with the top row containing the values of the x-coordinates and the bottom row containing the values of the y-coordinates. For example, given a planar triangular figure with coordinates (x_1, y_1), (x_2, y_2), and (x_3, y_3), the corresponding matrix is $\begin{bmatrix} x_1 & x_2 & x_3 \\ y_1 & y_2 & y_3 \end{bmatrix}$. You can then perform the necessary transformations on this matrix to determine the coordinates of the resulting figure.

Review Video: Matrices: Geometric Transformations
Visit mometrix.com/academy and enter code: 612781

Translation

A **translation** moves a figure along the x-axis, the y-axis, or both axes without changing the size or shape of the figure. To calculate the new coordinates of a planar figure following a translation, set up a matrix of the coordinates and a matrix of the translation values and add the two matrices.

$$\begin{bmatrix} h & h & h \\ v & v & v \end{bmatrix} + \begin{bmatrix} x_1 & x_2 & x_3 \\ y_1 & y_2 & y_3 \end{bmatrix} = \begin{bmatrix} h + x_1 & h + x_2 & h + x_3 \\ v + y_1 & v + y_2 & v + y_3 \end{bmatrix}$$

where h is the number of units the figure is moved along the x-axis (horizontally) and v is the number of units the figure is moved along the y-axis (vertically).

REFLECTION

To find the **reflection** of a planar figure over the x-axis, set up a matrix of the coordinates of the vertices and pre-multiply the matrix by the 2×2 matrix $\begin{bmatrix} 1 & 0 \\ 0 & -1 \end{bmatrix}$ so that $\begin{bmatrix} 1 & 0 \\ 0 & -1 \end{bmatrix}\begin{bmatrix} x_1 & x_2 & x_3 \\ y_1 & y_2 & y_3 \end{bmatrix} = \begin{bmatrix} x_1 & x_2 & x_3 \\ -y_1 & -y_2 & -y_3 \end{bmatrix}$. To find the reflection of a planar figure over the y-axis, set up a matrix of the coordinates of the vertices and pre-multiply the matrix by the 2×2 matrix $\begin{bmatrix} -1 & 0 \\ 0 & 1 \end{bmatrix}$ so that $\begin{bmatrix} -1 & 0 \\ 0 & 1 \end{bmatrix}\begin{bmatrix} x_1 & x_2 & x_3 \\ y_1 & y_2 & y_3 \end{bmatrix} = \begin{bmatrix} -x_1 & -x_2 & -x_3 \\ y_1 & y_2 & y_3 \end{bmatrix}$. To find the reflection of a planar figure over the line $y = x$, set up a matrix of the coordinates of the vertices and pre-multiply the matrix by the 2×2 matrix $\begin{bmatrix} 0 & 1 \\ 1 & 0 \end{bmatrix}$ so that $\begin{bmatrix} 0 & 1 \\ 1 & 0 \end{bmatrix}\begin{bmatrix} x_1 & x_2 & x_3 \\ y_1 & y_2 & y_3 \end{bmatrix} = \begin{bmatrix} y_1 & y_2 & y_3 \\ x_1 & x_2 & x_3 \end{bmatrix}$. Remember that the order of multiplication is important when multiplying matrices. The commutative property does not apply.

ROTATION

To find the coordinates of the figure formed by rotating a planar figure about the origin θ degrees in a counterclockwise direction, set up a matrix of the coordinates of the vertices and pre-multiply the matrix by the 2×2 matrix $\begin{bmatrix} \cos\theta & -\sin\theta \\ \sin\theta & \cos\theta \end{bmatrix}$. For example, if you want to rotate a figure 90° clockwise around the origin, you would have to convert the degree measure to 270° counterclockwise and solve the 2×2 matrix you have set as the pre-multiplier: $\begin{bmatrix} \cos 270° & \sin 270° \\ -\sin 270° & \cos 270° \end{bmatrix} = \begin{bmatrix} 0 & -1 \\ 1 & 0 \end{bmatrix}$. Use this as the pre-multiplier for the matrix $\begin{bmatrix} x_1 & x_2 & x_3 \\ y_1 & y_2 & y_3 \end{bmatrix}$ and solve to find the new coordinates.

DILATION

To find the **dilation** of a planar figure by a scale factor of k, set up a matrix of the coordinates of the vertices of the planar figure and pre-multiply the matrix by the 2×2 matrix $\begin{bmatrix} k & 0 \\ 0 & k \end{bmatrix}$ so that $\begin{bmatrix} k & 0 \\ 0 & k \end{bmatrix}\begin{bmatrix} x_1 & x_2 & x_3 \\ y_1 & y_2 & y_3 \end{bmatrix} = \begin{bmatrix} kx_1 & kx_2 & kx_3 \\ ky_1 & ky_2 & ky_3 \end{bmatrix}$. This is effectively the same as multiplying the matrix by the scalar k, but the matrix equation would still be necessary if the figure were being dilated by different factors in vertical and horizontal directions. The scale factor k will be greater than 1 if the figure is being enlarged, and between 0 and 1 if the figure is being shrunk. Again, remember that when multiplying matrices, the order of the matrices is important. The commutative property does not apply, and the matrix with the coordinates of the figure must be the second matrix.

MATRIX SYSTEMS

SOLVING SYSTEMS OF EQUATIONS

Matrices can be used to represent the coefficients of a system of linear equations and can be very useful in solving those systems. Take for instance three equations with three variables where all a, b, c, and d are known constants:

$$a_1x + b_1y + c_1z = d_1$$
$$a_2x + b_2y + c_2z = d_2$$
$$a_3x + b_3y + c_3z = d_3$$

To solve this system, define three matrices:

$$A = \begin{bmatrix} a_1 & b_1 & c_1 \\ a_2 & b_2 & c_2 \\ a_3 & b_3 & c_3 \end{bmatrix};\ D = \begin{bmatrix} d_1 \\ d_2 \\ d_3 \end{bmatrix};\ X = \begin{bmatrix} x \\ y \\ z \end{bmatrix}$$

The three equations in our system can be fully represented by a single matrix equation:

$$AX = D$$

We know that the identity matrix times X is equal to X, and we know that any matrix multiplied by its inverse is equal to the identity matrix.

$$A^{-1}AX = IX = X; \text{thus } X = A^{-1}D$$

Our goal then is to find the inverse of A, or A^{-1}. Once we have that, we can pre-multiply matrix D by A^{-1} (post-multiplying here is an undefined operation) to find matrix X.

Systems of equations can also be solved using the transformation of an augmented matrix in a process similar to that for finding a matrix inverse. Begin by arranging each equation of the system in the following format:

$$\begin{aligned} a_1x + b_1y + c_1z &= d_1 \\ a_2x + b_2y + c_2z &= d_2 \\ a_3x + b_3y + c_3z &= d_3 \end{aligned}$$

Define matrices A and D and combine them into augmented matrix A_a:

$$A = \begin{bmatrix} a_1 & b_1 & c_1 \\ a_2 & b_2 & c_2 \\ a_3 & b_3 & c_3 \end{bmatrix};\ D = \begin{bmatrix} d_1 \\ d_2 \\ d_3 \end{bmatrix};A_a = \begin{bmatrix} a_1 & b_1 & c_1 & d_1 \\ a_2 & b_2 & c_2 & d_2 \\ a_3 & b_3 & c_3 & d_3 \end{bmatrix}$$

To solve the augmented matrix and the system of equations, use elementary row operations to form an identity matrix in the first 3×3 section. When this is complete, the values in the last column are the solutions to the system of equations:

$$\begin{bmatrix} 1 & 0 & 0 & x \\ 0 & 1 & 0 & y \\ 0 & 0 & 1 & z \end{bmatrix}$$

If an identity matrix is not possible, the system of equations has no unique solution. Sometimes only a partial solution will be possible. The following are partial solutions you may find:

$\begin{bmatrix} 1 & 0 & k_1 & x_0 \\ 0 & 1 & k_2 & y_0 \\ 0 & 0 & 0 & 0 \end{bmatrix}$ gives the non-unique solution $x = x_0 - k_1z;\ y = y_0 - k_2z$

$\begin{bmatrix} 1 & j_1 & k_1 & x_0 \\ 0 & 0 & 0 & 0 \\ 0 & 0 & 0 & 0 \end{bmatrix}$ gives the non-unique solution $x = x_0 - j_1y - k_1z$

This process can be used to solve systems of equations with any number of variables, but three is the upper limit for practical purposes. Anything more ought to be done with a graphing calculator.

Review Video: Matrices: Data Systems
Visit mometrix.com/academy and enter code: 579763

Trigonometry

The Unit Circle

Degrees, Radians, and the Unit Circle

It is important to understand the deep connection between trigonometry and circles. Specifically, the two main units, **degrees** (°) and **radians** (rad), that are used to measure angles are related this way: 360° in one full circle and 2π radians in one full circle: ($360° = 2\pi$ rad). The conversion factor relating the two is often stated as $\frac{180°}{\pi}$. For example, to convert $\frac{3\pi}{2}$ radians to degrees, multiply by the conversion factor: $\frac{3\pi}{2} \times \frac{180°}{\pi} = 270°$. As another example, to convert 60° to radians, divide by the conversion factor or multiply by the reciprocal: $60° \times \frac{\pi}{180°} = \frac{\pi}{3}$ radians.

Recall that the standard equation for a circle is $(x - h)^2 + (y - k)^2 = r^2$. A **unit circle** is a circle with a radius of 1 ($r = 1$) that has its center at the origin ($h = 0, k = 0$). Thus, the equation for the unit circle simplifies from the standard equation down to $x^2 + y^2 = 1$.

Standard position is the position of an angle of measure θ whose vertex is at the origin, the initial side crosses the unit circle at the point $(1, 0)$, and the terminal side crosses the unit circle at some other point (a, b). In the standard position, $\sin\theta = b$, $\cos\theta = a$, and $\tan\theta = \frac{b}{a}$.

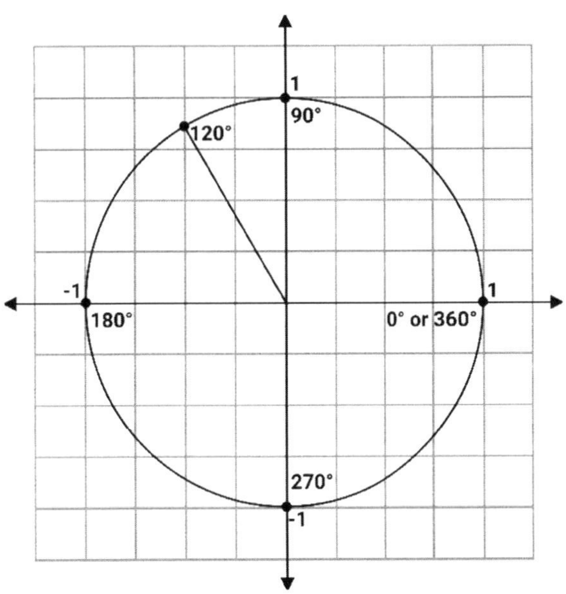

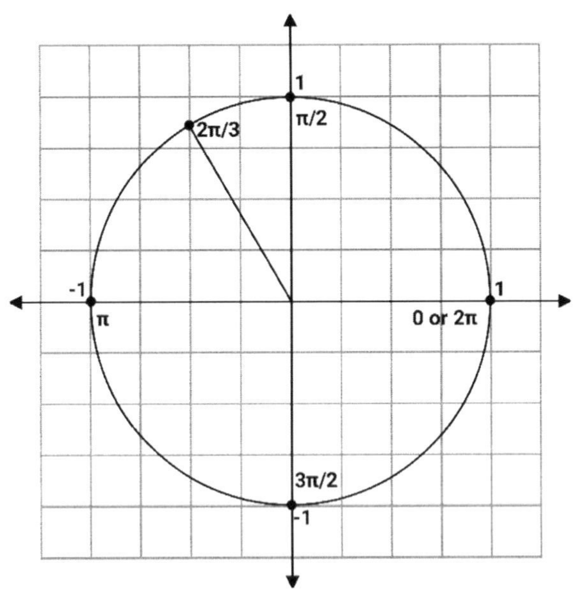

Review Video: Unit Circle
Visit mometrix.com/academy and enter code: 333922

Table of Commonly Encountered Angles

$0° = 0$ radians, $30° = \frac{\pi}{6}$ radians, $45° = \frac{\pi}{4}$ radians, $60° = \frac{\pi}{3}$ radians, and $90° = \frac{\pi}{2}$ radians

$\sin 0° = 0$	$\cos 0° = 1$	$\tan 0° = 0$
$\sin 30° = \frac{1}{2}$	$\cos 30° = \frac{\sqrt{3}}{2}$	$\tan 30° = \frac{\sqrt{3}}{3}$
$\sin 45° = \frac{\sqrt{2}}{2}$	$\cos 45° = \frac{\sqrt{2}}{2}$	$\tan 45° = 1$
$\sin 60° = \frac{\sqrt{3}}{2}$	$\cos 60° = \frac{1}{2}$	$\tan 60° = \sqrt{3}$
$\sin 90° = 1$	$\cos 90° = 0$	$\tan 90° =$ undefined
$\csc 0° =$ undefined	$\sec 0° = 1$	$\cot 0° =$ undefined
$\csc 30° = 2$	$\sec 30° = \frac{2\sqrt{3}}{3}$	$\cot 30° = \sqrt{3}$
$\csc 45° = \sqrt{2}$	$\sec 45° = \sqrt{2}$	$\cot 45° = 1$
$\csc 60° = \frac{2\sqrt{3}}{3}$	$\sec 60° = 2$	$\cot 60° = \frac{\sqrt{3}}{3}$
$\csc 90° = 1$	$\sec 90° =$ undefined	$\cot 90° = 0$

The values in the upper half of this table are values you should have memorized or be able to find quickly and those in the lower half can easily be determined as the reciprocal of the corresponding function.

Defined and Reciprocal Functions

The tangent function is defined as the ratio of the sine to the cosine: $\tan x = \frac{\sin x}{\cos x}$.

To take the reciprocal of a number means to place that number as the denominator of a fraction with a numerator of 1. The reciprocal functions are thus defined quite simply.

Cosecant	$\csc x$	$\frac{1}{\sin x}$
Secant	$\sec x$	$\frac{1}{\cos x}$
Cotangent	$\cot x$	$\frac{1}{\tan x}$

It is important to know these reciprocal functions, but they are not as commonly used as the three basic functions.

Review Video: Defined and Reciprocal Functions
Visit mometrix.com/academy and enter code: 996431

Inverse Trigonometric Functions

Inverse Functions

Each of the trigonometric functions accepts an angular measure, either degrees or radians, and gives a numerical value as the output. The inverse functions do the opposite; they accept a numerical value and give an angular measure as the output.

The inverse of sine, or arcsine, commonly written as either $\sin^{-1} x$ or $\arcsin x$, gives the angle whose sine is x. Similarly:

The inverse of $\cos x$ is written as $\cos^{-1} x$ or $\arccos x$ and means the angle whose cosine is x.
The inverse of $\tan x$ is written as $\tan^{-1} x$ or $\arctan x$ and means the angle whose tangent is x.
The inverse of $\csc x$ is written as $\csc^{-1} x$ or $\text{arccsc}\, x$ and means the angle whose cosecant is x.
The inverse of $\sec x$ is written as $\sec^{-1} x$ or $\text{arcsec}\, x$ and means the angle whose secant is x.
The inverse of $\cot x$ is written as $\cot^{-1} x$ or $\text{arccot}\, x$ and means the angle whose cotangent is x.

Review Video: Inverse Trig Functions
Visit mometrix.com/academy and enter code: 156054

Important Note About Solving Trigonometric Equations

When solving for an angle with a known trigonometric value, you must consider the sign and include all angles with that value. Your calculator will probably only give one value as an answer, typically in the following ranges:

- For $\sin^{-1} x$, $\left[-\frac{\pi}{2}, \frac{\pi}{2}\right]$ or $[-90°, 90°]$
- For $\cos^{-1} x$, $[0, \pi]$ or $[0°, 180°]$
- For $\tan^{-1} x$, $\left[-\frac{\pi}{2}, \frac{\pi}{2}\right]$ or $[-90°, 90°]$

It is important to determine if there is another angle in a different quadrant that also satisfies the problem. To do this, find the other quadrant(s) with the same sign for that trigonometric function and find the angle that has the same reference angle. Then check whether this angle is also a solution.

- In the first quadrant, all six trigonometric functions are positive.
- In the second quadrant, sin and csc are positive.
- In the third quadrant, tan and cot are positive.
- In the fourth quadrant, cos and sec are positive.

If you remember the phrase, "ALL Students Take Classes," you will be able to remember the sign of each trigonometric function in each quadrant. ALL represents all the signs in the first quadrant. The "S" in "Students" represents the sine function and its reciprocal in the second quadrant. The "T" in "Take" represents the tangent function and its reciprocal in the third quadrant. The "C" in "Classes" represents the cosine function and its reciprocal.

TRIGONOMETRIC IDENTITIES

SUM AND DIFFERENCE

To find the sine, cosine, or tangent of the sum or difference of two angles, use one of the following formulas where α and β are two angles with known sine, cosine, or tangent values as needed:

$$\sin(\alpha \pm \beta) = \sin\alpha\cos\beta \pm \cos\alpha\sin\beta$$
$$\cos(\alpha \pm \beta) = \cos\alpha\cos\beta \mp \sin\alpha\sin\beta$$
$$\tan(\alpha \pm \beta) = \frac{\tan\alpha \pm \tan\beta}{1 \mp \tan\alpha\tan\beta}$$

HALF ANGLE

To find the sine or cosine of half of a known angle, use the following formulas where θ is an angle with a known exact cosine value:

$$\sin\left(\frac{\theta}{2}\right) = \pm\sqrt{\frac{(1 - cos\theta)}{2}}$$
$$\cos\left(\frac{\theta}{2}\right) = \pm\sqrt{\frac{(1 + \cos\theta)}{2}}$$

To determine the sign of the answer, you must recognize which quadrant the given angle is in and apply the correct sign for the trigonometric function you are using. If you need to find an expression for the exact sine or cosine of an angle that you do not know, such as sine 22.5°, you can rewrite the given angle as a half angle, such as $\sin\left(\frac{45°}{2}\right)$, and use the formula above:

$$\sin\left(\frac{45°}{2}\right) = \pm\sqrt{\frac{(1 - \cos(45°))}{2}} = \pm\sqrt{\frac{\left(1 - \frac{\sqrt{2}}{2}\right)}{2}} = \pm\sqrt{\frac{(2 - \sqrt{2})}{4}} = \pm\frac{1}{2}\sqrt{(2 - \sqrt{2})}$$

To find the tangent or cotangent of half of a known angle, use the following formulas where θ is an angle with known exact sine and cosine values:

$$\tan\frac{\theta}{2} = \frac{sin\theta}{1 + \cos\theta}$$
$$\cot\frac{\theta}{2} = \frac{\sin\theta}{1 - \cos\theta}$$

These formulas will work for finding the tangent or cotangent of half of any angle unless the cosine of θ happens to make the denominator of the identity equal to 0.

The Pythagorean theorem states that $a^2 + b^2 = c^2$ for all right triangles. The trigonometric identity that derives from this principle is stated in this way: $\sin^2\theta + \cos^2\theta = 1$.

Dividing each term by either $\sin^2\theta$ or $\cos^2\theta$ yields two other identities, respectively:

$$1 + \cot^2\theta = \csc^2\theta$$
$$\tan^2\theta + 1 = \sec^2\theta$$

Review Video: Sum and Difference Trigonometric Identities
Visit mometrix.com/academy and enter code: 468838

Double Angles

In each case, use one of the double angle formulas. To find the sine or cosine of twice a known angle, use one of the following formulas:

$$\sin(2\theta) = 2\sin\theta\cos\theta$$

$$\begin{aligned}\cos(2\theta) &= \cos^2\theta - \sin^2\theta \\ &= 2\cos^2\theta - 1 \\ &= 1 - 2\sin^2\theta\end{aligned}$$

To find the tangent or cotangent of twice a known angle, use the formulas where θ is an angle with known exact sine, cosine, tangent, and cotangent values:

$$\tan(2\theta) = \frac{2\tan\theta}{1 - \tan^2\theta}$$
$$\cot(2\theta) = \frac{\cot\theta - \tan\theta}{2}$$

Products

To find the product of the sines and cosines of two different angles, use one of the following formulas where α and β are two unique angles:

$$\sin\alpha\sin\beta = \frac{1}{2}[\cos(\alpha - \beta) - \cos(\alpha + \beta)]$$
$$\cos\alpha\cos\beta = \frac{1}{2}[\cos(\alpha + \beta) + \cos(\alpha - \beta)]$$
$$\sin\alpha\cos\beta = \frac{1}{2}[\sin(\alpha + \beta) + \sin(\alpha - \beta)]$$
$$\cos\alpha\sin\beta = \frac{1}{2}[\sin(\alpha + \beta) - \sin(\alpha - \beta)]$$

Review Video: Half-Angle, Double Angle, and Product Trig Identities
Visit mometrix.com/academy and enter code: 274252

Complementary

The trigonometric cofunction identities use the trigonometric relationships of complementary angles (angles whose sum is 90°). These are:

$$\cos x = \sin(90° - x)$$
$$\csc x = \sec(90° - x)$$
$$\cot x = \tan(90° - x)$$

Domain, Range, and Asymptotes in Trigonometry

The domain is the set of all possible real number values of x on the graph of a trigonometric function. Some graphs will impose limits on the values of x.

The range is the set of all possible real number values of y on the graph of a trigonometric function. Some graphs will impose limits on the values of y.

Asymptotes are lines that the graph of a trigonometric function approaches but never reaches. Asymptotes exist for values of x in the graphs of the tangent, cotangent, secant, and cosecant. The sine and cosine graphs do not have any asymptotes.

Domain, Range, and Asymptotes of the Six Trigonometric Functions

The domain, range, and asymptotes for each of the trigonometric functions are as follows:

- In the **sine** function, the domain is all real numbers, the range is $-1 \leq y \leq 1$, and there are no asymptotes.
- In the **cosine** function, the domain is all real numbers, the range is $-1 \leq y \leq 1$, and there are no asymptotes.
- In the **tangent** function, the domain is $x \in \mathbb{R}; x \neq \frac{\pi}{2} + k\pi$, the range is all real numbers, and the asymptotes are the lines $x = \frac{\pi}{2} + k\pi$.
- In the **cosecant** function, the domain is $x \in \mathbb{R}; x \neq k\pi$, the range is $(-\infty, -1]$ and $[1, \infty)$, and the asymptotes are the lines $x = k\pi$.
- In the **secant** function, the domain is $x \in \mathbb{R}; x \neq \frac{\pi}{2} + k\pi$, the range is $(-\infty, 1]$ and $[1, \infty)$, and the asymptotes are the lines $x = \frac{\pi}{2} + k\pi$.
- In the **cotangent** function, the domain is $x \in \mathbb{R}; x \neq k\pi$, the range is all real numbers, and the asymptotes are the lines $x = k\pi$.

In each of the above cases, k represents any integer.

Rectangular and Polar Coordinates

Rectangular coordinates are those that lie on the square grids of the Cartesian plane. They should be quite familiar to you. The polar coordinate system is based on a circular graph, rather than the square grid of the Cartesian system. Points in the polar coordinate system are in the format (r, θ), where r is the distance from the origin (think radius of the circle) and θ is the smallest positive angle (moving counterclockwise around the circle) made with the positive horizontal axis.

To convert a point from rectangular (x, y) format to polar (r, θ) format, use the formula (x, y) to $(r, \theta) \Rightarrow r = \sqrt{x^2 + y^2}; \theta = \arctan\frac{y}{x}$ when $x \neq 0$.

If x is positive, use the positive square root value for r. If x is negative, use the negative square root value for r. If $x = 0$, use the following rules:

- If $y = 0$, then $\theta = 0$.
- If $y > 0$, then $\theta = \frac{\pi}{2}$.
- If $y < 0$, then $\theta = \frac{3\pi}{2}$.

To convert a point from polar (r, θ) format to rectangular (x, y) format, use the formula (r, θ) to $(x, y) \Rightarrow x = r\cos\theta\,;\, y = r\sin\theta$.

De Moivre's Theorem

De Moivre's theorem is used to find the powers of complex numbers (numbers that contain the imaginary number i) written in polar form. Given a trigonometric expression that contains i, such as $z = r\cos x + ir\sin x$, where r is a real number and x is an angle measurement in polar form, use the formula $z^n = r^n(\cos nx + i\sin nx)$, where r and n are real numbers, x is the angle measure in polar form, and i is the imaginary number $i = \sqrt{-1}$. The expression $\cos x + i\sin x$ can be written cis x, making the formula appear in the format $z^n = r^n$ cis nx.

Note that De Moivre's theorem is only for angles in polar form. If you are given an angle in degrees, you must convert to polar form before using the formula.

Set Theory

Set Theory

Discrete Mathematics

Among mathematicians, there is not an agreed-upon definition of discrete math. What is agreed upon is the fact that discrete math deals with processes that use a finite, or countable, number of elements. In discrete math, the elements will be discontinuous, as this branch of mathematics does not involve the continuity that processes of calculus do. Generally, discrete math uses countable sets of rational numbers, although they do not use the set of all real numbers, as that would then make the math continuous and put it in the category of algebra or calculus. Discrete math has numerous applications in the fields of computer science and business.

Review Video: Introduction to Set Theory
Visit mometrix.com/academy and enter code: 397496

Element of a Set

A set is a mathematical collection of items, and an element is an item that is included in the set. These items are typically sets of numbers, or sets of geometrical points, or even sets of sets.

Whether an item is an **element of a set** is a binary property. In other words, a particular item either is or is not an element of a given set. There are not different degrees of belonging to a set, and one element of a set cannot be more an element than another. Additionally, the elements do not have any particular order, and there is no count of how many times an element appears in a set. For example, in the set $\{0, 2, 1, 2, 4\}$, the numbers 0, 1, 2, and 4 are elements of the set. Two is not more of an element than the others because it is listed twice. Any number other than these, such as 3, is not an element of the set.

The mathematical symbol $\in$ means "is an element of." for instance, "$1 \in A$" means that "the number 1 is an element of set A". The symbol can be negated with a diagonal slash, so "$1 \notin A$" means "the number 1 is *not* an element of set A."

Empty Set

The empty set contains no elements. The symbol for the **empty set** is a circle with a line through it, $\emptyset$, or the empty set can be written in roster form as $\{\quad\}$. Although it may seem trivial, the empty set is important for the same reason that zero is an important number—without the empty set, many set operations and definitions would be incomplete. For instance, the intersection of two nonoverlapping sets is the empty set. The set of all prime numbers that are perfect squares is the empty set, because there are no such numbers. Other sets can be constructed using the empty set. For instance, a set *containing* the empty set, $\{\{\ \}\}$ or $\{\emptyset\}$, is different from the empty set itself, since it's not actually empty—it contains one element, the empty set.

The empty set is, by definition, a subset of every set, including itself. This is because every element that is an element of the empty set is also an element of any other set, since the empty set contains no elements that could make this statement false.

Subset, Proper Subset, and Superset

Set A is a **subset** of set B if set A is contained entirely within set B. More formally, set A is a subset of set B if every element of set A is also in set B. We can write this as $\forall x(x \in A \Rightarrow x \in B)$. The symbol for subset is $\subseteq$, so we can write "$A \subseteq B$" to mean "set A is a subset of set B," or "$A \nsubseteq B$" to mean "set A is NOT a subset of set B".

Any set is a subset of itself, since naturally any element in a set is in that set. A **proper subset** means a subset that is not equal to the other set. In other words, set A is a proper subset of set B if set A is a subset of set B but they are not the same, so $A \subseteq B$ but $B \nsubseteq A$. For example, $\{0, 1, 2\}$ is a proper subset of $\{0, 1, 2, 3\}$ because every element in the first set is included in the second set but the two sets are not identical. The symbol for a proper subset is $\subset$, so we write "$A \subset B$" to mean "set A is a proper subset of set B," and "$A \not\subset B$" to mean "set A is not a proper subset of set B."

The converse of a subset is a **superset**. If A is a subset of B, then B is a superset of A. In the example above, $\{0, 1, 2, 3\}$ is a superset of $\{0, 1, 2\}$ because the first set contains every element of the second plus more.

Union of Two or More Sets

The **union** of two or more sets includes all the elements that are included in all of the sets. An element is in the union of sets A and B if it is in set A or in set B, or in both. The union is written with the symbol $\cup$, so "$A \cup B$" (read "A union B") means the union of sets A and B.

For example, given the sets $A = \{1, 2, 3, 4\}$ and $B = \{2, 4, 6, 8\}$, then $A \cup B = \{1, 2, 3, 4, 6, 8\}$. 1 and 3 are in $A \cup B$ because they are in set A, and 6 and 8 are in $A \cup B$ because they are in set B. 2 and 4 appear in both A and B, so they are in $A \cup B$, but they only appear once.

The union operation on sets is both commutative and associative. That is, $A \cup B = B \cup A$, and $(A \cup B) \cup C = A \cup (B \cup C)$.

Intersection of Two or More Sets

The intersection of two or more sets is a set including every element that appears in *all* of the sets. An element is in the intersection of sets A and B if and only if, the element appears in both set A and set B. For instance, if set $A = \{0, 1, 2, 3\}$ and set $B = \{2, 3, 4, 5\}$, the intersection of sets A and B includes the elements 2 and 3, because these are the only elements that appear in both sets. The intersection is written with the symbol $\cap$, so "$A \cap B$" (read "A intersection B") means the intersection of sets A and B.

The intersection operation on sets is both commutative and associative. That is, $A \cap B = B \cap A$, and $(A \cap B) \cap C = A \cap (B \cap C)$. The union and intersection operations also jointly have distributive properties: $A \cap (B \cup C) = (A \cap B) \cup (A \cap C)$ and $A \cup (B \cap C) = (A \cup B) \cap (A \cup C)$.

COMPLEMENT OF A SET

The complement of a set is a set containing all the elements that are *not* in the original set. To determine this, we must also define the **universe of discourse**—the set of all possible elements we're considering, abbreviated U. For mathematical applications, the universe of discourse is commonly the set of all integers (abbreviated $\mathbb{Z}$), or the set of all real numbers (abbreviated $\mathbb{R}$). If U is the set of all integers, for example, then the complement of the set $A = \{1, 2, 3\}$ would include elements such as -3, 0, or 6, but it would not include elements such as $\sqrt{7}$ or $\frac{1}{4}$, because these are not in the universe of discourse.

The **complement of a set** is often written either by drawing a line over the name of the original set, or by adding an apostrophe or a superscripted C. The complement of set A, for instance, could be written as $\bar{A}$, as A', or as A^C.

For example, given set $A = \{2, 4, 6, 8\}$ with a universe of discourse of $U = \{1, 2, 3, 4, 5, 6, 7, 8, 9, 10\}$, the complement of set A would be $\{1, 3, 5, 7, 9, 10\}$—all the elements of U that are not in A.

DIFFERENCE OF TWO SETS

The difference of two sets is a set containing all the elements that are in the first set but not in the second. The difference of sets A and B is also referred to as the **relative complement** of set A with respect to set B, and is written $A \setminus B$ or $A - B$. The difference is always a subset of the first set: $A \setminus B \subseteq A$. However, it is *not* necessarily the case that $A \setminus B \subseteq B$. In fact, because any element of $A \setminus B$ is by definition not an element of B, the only time that $A \setminus B$ can be a subset of B is if $A \setminus B$ has no elements, i.e., if $A \setminus B = \emptyset$, which is true if and only if, $A \subseteq B$.

Unlike the union and intersection, the operation of the difference between sets is neither commutative nor associative. In general, $A \setminus B \neq B \setminus A$, and $A \setminus (B \setminus C) \neq (A \setminus B) \setminus C$.

For example, consider the sets $A = \{1, 2, 3\}$, $B = \{2, 4\}$, and $C = \{1, 2\}$. Then $A \setminus B = \{1, 3\}$ since 1 and 3 are in set A but not in set B. Similarly, $B \setminus A = \{4\}$, $B \setminus C = \{4\}$, $C \setminus B = \{1\}$, and $A \setminus C = \{3\}$. However, $C \setminus A = \emptyset$, i.e., set C is a subset of set A, so there are no elements that appear in C but not in A, which means the difference between C and A is the empty set.

SYMBOLS FOR SETS COMMONLY USED IN MATHEMATICS

Certain sets are used frequently enough in mathematics to have their own symbols. The standard symbols for these sets resemble upper-case letters of the Latin alphabet, but in a typeface with double lines. Among the most commonly used **sets** are:

- $\mathbb{R}$ - the set of all real numbers
- $\mathbb{Z}$ - the set of all integers
- $\mathbb{N}$ - the set of all natural numbers
- $\mathbb{Q}$ - the set of all rational numbers (numbers that can be written as the ratio of two integers, $\frac{p}{q}$, where $q \neq 0$)
- $\mathbb{C}$ - the set of all complex numbers (numbers of the form $a + bi$, where a and b are real numbers and $i = \sqrt{-1}$)

A superscripted plus or minus sign is used to restrict the set to positive or negative numbers. for instance, $\mathbb{R}^+$ would be the set of all positive real numbers, and $\mathbb{Z}^-$ would be the set of all negative integers.

Some of these sets are, of course, subsets of others. Specifically, $\mathbb{N} \subset \mathbb{Z} \subset \mathbb{Q} \subset \mathbb{R} \subset \mathbb{C}$.

Recursive and Explicit Formulas

Sets of numbers can have a consistent relationship between the elements of the set. Some of these relationships can be represented with simple recursive or explicit formulas. For example, consider the set of all positive, even numbers (a) and the set of all positive, odd numbers (b):

Positive, Even Numbers:

Recursive: $a_n = a_{n-1} + 2, n \geq 2, a_1 = 0$
Explicit: $a_n = 2n, n \geq 0$

Positive, Odd Numbers:

Recursive: $b_n = b_{n-1} + 2, n \geq 2, b_1 = 1$
Explicit: $b_n = 2n + 1, n \geq 0$

Each set of numbers represents a linear function, with a constant rate of change of 2. The positive, even numbers represent a linear function that is proportional, whereas the positive, odd numbers represent a linear function that is not proportional. The set of even, positive numbers is represented by a function with a y-intercept of 0. The set of odd, positive numbers is represented by a function with a y-intercept of 1.

Venn Diagrams

Set Operations with Venn Diagrams

A Venn diagram is a useful visual tool for representing two or three sets and their common elements. Each set is drawn as a **circle**, with the different circles overlapping. Elements are placed in the circle corresponding to the appropriate set or sets—or placed outside all the circles if they belong to the universe of discourse but not to any of the sets.

For example, suppose our universe of discourse is the integers from 1 to 9, and we have the three sets $A = \{1, 2, 3, 4, 5, 6\}$, $B = \{4, 5, 6, 7\}$, and $C = \{3, 6, 9\}$. This could be illustrated with the following **Venn diagram**:

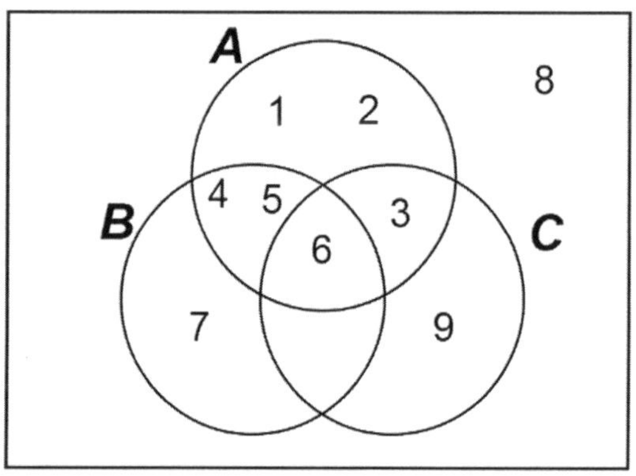

Note, for example, that 6 appears in the center of the diagram where all three circles overlap, because it is an element of all three sets. On the other hand, 8 is placed outside the three circles because it is not an element of any of the sets. Sometimes, instead of writing the elements themselves in the diagram, the total *number* of elements in each part of the Venn diagram is noted. This is especially useful for solving problems involving these numbers of elements.

Using Venn Diagrams to Solve Problems

Venn diagrams are useful for solving problems involving the numbers of elements in sets and in their intersections. By putting those numbers into a Venn diagram, it's simple to see how many must be in the "leftover" parts.

For example, suppose we're told that 200 voters were polled about two propositions, Proposition 1 and Proposition 2. Further,120 support Proposition 1, 85 support Proposition 2, and 50 support both propositions. To find how many of the voters support neither proposition, we can draw a Venn diagram with a circle representing the supporters of each proposition. We know 50 voters support both propositions, so we can write a 50 in the center of the diagram.

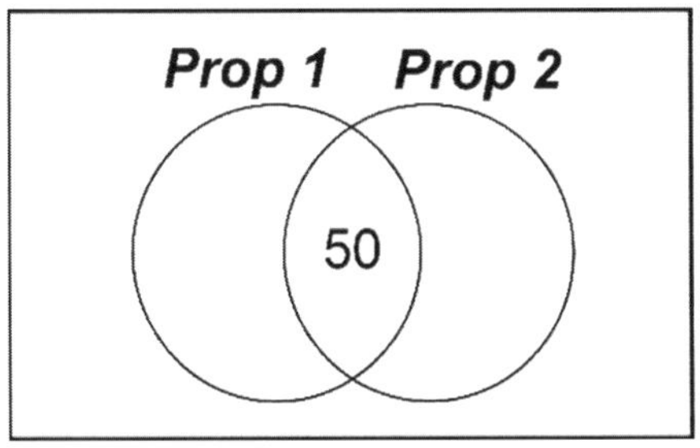

The Proposition 1 circle should contain 120 voters total, so subtracting the 50 voters in the overlap, the other section of the circle must contain $120 - 50 = 70$. Similarly, the nonoverlapping part of the Proposition 2 circle should contain $85 - 50 = 35$.

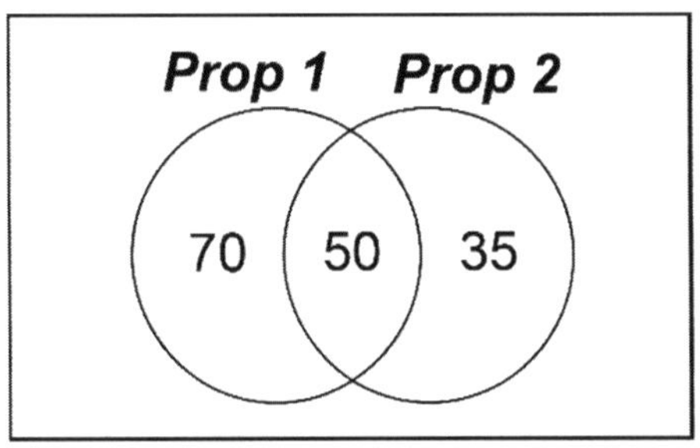

Adding all three sections, the total number of voters supporting either proposition is $70 + 50 + 35 = 155$, so there must be $200 - 155 = 45$ voters who support neither.

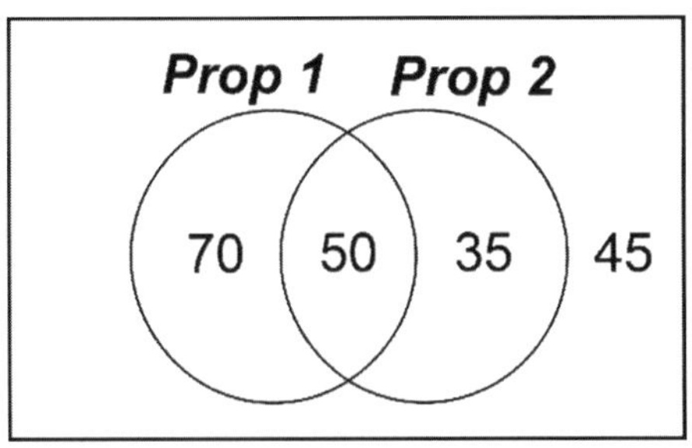

Advanced Set Theory

Properties of Infinite Sets

An infinite set has an infinite number of elements. a more technical definition is that a set is **infinite** if its elements can be put in one-to-one correspondence with the elements of one of its proper subsets. For instance, consider the set of all positive integers, $\mathbb{Z}^+$. If we remove the number 1, we can still match up every positive integer to an element of the remaining subset (by simply matching the number n to the number $n + 1$). $\mathbb{Z}^+$ is therefore an infinite set.

The union of an infinite set and any other set is always infinite. The intersection of two infinite sets may or may not be infinite. For instance, consider the set P of prime numbers, the set O of positive odd integers, and the set E of positive even integers—all infinite sets. $P \cap O$ is another infinite set, because there are infinitely many odd prime numbers. $P \cap E$ is finite, because there is only one even prime number. $E \cap O$ is the empty set. Likewise, the complement of an infinite set may be infinite, finite, or the empty set (if the set equals the universe of discourse).

Cardinality

Although all infinite sets have infinitely many members, they may still have different sizes. Two sets are defined to have the same size—or more technically the same **cardinality**—if each element of one set can be matched up to a unique element of the other, with none left over. For example, the set of all integers, $\mathbb{Z}$, and the set of all *even* integers have the same cardinality, even though the latter is a proper subset of the former: every number n in $\mathbb{Z}$ can be matched to a unique number $2n$ in the set of all *even* integers. Although it's more difficult to prove, the set of all rational numbers, $\mathbb{Q}$, also has the same cardinality as $\mathbb{Z}$. However, the set of all real numbers, $\mathbb{R}$, does *not* have the same cardinality—it is impossible to match each integer to a unique real number without any real numbers left over. The most famous proof of this fact was developed by Georg Cantor, and is called the *diagonal argument.*

Sets with the same cardinality as $\mathbb{Z}$ are said to be "countably infinite," or simply **countable**. Sets with a larger cardinality are said to be "uncountably infinite," or **uncountable**.

Cartesian Products and Binary Relations

A **Cartesian product** is the product of two sets of data, X and Y, such that all elements x are a member of set X, and all elements y are a member of set Y. The product of the two sets, $X \times Y$ is the set of all ordered pairs (x, y). For example, given a standard deck of 52 playing cards, there are four possible suits (hearts, diamonds, clubs, and spades) and thirteen possible card values (the numbers 2 through 10, ace, jack, queen, and king). If the card suits are set X and the card values are set Y, then there are $4 \times 13 = 52$ possible different (x, y) combinations, as seen in the 52 cards of a standard deck.

A **binary relation**, also referred to as a relation, dyadic relation, or 2-place relation, is a subset of a Cartesian product. It shows the relation between one set of objects and a second set of objects, or between one set of objects and itself. The prefix *bi-* means *two*, so there are always two sets involved—either two different sets, or the same set used twice. The ordered pairs of the Cartesian product are used to indicate a binary relation. Relations are possible for situations involving more than two sets, but those are not called binary relations.

The five types of relations are reflexive, symmetric, transitive, antisymmetric, and equivalence. A **reflexive relation** has $x\Re x$ (x related to x) for all values of x in the set. A **symmetric relation** has $x\Re y \Rightarrow y\Re x$ for all values of x and y in the set. A **transitive relation** has $(x\Re y \text{ and } y\Re z) \Rightarrow x\Re z$ for all values of x, y, and z in the set. An **antisymmetric relation** has $(x\Re y \text{ and } y\Re x) \Rightarrow x = y$ for all values of x and y in the set. A relation that is reflexive, symmetric, and transitive is called an **equivalence relation**.

VERTEX-EDGE GRAPHS

A **vertex-edge graph** is a set of items or objects connected by pathways or links. As an example, consider the following set of nodes and a few graphs representing ways of connecting them with edges.

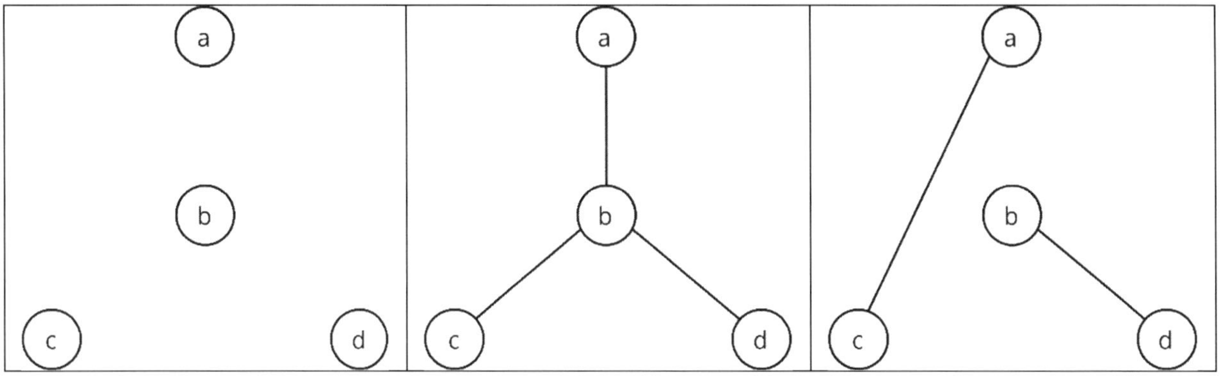

Vertex-edge graphs are useful for solving problems involving schedules, relationships, networks, or paths among a set number of objects. The number of objects may be large, but it will never be infinite. The **vertices** or points on the graph represent the objects and may also be referred to as **nodes**. The nodes are joined by line segments called **edges** or links that show the specific paths that connect the various elements represented by the nodes. The number of nodes does not have to equal the number of edges. There may be more or less, depending on the number of allowable paths.

An **endpoint** on a vertex-edge graph is a vertex on exactly one edge. In the case of a vertex that is an endpoint, the edge that the vertex is on is incident with the vertex. Two edges are considered to be adjacent if they share a vertex. Two vertices are considered to be adjacent if they share an edge.

In a vertex-edge graph, a **loop** is an edge that has the same vertex as both endpoints. To calculate the **degree of a vertex** in a vertex-edge graph, count the number of edges that are incident with the vertex, counting loops twice since they meet the vertex at both ends. The **degree sum formula** states that the sum of the degrees of all vertices on a vertex-edge graph is always equal to twice the number of edges on the graph. Thus, the sum of the degrees will never be odd, even if there are an odd number of vertices. Consider the following graph. Node d is an endpoint, there is a loop on node b, and the degree sum of the graph is $2 \times 5 = 10$.

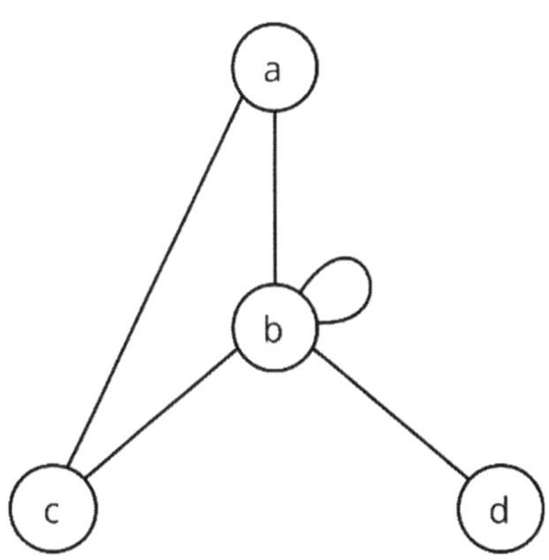

In a vertex-edge graph, a **path** is a given sequence of vertices that follows one or more edges to get from vertex to vertex. There is no jumping over spaces to get from one vertex to the next, although doubling back over an edge already traveled is allowed. A **simple path** is a path that does not repeat an edge in traveling from beginning to end. Think of the vertex-edge graph as a map, with the vertices as cities on the map, and the edges as roads between the cities. To get from one city to another, you must drive on the roads. A simple path allows you to complete your trip without driving on the same road twice.

In a vertex-edge graph, a **circuit** is a path that has the same starting and stopping point. Picturing the vertex-edge graph as a map with cities and roads, a circuit is like leaving home on vacation and then returning home after you have visited your intended destinations. You may go in one direction and then turn around, or you may go in a circle. A **simple circuit** on the graph completes the circuit without repeating an edge. This is like going on vacation and returning home without driving on the same road twice.

Graph	**Example Paths**
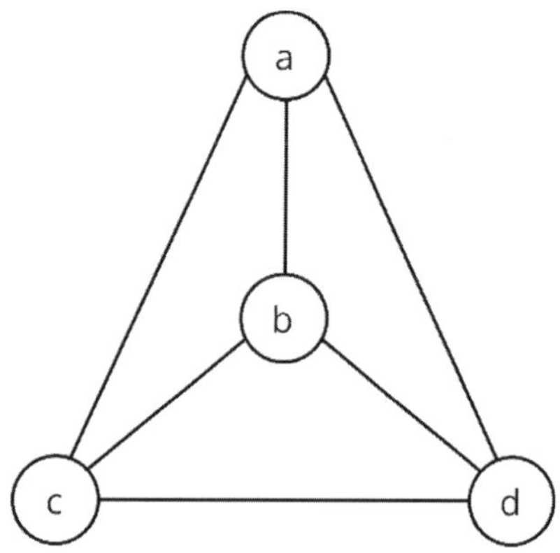	Path: **a-b-c-b-d** Simple path: **a-b-d** Circuit: **b-a-c-a-b** Simple circuit: **a-b-c-a**

On a vertex-edge graph, any path that uses each edge exactly one time is called an **Euler path**. One simple way to rule out the possibility of an Euler path is to calculate the degree of each vertex. If more than two vertices have an odd degree, an Euler path is impossible. A path that uses each vertex exactly one time is called a **Hamiltonian path**.

Graph	**Example Paths**
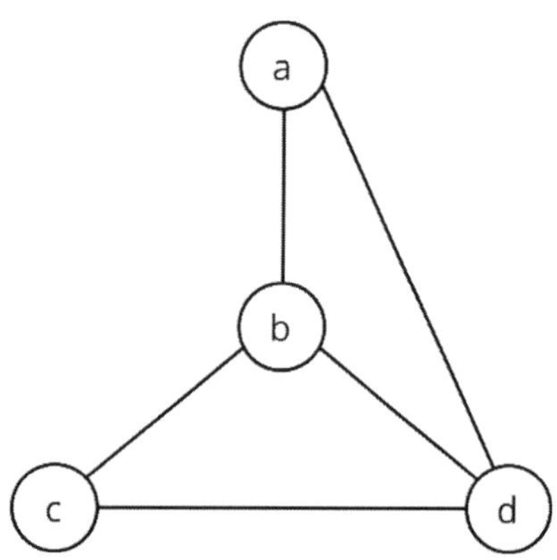	Euler path: **b-c-d-a-b-d** Hamiltonian path: **a-b-c-d**

If every pair of vertices is joined by an edge, the vertex-edge graph is said to be **complete**. If the vertex-edge graph has no simple circuits in it, then the graph is said to be a **tree**. If every vertex is connected to every other vertex by some *path*, then the graph is said to be **connected**, otherwise it is **disconnected**.

Complete and Connected **Tree and Connected** **Disconnected**

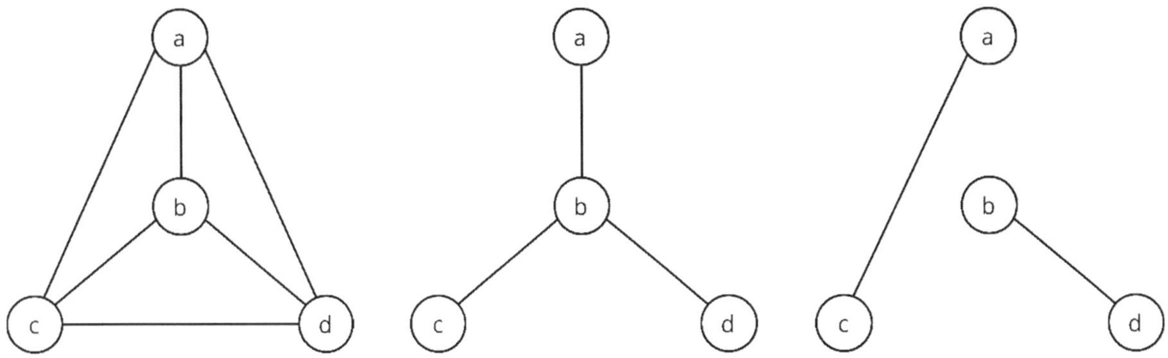

Complex Numbers

Complex Numbers

Complex numbers consist of a real component and an imaginary component. Complex numbers are expressed in the form $a + bi$ with real component a and imaginary component bi. The imaginary unit i is equal to $\sqrt{-1}$. That means $i^2 = -1$. The imaginary unit provides a way to find the square root of a negative number. For example, $\sqrt{-25}$ is $5i$. You should expect questions asking you to add, subtract, multiply, divide, and simplify complex numbers. You may see a question that says, "Add $3 + 2i$ and $5 - 7i$" or "Subtract $4 + i\sqrt{5}$ from $2 + i\sqrt{5}$." Or you may see a question that says, "Multiply $6 + 2i$ by $8 - 4i$" or "Divide $1 - 3i$ by $9 - 7i$."

Operations on Complex Numbers

Operations with complex numbers resemble operations with variables in algebra. When adding or subtracting complex numbers, you can only combine like terms—real terms with real terms and imaginary terms with imaginary terms. For example, if you are asked to simplify the expression $-2 + 4i - (-3 + 7i) - 5i$, you should first remove the parentheses to yield $-2 + 4i + 3 - 7i - 5i$. Combining like terms yields $1 - 8i$. One interesting aspect of imaginary numbers is that if i has an exponent greater than 1, it can be simplified. Example: $i^2 = -1$, $i^3 = -i$, and $i^4 = 1$. When multiplying complex numbers, remember to simplify each i with an exponent greater than 1. For example, you might see a question that says, "Simplify $(2 - i)(3 + 2i)$." You need to distribute and multiply to get $6 + 4i - 3i - 2i^2$. This is further simplified to $6 + i - 2(-1)$, or $8 + i$.

Simplifying Expressions with Complex Denominators

If an expression contains an i in the denominator, it must be simplified. Remember, roots cannot be left in the denominator of a fraction. Since i is equivalent to $\sqrt{-1}$, i cannot be left in the denominator of a fraction. You must rationalize the denominator of a fraction that contains a complex denominator by multiplying the numerator and denominator by the conjugate of the denominator. The conjugate of the complex number $a + bi$ is $a - bi$. You can simplify $\frac{2}{5i}$ by simply multiplying $\frac{2}{5i} \times \frac{i}{i}$, which yields $-\frac{2}{5}i$. And you can simplify $\frac{5+3i}{2-4i}$ by multiplying $\frac{5+3i}{2-4i} \times \frac{2+4i}{2+4i}$. This yields $\frac{10+20i+6i-12}{4-8i+8i+16}$ which simplifies to $\frac{-2+26i}{20}$ or $\frac{-1+13i}{10}$, which can also be written as $-\frac{1}{10} + \frac{13}{10}i$.

Calculus

Calculus

Calculus, also called analysis, is the branch of mathematics that studies the length, area, and volume of objects, and the rate of change of quantities (which can be expressed as slopes of curves). The two principal branches of calculus are differential and integral. **Differential calculus** is based on derivatives and takes the form,

$$\frac{d}{dx}f(x)$$

Integral calculus is based on integrals and takes the form,

$$\int f(x)dx$$

Some of the basic ideas of calculus were utilized as far back in history as Archimedes. However, its modern forms were developed by Newton and Leibniz.

Limits

The **limit of a function** is represented by the notation $\lim_{x \to a} f(x)$. It is read as "the limit of f of x as x approaches a." In many cases, $\lim_{x \to a} f(x)$ will simply be equal to $f(a)$, but not always. Limits are important because some functions are not defined or are not easy to evaluate at certain values of x.

The limit at the point is said to exist only if the limit is the same when approached from the right side as from the left: $\lim_{x \to a^+} f(x) = \lim_{x \to a^-} f(x)$). Notice the symbol by the a in each case. When x approaches a from the right, it approaches from the positive end of the number line. When x approaches a from the left, it approaches from the negative end of the number line.

If the limit as x approaches a differs depending on the direction from which it approaches, then the limit does not exist at a. In other words, if $\lim_{x \to a^+} f(x)$ does not equal $\lim_{x \to a^-} f(x)$, then the limit does not exist at a. The limit also does not exist if either of the one-sided limits does not exist.

Situations in which the limit does not exist include a function that jumps from one value to another at a, one that oscillates between two different values as x approaches a, or one that increases or decreases without bounds as x approaches a. If the limit you calculate has a value of $\frac{c}{0}$, where c is any constant, this means the function goes to infinity and the limit does not exist.

It is possible for two functions that do not have limits to be multiplied to get a new function that does have a limit. Just because two functions do not have limits, do not assume that the product will not have a limit.

Direct Substitution

The first thing to try when looking for a limit is direct substitution. To find the limit of a function $\lim_{x \to a} f(x)$ by direct substitution, substitute the value of a for x in the function and solve. The following patterns apply to finding the limit of a function by direct substitution:

$$\lim_{x \to a} b = b\text{, where } b \text{ is any real number}$$

$$\lim_{x \to a} x = a$$

$$\lim_{x \to a} x^n = a^n\text{, where } n \text{ is any positive integer}$$

$$\lim_{x \to a} \sqrt{x} = \sqrt{a}; a > 0$$

$$\lim_{x \to a} \sqrt[n]{x} = \sqrt[n]{a}\text{, where } n \text{ is a positive integer and } a > 0 \text{ for all even values of } n$$

$$\lim_{x \to a} \frac{1}{x} = \frac{1}{a}; a \neq 0$$

You can also use substitution for finding the limit of a trigonometric function, a polynomial function, or a rational function. Be sure that in manipulating an expression to find a limit that you do not divide by terms equal to zero.

In finding the limit of a composite function, begin by finding the limit of the innermost function. For example, to find $\lim_{x \to a} f(g(x))$, first find the value of $\lim_{x \to a} g(x)$. Then substitute this value for x in $f(x)$ and solve. The result is the limit of the original problem.

Limits and Operations

When finding the limit of the sum or difference of two functions, find the limit of each individual function and then add or subtract the results. Example:

$$\lim_{x \to a} [f(x) \pm g(x)] = \lim_{x \to a} f(x) \pm \lim_{x \to a} g(x)$$

To find the limit of the product or quotient of two functions, find the limit of each individual function and then multiply or divide the results. Example:

$$\lim_{x \to a} [f(x) \times g(x)] = \lim_{x \to a} f(x) \times \lim_{x \to a} g(x)$$

$$\lim_{x \to a} \frac{f(x)}{g(x)} = \frac{\lim_{x \to a} f(x)}{\lim_{x \to a} g(x)}\text{, where } g(x) \neq 0$$

$$\lim_{x \to a} g(x) \neq 0$$

When finding the quotient of the limits of two functions, make sure the denominator is not equal to zero. If it is, use differentiation or L'Hôpital's rule to find the limit.

To find the limit of a power of a function or a root of a function, find the limit of the function and then raise the limit to the original power or take the root of the limit. Example:

$$\lim_{x\to a}[f(x)]^n = \left[\lim_{x\to a} f(x)\right]^n$$

$$\lim_{x\to a} \sqrt[n]{f(x)} = \sqrt[n]{\lim_{x\to a} f(x)}, \text{ where } n \text{ is a positive integer}$$

$$\lim_{x\to a} f(x) > 0 \text{ for all even values of } n$$

To find the limit of a function multiplied by a scalar, find the limit of the function and multiply the result by the scalar. Example:

$$\lim_{x\to a} kf(x) = k \lim_{x\to a} f(x), \text{ where } k \text{ is a real number.}$$

Review Video: Limits
Visit mometrix.com/academy and enter code: 554961

L'HÔPITAL'S RULE

Sometimes solving $\lim_{x\to a} \frac{f(x)}{g(x)}$ by the direct substitution method will result in the numerator and denominator both being equal to zero, or both being equal to infinity. This outcome is called an indeterminate form. The limit cannot be directly found by substitution in these cases. L'Hôpital's rule is a useful method for finding the limit of a problem in the indeterminate form. L'Hôpital's rule allows you to find the limit using derivatives. Assuming both the numerator and denominator are differentiable, and that both are equal to zero when the direct substitution method is used, take the derivative of both the numerator and the denominator and then use the direct substitution method. For example, if $\lim_{x\to a} \frac{f(x)}{g(x)} = \frac{0}{0}$, take the derivatives of $f(x)$ and $g(x)$ and then find $\lim_{x\to a} \frac{f'(x)}{g'(x)}$. If $g'(x) \neq 0$, then you have found the limit of the original function. If $g'(x) = 0$ and $f'(x) = 0$, L'Hôpital's rule may be applied to the function $\frac{f'(x)}{g'(x)}$, and so on until either a limit is found, or it can be determined that the limit does not exist.

Review Video: L'Hopital's Rule
Visit mometrix.com/academy and enter code: 624400

SQUEEZE THEOREM

The squeeze theorem is known by many names, including the sandwich theorem, the sandwich rule, the squeeze lemma, the squeezing theorem, and the pinching theorem. No matter what you call it, the principle is the same. To prove the limit of a difficult function exists, find the limits of two functions, one on either side of the unknown, that are easy to compute. If the limits of these functions are equal, then that is also the limit of the unknown function. In mathematical terms, the theorem is:

If $g(x) \leq f(x) \leq h(x)$ for all values of x where $f(x)$ is the function with the unknown limit, and if $\lim_{x \to a} g(x) = \lim_{x \to a} h(x)$, then this limit is also equal to $\lim_{x \to a} f(x)$.

To find the limit of an expression containing an absolute value sign, take the absolute value of the limit. If $\lim_{n \to \infty} a_n = L$, where L is the numerical value for the limit, then $\lim_{n \to \infty} |a_n| = |L|$. Also, if $\lim_{n \to \infty} |a_n| = 0$, then $\lim_{n \to \infty} a_n = 0$. The trick comes when you are asked to find the limit as n approaches from the left. Whenever the limit is being approached from the left, it is being approached from the negative end of the domain. The absolute value sign makes everything in the equation positive, essentially eliminating the negative side of the domain. In this case, rewrite the equation without the absolute value signs and add a negative sign in front of the expression. Example:

$$\lim_{n \to 0^-} |x| \text{ becomes } \lim_{n \to 0^-} (-x)$$

Review Video: Squeeze Theorem
Visit mometrix.com/academy and enter code: 383104

DERIVATIVES

The derivative of a function is a measure of how much that function is changing at a specific point, and is the slope of a line tangent to a curve at the specific point. The derivative of a function $f(x)$ is written $f'(x)$, and read, "f prime of x." Other notations for the derivative include $D_x f(x)$, y', $D_x y$, $\frac{dy}{dx}$, and $\frac{d}{dx} f(x)$. The definition of the derivative of a function is $f'(x) = \lim_{h \to 0} \frac{f(x+h) - f(x)}{h}$. However, this formula is rarely used.

There is a simpler method you can use to find the derivative of a polynomial. Given a function $f(x) = a_n x^n + a_{n-1} x^{n-1} + a_{n-2} x^{n-2} + \cdots + a_1 x + a_0$, multiply each exponent by its corresponding coefficient to get the new coefficient and reduce the value of the exponent by one. Coefficients with no variable are dropped. This gives $f'(x) = n a_n x^{n-1} + (n-1) a_{n-1} x^{n-2} + \cdots + a_1$, a pattern that can be repeated for each successive derivative.

Review Video: Definition of a Derivative
Visit mometrix.com/academy and enter code: 787269

Differentiable functions are functions that have a derivative. Some basic rules for finding derivatives of functions are:

$$f(x) = c \Rightarrow f'(x) = 0; \text{ where } c \text{ is a constant}$$
$$f(x) = x \Rightarrow f'(x) = 1$$
$$f(x) = x^n \Rightarrow f'(x) = nx^{n-1}; \text{ where } n \text{ is a real number}$$

$$\left(cf(x)\right)' = cf'(x); \text{ where } c \text{ is a constant}$$
$$(f+g)'(x) = f'(x) + g'(x)$$
$$(fg)'(x) = f(x)g'(x) + f'(x)g(x)$$
$$\left(\frac{f}{g}\right)'(x) = \frac{f'(x)g(x) - f(x)g'(x)}{[g(x)]^2}$$
$$(f \circ g)'(x) = f'\left(g(x)\right) \times g'(x)$$

This last formula is also known as the **chain rule**. If you are finding the derivative of a polynomial that is raised to a power, let the polynomial be represented by $g(x)$ and use the chain rule. The chain rule is one of the most important concepts to grasp in the early stages of learning calculus. Many other rules and shortcuts are based upon the chain rule.

Review Video: Derivative Properties and Formulas
Visit mometrix.com/academy and enter code: 735227

Review Video: Product and Quotient Rules in Calculus
Visit mometrix.com/academy and enter code: 649197

Review Video: The Chain Rule - An Integral Part of Calculus
Visit mometrix.com/academy and enter code: 938732

Difference Quotient and Derivative

A secant is a line that connects two points on a curve. The **difference quotient** gives the slope of an arbitrary secant line that connects the point $\left(x, f(x)\right)$ with a nearby point $\left(x+h, f(x+h)\right)$ on the graph of the function f. The difference quotient is the same formula that is always used to determine a slope—the change in y divided by the change in x. It is written as $\frac{f(x+h)-f(x)}{h}$.

A tangent is a line that touches a curve at one point. The tangent and the curve have the same slope at the point where they touch. The derivative is the function that gives the slope of both the tangent and the curve of the function at that point. The derivative is written as the limit of the difference quotient, or:

$$\lim_{h \to 0} \frac{f(x+h) - f(x)}{h}$$

If the function is f, the derivative is denoted as $f'(x)$, and it is the slope of the function f at point $\left(x, f(x)\right)$. It is expressed as:

$$f'(x) = lim_{h \to 0} \frac{f(x+h) - f(x)}{h}$$

Implicit Functions

An **implicit function** is one where it is impossible, or very difficult, to express one variable in terms of another by normal algebraic methods. This would include functions that have both variables raised to a power greater than 1, functions that have two variables multiplied by each other, or a combination of the two. To differentiate such a function with respect to x, take the derivative of each term that contains a variable, either x or y. When differentiating a term with y, use the chain rule, first taking the derivative with respect to y, and then multiplying by $\frac{dy}{dx}$. If a term contains both

x and y, you will have to use the product rule as well as the chain rule. Once the derivative of each individual term has been found, use the rules of algebra to solve for $\frac{dy}{dx}$ to get the final answer.

Review Video: Implicit Differentiation
Visit mometrix.com/academy and enter code: 102151

DERIVATIVES OF TRIGONOMETRIC FUNCTIONS

Trigonometric functions are any functions that include one of the six trigonometric expressions. The following rules for derivatives apply for all trigonometric differentiation:

$$\frac{d}{dx}(\sin x) = \cos x, \qquad \frac{d}{dx}(\cos x) = -\sin x, \qquad \frac{d}{dx}(\tan x) = \sec^2 x$$

For functions that are a combination of trigonometric and algebraic expressions, use the chain rule:

$$\frac{d}{dx}(\sin u) = \cos u\,\frac{du}{dx} \qquad \frac{d}{dx}(\sec u) = \tan u \sec u\,\frac{du}{dx}$$

$$\frac{d}{dx}(\cos u) = -\sin u\,\frac{du}{dx} \qquad \frac{d}{dx}(\csc u) = -\csc u \cot u\,\frac{du}{dx}$$

$$\frac{d}{dx}(\tan u) = \sec^2 u\,\frac{du}{dx} \qquad \frac{d}{dx}(\cot u) = -\csc^2 u\,\frac{du}{dx}$$

Functions involving the inverses of the trigonometric functions can also be differentiated.

$$\frac{d}{dx}(\sin^{-1} u) = \frac{1}{\sqrt{1-u^2}}\frac{du}{dx} \qquad \frac{d}{dx}(\csc^{-1} u) = \frac{-1}{|u|\sqrt{u^2-1}}\frac{du}{dx}$$

$$\frac{d}{dx}(\cos^{-1} u) = \frac{-1}{\sqrt{1-u^2}}\frac{du}{dx} \qquad \frac{d}{dx}(\sec^{-1} u) = \frac{1}{|u|\sqrt{u^2-1}}\frac{du}{dx}$$

$$\frac{d}{dx}(\tan^{-1} u) = \frac{1}{1+u^2}\frac{du}{dx} \qquad \frac{d}{dx}(\cot^{-1} u) = \frac{-1}{1+u^2}\frac{du}{dx}$$

In each of the above expressions, u represents a differentiable function. Also, the value of u must be such that the radicand, if applicable, is a positive number. Remember the expression $\frac{du}{dx}$ means to take the derivative of the function u with respect to the variable x.

Review Video: Derivatives of Trigonometry Functions
Visit mometrix.com/academy and enter code: 132724

DERIVATIVES OF EXPONENTIAL AND LOGARITHMIC FUNCTIONS

Exponential functions are in the form e^x, which has itself as its derivative: $\frac{d}{dx}\, e^x = e^x$. For functions that have a function as the exponent rather than just an x, use the formula $\frac{d}{dx}\, e^u = e^u \frac{du}{dx}$. The inverse of the exponential function is the natural logarithm. To find the derivative of the natural logarithm, use the formula $\frac{d}{dx}\ln u = \frac{1}{u}\frac{du}{dx}$.

If you are trying to solve an expression with a variable in the exponent, use the formula $a^x = e^{x \ln a}$, where a is a positive real number and x is any real number. To find the derivative of a function in this format, use the formula $\frac{d}{dx}a^x = a^x \ln a$. If the exponent is a function rather than a single variable x, use the formula $\frac{d}{dx}a^u = a^u \ln a \frac{du}{dx}$. If you are trying to solve an expression involving a logarithm, use the formula $\frac{d}{dx}(\log_a x) = \frac{1}{x \ln a}$ or $\frac{d}{dx}(\log_a |u|) = \frac{1}{u \ln a}\frac{du}{dx}; u \neq 0$.

Review Video: Derivatives of Exponential and Logarithmic Functions
Visit mometrix.com/academy and enter code: 594367

Continuity

A function can be either continuous or discontinuous. A conceptual way to describe continuity is this: A function is continuous if its graph can be traced with a pen without lifting the pen from the page. In other words, there are no breaks or gaps in the graph of the function. However, this is only a description, not a technical definition. A function is continuous at the point $x = a$ if the three following conditions are met:

1. $f(a)$ is defined
2. $\lim_{x \to a} f(x)$ exists
3. $\lim_{x \to a} f(x) = f(a)$

If any of these conditions are not met, the function is discontinuous at the point $x = a$.

A function can be continuous at a point, continuous over an interval, or continuous everywhere. The above rules define continuity at a point. A function that is continuous over an interval $[a, b]$ is continuous at the points a and b and at every point between them. A function that is continuous everywhere is continuous for every real number, that is, for all points in its domain.

Discontinuity

Discontinuous functions are categorized according to the type or cause of discontinuity. Three examples are point, infinite, and jump discontinuity. A function with a point discontinuity has one value of x for which it is not continuous. A function with infinite discontinuity has a vertical asymptote at $x = a$ and $f(a)$ is undefined. It is said to have an infinite discontinuity at $x = a$. A function with jump discontinuity has one-sided limits from the left and from the right, but they are not equal to one another, that is, $\lim_{x \to a^-} f(x) \neq \lim_{x \to a^+} f(x)$. It is said to have a jump discontinuity at $x = a$.

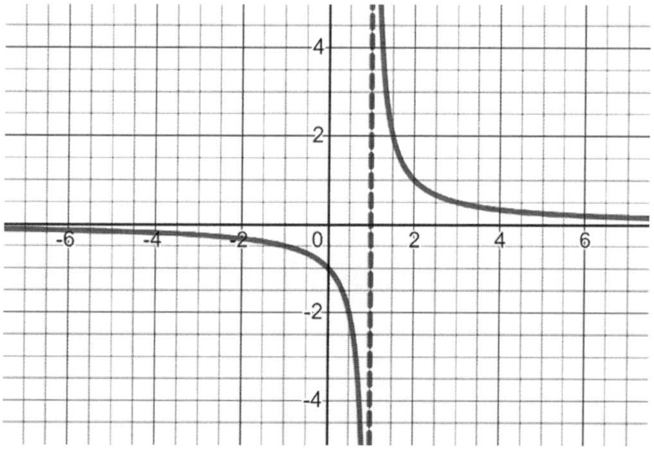

The function $f(x) = \sqrt{x}$ is not differentiable because its domain is $[0, \infty)$ and it has a discontinuity at $x = 0$. Therefore, a tangent could not be drawn at that point.

DIFFERENTIABILITY

A function is said to be differentiable at point $x = a$ if it has a derivative at that point, that is, if $f'(a)$ exists. For a function to be differentiable, it must be continuous because the slope cannot be defined at a point of discontinuity. Furthermore, for a function to be differentiable, its graph must not have any sharp turn for which it is impossible to draw a tangent line. The sine function is an example of a differentiable function. It is continuous, and a tangent line can be drawn anywhere along its graph.

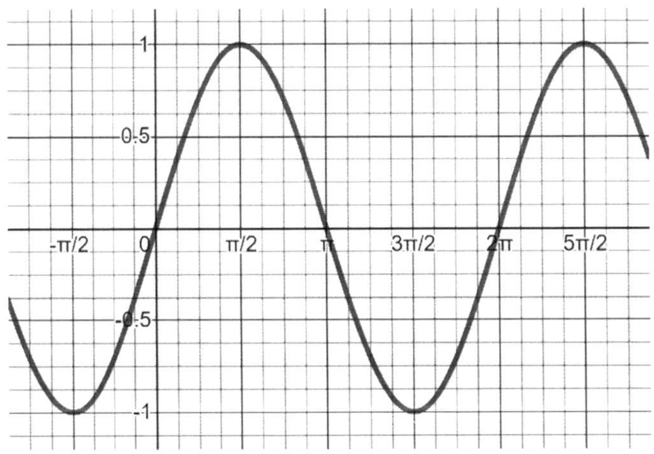

The absolute value function, $f(x) = |x|$, is an example of a function that is not differentiable:

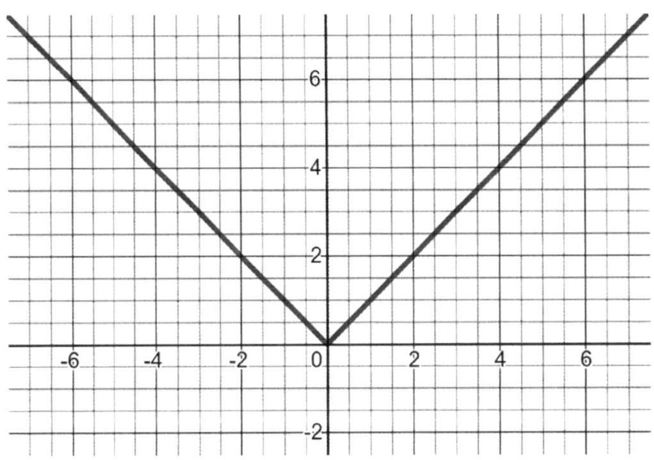

It is continuous, but it has a sharp turn at $x = 0$ which prohibits the drawing of a tangent at that point. All differentiable functions are continuous, but not all continuous functions are differentiable, as the absolute value function demonstrates.

The function $f(x) = \sqrt{x}$ is not differentiable because its domain is $[0, \infty)$ and it has a discontinuity at $x = 0$. Therefore, a tangent could not be drawn at that point.

APPROXIMATING A DERIVATIVE FROM A TABLE OF VALUES

The derivative of a function at a particular point is equal to the slope of the graph of the function at that point. For a nonlinear function, it can be thought of as the limit of the slope of a line drawn between two other points on the function as those points become closer to the point in question. Such a line drawn through two points on the function is called a **secant** of the function.

This definition of the derivative in terms of the secant allows us to approximate the derivative of a function at a point from a table of values: we take the slope of the line through the points on either side. That is, if the point lies between (x_1, y_1) and (x_2, y_2), the slope of the secant—the approximate derivative—is $\frac{y_2 - y_1}{x_2 - x_1}$. (This is also equal to the average slope over the interval $[x_1, x_2]$.)

For example, consider the function represented by the following table:

x	0	2	4	6	8	10
y	1	5	8	9	7	4

Suppose we want to know the derivative of the function when $x = 3$. This lies between the points $(2, 5)$ and $(4, 8)$; the approximate derivative is $\frac{8-5}{4-2} = \frac{3}{2}$.

Position, Velocity, and Acceleration

Velocity is a specific type of rate of change. It refers to the rate of change of the position of an object with relation to a reference frame. **Acceleration** is the rate of change of velocity.

Average velocity over a period of time is found using the formula $\bar{v} = \frac{s(t_2) - s(t_1)}{t_2 - t_1}$, where t_1 and t_2 are specific points in time and $s(t_1)$ and $s(t_2)$ are the distances traveled at those points in time.

Instantaneous velocity at a specific time, t, is found using the limit $v = \lim_{h \to 0} \frac{s(t+h) - s(t)}{h}$, or $v = s'(t)$.

Remember that velocity at a given point is found using the first derivative, and acceleration at a given point is found using the second derivative. Therefore, the formula for acceleration at a given point in time is found using the formula $a(t) = v'(t) = s''(t)$, where a is acceleration, v is velocity, and s is displacement.

Review Video: Position, Velocity, and Acceleration
Visit mometrix.com/academy and enter code: 714040

Using First and Second Derivatives

The **first derivative** of a function is equal to the **rate of change** of the function. The sign of the rate of change shows whether the value of the function is **increasing** or **decreasing**. A positive rate of change—and therefore a positive first derivative—represents that the function is increasing at that point. A negative rate of change represents that the function is decreasing. If the rate of change is zero, the function is not changing, i.e., it is constant.

For example, consider the function $f(x) = x^3 - 6x^2 - 15x + 12$. The derivative of this function is $f'(x) = 3x^2 - 12x - 15 = 3(x^2 - 4x - 5) = 3(x - 5)(x + 1)$. This derivative is a quadratic function with zeroes at $x = 5$ and $x = -1$; by plugging in points in each interval we can find that $f'(x)$ is positive when $x < -1$ and when $x > 5$ and negative when $-1 < x < 5$. Thus $f(x)$ is increasing in the interval $(-\infty, -1) \cup (5, \infty)$ and decreasing in the interval $(-1, 5)$.

Review Video: Rate of Change
Visit mometrix.com/academy and enter code: 100367

EXTREMA

The **maximum** and **minimum** values of a function are collectively called the **extrema** of the function. Both maxima and minima can be local, also known as relative, or absolute. A local maximum or minimum refers to the value of a function near a certain value of x. An absolute maximum or minimum refers to the value of a function on a given interval.

The local maximum of a function is the largest value that the function attains near a certain value of x. For example, function f has a local maximum at $x = b$ if $f(b)$ is the largest value that f attains as it approaches b.

Conversely, the local minimum is the smallest value that the function attains near a certain value of x. In other words, function f has a local minimum at $x = b$ if $f(b)$ is the smallest value that f attains as it approaches b.

The absolute maximum of a function is the largest value of the function over a certain interval. The function f has an absolute maximum at $x = b$ if $f(b) \geq f(x)$ for all x in the domain of f.

The absolute minimum of a function is the smallest value of the function over a certain interval. The function f has an absolute minimum at $x = b$ if $f(b) \leq f(x)$ for all x in the domain of f.

CRITICAL POINTS

Remember Rolle's theorem, which states that if two points have the same value in the range that there must be a point between them where the slope of the graph is zero. This point is located at a peak or valley on the graph. A **peak** is a maximum point, and a **valley** is a minimum point. The relative minimum is the lowest point on a graph for a given section of the graph. It may or may not be the same as the absolute minimum, which is the lowest point on the entire graph. The relative maximum is the highest point on one section of the graph. Again, it may or may not be the same as the absolute maximum. A relative extremum (plural extrema) is a relative minimum or relative maximum point on a graph.

A **critical point** is a point $(x, f(x))$ that is part of the domain of a function, such that either $f'(x) = 0$ or $f'(x)$ does not exist. If either of these conditions is true, then x is either an inflection point or a point at which the slope of the curve changes sign. If the slope changes sign, then a relative minimum or maximum occurs.

In graphing an equation with relative extrema, use a sign diagram to approximate the shape of the graph. Once you have determined the relative extrema, calculate the sign of a point on either side of each critical point. This will give a general shape of the graph, and you will know whether each critical point is a relative minimum, a relative maximum, or a point of inflection.

FIRST DERIVATIVE TEST

Remember that critical points occur where the slope of the curve is 0. Also remember that the **first derivative** of a function gives the slope of the curve at a particular point on the curve. Because of this property of the first derivative, the first derivative test can be used to determine if a critical point is a minimum or maximum. If $f'(x)$ is negative at a point to the left of a critical number and $f'(x)$ is positive at a point to the right of a critical number, then the critical number is a relative minimum. If $f'(x)$ is positive to the left of a critical number and $f'(x)$ is negative to the right of a critical number, then the critical number is a relative maximum. If $f'(x)$ has the same sign on both sides, then the critical number is a point of inflection.

Review Video: First Derivative Test
Visit mometrix.com/academy and enter code: 205981

Second Derivative Test

The **second derivative**, designated by $f''(x)$, is helpful in determining whether the relative extrema of a function are relative maximums or relative minimums. If the second derivative at the critical point is greater than zero, the critical point is a relative minimum. If the second derivative at the critical point is less than zero, the critical point is a relative maximum. If the second derivative at the critical point is equal to zero, you must use the first derivative test to determine whether the point is a relative minimum or a relative maximum.

There are a couple of ways to determine the concavity of the graph of a function. To test a portion of the graph that contains a point with domain p, find the second derivative of the function and evaluate it for p. If $f''(p) > 0$, then the graph is concave upward at that point. If $f''(p) < 0$, then the graph is concave downward at that point.

The **point of inflection** on the graph of a function is the point at which the concavity changes from concave downward to concave upward or from concave upward to concave downward. The easiest way to find the points of inflection is to find the second derivative of the function and then solve the equation $f''(x) = 0$. Remember that if $f''(p) > 0$, the graph is concave upward, and if $f''(p) < 0$, the graph is concave downward. Logically, the concavity changes at the point when $f''(p) = 0$:

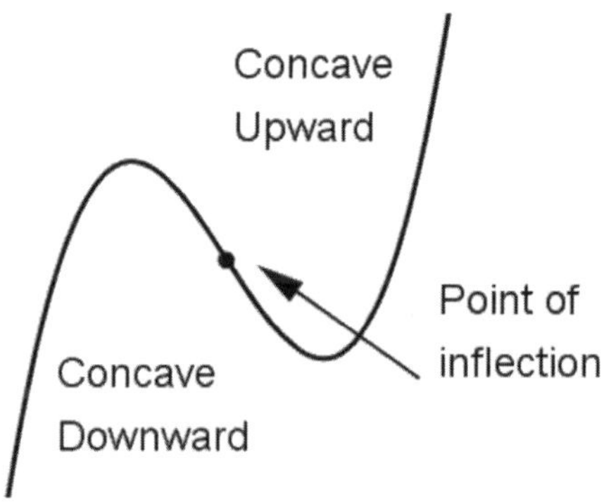

It is important to note in situations where $f'(p) = f''(p) = 0$ it is necessary to use the first derivative test to determine if p is an inflection point.

The derivative tests that have been discussed thus far can help you get a rough picture of what the graph of an unfamiliar function looks like. Begin by solving the equation $f(x) = 0$ to find all the zeros of the function, if they exist. Plot these points on the graph. Then, find the first derivative of the function and solve the equation $f'(x) = 0$ to find the critical points. Remember the numbers obtained here are the x portions of the coordinates. Substitute these values for x in the original function and solve for y to get the full coordinates of the points. Plot these points on the graph. Take the second derivative of the function and solve the equation $f''(x) = 0$ to find the points of inflection. Substitute in the original function to get the coordinates and graph these points. Test points on both sides of the critical points to test for concavity and draw the curve.

Review Video: Second Derivative Test
Visit mometrix.com/academy and enter code: 655614

Derivative Problems

A derivative represents the rate of change of a function; thus, derivatives are a useful tool for solving any problem that involves finding the rate at which a function is changing. In its simplest form, such a problem might provide a formula for a quantity as a function of time and ask for its rate of change at a particular time.

If the temperature in a chamber in degrees Celsius is equal to $T(t) = 20 + e^{-\left(\frac{t}{2}\right)}$, where t is the time in seconds, then the derivative of the function represents the rate of change of the temperature over time. The rate of change is equal to $\frac{dT}{dt} = \frac{d}{dt}\left(20 + e^{-\left(\frac{t}{2}\right)}\right) = -\frac{1}{2}e^{-\left(\frac{t}{2}\right)}$, and the initial rate of change is $T'(0) = -\frac{1}{2}e^{-\left(\frac{0}{2}\right)} = -\frac{1}{2}\frac{°C}{s}$.

Suppose we are told that the net profit that a small company makes when it produces and sells x units of a product is equal to $P(x) = 200x - 20{,}000$. The derivative of this function would be the *additional profit for each additional unit sold*, a quantity known as the marginal profit. The marginal profit in this case is $P'(x) = 200$.

Solving Related Rates Problems

A **related rate problem** is one in which one variable has a relation with another variable, and the rate of change of one of the variables is known. With that information, the rate of change of the other variable can be determined. The first step in solving related rates problems is defining the known rate of change. Then, determine the relationship between the two variables, then the derivatives (the rates of change), and finally substitute the problem's specific values. Consider the following example:

The side of a cube is increasing at a rate of 2 feet per second. Determine the rate at which the volume of the cube is increasing when the side of the cube is 4 feet long.

For the problem in question, the known rate of change can be expressed as $s'(t) = \frac{ds}{dt} = 2\frac{\text{ft}}{\text{s}}$, where s is the length of the side and t is the elapsed time in seconds. The relationship between the two variables of the cube is $v = s^3$, where v is the volume of the cube and s is the length of the side. The unknown rate of change to determine is the volume. As both v and s change with time, $v = s^3$ becomes $v(t) = [s(t)]^3$

Now, the chain rule is applied to differentiate both sides of the equation with respect to t.

$$d\frac{v(t)}{dt} = \frac{d[s(t)]^3}{dt};\ \frac{dv}{dt} = \frac{(3[s(t)]^2)ds}{dt}$$

Finally, the specific value of $s = 4$ feet is substituted, and the equation is evaluated.

$$\begin{aligned}\frac{dv}{dt} &= \frac{(3[s(t)]^2)ds}{dt}\\ &= 3(4)^2 \times 2 = 96\frac{\text{ft}^3}{\text{s}}\\ &= 96\text{ cubic}\frac{\text{ft}}{\text{s}}\end{aligned}$$

Therefore, when a side of the cube is 4 feet long, the volume of the cube is increasing at a rate of 96 cubic $\frac{\text{feet}}{\text{second}}$.

Review Video: Solving Related Rates Problems
Visit mometrix.com/academy and enter code: 321959

Solving Optimization Problems

An **optimization problem** is a problem in which we are asked to find the value of a variable that maximizes or minimizes a particular value. Because the minimum or maximum occurs at a critical point, and because the critical point occurs when the derivative of the function is zero, we can solve an optimization problem by setting the derivative of the function to zero and solving for the desired variable.

For example, suppose a farmer has 720 m of fencing, and wants to use it to fence in a 2 by 3 block of identical rectangular pens. What dimensions of the pens will maximize their area?

We can draw a diagram:

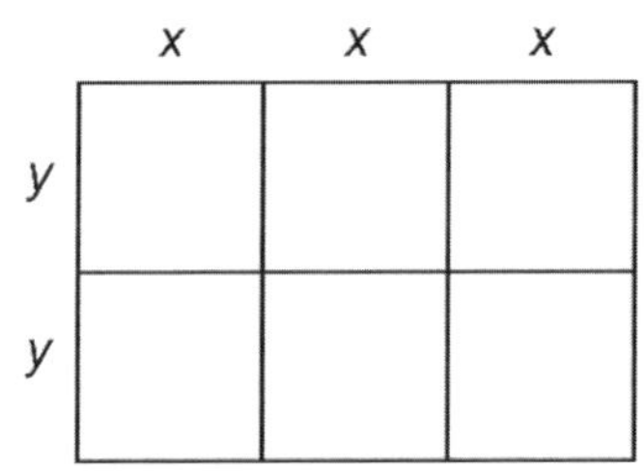

We want to maximize the area of each pen, $A(x, y) = xy$. However, we have the additional constraint that the farmer has only 720 m of fencing. In terms of x and y, we can count the number of segments of each length, 9 for x and 8 for y, so the total amount of fencing required will be $9x + 8y$. Our constraint becomes $9x + 8y = 720$; solving for y yields $y = -\frac{9}{8}x + 90$. We can substitute that into the area equation to get $A(x) = x\left(-\frac{9}{8}x + 90\right) = -\frac{9}{8}x^2 + 90x$. Taking the derivative yields $A'(x) = -\frac{9}{4}x + 90$; setting that equal to zero and solving for x yields $x = 40$. $y = -\frac{9}{8}(40) + 90 = 45$; thus, the maximum dimensions of the pen are 40 by 45 meters.

Review Video: Solving Optimization Problems
Visit mometrix.com/academy and enter code: 628734

Characteristics of Functions (Using Calculus)

Rolle's theorem states that if a differentiable function has two different values in the domain that correspond to a single value in the range, then the function must have a point between them where the slope of the tangent to the graph is zero. This point will be a maximum or a minimum value of the function between those two points. The maximum or minimum point is the point at which $f'(c) = 0$, where c is within the appropriate interval of the function's domain. The following graph shows a function with one maximum in the second quadrant and one minimum in the fourth quadrant.

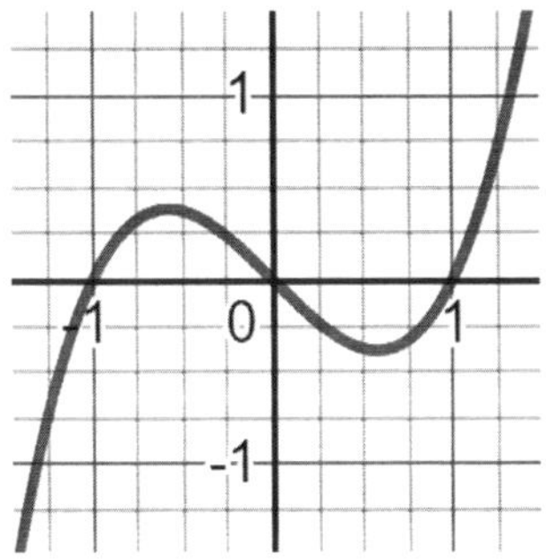

Mean Value Theorem

According to the **mean value theorem**, between any two points on a curve, there exists a tangent to the curve whose slope is parallel to the chord formed by joining those two points. Remember the formula for slope: $m = \frac{\Delta y}{\Delta x}$. In a function, $f(x)$ represents the value for y. Therefore, if you have two points on a curve, m and n, the corresponding points are $(m, f(m))$ and $(n, f(n))$. Assuming $m < n$, the formula for the slope of the chord joining those two points is $\frac{f(n)-f(m)}{n-m}$. This must also be the slope of a line parallel to the chord, since parallel lines have equal slopes. Therefore, there must be a value p between m and n such that $f'(p) = \frac{f(n)-f(m)}{n-m}$.

For a function to have continuity, its graph must be an unbroken curve. That is, it is a function that can be graphed without having to lift the pencil to move it to a different point. To say a function is continuous at point p, you must show the function satisfies three requirements. First, $f(p)$ must exist. If you evaluate the function at p, it must yield a real number. Second, there must exist a relationship such that $\lim_{x\to p} f(x) = f(p)$. Finally, the following relationship must be true:

$$\lim_{x\to p^+} F(x) = \lim_{x\to p^-} F(x) = F(p)$$

If all three of these requirements are met, a function is considered continuous at p. If any one of them is not true, the function is not continuous at p.

> **Review Video: Mean Value Theorem**
> Visit mometrix.com/academy and enter code: 633482

Tangents

Tangents are lines that touch a curve in exactly one point and have the same slope as the curve at that point. To find the slope of a curve at a given point and the slope of its tangent line at that point, find the derivative of the function of the curve. If the slope is undefined, the tangent is a vertical line. If the slope is zero, the tangent is a horizontal line.

A line that is normal to a curve at a given point is perpendicular to the tangent at that point. Assuming $f'(x) \neq 0$, the equation for the normal line at point (a, b) is: $y - b = -\frac{1}{f'(a)}(x - a)$. The easiest way to find the slope of the normal is to take the negative reciprocal of the slope of the tangent. If the slope of the tangent is zero, the slope of the normal is undefined. If the slope of the tangent is undefined, the slope of the normal is zero.

ANTIDERIVATIVES (INTEGRALS)

The antiderivative of a function is the function whose first derivative is the original function. Antiderivatives are typically represented by capital letters, while their first derivatives are represented by lower case letters. For example, if $F' = f$, then F is the antiderivative of f. Antiderivatives are also known as indefinite integrals. When taking the derivative of a function, any constant terms in the function are eliminated because their derivative is 0. To account for this possibility, when you take the indefinite integral of a function, you must add an unknown constant C to the end of the function. Because there is no way to know what the value of the original constant was when looking just at the first derivative, the integral is indefinite.

To find the indefinite integral, reverse the process of differentiation. Below are the formulas for constants and powers of x.

$$\int 0\,dx = C$$

$$\int k\,dx = kx + C$$

$$\int x^n\,dx = \frac{x^{n+1}}{n+1} + C, \text{where } n \neq -1$$

Recall that in the differentiation of powers of x, you multiplied the coefficient of the term by the exponent of the variable and then reduced the exponent by one. In integration, the process is reversed: add one to the value of the exponent, and then divide the coefficient of the term by this number to get the integral. Because you do not know the value of any constant term that might have been in the original function, add C to the end of the function once you have completed this process for each term.

Review Video: Indefinite Integrals
Visit mometrix.com/academy and enter code: 541913

Finding the integral of a function is the opposite of finding the derivative of the function. Where possible, you can use the trigonometric or logarithmic differentiation formulas in reverse, and add C to the end to compensate for the unknown term. In instances where a negative sign appears in the differentiation formula, move the negative sign to the opposite side (multiply both sides by -1) to reverse for the integration formula. You should end up with the following formulas:

$$\int \cos x\ dx = \sin x + C$$

$$\int \sec x \tan x\ dx = \sec x + C$$

$$\int \sin x\ dx = -\cos x + C$$

$$\int \csc x \cot x\ dx = -\csc x + C$$

$$\int \sec^2 x\ dx = \tan x + C$$

$$\int \csc^2 x\ dx = -\cot x + C$$

$$\int \frac{1}{x}\ dx = \ln|x| + C$$

$$\int e^x\ dx = e^x + C$$

Integration by substitution is the integration version of the chain rule for differentiation. The formula for integration by substitution is given by the equation

$$\int f(g(x))g'(x)dx = \int f(u)du\,; \quad u = g(x) \text{ and } du = g'(x)dx$$

When a function is in a format that is difficult or impossible to integrate using traditional integration methods and formulas due to multiple functions being combined, use the formula shown above to convert the function to a simpler format that can be integrated directly.

Integration by parts is the integration version of the product rule for differentiation. Whenever you are asked to find the integral of the product of two different functions or parts, integration by parts can make the process simpler. Recall for differentiation $(fg)'(x) = f(x)g'(x) + g(x)f'(x)$. This can also be written $\frac{d}{dx}(u \times v) = u\frac{dv}{dx} + v\frac{du}{dx}$, where $u = f(x)$ and $v = g(x)$. Rearranging to integral form gives the formula:

$$\int u\,dv = uv - \int v\,du$$

$$\int f(x)g'(x)\,dx = f(x)g(x) - \int f'(x)g(x)\,dx$$

When using integration by parts, the key is selecting the best functions to substitute for u and v so that you make the integral easier to solve and not harder.

While the indefinite integral has an undefined constant added at the end, the definite integral can be calculated as an exact real number. To find the definite integral of a function over a closed interval, use the formula $\int_n^m f(x)\,dx = F(m) - F(n)$ where F is the integral of f. Because you have been given the boundaries of n and m, no undefined constant C is needed.

Review Video: Integration by Parts
Visit mometrix.com/academy and enter code: 459972

Review Video: Integration by Substitution
Visit mometrix.com/academy and enter code: 740649

First Fundamental Theorem of Calculus

The **first fundamental theorem of calculus** shows that the process of indefinite integration can be reversed by finding the first derivative of the resulting function. It also gives the relationship between differentiation and integration over a closed interval of the function. For example, assuming a function is continuous over the interval $[m, n]$, you can find the definite integral by using the formula

$$\int_m^n f(x)\,dx = F(n) - F(m)$$

To find the **average value** of the function over the given interval, use the formula:

$$\frac{1}{n-m}\int_m^n f(x)\,dx$$

Review Video: First Fundamental Theorem of Calculus
Visit mometrix.com/academy and enter code: 248431

Second Fundamental Theorem of Calculus

The **second fundamental theorem of calculus** is related to the first. This theorem states that, assuming the function is continuous over the interval you are considering, taking the derivative of the integral of a function will yield the original function. The general format for this theorem for any point having a domain value equal to c in the given interval is:

$$\frac{d}{dx}\int_c^x f(t)\,dt = f(x)$$

For each of the following **properties of integrals** of function f, the variables m, n, and p represent values in the domain of the given interval of $f(x)$. The function is assumed to be integrable across all relevant intervals.

Swapping the limits of integration:	$\int_m^n f(x)\,dx = -\int_n^m f(x)\,dx$
Function multiplied by a constant:	$\int_m^n kf(x)dx = k\int_m^n f(x)\,dx$
Separating the integral into parts:	$\int_m^n f(x)\,dx = \int_m^p f(x)\,dx + \int_p^n f(x)\,dx$
If the limits of integration are equivalent:	$\int_n^n f(x)\,dx = 0$
If $f(x)$ is an even function and the limits of integration are symmetric:	$\int_{-m}^m f(x)\,dx = 2\int_0^m f(x)\,dx$
If $f(x)$ is an odd function and the limits of integration are symmetric:	$\int_{-m}^m f(x)\,dx = 0$

Review Video: Second Fundamental Theorem of Calculus
Visit mometrix.com/academy and enter code: 524689

Matching Functions to Derivatives or Accumulations

Derivatives

We can use what we know about the meaning of a derivative to match the graph of a function with a graph of its derivative. For one thing, we know that where the function has a critical point, the derivative is zero. Therefore, at every x value at which the graph of a function has a maximum or minimum, the derivative must cross the *x-axis*—and conversely, everywhere the graph of the derivative crosses the x axis, the function must have a critical point: either a maximum, a minimum, or an inflection point. If this is still not enough to identify the correct match, we can also use the fact that the sign of the derivative corresponds to whether the function is increasing or decreasing: everywhere the graph of the derivative is above the x-axis, the function must be increasing (its slope is positive), and everywhere the graph of the derivative is below the x-axis, the function must be decreasing (its slope is negative).

For example, below are graphs of the function and its derivative. The maxima and minima of the function (left) are circled, and the zeroes of the derivative (right) are circled.

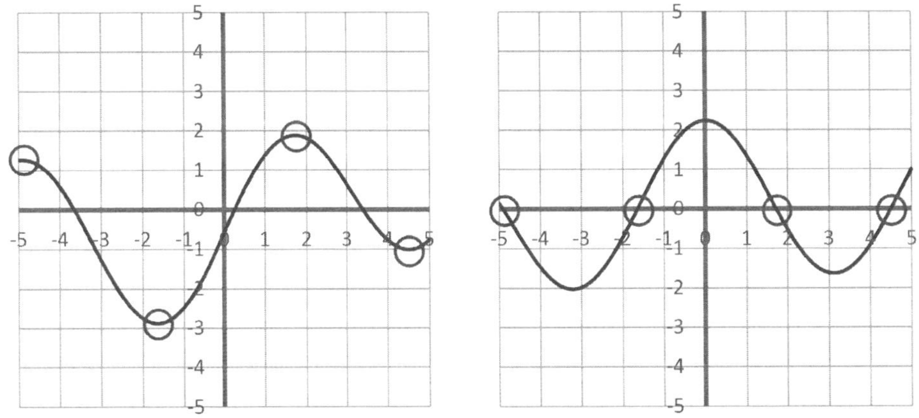

ACCUMULATIONS

The **accumulation** of a function is another name for its antiderivative, or integral. We can use the relationship between a function and its antiderivative to match the corresponding graphs. For example, we know that where the graph of the function is above the x-axis, the function is positive, thus the accumulation must be increasing (its slope is positive); where the graph of the function is below the x-axis, the accumulation must be decreasing (its slope is negative). It follows that where the function changes from positive to negative—where the graph crosses the x-axis with a negative slope—, its accumulation changes from increasing to decreasing—so the accumulation has a local maximum. Where the function changes from negative to positive—where its graph crosses the x-axis with a positive slope—, the accumulation has a local minimum.

For example, below are graphs of a function and its accumulation. The points on the function (left) where the graph crosses the x-axis are circled; the local minima and maxima of the accumulation (right) are circled.

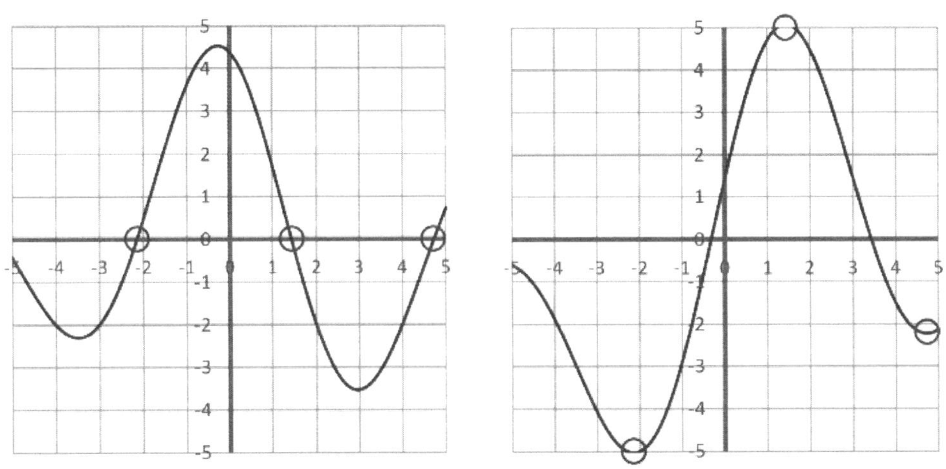

RIEMANN SUMS

A **Riemann sum** is a sum used to approximate the definite integral of a function over a particular interval by dividing the area under the function into vertical rectangular strips and adding the areas of the strips. The height of each strip is equal to the value of the function at some point within the interval covered by the strip. Formally, if we divide the interval over which we are finding the area into n intervals bounded by the $n+1$ points $\{x_i\}$ (where x_0 and x_n are the left and right bounds of the interval), then the Riemann sum is $\sum_{i=1}^{n} f(x_i^*)\Delta x_i$, where $\Delta x_i = x_i - x_{i-1}$ and x_i^* is some point in the interval $[x_{i-1}, x_i]$. In principle, any point in the interval can be chosen, but common choices include the left endpoint of the interval (yielding the **left Riemann sum**), the right endpoint (yielding the **right Riemann sum**), and the midpoint of the interval (the basis of the **midpoint rule**). Usually, it is convenient to set all the intervals to the same width, although the definition of the Riemann sum does not require this.

The following graphic shows the rectangular strips used for one possible Riemann sum of a particular function:

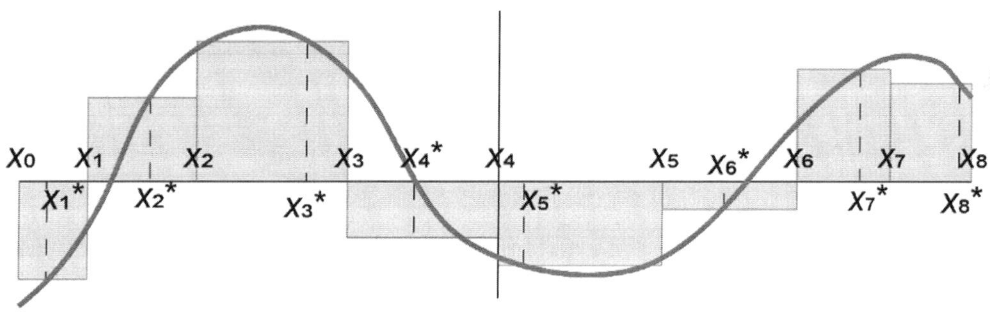

LEFT AND RIGHT RIEMANN SUMS

A **Riemann sum** is an approximation to the definite integral of a function over a particular interval performed by dividing it into smaller intervals and summing the products of the width of each interval and the value of the function evaluated at some point within the interval. The **left Riemann sum** is a Riemann sum in which the function is evaluated at the left endpoint of each interval. In the **right Riemann sum**, the function is evaluated at the right endpoint of each interval.

Review Video: Left and Right Riemann Sums
Visit mometrix.com/academy and enter code: 998275

When the function is increasing, the left Riemann sum will always underestimate the function. This is because we are evaluating the function at the minimum point within each interval; the integral of the function in the interval will be larger than the estimate. Conversely, the right Riemann sum is evaluating the function at the maximum point within each interval, thus it will always overestimate the function. Consider the following diagrams, in which the area under the same increasing function is shown approximated by a left Riemann sum and a right Riemann sum:

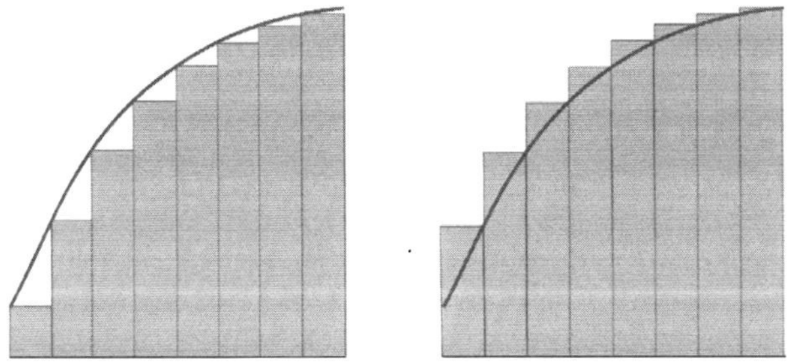

For a decreasing function these considerations are reversed: a left Riemann sum will overestimate the integral, and a right Riemann sum will underestimate it.

Midpoint Rule

The **midpoint rule** is a way of approximating the definite integral of a function over an interval by dividing the interval into smaller sub-intervals, multiplying the width of each sub-interval by the value of the function at the midpoint of the sub-interval, and then summing these products. This is a special case of the Riemann sum, specifying the midpoint of the interval as the point at which the function is to be evaluated. The approximation found using the midpoint rule is usually more accurate than that found using the left or right Riemann sum, though as the number of intervals becomes very large the difference becomes negligible.

For example, suppose we are asked to estimate by the midpoint rule the integral of $f(x) = \frac{1}{x}$ in the interval [2, 4]. We can divide this interval into four intervals of width $\frac{1}{2}$: [2, 2.5], [2.5, 3], [3, 3.5], and [3.5, 4]. (The more intervals, the more accurate the estimate, but we'll use a small number of intervals in this example to keep it simple.) The midpoint rule then gives an estimate of $\frac{1}{2}\left(f(2.25)\right) + \frac{1}{2}\left(f(2.75)\right) + \frac{1}{2}\left(f(3.25)\right) + \frac{1}{2}\left(f(3.75)\right) = \frac{1}{2}\left(\frac{4}{9}\right) + \frac{1}{2}\left(\frac{4}{11}\right) + \frac{1}{2}\left(\frac{4}{13}\right) + \frac{1}{2}\left(\frac{4}{15}\right) \approx 0.691$, not far from the actual value of $\int_2^4 \frac{1}{x}dx = [\ln x]_2^4 \approx 0.693$.

Review Video: Midpoint Rule
Visit mometrix.com/academy and enter code: 790070

Trapezoid Rule

The **trapezoid rule** is a method of approximating the definite integral of a function by dividing the area under the function into a series of trapezoidal strips, the upper corners of the trapezoid touching the function, and adding the areas of the strips. The following diagram shows the use of the trapezoid rule to estimate the integral of the function $y = 2^x$ in the interval $[0, 3]$:

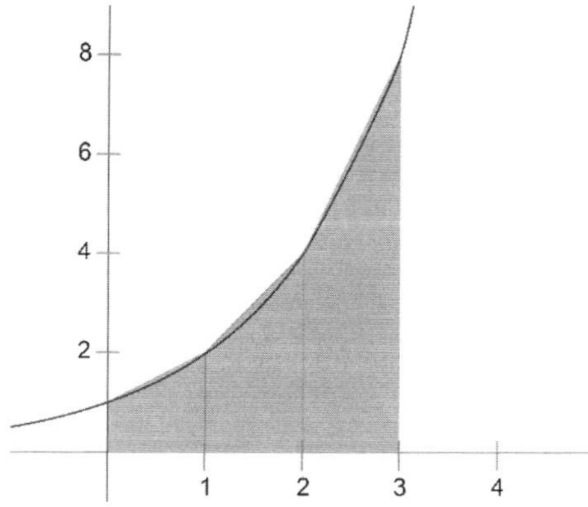

Mathematically, if we define the endpoints of the n subdivisions to be $\{x_{i-1}, x_i\}$: $(1 \le i \le n)$, where x_0 and x_n are the endpoints of the entire interval over which we are estimating the integral, then the result of the application of the trapezoid rule is equal to $\sum_{i=1}^{n}\left(\frac{f(x_{i-1})+f(x_i)}{2}\right)(x_i - x_{i-1})$. For the example shown above, that yields $\left(\frac{2^1+2^0}{2}\right)(1-0) + \left(\frac{2^2+2^1}{2}\right)(2-1) + \left(\frac{2^3+2^2}{2}\right)(3-2) = \frac{21}{2}$, or 10.5—not far from the actual value of $\int_0^3 2^x dx = \int_0^3 e^{x\ln 2}\, dx = \left[\frac{2^x}{\ln 2}\right]_0^3 \approx 10.1$. (Of course, we could have achieved more accuracy by using smaller subdivisions.)

The trapezoid rule is related to the Riemann sum, but usually gives more accurate results than the left or right Riemann sum for the same number of intervals. In fact, it isn't hard to prove that the answer given by the trapezoid rule is equal to the average of the left and right Riemann sums using the same partition.

Review Video: Trapezoid Rule
Visit mometrix.com/academy and enter code: 170482

Limit of Riemann Sums

As the number of sub-intervals becomes larger, and the width of each sub-interval becomes smaller, the approximation becomes increasingly accurate, and at the limit as the number of sub-intervals approaches infinity and their width approaches zero, the value becomes exact. In fact, the definite integral is often defined as a limit of Riemann sums.

It's possible to find the definite integral by this method. Suppose we want to find the integral of $f(x) = x^2$ over the interval [0, 2]. We'll divide this interval into n sub-intervals of equal width and evaluate the function at the right endpoint of each sub-interval. (This choice is arbitrary; at the limit the answer would be the same if we chose the left endpoint, or any other point within the interval.) Our Riemann sum becomes $\sum_{i=1}^{n}\frac{2}{n}\left(\frac{2}{n}i\right)^2 = \frac{8}{n^3}\sum_{i=1}^{n} i^2$, where $\sum_{i=1}^{n} i^2 = \frac{1}{6}n(n+1)(2n+1)$, thus this becomes $\frac{8}{n^3}\cdot\frac{1}{6}n(n+1)(2n+1) = \frac{4}{3}\left(1+\frac{1}{n}\right)\left(2+\frac{1}{n}\right)$. At the limit as $n \to \infty$, this becomes $\frac{4}{3}(1)(2) = \frac{8}{3}$. This is the same result as we get by integrating directly: $\int_0^2 x^2 dx = \left[\frac{1}{3}x^3\right]_0^2 = \frac{1}{3}(2)^3 - \frac{1}{3}(0)^3 = \frac{8}{3}$.

Uses for Integration

Calculating Distances

When given the velocity of an object over time, it's possible to find a distance by integration. The velocity is the rate of change of the position; therefore, the displacement is the accumulation of the velocity: that is, the integral of the velocity is the displacement. However, if asked to find the total distance traveled (as opposed to the displacement), it's important to take the sign into account: we must integrate not just the velocity, but the absolute value of the velocity, which essentially means integrating separately over each interval in which the velocity has a different sign.

For example, suppose we're asked to find the total distance traveled from $t = 0$ to $t = 8$ by an object moving with a velocity in meters per second given by the equation $v(t) = 2\sqrt{t} - t$. This function is zero when $2\sqrt{t} - t = 0 \Rightarrow \sqrt{t}(2 - \sqrt{t}) = 0 \Rightarrow t = 0$ or 4. $v(t)$ is positive when $0 < t < 4$ and negative when $t > 4$. Thus, the distance travelled is

$$\begin{aligned}
\int_0^8 |v(t)|dt &= \int_0^8 \left|2\sqrt{t} - t\right|dt \\
&= \int_0^4 \left(2\sqrt{t} - t\right)dt - \int_4^8 \left(2\sqrt{t} - t\right)dt \\
&= \left[\frac{4}{3}t^{\frac{3}{2}} - \frac{1}{2}t^2\right]_0^4 - \left[\frac{4}{3}t^{\frac{3}{2}} - \frac{1}{2}t^2\right]_4^8 \\
&= \left(\left[\frac{4}{3}(4)^{\frac{3}{2}} - \frac{1}{2}4^2\right] - \left[\frac{4}{3}(0)^{\frac{3}{2}} - \frac{1}{2}(0)^2\right]\right) - \left(\left[\frac{4}{3}(8)^{\frac{3}{2}} - \frac{1}{2}(8)^2\right] - \left[\frac{4}{3}(4)^{\frac{3}{2}} - \frac{1}{2}(4)^2\right]\right) \\
&= \left(\left[\frac{32}{3} - 8\right] - 0\right) - \left(\left[\frac{64}{3}\sqrt{2} - 32\right] - \left[\frac{32}{3} - 8\right]\right) \\
&= \frac{8}{3} - \frac{64}{3}\sqrt{2} + \frac{96}{3} + \frac{8}{3} \\
&= \frac{8}{3}\left(1 - 8\sqrt{2} + 12 + 1\right) \\
&= \frac{8}{3}\left(14 - 8\sqrt{2}\right) \approx 7.16 \text{ meters}
\end{aligned}$$

Review Video: Calculating Distances Using Integration
Visit mometrix.com/academy and enter code: 866719

Calculating Areas

One way to calculate the area of an irregular shape is to find a formula for the width of the shape along the x direction as a function of the y coordinate, and then integrate over y, or vice versa. What this amounts to is dividing the area into thin strips and adding the areas of the strips—and then taking the limit as the width of the strips approaches zero.

For example, suppose we want to find the area enclosed by the functions $y_1 = x^2$ and $y_2 = (2 - x^2)$. The height of this enclosure is equal to $y_2 - y_1 = 2 - 2x^2$; we can find the area by integrating this height over x. The two shapes intersect at the points $(1, 1)$ and $(-1, 1)$, thus our limits of integration are –1 and 1. Thus the area can be found as:

$$\int_{-1}^{1}(2-2x^2)dx = \left[2x - \frac{2}{3}x^3\right]_{-1}^{1} = \left(2(1) - \frac{2}{3}(1)\right) - \left(2(-1) - \frac{2}{3}(-1)\right) = \frac{8}{3}$$

Review Video: Calculating Areas Using Integration
Visit mometrix.com/academy and enter code: 118949

Calculating Volumes

One way to calculate the volume of a three-dimensional shape is to find a formula for its cross-sectional area perpendicular to some axis and then integrate over that axis. Effectively, this divides the shape into thin, flat slices and adds the volumes of the slices—and then takes the limit as the thickness of the slices approaches zero.

For example, suppose we want to find the volume of the ellipsoid $4x^2 + 4y^2 + z^2 = 36$. If we take a cross-section perpendicular to the z-axis, this has the formula $4x^2 + 4y^2 = 36 - z^2$, or $x^2 + y^2 = 9 - \frac{z^2}{4}$; this is the formula of a circle with a radius of $\sqrt{9 - \frac{z^2}{4}}$, and thus has an area of $\pi\left(9 - \frac{z^2}{4}\right)$. To find the volume, we integrate this formula over z. The maximum and minimum values of z occur when $x = y = 0$, and then $z^2 = 36$, thus $z = \pm 6$; these are our limits of integration. Thus, the volume is:

$$\begin{aligned}\int_{-6}^{6}\pi\left(9 - \frac{z^2}{4}\right)dz &= \pi\left[9z - \frac{z^3}{12}\right]_{-6}^{6} \\ &= \pi\left[\left(9(6) - \frac{6^3}{12}\right) - \left(9(-6) - \frac{(-6)^3}{12}\right)\right] \\ &= \pi[(54 - 18) - (-54 + 18)] \\ &= 72\pi \approx 226.2\end{aligned}$$

Review Video: Calculating Volume Using Integration
Visit mometrix.com/academy and enter code: 100341

Chapter Quiz

Ready to see how well you retained what you just read? Scan the QR code to go directly to the chapter quiz interface for this study guide. If you're using a computer, simply visit the online resources page at **mometrix.com/resources719/texesmathpse** and click the Chapter Quizzes link.

Mometrix
TEST PREPARATION

TExES

Mathematics/Physical Science/Engineering 6-12 (274) Secrets Study Guide

Part 2 of 3

Dear Future Exam Success Story

First of all, **THANK YOU** for purchasing Mometrix study materials!

Second, congratulations! You are one of the few determined test-takers who are committed to doing whatever it takes to excel on your exam. **You have come to the right place.** We developed these study materials with one goal in mind: to deliver you the information you need in a format that's concise and easy to use.

In addition to optimizing your guide for the content of the test, we've outlined our recommended steps for breaking down the preparation process into small, attainable goals so you can make sure you stay on track.

We've also analyzed the entire test-taking process, identifying the most common pitfalls and showing how you can overcome them and be ready for any curveball the test throws you.

Standardized testing is one of the biggest obstacles on your road to success, which only increases the importance of doing well in the high-pressure, high-stakes environment of test day. Your results on this test could have a significant impact on your future, and this guide provides the information and practical advice to help you achieve your full potential on test day.

Your success is our success

We would love to hear from you! If you would like to share the story of your exam success or if you have any questions or comments in regard to our products, please contact us at **800-673-8175** or **support@mometrix.com**.

Thanks again for your business and we wish you continued success!

Sincerely,
The Mometrix Test Preparation Team

Need more help? Check out our flashcards at:
http://mometrixflashcards.com/TExES

TABLE OF CONTENTS

Geometry and Measurement

Measurements

ROUNDING AND ESTIMATION

Rounding is reducing the digits in a number while still trying to keep the value similar. The result will be less accurate but in a simpler form and easier to use. Whole numbers can be rounded to the nearest ten, hundred, or thousand, for instance.

To round a number, we make it a little smaller (rounding down) or a little larger (rounding up) to get a number that ends in zeros. We specify the number of zeros by naming the last place that we will not "zero out." For example, to round 8,327 to the nearest hundred, we round down to 8,300, zeroing out every digit to the right of the hundreds place. To round 4,728 to the nearest thousand, we round up to 5,000, increasing the thousands digit by one (to make the number larger) and zeroing out every digit to the right of the thousands place.

We decide whether to round down or up by looking at the first digit we are going to zero out. If it is less than 5 (namely, 0, 1, 2, 3, or 4) we round down. If it is greater than or equal to 5 (namely, 5, 6, 7, 8, or 9) we round up by adding 1 to the place we are rounding to. So, rounding 8,327 to the nearest hundred, we round down to 8,300 because the tens digit, 2, is less than 5. And rounding 4,728 to the nearest thousand, we round up to 5,000, increasing the thousands digit by 1, because the hundreds digit, 7, is greater than or equal to 5.

This even works with decimals. For example, rounding 39.7426 to the nearest tenth, we round down to 39.7000 (or simply 39.7) because the hundredths digit, 4, is less than 5. And rounding 0.019823 to the nearest thousandth, we round up to 0.020000 (or simply 0.02) by increasing the thousandths digit by 1, because the ten-thousandths digit, 8, is greater than or equal to 5.

When you are asked to estimate the solution to a problem, you will need to provide only an approximate figure or **estimation** for your answer. In this situation, you will need to round each number in the calculation to the level indicated (nearest hundred, nearest thousand, etc.) or to a level that makes sense for the numbers involved. When estimating a sum **all numbers must be rounded to the same level**. You cannot round one number to the nearest thousand while rounding another to the nearest hundred.

For instance, suppose you are considering buying four pieces of equipment for your home office. Their prices are \$485, \$1,217, \$750, and \$643. To estimate their total cost, you might round each price to the nearest hundred and add the rounded figures, getting an estimate of \$500 + \$1,200 + \$800 + \$600 = \$3,100. By estimating instead of making an exact calculation, you give up a little accuracy to get a simpler calculation.

Review Video: Rounding and Estimation
Visit mometrix.com/academy and enter code: 126243

SCIENTIFIC NOTATION

Scientific notation is a way of writing large numbers in a shorter form. The form $a \times 10^n$ is used in scientific notation, where a is greater than or equal to 1 but less than 10, and n is the number of places the decimal must move to get from the original number to a. Example: The number 230,400,000 is cumbersome to write. To write the value in scientific notation, place a decimal point between the first and second numbers, and include all digits through the last non-zero digit ($a = 2.304$). To find the appropriate power of 10, count the number of places the decimal point had to move ($n = 8$). The number is positive if the decimal moved to the left, and negative if it moved to the right. We can then write 230,400,000 as 2.304×10^8. If we look instead at the number 0.00002304, we have the same value for a, but this time the decimal moved 5 places to the right ($n = -5$). Thus, 0.00002304 can be written as 2.304×10^{-5}. Using this notation makes it simple to compare very large or very small numbers. By comparing exponents, it is easy to see that 3.28×10^4 is smaller than 1.51×10^5, because 4 is less than 5.

Review Video: Scientific Notation
Visit mometrix.com/academy and enter code: 976454

Metric and Customary Measurements

Metric Measurement Prefixes

Giga-	One billion	1 *giga*watt is one billion watts
Mega-	One million	1 *mega*hertz is one million hertz
Kilo-	One thousand	1 *kilo*gram is one thousand grams
Deci-	One-tenth	1 *deci*meter is one-tenth of a meter
Centi-	One-hundredth	1 *centi*meter is one-hundredth of a meter
Milli-	One-thousandth	1 *milli*liter is one-thousandth of a liter
Micro-	One-millionth	1 *micro*gram is one-millionth of a gram

Review Video: How the Metric System Works
Visit mometrix.com/academy and enter code: 163709

Measurement Conversion

When converting between units, the goal is to maintain the same meaning but change the way it is displayed. In order to go from a larger unit to a smaller unit, multiply the number of the known amount by the equivalent amount. When going from a smaller unit to a larger unit, divide the number of the known amount by the equivalent amount.

For complicated conversions, it may be helpful to set up conversion fractions. In these fractions, one fraction is the **conversion factor**. The other fraction has the unknown amount in the numerator. So, the known value is placed in the denominator. Sometimes, the second fraction has the known value from the problem in the numerator and the unknown in the denominator. Multiply the two fractions to get the converted measurement. Note that since the numerator and the denominator of the factor are equivalent, the value of the fraction is 1. That is why we can say that the result in the new units is equal to the result in the old units even though they have different numbers.

It can often be necessary to chain known conversion factors together. As an example, consider converting 512 square inches to square meters. We know that there are 2.54 centimeters in an inch and 100 centimeters in a meter, and we know we will need to square each of these factors to achieve the conversion we are looking for.

$$\frac{512\text{ in}^2}{1} \times \left(\frac{2.54\text{ cm}}{1\text{ in}}\right)^2 \times \left(\frac{1\text{ m}}{100\text{ cm}}\right)^2 = \frac{512\ \cancel{\text{in}^2}}{1} \times \left(\frac{6.4516\ \cancel{\text{cm}^2}}{1\ \cancel{\text{in}^2}}\right) \times \left(\frac{1\text{ m}^2}{10{,}000\ \cancel{\text{cm}^2}}\right) = 0.330\text{ m}^2$$

Review Video: Measurement Conversions
Visit mometrix.com/academy and enter code: 316703

Review Video: Converting Kilograms to Pounds
Visit mometrix.com/academy and enter code: 241463

Common Units and Equivalents

Metric Equivalents

1000 μg (microgram)	1 mg
1000 mg (milligram)	1 g
1000 g (gram)	1 kg
1000 kg (kilogram)	1 metric ton
1000 mL (milliliter)	1 L
1000 μm (micrometer)	1 mm
1000 mm (millimeter)	1 m
100 cm (centimeter)	1 m
1000 m (meter)	1 km

Distance and Area Measurement

Unit	Abbreviation	US equivalent	Metric equivalent
Inch	in	1 inch	2.54 centimeters
Foot	ft	12 inches	0.305 meters
Yard	yd	3 feet	0.914 meters
Mile	mi	5280 feet	1.609 kilometers
Acre	ac	4840 square yards	0.405 hectares
Square Mile	sq. mi. or $mi.^2$	640 acres	2.590 square kilometers

Capacity Measurements

Unit	Abbreviation	US equivalent	Metric equivalent
Fluid Ounce	fl oz	8 fluid drams	29.573 milliliters
Cup	c	8 fluid ounces	0.237 liter
Pint	pt.	16 fluid ounces	0.473 liter
Quart	qt.	2 pints	0.946 liter
Gallon	gal.	4 quarts	3.785 liters
Teaspoon	t or tsp.	1 fluid dram	5 milliliters
Tablespoon	T or tbsp.	4 fluid drams	15 or 16 milliliters
Cubic Centimeter	cc or cm^3	0.271 drams	1 milliliter

Weight Measurements

Unit	Abbreviation	US equivalent	Metric equivalent
Ounce	oz	16 drams	28.35 grams
Pound	lb	16 ounces	453.6 grams
Ton	tn.	2,000 pounds	907.2 kilograms

Volume and Weight Measurement Clarifications

Always be careful when using ounces and fluid ounces. They are not equivalent.

1 pint = 16 fluid ounces	1 fluid ounce ≠ 1 ounce
1 pound = 16 ounces	1 pint ≠ 1 pound

Having one pint of something does not mean you have one pound of it. In the same way, just because something weighs one pound does not mean that its volume is one pint.

In the United States, the word "ton" by itself refers to a short ton or a net ton. Do not confuse this with a long ton (also called a gross ton) or a metric ton (also spelled *tonne*), which have different measurement equivalents.

$$1 \text{ US ton} = 2000 \text{ pounds} \quad \neq \quad 1 \text{ metric ton} = 1000 \text{ kilograms}$$

Precision, Accuracy, and Error

Measurements of physical quantities (e.g., length, area, volume, weight, mass, and time) in the real world are never perfect. Measurements miss the true value, and repeated measurements produce different values. For this reason, fields that depend on good measurement have technical terms, precision and accuracy, that describe how particular ways of measuring a quantity produce good or bad results. Note that these terms apply not to single measurements but to repeated measurements of the same quantity using the same procedure.

Precision describes the consistency of measurements. Measurements that cluster closely together, with little variation from one measurement to the next, have high precision. Measurements that vary a great deal from one measurement to the next have low precision.

Accuracy describes the closeness of measurements to the true value of the quantity being measured or, more technically, the tendency of measurements to cluster around the true value (though we do not usually know the true value; otherwise, we would not bother to measure it).

An analogy from archery may help. An outstanding archer aiming at the center of the target (the true value) produces a tight cluster of arrows around the center (high accuracy, high precision). Under the same circumstances a modestly good archer produces a loose cluster around the center (high accuracy, low precision). If, however, there is a strong crosswind and the archers do nothing to compensate for it, the outstanding archer's shots will cluster tightly around a point away from the center (low accuracy, high precision); and the modestly good archer's shots will cluster loosely around a point away from the center (low accuracy, low precision).

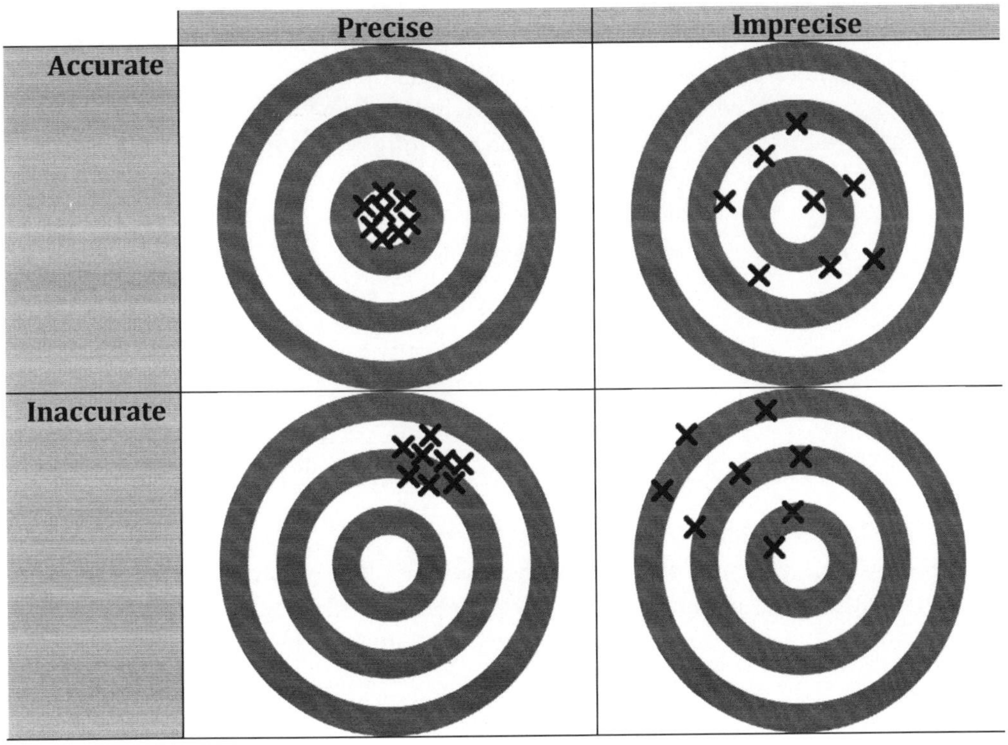

Error in measurement is not a mistake but simply the difference between the true value and the measured value. Since we seldom know the true value, we seldom know the exact error; but sometimes we know a limit on how big the error can be (an error bound), in which case we can use the plus-or-minus sign, $\pm$, to indicate how far the true value might lie from the measured value. For instance, if we measure the length of a metal bar as 25.6 cm and we know the error in our measurement is no more than 0.03 cm (some sources call this **approximate error**), then we might report the length of the bar as 25.6 ± 0.03 cm, which means it lies between 25.57 cm and 25.63 cm.

A particularly important application of this comes from the necessity of rounding whenever we make a measurement. For instance, if we measure the length of a pencil using a ruler marked off in whole inches (no fractions), then we must round our measurement to the nearest inch. Thus, if we report the length as 8 inches, it means that the actual value lies somewhere between 7.5 inches and 8.5 inches, which is to say 8 ± 0.5 inches. This built-in error bound due to rounding is called the **maximum possible error**, and it is always half the magnitude of the smallest unit used in the measurement. Determining the smallest unit can be somewhat subtle, involving the rules for significant figures commonly used in physics, chemistry, and other fields.

Review Video: Precision, Accuracy, and Error
Visit mometrix.com/academy and enter code: 520377

Trigonometry

Pythagorean Theorem

The side of a triangle opposite the right angle is called the **hypotenuse**. The other two sides are called the legs. The Pythagorean theorem states a relationship among the legs and hypotenuse of a right triangle: $(a^2 + b^2 = c^2)$, where a and b are the lengths of the legs of a right triangle, and c is the length of the hypotenuse. Note that this formula will only work with right triangles.

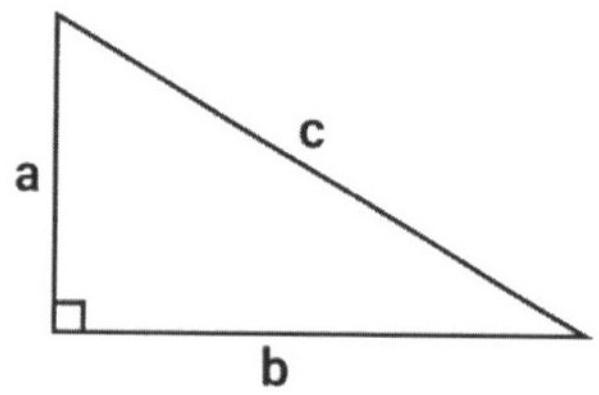

Review Video: Pythagorean Theorem
Visit mometrix.com/academy and enter code: 906576

Trigonometric Formulas

In the diagram below, angle C is the right angle, and side c is the hypotenuse. Side a is the side opposite to angle A and side b is the side opposite to angle B. Using ratios of side lengths as a means to calculate the sine, cosine, and tangent of an acute angle only works for right triangles.

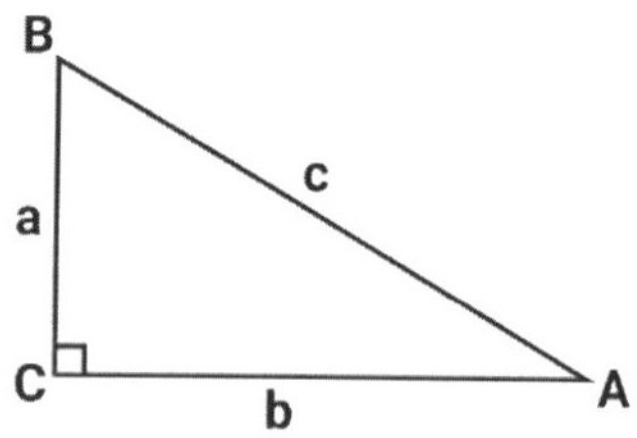

$$\sin A = \frac{\text{opposite side}}{\text{hypotenuse}} = \frac{a}{c} \qquad \csc A = \frac{1}{\sin A} = \frac{\text{hypotenuse}}{\text{opposite side}} = \frac{c}{a}$$

$$\cos A = \frac{\text{adjacent side}}{\text{hypotenuse}} = \frac{b}{c} \qquad \sec A = \frac{1}{\cos A} = \frac{\text{hypotenuse}}{\text{adjacent side}} = \frac{c}{b}$$

$$\tan A = \frac{\text{opposite side}}{\text{adjacent side}} = \frac{a}{b} \qquad \cot A = \frac{1}{\tan A} = \frac{\text{adjacent side}}{\text{opposite side}} = \frac{b}{a}$$

Laws of Sines and Cosines

The **law of sines** states that $\frac{\sin A}{a} = \frac{\sin B}{b} = \frac{\sin C}{c}$, where A, B, and C are the angles of a triangle, and a, b, and c are the sides opposite their respective angles. This formula will work with all triangles, not just right triangles.

The **law of cosines** is given by the formula $c^2 = a^2 + b^2 - 2ab(\cos C)$, where a, b, and c are the sides of a triangle, and C is the angle opposite side c. This is a generalized form of the Pythagorean theorem that can be used on any triangle.

Review Video: Law of Sines
Visit mometrix.com/academy and enter code: 206844

Review Video: Law of Cosines
Visit mometrix.com/academy and enter code: 158911

Points, Lines, and Planes

POINTS, LINES, AND PLANES

POINTS AND LINES

A **point** is a fixed location in space, has no size or dimensions, and is commonly represented by a dot. A **line** is a set of points that extends infinitely in two opposite directions. It has length, but no width or depth. A line can be defined by any two distinct points that it contains. A **line segment** is a portion of a line that has definite endpoints. A **ray** is a portion of a line that extends from a single point on that line in one direction along the line. It has a definite beginning, but no ending.

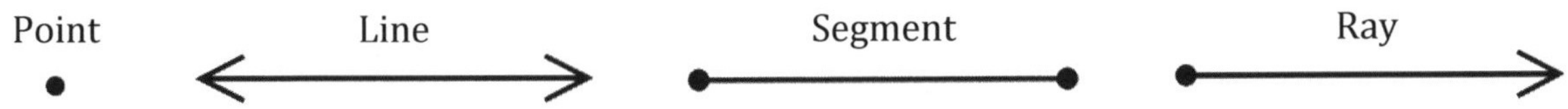

Points are **collinear** if there is a single line that passes through all of them. Otherwise, they are noncollinear. Two points are always collinear since two points define a line. Three points may be noncollinear. For example, the three vertices of a triangle are noncollinear since there is no line that goes through all three of them.

INTERACTIONS BETWEEN LINES

Intersecting lines are lines that have exactly one point in common. **Concurrent lines** are multiple lines that intersect at a single point. **Perpendicular lines** are lines that intersect at right angles. They are represented by the symbol $\perp$. The shortest distance from a line to a point not on the line is a perpendicular segment from the point to the line. **Parallel lines** are lines in the same plane that have no points in common and never meet. Two distinct lines in a given plane are always either intersecting or parallel. **Skew lines** are two distinct lines in a three dimensional space that do not intersect and may also not be parallel because there is no single plane that contains them both.

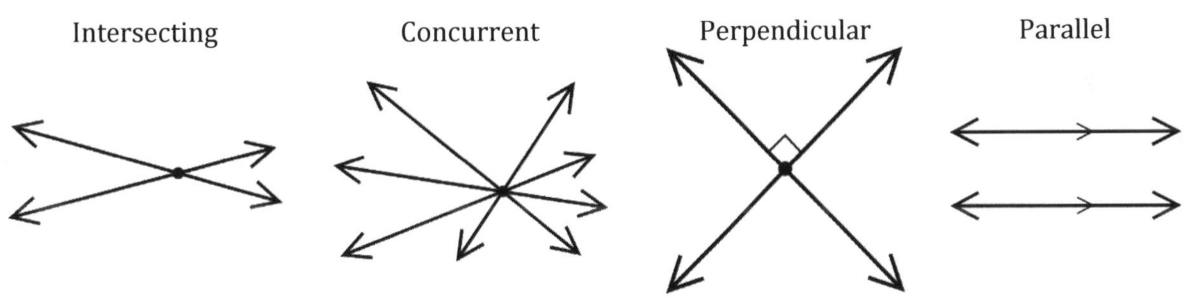

Review Video: Parallel and Perpendicular Lines
Visit mometrix.com/academy and enter code: 815923

A **transversal** is a line that intersects at least two other lines, which may or may not be parallel to one another. A transversal that intersects parallel lines is a common occurrence in geometry. A **bisector** is a line or line segment that divides another line segment into two equal lengths. A

perpendicular bisector of a line segment is composed of points that are equidistant from the endpoints of the segment it is dividing.

Transversal

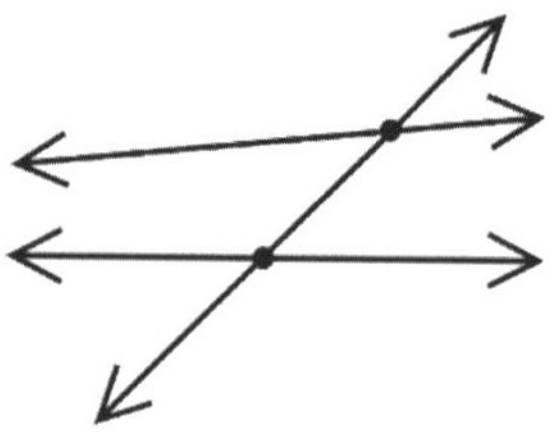

Bisector

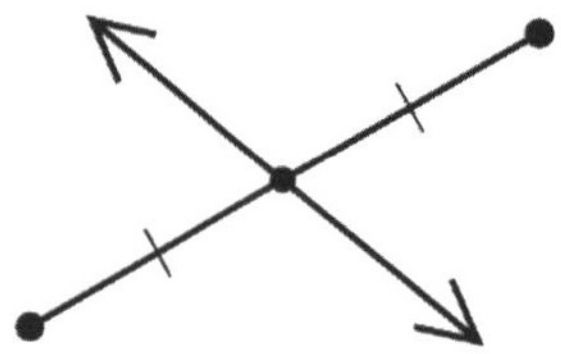

Perpendicular bisector

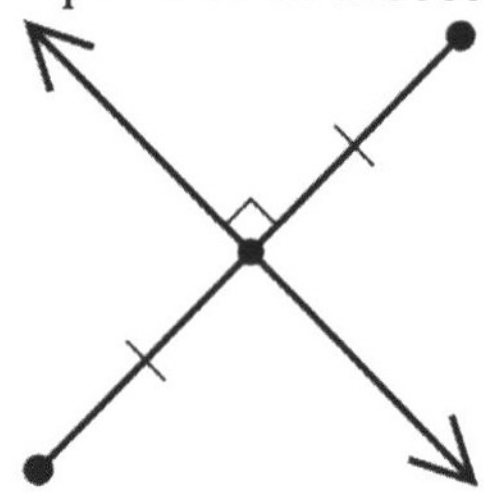

The **projection of a point on a line** is the point at which a perpendicular line drawn from the given point to the given line intersects the line. This is also the shortest distance from the given point to the line. The **projection of a segment on a line** is a segment whose endpoints are the points formed when perpendicular lines are drawn from the endpoints of the given segment to the given line. This is similar to the length a diagonal line appears to be when viewed from above.

Projection of a point on a line

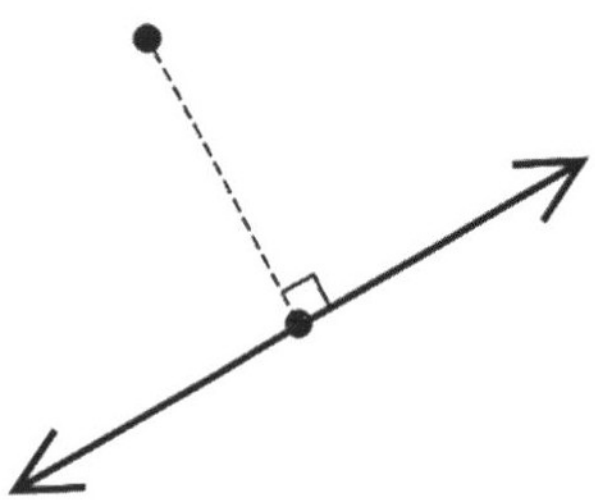

Projection of a segment on a line

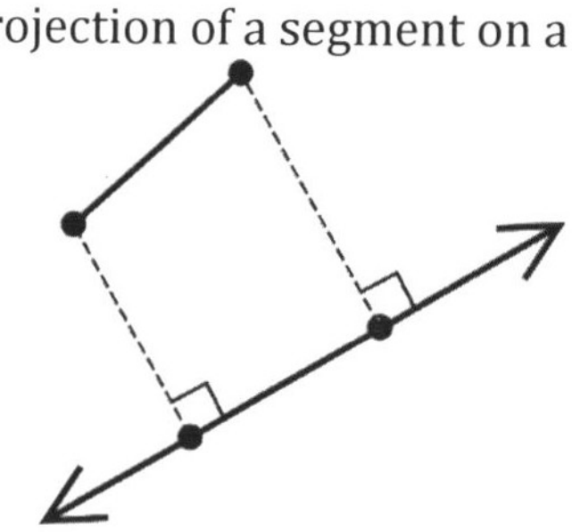

PLANES

A **plane** is a two-dimensional flat surface defined by three non-collinear points. A plane extends an infinite distance in all directions in those two dimensions. It contains an infinite number of points, parallel lines and segments, intersecting lines and segments, as well as parallel or intersecting rays. A plane will never contain a three-dimensional figure or skew lines. Two given planes are either parallel or they intersect at a line. A plane may intersect a circular conic surface to form **conic sections**, such as a parabola, hyperbola, circle or ellipse.

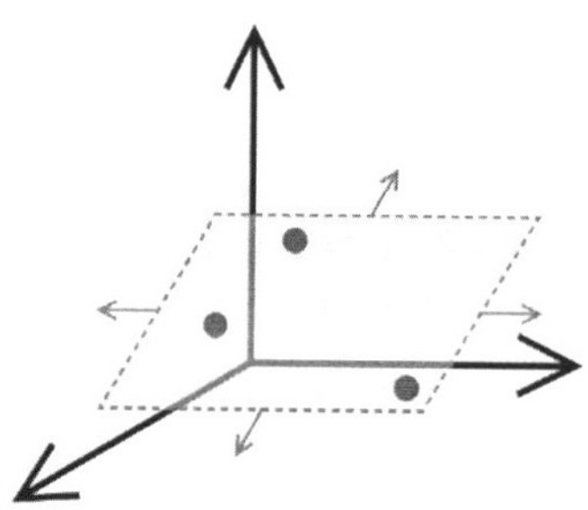

Review Video: Lines and Planes
Visit mometrix.com/academy and enter code: 554267

Angles

ANGLES

ANGLES AND VERTICES

An **angle** is formed when two lines or line segments meet at a common point. It may be a common starting point for a pair of segments or rays, or it may be the intersection of lines. Angles are represented by the symbol ∠.

The **vertex** is the point at which two segments or rays meet to form an angle. If the angle is formed by intersecting rays, lines, and/or line segments, the vertex is the point at which four angles are formed. The pairs of angles opposite one another are called vertical angles, and their measures are equal.

- An **acute** angle is an angle with a degree measure less than 90°.
- A **right** angle is an angle with a degree measure of exactly 90°.
- An **obtuse** angle is an angle with a degree measure greater than 90° but less than 180°.
- A **straight angle** is an angle with a degree measure of exactly 180°.
- A **reflex angle** is an angle with a degree measure greater than 180° but less than 360°.
- A **full angle** is an angle with a degree measure of exactly 360°.

Review Video: Angles
Visit mometrix.com/academy and enter code: 264624

RELATIONSHIPS BETWEEN ANGLES

Two angles whose sum is exactly 90° are said to be **complementary**. The two angles may or may not be adjacent. In a right triangle, the two acute angles are complementary.

Two angles whose sum is exactly 180° are said to be **supplementary**. The two angles may or may not be adjacent. Two intersecting lines always form two pairs of supplementary angles. Adjacent supplementary angles will always form a straight line.

Two angles that have the same vertex and share a side are said to be **adjacent**. Vertical angles are not adjacent because they share a vertex but no common side.

Review Video: Adjacent Angles
Visit mometrix.com/academy and enter code: 100375

Adjacent
Share vertex and side

Not adjacent
Share part of a side, but not vertex

When two lines are cut by a transversal, the angles that are between the two lines are **interior angles**. In the diagram below, angles 3, 4, 5, and 6 are interior angles.

When two lines are cut by a transversal, the angles that are outside the lines are **exterior angles**. In the diagram below, angles 1, 2, 7, and 8 are exterior angles.

When two lines are cut by a transversal, the angles that are in the same position relative to the transversal and the cut lines are **corresponding angles**. The diagram below has four pairs of corresponding angles: angles 1 and 5, angles 2 and 6, angles 3 and 7, and angles 4 and 8. Corresponding angles formed by parallel lines are congruent.

When two lines are cut by a transversal, the two interior angles that are on opposite sides of the transversal are called **alternate interior angles**. In the diagram below, there are two pairs of alternate interior angles: angles 3 and 6, and angles 4 and 5. Alternate interior angles formed by parallel lines are congruent. Similarly, the two interior angles on the same side of the transversal (angles 3 and 5, and angles 4 and 6) are supplementary when the transversed lines are parallel. Some books call these angles **same side interior angles**.

When two lines are cut by a transversal, the two exterior angles that are on opposite sides of the transversal are called **alternate exterior angles**. In the diagram below, there are two pairs of alternate exterior angles: angles 1 and 8, and angles 2 and 7. Alternate exterior angles formed by parallel lines are congruent. Similarly, the two exterior angles on the same side of the transversal (angles 1 and 7, and angles 2 and 8) are supplementary when the transversed lines are parallel. Some books call these angles **same side exterior angles**.

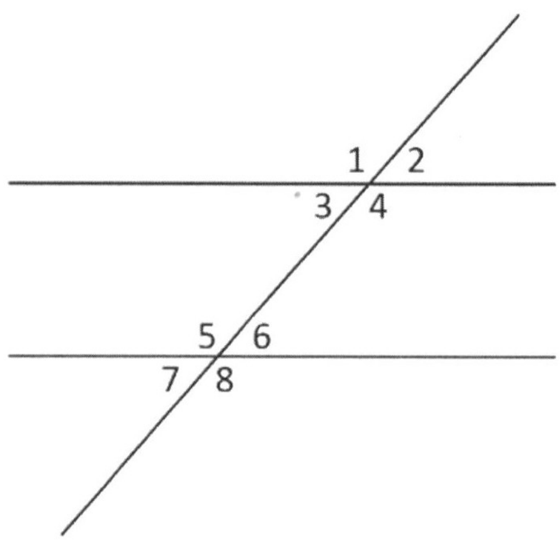

When two lines intersect, four angles are formed. The non-adjacent angles at this vertex are called vertical angles. Vertical angles are congruent. In the diagram, $\angle ABD \cong \angle CBE$ and $\angle ABC \cong \angle DBE$. The other pairs of angles, $(\angle ABC, \angle CBE)$ and $(\angle ABD, \angle DBE)$, are supplementary, meaning the pairs sum to 180°.

Review Video: Congruent Angles
Visit mometrix.com/academy and enter code: 642874

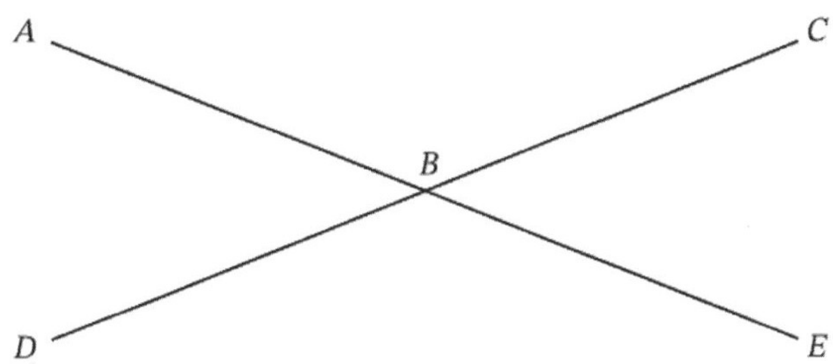

Polygons

POLYGONS

A **polygon** is a closed, two-dimensional figure with three or more straight line segments called **sides**. The point at which two sides of a polygon intersect is called the **vertex**. In a polygon, the number of sides is always equal to the number of vertices. A polygon with all sides congruent and all angles equal is called a **regular polygon**. Common polygons are:

Triangle = 3 sides
Quadrilateral = 4 sides
Pentagon = 5 sides
Hexagon = 6 sides
Heptagon = 7 sides
Octagon = 8 sides
Nonagon = 9 sides
Decagon = 10 sides
Dodecagon = 12 sides

More generally, an n-gon is a polygon that has n angles and n sides.

Review Video: Intro to Polygons
Visit mometrix.com/academy and enter code: 271869

The sum of the interior angles of an n-sided polygon is $(n - 2) \times 180°$. For example, in a triangle $n = 3$. So the sum of the interior angles is $(3 - 2) \times 180° = 180°$. In a quadrilateral, $n = 4$, and the sum of the angles is $(4 - 2) \times 180° = 360°$.

Review Video: Sum of Interior Angles
Visit mometrix.com/academy and enter code: 984991

CONVEX AND CONCAVE POLYGONS

A **convex polygon** is a polygon whose diagonals all lie within the interior of the polygon. A **concave polygon** is a polygon with at least one diagonal that is outside the polygon. In the diagram below, quadrilateral $ABCD$ is concave because diagonal $\overline{AC}$ lies outside the polygon and quadrilateral $EFGH$ is convex because both diagonals lie inside the polygon.

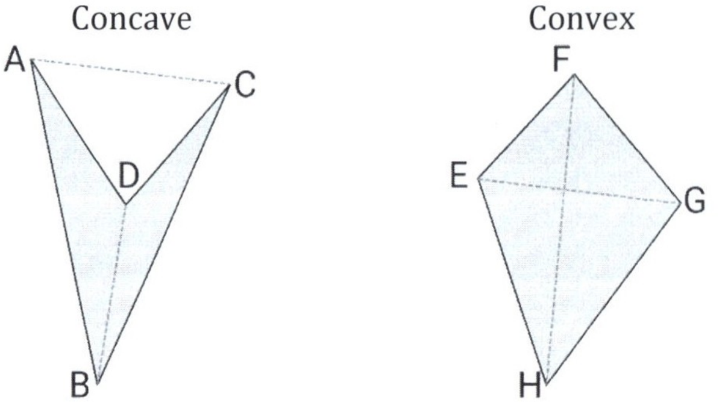

Apothem and Radius

A line segment from the center of a regular polygon that is perpendicular to a side of the polygon is called the **apothem**. A line segment from the center of a regular polygon to a vertex of the polygon is called a **radius**. In a regular polygon, the apothem can be used to find the area of the polygon using the formula $A = \frac{1}{2}ap$, where a is the apothem, and p is the perimeter.

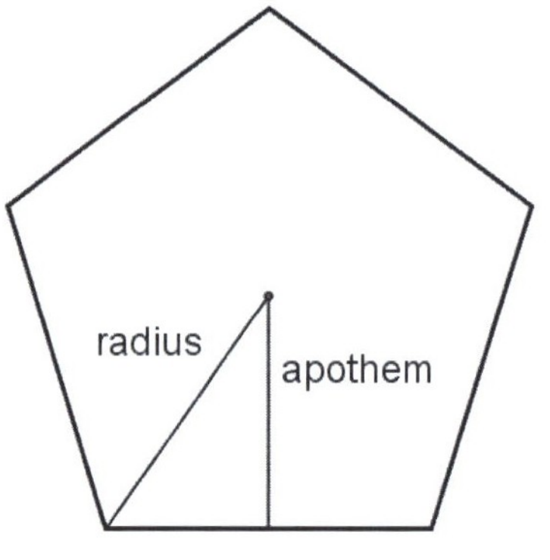

A **diagonal** is a line segment that joins two non-adjacent vertices of a polygon. The number of diagonals a polygon has can be found by using the formula:

$$\text{number of diagonals} = \frac{n(n-3)}{2}$$

Note that n is the number of sides in the polygon. This formula works for all polygons, not just regular polygons.

Congruence and Similarity

Congruent figures are geometric figures that have the same size and shape. For congruent polygons all corresponding angle measures are equal, and all corresponding side lengths are equal. Congruence is indicated by the symbol $\cong$. For instance, the expression $ABC \cong DEF$ indicates that the triangles below are congruent. The order of the letters is important, indicating which parts of the polygons correspond to each other. For example, since the letters A and D both come first, $\angle A$ and $\angle D$ have the same measure.

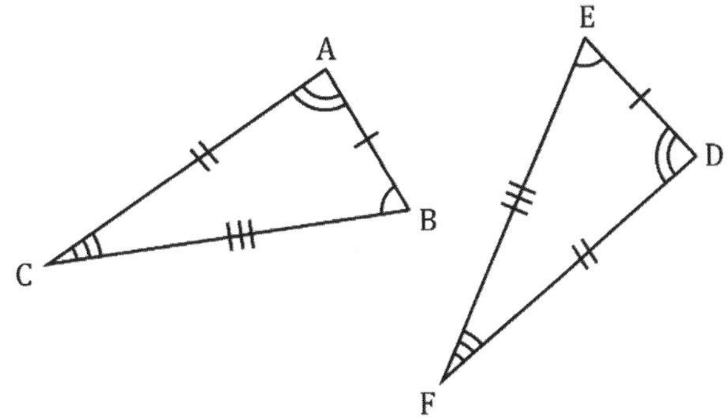

Similar figures are geometric figures that have the same shape, but do not necessarily have the same size. For similar polygons all corresponding angle measures are equal, and all corresponding side lengths are proportional, but they do not have to be equal. It is indicated by the symbol ~. For instance, the expression $ABC{\sim}DEF$ indicates that the triangles below are similar. Again, the order of the letters indicates which parts of the polygons correspond to each other.

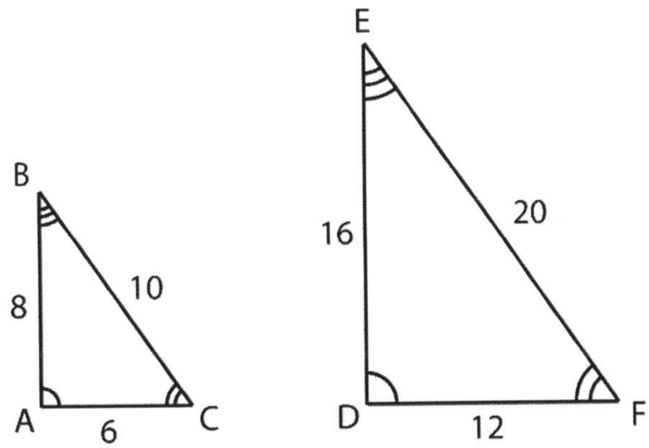

Note that all congruent figures are also similar, but not all similar figures are congruent.

Review Video: Congruent Shapes
Visit mometrix.com/academy and enter code: 492281

LINE OF SYMMETRY

A line that divides a figure or object into congruent parts that are mirror images of each other across the line is called a **line of symmetry**. An object may have no lines of symmetry, one line of symmetry, or multiple (i.e., more than one) lines of symmetry.

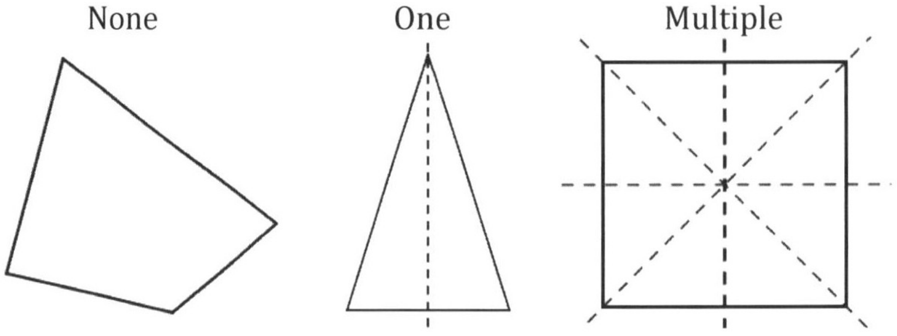

Review Video: Symmetry
Visit mometrix.com/academy and enter code: 528106

Quadrilaterals

QUADRILATERALS

A **quadrilateral** is a closed two-dimensional geometric figure that has four straight sides. The sum of the interior angles of any quadrilateral is 360°.

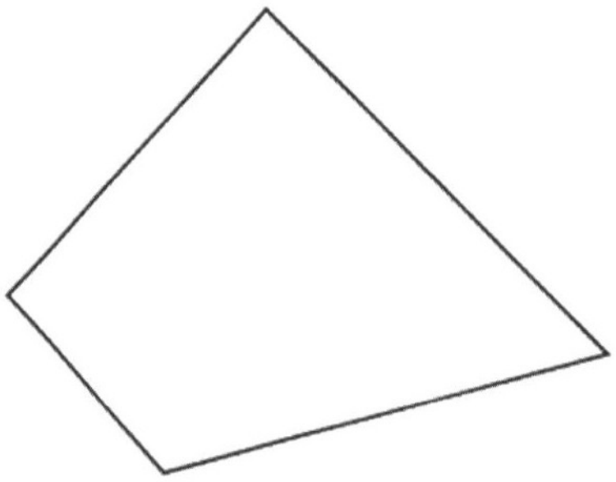

Review Video: Diagonals of Parallelograms, Rectangles, and Rhombi
Visit mometrix.com/academy and enter code: 320040

KITE

A **kite** is a quadrilateral with two pairs of adjacent sides that are congruent. A result of this is perpendicular diagonals. A kite can be concave or convex and has one line of symmetry.

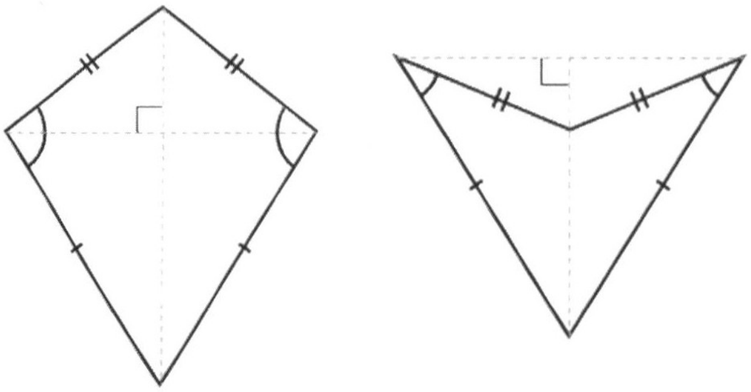

TRAPEZOID

Trapezoid: A trapezoid is defined as a quadrilateral that has at least one pair of parallel sides. There are no rules for the second pair of sides. So, there are no rules for the diagonals and no lines of symmetry for a trapezoid.

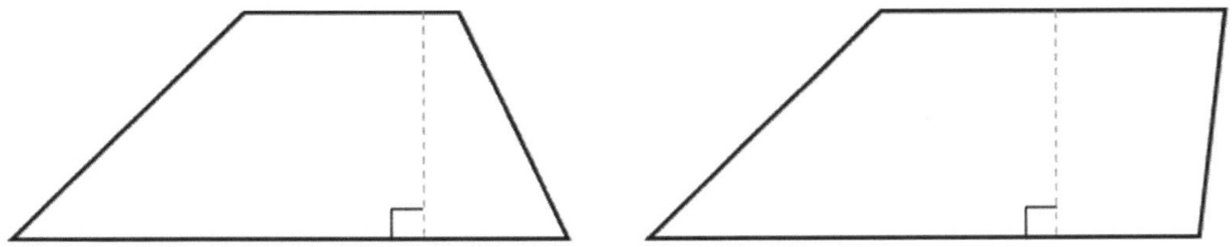

The **area of a trapezoid** is found by the formula $A = \frac{1}{2}h(b_1 + b_2)$, where h is the height (segment joining and perpendicular to the parallel bases), and b_1 and b_2 are the two parallel sides (bases). Do not use one of the other two sides as the height unless that side is also perpendicular to the parallel bases.

The **perimeter of a trapezoid** is found by the formula $P = a + b_1 + c + b_2$, where a, b_1, c, and b_2 are the four sides of the trapezoid.

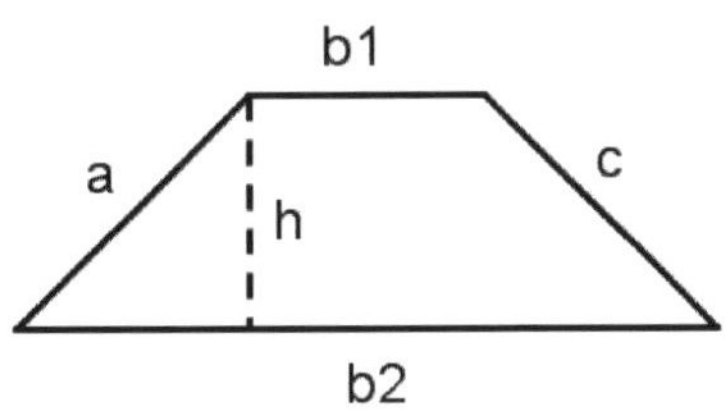

Review Video: Area and Perimeter of a Trapezoid
Visit mometrix.com/academy and enter code: 587523

Isosceles trapezoid: A trapezoid with equal base angles. This gives rise to other properties including: the two nonparallel sides have the same length, the two non-base angles are also equal, and there is one line of symmetry through the midpoints of the parallel sides.

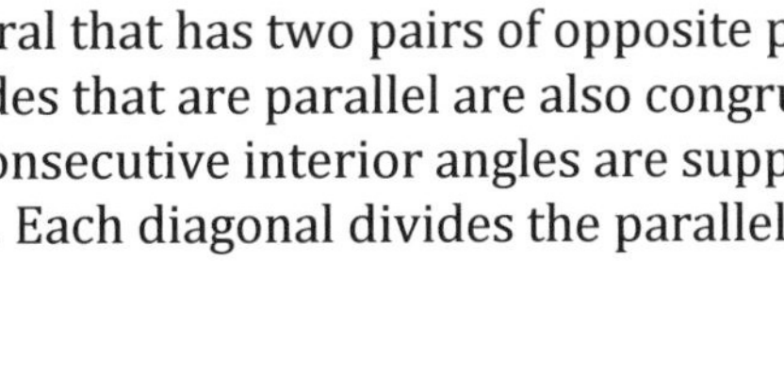

PARALLELOGRAM

A **parallelogram** is a quadrilateral that has two pairs of opposite parallel sides. As such it is a special type of trapezoid. The sides that are parallel are also congruent. The opposite interior angles are always congruent, and the consecutive interior angles are supplementary. The diagonals of a parallelogram divide each other. Each diagonal divides the parallelogram into two congruent triangles. A parallelogram has no line of symmetry, but does have 180-degree rotational symmetry about the midpoint.

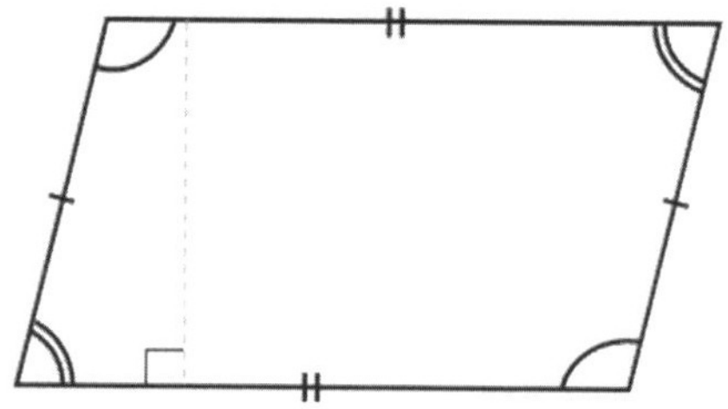

The **area of a parallelogram** is found by the formula $A = bh$, where b is the length of the base, and h is the height. Note that the base and height correspond to the length and width in a rectangle, so this formula would apply to rectangles as well. Do not confuse the height of a parallelogram with the length of the second side. The two are only the same measure in the case of a rectangle.

The **perimeter of a parallelogram** is found by the formula $P = 2a + 2b$ or $P = 2(a + b)$, where a and b are the lengths of the two sides.

Review Video: Area and Perimeter of a Parallelogram
Visit mometrix.com/academy and enter code: 718313

Rectangle

A **rectangle** is a quadrilateral with four right angles. All rectangles are parallelograms and trapezoids, but not all parallelograms or trapezoids are rectangles. The diagonals of a rectangle are congruent. Rectangles have two lines of symmetry (through each pair of opposing midpoints) and 180-degree rotational symmetry about the midpoint.

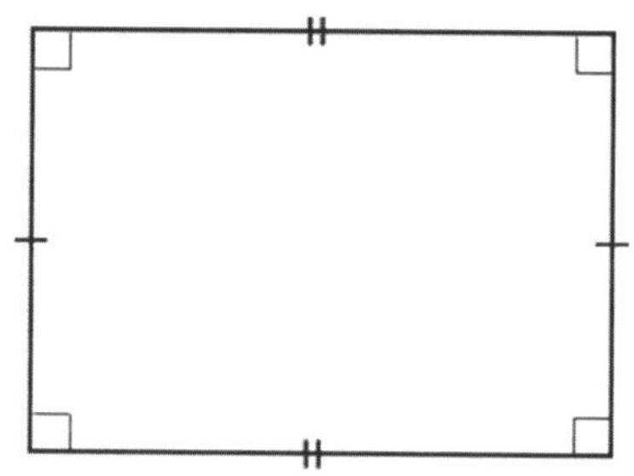

The **area of a rectangle** is found by the formula $A = lw$, where A is the area of the rectangle, l is the length (usually considered to be the longer side) and w is the width (usually considered to be the shorter side). The numbers for l and w are interchangeable.

The **perimeter of a rectangle** is found by the formula $P = 2l + 2w$ or $P = 2(l + w)$, where l is the length, and w is the width. It may be easier to add the length and width first and then double the result, as in the second formula.

Rhombus

A **rhombus** is a quadrilateral with four congruent sides. All rhombuses are parallelograms and kites; thus, they inherit all the properties of both types of quadrilaterals. The diagonals of a rhombus are perpendicular to each other. Rhombi have two lines of symmetry (along each of the diagonals) and 180° rotational symmetry. The **area of a rhombus** is half the product of the diagonals: $A = \frac{d_1 d_2}{2}$ and the perimeter of a rhombus is: $P = 2\sqrt{(d_1)^2 + (d_2)^2}$.

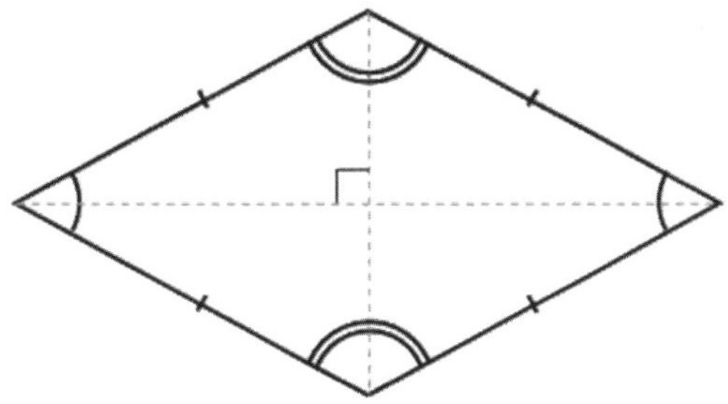

SQUARE

A **square** is a quadrilateral with four right angles and four congruent sides. Squares satisfy the criteria of all other types of quadrilaterals. The diagonals of a square are congruent and perpendicular to each other. Squares have four lines of symmetry (through each pair of opposing midpoints and along each of the diagonals) as well as 90° rotational symmetry about the midpoint.

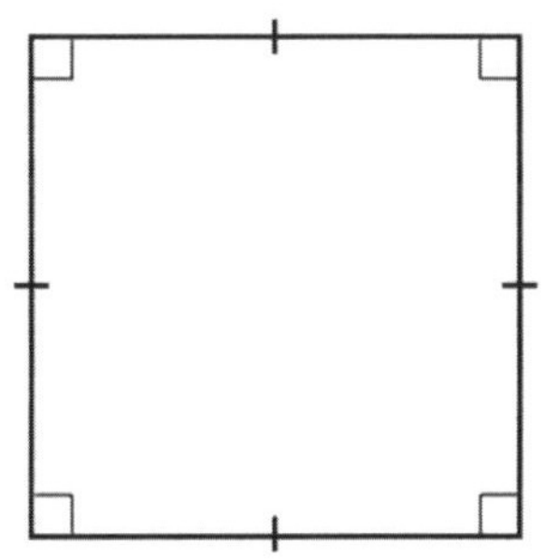

The **area of a square** is found by using the formula $A = s^2$, where s is the length of one side. The **perimeter of a square** is found by using the formula $P = 4s$, where s is the length of one side. Because all four sides are equal in a square, it is faster to multiply the length of one side by 4 than to add the same number four times. You could use the formulas for rectangles and get the same answer.

Review Video: Area and Perimeter of Rectangles and Squares
Visit mometrix.com/academy and enter code: 428109

HIERARCHY OF QUADRILATERALS

The hierarchy of quadrilaterals is as follows:

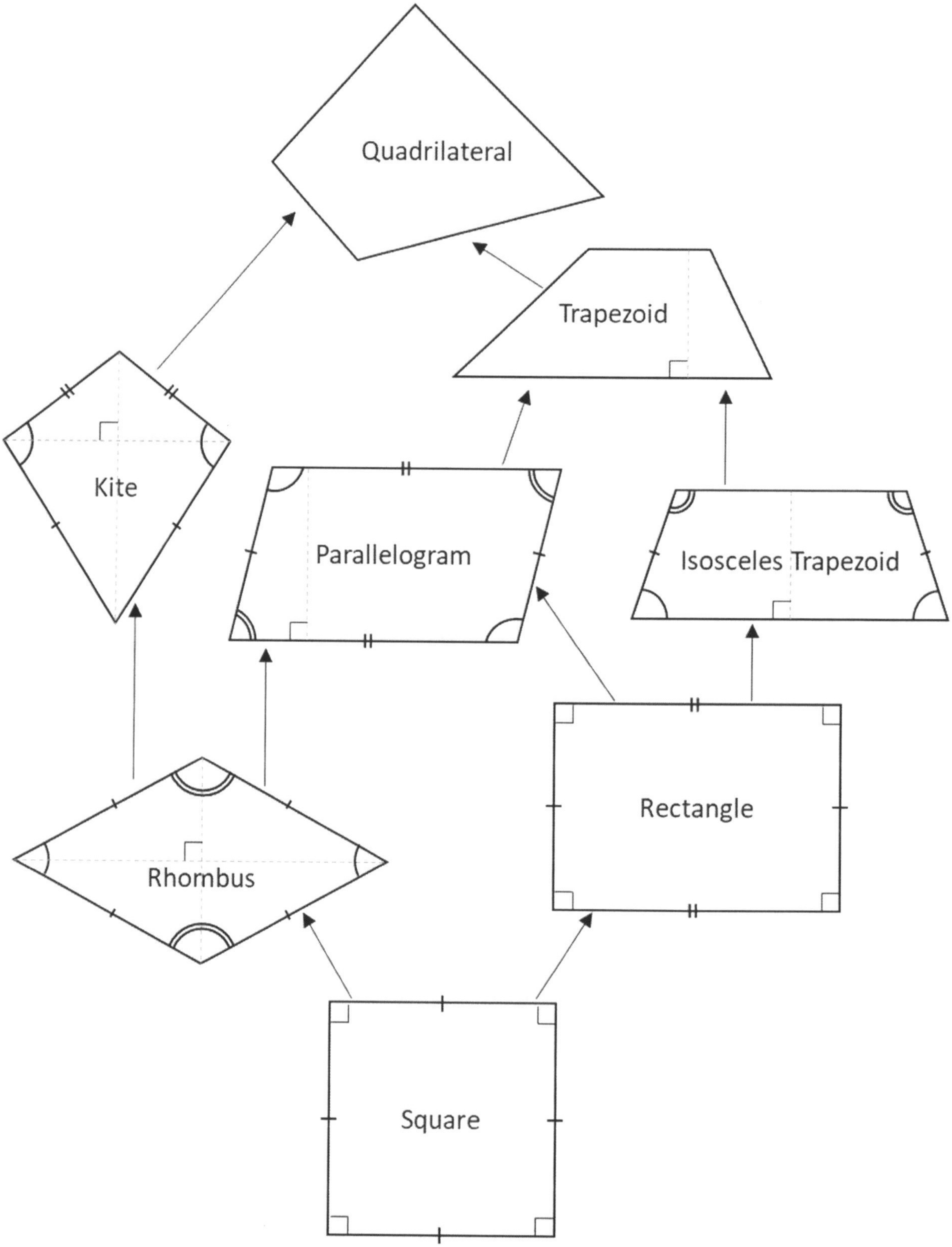

Triangles

TRIANGLES

A triangle is a three-sided figure with the sum of its interior angles being 180°. The **perimeter of any triangle** is found by summing the three side lengths; $P = a + b + c$. For an equilateral triangle, this is the same as $P = 3a$, where a is any side length, since all three sides are the same length.

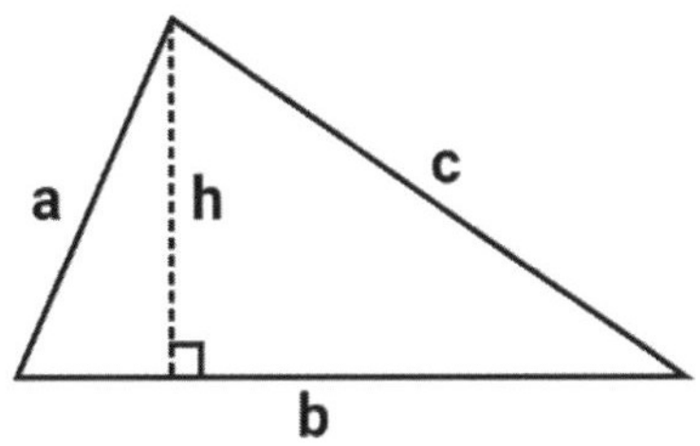

Review Video: Proof that a Triangle is 180 Degrees
Visit mometrix.com/academy and enter code: 687591

Review Video: Area and Perimeter of a Triangle
Visit mometrix.com/academy and enter code: 853779

The **area of any triangle** can be found by taking half the product of one side length referred to as the base, often given the variable b and the perpendicular distance from that side to the opposite vertex called the altitude or height and given the variable h. In equation form that is $A = \frac{1}{2}bh$. Another formula that works for any triangle is $A = \sqrt{s(s-a)(s-b)(s-c)}$, where s is the semiperimeter: $\frac{a+b+c}{2}$, and a, b, and c are the lengths of the three sides. Special cases include isosceles triangles, $A = \frac{1}{2}b\sqrt{a^2 - \frac{b^2}{4}}$, where b is the unique side and a is the length of one of the two congruent sides, and equilateral triangles, $A = \frac{\sqrt{3}}{4}a^2$, where a is the length of a side.

Review Video: Area of Any Triangle
Visit mometrix.com/academy and enter code: 138510

PARTS OF A TRIANGLE

An **altitude** of a triangle is a line segment drawn from one vertex perpendicular to the opposite side. In the diagram that follows, $\overline{BE}$, $\overline{AD}$, and $\overline{CF}$ are altitudes. The length of an altitude is also called the height of the triangle. The three altitudes in a triangle are always concurrent. The point of concurrency of the altitudes of a triangle, O, is called the **orthocenter**. Note that in an obtuse triangle, the orthocenter will be outside the triangle, and in a right triangle, the orthocenter is the vertex of the right angle.

A **median** of a triangle is a line segment drawn from one vertex to the midpoint of the opposite side. In the diagram that follows, $\overline{BH}$, $\overline{AG}$, and $\overline{CI}$ are medians. This is not the same as the altitude, except the altitude to the base of an isosceles triangle and all three altitudes of an equilateral triangle. The point of concurrency of the medians of a triangle, T, is called the **centroid**. This is the same point as the orthocenter only in an equilateral triangle. Unlike the orthocenter, the centroid is always inside the triangle. The centroid can also be considered the exact center of the triangle. Any shape triangle can be perfectly balanced on a tip placed at the centroid. The centroid is also the point that is two-thirds the distance from the vertex to the opposite side.

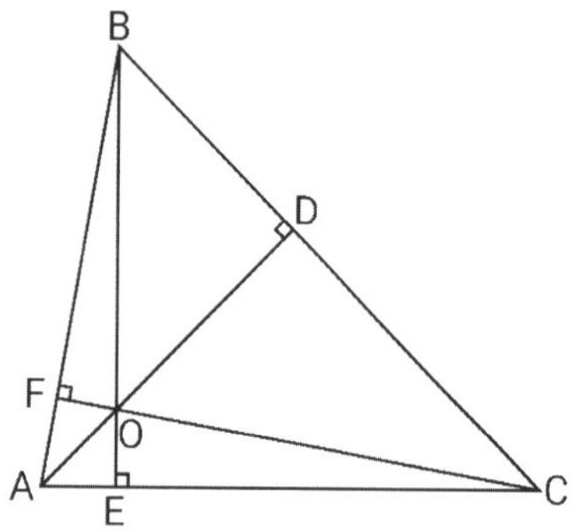

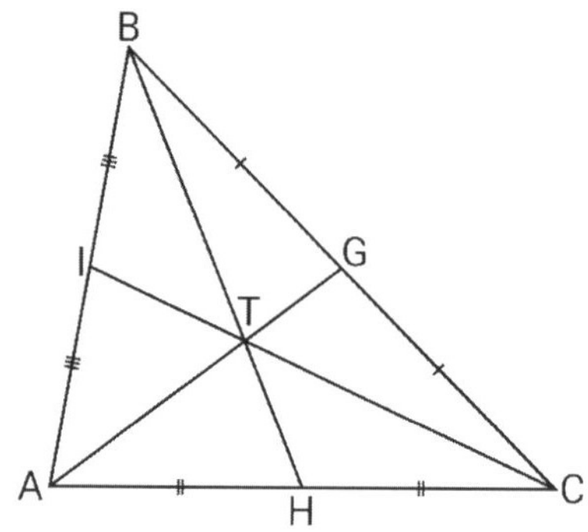

Review Video: Centroid, Incenter, Circumcenter, and Orthocenter
Visit mometrix.com/academy and enter code: 598260

TRIANGLE PROPERTIES

CLASSIFICATIONS OF TRIANGLES

A **scalene triangle** is a triangle with no congruent sides. A scalene triangle will also have three angles of different measures. The angle with the largest measure is opposite the longest side, and the angle with the smallest measure is opposite the shortest side. An **acute triangle** is a triangle whose three angles are all less than 90°. If two of the angles are equal, the acute triangle is also an **isosceles triangle**. An isosceles triangle will also have two congruent angles opposite the two congruent sides. If the three angles are all equal, the acute triangle is also an **equilateral triangle**. An equilateral triangle will also have three congruent angles, each 60°. All equilateral triangles are also acute triangles. An **obtuse triangle** is a triangle with exactly one angle greater than 90°. The other two angles may or may not be equal. If the two remaining angles are equal, the obtuse triangle is also an isosceles triangle. A **right triangle** is a triangle with exactly one angle equal to 90°. All right triangles follow the Pythagorean theorem. A right triangle can never be acute or obtuse.

The table below illustrates how each descriptor places a different restriction on the triangle:

Angles / Sides	Acute: All angles < 90°	Obtuse: One angle > 90°	Right: One angle = 90°
Scalene: No equal side lengths	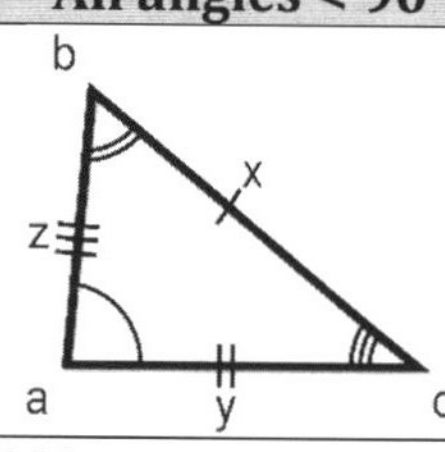	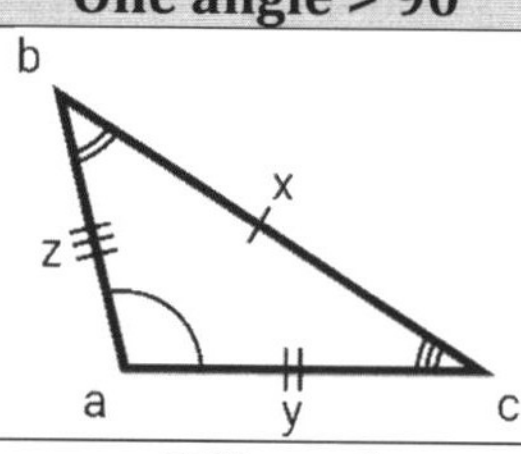	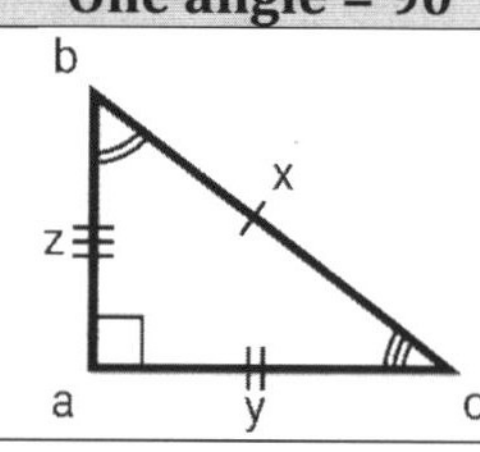
	$90° > \angle a > \angle b > \angle c$ $x > y > z$	$\angle a > 90° > \angle b > \angle c$ $x > y > z$	$90° = \angle a > \angle b > \angle c$ $x > y > z$

Angles / Sides	**Acute:** **All angles < 90°**	**Obtuse:** **One angle > 90°**	**Right:** **One angle = 90°**
Isosceles: Two equal side lengths	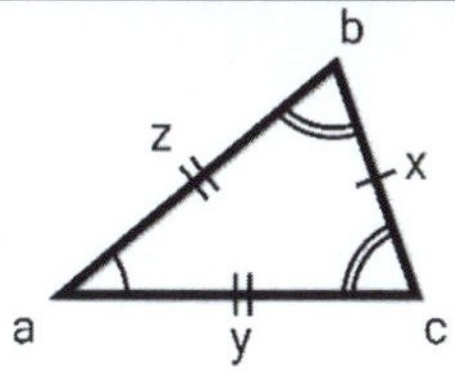 $90° > \angle a, \angle b, or\ \angle c$ $\angle b = \angle c, \quad y = z$	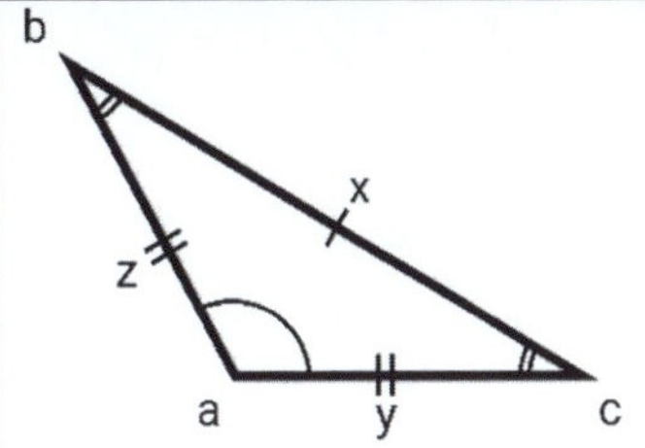 $\angle a > 90° > \angle b = \angle c$ $x > y = z$	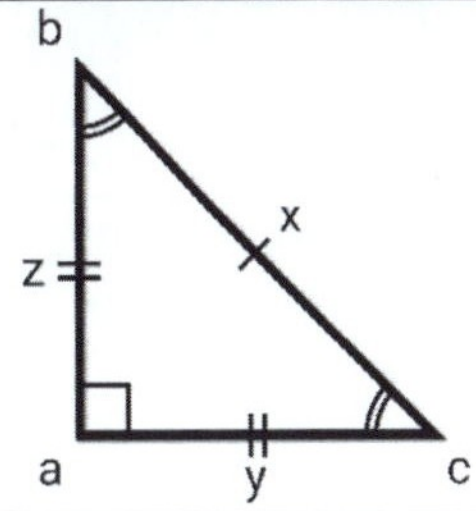 $\angle a = 90°$ $\angle b = \angle c = 45°$ $x > y = z$
Equilateral: Three equal side lengths	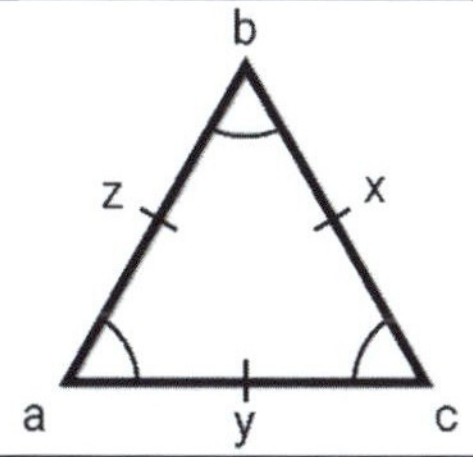 $60° = \angle a = \angle b = \angle c$ $x = y = z$		

Review Video: Introduction to Types of Triangles
Visit mometrix.com/academy and enter code: 511711

General Rules for Triangles

The **triangle inequality theorem** states that the sum of the measures of any two sides of a triangle is always greater than the measure of the third side. If the sum of the measures of two sides were equal to the third side, a triangle would be impossible because the two sides would lie flat across the third side and there would be no vertex. If the sum of the measures of two of the sides was less than the third side, a closed figure would be impossible because the two shortest sides would never meet. In other words, for a triangle with sides lengths A, B, and C: $A + B > C, B + C > A$, and $A + C > B$.

The sum of the measures of the interior angles of a triangle is always 180°. Therefore, a triangle can never have more than one angle greater than or equal to 90°.

In any triangle, the angles opposite congruent sides are congruent, and the sides opposite congruent angles are congruent. The largest angle is always opposite the longest side, and the smallest angle is always opposite the shortest side.

The line segment that joins the midpoints of any two sides of a triangle is always parallel to the third side and exactly half the length of the third side.

Review Video: General Rules (Triangle Inequality Theorem)
Visit mometrix.com/academy and enter code: 166488

SIMILARITY AND CONGRUENCE RULES

Similar triangles are triangles whose corresponding angles are equal and whose corresponding sides are proportional. Represented by AAA. Similar triangles whose corresponding sides are congruent are also congruent triangles.

Triangles can be shown to be **congruent** in 5 ways:

- **SSS**: Three sides of one triangle are congruent to the three corresponding sides of the second triangle.
- **SAS**: Two sides and the included angle (the angle formed by those two sides) of one triangle are congruent to the corresponding two sides and included angle of the second triangle.
- **ASA**: Two angles and the included side (the side that joins the two angles) of one triangle are congruent to the corresponding two angles and included side of the second triangle.
- **AAS**: Two angles and a non-included side of one triangle are congruent to the corresponding two angles and non-included side of the second triangle.
- **HL**: The hypotenuse and leg of one right triangle are congruent to the corresponding hypotenuse and leg of the second right triangle.

Review Video: Similar Triangles
Visit mometrix.com/academy and enter code: 398538

Circles

CIRCLES

The **center** of a circle is the single point from which every point on the circle is **equidistant**. The **radius** is a line segment that joins the center of the circle and any one point on the circle. All radii of a circle are equal. Circles that have the same center but not the same length of radii are **concentric**. The **diameter** is a line segment that passes through the center of the circle and has both endpoints on the circle. The length of the diameter is exactly twice the length of the radius. Point O in the diagram below is the center of the circle, segments $\overline{OX}$, $\overline{OY}$, and $\overline{OZ}$ are radii; and segment $\overline{XZ}$ is a diameter.

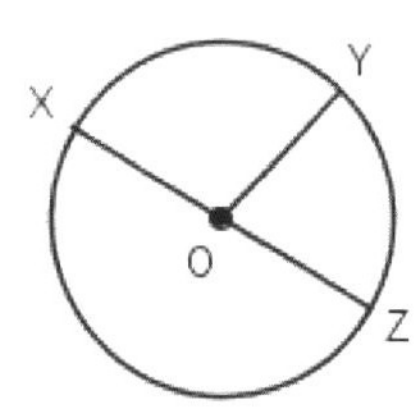

Review Video: Points of a Circle
Visit mometrix.com/academy and enter code: 420746

Review Video: Diameter, Radius, and Circumference
Visit mometrix.com/academy and enter code: 448988

The **area of a circle** is found by the formula $A = \pi r^2$, where r is the length of the radius. If the diameter of the circle is given, remember to divide it in half to get the length of the radius before proceeding.

The **circumference** of a circle is found by the formula $C = 2\pi r$, where r is the radius. Again, remember to convert the diameter if you are given that measure rather than the radius.

Review Video: Area and Circumference of a Circle
Visit mometrix.com/academy and enter code: 243015

Inscribed and Circumscribed Figures

These terms can both be used to describe a given arrangement of figures, depending on perspective. If each of the vertices of figure A lie on figure B, then it can be said that figure A is **inscribed** in figure B, but it can also be said that figure B is **circumscribed** about figure A. The following table and examples help to illustrate the concept. Note that the figures cannot both be circles, as they would be completely overlapping and neither would be inscribed or circumscribed.

Given	Description	Equivalent Description	Figures
Each of the sides of a pentagon is tangent to a circle	The circle is inscribed in the pentagon	The pentagon is circumscribed about the circle	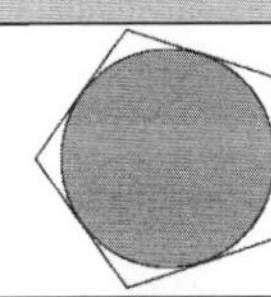
Each of the vertices of a pentagon lie on a circle	The pentagon is inscribed in the circle	The circle is circumscribed about the pentagon	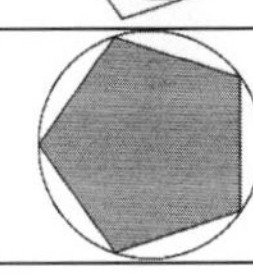

Circle Properties

Arcs

An **arc** is a portion of a circle. Specifically, an arc is the set of points between and including two points on a circle. An arc does not contain any points inside the circle. When a segment is drawn from the endpoints of an arc to the center of the circle, a sector is formed. A **minor arc** is an arc that has a measure less than 180°. A **major arc** is an arc that has a measure of at least 180°. Every minor arc has a corresponding major arc that can be found by subtracting the measure of the minor arc from 360°. A **semicircle** is an arc whose endpoints are the endpoints of the diameter of a circle. A semicircle is exactly half of a circle.

Arc length is the length of that portion of the circumference between two points on the circle. The formula for arc length is $s = \frac{\pi r\theta}{180^\circ}$, where s is the arc length, r is the length of the radius, and θ is the angular measure of the arc in degrees, or $s = r\theta$, where θ is the angular measure of the arc in radians (2π radians $=$ 360 degrees).

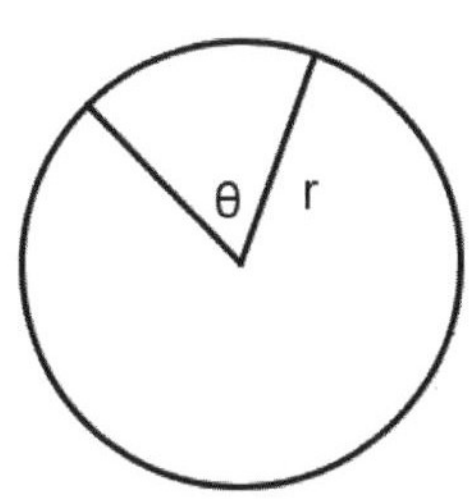

ANGLES OF CIRCLES

A **central angle** is an angle whose vertex is the center of a circle and whose legs intercept an arc of the circle. The measure of a central angle is equal to the measure of the minor arc it intercepts.

An **inscribed angle** is an angle whose vertex lies on a circle and whose legs contain chords of that circle. The portion of the circle intercepted by the legs of the angle is called the intercepted arc. The measure of the intercepted arc is exactly twice the measure of the inscribed angle. In the following diagram, angle ABC is an inscribed angle. $\widehat{AC} = 2(\text{m}\angle ABC)$.

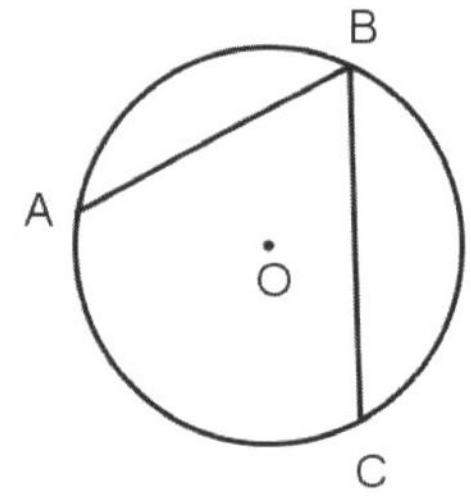

Any angle inscribed in a semicircle is a right angle. The intercepted arc is 180°, making the inscribed angle half that, or 90°. In the diagram below, angle ABC is inscribed in semicircle ABC, making angle ABC equal to 90°.

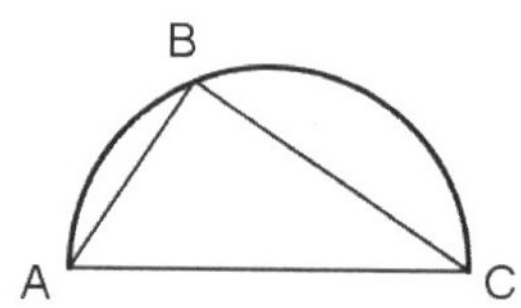

Review Video: Arcs and Angles of Circles
Visit mometrix.com/academy and enter code: 652838

SECANTS, CHORDS, AND TANGENTS

A **secant** is a line that intersects a circle in two points. The segment of a secant line that is contained within the circle is called a **chord**. Two secants may intersect inside the circle, on the circle, or outside the circle. When the two secants intersect on the circle, an inscribed angle is formed. When two secants intersect inside a circle, the measure of each of two vertical angles is equal to half the sum of the two intercepted arcs. Consider the following diagram where $\text{m}\angle AEB = \frac{1}{2}(\widehat{AB} + \widehat{CD})$ and $\text{m}\angle BEC = \frac{1}{2}(\widehat{BC} + \widehat{AD})$.

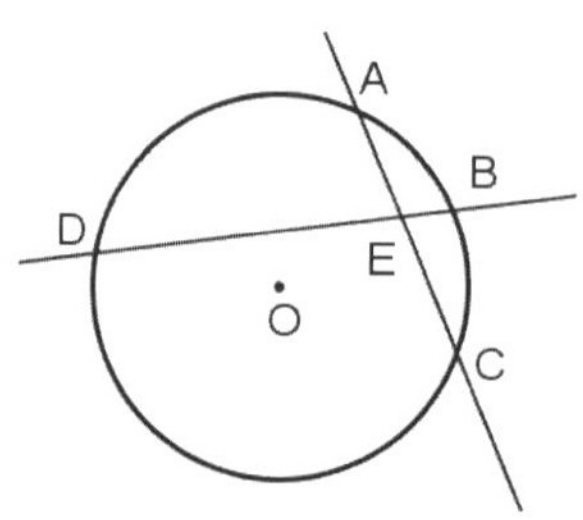

When two secants intersect outside a circle, the measure of the angle formed is equal to half the difference of the two arcs that lie between the two secants. In the diagram below, $m\angle AEB = \frac{1}{2}(\widehat{AB} - \widehat{CD})$.

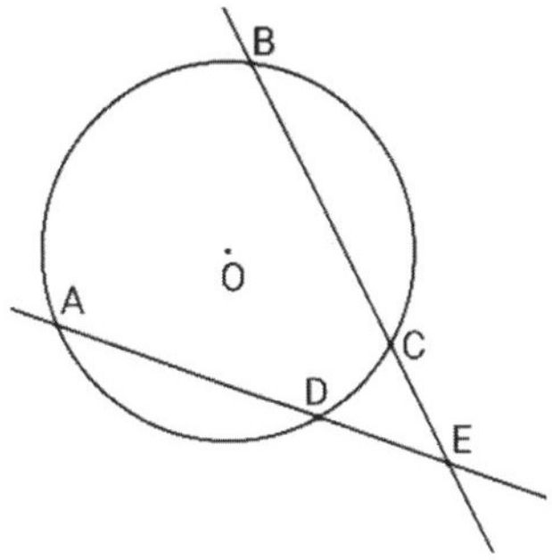

A **tangent** is a line in the same plane as a circle that touches the circle in exactly one point. The point at which a tangent touches a circle is called the **point of tangency**. While a line segment can be tangent to a circle as part of a line that is tangent, it is improper to say a tangent can be simply a line segment that touches the circle in exactly one point.

In the diagram below, $\overleftrightarrow{EB}$ is a secant and contains chord $\overline{EB}$, and $\overleftrightarrow{CD}$ is tangent to circle A. Notice that $\overline{FB}$ is not tangent to the circle. $\overline{FB}$ is a line segment that touches the circle in exactly one point, but if the segment were extended, it would touch the circle in a second point. In the diagram below, point B is the point of tangency.

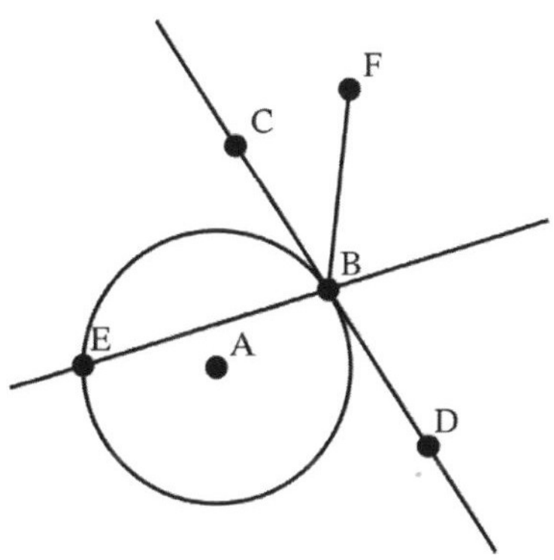

Review Video: Secants, Chords, and Tangents
Visit mometrix.com/academy and enter code: 258360

Review Video: Tangent Lines of a Circle
Visit mometrix.com/academy and enter code: 780167

SECTORS

A **sector** is the portion of a circle formed by two radii and their intercepted arc. While the arc length is exclusively the points that are also on the circumference of the circle, the sector is the entire area bounded by the arc and the two radii.

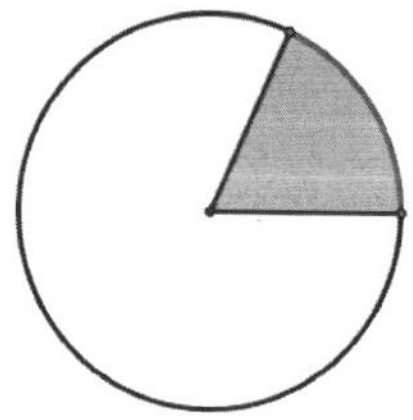

The **area of a sector** of a circle is found by the formula, $A = \frac{\theta r^2}{2}$, where A is the area, θ is the measure of the central angle in radians, and r is the radius. To find the area with the central angle in degrees, use the formula, $A = \frac{\theta \pi r^2}{360}$, where θ is the measure of the central angle and r is the radius.

Transformations

TRANSFORMATIONS

ROTATION

A **rotation** is a transformation that turns a figure around a point called the **center of rotation**, which can lie anywhere in the plane. If a line is drawn from a point on a figure to the center of rotation, and another line is drawn from the center to the rotated image of that point, the angle between the two lines is the **angle of rotation**. The vertex of the angle of rotation is the center of rotation.

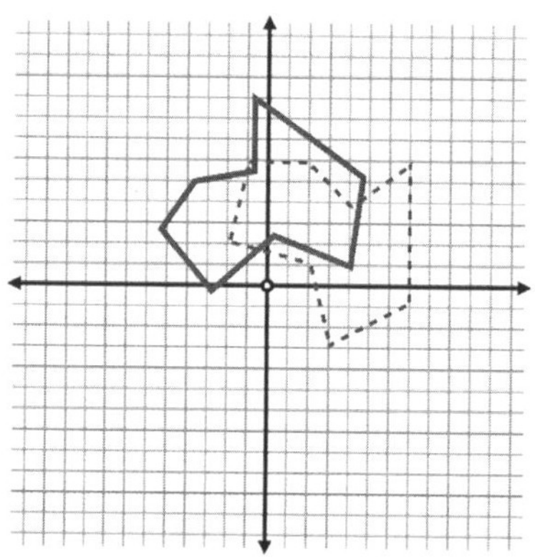

Review Video: Rotation
Visit mometrix.com/academy and enter code: 602600

TRANSLATION AND DILATION

A **translation** is a transformation which slides a figure from one position in the plane to another position in the plane. The original figure and the translated figure have the same size, shape, and orientation. A **dilation** is a transformation which proportionally stretches or shrinks a figure by a

scale factor. The dilated image is the same shape and orientation as the original image but a different size. A polygon and its dilated image are similar.

Translation

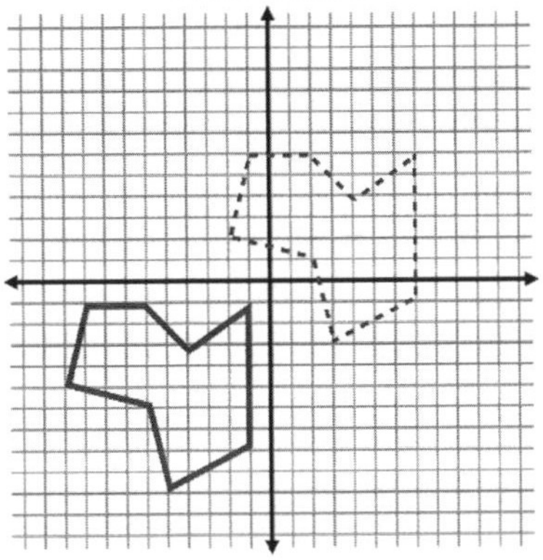

Dilation

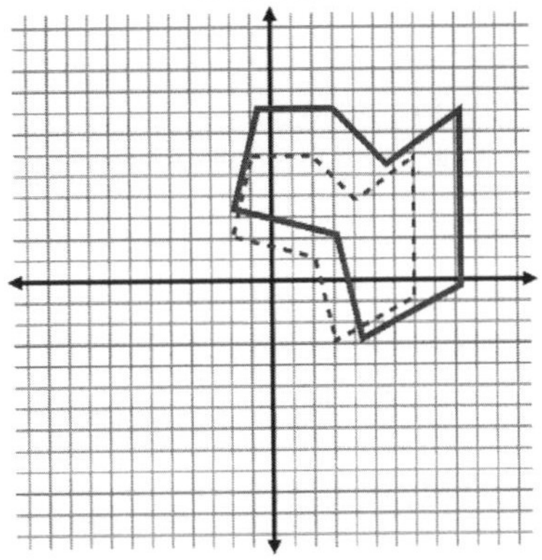

Review Video: Translation
Visit mometrix.com/academy and enter code: 718628

Review Video: Dilation
Visit mometrix.com/academy and enter code: 471630

A **reflection of a figure over a line** (a "flip") creates a congruent image that is the same distance from the line as the original figure but on the opposite side. The **line of reflection** is the perpendicular bisector of any line segment drawn from a point on the original figure to its reflected image (unless the point and its reflected image happen to be the same point, which happens when a figure is reflected over one of its own sides). A **reflection of a figure over a point** (an inversion) in two dimensions is the same as the rotation of the figure 180° about that point. The image of the figure is congruent to the original figure. The **point of reflection** is the midpoint of a line segment which connects a point in the figure to its image (unless the point and its reflected image happen to be the same point, which happens when a figure is reflected in one of its own points).

Reflection of a figure over a line

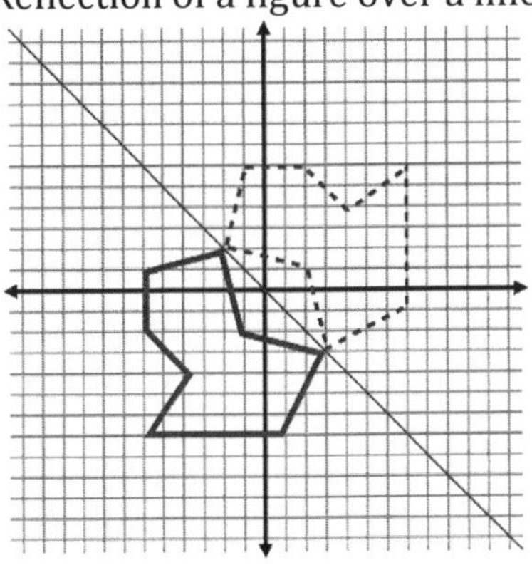

Reflection of a figure over a point

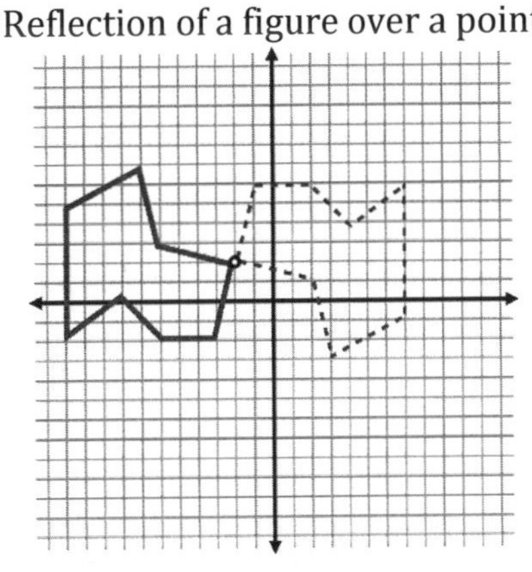

Review Video: Reflection
Visit mometrix.com/academy and enter code: 955068

3D Shapes

3D SHAPES

SOLIDS

The **surface area of a solid object** is the area of all sides or exterior surfaces. For objects such as prisms and pyramids, a further distinction is made between base surface area (B) and lateral surface area (LA). For a prism, the total surface area (SA) is $SA = LA + 2B$. For a pyramid or cone, the total surface area is $SA = LA + B$.

The **surface area of a sphere** can be found by the formula $A = 4\pi r^2$, where r is the radius. The volume is given by the formula $V = \frac{4}{3}\pi r^3$, where r is the radius. Both quantities are generally given in terms of π.

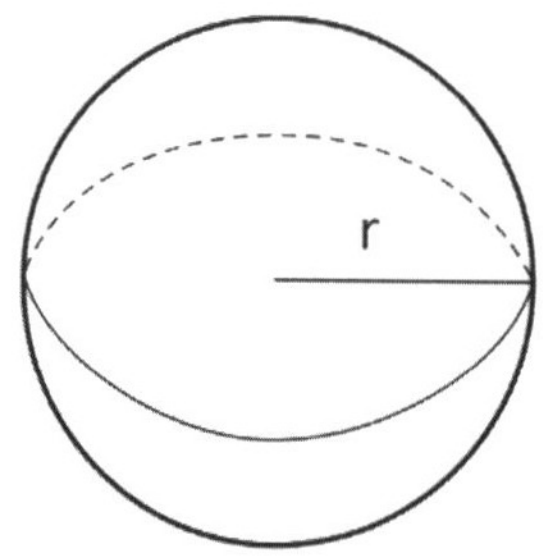

Review Video: Volume and Surface Area of a Sphere
Visit mometrix.com/academy and enter code: 786928

Review Video: How to Calculate the Volume of 3D Objects
Visit mometrix.com/academy and enter code: 163343

The **volume of any prism** is found by the formula $V = Bh$, where B is the area of the base, and h is the height (perpendicular distance between the bases). The surface area of any prism is the sum of the areas of both bases and all sides. It can be calculated as $SA = 2B + Ph$, where P is the perimeter of the base.

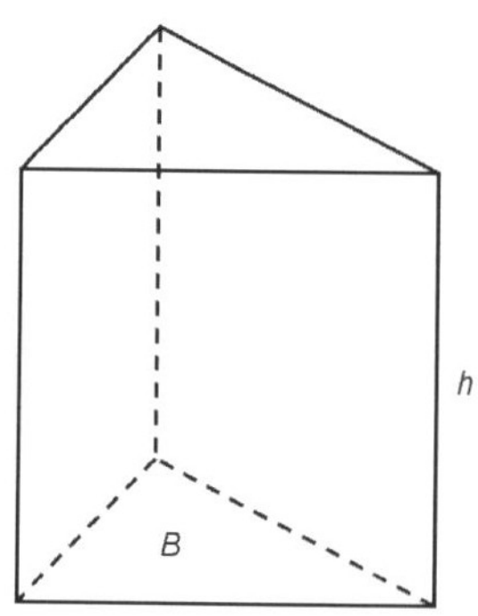

Review Video: Volume and Surface Area of a Prism
Visit mometrix.com/academy and enter code: 420158

For a **rectangular prism**, the volume can be found by the formula $V = lwh$, where V is the volume, l is the length, w is the width, and h is the height. The surface area can be calculated as $SA = 2lw + 2hl + 2wh$ or $SA = 2(lw + hl + wh)$.

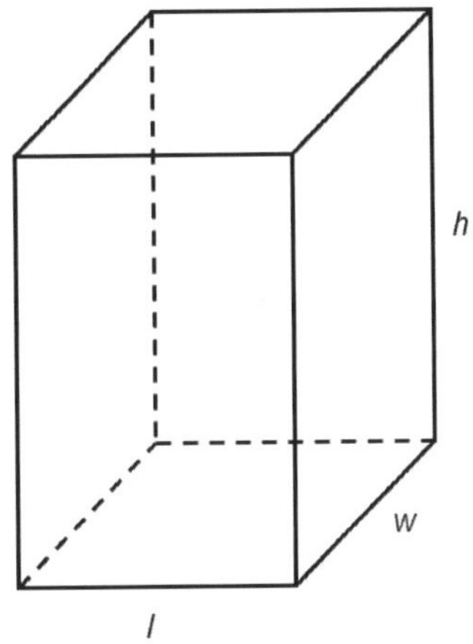

Review Video: Volume and Surface Area of a Rectangular Prism
Visit mometrix.com/academy and enter code: 282814

The **volume of a cube** can be found by the formula $V = s^3$, where s is the length of a side. The surface area of a cube is calculated as $SA = 6s^2$, where SA is the total surface area and s is the length of a side. These formulas are the same as the ones used for the volume and surface area of a rectangular prism, but simplified since all three quantities (length, width, and height) are the same.

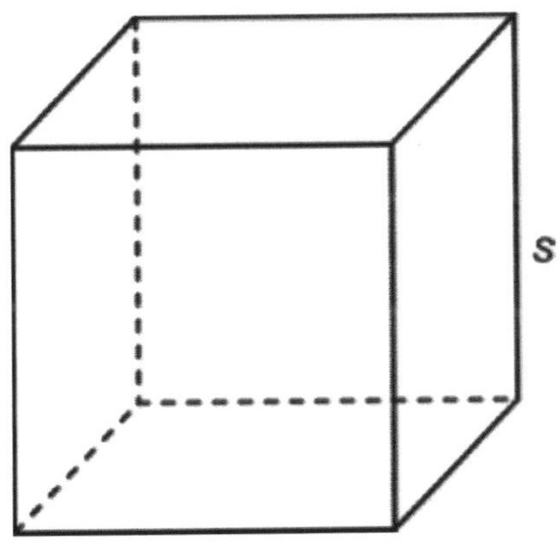

Review Video: Volume and Surface Area of a Cube
Visit mometrix.com/academy and enter code: 664455

The **volume of a cylinder** can be calculated by the formula $V = \pi r^2 h$, where r is the radius, and h is the height. The surface area of a cylinder can be found by the formula $SA = 2\pi r^2 + 2\pi rh$. The first term is the base area multiplied by two, and the second term is the perimeter of the base multiplied by the height.

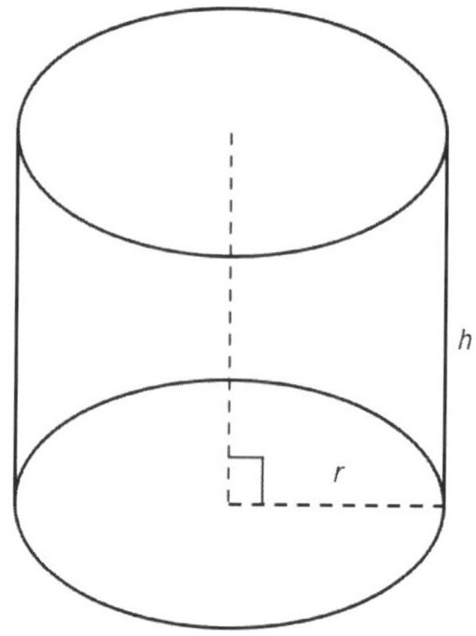

Review Video: Volume and Surface Area of a Right Circular Cylinder
Visit mometrix.com/academy and enter code: 226463

The **volume of a pyramid** is found by the formula $V = \frac{1}{3}Bh$, where B is the area of the base, and h is the height (perpendicular distance from the vertex to the base). Notice this formula is the same as $\frac{1}{3}$ times the volume of a prism. Like a prism, the base of a pyramid can be any shape.

Finding the **surface area of a pyramid** is not as simple as the other shapes we've looked at thus far. If the pyramid is a right pyramid, meaning the base is a regular polygon and the vertex is directly over the center of that polygon, the surface area can be calculated as $SA = B + \frac{1}{2}Ph_s$, where P is the perimeter of the base, and h_s is the slant height (distance from the vertex to the midpoint of one side of the base). If the pyramid is irregular, the area of each triangle side must be calculated individually and then summed, along with the base.

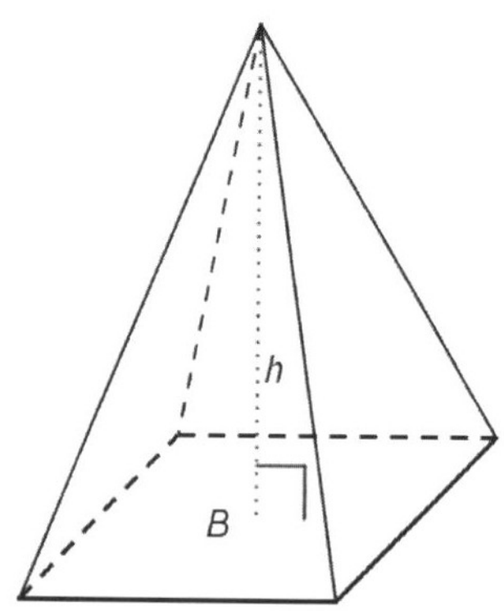

Review Video: Volume and Surface Area of a Pyramid
Visit mometrix.com/academy and enter code: 621932

The **volume of a cone** is found by the formula $V = \frac{1}{3}\pi r^2 h$, where r is the radius, and h is the height. Notice this is the same as $\frac{1}{3}$ times the volume of a cylinder. The surface area can be calculated as

$SA = \pi r^2 + \pi rs$, where s is the slant height. The slant height can be calculated using the Pythagorean theorem to be $\sqrt{r^2 + h^2}$, so the surface area formula can also be written as $SA = \pi r^2 + \pi r\sqrt{r^2 + h^2}$.

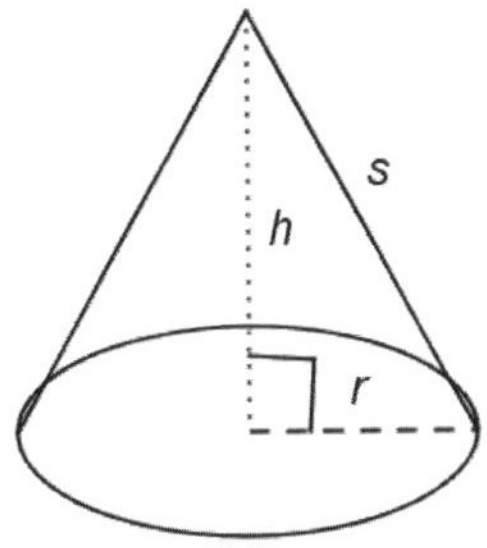

Review Video: Volume and Surface Area of a Right Circular Cone
Visit mometrix.com/academy and enter code: 573574

Conic Sections

Conic sections are a family of shapes that can be thought of as cross sections of a pair of infinite right cones stacked vertex to vertex. This is easiest to see with a visual representation:

A three-dimensional look at representative conic sections. (Note that a hyperbola intersects both cones.)

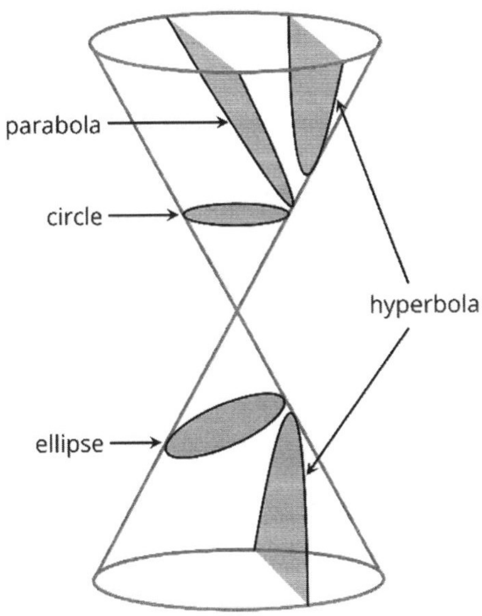

A side-on look at representative conic sections. (Note that the parabola is parallel to the slant of the cones.)

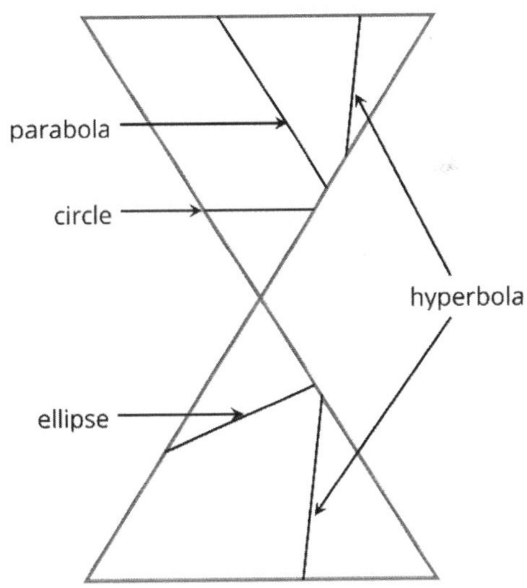

In short, a circle is a horizontal cross section, a parabola is a cross section parallel to the slant of the cone, an ellipse is a cross section at an angle *less than* the slant of the cone, and a hyperbola is a cross section at an angle *greater than* the slant of the cone.

Parabolas, Ellipses, and Hyperbolas

Parabolas

A **parabola** is the set of all points in a plane that are equidistant from a fixed line, called the **directrix**, and a fixed point not on the line, called the **focus**. The **axis** is the line perpendicular to the directrix that passes through the focus.

For parabolas that open up or down, the standard equation is $(x-h)^2 = 4c(y-k)$, where h, c, and k are coefficients. If c is positive, the parabola opens up. If c is negative, the parabola opens down. The vertex is the point (h, k). The directrix is the line having the equation $y = -c + k$, and the focus is the point $(h, c + k)$.

For parabolas that open left or right, the standard equation is $(y-k)^2 = 4c(x-h)$, where k, c, and h are coefficients. If c is positive, the parabola opens to the right. If c is negative, the parabola opens to the left. The vertex is the point (h, k). The directrix is the line having the equation $x = -c + h$, and the focus is the point $(c + h, k)$.

Review Video: Parabolas
Visit mometrix.com/academy and enter code: 129187

Review Video: Vertex of a Parabola
Visit mometrix.com/academy and enter code: 272300

Review Video: How to Convert Between Standard Form and Vertex Form
Visit mometrix.com/academy and enter code: 916601

Ellipses and Hyperbolas

Ellipse

An **ellipse** is the set of all points in a plane whose total distance from two fixed points called the **foci** (singular: focus) is constant, and whose center is the midpoint between the foci.

The standard equation of an ellipse that is wider than it is tall is $\frac{(x-h)^2}{a^2} + \frac{(y-k)^2}{b^2} = 1$, where a and b are coefficients. The center is the point (h, k) and the foci are the points $(h + c, k)$ and $(h - c, k)$, where $c^2 = a^2 - b^2$ and $a^2 > b^2$.

The major axis has length $2a$, and the minor axis has length $2b$.

Eccentricity (e) is a measure of how elongated an ellipse is, and is the ratio of the distance between the foci to the length of the major axis. Eccentricity will have a value between 0 and 1. The closer to 0 the eccentricity is, the closer the ellipse is to being a circle. The formula for eccentricity is $e = \frac{c}{a}$.

Review Video: Ellipse
Visit mometrix.com/academy and enter code: 703899

Hyperbola

A **hyperbola** is the set of all points in a plane, whose distance from two fixed points, called foci, has a constant difference.

The standard equation of a horizontal hyperbola is $\frac{(x-h)^2}{a^2} - \frac{(y-k)^2}{b^2} = 1$, where a, b, h, and k are real numbers. The center is the point (h, k), the vertices are the points $(h + a, k)$ and $(h - a, k)$, and the foci are the points that every point on one of the parabolic curves is equidistant from. The foci are found using the formulas $(h + c, k)$ and $(h - c, k)$, where $c^2 = a^2 + b^2$. The asymptotes are two lines the graph of the hyperbola approaches but never reaches, and are given by the equations $y = \left(\frac{b}{a}\right)(x - h) + k$ and $y = -\left(\frac{b}{a}\right)(x - h) + k$.

The standard equation of a vertical hyperbola is $\frac{(y-k)^2}{a^2} - \frac{(x-h)^2}{b^2} = 1$, where a, b, k, and h are real numbers. The center is the point (h, k), the vertices are the points $(h, k + a)$ and $(h, k - a)$, and the foci are the points that every point on one of the hyperbolic curves is equidistant from and are found using the formulas $(h, k + c)$ and $(h, k - c)$, where $c^2 = a^2 + b^2$. The asymptotes are two lines the graph of the hyperbola approaches but never reaches, and are given by the equations $y = \left(\frac{a}{b}\right)(x - h) + k$ and $y = -\left(\frac{a}{b}\right)(x - h) + k$.

Review Video: Hyperbolas
Visit mometrix.com/academy and enter code: 509429

Chapter Quiz

Ready to see how well you retained what you just read? Scan the QR code to go directly to the chapter quiz interface for this study guide. If you're using a computer, simply visit the online resources page at **mometrix.com/resources719/texesmathpse** and click the Chapter Quizzes link.

Probability and Statistics

Displaying Data

Tree Diagrams

For a simple sample space, possible outcomes may be determined by using a **tree diagram** or an organized chart. In either case, you can easily draw or list out the possible outcomes. For example, to determine all the possible ways three objects can be ordered, you can draw a tree diagram:

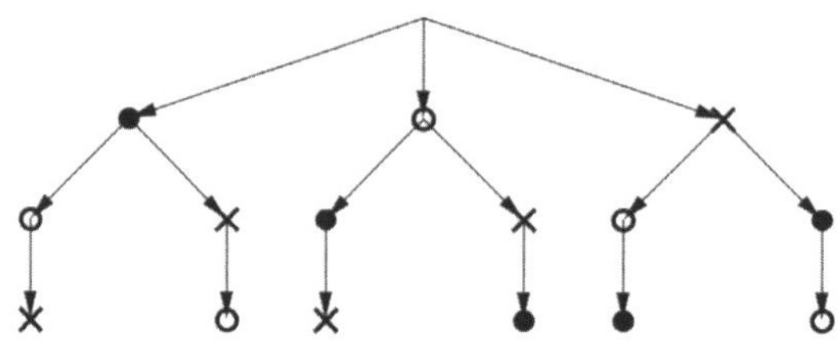

Review Video: Tree Diagrams
Visit mometrix.com/academy and enter code: 829158

You can also make a chart to list all the possibilities:

First object	Second object	Third object
●	x	o
●	o	x
o	●	x
o	x	●
x	●	o
x	o	●

Either way, you can easily see there are six possible ways the three objects can be ordered.

If two events have no outcomes in common, they are said to be **mutually exclusive**. For example, in a standard deck of 52 playing cards, the event of all card suits is mutually exclusive to the event of all card values. If two events have no bearing on each other so that one event occurring has no influence on the probability of another event occurring, the two events are said to be independent. For example, rolling a standard six-sided die multiple times does not change that probability that a particular number will be rolled from one roll to the next. If the outcome of one event does affect the probability of the second event, the two events are said to be dependent. For example, if cards are drawn from a deck, the probability of drawing an ace after an ace has been drawn is different than the probability of drawing an ace if no ace (or no other card, for that matter) has been drawn.

In probability, the **odds in favor of an event** are the number of times the event will occur compared to the number of times the event will not occur. To calculate the odds in favor of an event, use the formula $\frac{P(A)}{1-P(A)}$, where $P(A)$ is the probability that the event will occur. Many times, odds in favor is given as a ratio in the form $\frac{a}{b}$ or $a:b$, where a is the probability of the event occurring and b is the complement of the event, the probability of the event not occurring. If the odds in favor are given as 2:5, that means that you can expect the event to occur two times for every 5 times that it does not occur. In other words, the probability that the event will occur is $\frac{2}{2+5} = \frac{2}{7}$.

In probability, the **odds against an event** are the number of times the event will not occur compared to the number of times the event will occur. To calculate the odds against an event, use the formula $\frac{1-P(A)}{P(A)}$, where $P(A)$ is the probability that the event will occur. Many times, odds against is given as a ratio in the form $\frac{b}{a}$ or $b: a$, where b is the probability the event will not occur (the complement of the event) and a is the probability the event will occur. If the odds against an event are given as 3:1, that means that you can expect the event to not occur 3 times for every one time it does occur. In other words, 3 out of every 4 trials will fail.

Two-Way Frequency Tables

If we have a two-way frequency table, it is generally a straightforward matter to read off the probabilities of any two events A and B, as well as the joint probability of both events occurring, $P(A \cap B)$. We can then find the conditional probability $P(A|B)$ by calculating $P(A|B) = \frac{P(A \cap B)}{P(B)}$. We could also check whether or not events are independent by verifying whether $P(A)P(B) = P(A \cap B)$.

For example, a certain store's recent T-shirt sales:

	Small	Medium	Large	Total
Blue	25	40	35	100
White	27	25	22	74
Black	8	23	15	46
Total	60	88	72	220

Suppose we want to find the conditional probability that a customer buys a black shirt (event A), given that the shirt he buys is size small (event B). From the table, the probability $P(B)$ that a customer buys a small shirt is $\frac{60}{220} = \frac{3}{11}$. The probability $P(A \cap B)$ that he buys a small, black shirt is $\frac{8}{220} = \frac{2}{55}$. The conditional probability $P(A|B)$ that he buys a black shirt, given that he buys a small shirt, is therefore $P(A|B) = \frac{2/55}{3/11} = \frac{2}{15}$.

Similarly, if we want to check whether the event a customer buys a blue shirt, A, is independent of the event that a customer buys a medium shirt, B. From the table, $P(A) = \frac{100}{220} = \frac{5}{11}$ and $P(B) = \frac{88}{220} = \frac{4}{10}$. Also, $P(A \cap B) = \frac{40}{220} = \frac{2}{11}$. Since $\left(\frac{5}{11}\right)\left(\frac{4}{10}\right) = \frac{20}{110} = \frac{2}{11}$, $P(A)P(B) = P(A \cap B)$ and these two events are indeed independent.

DISPLAYING INFORMATION

FREQUENCY TABLES

Frequency tables show how frequently each unique value appears in a set. A **relative frequency table** is one that shows the proportions of each unique value compared to the entire set. Relative frequencies are given as percentages; however, the total percent for a relative frequency table will not necessarily equal 100 percent due to rounding. An example of a frequency table with relative frequencies is below.

Favorite Color	Frequency	Relative Frequency
Blue	4	13%
Red	7	22%
Green	3	9%
Purple	6	19%
Cyan	12	38%

Review Video: Data Interpretation of Graphs
Visit mometrix.com/academy and enter code: 200439

CIRCLE GRAPHS

Circle graphs, also known as *pie charts*, provide a visual depiction of the relationship of each type of data compared to the whole set of data. The circle graph is divided into sections by drawing radii to create central angles whose percentage of the circle is equal to the individual data's percentage of the whole set. Each 1% of data is equal to 3.6° in the circle graph. Therefore, data represented by a 90° section of the circle graph makes up 25% of the whole. When complete, a circle graph often looks like a pie cut into uneven wedges. The pie chart below shows the data from the frequency table referenced earlier where people were asked their favorite color.

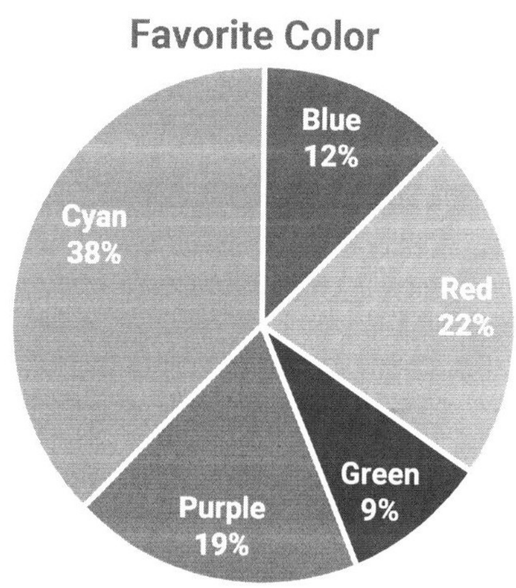

PICTOGRAPHS

A **pictograph** is a graph, generally in the horizontal orientation, that uses pictures or symbols to represent the data. Each pictograph must have a key that defines the picture or symbol and gives the quantity each picture or symbol represents. Pictures or symbols on a pictograph are not always shown as whole elements. In this case, the fraction of the picture or symbol shown represents the same fraction of the quantity a whole picture or symbol stands for. For example, a row with $3\frac{1}{2}$ ears of corn, where each ear of corn represents 100 stalks of corn in a field, would equal $3\frac{1}{2} \times 100 = 350$ stalks of corn in the field.

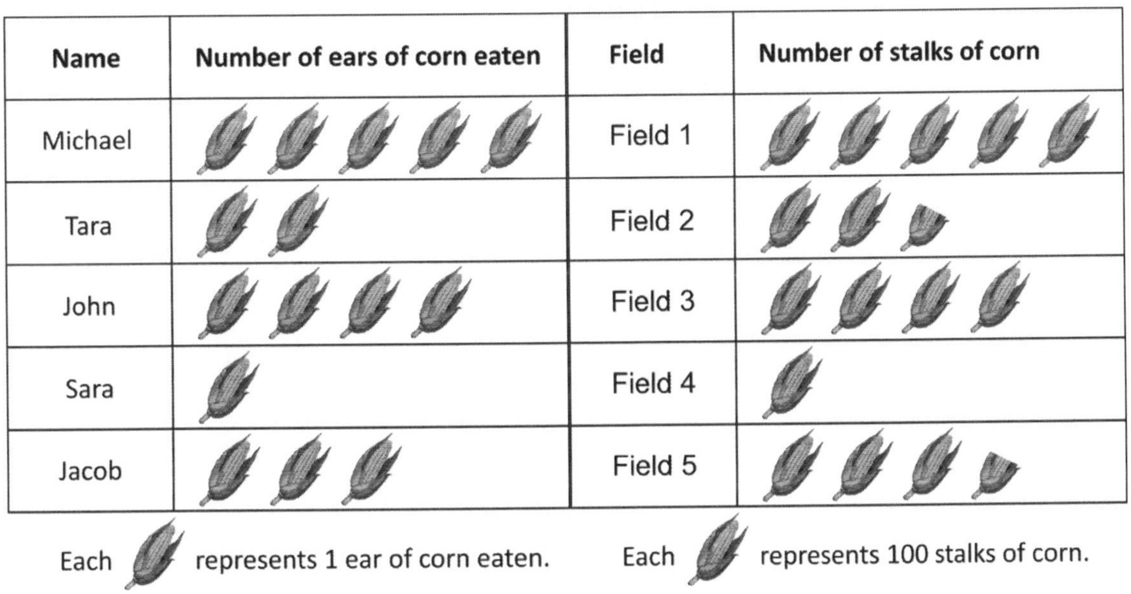

Review Video: Pictographs
Visit mometrix.com/academy and enter code: 147860

LINE GRAPHS

Line graphs have one or more lines of varying styles (solid or broken) to show the different values for a set of data. The individual data are represented as ordered pairs, much like on a Cartesian plane. In this case, the x- and y-axes are defined in terms of their units, such as dollars or time. The individual plotted points are joined by line segments to show whether the value of the data is increasing (line sloping upward), decreasing (line sloping downward), or staying the same (horizontal line). Multiple sets of data can be graphed on the same line graph to give an easy visual comparison. An example of this would be graphing achievement test scores for different groups of students over the same time period to see which group had the greatest increase or decrease in performance from year to year (as shown below).

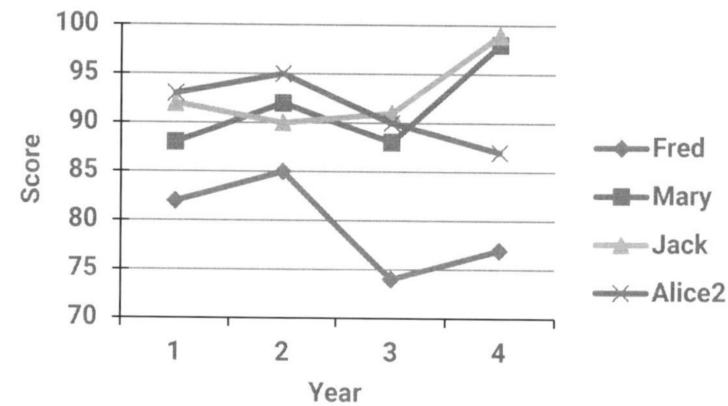

Review Video: How to Create a Line Graph
Visit mometrix.com/academy and enter code: 480147

Line Plots

A **line plot**, also known as a *dot plot*, has plotted points that are not connected by line segments. In this graph, the horizontal axis lists the different possible values for the data, and the vertical axis lists the number of times the individual value occurs. A single dot is graphed for each value to show the number of times it occurs. This graph is more closely related to a bar graph than a line graph. Do not connect the dots in a line plot or it will misrepresent the data.

Review Video: Line Plot
Visit mometrix.com/academy and enter code: 754610

Stem and Leaf Plots

A **stem and leaf plot** is useful for depicting groups of data that fall into a range of values. Each piece of data is separated into two parts: the first, or left, part is called the stem; the second, or right, part is called the leaf. Each stem is listed in a column from smallest to largest. Each leaf that has the common stem is listed in that stem's row from smallest to largest. For example, in a set of two-digit numbers, the digit in the tens place is the stem, and the digit in the ones place is the leaf. With a stem and leaf plot, you can easily see which subset of numbers (10s, 20s, 30s, etc.) is the largest. This information is also readily available by looking at a histogram, but a stem and leaf plot also allows you to look closer and see exactly which values fall in that range. Using a sample set of test scores (82, 88, 92, 93, 85, 90, 92, 95, 74, 88, 90, 91, 78, 87, 98, 99), we can assemble a stem and leaf plot like the one below.

Test Scores

7	4	8							
8	2	5	7	8	8				
9	0	0	1	2	2	3	5	8	9

Review Video: Stem and Leaf Plots
Visit mometrix.com/academy and enter code: 302339

BAR GRAPHS

A **bar graph** is one of the few graphs that can be drawn correctly in two different configurations – both horizontally and vertically. A bar graph is similar to a line plot in the way the data is organized on the graph. Both axes must have their categories defined for the graph to be useful. Rather than placing a single dot to mark the point of the data's value, a bar, or thick line, is drawn from zero to the exact value of the data, whether it is a number, percentage, or other numerical value. Longer bar lengths correspond to greater data values. To read a bar graph, read the labels for the axes to find the units being reported. Then, look where the bars end in relation to the scale given on the corresponding axis and determine the associated value.

The bar chart below represents the responses from our favorite-color survey.

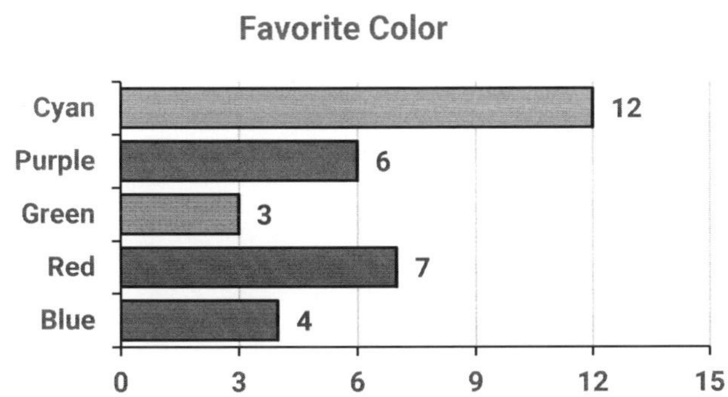

HISTOGRAMS

At first glance, a **histogram** looks like a vertical bar graph. The difference is that a bar graph has a separate bar for each piece of data and a histogram has one continuous bar for each *range* of data. For example, a histogram may have one bar for the range 0–9, one bar for 10–19, etc. While a bar graph has numerical values on one axis, a histogram has numerical values on both axes. Each range is of equal size, and they are ordered left to right from lowest to highest. The height of each column on a histogram represents the number of data values within that range. Like a stem and leaf plot, a histogram makes it easy to glance at the graph and quickly determine which range has the greatest quantity of values. A simple example of a histogram is below.

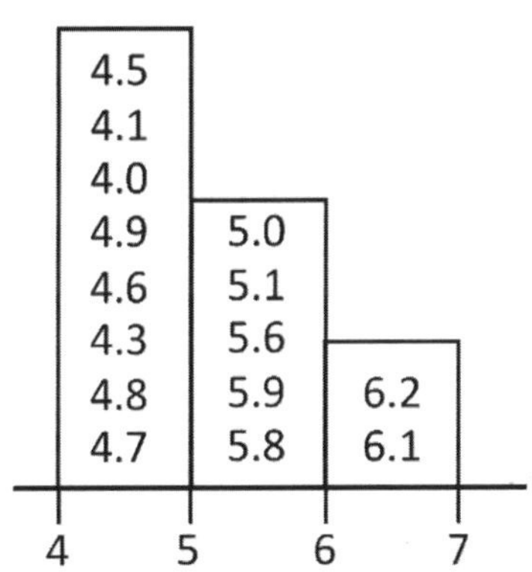

5-NUMBER SUMMARY

The **5-number summary** of a set of data gives a very informative picture of the set. The five numbers in the summary include the minimum value, maximum value, and the three quartiles. This information gives the reader the range and median of the set, as well as an indication of how the data is spread about the median.

Box and Whisker Plots

A **box-and-whiskers plot** is a graphical representation of the 5-number summary. To draw a box-and-whiskers plot, plot the points of the 5-number summary on a number line. Draw a box whose ends are through the points for the first and third quartiles. Draw a vertical line in the box through the median to divide the box in half. Draw a line segment from the first quartile point to the minimum value, and from the third quartile point to the maximum value.

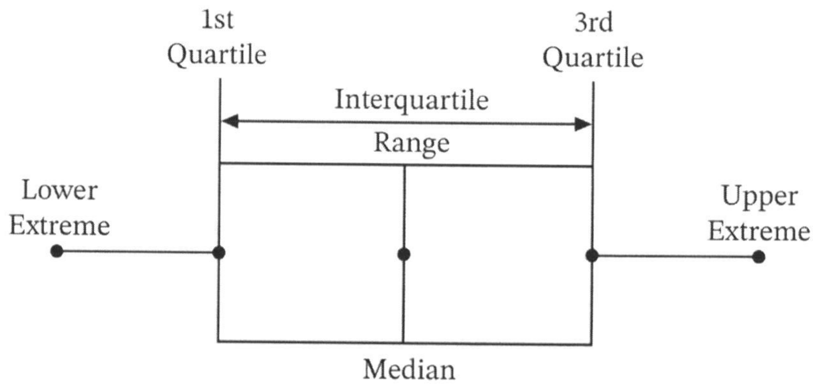

> **Review Video: Box and Whisker Plots**
> Visit mometrix.com/academy and enter code: 810817

Example

Given the following data (32, 28, 29, 26, 35, 27, 30, 31, 27, 32), we first sort it into numerical order: 26, 27, 27, 28, 29, 30, 31, 32, 32, 35. We can then find the median. Since there are ten values, we take the average of the 5th and 6th values to get 29.5. We find the lower quartile by taking the median of the data smaller than the median. Since there are five values, we take the 3rd value, which is 27. We find the upper quartile by taking the median of the data larger than the overall median, which is 32. Finally, we note our minimum and maximum, which are simply the smallest and largest values in the set: 26 and 35, respectively. Now we can create our box plot:

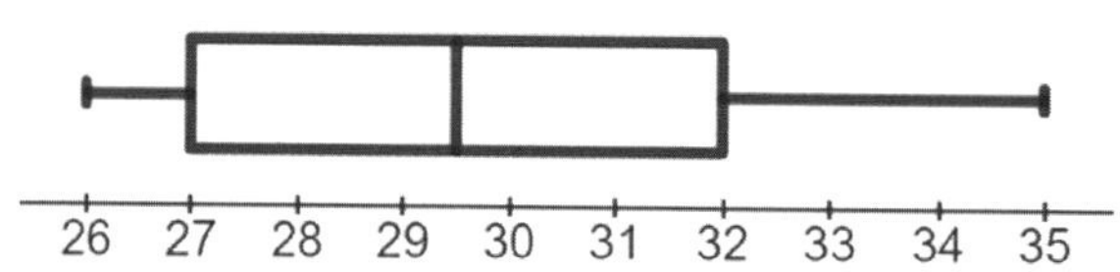

This plot is fairly "long" on the right whisker, showing one or more unusually high values (but not quite outliers). The other quartiles are similar in length, showing a fairly even distribution of data.

Interquartile Range

The **interquartile range, or IQR**, is the difference between the upper and lower quartiles. It measures how the data is dispersed: a high IQR means that the data is more spread out, while a low IQR means that the data is clustered more tightly around the median. To find the IQR, subtract the lower quartile value (Q_1) from the upper quartile value (Q_3).

EXAMPLE

To find the upper and lower quartiles, we first find the median and then take the median of all values above it and all values below it. In the following data set (16, 18, 13, 24, 16, 51, 32, 21, 27, 39), we first rearrange the values in numerical order: 13, 16, 16, 18, 21, 24, 27, 32, 39, 51. There are 10 values, so the median is the average of the 5th and 6th: $\frac{21+24}{2} = \frac{45}{2} = 22.5$. We do not actually need this value to find the upper and lower quartiles. We look at the set of numbers below the median: 13, 16, 16, 18, 21. There are five values, so the 3rd is the median (16), or the value of the lower quartile (Q_1). Then we look at the numbers above the median: 24, 27, 32, 39, 51. Again there are five values, so the 3rd is the median (32), or the value of the upper quartile (Q_3). We find the IQR by subtracting Q_1 from Q_3: $32 - 16 = 16$.

68-95-99.7 RULE

The **68–95–99.7 rule** describes how a normal distribution of data should appear when compared to the mean. This is also a description of a normal bell curve. According to this rule, 68 percent of the data values in a normally distributed set should fall within one standard deviation of the mean (34 percent above and 34 percent below the mean), 95 percent of the data values should fall within two standard deviations of the mean (47.5 percent above and 47.5 percent below the mean), and 99.7 percent of the data values should fall within three standard deviations of the mean, again, equally distributed on either side of the mean. This means that only 0.3 percent of all data values should fall more than three standard deviations from the mean. On the graph below, the normal curve is centered on the y-axis. The x-axis labels are how many standard deviations away from the center you are. Therefore, it is easy to see how the 68-95-99.7 rule can apply.

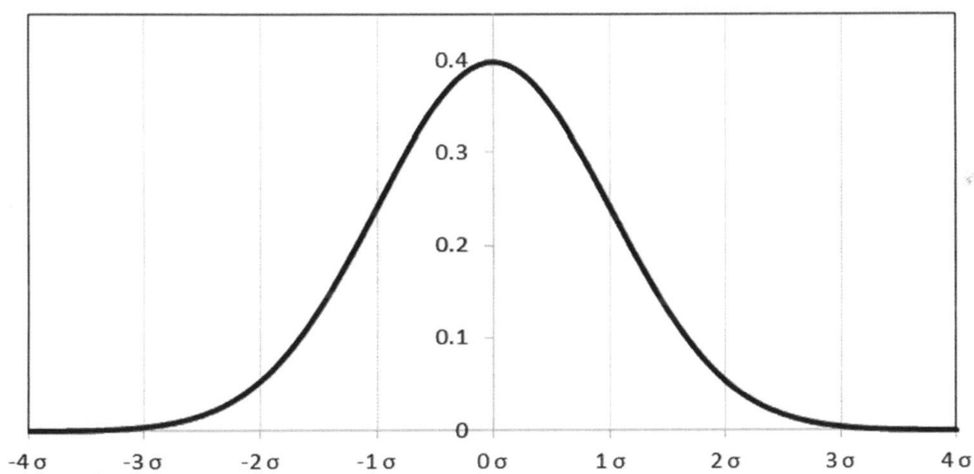

Scatter Plots

Bivariate Data

Bivariate data is simply data from two different variables. (The prefix *bi-* means *two.*) In a *scatter plot,* each value in the set of data is plotted on a grid similar to a Cartesian plane, where each axis represents one of the two variables. By looking at the pattern formed by the points on the grid, you can often determine whether or not there is a relationship between the two variables, and what that relationship is, if it exists. The variables may be directly proportionate, inversely proportionate, or show no proportion at all. It may also be possible to determine if the data is linear, and if so, to find an equation to relate the two variables. The following scatter plot shows the relationship between preference for brand "A" and the age of the consumers surveyed.

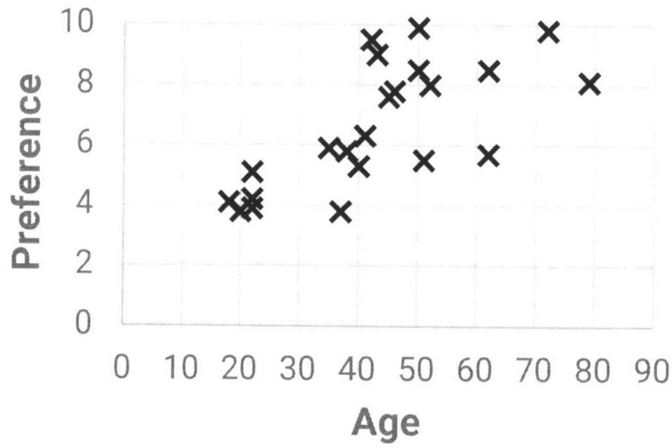

SCATTER PLOTS

Scatter plots are also useful in determining the type of function represented by the data and finding the simple regression. Linear scatter plots may be positive or negative. Nonlinear scatter plots are generally exponential or quadratic. Below are some common types of scatter plots:

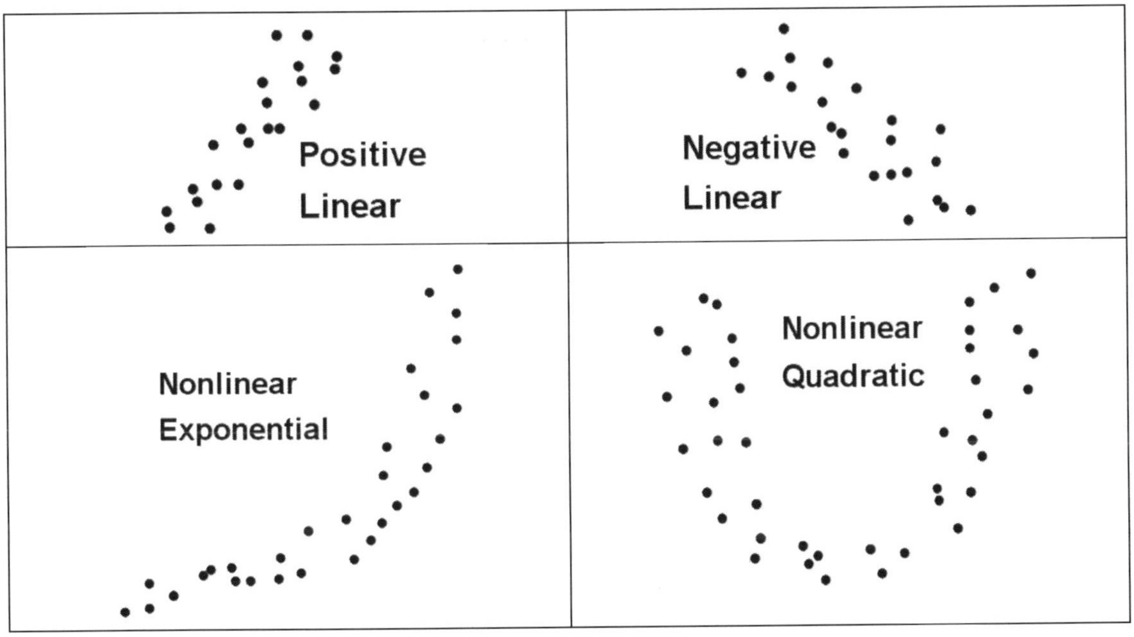

Review Video: Scatter Plot
Visit mometrix.com/academy and enter code: 596526

Statistics

INTRODUCTION TO STATISTICS

Statistics is the branch of mathematics that deals with collecting, recording, interpreting, illustrating, and analyzing large amounts of **data**. The following terms are often used in the discussion of data and **statistics**:

- **Data** – the collective name for pieces of information (singular is datum)
- **Quantitative data** – measurements (such as length, mass, and speed) that provide information about quantities in numbers
- **Qualitative data** – information (such as colors, scents, tastes, and shapes) that cannot be measured using numbers
- **Discrete data** – information that can be expressed only by a specific value, such as whole or half numbers. (e.g., since people can be counted only in whole numbers, a population count would be discrete data.)
- **Continuous data** – information (such as time and temperature) that can be expressed by any value within a given range
- **Primary data** – information that has been collected directly from a survey, investigation, or experiment, such as a questionnaire or the recording of daily temperatures. (Primary data that has not yet been organized or analyzed is called **raw data**.)
- **Secondary data** – information that has been collected, sorted, and processed by the researcher

- **Ordinal data** – information that can be placed in numerical order, such as age or weight
- **Nominal data** – information that *cannot* be placed in numerical order, such as names or places

Data Collection

Population

In statistics, the **population** is the entire collection of people, plants, etc., that data can be collected from. For example, a study to determine how well students in local schools perform on a standardized test would have a population of all the students enrolled in those schools, although a study may include just a small sample of students from each school. A **parameter** is a numerical value that gives information about the population, such as the mean, median, mode, or standard deviation. Remember that the symbol for the mean of a population is μ and the symbol for the standard deviation of a population is σ.

Sample

A **sample** is a portion of the entire population. Whereas a parameter helped describe the population, a **statistic** is a numerical value that gives information about the sample, such as mean, median, mode, or standard deviation. Keep in mind that the symbols for mean and standard deviation are different when they are referring to a sample rather than the entire population. For a sample, the symbol for mean is $\bar{x}$ and the symbol for standard deviation is s. The mean and standard deviation of a sample may or may not be identical to that of the entire population due to a sample only being a subset of the population. However, if the sample is random and large enough, statistically significant values can be attained. Samples are generally used when the population is too large to justify including every element or when acquiring data for the entire population is impossible.

Inferential Statistics

Inferential statistics is the branch of statistics that uses samples to make predictions about an entire population. This type of statistic is often seen in political polls, where a sample of the population is questioned about a particular topic or politician to gain an understanding of the attitudes of the entire population of the country. Often, exit polls are conducted on election days using this method. Inferential statistics can have a large margin of error if you do not have a valid sample.

Sampling Distribution

Statistical values calculated from various samples of the same size make up the **sampling distribution**. For example, if several samples of identical size are randomly selected from a large population and then the mean of each sample is calculated, the distribution of values of the means would be a sampling distribution.

The **sampling distribution of the mean** is the distribution of the sample mean, $\bar{x}$, derived from random samples of a given size. It has three important characteristics. First, the mean of the sampling distribution of the mean is equal to the mean of the population that was sampled. Second, assuming the standard deviation is non-zero, the standard deviation of the sampling distribution of the mean equals the standard deviation of the sampled population divided by the square root of the sample size. This is sometimes called the standard error. Finally, as the sample size gets larger, the sampling distribution of the mean gets closer to a normal distribution via the central limit theorem.

Survey Study

A **survey study** is a method of gathering information from a small group in an attempt to gain enough information to make accurate general assumptions about the population. Once a survey study is completed, the results are then put into a summary report.

Survey studies are generally in the format of surveys, interviews, or questionnaires as part of an effort to find opinions of a particular group or to find facts about a group.

It is important to note that the findings from a survey study are only as accurate as the sample chosen from the population.

Correlational Studies

Correlational studies seek to determine how much one variable is affected by changes in a second variable. For example, correlational studies may look for a relationship between the amount of time a student spends studying for a test and the grade that student earned on the test or between student scores on college admissions tests and student grades in college.

It is important to note that correlational studies cannot show a cause and effect, but rather can show only that two variables are or are not potentially correlated.

Experimental Studies

Experimental studies take correlational studies one step farther, in that they attempt to prove or disprove a cause-and-effect relationship. These studies are performed by conducting a series of experiments to test the hypothesis. For a study to be scientifically accurate, it must have both an experimental group that receives the specified treatment and a control group that does not get the treatment. This is the type of study pharmaceutical companies do as part of drug trials for new medications. Experimental studies are only valid when the proper scientific method has been followed. In other words, the experiment must be well-planned and executed without bias in the testing process, all subjects must be selected at random, and the process of determining which subject is in which of the two groups must also be completely random.

Observational Studies

Observational studies are the opposite of experimental studies. In observational studies, the tester cannot change or in any way control all of the variables in the test. For example, a study to determine which gender does better in math classes in school is strictly observational. You cannot change a person's gender, and you cannot change the subject being studied. The big downfall of observational studies is that you have no way of proving a cause-and-effect relationship because you cannot control outside influences. Events outside of school can influence a student's performance in school, and observational studies cannot take that into consideration.

Random Samples

For most studies, a **random sample** is necessary to produce valid results. Random samples should not have any particular influence to cause sampled subjects to behave one way or another. The goal is for the random sample to be a **representative sample**, or a sample whose characteristics give an accurate picture of the characteristics of the entire population. To accomplish this, you must make sure you have a proper **sample size**, or an appropriate number of elements in the sample.

Biases

In statistical studies, biases must be avoided. **Bias** is an error that causes the study to favor one set of results over another. For example, if a survey to determine how the country views the president's job performance only speaks to registered voters in the president's party, the results will be skewed because a disproportionately large number of responders would tend to show approval, while a disproportionately large number of people in the opposite party would tend to express disapproval. **Extraneous variables** are, as the name implies, outside influences that can affect the outcome of a study. They are not always avoidable but could trigger bias in the result.

DATA ANALYSIS

DISPERSION

A **measure of dispersion** is a single value that helps to "interpret" the measure of central tendency by providing more information about how the data values in the set are distributed about the measure of central tendency. The measure of dispersion helps to eliminate or reduce the disadvantages of using the mean, median, or mode as a single measure of central tendency, and give a more accurate picture of the dataset as a whole. To have a measure of dispersion, you must know or calculate the range, standard deviation, or variance of the data set.

RANGE

The **range** of a set of data is the difference between the greatest and lowest values of the data in the set. To calculate the range, you must first make sure the units for all data values are the same, and then identify the greatest and lowest values. If there are multiple data values that are equal for the highest or lowest, just use one of the values in the formula. Write the answer with the same units as the data values you used to do the calculations.

Review Video: Statistical Range
Visit mometrix.com/academy and enter code: 778541

SAMPLE STANDARD DEVIATION

Standard deviation is a measure of dispersion that compares all the data values in the set to the mean of the set to give a more accurate picture. To find the **standard deviation of a sample**, use the formula

$$s = \sqrt{\frac{\sum_{i=1}^{n}(x_i - \bar{x})^2}{n-1}}$$

Note that s is the standard deviation of a sample, x_i represents the individual values in the data set, $\bar{x}$ is the mean of the data values in the set, and n is the number of data values in the set. The higher the value of the standard deviation is, the greater the variance of the data values from the mean. The units associated with the standard deviation are the same as the units of the data values.

Review Video: Standard Deviation
Visit mometrix.com/academy and enter code: 419469

SAMPLE VARIANCE

The **variance of a sample** is the square of the sample standard deviation (denoted s^2). While the mean of a set of data gives the average of the set and gives information about where a specific data value lies in relation to the average, the variance of the sample gives information about the degree to which the data values are spread out and tells you how close an individual value is to the average compared to the other values. The units associated with variance are the same as the units of the data values squared.

PERCENTILE

Percentiles and quartiles are other methods of describing data within a set. **Percentiles** tell what percentage of the data in the set fall below a specific point. For example, achievement test scores are often given in percentiles. A score at the 80th percentile is one which is equal to or higher than 80 percent of the scores in the set. In other words, 80 percent of the scores were lower than that score.

Quartiles are percentile groups that make up quarter sections of the data set. The first quartile is the 25th percentile. The second quartile is the 50th percentile; this is also the median of the dataset. The third quartile is the 75th percentile.

SKEWNESS

Skewness is a way to describe the symmetry or asymmetry of the distribution of values in a dataset. If the distribution of values is symmetrical, there is no skew. In general the closer the mean of a data set is to the median of the data set, the less skew there is. Generally, if the mean is to the right of the median, the data set is *positively skewed*, or right-skewed, and if the mean is to the left of the median, the data set is *negatively skewed*, or left-skewed. However, this rule of thumb is not infallible. When the data values are graphed on a curve, a set with no skew will be a perfect bell curve.

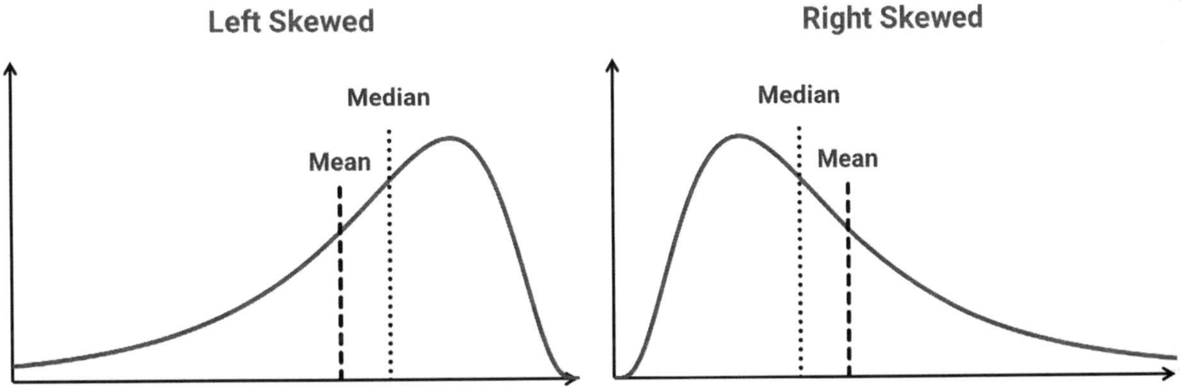

To estimate skew, use the formula:

$$\text{skew} = \frac{\sqrt{n(n-1)}}{n-2}\left(\frac{\frac{1}{n}\sum_{i=1}^{n}(x_i-\bar{x})^3}{\left(\frac{1}{n}\sum_{i=1}^{n}(x_i-\bar{x})^2\right)^{\frac{3}{2}}}\right)$$

Note that n is the datapoints in the set, x_i is the ith value in the set, and $\bar{x}$ is the mean of the set.

Review Video: Skew
Visit mometrix.com/academy and enter code: 661486

UNIMODAL VS. BIMODAL

If a distribution has a single peak, it would be considered **unimodal**. If it has two discernible peaks it would be considered **bimodal**. Bimodal distributions may be an indication that the set of data being considered is actually the combination of two sets of data with significant differences. A

uniform distribution is a distribution in which there is *no distinct peak or variation* in the data. No values or ranges are particularly more common than any other values or ranges.

Outlier

An outlier is an extremely high or extremely low value in the data set. It may be the result of measurement error, in which case, the outlier is not a valid member of the data set. However, it may also be a valid member of the distribution. Unless a measurement error is identified, the experimenter cannot know for certain if an outlier is or is not a member of the distribution. There are arbitrary methods that can be employed to designate an extreme value as an outlier. One method designates an outlier (or possible outlier) to be any value less than $Q_1 - 1.5(IQR)$ or any value greater than $Q_3 + 1.5(IQR)$.

Data Analysis

Simple Regression

In statistics, **simple regression** is using an equation to represent a relation between independent and dependent variables. The independent variable is also referred to as the explanatory variable or the predictor and is generally represented by the variable x in the equation. The dependent variable, usually represented by the variable y, is also referred to as the response variable. The equation may be any type of function - linear, quadratic, exponential, etc. The best way to handle this task is to use the regression feature of your graphing calculator. This will easily give you the curve of best fit and provide you with the coefficients and other information you need to derive an equation.

Line of Best Fit

In a scatter plot, the **line of best fit** is the line that best shows the trends of the data. The line of best fit is given by the equation $\hat{y} = ax + b$, where a and b are the regression coefficients. The regression coefficient a is also the slope of the line of best fit, and b is also the y-coordinate of the point at which the line of best fit crosses the y-axis. Not every point on the scatter plot will be on the line of best fit. The differences between the y-values of the points in the scatter plot and the corresponding y-values according to the equation of the line of best fit are the residuals. The line of best fit is also called the least-squares regression line because it is also the line that has the lowest sum of the squares of the residuals.

Correlation Coefficient

The **correlation coefficient** is the numerical value that indicates how strong the relationship is between the two variables of a linear regression equation. A correlation coefficient of -1 is a perfect negative correlation. A correlation coefficient of +1 is a perfect positive correlation. Correlation coefficients close to -1 or +1 are very strong correlations. A correlation coefficient equal to zero indicates there is no correlation between the two variables. This test is a good indicator of whether or not the equation for the line of best fit is accurate. The formula for the correlation coefficient is

$$r = \frac{\sum_{i=1}^{n}(x_i - \bar{x})(y_i - \bar{y})}{\sqrt{\sum_{i=1}^{n}(x_i - \bar{x})^2}\sqrt{\sum_{i=1}^{n}(y_i - \bar{y})^2}}$$

where r is the correlation coefficient, n is the number of data values in the set, (x_i, y_i) is a point in the set, and $\bar{x}$ and $\bar{y}$ are the means.

Z-Score

A **z-score** is an indication of how many standard deviations a given value falls from the sample mean. To calculate a z-score, use the formula:

$$\frac{x - \bar{x}}{\sigma}$$

In this formula x is the data value, $\bar{x}$ is the mean of the sample data, and σ is the standard deviation of the population. If the z-score is positive, the data value lies above the mean. If the z-score is negative, the data value falls below the mean. These scores are useful in interpreting data such as standardized test scores, where every piece of data in the set has been counted, rather than just a small random sample. In cases where standard deviations are calculated from a random sample of the set, the z-scores will not be as accurate.

Central Limit Theorem

According to the **central limit theorem**, regardless of what the original distribution of a sample is, the distribution of the means tends to get closer and closer to a normal distribution as the sample size gets larger and larger (this is necessary because the sample is becoming more all-encompassing of the elements of the population). As the sample size gets larger, the distribution of the sample mean will approach a normal distribution with a mean of the population mean and a variance of the population variance divided by the sample size.

Measures of Central Tendency

A **measure of central tendency** is a statistical value that gives a reasonable estimate for the center of a group of data. There are several different ways of describing the measure of central tendency. Each one has a unique way it is calculated, and each one gives a slightly different perspective on the data set. Whenever you give a measure of central tendency, always make sure the units are the same. If the data has different units, such as hours, minutes, and seconds, convert all the data to the same unit, and use the same unit in the measure of central tendency. If no units are given in the data, do not give units for the measure of central tendency.

Mean

The **statistical mean** of a group of data is the same as the arithmetic average of that group. To find the mean of a set of data, first convert each value to the same units, if necessary. Then find the sum of all the values, and count the total number of data values, making sure you take into consideration each individual value. If a value appears more than once, count it more than once. Divide the sum of the values by the total number of values and apply the units, if any. Note that the mean does not have to be one of the data values in the set, and may not divide evenly.

$$\text{mean} = \frac{\text{sum of the data values}}{\text{quantity of data values}}$$

For instance, the mean of the data set $\{88, 72, 61, 90, 97, 68, 88, 79, 86, 93, 97, 71, 80, 84, 89\}$ would be the sum of the fifteen numbers divided by 15:

$$\frac{88 + 72 + 61 + 90 + 97 + 68 + 88 + 79 + 86 + 93 + 97 + 71 + 80 + 84 + 89}{15} = \frac{1242}{15} = 82.8$$

While the mean is relatively easy to calculate and averages are understood by most people, the mean can be very misleading if it is used as the sole measure of central tendency. If the data set has outliers (data values that are unusually high or unusually low compared to the rest of the data values), the mean can be very distorted, especially if the data set has a small number of values. If unusually high values are countered with unusually low values, the mean is not affected as much. For example, if five of twenty students in a class get a 100 on a test, but the other 15 students have an average of 60 on the same test, the class average would appear as 70. Whenever the mean is skewed by outliers, it is always a good idea to include the median as an alternate measure of central tendency.

A **weighted mean**, or weighted average, is a mean that uses "weighted" values. The formula is weighted mean $= \frac{w_1x_1+w_2x_2+w_3x_3...+w_nx_n}{w_1+w_2+w_3+\cdots+w_n}$. Weighted values, such as $w_1, w_2, w_3, ... w_n$ are assigned to each member of the set $x_1, x_2, x_3, ... x_n$. When calculating the weighted mean, make sure a weight value for each member of the set is used.

Review Video: All About Averages
Visit mometrix.com/academy and enter code: 176521

MEDIAN

The **statistical median** is the value in the middle of the set of data. To find the median, list all data values in order from smallest to largest or from largest to smallest. Any value that is repeated in the set must be listed the number of times it appears. If there are an odd number of data values, the median is the value in the middle of the list. If there is an even number of data values, the median is the arithmetic mean of the two middle values.

For example, the median of the data set {88, 72, 61, 90, 97, 68, 88, 79, 86, 93, 97, 71, 80, 84, 88} is 86 since the ordered set is {61, 68, 71, 72, 79, 80, 84, **86**, 88, 88, 88, 90, 93, 97, 97}.

The big disadvantage of using the median as a measure of central tendency is that is relies solely on a value's relative size as compared to the other values in the set. When the individual values in a set of data are evenly dispersed, the median can be an accurate tool. However, if there is a group of rather large values or a group of rather small values that are not offset by a different group of values, the information that can be inferred from the median may not be accurate because the distribution of values is skewed.

MODE

The **statistical mode** is the data value that occurs the greatest number of times in the data set. It is possible to have exactly one mode, more than one mode, or no mode. To find the mode of a set of data, arrange the data like you do to find the median (all values in order, listing all multiples of data values). Count the number of times each value appears in the data set. If all values appear an equal number of times, there is no mode. If one value appears more than any other value, that value is the mode. If two or more values appear the same number of times, but there are other values that appear fewer times and no values that appear more times, all of those values are the modes.

For example, the mode of the data set {**88**, 72, 61, 90, 97, 68, **88**, 79, 86, 93, 97, 71, 80, 84, **88**} is 88.

The main disadvantage of the mode is that the values of the other data in the set have no bearing on the mode. The mode may be the largest value, the smallest value, or a value anywhere in between in the set. The mode only tells which value or values, if any, occurred the greatest number of times. It does not give any suggestions about the remaining values in the set.

Review Video: Mean, Median, and Mode
Visit mometrix.com/academy and enter code: 286207

Probability

PROBABILITY

Probability is the likelihood of a certain outcome occurring for a given event. An **event** is any situation that produces a result. It could be something as simple as flipping a coin or as complex as launching a rocket. Determining the probability of an outcome for an event can be equally simple or complex. As such, there are specific terms used in the study of probability that need to be understood:

- **Compound event**—an event that involves two or more independent events (rolling a pair of dice and taking the sum)
- **Desired outcome** (or success)—an outcome that meets a particular set of criteria (a roll of 1 or 2 if we are looking for numbers less than 3)
- **Independent events**—two or more events whose outcomes do not affect one another (two coins tossed at the same time)
- **Dependent events**—two or more events whose outcomes affect one another (two cards drawn consecutively from the same deck)
- **Certain outcome**—probability of outcome is 100% or 1
- **Impossible outcome**—probability of outcome is 0% or 0
- **Mutually exclusive outcomes**—two or more outcomes whose criteria cannot all be satisfied in a single event (a coin coming up heads and tails on the same toss)
- **Random variable**—refers to all possible outcomes of a single event which may be discrete or continuous.

Review Video: Intro to Probability
Visit mometrix.com/academy and enter code: 212374

SAMPLE SPACE

The total set of all possible results of a test or experiment is called a **sample space**, or sometimes a universal sample space. The sample space, represented by one of the variables S, Ω, or U (for universal sample space) has individual elements called outcomes. Other terms for outcome that may be used interchangeably include elementary outcome, simple event, or sample point. The number of outcomes in a given sample space could be infinite or finite, and some tests may yield multiple unique sample sets. For example, tests conducted by drawing playing cards from a standard deck would have one sample space of the card values, another sample space of the card suits, and a third sample space of suit-denomination combinations. For most tests, the sample spaces considered will be finite.

An **event**, represented by the variable E, is a portion of a sample space. It may be one outcome or a group of outcomes from the same sample space. If an event occurs, then the test or experiment will generate an outcome that satisfies the requirement of that event. For example, given a standard deck of 52 playing cards as the sample space, and defining the event as the collection of face cards, then the event will occur if the card drawn is a J, Q, or K. If any other card is drawn, the event is said to have not occurred.

For every sample space, each possible outcome has a specific likelihood, or probability, that it will occur. The probability measure, also called the **distribution**, is a function that assigns a real number probability, from zero to one, to each outcome. For a probability measure to be accurate, every outcome must have a real number probability measure that is greater than or equal to zero and less than or equal to one. Also, the probability measure of the sample space must equal one, and the probability measure of the union of multiple outcomes must equal the sum of the individual probability measures.

Probabilities of events are expressed as real numbers from zero to one. They give a numerical value to the chance that a particular event will occur. The probability of an event occurring is the sum of the probabilities of the individual elements of that event. For example, in a standard deck of 52 playing cards as the sample space and the collection of face cards as the event, the probability of drawing a specific face card is $\frac{1}{52} = 0.019$, but the probability of drawing any one of the twelve face cards is $12(0.019) = 0.228$. Note that rounding of numbers can generate different results. If you multiplied 12 by the fraction $\frac{1}{52}$ before converting to a decimal, you would get the answer $\frac{12}{52} = 0.231$.

THEORETICAL AND EXPERIMENTAL PROBABILITY

Theoretical probability can usually be determined without actually performing the event. The likelihood of an outcome occurring, or the probability of an outcome occurring, is given by the formula:

$$P(A) = \frac{\text{Number of acceptable outcomes}}{\text{Number of possible outcomes}}$$

Note that $P(A)$ is the probability of an outcome A occurring, and each outcome is just as likely to occur as any other outcome. If each outcome has the same probability of occurring as every other possible outcome, the outcomes are said to be equally likely to occur. The total number of acceptable outcomes must be less than or equal to the total number of possible outcomes. If the two are equal, then the outcome is certain to occur and the probability is 1. If the number of acceptable outcomes is zero, then the outcome is impossible and the probability is 0. For example, if there are 20 marbles in a bag and 5 are red, then the theoretical probability of randomly selecting a red marble is 5 out of 20, $\left(\frac{5}{20} = \frac{1}{4}, 0.25, \text{or } 25\%\right)$.

If the theoretical probability is unknown or too complicated to calculate, it can be estimated by an experimental probability. **Experimental probability**, also called empirical probability, is an estimate of the likelihood of a certain outcome based on repeated experiments or collected data. In other words, while theoretical probability is based on what *should* happen, experimental probability is based on what *has* happened. Experimental probability is calculated in the same way as theoretical probability, except that actual outcomes are used instead of possible outcomes. The more experiments performed or datapoints gathered, the better the estimate should be.

Theoretical and experimental probability do not always line up with one another. Theoretical probability says that out of 20 coin-tosses, 10 should be heads. However, if we were actually to toss 20 coins, we might record just 5 heads. This doesn't mean that our theoretical probability is incorrect; it just means that this particular experiment had results that were different from what was predicted. A practical application of empirical probability is the insurance industry. There are no set functions that define lifespan, health, or safety. Insurance companies look at factors from hundreds of thousands of individuals to find patterns that they then use to set the formulas for insurance premiums.

Review Video: Empirical Probability
Visit mometrix.com/academy and enter code: 513468

Objective and Subjective Probability

Objective probability is based on mathematical formulas and documented evidence. Examples of objective probability include raffles or lottery drawings where there is a pre-determined number of possible outcomes and a predetermined number of outcomes that correspond to an event. Other cases of objective probability include probabilities of rolling dice, flipping coins, or drawing cards. Most gambling games are based on objective probability.

In contrast, **subjective probability** is based on personal or professional feelings and judgments. Often, there is a lot of guesswork following extensive research. Areas where subjective probability is applicable include sales trends and business expenses. Attractions set admission prices based on subjective probabilities of attendance based on varying admission rates in an effort to maximize their profit.

Complement of an Event

Sometimes it may be easier to calculate the possibility of something not happening, or the **complement of an event**. Represented by the symbol $\bar{A}$, the complement of A is the probability that event A does not happen. When you know the probability of event A occurring, you can use the formula $P(\bar{A}) = 1 - P(A)$, where $P(\bar{A})$ is the probability of event A not occurring, and $P(A)$ is the probability of event A occurring.

Addition Rule

The **addition rule** for probability is used for finding the probability of a compound event. Use the formula $P(A \cup B) = P(A) + P(B) - P(A \cap B)$, where $P(A \cap B)$ is the probability of both events occurring to find the probability of a compound event. The probability of both events occurring at the same time must be subtracted to eliminate any overlap in the first two probabilities.

Conditional Probability

Given two events A and B, the **conditional probability** $P(A|B)$ is the probability that event A will occur, given that event B has occurred. The conditional probability cannot be calculated simply from $P(A)$ and $P(B)$; these probabilities alone do not give sufficient information to determine the conditional probability. It can, however, be determined if you are also given the probability of the intersection of events A and B, $P(A \cap B)$, the probability that events A and B both occur. Specifically, $P(A|B) = \frac{P(A \cap B)}{P(B)}$. For instance, suppose you have a jar containing two red marbles and two blue marbles, and you draw two marbles at random. Consider event A being the event that the first marble drawn is red, and event B being the event that the second marble drawn is blue. If we want to find the probability that B occurs given that A occurred, $P(B|A)$, then we can compute it using the fact that $P(A)$ is $\frac{1}{2}$, and $P(A \cap B)$ is $\frac{1}{3}$. (The latter may not be obvious, but may be determined by finding the product of $\frac{1}{2}$ and $\frac{2}{3}$). Therefore $P(B|A) = \frac{P(A \cap B)}{P(A)} = \frac{1/3}{1/2} = \frac{2}{3}$.

Conditional Probability in Everyday Situations

Conditional probability often arises in everyday situations in, for example, estimating the risk or benefit of certain activities. The conditional probability of having a heart attack given that you exercise daily may be smaller than the overall probability of having a heart attack. The conditional probability of having lung cancer given that you are a smoker is larger than the overall probability of having lung cancer. Note that changing the order of the conditional probability changes the meaning: the conditional probability of having lung cancer given that you are a smoker is a very different thing from the probability of being a smoker given that you have lung cancer. In an extreme case, suppose that a certain rare disease is caused only by eating a certain food, but even then, it is unlikely. Then the conditional probability of having that disease given that you eat the dangerous food is nonzero but low, but the conditional probability of having eaten that food given that you have the disease is 100%!

Review Video: Conditional Probability
Visit mometrix.com/academy and enter code: 397924

INDEPENDENCE

The conditional probability $P(A|B)$ is the probability that event A will occur given that event B occurs. If the two events are independent, we do not expect that whether or not event B occurs should have any effect on whether or not event A occurs. In other words, we expect $P(A|B) = P(A)$.

This can be proven using the usual equations for conditional probability and the joint probability of independent events. The conditional probability $P(A|B) = \frac{P(A \cap B)}{P(B)}$. If A and B are independent, then $P(A \cap B) = P(A)P(B)$. So $P(A|B) = \frac{P(A)P(B)}{P(B)} = P(A)$. By similar reasoning, if A and B are independent then $P(B|A) = P(B)$.

MULTIPLICATION RULE

The **multiplication rule** can be used to find the probability of two independent events occurring using the formula $P(A \cap B) = P(A) \times P(B)$, where $P(A \cap B)$ is the probability of two independent events occurring, $P(A)$ is the probability of the first event occurring, and $P(B)$ is the probability of the second event occurring.

The multiplication rule can also be used to find the probability of two dependent events occurring using the formula $P(A \cap B) = P(A) \times P(B|A)$, where $P(A \cap B)$ is the probability of two dependent events occurring and $P(B|A)$ is the probability of the second event occurring after the first event has already occurred.

Use a **combination of the multiplication** rule and the rule of complements to find the probability that at least one outcome of the element will occur. This is given by the general formula $P(\text{at least one event occurring}) = 1 - P(\text{no outcomes occurring})$. For example, to find the probability that at least one even number will show when a pair of dice is rolled, find the probability that two odd numbers will be rolled (no even numbers) and subtract from one. You can always use a tree diagram or make a chart to list the possible outcomes when the sample space is small, such as in the dice-rolling example, but in most cases it will be much faster to use the multiplication and complement formulas.

Review Video: Multiplication Rule
Visit mometrix.com/academy and enter code: 782598

UNION AND INTERSECTION OF TWO SETS OF OUTCOMES

If A and B are each a set of elements or outcomes from an experiment, then the **union** (symbol $\cup$) of the two sets is the set of elements found in set A or set B. For example, if $A = \{2, 3, 4\}$ and $B = \{3, 4, 5\}$, $A \cup B = \{2, 3, 4, 5\}$. Note that the outcomes 3 and 4 appear only once in the union. For statistical events, the union is equivalent to "or"; $P(A \cup B)$ is the same thing as $P(A \text{ or } B)$. The **intersection** (symbol $\cap$) of two sets is the set of outcomes common to both sets. For the above sets

A and B, $A \cap B = \{3, 4\}$. For statistical events, the intersection is equivalent to "and"; $P(A \cap B)$ is the same thing as $P(A \text{ and } B)$. It is important to note that union and intersection operations commute. That is:

$$A \cup B = B \cup A \text{ and } A \cap B = B \cap A$$

Permutations and Combinations in Probability

When trying to calculate the probability of an event using the $\frac{\text{desired outcomes}}{\text{total outcomes}}$ formula, you may frequently find that there are too many outcomes to individually count them. **Permutation** and **combination formulas** offer a shortcut to counting outcomes. A permutation is an arrangement of a specific number of a set of objects in a specific order. The number of **permutations** of r items given a set of n items can be calculated as ${}_nP_r = \frac{n!}{(n-r)!}$. Combinations are similar to permutations, except there are no restrictions regarding the order of the elements. While ABC is considered a different permutation than BCA, ABC and BCA are considered the same combination. The number of **combinations** of r items given a set of n items can be calculated as ${}_nC_r = \frac{n!}{r!(n-r)!}$ or ${}_nC_r = \frac{{}_nP_r}{r!}$.

Suppose you want to calculate how many different 5-card hands can be drawn from a deck of 52 cards. This is a combination since the order of the cards in a hand does not matter. There are 52 cards available, and 5 to be selected. Thus, the number of different hands is ${}_{52}C_5 = \frac{52!}{5! \times 47!} =$ 2,598,960.

Review Video: Probability - Permutation and Combination
Visit mometrix.com/academy and enter code: 907664

Expected Value

Expected value is a method of determining the expected outcome in a random situation. It is a sum of the weighted probabilities of the possible outcomes. Multiply the probability of an event occurring by the weight assigned to that probability (such as the amount of money won or lost). A practical application of the expected value is to determine whether a game of chance is really fair. If the sum of the weighted probabilities is equal to zero, the game is generally considered fair because the player has a fair chance to at least break even. If the expected value is less than zero, then players are expected to lose more than they win. For example, a lottery drawing might allow the player to choose any three-digit number, 000–999. The probability of choosing the winning number is 1:1000. If it costs \$1 to play, and a winning number receives \$500, the expected value is $\left(-\$1 \times \frac{999}{1{,}000}\right) + \left(\$499 \times \frac{1}{1{,}000}\right) = -\$0.50$. You can expect to lose on average 50 cents for every dollar you spend.

Review Video: Expected Value
Visit mometrix.com/academy and enter code: 643554

Expected Value and Simulators

A die roll simulator will show the results of n rolls of a die. The result of each die roll may be recorded. For example, suppose a die is rolled 100 times. All results may be recorded. The numbers of 1s, 2s, 3s, 4s, 5s, and 6s, may be counted. The experimental probability of rolling each number will equal the ratio of the frequency of the rolled number to the total number of rolls. As the number of rolls increases, or approaches infinity, the experimental probability will approach the theoretical probability of $\frac{1}{6}$. Thus, the expected value for the roll of a die is shown to be $\left(1 \times \frac{1}{6}\right) + \left(2 \times \frac{1}{6}\right) + \left(3 \times \frac{1}{6}\right) + \left(4 \times \frac{1}{6}\right) + \left(5 \times \frac{1}{6}\right) + \left(6 \times \frac{1}{6}\right)$, or 3.5.

Chapter Quiz

Ready to see how well you retained what you just read? Scan the QR code to go directly to the chapter quiz interface for this study guide. If you're using a computer, simply visit the online resources page at **mometrix.com/resources719/texesmathpse** and click the Chapter Quizzes link.

Mathematical Processes and Perspectives

PREMISE AND ARGUMENT

A premise is a statement that precedes a conclusion, in an argument. It is the proposition, or assumption, of an argument. An argument will have two or more premises.

Example:

If it is hot, then I will go swimming. (Premise)
It is hot. (Premise)
____
Therefore, I will go swimming. (Conclusion)

SIMPLE AND COMPOUND STATEMENTS

A **statement** in propositional logic is any sentence or expression that has a truth value—that is, that may in principle be considered true or false. "Hello!", for example, is not a statement; there's no sense in which it could be considered true or false. On the other hand, "$2 = 3$" *is* a statement, albeit a clearly false one. A **compound statement** is a statement that contains one or more other statements, combined or modified in some way. A **simple statement**, or a **proposition**, is a statement that cannot be broken down further into smaller statements.

For example, consider the statement, "If it rains tomorrow, then the streets will be flooded and traffic will be slow." This is a compound statement, because two smaller statements are embedded within it: "it rains tomorrow" and "the streets will be flooded and traffic will be slow." the former cannot be broken down further, and is therefore a simple statement, but the latter is another compound statement, because it includes two simple statements: "the streets will be flooded" and "traffic will be slow."

Common operations used to combine and modify simple statements into compound statements include conjunction, disjunction, negation, and implication.

CONJUNCTION

Conjunction is an operation that combines two or more statements into a compound statement that is true if and only if all of the component statements are true. When the statements are written out, conjunction is marked by the word "and." For example, the statement "Roses are red and violets are blue" is a compound statement that is a conjunction of the two simple statements "roses are red" and "violets are blue."

Conjunction is represented by the operator $\wedge$. In the previous example, if proposition P is "roses are red" and proposition Q is "violets are blue," then the compound statement "roses are red and violets are blue" would be written as "$P \wedge Q$."

DISJUNCTION

Disjunction is an operation that combines two or more statements into a compound statement that is true if and only if at least one of the component statements is true. When the statements are written out, disjunction is marked by the word "or." For example, the statement "I'll clean the closet today, or you'll clean it tomorrow" is a compound statement that is a disjunction of the simple statements "I'll clean the closet today" and "you'll clean the closet tomorrow."

Disjunction is represented by the operator $\vee$. In the previous example, if proposition P is "I'll clean the closet today" and proposition Q is "you'll clean the closet tomorrow," then the compound statement "I'll clean the closet today, or you'll clean it tomorrow" would be written as "$P \vee Q$."

Note that while in everyday language "or" implies exclusivity, as one or the other option but not both, in formal logic disjunction includes the possibility of both propositions being true. If I clean the closet today *and* you clean it tomorrow, then the sample statement "I'll clean the closet today, or you'll clean it tomorrow" is true.

Conditional and Biconditional Statements

A conditional statement, or **implication**, is a compound statement of the form "if P, then Q." for instance, the statement "if a snake has rattles, then it's venomous" is a conditional statement. It can also be written "P implies Q" ("that a snake has rattles implies that it's venomous") or "P only if Q" ("a snake has rattles only if it's venomous"). the conditional statement is true when both P and Q are true, and even when P is false, regardless of Q. In other words, the conditional statement is false only when P is true and Q is false. the conditional statement is written as "$P \rightarrow Q$." P is called the **premise** of the statement, and Q the **conclusion**.

A **biconditional statement** is a combination of two conditional statements: both "if P, then Q" and "if Q, then P." To state it more concisely, "P if and only if Q." an example is "A number is even if and only if it is divisible by 2." the biconditional statement is true when P and Q are either both true or both false; it is false if P is true and Q is false or vice versa. the biconditional statement is written "$P \leftrightarrow Q$."

A **quantifier** is a logical construct used in a compound statement to give information on the number of subjects for which a statement is true. The **existential quantifier** specifies that the statement is true for at least one subject. It is usually introduced as "there exists," such as "there exists a real number that is equal to its own square." The symbol $\exists$ is used to signify the existential quantifier. For example, the preceding statement could be written as "$\exists x \in \mathbb{R}\ x = x^2$." The **universal quantifier** specifies that the statement is true for *every* subject. It is usually said as "all" or "for all", such as "all real numbers are less than their own squares plus one." The symbol $\forall$ is used to signify the universal quantifier. For example, the preceding statement could be written as

$$\forall x \in \mathbb{R}\ x < x^2 + 1$$

Sometimes it is useful to specify that there exists *exactly* one subject that meets a given criterion. In other words, there exists a *unique* such subject. This can be signified by adding an exclamation mark after the existential quantifier: "$\exists!\, x \in \mathbb{R}\ |x| = 0$" means "there exists a unique real number that has an absolute value of zero."

A truth table shows the truth value of one or more compound statements for each possible combination of truth values of the propositions within it. The truth table contains one column for each **proposition**, and one column for each of the **compound statements** to be analyzed. It has one row for each combination of **truth values** of the propositions. Since each proposition has two possible truth values, the number of possible combinations for N propositions is 2^N, so the truth table will have 2^N rows.

The table below is a simple truth table for some common compound statements involving two propositions.

P	Q	$P \wedge Q$	$P \vee Q$	$\neg P$	$\neg Q$	$P \rightarrow Q$	$Q \rightarrow P$	$P \leftrightarrow Q$
T	T	T	T	F	F	T	T	T
T	F	F	T	F	T	F	T	F
F	T	F	T	T	F	T	F	F
F	F	F	F	T	T	T	T	T

Truth tables are useful for comparing two compound statements to see if they are equivalent. They are also useful for analyzing whether complicated compound statements are true or false. A table can have a column for each of the increasingly complex compound statements that combine to form the total statement.

Review Video: Truth Tables
Visit mometrix.com/academy and enter code: 293095

Truth Table to Validate the Rule of Detachment

The Rule of Detachment states that given the premises, $P \rightarrow Q$ and P, the valid conclusion is Q.

In other words, for every case where $(P \rightarrow Q) \wedge P$ is true, Q will also be true. The truth table below illustrates this fact:

P	Q	$P \rightarrow Q$	$(P \rightarrow Q) \wedge P$
T	T	T	T
T	F	F	F
F	T	T	F
F	F	T	F

Notice the first cell under $(P \rightarrow Q) \wedge P$ is true, while the first cell under Q is also true. Thus, for every case where $(P \rightarrow Q) \wedge P$ was true, Q was also true.

Truth Table to Validate the Chain Rule

The Chain Rule states that given the premises, $P \rightarrow Q$ and $Q \rightarrow R$, the valid conclusion is $P \rightarrow R$.

In other words, for every case where $(P \rightarrow Q) \wedge (Q \rightarrow R)$ is true, $P \rightarrow R$ will also be true. The truth table below illustrates this fact:

P	Q	R	$P \rightarrow Q$	$Q \rightarrow R$	$(P \rightarrow Q) \wedge (Q \rightarrow R)$	$P \rightarrow R$
T	T	T	T	T	T	T
T	T	F	T	F	F	F
T	F	T	F	T	F	T
T	F	F	F	T	F	F
F	T	T	T	T	T	T
F	T	F	T	F	F	T
F	F	T	T	T	T	T
F	F	F	T	T	T	T

Notice that for every case where $(P \rightarrow Q) \wedge (Q \rightarrow R)$ was true, $P \rightarrow R$ was also true.

For example, consider the premises below:

If I hike a mountain, I will not eat a sandwich.
If I do not eat a sandwich, I will drink some water.
I will not drink some water.

Write a valid conclusive statement. Explain how you arrived at your answer. Be specific in your explanation.

Valid conclusive statement: I will not hike a mountain.

Application of the chain rule and rule of contraposition give the valid conclusion of $\neg P$. According to the chain rule, given $P \rightarrow \neg Q$ and $\neg Q \rightarrow R$, then $P \rightarrow R$. According to the rule of contraposition, $P \rightarrow R$ and $\neg R$ yields $\neg P$. On a truth table, for every place where $(P \rightarrow R) \wedge \neg R$ is true, $\neg P$ is also true. Thus, this is a valid conclusive statement.

The converse of a conditional statement is a conditional statement with the premise and conclusion interchanged. the converse of $P \rightarrow Q$ is $Q \rightarrow P$. The **inverse** has the premise and conclusion both negated. The inverse of $P \rightarrow Q$ is $\neg P \rightarrow \neg Q$. The **contrapositive** has the premise and conclusion both negated *and* interchanged. The contrapositive of $P \rightarrow Q$ is $\neg Q \rightarrow \neg P$.

For example, given the **conditional statement**, "If there is a key in the lock, then someone is home," the **converse** is "if someone is home, then there is a key in the lock," the **inverse** is "if there is not a key in the lock, then no one is home," and the **contrapositive** is "if no one is home, then there is not a key in the lock."

Note that the converse and inverse of a statement are *not* logically equivalent to the original statement. For instance, the statement "if $x = 4$, then $x > 2$" is true, but its converse "if $x > 2$, then $x = 4$" is not, because there are many numbers greater than 2, not just 4. A statement *is*, however, logically equivalent to its contrapositive—and the converse and inverse, while not equivalent to the original statement, are equivalent to each other. The following truth table summarizes the relationships:

P	Q	$\neg P$	$\neg Q$	$P \rightarrow Q$ (statement)	$Q \rightarrow P$ (converse)	$\neg P \rightarrow \neg Q$ (inverse)	$\neg Q \rightarrow \neg P$ (contrapositive)
T	T	F	F	T	T	T	T
T	F	F	T	F	T	T	F
F	T	T	F	T	F	F	T
F	F	T	T	T	T	T	T

Review Video: Converse, Inverse, and Contrapositive
Visit mometrix.com/academy and enter code: 822844

In propositional logic, negation refers to the inversion of the truth value of a statement. The **negation** of a statement is true if the original statement is false, and false if the original statement is true. Negation can be signified by the word "not." For instance, the negation of the statement "Bob's cat is black" is "Bob's cat is not black." the symbol for negation is $\neg$. So, if the proposition P is "Bob's cat is black," then $\neg P$ would be "Bob's cat is not black." Two negations cancel each other out: $\neg\neg P = P$, or "not not P equals P."

It's important to be careful when combining negation with **quantifiers**. The negation of "there exists a cow that has a blue horn" is not "there exists a cow that does not have a blue horn." Rather, the negation is "there does not exist a cow that has a blue horn." the statements $\neg\exists x\ P(x)$ and

$\exists x \neg P(x)$ are not equivalent. The same is true for the universal quantifier: $\neg\forall x\, P(x)$ and $\forall x \neg P(x)$ do not mean the same thing. There is, however, a connection between the negated quantifiers: $\neg\exists x\, P(x)$ is equivalent to $\forall x \neg P(x)$, and $\exists x \neg P(x)$ is equivalent to $\neg\forall x\, P(x)$.

Review Video: Negation
Visit mometrix.com/academy and enter code: 429150

De Morgan's Laws

De Morgan's Laws are a set of useful relations connecting negation, conjunction, and disjunction. They can be stated briefly as "the negation of a conjunction is the disjunction of the negations" and "the negation of a disjunction is the conjunction of the negations." This can be written as:

$$\neg(P \wedge Q) \leftrightarrow (\neg P) \vee (\neg Q) \text{ and } \neg(P \vee Q) \leftrightarrow (\neg P) \wedge (\neg Q)$$

For instance, if proposition P is "$x > 3$" and proposition Q is "$y > 3$", then De Morgan's Laws state that "it is not true that both x and y are greater than 3" is equivalent to "either x is not greater than 3, or y is not greater than 3."

The validity of **De Morgan's Laws** can be shown with truth tables. Note that the columns highlighted in the same color match:

P	Q	$\neg P$	$\neg Q$	$(\neg P) \wedge (\neg Q)$	$(\neg P) \vee (\neg Q)$	$P \wedge Q$	$P \vee Q$	$\neg(P \wedge Q)$	$\neg(P \vee Q)$
T	T	F	F	F	F	T	T	F	F
T	F	F	T	F	T	F	T	T	F
F	T	T	F	F	T	F	T	T	F
F	F	T	T	T	T	F	F	T	T

Inductive Reasoning

Inductive reasoning is a method used to make a conjecture, based on patterns and observations. The conclusion of an inductive argument may be true or false.

Mathematical Example:

A cube has 6 faces, 8 vertices, and 12 edges. A square pyramid has 5 faces, 5 vertices, and 8 edges. A triangular prism has 5 faces, 6 vertices, and 9 edges. Thus, the sum of the numbers of faces and vertices, minus the number of edges, will always equal 2, for any solid.

Non-Mathematical Example:

Almost all summer days in Tucson are hot. It is a summer day in Tucson. Therefore, it will probably be hot.

Deductive Reasoning

Deductive reasoning is a method that proves a hypothesis or set of premises. The conclusion of a valid deductive argument will be true, given that the premises are true. Deductive reasoning utilizes logic to determine a conclusion. For instance, consider the following application of the chain rule:

If a ding is a dong, then a ping is a pong.	$p \rightarrow q$
If a ping is a pong, then a ring is a ting.	$q \rightarrow r$
A ding is a dong.	p
Therefore, a ring is a ting.	$\therefore r$

Formal Reasoning

Formal reasoning, in mathematics, involves justification using formal steps and processes to arrive at a conclusion. Formal reasoning is utilized when writing proofs and using logic. For example, when applying logic, validity of a conclusion is determined by truth tables. A set of premises will yield a given conclusion. This type of thinking is formal reasoning. Writing a geometric proof also employs formal reasoning. Example:

If a quadrilateral has four congruent sides, it is a rhombus.
If a shape is a rhombus, then the diagonals are perpendicular.
A quadrilateral has four congruent sides.
Therefore, the diagonals are perpendicular.

Informal Reasoning

Informal reasoning, in mathematics, uses patterns and observations to make conjectures. The conjecture may be true or false. Several, or even many, examples may show a certain pattern, shedding light on a possible conclusion. However, informal reasoning does not provide a justifiable conclusion. A conjecture may certainly be deemed as likely or probable. However, informal reasoning will not reveal a certain conclusion. Consider the following example:

Mathematical Idea – Given a sequence that starts with 1 and each term decreases by a factor of $\frac{1}{2}$, the limit of the sum of the sequence will be 2.

Informal Reasoning – The sum of 1 and $\frac{1}{2}$ is $1\frac{1}{2}$. The sum of 1, $\frac{1}{2}$, and $\frac{1}{4}$ is $1\frac{3}{4}$. The sum of 1, $\frac{1}{2}$, $\frac{1}{4}$, and $\frac{1}{8}$ is $1\frac{7}{8}$. Thus, it appears that as the sequence approaches infinity, the sum of the sequence approaches 2.

A **proof** serves to show the deductive or inductive process that relates the steps leading from a hypothesis to a conclusion. A proof may be direct ($p \rightarrow q$), meaning that a conclusion is shown to be true, given a hypothesis. There are also proofs by contradiction ($p \wedge \sim q$), whereby the hypothesis is assumed to be true, and the negation of the conclusion is assumed to be true. (In other words, the statement is assumed to be false.) Proofs by contraposition ($\sim q \rightarrow \sim p$) show that the negation of the conclusion leads to the negation of the hypothesis. (In other words, the negation of the conclusion is assumed to be true, and it must be shown that the negation of the hypothesis is also true.) A mathematical induction proof seeks to show that $P(1)$ is true and that $P(k+1)$ is true, given that $P(k)$ is true. Direct proofs, proofs by contradiction, and proofs by contraposition use deductive methods, while a mathematical induction proof uses an inductive method.

Direct proofs are those that assume a statement to be true. The purpose of such a proof is to show that the conclusion is true, given that the hypothesis is true. A sample of a direct proof is shown below:

Prove "If m divides a and m divides b, then m divides $a + b$."

Proof:

- Assume m divides a and m divides b.
- Thus, a equals the product of m and some integer factor, p, by the definition of division, and b equals the product of m and some integer factor, q, by the definition of division. According to substitution, $a + b$ may be rewritten as $(m \times p) + (m \times q)$. Factoring out the m gives $m(p + q)$. Since m divides $p + q$, and $p + q$ is an integer, according to the closure property, we have shown that m divides $a + b$, by the definition of division.

Indirect proofs (or proofs by contradiction) are those that assume a statement to be false. The purpose of such a proof is to show that a hypothesis is false, given the negation of the conclusion, indicating that the conclusion must be true. A sample of an indirect proof is shown below:

Prove "If $3x + 7$ is odd, then x is even."

Proof:

- Assume $3x + 7$ is odd and x is odd.
- According to the definition of odd, $x = 2a + 1$, where a is an element of the integers.
- Thus, by substitution, $3x + 7 = 3(2a + 1) + 7$, which simplifies as $6a + 3 + 7$, or $6a + 10$, which may be rewritten as $2(3a + 5)$. Any even integer may be written as the product of 2 and some integer, k. Thus, we have shown the hypothesis to be false, meaning that the conditional statement must be true.

A **proof by contraposition** is one written in the form, $\sim Q \to \sim P$. In other words, a proof by contraposition seeks to show that the negation of Q will yield the negation of P. A sample of a proof by contraposition is shown below:

Prove "If $5x + 7$ is even, then x is odd."

Proof:

- Assume that if x is even, then $5x + 7$ is odd.
- Assume x is even.
- Thus, by the definition of an even integer, $x = 2a$.

By substitution, $5x + 7$ may be rewritten as $5(2a) + 7$, which simplifies as $10a + 7$. This expression cannot be written as the product of 2 and some factor, k. Thus, $5x + 7$ is odd, by definition of an odd integer. So, when $5x + 7$ is even, x is odd, according to contraposition.

A **proof by contradiction** is one written in the form, $p \wedge \sim q$. In other words, a proof by contradiction seeks to show the negation of q will result in a false hypothesis, indicating that the conclusion of the statement, as written, must be true. In other words, the conditional statement of $p \to q$ is true.

Mathematical Induction Proof Utilizing Inductive Reasoning

A mathematical induction proof utilizes inductive reasoning in its assumption that if $P(k)$ is true, then $P(k+1)$ is also true. The induction hypothesis is $P(k)$. This step utilizes inductive reasoning because an observation is used to make the conjecture that $P(k+1)$ is also true.

Example:

For all natural numbers, n, the sum is equal to $(n+1)\left(\frac{n}{2}\right)$.
Show that $P(1)$ is true.
$1 = (1+1)\left(\frac{1}{2}\right)$.
Assume $P(k)$ is true.
$1+2+3+4+\cdots+k = (k+1)\left(\frac{k}{2}\right)$.

This previous step is the inductive hypothesis. This hypothesis may be used to write the conjecture that $P(k+1)$ is also true: $(1+2+3+4+\cdots+k)+(k+1) = [(k+1)+1]\left(\frac{k+1}{2}\right)$

$$(k+1)\left(\frac{k}{2}\right)+(k+1) = [(k+1)+1]\left(\frac{k}{2}+\frac{1}{2}\right)$$
$$(k+1)\left(\frac{k}{2}\right)+(k+1) = \left(\frac{k}{2}(k+1)+\frac{k}{2}\right)+\left(\frac{1}{2}(k+1)+\frac{1}{2}(1)\right)$$
$$(k+1)\left(\frac{k}{2}\right)+(k+1) = \frac{k}{2}(k+1)+\frac{k}{2}+\frac{k+1}{2}+\frac{1}{2}$$
$$(k+1)\left(\frac{k}{2}\right)+(k+1) = \frac{k}{2}(k+1)+\frac{2k+2}{2}$$
$$(k+1)\left(\frac{k}{2}\right)+(k+1) = \frac{k}{2}(k+1)+(k+1)$$

Mathematical Learning, Instruction, and Assessment

INSTRUCTION

MATHEMATICAL JARGON

Mathematical language is hard for beginners. Words such as "or" and "only" have more precise meanings than in everyday speech. Also confusing to beginners are words such as "open" and "field" that have been given specific mathematical meanings. **Mathematical jargon** includes technical terms such as homeomorphism and integrable. But there is a reason for special notation and technical jargon. Mathematics requires more precision than everyday speech. Mathematicians refer to this precision of language and logic as rigor.

RIGOR

Rigor is fundamentally a matter of mathematical proof. Mathematicians want their theorems to follow from axioms by means of systematic reasoning. This is to avoid mistaken "theorems", based upon fallible intuitions, of which many instances have occurred in the history of the subject. The level of rigor expected in mathematics has varied over time; the Greeks expected detailed arguments, but at the time of Isaac Newton the methods employed were less rigorous. Problems inherent in the definitions used by Newton would lead to a resurgence of careful analysis and formal proof in the 19th century. Today, mathematicians continue to argue amongst themselves about computer-assisted proofs. Because large computations are hard to verify, such proofs may not be sufficiently rigorous. Axioms in traditional thought were "self-evident truths," but that conception is problematic. At a formal level, an axiom is just a string of symbols which has an intrinsic meaning only in the context of all derivable formulas of an axiomatic system. It was the goal of Hilbert's program to put all of mathematics on a firm axiomatic basis, but according to Gödel's incompleteness theorem every (sufficiently powerful) axiomatic system has undecidable formulas; and thus, a final axiomatization of mathematics is impossible. Nonetheless mathematics is often imagined to be (as far as its formal content) nothing but set theory in some axiomatization, in the sense that every mathematical statement or proof could be cast into formulas within set theory.

NUMERALS AND NAMING SYSTEMS

Some of the systems for representing numbers in previous and present cultures are well known. Roman numerals use a few letters of the alphabet to represent numbers up to the thousands, but are not intended for arbitrarily large numbers and can only represent positive integers. Arabic numerals are a family of systems originating in India, passing to medieval Islamic civilization and then to Europe, and now are the standard in global culture. They have undergone many curious changes with time and geography, but can represent arbitrarily large numbers and have been adapted to negative numbers, fractions, and other real numbers.

Less-well-known systems include some that are written and can be read today, such as the Hebrew and Greek method of using the letters of the alphabet, in order, for digits 1–9, tens 10–90, and hundreds 100–900.

A completely different system is that of the quipu, which the Inca used to record numbers on knotted strings.

FINGER COUNTING

Many systems of finger counting have been, and still are, used in various parts of the world. Most are not as obvious as holding up a number of fingers. The position of fingers may be most important. One continuing use for finger counting is for people who speak different languages to communicate prices in the marketplace.

COGNITIVE THEORISTS AND CONSTRUCTIVISTS

Constructivists believe that students may construct knowledge by themselves. In other words, students are actively engaged in the construction of their own knowledge. Students will assimilate and accommodate in order to build new knowledge, based on previous knowledge. Thus, in planning instruction based on constructivism, a teacher would focus on grouping designs, environment, problem-solving tasks, and inclusion of multiple representations. The goal in such a classroom would be for students to construct knowledge on their own. There are different levels of constructivism, including weak constructivism and radical constructivism.

Cognitivists differ from constructivists in that they believe that active exploration is important in helping students make sense of observations and experiences. However, the students are not expected to invent or construct knowledge by themselves. They are only expected to make sense of the mathematics. In planning instruction based on cognitivism, a teacher would employ similar methods to those discussed above, with the focus on active exploration. Students would do a lot of comparisons of mathematical methods in making sense of ideas.

CONSTRUCTIVISM

Three types of constructivism are weak constructivism, social constructivism, and radical constructivism. **Weak constructivists** believe that students construct their own knowledge, but also accept certain preconceived notions or facts. **Social constructivists** believe that students construct knowledge by interacting with one another and holding discussions and conversations. **Radical constructivists** believe that all interpretations of knowledge are subjective, based on the individual learner. In other words, there is no real truth; it is all subjective. Classroom instructional planning based on a weak constructivist viewpoint might involve incorporation of some accepted theorems and definitions, while continuing to plan active explorations and discussions. Planning based on a social constructivist viewpoint might involve group activities, debates, discussion forums, etc. Planning based on a radical constructivist viewpoint would involve activities that are open-ended, where there is more than one correct answer. The problems would invite more than one correct answer.

PROJECT-BASED LEARNING

Project-based learning is learning that centers on the solving of a problem. Students learn many different ideas by solving one "big" problem. For example, for a unit on sine and cosine functions, a teacher may design a problem whereby the students are asked to model a real-world phenomenon using both types of functions. Students must investigate the effects of changes in amplitude, period, shifts, etc., on the graphs of the functions. Students will also be able to make connections between the types of functions when modeling the same phenomenon. Such a problem will induce high-level thinking.

Project-based learning is derived from constructivist theory, which contends that students learn by doing and constructing their own knowledge.

Cooperative Learning

Cooperative learning simply means that students will learn by cooperating with one another. Students will be placed into groups of a size determined by the teacher. With such an approach, students work together to succeed in learning. Students may work together to learn a topic, complete an assignment, or compete with other groups.

Examples of cooperative learning include Think-Pair-Share and Jigsaw. **Think-Pair-Share** is a cooperative learning strategy that involves thinking about some given topic, sharing ideas, thoughts, or questions with a partner, and then sharing the partner discussion with the whole group. For example, in the mathematics classroom, a teacher may ask the class to think about the meaning of a proportional relationship. Each student would think for a set period of time, share ideas with a partner, and then each partner group would share their ideas regarding the meaning of proportionality. **Jigsaw** is another cooperative learning strategy that involves dividing among each group member reading material or ideas to be learned. Each student will then read his or her information, summarize it, and share the findings or ideas with the group. In mathematics, students might be given information on modeling with cosine and sine functions. Students could then share what they learned about real-world phenomena modeled by each. Different students may also be assigned to read in-depth material on amplitude, period, shifts, etc.

Control Strategies

"**Control strategies**" is another name for "metacognitive learning strategies," which indicate any strategy that promotes a learner's awareness of his or her level of learning. With such strategies, the student will work to determine what he or she knows and does not know regarding a subject. Possible control strategies are thinking, self-regulation, and discussing ideas with peers.

Example:

> A student may discover his or her level of "knowing" about functions by keeping a journal of any questions he or she might have regarding the topic. The student may list everything that he or she understands, as well as aspects not understood. As the student progresses through the course, he or she may go back and reconfirm any correct knowledge and monitor progress on any previous misconceptions.

Memorization and Elaboration Strategies

Memorization is simply a technique whereby rote repetition is used to learn information. **Elaboration** strategies involve the connection of new information to some previously learned information. In mathematics, for example, students may use elaboration strategies when learning how to calculate the volume of a cone, based on their understood approach for calculating the volume of a cylinder. The student would be making connections in his or her mind between this new skill and other previously acquired skills. A memorization technique would simply involve memorization of the volume of a cone formula, as well as ways to evaluate the formula.

Prior Knowledge

Three ways of activating students' prior knowledge are concept mapping, visual imagery, and comparing and contrasting. With **concept mapping**, a student would detail and connect all known aspects of a mathematics topic. Ideas would be grouped into subgroups. Such an approach would allow a student to see what he or she does not know, prompting the activation of any prior knowledge on the subject. **Visual imagery** is simply the use of any pictures or diagrams to promote activation of prior knowledge. For example, giving a picture of Pascal's triangle would likely activate students' prior knowledge regarding the binomial theorem. **Comparing and contrasting** means that the student will compare and contrast ideas or approaches. For example, a student might be given a mapping of an inverse function. He or she could then compare and contrast this mapping to a known mapping of a function, in order to decide how they are the same and different. This would activate a student's prior understanding of functions and the definition thereof.

Three methods for ascertaining, or assessing, students' prior knowledge are portfolios, pre-tests, and self-inventories. **Portfolios** are simply a compilation of prior student activity related to mathematics topics. For example, a portfolio might show a student's work with transforming functions. **Pre-tests** are designed to measure a student's understanding of mathematics topics that will be taught in the course during the year. **Self-inventories** are just what the name implies: inventories that ask the students to name, list, describe, and explain information understood about various mathematics topics.

Once a teacher has assessed students' level of prior knowledge regarding some mathematics topic, he or she may use that information to scaffold the instruction. In other words, the teacher may decide to further break down the mathematics material into more integral parts. Exact processes or steps may be shown, including justification for using certain properties or theorems. More examples may be shown, while including examples of many different variations of problems, in order to ensure that students are not simply memorizing one approach that will be incorrectly applied to any problem of that sort. The teacher may also decide that more group work, peer cooperation, and discussion are needed.

For example, suppose a teacher determines that students have very little understanding of logic and valid arguments. The teacher may decide to re-teach the creation of truth tables, including truth values for intersections and "if p, then q" statements. The teacher may also decide to re-teach how a truth table may be used to show if an argument is valid. Students may be placed into groups and asked to determine the validity of several simple arguments. Once students understand the concept, they may move on to more rigorous arguments, including equivalence relations.

Concept Whereby Usage of Manipulatives Would Increase Conceptual Understanding

Understanding of how to solve one-variable equations would certainly be enhanced by using rods and counters. With this manipulative, the rod would represent the variable, or x, while the counters would represent the constants on each side of the equation. A sample diagram of the equation, $x + 4 = 8$, is shown below. Note that the vertical line represents the equals sign.

In order to solve the equation (and isolate x), four counters may be removed from each side of the mat. This process is shown below:

Now, the final illustration is:

Thus, the solution is $x = 4$. The manipulative helps students understand the meaning of the subtraction property of equality in action, without simply memorizing its meaning.

Piaget's Cognitive Development Theory

Piaget's cognitive development theory is aligned with **constructivism**. In fact, constructivism is built on his ideas. Piaget's cognitive development theory indicates that students actively participate in the construction of their own knowledge via assimilation and accommodation. Current cognitive theorists do not believe that students have to construct their own knowledge, but instead that they only have to make sense of what they are observing.

The four stages of learning, as developed by Piaget, are sensorimotor, preoperational, concrete operational, and formal operational. The defined stages show the progression from concrete thinking to abstract thinking. In other words, a child would need an object to understand properties, in the first stage. By the fourth stage, the child would be able to think abstractly, without some concrete form. In mathematics, this idea might be illustrated by first working with diagrams and manipulatives of numbers and then later writing symbolic forms of the numbers, including the numerals. This would illustrate the progression from 0 to 7 years. In the years of 11 to adulthood, much deeper abstraction is utilized. For example, people would be able to discuss functions and general properties, without looking at any concrete graphs or representations.

Review Video: Piaget's Cognitive Development Theory
Visit mometrix.com/academy and enter code: 100376

Progression That a Student Undergoes as He or She Learns Mathematics

When learning mathematics, students begin with concrete representations and ideas. Later, students are able to abstract meaning and make generalizations. Students will also be asked to apply abstract ideas from one topic to another mathematics topic. In other words, students would move from concrete representations, ideas, and facts to symbolic representations and generalizations. Piaget outlined such a progression in his general four stages of cognitive learning. For example, a student may first learn about solving equations by using a balance scale. After the student understands the process, he or she can solve alone, using the symbolic equations. He or she would also be able to describe the process for solving any equation.

Direct Instruction Versus Student-Centered Instruction

Direct instruction is instruction whereby the teacher delivers all content knowledge to be learned, and students, more or less, passively listen. The teacher employs a step-by-step instruction method for learning content. Student-centered instruction is learning whereby the teacher serves as a facilitator of learning and students actively participate in their own learning. Research has shown that students show a higher level of procedural and conceptual understanding when learning in a student-centered approach. Direct instruction might be more appropriate when teaching basic or fundamental theorems. Student-centered learning might be more appropriate when helping students make connections or develop higher-level thinking regarding a topic.

Cooperative Learning Task Versus Traditional Task

Think-Pair-Share is an activity whereby a topic is first given for consideration on an individual basis. Next, the students are arranged in pairs and asked to discuss the topic (e.g., any questions, comments, generalizations, etc.). Finally, each pair will contribute to a whole-class discussion on the topic.

In mathematics, students would likely develop a higher level of understanding by using such an activity as Think-Pair-Share when learning about trigonometric functions. For example, students might be asked to consider different real-world situations that may be modeled with sine and cosine functions. Students could individually make a list and then share with a partner. Each partner group could then contribute to a whole class list. This list could be used as a reference sheet.

Implementing Technology in Classroom Instruction

Technology may be implemented in the mathematics classroom in many ways. For example, Excel may be used to perform regressions, calculate lines of best fit, calculate correlation coefficients, plot residuals, show convergence or divergence of a sequence, etc. Calculators may be used to evaluate and graph functions, find area under the normal curve, calculate combinations and permutations, perform statistical tests, etc. Graphing software, such as GeoGebra, may be used to graph and explore many shapes and functions. Students may also use it to graph reflections, rotations, translations, and dilations.

Modifying Instruction to Accommodate English-Language Learners

In mathematics specifically, instruction may be modified to include illustrations of ideas, in addition to given words. Audio may also be included for problem tasks. English-language learners may also be grouped with other fluent English-speaking students in order to assist with learning of the mathematics topic. Students will be able to hear the conversation, in addition to seeing the topic in print. In addition, problems may be broken down into smaller pieces, which can help the student focus on one step at a time. Further, additional one-on-one time with the teacher may be needed, whereby the teacher reads aloud and illustrates examples to be learned.

Effective Learning Environment for ELL Students

Characteristics of an effective learning environment for ELL students include creation of a low threshold for anxiety, use of pictures to teach vocabulary and mathematics ideas, implementation of graphic organizers, explicit teaching of vocabulary words, and use of active learning strategies. The latter two are extremely important, since ELL students need to learn exact terms and exact definitions while also engaging with fellow students, as opposed to sitting alone at a desk. Research completed by professors at the University of Houston and University of California list collaborative learning, use of multiple representations, and technology integration as important facets of an effective learning environment for ELL students (Waxman & Tellez, 2002).

Closed-Ended Mathematics Question and Then Rewritten in an Open-Ended Manner

Closed-Ended:

- Look at the graph of $y = x^2 + 2$. Decide if the graph represents a function.

Open-Ended:

- Provide an example of an equation that represents a function. Provide an example of an equation that does not represent a function. Explain how the graphs of the two equations compare to one another.

The first question will elicit a simple, straightforward response, or "Yes, it is a function."

The second question prompts the student to come up with two equations and then describe how the graphs of the two equations would compare. There is more than one possible answer, and the student has to make a comparison as well.

Good Questioning Response Techniques

A few good questioning response techniques are:

- Make sure the wait time is sufficient;
- Do not include leading prompts within questions;
- Ask more questions based on student answers;
- Confirm or restate correct student comments.

The key to good questioning response techniques is to show the student that his or her comments are important and to connect those comments to other student comments. The student should feel that he or she has made a contribution to the community of learners. A teacher should always ask a meaningful, thought-provoking question and provide sufficient time for the student to provide a meaningful and well-thought-out response. Student answers should lead to more questions and ideas and not serve as an endpoint.

NCTM Categories of Questions That Teachers Should Ask

The professional standards describe five categories of questions that teachers should ask. These categories are: 1) working together to make sense of problems; 2) individually making sense of problems; 3) reasoning about mathematics; 4) providing conjectures about mathematics; and 5) making connections within and outside of mathematics. Sample questions include "What does this mean?," "How can you prove that?," and "What does this relate to?". Categories 4 and 5 are high level and include questions that prompt students to invent ideas and make meaningful connections.

Accountants and Mathematical Modeling

Accountants use mathematical modeling in a variety of ways. For example, an accountant models the future value of a certificate of deposit (CD) using the compound interest formula. An accountant also may fit a regression line to a client's overall savings over x years. An accountant may model tax payments with residual plots. Accountants may use past income tax returns to predict future tax expenses. Accountants may compare rates of return when investing in different mutual funds, by fitting and comparing regression lines.

Scientists and Functions

Scientists use functions to model real-world phenomena. For example, scientists use quadratic functions to model the height of an object tossed into the air or dropped from a certain height. Scientists use sine and cosine functions to model real-world occurrences such as the depth of water at various times of the day, the movement of a pendulum, etc. Scientists use exponential functions to analyze and predict the number of bacteria present after x amount of time. Scientists also use functions when analyzing the time it takes a rocket to reach a destination.

Making Mathematics Relevant to Students' Lives

Teachers can make mathematics relevant to students, using a variety of strategies. Teachers may include items relevant and pertinent to students within question stems, such as including "iPad," "apps," and video game names. Teachers should pose questions that are similar to what students may have asked themselves, such as, "If I invest this much money in an account and save for x years, after how many years will I have y dollars?" Teachers should include real-world problems to solve, and not simply include rote solving of equations. Students should know what sorts of scenarios may be modeled with rational expressions. Many researchers believe that curricula should be centered on the "real world," with all facets of mathematics learning spawning from that center. In other words, students often know how to convert a decimal to a percentage, but when reading *The Wall Street Journal*, they may not be able to interpret a percentage yield.

Assessment

Assessment Tool

A **mathematics assessment tool** is used to assess a student's prior knowledge, current knowledge, skill set, procedural knowledge, conceptual understanding, depth of understanding, and ability to make abstractions and generalizations. Perhaps the most important purpose of such a tool is to help the student develop and modify instruction. A teacher may determine that students are ready to surpass the current lesson or need it to be much more scaffolded. A teacher may also use the assessment to track students' progress. For example, a portfolio might show students' initial understanding of functions and end with their work with function modeling.

When a teacher needs to decide on an appropriate assessment tool, he or she needs to consider the purpose of the assessment. For example, if the purpose of an assessment is to direct the instruction, a pre-test may be a good assessment to use. If the purpose of the assessment is to determine the level of student understanding, then a whole-class discussion may be desired. If the purpose of an assessment is to assess student understanding of a unit of material, then an exam would be appropriate. If a teacher wishes to analyze student understanding and ability to abstract knowledge, then a performance assessment may be used. If a teacher wishes to check off skills mastered by students, then a checklist would be appropriate.

Valid Test

A test is valid if it tests what it is supposed to test. In other words, a test is valid if it appropriately covers the material it is supposed to cover. For example, a topic not taught in class should not be included on a valid test. In order to construct a valid test, a teacher should make a list of all standards covered during that time period. The teacher should also closely mirror the design of problems examined in class, for homework, and in group discussions. Finally, the teacher should make sure that there is an even balance of questions to cover all of the material.

Valid Exam

In order to select a **valid exam**, a teacher should make sure that the test aligns with the objectives and standards covered in the unit. The teacher should also make sure that the test problems are similar to those covered during class time. The teacher should make sure the percentages of questions devoted to each objective are balanced. In order for a test to be valid, it must be reliable, meaning that it produces similar results with different groups. A teacher may wish to check the validity and reliability results of an exam.

In general, an exam is considered **invalid** if it does not measure what it is supposed to measure. The exam may include questions from another unit. It may include questions with different wording techniques, making it much more difficult. The exam may include representations different from those covered in class. An invalid exam would not be reliable, meaning the results would not be consistent with different administrations of the exam. Biased questions and wording may also make an exam invalid.

Assessing Students' Understanding of What Has Been Taught

In order to assess thought processes, **open-ended questions** are needed. The teacher may wish to have students write an essay, write entries in a mathematics journal, undergo a performance task, or participate in a debate or discussion. The teacher may also design a pre-test that includes all constructed response questions. In particular, a performance task requires students to justify solutions, which provide the teacher with insight into students' understanding and reasoning. In general, the assessment should include questions that ask students to make abstractions and justify their thinking.

Testing Issue

Example: A student claims that an exam is more difficult and includes more content than what was presented in class. How might a teacher determine if the student's claim is true?

The teacher would need to make a list of all objectives and standards covered during the time period. The teacher would also need to compile all problems and examples covered in class and as homework. Finally, the teacher would need to do a careful analysis of the wording of the problems covered in class and as homework. If any of these items are not aligned to the exam, the teacher would need to go back and re-teach the material, using the created test as a guide for instruction.

Performance Task

A **performance task** allows the teacher to assess process as well as product, meaning that a teacher can assess students' thought processes as well as their final answer. The level of student learning will be much clearer when reviewing a performance task. A performance task goes beyond a multiple-choice format, allowing for oral and tactile-kinesthetic performances. Furthermore, a performance task may combine several mathematics concepts into one assessment instrument. This type of assessment often includes real-world problems, which helps the student connect mathematics to the outside world.

Formative and Summative Assessments

Formative assessments are those given during the learning process. Formative assessments provide the teacher with information related to a student's progress at various stages throughout a time period. Formative assessments are used to modify instruction as needed. In other words, formative assessments inform instruction. Summative assessments are those given at the end of a learning period. Summative assessments serve to measure the cumulative knowledge gained. Examples of formative assessments include quizzes, checklists, observations, and discussion. Examples of summative assessments include exams, portfolios, performance tasks, and standardized tests.

Four formative assessments include quizzes, checklists, observations, and discussion. **Quizzes** are often short assessments that may include multiple-choice items, short response items, or essay items. Quizzes are often administered following presentation of a portion of a mathematics unit. **Checklists** include a list of skills or concepts that should be mastered or understood. A teacher will check off all items mastered by a student. **Observations** are informal means of assessing students' understanding of a topic. A teacher may observe students' questions, engagement, and performance on projects. **Discussion** is another informal formative assessment. Discussions, both in groups and whole-class formats, allow the teacher to analyze students' thinking.

Four summative assessments include exams, portfolios, performance tasks, and standardized tests. **Exams** may include closed-ended or open-ended questions. Exams may be administered after each unit, semester, or at the end of the year. **Portfolios** include tasks created by a student and may include writing pieces and other large projects. Although the portfolio contains formative work, the tool itself may be used as a summative assessment piece. **Performance tasks** are large-scale problems that include many different components that relate to some big idea. For example, a student may be asked to formulate a plan for modeling a real-world phenomenon with a sine function. The student may be asked to explain how the function would change, given changes to the amplitude, period, shifts, etc. The student may then explain how these components would need to change to fit a new function. **Standardized tests** are tests that compare a student's performance to that of other students. They are often given at the end of the school year.

Review Video: Formative and Summative Assessments
Visit mometrix.com/academy and enter code: 804991

Review Video: Assessment Reliability and Validity
Visit mometrix.com/academy and enter code: 424680

Scoring Rubric

A **strong rubric** will include unique performance criteria for each bullet. In other words, a portion of one criteria statement should not be included in a portion of another criteria statement. Each criteria statement should be clearly delineated, describing exactly what the student must be able to do. Furthermore, a strong rubric will often have scoring options, ranging from 0 to 4. When designing the rubric, it is helpful to create a model student response that will warrant each rubric score. It is also helpful to provide a space to provide feedback to students.

Enhancing Student Understanding

In order for an assessment to enhance student understanding, it should provide an opportunity for the student to learn something. The assessment should be a learning opportunity for the student. It should prompt the student to think deeper about a mathematics topic. In other words, the student should think, "Okay. I understand this. I wonder how the process/solution would change if I did this." The assessment might prompt the student to ask deeper questions in the next class session or complete research on a certain topic. In order to create such an assessment, open-ended and challenging questions should be included on the exam. The exam should not consist of simple, lower-level, one-answer questions.

Testing Mathematical Misconceptions

In order to design such an assessment, the teacher should include mathematical error-type problems, whereby the student must look at a solution process or conjecture and determine if he or she agrees, of if and where an error occurred. The student would need to identify the error, correct it, and explain why it was erroneous. The assessment should include a variety of mathematical misconceptions. One solution process may include more than one error. A teacher may also simply ask students to participate in a collaborative learning activity, whereby the students must share ideas and thoughts regarding a new mathematical topic.

Assessing Prior Knowledge

Such a pre-test must not include any leading prompts. It should include open-ended and constructed-response items as well. A pre-test with solely multiple-choice items will not be sufficient, since a student has the option of guessing. The test should include higher-level questions that require connections within the field of mathematics. In other words, the questions should not all be mutually exclusive. They should build on one another. Finally, the test might include student error problems as well.

Assessing Both Procedural Knowledge and Conceptual Understanding

The assessment should include rote, algorithmic-type problems, as well as those that ask the student to utilize higher-level thinking, abstractions, and generalizations. The test should include open-ended, constructed-response-type problems. A performance task is an excellent assessment for assessing a student's ability to solve a problem, while also examining the student's thought processes, rationales, etc. In order to assess both types of understanding, the assessment will need to ask students to justify and explain solutions. In other words, the assessments should include questions at both ends of Bloom's Taxonomy.

Pre-Test and Post-Test

A **post-test** should be exactly the same as an administered pre-test. If the teacher is to compare the results of a post-test to a pre-test, then the test and testing conditions should be identical. The **pre-test** assesses students' prior knowledge, while a post-test assesses students post knowledge. Comparing the results, side by side, allows the teacher to track student progress. The teacher may wish to add additional questions to the post-test, but the original questions should remain.

Assessment That Will Show What Students Do and Do Not Know

The teacher should include questions that are straightforward, involve errors, require justification, and require shown work. A student self-assessment is one such tool that would show misconceptions, understood material, and advanced knowledge. The assessment should include more than multiple-choice questions. Designing a performance assessment with scaffolded questions, whereby only one solution may be found based on a previous answer, will also show students' exact level of understanding. A debate format is one type of assessment whereby the teacher will be able to see a student's level of understanding, as he or she seeks to respond with a rebuttal.

Assessment to Hone in on Any Error Patterns Evident in Students' Work

A **portfolio** would be an excellent assessment for monitoring any student error patterns. The teacher would be able to track student errors as the course progressed. The teacher would be given insight into how, and if, errors improved, or if some knowledge was acquired but other knowledge was still incorrect. The portfolio might include a series of similar questions related to a certain topic. For example, a portfolio may include function transformation questions. A student's ability to transform functions may be tracked, starting with simple linear functions and ending with complex sine functions.

Components That Must Be Present in an Assessment That Supports Student Learning

The assessment must require students to **think deeper** than what they have covered in class. It should prompt them to make connections between topics. It should invite different ways of thinking about problem solving. In other words, the student may think, "Okay. I have seen a similar version in class. This problem is slightly different, in that the parabola is shifted left. This is the opposite of shifting right, so I will add the constant to the x-term." The assessment will thus solidify the student's understanding of how to shift any function.

Using Assessment Results from ELL Learners in Order to Modify Instruction

The teacher would be able to see if language itself is a barrier in learning. In other words, if the group of ELL students, as a whole, show difficulty with a mathematics topic, the teacher may deduce that the content was not clear due to minimal supporting pictures, diagrams, and auditory support. The teacher may decide to reteach the lesson, using more visual cues, verbal pronunciations, explicit vocabulary usage, and peer-group placement. Collaborative learning may be employed.

A Teacher's Questions Regarding the Results of an Administered Exam

The teacher may ask the following:

- Did I cover the content in an explicit manner?
- Did I show plenty of examples?
- Did I use multiple representations when teaching the concepts?
- Did I design instruction such as to accommodate all modes of learning?
- Was the test valid?
- Did students have an adequate amount of time to complete the test?
- Why did some groups of students score lower or higher?
- Did any biased questions affect the results?

Effects of Focus on Career and College Readiness

The focus on college and career-readiness standards prompts publishers and teachers to utilize more real-world problems in instruction and assessments. The focus in mathematics classrooms is shifting to more real-world, cumulative problems that require understanding of many different mathematics concepts in order to solve. Problems are related to science, finance, medicine, etc. The focus includes the ability to apply the algorithms to many different career situations. In summary, the recent focus shifts the instructional design to an application-based status.

Role of Assessment in a Classroom Focused on Cognitive Instruction

A cognitively guided classroom would be similar to a constructivist classroom, in that **active participation** would be present. However, in a cognitive classroom (as advocated by current cognitive theorists), students are not required to invent their own knowledge. Instead, they must simply make sense of what they are observing and experiencing. They may be assisted by the teacher. Thus, the role of an assessment in such a classroom is to ascertain student thought processes. Such an assessment would ask students to describe thinking and perhaps make connections to other mathematics topics. The assessment must ascertain students' reasoning abilities.

Instructional Cycle Described by a Learning Theorist

The **5E Learning Model** is based on the thinking of Jean Piaget. It is a constructivist learning model. Piaget believed that students construct their own knowledge via active participation and experiences. Problem solving is integral to student learning. The cycle is listed as engagement, exploration, explanation, elaboration, and evaluation. Thus, with active engagement and exploration, the student is able to develop his or her own explanation, use assimilation and accommodation to make sense of the information, and then evaluate the material and make conjectures, etc.

Scientific Inquiry and Processes

Safety and Equipment

Laboratory Accidents

Any spills or accidents should be **reported** to the teacher so that the teacher can determine the safest clean-up method. The student should start to wash off a **chemical** spilled on the skin while reporting the incident. Some spills may require removal of contaminated clothing and use of the **safety shower**. Broken glass should be disposed of in a designated container. If someone's clothing catches fire they should walk to the safety shower and use it to extinguish the flames. A fire blanket may be used to smother a **lab fire**. A fire extinguisher, phone, spill neutralizers, and a first aid box are other types of **safety equipment** found in the lab. Students should be familiar with **routes** out of the room and the building in case of fire. Students should use the **eye wash station** if a chemical gets in the eyes.

Safety Procedures

Students should wear a **lab apron** and **safety goggles**. Loose or dangling clothing and jewelry, necklaces, and earrings should not be worn. Those with long hair should tie it back. Care should always be taken not to splash chemicals. Open-toed shoes such as sandals and flip-flops should not be worn, nor should wrist watches. Glasses are preferable to contact lenses since the latter carry a risk of chemicals getting caught between the lens and the eye. Students should always be supervised. The area where the experiment is taking place and the surrounding floor should be free of clutter. Only the lab book and the items necessary for the experiment should be present. Smoking, eating, and chewing gum are not permitted in the lab. Cords should not be allowed to dangle from work stations. There should be no rough-housing in the lab. Hands should be washed after the lab is complete.

Fume Hoods

Because of the potential safety hazards associated with chemistry lab experiments, such as fire from vapors and the inhalation of toxic fumes, a **fume hood** should be used in many instances. A fume hood carries away vapors from reagents or reactions. Equipment or reactions are placed as far back in the hood as practical to help enhance the collection of the fumes. The **glass safety shield** automatically closes to the appropriate height, and it should be low enough to protect the face and body. The safety shield should only be raised to move equipment in and out of the hood. One should not climb inside a hood or stick one's head inside. All spills should be wiped up immediately, and the glass should be cleaned if a splash occurs.

Common Safety Hazards

Some specific safety hazards possible in a chemistry lab include:

- **Fire**: Fire can be caused by volatile solvents such as ether, acetone, or benzene being kept in an open beaker or Erlenmeyer flask. Vapors can creep along the table and ignite if they reach a flame or spark. Solvents should be heated in a hood with a steam bath, not on a hot plate.
- **Explosion**: Heating or creating a reaction in a closed system can cause an explosion, resulting in flying glass and chemical splashes. The system should be vented to prevent this.
- **Chemical and thermal burns**: Many chemicals are corrosive to the skin and eyes.

- **Inhalation of toxic fumes**: Some compounds severely irritate membranes in the eyes, nose, throat, and lungs.
- **Absorption** of toxic chemicals such as dimethyl sulfoxide (DMSO) and nitrobenzene through the skin.
- **Ingestion** of toxic chemicals.

Safety Gloves

There are many types of **gloves** available to help protect the skin from cuts, burns, and chemical splashes. There are many considerations when choosing a glove. For example, gloves that are highly protective may limit dexterity. Some gloves may not offer appropriate protection against a specific chemical. Other considerations include degradation rating, which indicates how effective a glove is when exposed to chemicals; breakthrough time, which indicates how quickly a chemical can break through the surface of the glove; and permeation rate, which indicates how quickly chemicals seep through after the initial breakthrough. Disposable latex, vinyl, or nitrile gloves are usually appropriate for most circumstances, and offer protection from incidental splashes and contact. Other types of gloves include butyl, neoprene, PVC, PVA, Viton, Silver Shield, and natural rubber. Each offers its own type of protection but may have drawbacks as well.

Proper Handling and Storage of Chemicals

Students should take care when **carrying chemicals** from one place to another. Chemicals should never be taken from the room, tasted, or touched with bare hands. **Safety gloves** should be worn when appropriate and glove/chemical interactions and glove deterioration should be considered. Hands should always be **washed** thoroughly after a lab. Potentially hazardous materials intended for use in chemistry, biology, or other science labs should be secured in a safe area where relevant **Safety Data Sheets (SDS)** can be accessed. Chemicals and solutions should be used as directed and labels should be read before handling solutions and chemicals. Extra chemicals should not be returned to their original containers, but should be disposed of as directed by the school district's rules or local ordinances. Local municipalities often have hazardous waste disposal programs. Acids should be stored separately from other chemicals. Flammable liquids should be stored away from acids, bases, and oxidizers.

Bunsen Burners

When using a **Bunsen burner**, loose clothing should be tucked in, long hair should be tied back, and safety goggles and aprons should be worn. Students should know what to do in case of a fire or accident. When lighting the burner, strikers should always be used instead of matches. Do not touch the hot barrel. Tongs (never fingers) should be used to hold the material in the flame. To heat liquid, a flask may be set upon wire gauze on a tripod and secured with an iron ring or clamp on a stand. The flame is extinguished by turning off the gas at the source.

Safety Procedures Related to Animals

Animals to be used for **dissections** should be obtained from a company that provides animals for this purpose. Road kill or decaying animals that a student brings in should not be used. It is possible that such an animal may have a pathogen or a virus, such as rabies, which can be transmitted via the saliva of even a dead animal. Students should use gloves and should not participate if they have open sores or moral objections to dissections. It is generally accepted that biological experiments may be performed on lower-order life forms and invertebrates, but not on mammalian vertebrates and birds. No animals should be harmed physiologically. Experimental animals should be kept, cared for, and handled in a safe manner and with compassion. Pathogenic (anything able to cause a disease) substances should not be used in lab experiments.

Lab Notebooks

A **lab notebook** is a record of all pre-lab work and lab work. It differs from a lab report, which is prepared after lab work is completed. A lab notebook is a formal record of lab preparations and what was done. **Observational recordings** should not be altered, erased, or whited-out to make corrections. Drawing a single line through an entry is sufficient to make changes. Pages should be numbered and should not be torn out. Entries should be made neatly, but don't necessarily have to be complete sentences. **Entries** should provide detailed information and be recorded in such a way that another person could use them to replicate the experiment. **Quantitative data** may be recorded in tabular form, and may include calculations made during an experiment. Lab book entries can also include references and research performed before the experiment. Entries may also consist of information about a lab experiment, including the objective or purpose, the procedures, data collected, and the results.

Lab Reports

A **lab report** is an item developed after an experiment that is intended to present the results of a lab experiment. Generally, it should be prepared using a word processor, not hand-written or recorded in a notebook. A lab report should be formally presented. It is intended to persuade others to accept or reject a hypothesis. It should include a brief but descriptive **title** and an **abstract**. The abstract is a summary of the report. It should include a purpose that states the problem that was explored or the question that was answered. It should also include a **hypothesis** that describes the anticipated results of the experiment. The experiment should include a **control** and one **variable** to ensure that the results can be interpreted correctly. Observations and results can be presented using written narratives, tables, graphs, and illustrations. The report should also include a **summation** or **conclusion** explaining whether the results supported the hypothesis.

Types of Laboratory Glassware

Two types of flasks are Erlenmeyer flasks and volumetric flasks. **Volumetric flasks** are used to accurately prepare a specific volume and concentration of a solution. **Erlenmeyer flasks** can be used for mixing, transporting, and reacting, but are not appropriate for accurate measurements.

A **pipette** can be used to accurately measure small amounts of liquid. Liquid is drawn into the pipette through a bulb. The liquid measurement is read at the **meniscus**. There are also plastic disposable pipettes. A **repipette** is a hand-operated pump that dispenses solutions.

Beakers can be used to measure mass or dissolve a solvent into a solute. They do not measure volume as accurately as a volumetric flask, pipette, graduated cylinder, or burette.

Graduated cylinders are used for precise measurements and are considered more accurate than Erlenmeyer flasks or beakers. To read a graduated cylinder, it should be placed on a flat surface and read at eye level. The surface of a liquid in a graduated cylinder forms a lens-shaped curve. The measurement should be taken from the bottom of the curve. A ring may be placed at the top of tall, narrow cylinders to help avoid breakage if they are tipped over.

A **burette**, or buret, is a piece of lab glassware used to accurately dispense liquid. It looks similar to a narrow graduated cylinder, but it includes a stopcock and tip. It may be filled with a funnel or pipette.

Microscopes

There are different kinds of microscopes, but **optical** or **light microscopes** are the most commonly used in lab settings. Light and lenses are used to magnify and view samples. A specimen or sample is placed on a slide, and the slide is placed on a stage with a hole in it. Light passes through the hole and illuminates the sample. The sample is magnified by lenses and viewed through the eyepiece. A simple microscope has one lens, while a typical compound microscope has three lenses. The light source can be room light redirected by a mirror, or the microscope can have its own independent light source that passes through a condenser. In this case, there are diaphragms and filters to allow light intensity to be controlled. Optical microscopes also have coarse and fine adjustment knobs.

Other types of microscopes include **digital microscopes**, which use a camera and a monitor to allow viewing of the sample. **Scanning electron microscopes (SEMs)** provide greater detail in terms of a sample's surface topography and can produce magnifications much greater than those possible with optical microscopes. The technology of an SEM is quite different from an optical microscope in that it does not rely on lenses to magnify objects, but uses samples placed in a chamber. In one type of SEM, a beam of electrons from an electron gun scans and actually interacts with the sample to produce an image.

Wet mount slides designed for use with a light microscope typically require a thin portion of the specimen to be placed on a standard glass slide. A drop of water is added, and a cover slip or cover glass is placed on top. Air bubbles and fingerprints can make viewing difficult. Placing the cover slip at a 45-degree angle and allowing it to drop into place can help avoid the problem of air bubbles. A **cover slip** should always be used when viewing wet mount slides. The viewer should start with the objective in its lowest position and then fine-focus. The microscope should be carried with two hands and stored with the low-power objective in the down position. **Lenses** should be cleaned with lens paper only. A **graticule slide** is marked with a grid line, and is useful for counting or estimating a quantity.

BALANCES

Balances such as triple-beam balances, spring balances, and electronic balances measure mass and force. An **electronic balance** is the most accurate, followed by a **triple-beam balance** and then a **spring balance**. One part of a **triple-beam balance** is the plate, which is where the item to be weighed is placed. There are also three beams, which have hash marks indicating amounts and which hold the weights that rest in the notches. The front beam measures weights between 0 and 10 grams, the middle beam measures weights in 100-gram increments, and the far beam measures weights in 10-gram increments. The sum of the weight of each beam is the total weight of the object. A triple beam balance also includes a set screw to calibrate the equipment, as well as a mark indicating that the object and counterweights are in balance.

CHROMATOGRAPHY

Chromatography refers to a set of laboratory techniques used to separate or analyze **mixtures**. Mixtures are dissolved in their mobile phases. In the stationary or bonded phase, the desired component is separated from other molecules in the mixture. In chromatography, the analyte is the substance to be separated. **Preparative chromatography** refers to the type of chromatography that involves purifying a substance for further use rather than further analysis. **Analytical chromatography** involves analyzing the isolated substance. Other types of chromatography include column, planar, paper, thin layer, displacement, supercritical fluid, affinity, ion exchange, and size exclusion chromatography. Reversed phase, two-dimensional, simulated moving bed, pyrolysis, fast protein, counter current, and chiral are also types of chromatography. **Gas**

chromatography refers to the separation technique in which the mobile phase of a substance is in gas form.

Review Video: Paper Chromatography
Visit mometrix.com/academy and enter code: 543963

REAGENTS AND REACTANTS

A **reagent** or **reactant** is a chemical agent for use in chemical reactions. When preparing for a lab, it should be confirmed that glassware and other equipment have been cleaned and/or sterilized. There should be enough materials, reagents, or other solutions needed for the lab for every group of students completing the experiment. Distilled water should be used instead of tap water when performing lab experiments because distilled water has most of its impurities removed. Other needed apparatus such as funnels, filter paper, balances, Bunsen burners, ring stands, and/or microscopes should also be set up. After the lab, it should be confirmed that sinks, workstations, and any equipment used have been cleaned. If chemicals or specimens need to be kept at a certain temperature by refrigerating them or using another storage method, the temperature should be checked periodically to ensure the sample does not spoil.

DILUTING ACIDS

When preparing a solution of **dilute acid**, always add the concentrated acid solution to water, not water to concentrated acid. Start by adding approximately $\frac{2}{3}$ of the total volume of water to the graduated cylinder or volumetric flask. Next, add the concentrated acid to the water. Add additional water to the diluted acid to bring the solution to the final desired volume.

CLEANING AFTER ACID SPILLS

In the event of an **acid spill**, any clothes that have come into contact with the acid should be removed and any skin contacted with acid must be rinsed with clean water. To the extent a window can be opened or a fume hood can be turned on, do so. Do not try to force air circulation, such as by adding a fan, as acid fumes can be harmful if spread.

Next, pour one of the following over the spill area: sodium bicarbonate, baking soda, soda ash, or cat litter. Start from the outside of the spill and then move towards the center, in order to prevent splashing. When the clumps have thoroughly dried, sweep up the clumps and dispose of them as chemical waste.

CENTRIFUGES

A centrifuge is used to separate the components of a heterogeneous mixture (consisting of two or more compounds) by spinning it. The solid precipitate settles in the bottom of the container, and the liquid component of the solution, called the **centrifugate**, is at the top. A well-known application of this process is using a centrifuge to separate blood cells and plasma. The heavier cells settle on the bottom of the test tube, and the lighter plasma stays on top. Another example is using a salad spinner to help dry lettuce.

Electrophoresis, Calorimetry, and Titration

- **Electrophoresis** is the separation of molecules based on electrical charge. This is possible because particles dispersed in a fluid usually carry electric charges on their surfaces. Molecules are pulled through the fluid toward the positive end if the molecules have a negative charge and are pulled through the fluid toward the negative end if the molecules have a positive charge.
- **Calorimetry** is used to determine the heat released or absorbed in a chemical reaction.
- **Titration** helps determine the precise endpoint of a reaction. With this information, the precise quantity of reactant in the titration flask can be determined. A burette is used to deliver the second reactant to the flask and an indicator or pH meter is used to detect the endpoint of the reaction.

Field Studies and Research Projects

Field studies may facilitate scientific inquiry in a manner similar to indoor lab experiments. Field studies can be interdisciplinary in nature and can help students learn and apply scientific concepts and processes. **Research projects** can be conducted in any number of locations, including school campuses, local parks, national parks, beaches, or mountains. Students can practice the general techniques of observation, data collection, collaborative planning, and analysis of experiments. Field studies give students the chance to learn through hands-on applications of scientific processes, such as map making in geography, observation of stratification in geology, observation of life cycles of plants and animals, and analysis of water quality.

Students should watch out for obvious outdoor **hazards**. These include poisonous flora and fauna such as poison ivy, poison oak, and sumac. Depending on the region of the United States in which the field study is being conducted, hazards may also include rattlesnakes and black widow or brown recluse spiders. Students should also be made aware of potentially hazardous situations specific to **geographic locales** and the possibility of coming into contact with **pathogens**.

Field studies allow for great flexibility in the use of traditional and technological methods for **making observations** and **collecting data**. For example, a nature study could consist of a simple survey of bird species within a given area. Information could be recorded using still photography or a video camera. This type of activity gives students the chance to use technologies other than computers. Computers could still be used to create a slide show of transferred images or a digital lab report. If a quantitative study of birds was being performed, the simple technique of using a pencil and paper to tabulate the number of birds counted in the field could also be used. Other techniques used during field studies could include collecting specimens for lab study, observing coastal ecosystems and tides, and collecting weather data such as temperature, precipitation amounts, and air pressure in a particular locale.

Scientific Inquiry and Reasoning

Scientific Inquiry

The concept of **scientific inquiry** refers to the idea of how one thinks and asks questions in a logical way to gain trustworthy information. The underlying motivation of science is to try to understand the natural world. Much of human thought is based on assumptions about how things work that may or may not be true. The goal of scientific inquiry is to test those assumptions to gain a greater understanding of the world with good questions and objective tests, and then re-use what was learned to ask better questions. The more we understand about the natural world, the better the questions we can ask, and that is the general idea behind scientific inquiry. The applied practice of scientific inquiry is to ask questions in a systematic method, called the scientific method.

Scientific Knowledge

Scientific knowledge refers to any topic that is studied **empirically**, meaning that it is based on observation of a **phenomenon** in an objective way. The body of **scientific knowledge** is often broken down into several domains including biology, ecology, Earth science, space science, physics, and chemistry. These each have further subdomains and are overlapping in many ways. For instance, ecology is the study of ecosystems, which are made up of biological factors and geological factors, so it contains elements of both biology and Earth science. Each of these domains is subject to the concepts of scientific inquiry, such as the scientific method, scientific facts, hypotheses, and scientific laws.

Important Terminology

- A **phenomenon** is an event or effect that is observed.
- A **scientific fact** is considered an objective and verifiable observation. Usually, a fact can be repeated or demonstrated to others.
- A **scientific theory** is a proposition explaining why or how something happens and is built on scientific facts and laws. Scientific theories can be tested, but are not fully proven. If new evidence is found that disproves the theory, it is no longer considered true.
- A **hypothesis** is an educated guess that is not yet proven. It is used to predict the outcome of an experiment in an attempt to solve a problem or answer a question.
- A **law** is an explanation of events that always leads to the same outcome. It is a fact that an object falls. The law of gravity explains why an object falls. The theory of relativity, although generally accepted, has been neither proven nor disproved.
- A **model** is used to explain something on a smaller scale or in simpler terms to provide an example. It is a representation of an idea that can be used to explain events or applied to new situations to predict outcomes or determine results.

History of Scientific Knowledge

When one examines the history of **scientific knowledge**, it is clear that it is constantly **evolving**. The body of facts, models, theories, and laws grows and changes over time. In other words, one scientific discovery leads to the next. Some advances in science and technology have important and long-lasting effects on science and society. Some discoveries were so alien to the accepted beliefs of the time that not only were they rejected as wrong, but were also considered outright blasphemy. Today, however, many beliefs once considered incorrect have become an ingrained part of scientific knowledge, and have also been the basis of new advances. Examples of advances include: Copernicus's heliocentric view of the universe, Newton's laws of motion and planetary orbits, relativity, geologic time scale, plate tectonics, atomic theory, nuclear physics, biological evolution, germ theory, industrial revolution, molecular biology, information and communication, quantum theory, galactic universe, and medical and health technology.

Scientific Inquiry and Scientific Method

Scientists use a number of generally accepted techniques collectively known as the **scientific method**. The scientific method generally involves carrying out the following steps:

- Identifying a problem or posing a question
- Formulating a hypothesis or an educated guess
- Conducting experiments or tests that will provide a basis to solve the problem or answer the question
- Observing the results of the test
- Drawing conclusions

An important part of the scientific method is using acceptable experimental techniques. Objectivity is also important if valid results are to be obtained. Another important part of the scientific method is peer review. It is essential that experiments be performed and data be recorded in such a way that experiments can be reproduced to verify results. Historically, the scientific method has been taught with a more linear approach, but it is important to recognize that the scientific method should be a cyclical or **recursive process**. This means that as hypotheses are tested and more is learned, the questions should continue to change to reflect the changing body of knowledge. One cycle of experimentation is not enough.

Review Video: The Scientific Method
Visit mometrix.com/academy and enter code: 191386

Metric and International System of Units

The **metric system** is the accepted standard of measurement in the scientific community. The **International System of Units (SI)** is a set of measurements (including the metric system) that is almost globally accepted. The United States, Liberia, and Myanmar have not accepted this system. **Standardization** is important because it allows the results of experiments to be compared and reproduced without the need to laboriously convert measurements. The SI is based partially on the **meter-kilogram-second (MKS) system** rather than the **centimeter-gram-second (CGS) system**. The MKS system considers meters, kilograms, and seconds to be the basic units of measurement, while the CGS system considers centimeters, grams, and seconds to be the basic units of measurement. Under the MKS system, the length of an object would be expressed as 1 meter instead of 100 centimeters, which is how it would be described under the CGS system.

Review Video: Metric System Conversions
Visit mometrix.com/academy and enter code: 163709

Basic Units of Measurement

Using the **metric system** is generally accepted as the preferred method for taking measurements. Having a **universal standard** allows individuals to interpret measurements more easily, regardless of where they are located. The basic units of measurement are: the **meter**, which measures length; the **liter**, which measures volume; and the **gram**, which measures mass. The metric system starts with a base unit and increases or decreases in units of 10. The prefix and the base unit combined are used to indicate an amount. For example, deka- is 10 times the base unit. A dekameter is 10 meters; a dekaliter is 10 liters; and a dekagram is 10 grams. The prefix hecto- refers to 100 times the base amount; kilo- is 1,000 times the base amount. The prefixes that indicate a fraction of the base unit are deci-, which is $\frac{1}{10}$ of the base unit; centi-, which is $\frac{1}{100}$ of the base unit; and milli-, which is $\frac{1}{1,000}$ of the base unit.

Common Prefixes

The prefixes for multiples are as follows:

Deka	(da)	$\mathbf{10^1}$ (deka is the American spelling, but deca is also used)
Hecto	(h)	10^2
Kilo	(k)	10^3
Mega	(M)	10^6
Giga	(G)	10^9
Tera	(T)	10^{12}

The prefixes for subdivisions are as follows:

Deci	(d)	$\mathbf{10^{-1}}$
Centi	(c)	10^{-2}
Milli	(m)	10^{-3}
Micro	(μ)	10^{-6}
Nano	(n)	10^{-9}
Pico	(p)	10^{-12}

The rule of thumb is that prefixes greater than 10^3 are capitalized when abbreviating. Abbreviations do not need a period after them. A decimeter (dm) is a tenth of a meter, a deciliter (dL) is a tenth of a liter, and a decigram (dg) is a tenth of a gram. Pluralization is understood. For example, when referring to 5 mL of water, no "s" needs to be added to the abbreviation.

Basic SI Units of Measurement

SI uses **second(s)** to measure time. Fractions of seconds are usually measured in metric terms using prefixes such as millisecond ($\frac{1}{1,000}$ of a second) or nanosecond ($\frac{1}{1,000,000,000}$ of a second). Increments of time larger than a second are measured in **minutes** and **hours**, which are multiples of 60 and 24. An example of this is a swimmer's time in the 800-meter freestyle being described as 7:32.67, meaning 7 minutes, 32 seconds, and 67 one-hundredths of a second. One second is equal to $\frac{1}{60}$ of a minute, $\frac{1}{3,600}$ of an hour, and $\frac{1}{86,400}$ of a day. Other SI base units are the **ampere** (A) (used to measure electric current), the **kelvin** (K) (used to measure thermodynamic temperature), the **candela** (cd) (used to measure luminous intensity), and the **mole** (mol) (used to measure the amount of a substance at a molecular level). **Meter** (m) is used to measure length and **kilogram** (kg) is used to measure mass.

Significant Figures

The mathematical concept of **significant figures** or **significant digits** is often used to determine the accuracy of measurements or the level of confidence one has in a specific measurement. The significant figures of a measurement include all the digits known with certainty plus one estimated or uncertain digit. There are a number of rules for determining which digits are considered "important" or "interesting." They are:

- All non-zero digits are *significant.*
- Zeros between digits are *significant.*
- Leading and trailing zeros are *not significant* unless they appear to the right of the non-zero digits in a decimal.

For example, in 0.01230, the significant digits are 1230, and this number would be said to be accurate to the hundred-thousandths place. The zero indicates that the amount has actually been measured as 0. Other zeros are considered placeholders and are not important. A decimal point may be placed after zeros to indicate their importance (in "100." for example).

Graphs and Charts

Graphs and charts are effective ways to present scientific data such as observations, statistical analyses, and comparisons between dependent variables and independent variables. On a line chart, the **independent variable** (the one that is being manipulated for the experiment) is represented on the horizontal axis (the x-axis). Any **dependent variables** (the ones that may change as the independent variable changes) are represented on the y-axis. An **XY** or **scatter plot** is often used to plot many points. A "best fit" line is drawn, which allows outliers to be identified more easily. Charts and their axes should have titles. The x and y interval units should be evenly spaced and labeled. Other types of charts are **bar charts** and **histograms**, which can be used to compare differences between the data collected for two variables. A **pie chart** can graphically show the relation of parts to a whole.

Review Video: Identifying Variables
Visit mometrix.com/academy and enter code: 627181

Review Video: Data Interpretation of Graphs
Visit mometrix.com/academy and enter code: 200439

Data Presentation

Data collected during a science lab can be organized and **presented** in any number of ways. While **straight narrative** is a suitable method for presenting some lab results, it is not a suitable way to present numbers and quantitative measurements. These types of observations can often be better presented with **tables** and **graphs**. Data that is presented in tables and organized in rows and columns may also be used to make graphs quite easily. Other methods of presenting data include illustrations, photographs, video, and even audio formats. In a **formal report**, tables and figures are labeled and referred to by their labels. For example, a picture of a bubbly solution might be labeled Figure 1, Bubbly Solution. It would be referred to in the text in the following way: "The reaction created bubbles 10 mm in size, as shown in Figure 1, Bubbly Solution." Graphs are also labeled as figures. Tables are labeled in a different way. Examples include: Table 1, Results of Statistical Analysis, or Table 2, Data from Lab 2.

Statistical Precision and Errors

Errors that occur during an experiment can be classified into two categories: random errors and systematic errors. **Random errors** can result in collected data that is wildly different from the rest of the data, or they may result in data that is indistinguishable from the rest. Random errors are not consistent across the data set. In large data sets, random errors may contribute to the variability of data, but they will not affect the average. Random errors are sometimes referred to as noise. They may be caused by a student's inability to take the same measurement in exactly the same way or by outside factors that are not considered variables, but influence the data. A **systematic error** will show up consistently across a sample or data set, and may be the result of a flaw in the experimental design. This type of error affects the average, and is also known as bias.

Scientific Notation

Scientific notation is used because values in science can be very large or very small, which makes them unwieldy. A number in **decimal notation** is 93,000,000. In **scientific notation**, it is 9.3×10^7. The first number, 9.3, is the **coefficient**. It is always greater than or equal to 1 and less than 10. This number is followed by a multiplication sign. The base is always 10 in scientific notation. If the number is greater than ten, the exponent is positive. If the number is between zero and one, the exponent is negative. The first digit of the number is followed by a decimal point and then the rest of the number. In this case, the number is 9.3, and the decimal point was moved seven places to the right from the end of the number to get 93,000,000. The number of places moved, seven, is the exponent.

Statistical Terminology

- **Mean**—The average, found by taking the sum of a set of numbers and dividing by the number of numbers in the set.
- **Median**—The middle number in a set of numbers sorted from least to greatest. If the set has an even number of entries, the median is the average of the two in the middle.
- **Mode**—The value that appears most frequently in a data set. There may be more than one mode. If no value appears more than once, there is no mode.
- **Range**—The difference between the highest and lowest numbers in a data set.
- **Standard deviation**—Measures the dispersion of a data set, or how far from the mean a single data point is likely to be.
- **Regression analysis**—A method of analyzing sets of data and sets of variables. It involves studying how the typical value of the dependent variable changes when any one of the independent variables is varied and the other independent variables remain fixed.

Review Video: Mean, Median, and Mode
Visit mometrix.com/academy and enter code: 286207

Review Video: Standard Deviation
Visit mometrix.com/academy and enter code: 419469

Chapter Quiz

Ready to see how well you retained what you just read? Scan the QR code to go directly to the chapter quiz interface for this study guide. If you're using a computer, simply visit the online resources page at **mometrix.com/resources719/texesmathpse** and click the Chapter Quizzes link.

Physics

Mechanics

Work, Energy, and Power

Basic Equation for Work

The equation for **work** (W) is $W = \boldsymbol{Fd}$, where $\boldsymbol{F}$ is the force exerted and $\boldsymbol{d}$ is the displacement of the object on which the force is exerted. For the simplest case, when the vectors of force and displacement have the same direction, the work done is equal to the product of the magnitudes of the force and displacement. If this is not the case, then the work may be calculated as $W = \boldsymbol{Fd}\cos\theta$, where θ is the angle between the force and displacement vectors. If force and displacement have the same direction, then work is positive; if they are in opposite directions, however, work is negative; and if they are perpendicular, the work done by the force is zero.

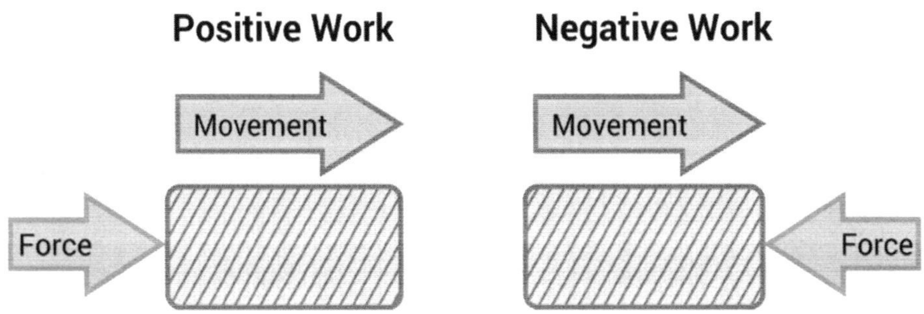

Review Video: Work
Visit mometrix.com/academy and enter code: 681834

For example, if a man pushes a block horizontally across a surface with a constant force of 10 N for a distance of 20 m, the work done by the man is 200 N-m or 200 J. If instead the block is sliding and the man tries to **slow its progress** by pushing against it, his work done is –200 J, since he is pushing in the direction opposite the motion. Also, if the man pushes vertically downward on the block while it slides, his work done is zero, since his force vector is perpendicular to the displacement vector of the block. It is important to note in each of these cases that neither the mass of the block nor the elapsed time is considered when calculating the amount of work done by the man.

Review Video: Push and Pull Forces
Visit mometrix.com/academy and enter code: 104731

Power

Put simply, **power** is the **rate at which work is done**. Power, like work, is a scalar quantity. If we know the amount of work, W, that has been performed in a given amount of time, Δt, then we may find average power, $P_{avg} = \frac{W}{\Delta t}$. If we are instead looking for the instantaneous power, there are two possibilities. If the force on an object is constant, and the object is moving at a constant velocity, then the instantaneous power is the same as the average power. If either the force or the velocity is varying, the instantaneous power should be computed by the equation $P = \boldsymbol{F}\boldsymbol{v}$, where $\boldsymbol{F}$ and $\boldsymbol{v}$ are the instantaneous force and velocity, respectively. This equation may also be used to compute average power if the force and velocity are constant. Power is typically expressed in joules per second, or watts.

SIMPLE MACHINES

Simple machines include the pulley, lever, wheel and axle, wedge, inclined plane, and screw. These simple machines have no internal source of energy. More complex or compound machines can be formed from them. Simple machines provide a mechanical advantage and make it easier to accomplish a task. Single or double pulleys allow for easier direction of force. A lever enables a multiplication of force. The wheel and axle allows for movement with less resistance. The inclined plane enables a force less than an object's weight to be used to push it to a greater height. The wedge and screw are forms of the inclined plane. A wedge turns a smaller force working over a greater distance into a larger force. The screw is similar to an incline that is wrapped around a shaft.

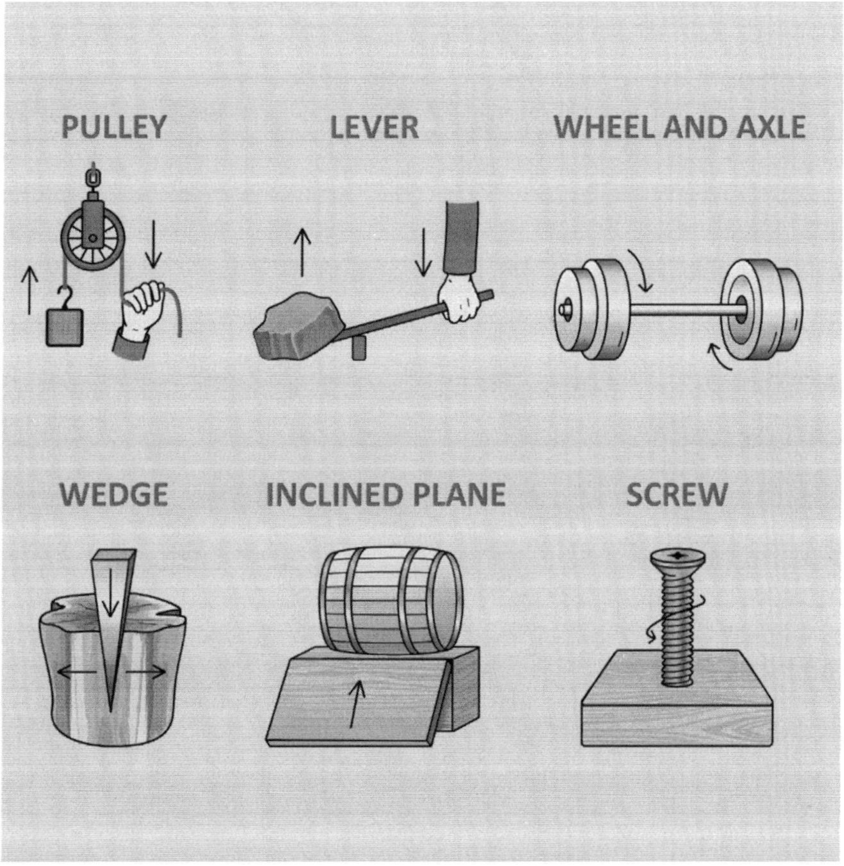

Review Video: Simple Machines
Visit mometrix.com/academy and enter code: 950789

MECHANICAL ADVANTAGE

There is a certain amount of **work** required to move an object that cannot be reduced. However, using one or more simple machines can increase either the distance or force needed. Since work is defined as a force multiplied by a distance, force and distance are inversely proportional.

$$\mathbf{Work_{input} = Work_{output}}$$

$$\mathbf{force_{input} \times distance_{input} = force_{output} \times distance_{output}}$$

Simple machines can either reduce the amount of input force needed by increasing the input distance or they can reduce the input distance needed by increasing the required input force. The ratio of the output force over the input force is a measure of the **mechanical advantage** of a machine. Due to the inverse relationship between force and distance for these machines, mechanical advantage can also be expressed as the ratio of input distance over the output distance.

$$\mathbf{Mechanical\ Advantage} = \frac{\mathbf{force_{output}}}{\mathbf{force_{input}}} = \frac{\mathbf{distance_{input}}}{\mathbf{distance_{output}}}$$

LEVERS

The **lever** is the most common kind of simple machine. See-saws, shovels, and baseball bats are all examples of levers. There are three classes of levers which are differentiated by the relative orientations of the fulcrum, resistance, and effort. The **fulcrum** is the point at which the lever rotates, the **effort** is the point on the lever where force is applied, and the **resistance** is the part of the lever that acts in response to the effort.

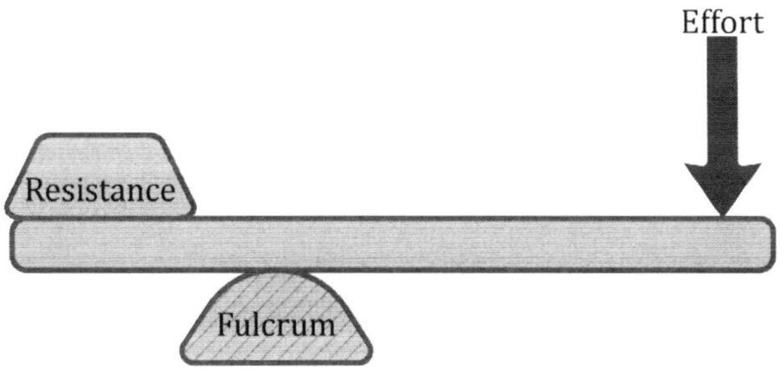

The mechanical advantage of a lever depends on the distances of the effort and resistance from the fulcrum.

$$\mathbf{Mechanical\ Advantage} = \frac{\mathbf{effort\ distance}}{\mathbf{resistance\ distance}}$$

In a **first-class lever**, the fulcrum is between the effort and the resistance. A seesaw is a good example of a first-class lever when effort is applied to force one end up, the other end goes down, and vice versa. The shorter the distance between the fulcrum and the resistance, the easier it will be to move the resistance. As an example, consider whether it is easier to lift another person on a seesaw when they are sitting close to the middle or all the way at the end. A little practice will show you that it is much more difficult to lift a person the farther away he or she is on the see-saw.

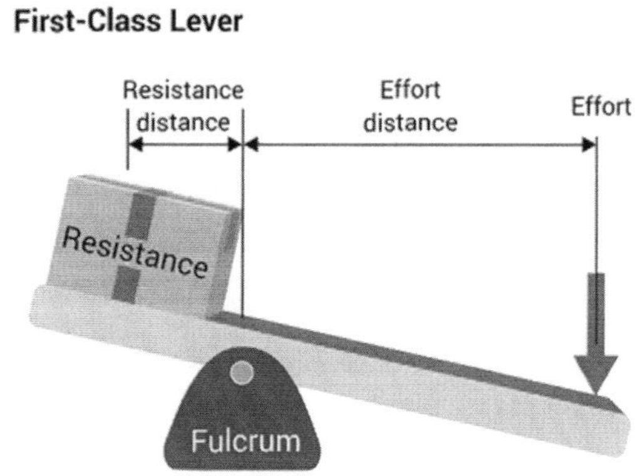

In a **second-class lever**, the resistance is in between the fulcrum and the effort. While a first-class lever is able to increase force and distance through mechanical advantage, a second-class lever is only able to increase force. A common example of a second-class lever is the wheelbarrow; the force exerted by your hand at one end of the wheelbarrow is magnified at the load. Basically, with a second-class lever, you are trading distance for force; by moving your end of the wheelbarrow a bit farther, you produce greater force at the load.

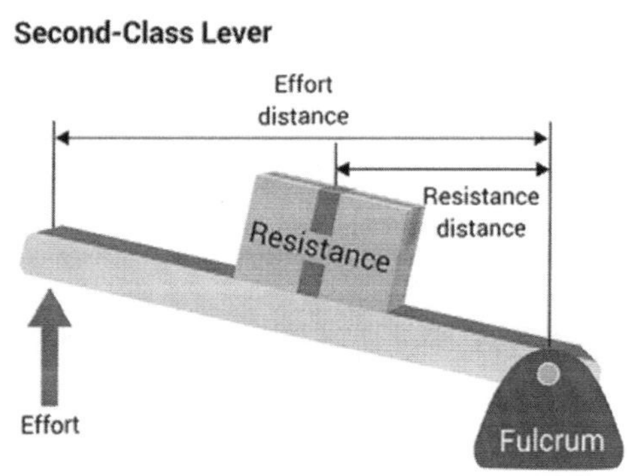

Third-class levers are used to produce greater distance. In a third-class lever, the force is applied in between the fulcrum and the resistance. A baseball bat is a classic example of a third-class lever; the bottom of the bat, below where you grip it, is considered the fulcrum. The end of the bat, where the ball is struck, is the resistance. By exerting effort at the base of the bat, close to the fulcrum, you are able to make the end of the bat fly quickly through the air. The closer your hands are to the base of the bat, the faster you will be able to make the other end of the bat travel.

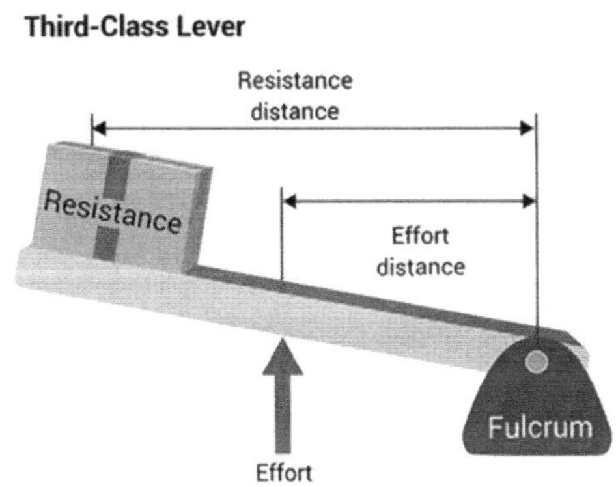

Review Video: Levers
Visit mometrix.com/academy and enter code: 103910

Wheel and Axle

Another basic arrangement that makes use of simple machines is called the wheel and axle. When most people think of a wheel and axle, they immediately envision an automobile tire. The steering wheel of the car, however, operates on the same mechanical principle, namely that the force required to move the center of a circle is much greater than the force required to move the outer rim of a circle. When you turn the steering wheel, you are essentially using a second-class lever by increasing the output force by increasing the input distance. The force required to turn the wheel from the outer rim is much less than would be required to turn the wheel from its center.

The equation for the mechanical advantage of a wheel and axle is:

$$\textbf{Mechanical Advantage} = \frac{\textbf{radius}_{\textbf{wheel}}}{\textbf{radius}_{\textbf{axle}}}$$

For instance, a steering wheel with a radius of 12 inches has a greater mechanical advantage than a steering wheel with a radius of 10 inches; the same amount of force exerted on the rim of each wheel will produce greater force on the axle of the larger wheel.

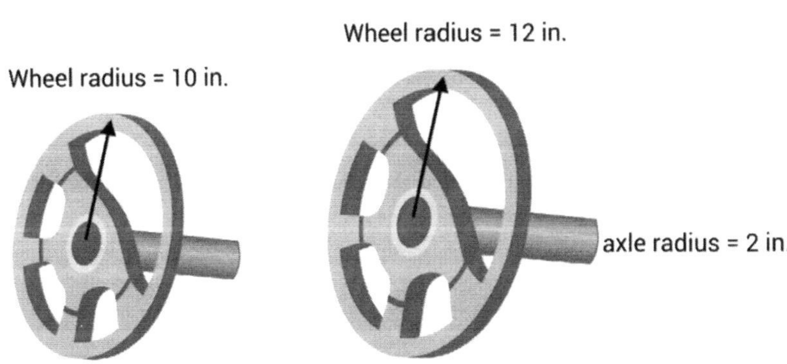

Thus, the mechanical advantage for each is:

$$\frac{10 \text{ inches}}{2 \text{ inches}} = 5 \qquad \frac{12 \text{ inches}}{2 \text{ inches}} = 6$$

Review Video: Wheel and Axle
Visit mometrix.com/academy and enter code: 574045

PULLEYS

The pulley is a simple machine in which a rope is carried by the rotation of a wheel. Another name for a pulley is a block. Pulleys are typically used to allow the force to be directed from a convenient location. For instance, imagine you are given the task of lifting a heavy and tall bookcase. Rather than tying a rope to the bookcase and trying to lift it, it would make sense to tie a pulley system to a rafter above the bookcase and run the rope through it, so that you could pull down on the rope and lift the bookcase. Pulling down allows you to incorporate your weight (normal force) into the act of lifting, thereby making it easier.

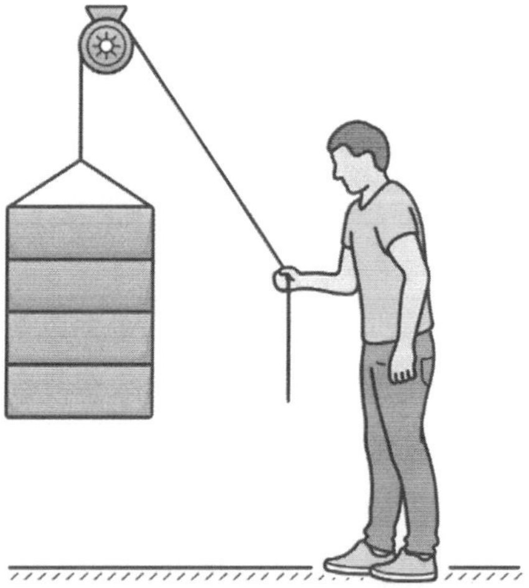

If there is just one pulley above the bookcase, you have created a first-class lever that will not diminish the amount of force that needs to be applied to lift the bookcase. There is another way to use a pulley, however, that can make the job of lifting a heavy object considerably easier. First, tie the rope directly to the rafter. Then, attach a pulley to the top of the bookcase and run the rope through it. If you can then stand so that you are above the bookcase, you will have a much easier time lifting this heavy object. This is because the weight of the bookcase is now being distributed: half of it is acting on the rafter, and half of it is acting on you. In other words, this arrangement allows you to lift an object with half the force. This simple pulley system, therefore, has a mechanical advantage of 2. Note that in this arrangement, the unfixed pulley is acting like a second-class lever. The price you pay for your mechanical advantage is that whatever distance you raise your end of the rope, the bookcase will only be lifted half as much.

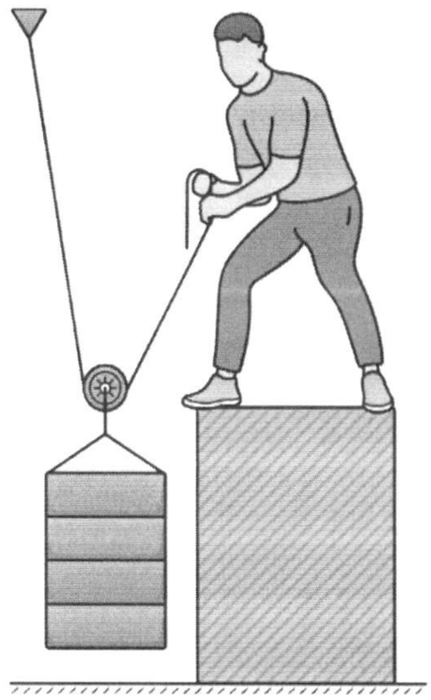

Of course, it might be difficult for you to find a place high enough to enact this system. If this is the case, you can always tie another pulley to the rafter and run the rope through it and back down to the floor. Since this second pulley is fixed, the mechanical advantage will remain the same.

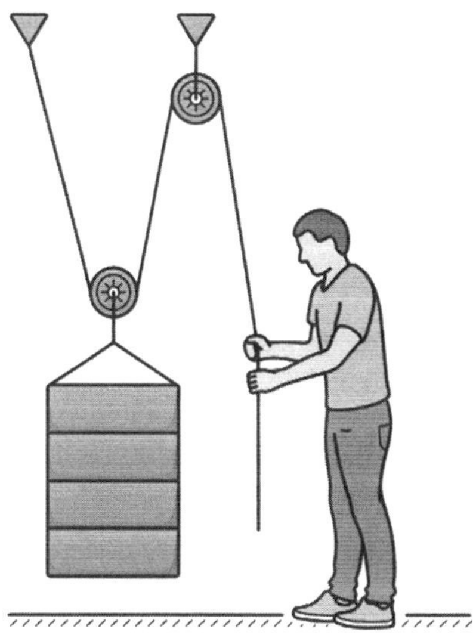

INCLINED PLANE

The inclined plane is perhaps the most common of the simple machines. It is simply a flat surface that elevates as you move from one end to the other. Consider how much easier it is for a person to walk up a long ramp than to climb a shorter but steeper flight of stairs; this is because the force required is diminished as the distance increases. Indeed, the longer the ramp, the easier it is to ascend.

Inclined planes often used to move heavy objects. For instance, moving a heavy box onto the back of a truck requires less force when pushing it up a ramp than when lifting it directly onto the truck bed. The longer the ramp, the greater the mechanical advantage, and the easier it will be to move the box. The mechanical advantage of an inclined plane is equal to the slant length divided by the rise of the plane.

$$\textbf{Mechanical Advantage} = \frac{\textbf{slant length}}{\textbf{rise}}$$

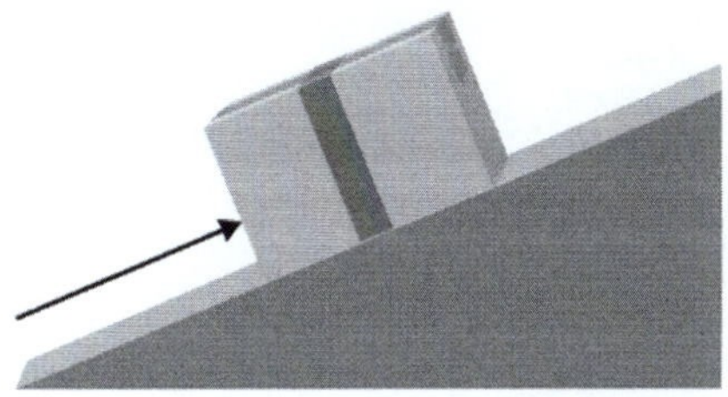

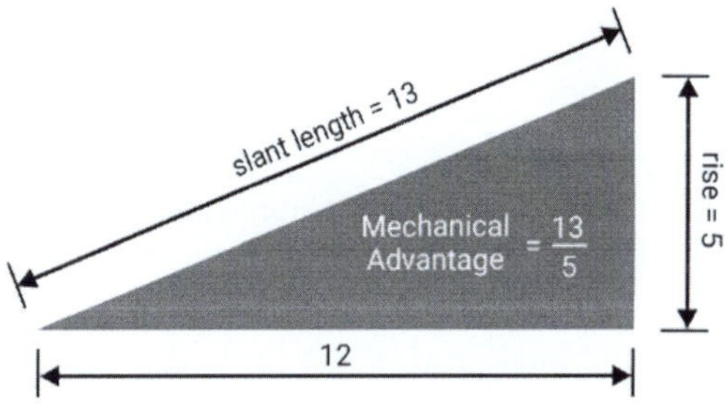

Screw

A screw is simply an inclined plane that has been wound around a cylinder so that it forms a sort of spiral.

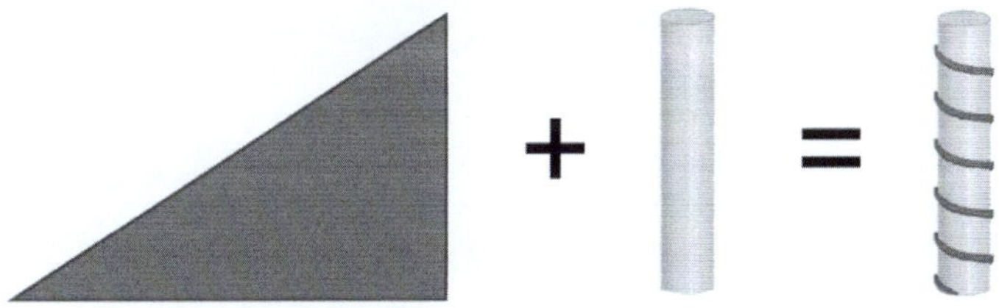

When it is placed into some medium, as for instance wood, the screw will move either forward or backward when it is rotated. The principle of the screw is used in a number of different objects, from jar lids to flashlights. The equation for the mechanical advantage is a modification of the inclined plane's equation. Because the rise of the inclined plane is the length along a screw, length between rotations is the rise. The slant length is equal the circumference of one rotation ($2\pi r$).

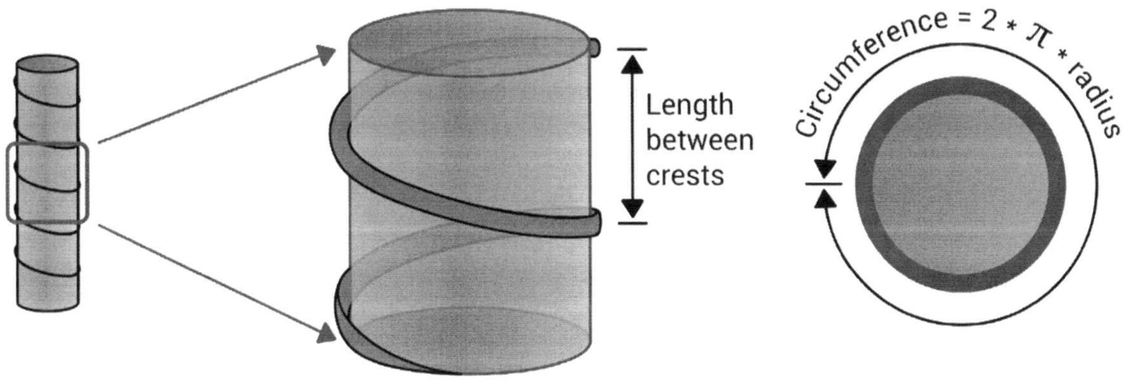

$$\text{Mechanical Advantage} = \frac{2 \times \pi \times \text{radius}}{\text{length between crests}}$$

WEDGE

A wedge is a variation on the inclined plane, in which the wedge moves between objects or parts and forces them apart. The unique characteristic of a wedge is that, unlike an inclined plane, it is designed to move. Perhaps the most familiar use of the wedge is in splitting wood. A wedge is driven into the wood by hitting the flat back end. The thin end of a wedge is easier to drive into the wood since it has less surface area and, therefore, transmits more force per area. As the wedge is driven in, the increased width helps to split the wood.

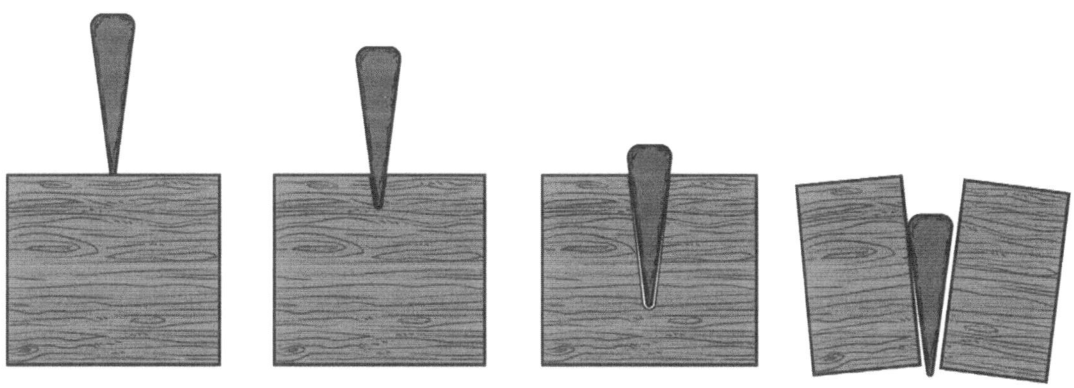

The longer and thinner the wedge, the greater the mechanical advantage. The equation for mechanical advantage of a wedge is:

$$\text{Mechanical Advantage} = \frac{\text{length}}{\text{width}}$$

GEARS

Gears are a system of interlocking wheels that can create immense mechanical advantages. The amount of mechanical advantage, however, will depend on the gear ratio; that is, on the relation in size between the gears.

When a small gear is driving a big gear, the speed of the big gear is relatively slow; when a big gear is driving a small gear, the speed of the small gear is relatively fast.

The equation for the mechanical advantage is:

$$\textbf{Mechanical Advantage} = \frac{\textbf{torque}_{\textbf{output}}}{\textbf{torque}_{\textbf{input}}} = \frac{\textbf{r}_{\textbf{output}}}{\textbf{r}_{\textbf{input}}} = \frac{\textbf{\# of teeth}_{\textbf{output}}}{\textbf{\# of teeth}_{\textbf{input}}}$$

Note that mechanical advantage is greater than 1 when the output gear is larger. In these cases, the output velocity ($\boldsymbol{\omega}$) will be lower. The equation for the relative speed of a gear system is:

$$\frac{\omega_{\text{input}}}{\omega_{\text{output}}} = \frac{r_{\text{output}}}{r_{\text{input}}}$$

$$\textit{Mechanical Advantage} = \frac{\textit{teeth}_{\textit{output}}}{\textit{teeth}_{\textit{input}}} = \frac{20}{10} = 2$$

$$\textit{Mechanical Advantage} = \frac{\textit{teeth}_{\textit{output}}}{\textit{teeth}_{\textit{input}}} = \frac{16}{8} = 2$$

Gear Ratios

A gear ratio is a measure of how much the speed and torque are changing in a gear system. It is the ratio of output speed to input speed. Because the number of teeth is directly proportional to the speed in meshing gears, a gear ratio can also be calculated using the number of teeth on the gears. When the driving gear has 30 teeth and the driven gear has 10 teeth, the gear ratio is 3:1.

$$\text{Gear Ratio} = \frac{\text{\# of teeth}_{\text{driving}}}{\text{\# of teeth}_{\text{driven}}} = \frac{30}{10} = \frac{3}{1} = 3:1$$

This means that the smaller, driven gear rotates 3 times for every 1 rotation of the driving gear.

USES OF GEARS

Gears are used to change the direction, location, and amount of output torque, as well as change the angular velocity of output.

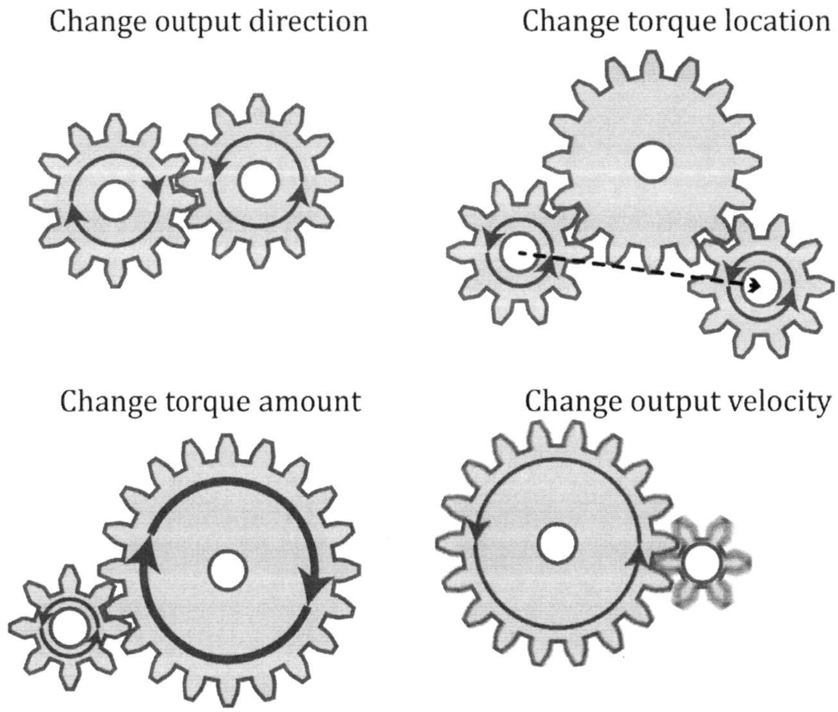

CAMS

In the study of motion, a final application often tested is the cam. A cam and follower system allows mechanical systems to have timed, specified, and repeating motion. Although cams come in varied forms, tests focus on rotary cams. In engines, a cam shaft coordinates the valves for intake and exhaust. Cams are often used to convert rotational motion into repeating linear motion.

Cams rotate around one point. The follower sits on the edge of the cam and moves along with the edge. To understand simple cams, count the number of bumps on the cam. Each bump will cause the follower to move outwards.

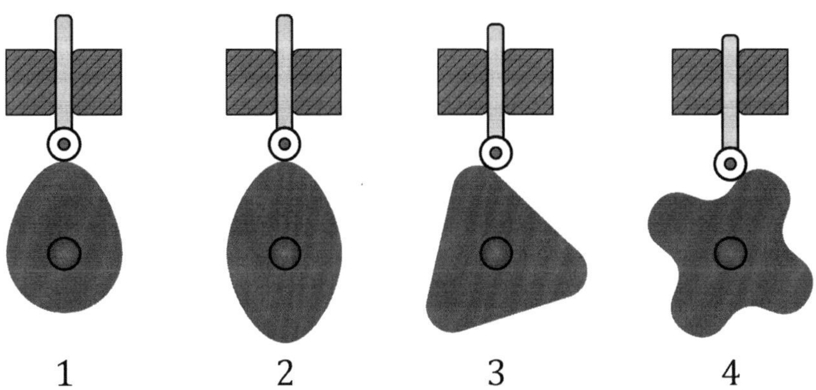

Another way to consider cams is to unravel the cam profile into a straight object. The follower will then follow the top of the profile.

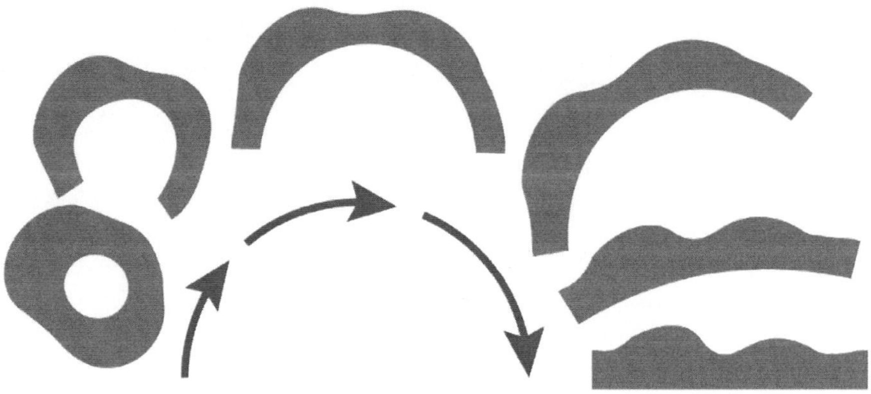

ENERGY

Energy is a word that has developed several different meanings in the English language, but in physics, it refers to the measure of a body's ability to do work. In physics, energy may not have a million meanings, but it does have many forms. Each of these forms, such as chemical, electric, and nuclear, is the capability of an object to perform work. However, the most commonly used concepts are mechanical energy and mechanical work. **Mechanical energy** is the sum of an object's kinetic and potential energies. While kinetic energy is linked to an object's motion, potential energy can be in a few different forms. The common forms of potential energy are gravitational and elastic.

KINETIC ENERGY

The **kinetic energy of an object** is that quality of its motion that can be related in a qualitative way to the amount of work performed on the object. Kinetic energy can be defined as $KE = \frac{mv^2}{2}$, in which m is the mass of an object and v is the magnitude of its velocity. Kinetic energy cannot be negative, since it depends on the square of velocity. Units for kinetic energy are the same as those for work: joules. Kinetic energy is a scalar quantity.

Changes in kinetic energy occur when a force does work on an object, such that the speed of the object is altered. This change in kinetic energy is equal to the amount of work that is done, and can be expressed as $W = KE_f - KE_i = \Delta KE$. This equation is commonly referred to as the work-kinetic energy theorem. If there are several different forces acting on the object, then W in this equation is the total work done by all the forces, or by the net force. This equation can be very helpful in solving some problems that would otherwise rely solely on Newton's laws of motion.

POTENTIAL ENERGY

Potential energy is the amount of energy that can be ascribed to a body or bodies based on configuration. There are a couple of different kinds of potential energy. **Gravitational potential energy** is the energy associated with the separation of bodies that are attracted to one another gravitationally. Any time you lift an object, you are increasing its gravitational potential energy. Gravitational potential energy can be found by the equation $PE = mgh$, where m is the mass of an object, g is the gravitational acceleration, and h is its height above a reference point, most often the ground.

Another kind of potential energy is **elastic potential energy**; elastic potential energy is associated with the compression or expansion of an elastic, or spring-like, object. Physicists will often refer to potential energy as being stored within a body, the implication being that it could emerge in the future.

Review Video: Potential and Kinetic Energy
Visit mometrix.com/academy and enter code: 491502

Elastic Potential Energy

Elastic potential energy is the potential for a certain amount of work to be done by one object on another using elastic compression or tension. The most common example is the spring. A spring will resist any compression or tension away from its equilibrium position (natural position). A small buggy is pressed into a large spring. The spring contains a large amount of elastic potential energy. If the buggy and spring are released, the spring will exert a force on the buggy, pushing it for a distance. This work will put kinetic energy into the buggy. The energy can be imagined as a liquid poured from one container into another. The spring pours its elastic energy into the buggy, which receives the energy as kinetic energy.

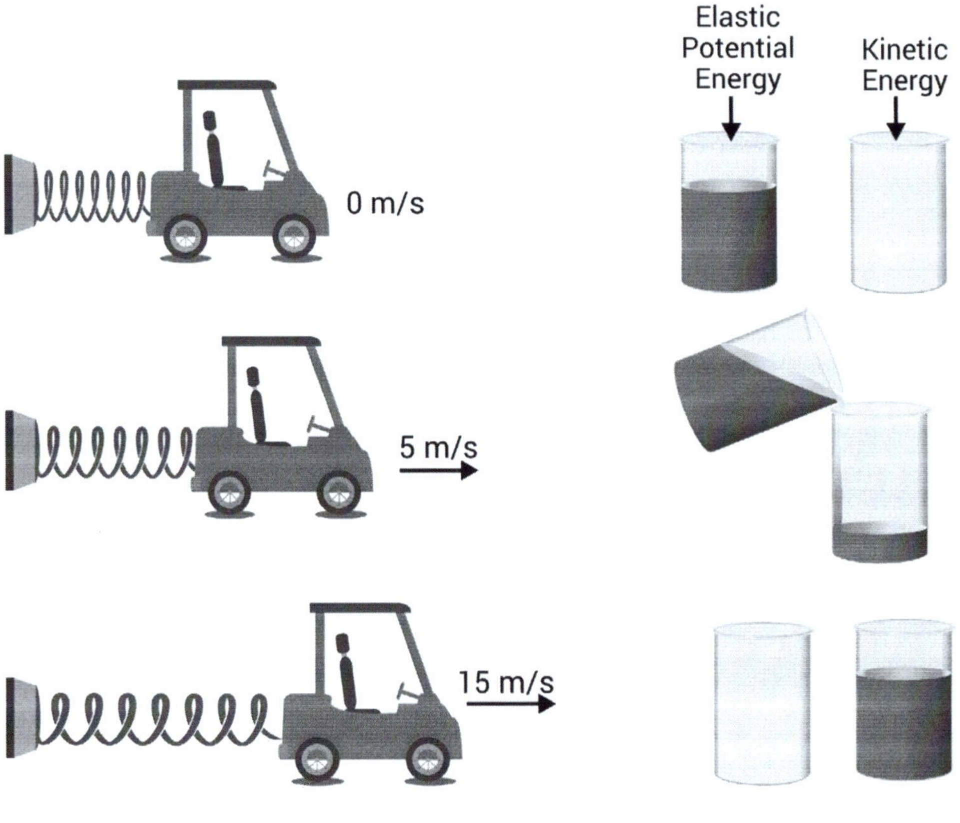

Conservative and Non-Conservative Forces

Forces that change the state of a system by changing kinetic energy into potential energy, or vice versa, are called **conservative forces**. This name arises because these forces conserve the total amount of kinetic and potential energy. Every other kind of force is considered non-conservative. One example of a conservative force is gravity. Consider the path of a ball thrown straight up into the air. Since the ball has the same amount of kinetic energy when it is thrown as it does when it returns to its original location (known as completing a closed path), gravity can be said to be a conservative force. More generally, a force can be said to be conservative if the work it does on an object through a closed path is zero. Frictional force would not meet this standard, of course, because it is only capable of performing negative work.

For example, imagine a ball moving perpendicular to the surface of the Earth, in other words straight up and down, with its weight being the only force acting on it. As the ball rises, the weight will be doing work on the ball, decreasing its speed and its kinetic energy and slowing it down until it momentarily stops. During this ascent, the potential energy of the ball will be rising. Once the ball begins to fall back down, it will lose potential energy as it gains kinetic energy. Mechanical energy is conserved throughout; the potential energy of the ball at its highest point is equal to the kinetic energy of the ball at its lowest point, just before to impact.

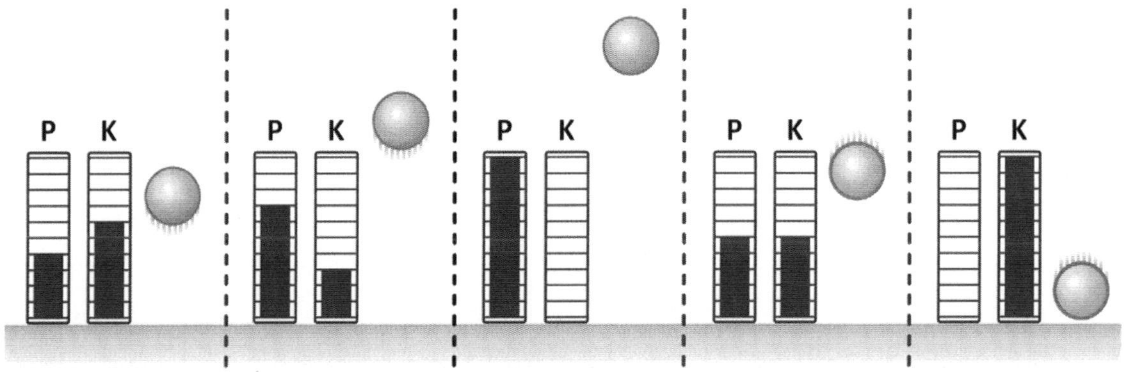

In systems where friction and air resistance are not negligible, we observe a different sort of result. For example, imagine a block sliding across the floor until it comes to a stop due to friction. Unlike a compressed spring or a ball flung into the air, there is no way for this block to regain its energy with a return trip. Therefore, we cannot say that the lost kinetic energy is being stored as potential energy. Instead, it has been dissipated and cannot be recovered. The total mechanical energy of the block-floor system has been not conserved in this case but rather reduced. The total energy of the system has not decreased, since the kinetic energy has been converted into thermal energy, but that energy is no longer useful for work.

One-Dimensional Analysis of Work Done By a Variable Force

If the force on an object varies across the distance the object is moved, then a simple product will not yield the work. If we consider the work performed by a variable force in one dimension, then we are assuming that the directions of the force and the displacement are the same. The magnitude of the force will depend on the position of the particle. In order to calculate the amount of work performed by a variable force over a given distance, we should first divide the total displacement into a number of intervals, each with a width of Δx. We may then say that the amount of work performed during any one interval is $\Delta W = \boldsymbol{F}_{avg}\Delta x$, where $\boldsymbol{F}_{avg}$ is the average force over the interval Δx. We can then say that the total amount of work performed is the sum of all work performed during the various intervals. By reducing the interval to an infinitesimal length, we obtain the integral:

$$W = \int_{x_1}^{x_2} \boldsymbol{F}_x dx$$

This integral requires that the force be a known function of x.

WORK PERFORMED BY A SPRING

If we move a block attached to a spring from point x_i to point x_f, we are doing work on the block, and the spring is also doing work on the block. To determine the work done by the spring on the block, we can substitute $\boldsymbol{F}$ from Hooke's law into our equation for work performed by a variable force, and arrive at this measure: $W = \frac{k(x_i{}^2 - x_f{}^2)}{2}$. This work will be positive if $x_i{}^2 > x_f{}^2$, and negative if the opposite is true. If $x_i = 0$ and we decide to call the final position x, then we may change our equation: $W = \frac{-kx^2}{2}$. It is important to keep in mind that this is the work done by the spring. The work done by the force that moves the block to its final position will be a positive quantity.

Like all simple harmonic oscillators, springs operate by **storing and releasing potential energy**. The amount of energy being stored or released by a spring is equal to the magnitude of the work done by the spring during that same operation. The total potential energy stored in a spring can be calculated as $PE = \frac{kx^2}{2}$. Neglecting the effects of friction and drag, an object oscillating on a spring will continue to do so indefinitely, since total mechanical energy (kinetic and potential) is conserved. In such a situation, the period of oscillation can be calculated as $T = 2\pi \times \sqrt{\frac{m}{k}}$.

DISPLACEMENT, VELOCITY, AND ACCELERATION

DISPLACEMENT

When something changes its location from one place to another, it is said to have undergone **displacement**. If we can determine the original and final position of the object, then we can determine the total displacement with the equation $\Delta\boldsymbol{x} = x_f - x_i$, where x_f is the final position and x_i is the initial position.

If the object has moved in the positive direction, then the final position will be greater than the original position, so we can say that the change was positive. If the final position is less than the original, however, displacement will be negative. Displacement along a straight line is an example of a vector quantity; it has both a magnitude and a direction. If an object travels from position $x = -5$ cm to $x = 5$ cm, it has undergone a displacement of 10 cm. If it traverses the same path in the opposite direction, its displacement is -10 cm. A vector that spans the object's displacement in the direction of travel is known as a displacement vector, with units of length.

Review Video: Displacement in Physics
Visit mometrix.com/academy and enter code: 236197

DETERMINING POSITION

In order to determine anything about the motion of an object, we must first locate it. In other words, we must be able to describe its position relative to some reference point, often called an **origin**. If we consider the origin as the zero point of an axis, then positive values correspond to the location of an object one direction, and negative values are locations in the exact opposite direction. If a particle is located 5 cm from the origin in the positive direction of the x-axis, its location is said to be $x = 5$ cm. If another particle is 5 cm from the origin in the negative direction of the x-axis, its position is $x = -5$ cm. These two particles are 10 cm apart. A vector whose starting point is the origin and whose endpoint is the location of an object is that object's position vector, with units of length.

Velocity

Difference between Speed and Velocity

Often, people confuse the words *speed* and *velocity*. There is a significant difference. The average velocity is based on the amount of displacement, a vector. Alternately, the average speed is based on the distance covered or the path length. The equation for speed is:

$$\textbf{average speed} = \frac{\textbf{total distance traveled}}{\textbf{change in time}}$$

Notice that we used total distance and *not* change in position, because speed is path-dependent.

If the plane traveling between cities had needed to fly around a storm on its way, making the distance traveled 50 miles greater than the distance the car traveled, the plane would still have the same total displacement as the car.

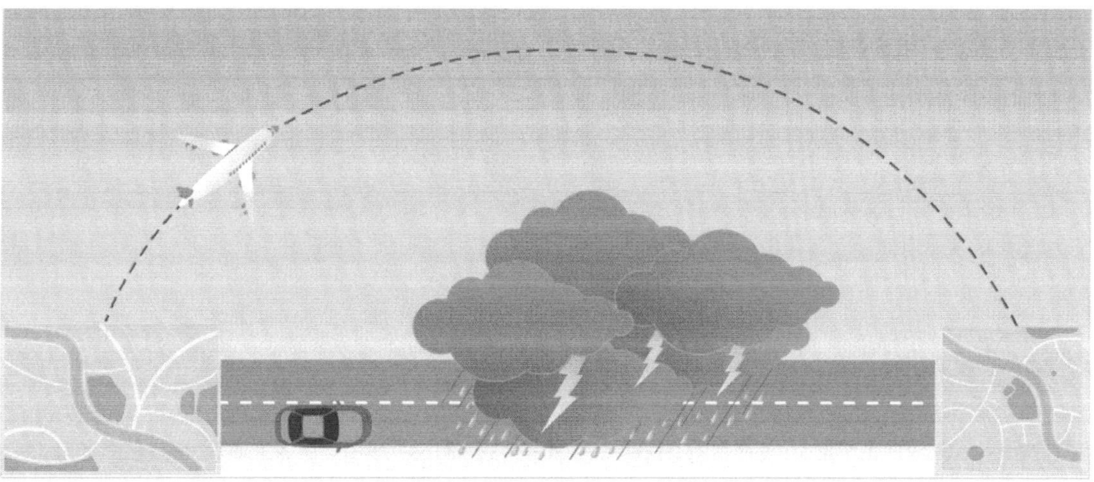

For this reason, the average speed can be calculated:

$$\text{plane average speed} = \frac{150 \text{ miles}}{1 \text{ hour}} = 150 \text{ miles per hour}$$

$$\text{car average speed} = \frac{100 \text{ miles}}{2 \text{ hours}} = 50 \text{ miles per hour}$$

Instantaneous Velocity

There are two types of velocity that are commonly considered in physics: average velocity and instantaneous velocity. In order to obtain the **instantaneous velocity** of an object, we must find its average velocity and then try to decrease Δt as close as possible to zero. As Δt decreases, it approaches what is known as a limiting value, bringing the average velocity very close to the instantaneous velocity. Instantaneous velocity is most easily discussed in the context of calculus-based physics.

Average Velocity

If we want to calculate the **average velocity** of an object, we must know two things. First, we must know its **displacement**, or the distance it has covered relative to a starting point. Second, we must know the **time it took to cover this distance**. Once we have this information, the formula for average velocity is: $\boldsymbol{v}_{avg} = \frac{(x_f - x_i)}{(t_f - t_i)}$, where the subscripts i and f denote the initial and final values of the position and time. In other words, the average velocity is equal to the change in position divided by the change in time. This calculation will indicate the average distance that was covered per unit of time. Average velocity is a vector and will always point in the same direction as the displacement vector (since time is a scalar and always positive).

Acceleration

Acceleration is the **change in the velocity** of an object. Like velocity, acceleration may be computed as an average or an instantaneous quantity. To calculate average acceleration, we may use the equation $\boldsymbol{a}_{avg} = \frac{v_f - v_i}{t_f - t_i}$, where the subscripts i and f denote the initial and final values of the velocity and time. The so-called instantaneous acceleration of an object can be found by reducing the time component to the limiting value until instantaneous velocity is approached. Acceleration will be expressed in units of distance divided by time squared; for instance, meters per second squared. Like position and velocity, acceleration is a vector quantity and will therefore have both magnitude and direction.

Review Video: Velocity and Acceleration
Visit mometrix.com/academy and enter code: 671849

Kinematics

Kinematic Equations

The phenomenon of constant acceleration allows physicists to construct a number of helpful equations. Perhaps the most fundamental equation of an object's motion is the **position equation**:

$$x_f = x_i + \boldsymbol{v}_i t + \frac{1}{2}\boldsymbol{a}t^2$$

If the object is starting from rest at the origin, this equation reduces to $x_f = \frac{\boldsymbol{a}t^2}{2}$. The position equation can be rearranged to give the **displacement equation**:

$$\Delta\boldsymbol{x} = \boldsymbol{v}_i t + \frac{1}{2}\boldsymbol{a}t^2$$

If the object's acceleration is unknown, the position or displacement may be found by the equation:

$$\Delta\boldsymbol{x} = \frac{(\boldsymbol{v}_f + \boldsymbol{v}_i)t}{2}$$

If the position of an object is unknown, the velocity may be found by the equation:

$$\boldsymbol{v}_f = \boldsymbol{v}_i + \boldsymbol{a}t$$

Similarly, if the time is unknown, the velocity after a given displacement may be found by the equation:

$$v_f = \sqrt{(v_i{}^2 + 2a\Delta x)}$$

Concept of Projectile Motion

When we discuss **projectile motion**, we are referring to the movement of an object through two dimensions during a free fall. Two-dimensional motion may be described using the same equations as one-dimensional motion, but two equations must be considered simultaneously. For basic equations for projectile motion, it is often assumed that the rate of gravitational acceleration on the Earth is $\boldsymbol{g} = 9.8\ \text{m/s}^2$, and that the effect of air resistance can be ignored (Note: take care with the sign on gravitational acceleration make sure that it always points toward the Earth). If a projectile is launched under such ideal conditions, we may say that its initial velocity is $\boldsymbol{v}_0 = v_0 \cos\theta\ \mathbf{i} + v_0 \sin\theta\ \mathbf{j}$. These two velocity components are sometimes written as $\boldsymbol{v}_{0x}$ and $\boldsymbol{v}_{0y}$, respectively.

Projectile Motion Example

Simple projectile motion occurs when an object is in the air and experiencing only the force of gravity. We will disregard drag for this topic. Some common examples of projectile motion are thrown balls, flying bullets, and falling rocks. The characteristics of projectile motion are:

1. The horizontal component of velocity doesn't change
2. The vertical acceleration due to gravity affects the vertical component of velocity

Because gravity only acts downwards, objects in projectile motion only experience acceleration in the y-direction (vertical). The horizontal component of the object's velocity does not change in flight. This means that if a rock is thrown out off a cliff, the horizontal velocity (think of the shadow if the sun is directly overhead) will not change until the ball hits the ground.

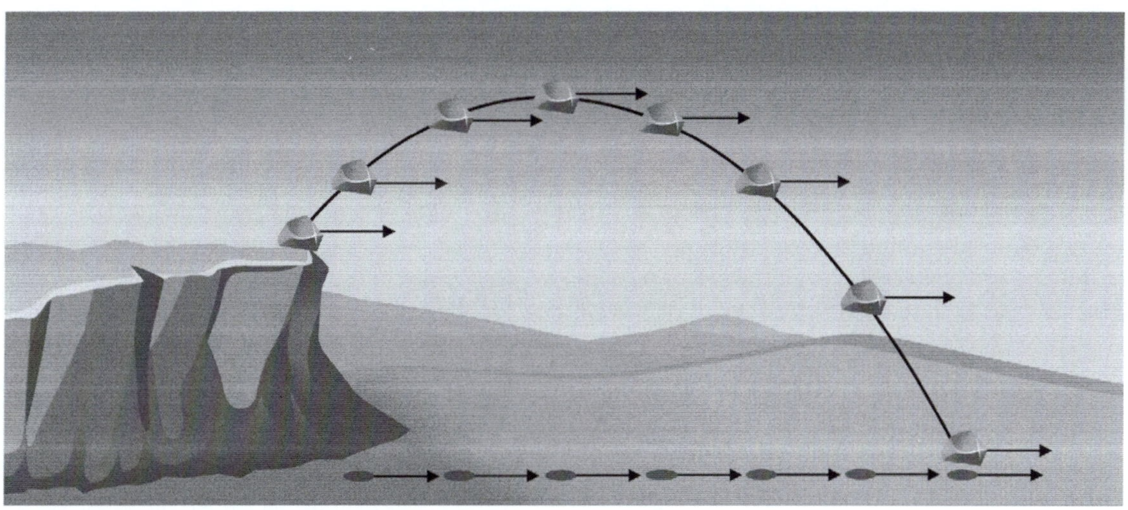

The velocity in the vertical direction is affected by gravity. Gravity imposes an acceleration of $g = 9.8\frac{\text{m}}{\text{s}^2}$ or $32\frac{\text{ft}}{\text{s}^2}$ downward on projectiles. The vertical component of velocity at any point is equal to:

$$\textbf{vertical velocity} = \textbf{original vertical velocity} - \textbf{g} \times \textbf{time}$$

When these characteristics are combined, there are three points of particular interest in a projectile's flight. At the beginning of a flight, the object has a horizontal component and a vertical component giving it a large speed. At the top of a projectile's flight, the vertical velocity equals zero, making the top the slowest part of travel. When the object passes the same height as the launch, the vertical velocity is opposite of the initial vertical velocity, making the speed equal to the initial speed.

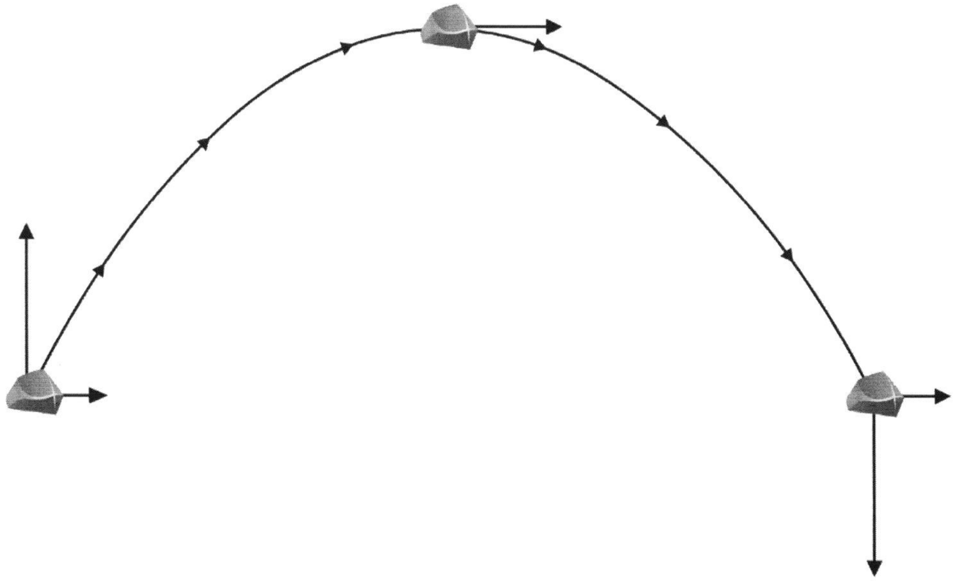

If the object continues falling below the initial height from which it was launched (e.g., it was launched from the edge of a cliff), it will have an even greater velocity than it did initially from that point until it hits the ground.

Review Video: Projectile Motion
Visit mometrix.com/academy and enter code: 719700

Example: If a cannon located at a height of 5 m above ground level fires a cannonball 250 m/s at an angle of $\frac{\pi}{6}$ from the horizontal, how far will the cannonball travel before hitting the ground?

When the cannonball hits the ground, it has been displaced by –5 m in the y-direction. Solving for the components of initial velocity yields $\boldsymbol{v}_{0x} = 216.5$ m/s and $\boldsymbol{v}_{0y} = 125$ m/s. Setting up the y-direction displacement equation results in the following: $-5 = 125t_f - 4.9{t_f}^2$. Solving for t_f yields an impact time of around 25.5 seconds. To find the horizontal distance covered, set up the displacement equation for the x-direction: $\Delta\boldsymbol{x} = \boldsymbol{v}_{0x}t_f + \frac{1}{2}\boldsymbol{a}_x(t_f)^2$. Since we ignore the effects of air resistance, acceleration in the x-direction is zero, yielding a flight distance of 5,530 m.

Uniform Circular Motion

We may say that a particle is in **uniform circular motion** when it is traveling in a circle, or circular arc, and at a constant speed. Crucially, we must note that such a particle is accelerating, even though the magnitude of its velocity does not change. This is because velocity is a vector, and consequently, any change in its direction is an acceleration. So, if we take two points on an arc of radius, r, separated by an angle, θ, and want to determine the time it will take a particle to move between these two points at a constant speed, $|\boldsymbol{v}|$, we can use the equation: $\Delta t = \frac{r\theta}{|\boldsymbol{v}|}$. The quantity $\frac{|\boldsymbol{v}|}{r}$ is often written as $\boldsymbol{\omega}$, or angular velocity, having units of radians per second, so the time may also be computed as $\Delta t = \frac{\theta}{\boldsymbol{\omega}}$. The speed, or absolute value of the velocity, of an object in uniform circular motion is also called the tangential speed, because the object is always moving in a direction tangent to the circle. Similarly, an increase in the magnitude of this velocity is called **tangential acceleration**.

A very important component of uniform motion is the centripetal acceleration. This is the acceleration that changes the direction of the velocity vector to follow the circular arc. It is directed toward the center of the circle or arc and is described by $\boldsymbol{a}_c = \frac{|\boldsymbol{v}|^2}{r} = r\boldsymbol{\omega}^2$.

Relative Motion and Inertial Reference Frames

When we describe motion as being **relative**, we mean that it can only be measured in relation to something else. If a moving object is considered as it relates to some stationary object or arbitrary location, it will have a different measured velocity than it would if it were compared to some other object that is itself in motion. In other words, the measure of an object's velocity depends entirely on the reference frame from which the measurement is taken. When performing measurements of this kind, we may use any reference point we like. However, once we have decided on a reference point, we must be consistent in using it as the basis for all of our measurements, or else we will go astray. Additionally, if we want to be able to apply Newton's laws of motion or Galilean principles of relativity, we must select an **inertial reference frame**: that is, a reference frame that is not accelerating or rotating. A car traveling at a constant speed in a straight line is an inertial reference frame. A car moving in uniform circular motion is not.

An object's velocity with respect to a frame fixed to the Earth can be computed by measuring its velocity from any inertial reference frame and combining that velocity by vector addition with the velocity of the inertial frame with respect to the Earth. For instance, if a man is traveling in the x-direction at 20 m/s, and he throws a rock out the window at a relative velocity of 15 m/s in the y-direction, the rock's velocity with respect to the Earth is found by adding the two vectors:

$$\boldsymbol{v}_r = 20\mathbf{i} + 15\mathbf{j} \text{ m/s}$$

LAWS OF MOTION

NEWTON'S LAWS

NEWTON'S FIRST LAW

Before Newton formulated his laws of mechanics, it was generally assumed that some force had to act on an object continuously in order to make the object move at a **constant velocity**. Newton, however, determined that unless some other force acted on the object (most notably friction or air resistance), it would continue in the direction it was pushed at the same velocity forever.

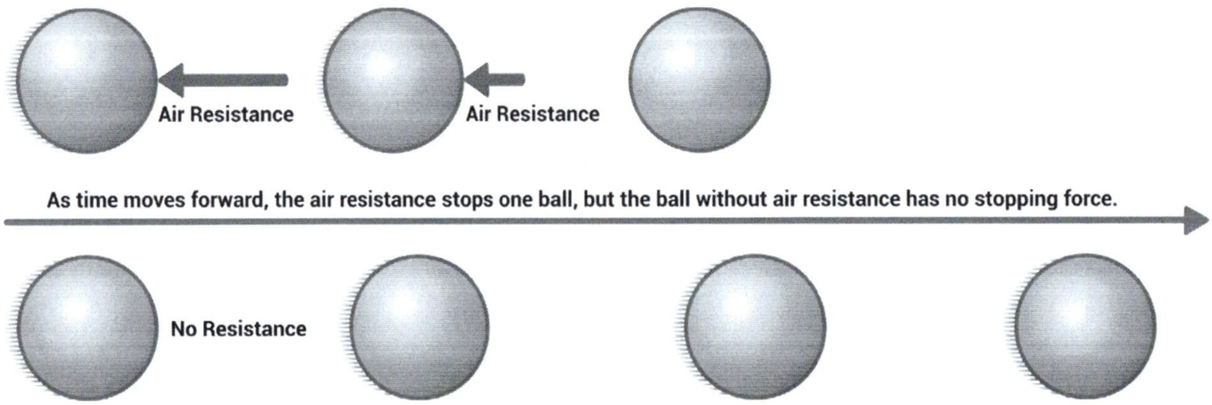

In this light, a body at rest and a body in motion are not all that different, and Newton's first law makes little distinction. It states that a body at rest will tend to remain at rest, while a body in motion will tend to remain in motion. This tendency of a body to remain in its present state of motion is referred to as **inertia**. In order for the body's state of motion to change, it must be acted on by a non-zero net force. **Net force** is the vector sum of all forces acting on a body. If this vector sum is zero, then there is no unbalanced force, and the body will remain in its present state of motion. It is important to remember that this law only holds in inertial reference frames.

Review Video: Newton's First Law of Motion
Visit mometrix.com/academy and enter code: 590367

NEWTON'S SECOND LAW

Newton's second law states that an **object's acceleration** is directly proportional to the net force acting on the object, and inversely proportional to the object's mass. It is generally written in equation form $\boldsymbol{F} = m\boldsymbol{a}$, where $\boldsymbol{F}$ is the net force acting on a body, m is the mass of the body, and $\boldsymbol{a}$ is its acceleration. It is important to note from this equation that since the mass is always a positive quantity, the acceleration vector is always pointed in the same direction as the net force vector. Of course, in order to apply this equation correctly, one must clearly identify the body to which it is being applied. Once this is done, we may say that $\boldsymbol{F}$ is the vector sum of all forces acting on that body, or the net force. This measure includes only those forces that are external to the body; any internal forces, in which one part of the body exerts force on another, are discounted.

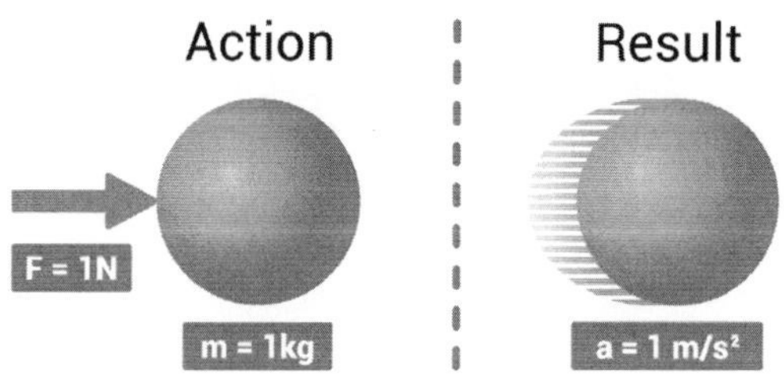

Newton's second law somewhat encapsulates his first, because it includes the principle that if no net force is acting on a body, the body will not accelerate. As was the case with his first law, Newton's second law may only be applied in inertial reference frames.

Review Video: Newton's Second Law of Motion
Visit mometrix.com/academy and enter code: 737975

NEWTON'S THIRD LAW

Newton's third law of motion can be stated as: **for every force, there is an equal and opposite force**. When a hammer strikes a nail, the nail hits the hammer just as hard. If we consider two objects, A and B, then we may express any contact between these two bodies with the equation $\boldsymbol{F}_{AB} = -\boldsymbol{F}_{BA}$. It is important to note in this kind of equation that the order of the subscripts denotes which body is exerting the force. Although the two forces are often referred to as the **action** and **reaction** forces, in physics there is really no such thing. There is no implication of cause and effect in the equation for Newton's third law. At first glance, this law might seem to forbid any movement at all. We must remember, however, that these equal, opposite forces are exerted on different bodies with different masses, so they will not cancel each other out.

As an example, consider two spring-based scales, both tipped on their sides, with the weighing surfaces facing each other. If scale #1 is pressing scale #2 into the wall, it exerts a force on scale #2, measurable by the reading on scale #2. However, because scale #1 is exerting a force on scale #2, scale #2 is exerting a force on scale #1 with an opposite direction, but the same magnitude.

Review Video: Newton's Third Law of Motion
Visit mometrix.com/academy and enter code: 838401

EQUILIBRIUM AND FRICTION

NORMAL FORCE

The word *normal* is used in mathematics to mean perpendicular, and so the force known as normal force should be remembered as the perpendicular force exerted on an object that is resting on some other surface. For instance, if a box is resting on a horizontal surface, we may say that the normal force is directed upwards through the box (the opposite, downward force is the weight of the box). If the box is resting on a wedge, the normal force from the wedge is not vertical but is perpendicular to the surface.

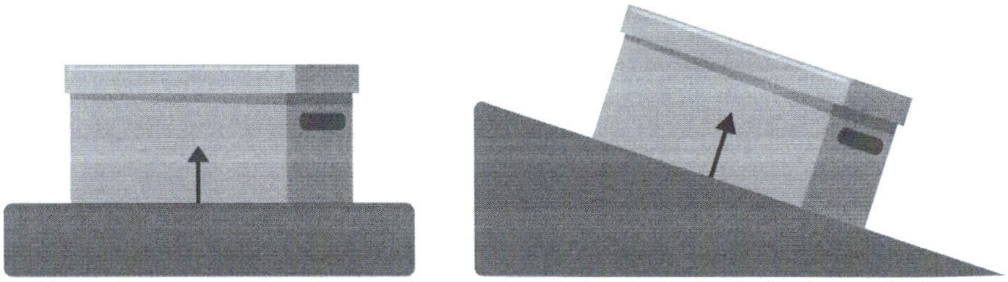

STATIC AND KINETIC FRICTIONAL FORCES

In order to illustrate the concept of friction, let us imagine a book resting on a table. As it sits there, the force of its weight ($\boldsymbol{W}$) is equal and opposite to the normal force ($\boldsymbol{N}$). If, however, we were to exert a force ($\boldsymbol{F}$) on the book, attempting to push it to one side, a frictional force ($\boldsymbol{f}$) would arise, equal and opposite to our force. This kind of frictional force is known as **static frictional force**.

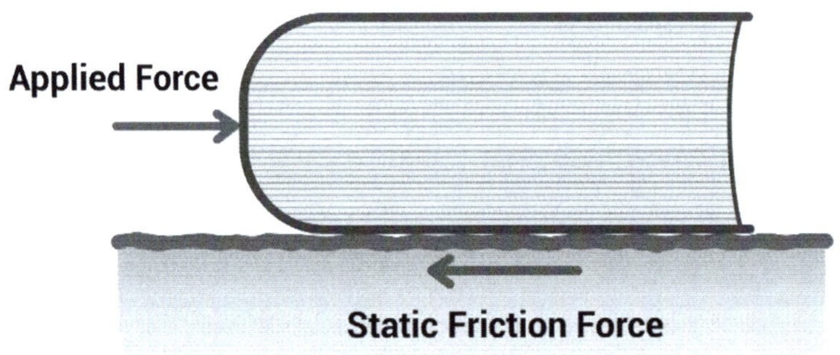

As we increase our force on the book, however, we will eventually cause it to accelerate in the direction of our force. At this point, the frictional force opposing us will be known as **kinetic frictional force**.

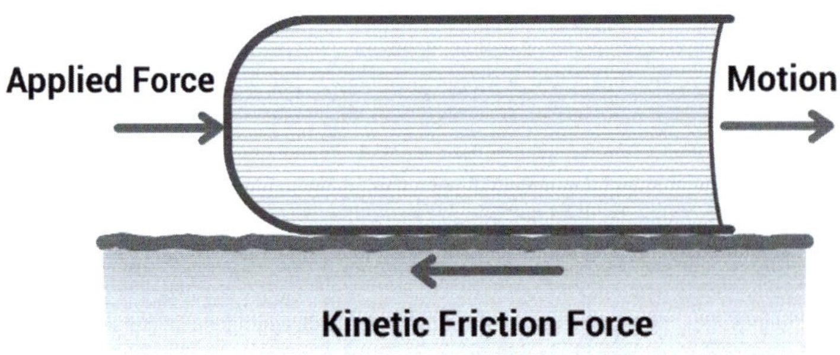

For the most part, kinetic frictional force is lower than static frictional force, and so the amount of force needed to maintain the movement of the book will be less than that needed to initiate movement. For wheels and spherical objects on a surface, static friction at the point of contact allows them to roll, but there is a frictional force that resists the rolling motion as well, due primarily to deformation effects in the rolling material. This is known as rolling friction, and tends to be much smaller than either static or kinetic friction.

Coefficient of Friction

If an object does not move when a horizontal force $\boldsymbol{F}$ is applied, then the **static frictional force ($\boldsymbol{f_s}$)** is exactly equal and opposite to $\boldsymbol{F}$, i.e., $\boldsymbol{f}_s = -\boldsymbol{F}$. Static frictional force has a maximum value, however, which is expressed as $\boldsymbol{f}_{s,max} = \mu_s N$, in which μ_s is the coefficient of static friction, and N is the magnitude of the normal force. If the magnitude of horizontal force applied to an object exceeds the maximum value of static friction, the object will begin to move. Once the object has begun to slide, the frictional force will generally decrease. The value to which the frictional force will diminish is expressed as $\boldsymbol{f}_k = \mu_k N$, in which μ_k is the coefficient of kinetic friction. For objects inclined to roll, such as balls or wheels, there is a rolling frictional force that resists the continued rolling of such an object. This force is expressed by $\boldsymbol{f}_r = \mu_r N$, in which μ_r is the coefficient of rolling friction. All of these frictional coefficients are dimensionless. Since the value of the frictional force depends on the interaction of the body and the surface, it is usually described as friction between the two.

Review Video: Friction
Visit mometrix.com/academy and enter code: 716782

Equilibrium

We may say that an object is in a **state of equilibrium** when it has a **constant linear momentum ($\boldsymbol{p}$)** at its center of mass, or when **angular momentum ($\boldsymbol{L}$) is also constant about the center of mass**. In other words, a wheel may be in equilibrium when it is spinning at a constant speed, and a hockey puck may be in equilibrium as it slides across ice. These are both examples of **dynamic equilibrium**. The phrase **static equilibrium**, however, is reserved for objects in which both linear and angular momentum are at zero. An object sitting on a table could be considered as being in static equilibrium.

Balanced Forces

An object is in equilibrium when the sum of all forces acting on the object is zero. When the forces on an object sum to zero, the object does not accelerate. Equilibrium can be obtained when forces in the y-direction sum to zero, forces in the x-direction sum to zero, or forces in both directions sum to zero.

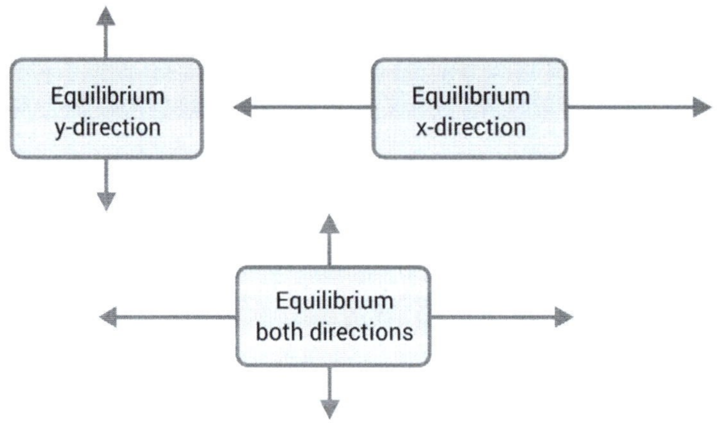

In most cases, a problem will provide one or more forces acting on an object and ask for a force to balance the system. The force will be the opposite of the current force or sum of current forces.

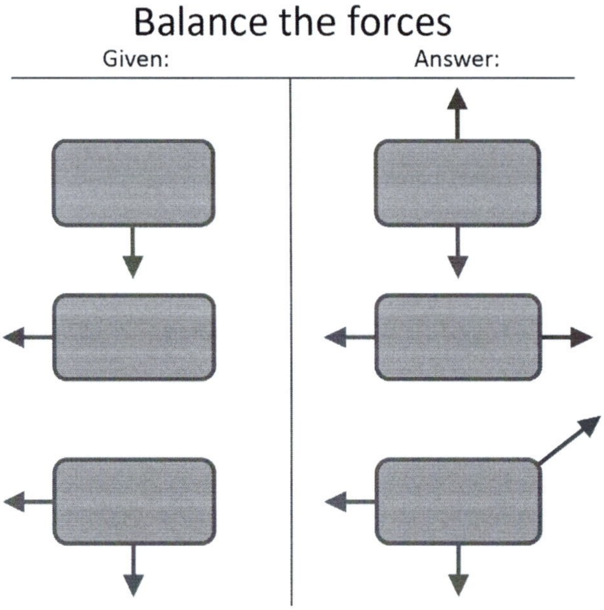

Using Equilibrium Conditions

For a **body in equilibrium**, the net force vector and the net torque vector will both be equal to zero. For the most common cases, two-dimensional systems, these conditions can be fully expressed by one or two force summation equations and one torque summation equation. Torque summations may be taken about any point on the body, though strategic placement can make calculations simpler. To determine the **torque exerted by a force**, multiply the magnitude of the force by the perpendicular distance to the point of interest. It will be necessary to decide in advance which direction of torque (clockwise or counterclockwise) will be considered positive.

For example, if we have a bar of known mass, m, that is suspended by cables at each end and whose center of mass is two thirds of the way along its length, L, we can use the equilibrium conditions to determine the tension in each cable. Gravity exerts a force of $-m\boldsymbol{g}$ on the bar's center of mass.

Translational equilibrium conditions tell us that $\boldsymbol{T}_1 + \boldsymbol{T}_2 - m\boldsymbol{g} = 0$. Setting the total torque about the center of mass equal to zero, considering counterclockwise torque to be positive, yields the equation $\boldsymbol{T}_2\left(\frac{L}{3}\right) - \boldsymbol{T}_1\left(\frac{2L}{3}\right) = 0$. Solving these equations results in $\boldsymbol{T}_1 = \frac{m\boldsymbol{g}}{3}$ and $\boldsymbol{T}_2 = \frac{2m\boldsymbol{g}}{3}$. This result makes sense since the center of mass is closer to the second cable.

Translational and Rotational Equilibrium

If a body is in **translational equilibrium**, then its linear momentum will be constant, and there will be a net force of zero. Likewise, a body in rotational equilibrium will have a constant angular momentum, and again there will be a net torque of zero. Both of these equations are vector equations, and as such are both equivalent to three scalar equations for the three dimensions of motion, though in most instances, only one or two dimensions will be considered at a time. We may say that the two requirements for a body to be in equilibrium are that the vector sum of all the external forces acting on the body must be zero, and the vector sum of all the external torques acting on the body must also be zero. Conversely, if we are told that a body is in equilibrium, we may assume that both of these conditions will hold, and that we can use them to find unknown forces or torques.

Conservation of Energy and Momentum

Applying Conservation of Rotational Energy and Angular Momentum

A metal hoop of mass m and radius r is released from rest at the top of a hill of height h. Assuming that it rolls without sliding and does not lose energy to friction or drag, what will be the hoop's angular and linear velocities upon reaching the bottom of the hill?

The hoop's initial energy is all potential energy, $PE = mgh$. As the hoop rolls down, all of its energy is converted to **translational** and **rotational kinetic energy**. Thus, $mgh = \frac{1}{2}m\boldsymbol{v}^2 + \frac{1}{2}I\boldsymbol{\omega}^2$. Since the moment for a hoop is $I = mr^2$, and $\boldsymbol{\omega} = \frac{\boldsymbol{v}}{r}$, the equation becomes $mgh = \frac{1}{2}m\boldsymbol{v}^2 + \frac{1}{2}mr^2\left(\frac{\boldsymbol{v}^2}{r^2}\right)$, which further simplifies to $gh = \boldsymbol{v}^2$. Thus, the resulting velocity of the hoop is $\boldsymbol{v}_f = \sqrt{gh}$, with an angular velocity of $\boldsymbol{\omega}_f = \frac{\boldsymbol{v}_f}{r}$. Note that if you were to forget about the energy converted to rotational motion, you would calculate a final velocity of $\boldsymbol{v}_f = \sqrt{2gh}$, which is the **impact velocity** of an object dropped from height h.

Angular momentum, $\boldsymbol{L}$, of an object is defined as its moment of inertia multiplied by its angular velocity, or $\boldsymbol{L} = I\boldsymbol{\omega}$. Consider a planet orbiting the sun with an elliptical orbit where the small radius is r_S and large radius is r_L. Find the angular velocity of the planet when it is at distance r_S from the sun if its velocity at r_L is $\boldsymbol{\omega}_L$.

Since the size of a planet is almost insignificant compared to the interplanetary distances, the planet may be treated as a single particle of mass m, giving it a moment about the sun of $I = mr^2$. Since the gravitational force is incapable of exerting a net torque on an object, we can assume that the planet's angular momentum about the sun is a constant, $\boldsymbol{L}_L = \boldsymbol{L}_S$. Thus, $m{r_L}^2\boldsymbol{\omega}_L = m{r_S}^2\boldsymbol{\omega}_S$. Solving this equation for $\boldsymbol{\omega}_S$ yields $\boldsymbol{\omega}_S = \boldsymbol{\omega}_L\left(\frac{r_L}{r_S}\right)^2$.

Mass-Energy Relationship

Because mass consists of atoms, which are themselves formed of subatomic particles, there is an energy inherent in the composition of all mass. In other words, it would require a significant input of energy to form all the atoms in a given mass from their most basic particles. This rest energy is the energy that Einstein refers to in his famous mass-energy relation $E = mc^2$, where c is the speed of light in a vacuum. In theory, if all the particles in a given mass were converted directly to energy (e.g., by matter-antimatter annihilation), it would give off energy $E = mc^2$. For example, if this were to happen to a single gram of mass, the resulting outburst of energy would be $E = 9 \times 10^{13}$ J, enough energy to provide power for over 2,000 average households for a whole year.

In some nuclear reactions, small amounts of mass are converted to energy. The amount of energy released can be calculated through the same relation, $E = mc^2$. Most such reactions involve mass losses on the order of 10^{-30} kg.

WEIGHT AND MASS

WEIGHT

Not to be confused with mass (quantity of matter), weight the term for the force due to the gravitational attraction between the masses of the two bodies. This force is described by the expression $\frac{Gm_1m_2}{r^2}$, where G is the gravitational constant, m_1 and m_2 are the masses of the two objects, and r is the distance between the centers of mass. Since the majority of humans are concerned with events close to the surface of the Earth, one of the masses (M_E) and the distance (R_E) are essentially constant and are combined into $\boldsymbol{g}$, which is the acceleration due to gravity near the surface of the Earth $\left(\boldsymbol{g} = \frac{GM_E}{(R_E)^2}\right)$. Thus, we can express weight as $\boldsymbol{W} = m\boldsymbol{g}$. Since it is a force, the SI unit for weight is the Newton. As a vector, $\boldsymbol{W}$ can be expressed as either $-mg\mathbf{j}$ or $-W\mathbf{j}$, in which $\mathbf{j}$ is the direction on the axis pointing away from the Earth.

Review Video: Mass, Weight, Volume, Density, and Specific Gravity
Visit mometrix.com/academy and enter code: 920570

Electricity and Magnetism

ELECTRICAL PROPERTIES OF MATERIALS

COMMON MEANS OF TRANSFERRING ELECTRICAL CHARGE

Charge is transferred in three common ways: conduction, induction, and friction. **Conduction**, as the name implies, takes place between conductive materials. There must be a point of contact between the two materials and a potential difference, such as when a battery is connected to a circuit. **Induction also requires conductive materials. It occurs when a conductive material encounters a changing magnetic field**. The change can be the result of a changing magnetic field or the material moving within a constant magnetic field. Charge transfer due to **friction** does not require conductive materials. When two materials are rubbed together, electrons may be transferred from one to the other, leaving the two materials with equal and opposite charges. This is observed when shoes are dragged across a carpeted floor.

Review Video: Charging by Conduction
Visit mometrix.com/academy and enter code: 502661

CONDUCTORS, INSULATORS, AND SEMICONDUCTORS

In many materials, electrons are able to move freely; these are known as **conductors**. Due to their atomic structure and delocalized electrons, **metals** tend to be the best conductors, particularly copper and silver. Highly conductive wires are instrumental in creating low-resistance pathways for electrons to travel along within a circuit.

Other materials naturally inhibit the movement of charge and are known as **insulators**. Their electrons are tightly held by the individual constituent atoms. Glass, pure water, wood, and plastic are all insulators. Insulators are necessary in circuits to prevent charge from escaping to undesirable places, such as an operator's hand. For this reason, most highly conductive materials are covered by insulators.

Semiconductors, as the name suggests, are materials that only partially conduct electrical charge. The elements silicon and germanium are both common semiconductors, and are frequently used in microelectronic devices because they allow for tight control of the rate of conduction. In many cases, the conduction ability of semiconductors can be controlled by adjusting the temperature of the material.

Doping Semiconductors

Resistivity is the physical property of resistance of different materials: metals, which easily conduct electricity, have low resistivity; insulators have high resistivity; and the resistivity of **semiconductors** falls in between (example: silicon). **Doping** is the process of mixing different semiconductor atoms in order to control conductivity of the material. **N-type semiconductors** have an excess of electrons as a result of the doping process; when an electric field is applied, a negative pole forms due to the buildup of negatively charged electrons (example: silicon doped with antimony). **P-type semiconductors** have a shortage of electrons; when an electric field is applied, a positive pole forms (example: silicon doped with boron).

Introduction to Circuits and Current

Electric Current

Charge is a physical property of particles. For the particles of an atom, protons have a positive charge of +1, neutrons have no charge, and **electrons** have a negative charge of −1. Like charges repel each other (positive and positive or negative and negative), and opposite charges attract (negative and positive). The **net charge** of an atom or molecule can be found by adding up all the protons and electrons that it contains. When dealing with charge on the macro level, it is helpful to aggregate the charges in a material with different units. The coulomb is the SI unit for charge and is equivalent to about 6.24×10^{18} charged particles.

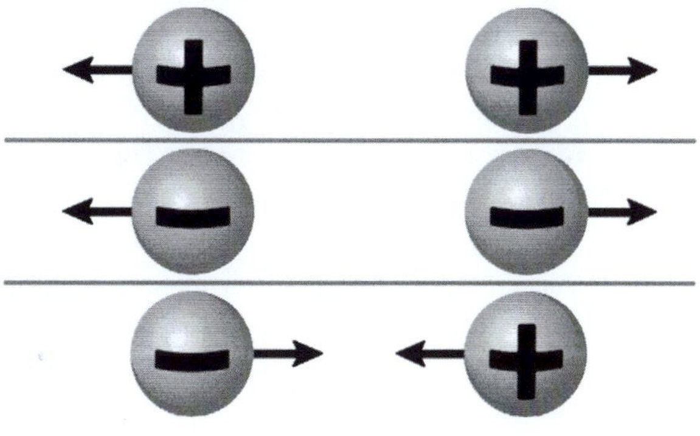

Electric current is the net rate of flow of charge (electrons) past a specific point, as in a wire or circuit. Current (represented by I in equations) is measured in amperes or amps (A). An ampere is equal to one coulomb per second $\left(\mathrm{A} = \frac{\mathrm{C}}{\mathrm{s}}\right)$. Ammeters are tools that can be used to measure current.

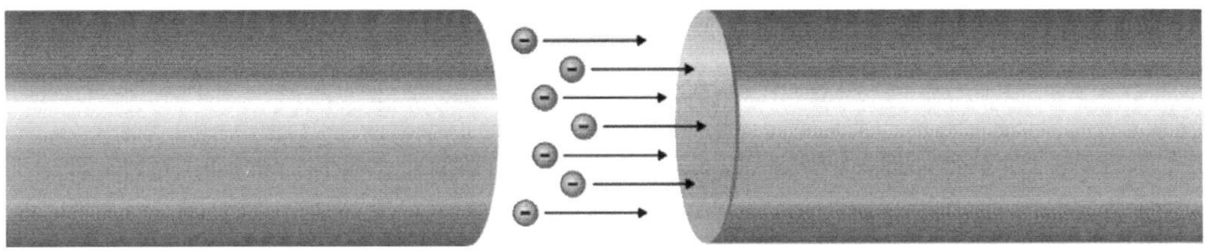

Electric current carries energy much like moving balls carry energy.

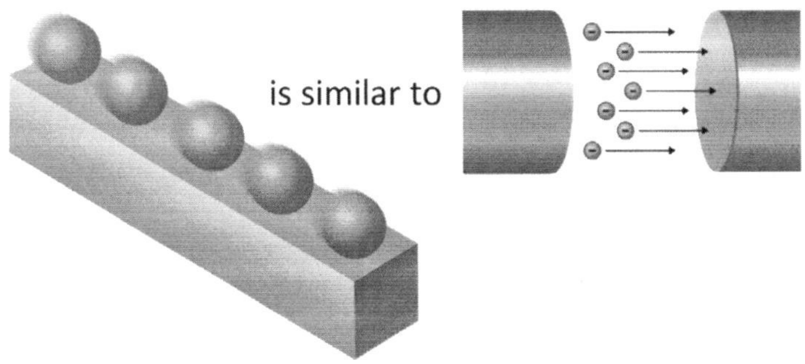

Electron flow theory states that electrons (e^-) flow from the negative terminal to the positive terminal. **Electricity** is the form of energy that exists statically (potential energy) with an accumulation of protons or electrons or dynamically with their movement (current).

Review Video: Electric Charge
Visit mometrix.com/academy and enter code: 323587

Alternating and Direct Current

For circuits with **direct current** (DC), when current flows in only one direction, the voltage and current are constant. Direct current is supplied by batteries and is used in cell phones, ships, and planes. **Alternating current** (AC), in which current periodically reverses direction, can be produced using generators and is used for land-based applications (including in homes) because less power is lost when electricity travels long distances. In the United States, AC electricity is supplied most commonly at 120 V and 240 V.

Electric Potential

Electric potential energy is the energy stored in a charge by virtue of its proximity to other charged regions. It can be calculated in the same way as calculating the amount of work required to move it to that location from an infinite distance away. The work required to move a charge of magnitude q from infinity to a distance r from another charge of magnitude Q is calculated to be $PE_e = W = \frac{kQq}{r}$, where k is the **electrostatic constant**.

Electric potential, V, is closely related to electric potential energy. The potential due to a charge Q can be found by dividing the electric potential energy of another charge q by its magnitude, $V = \frac{PE_e}{q}$, or by the equation $V = \frac{kQ}{r}$.

The difference between the electric potential of two points is known as **voltage**. It is measured in volts, or joules per coulomb. Since it is impractical to find a point of zero absolute electric potential, for each system a reference point or ground is defined, to which all other points in the system may be related. Voltage is similar to gravitational potential energy.

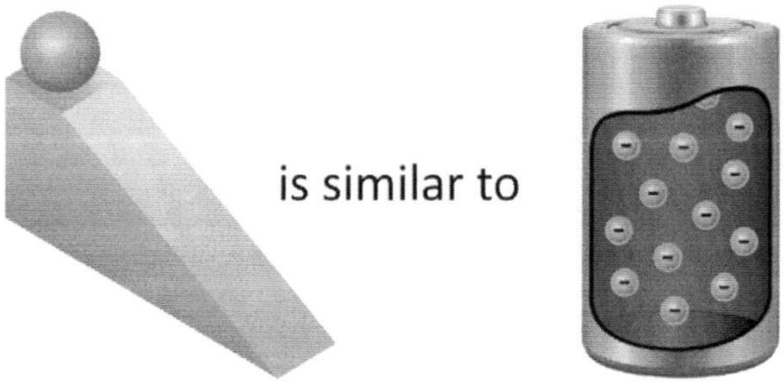

ELECTROMOTIVE FORCE AND COMMON EMF DEVICES

A force that maintains a potential difference between two locations in a circuit is known as an **electromotive force (emf)**. A device that creates this force is referred to as an **emf device**. The most common emf device is the battery. **Batteries** operate by converting chemical energy stored in the electrolyte, the internal chemical material, into electrical energy. The reaction causes a lack of electrons on the cathode, and when the circuit is connected, they flow from the anode, creating a flow of current. The electrolyte's composition also determines whether the battery is classified as acidic or alkaline, and wet or dry. Another emf device is the **photocell**, also commonly called the solar cell, since most photocells are powered by the sun. These operate by absorbing photons, which cause the electrons to be excited and flow in a current, a process of converting light energy into electrical energy. A third type of emf device is the **generator**. This device converts mechanical energy to electrical energy. A generator may be powered by such diverse sources as gasoline engines, flowing water, or even manually powered cranks. These devices utilize a rotating shaft to spin a coil within a magnetic field, creating a potential difference by induction.

OHM'S LAW

If we were to apply the exact same potential difference between the ends of two geometrically similar rods, one made of copper and one made of glass, we would create vastly different currents. This is because these two substances have different **resistances**. **Ohm's Law** describes the relation between applied voltage and induced current, $V = IR$. This is one of the most important tools of circuit analysis. Resistance, then, can be calculated as $R = \frac{V}{I}$. The SI unit for resistance is the **ohm** (Ω), equal to a volt per ampere. When a component is placed into a circuit to provide a specific resistance, it is known as a **resistor**. For a given potential difference, the greater the resistance is to the current, the smaller the current will be. Electrical resistance is much like friction, resisting flow and dissipating energy.

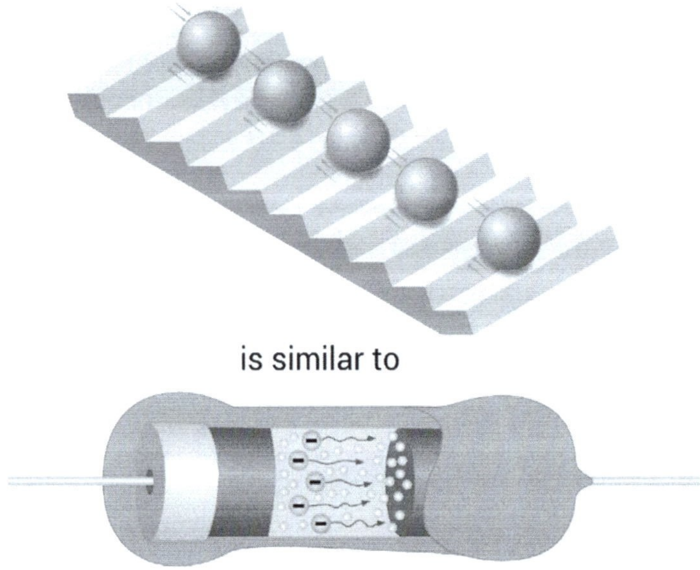

If we wish to look instead at the quality of the material of which the resistor is made, then we must consider resistivity. **Resistivity**, ρ, is a physical property of every material, which, if known, can be used to size a resistor for a specific resistance. Resistance is dictated by both the material and the dimensions of the resistor, given by the relation $R = \frac{\rho L}{A}$, where L is the effective length of the resistor and A is the effective cross-section. Alternatively, an unknown resistivity may be calculated by rearranging the equation as $\rho = \frac{RA}{L}$.

Resistivity will often change with temperature. In these cases, the relevant resistivity may be calculated $\rho = p_{ref}\left(1 + \alpha\left(T - T_{ref}\right)\right)$, where α is the resistivity proportionality constant and T is the material temperature.

Review Video: Resistance of Electric Currents
Visit mometrix.com/academy and enter code: 668423

Ground

Grounding is the process of neutralizing the charge of an object by removal of excess electrons to or donation of additional electrons by a much larger object (example: the Earth). This ground or large object can seemingly infinitely donate or accept electrons without mathematically significant changes to its net voltage. Examples of grounds include lighting rods and the round component of a three-pronged plug, as used for home appliances. Current does not usually flow through air, but lightning is the visible current that results when charge builds up in clouds; lightning rods provide a safe, low-resistance ground so the high-voltage current is less likely to be destructive. The round component of three-pronged plugs serves as one of the residential applications of this concept.

ENERGY AND POWER

Electric circuits operate by **transferring** electrical energy from one location in the circuit to another. Some devices in a circuit can store and release energy while other devices, like resistors, dissipate energy. **Power** is a measure of the rate at which energy is stored, released, transferred, or dissipated. It is measured in watts (W), or joules per second. Power is calculated by $P = VI$. The amount of power being released by a 9-V battery producing a current of 5 A is 45 W. When calculating the amount of power dissipated by a resistor, Ohm's Law can be combined with the power equation to form two other equations for power, $P = I^2R$ and $P = \frac{V^2}{R}$.

When power consumption over long periods of time needs to be measured, it will often be measured in units of kilowatt-hours, which is the amount of energy consumed at a rate of 1 kW over the course of an hour. One kilowatt-hour is equal to 3,600 kJ.

CAPACITORS AND DIELECTRICS

Capacitors are devices used in circuits to store energy in the form of electric fields. They are most often composed of two oppositely charged parallel plates separated by a medium, generally air. This medium is referred to as the capacitor's **dielectric**.

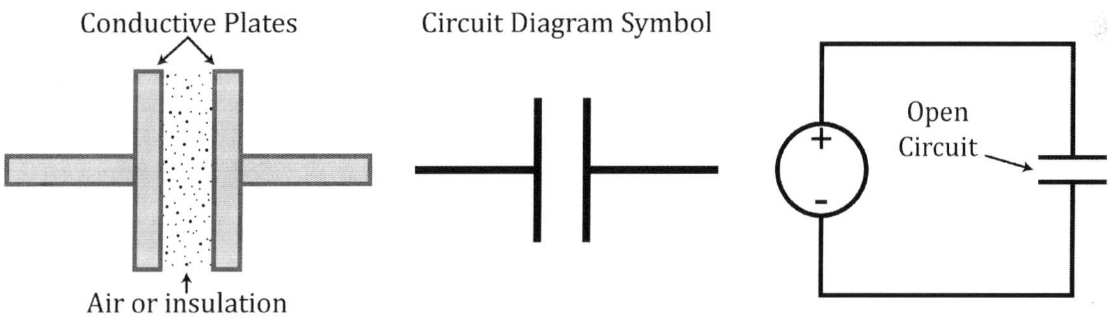

The dielectric material dictates the amount of energy in the electric field and, consequently, the amount of energy that can be stored by the capacitor. The measurable quality of a capacitor is known as its **capacitance**, which is defined as the amount of charge that it can store per volt of potential difference. This is given by the equation $C = \frac{Q}{V}$, with capacitance having units of farads or coulombs per volt. Physically, the capacitance depends on three things: the **area** of the parallel plates, the **separation distance** between them, and the **dielectric** material. For cases in which the separation distance is insignificant compared to the area, the capacitance can be found by the equation $C = \frac{\varepsilon A}{d}$, where ε is the permittivity of the dielectric material. Often, instead of being given the permittivity, we will be given the dielectric constant, κ, which is the ratio of the permittivities of the material and air, $\kappa = \frac{\varepsilon}{\varepsilon_{air}}$. This yields an obvious result of $\kappa_{air} = 1$.

The energy stored in a capacitor can be calculated in three different ways: $E = \frac{CV^2}{2} = \frac{Q^2}{2C} = \frac{VQ}{2}$. Another quantity associated with capacitors is the electric field energy density, η. This energy density is found by $\eta = \frac{\varepsilon E^2}{2}$.

INDUCTORS

When current passes through a wire coil, a magnetic field develops. An **inductor** is an electrical component made of a coil of wire that can store energy and opposes the rate of change of alternating current flowing through it; however, direct current passes through easily. They can be used as filters, sensors, motors, and transformers.

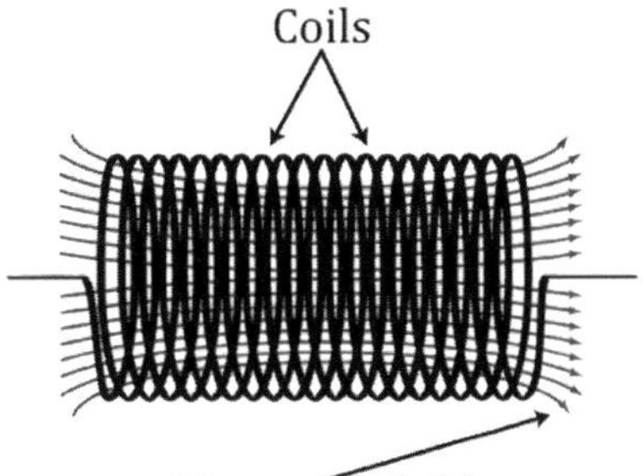

Circuit Diagram Symbol

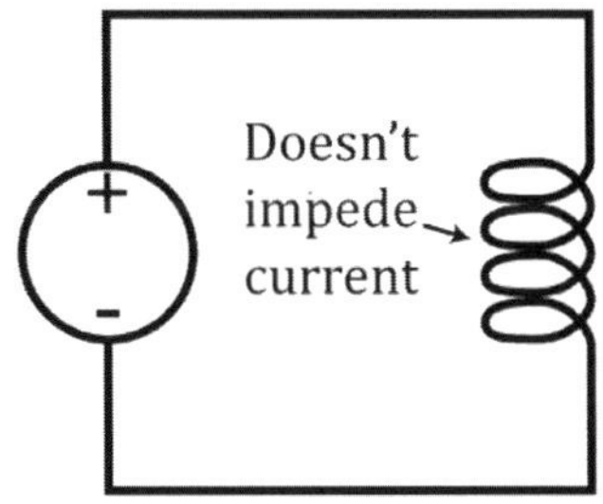

Inductance is the measure of ability of an inductor to resist changes in current. **Faraday's law of induction describes the ways voltage** or electromagnetic frequency can be generated by changing the magnetic environment in a coil of wire by moving a magnet within it, changing the external magnetic field of the magnet, or changing the area of the coil.

Capacitors and Inductors in AC Circuits

Capacitors and inductors both oppose immediate acceptance of the flow reversal of alternating current. This opposition is referred to as **impedance** and is similar to resistance, also having units of ohms, but unlike resistance, impedance is a complex value, meaning that it may have an **imaginary component** as well as a **real component**. For ideal capacitors and inductors, impedance is purely imaginary, and for ideal resistors, impedance is purely real. It is only when combining the effects of these devices that the full expression for impedance, Z, is necessary: $Z = R + X_i$, where $i = \sqrt{(-1)}$. X is a quantity known as reactance. For capacitors, $X_c = \frac{1}{\omega C}$, where ω is the angular frequency of the current, and for inductors, $X_L = \omega L$.

Other Electrical Components

Diodes

Diodes are a basic component of circuits, but they can't be described using Ohm's law; they operate as an electrical "valve", only allowing current to pass in one direction. This allows them to rectify alternating current by converting it to direct current, which is preferred or necessary for some applications. A common example is the light-emitting diode (LED) bulb, which emits light when powered more efficiently than regular light bulbs.

Circuit Diagram Symbol

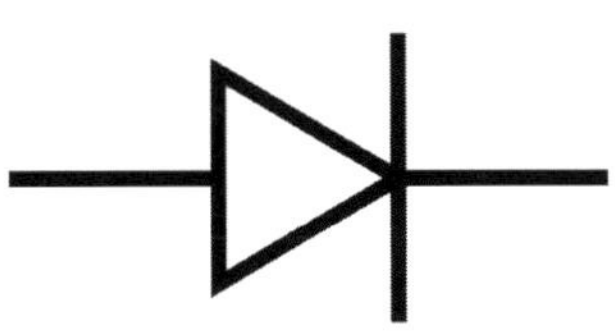

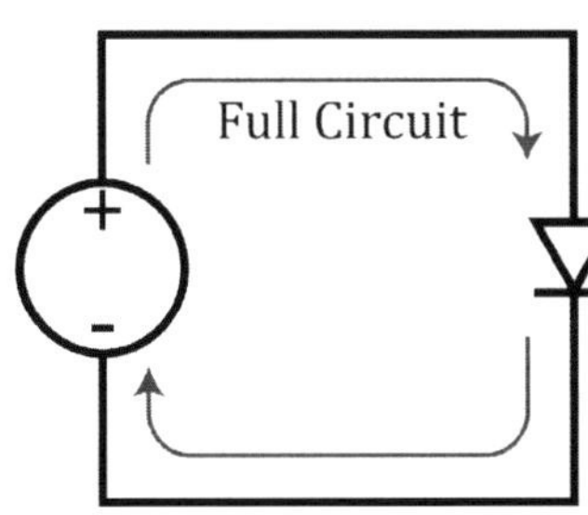

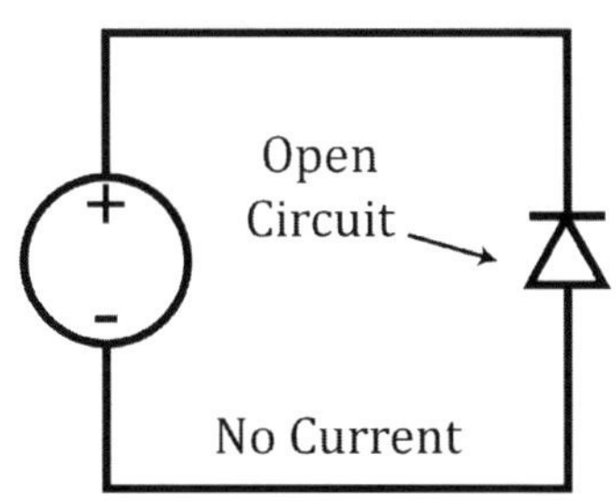

A p-n junction diode is formed by fusing a p-type semiconductor and an n-type semiconductor. It is considered a solid-state device because electricity flows through solid material rather than a vacuum tube. The p-region of the junction is positively charged and the n-region is negatively charged. Reverse bias occurs when the diode is connected such that the positive voltage is applied to the n-region; forward bias occurs when the positive voltage is applied to the p-region.

Transistors

A bipolar junction transistor, p-n-p or n-p-n, consists of two p-n junction diodes arranged back-to-back with three electrical leads or terminals: the emitter, the collector, and the base. Transistors are used to boost electrical signals or switch them on or off at high speeds. A large current flows from the emitter to the collector, and a smaller current entering through the base lead can be used to control the larger collector current.

Transformers

Transformers are devices made of two or more coils of wire that use induction to transfer electricity between circuits. A **step-up transformer**'s input (primary) voltage is lower than its output (secondary) voltage; and a **step-down transformer**'s input voltage is higher than its output voltage. This allows for electricity to be to be generated safely at a lower voltage (example: 12 kV), passed through a step-up transformer for transport through power lines at high voltage (example: 400 kV), and passed through step-down transformers for distribution and use (example: 240 V residential use).

Motors and Generators

Motors use electromagnetic induction to convert electrical energy (electricity) to mechanical energy (motion). In a **DC motor**, torque is produced by magnetic force, which results from current passing through coil located in a magnetic field. They have been around for more than 100 years and are simple, inexpensive, and easy to maintain. In **AC (synchronous) motors**, torque is produced the same way as in DC motors, but much higher current is required, and they are inefficient. **Induction (asynchronous) motors** are more common, and they rotate a magnetic field in order to induce alternating current.

Generators use electromagnetic induction to convert mechanical energy to electrical energy. **AC generators** mechanically turn a coil in a magnetic field to produce voltage output and induce alternating current.

Simple Circuits

The Use of Ohm's Law and Kirchhoff's Laws

Circuit analysis is the process of determining the **current** or **voltage drop** across devices of interest in a circuit. Ohm's Law is useful in doing this since it definitively relates the current to the voltage drop for resistors, $V = IR$. Kirchhoff's voltage law (KVL) states that if you sum the voltage drops across all devices in any closed loop of a circuit, the sum will always be zero, $V_1 + V_2 + \cdots + V_n = 0$. This law is particularly useful if there are multiple closed-loop pathways in a circuit. Kirchhoff's current law (KCL) states that the amount of current entering a point must equal the amount of current leaving, $I_{in} = I_{out}$. This law may also be expanded to apply to the current entering and leaving a larger region of a circuit. In any given circuit analysis, it may be necessary to use all three of these laws.

Another important principle to remember in an ideal circuit is that any two points connected by only wire are at equal voltage. Only devices on the circuit may change the voltage. In actual practice, however, all wire has some amount of resistance. A battery that provides an EMF of V_B is only able to deliver a voltage to the circuit of $V = V_\text{B} - IR_\text{B}$, where R_B is the internal resistance of the battery.

To express this concept in an ideal circuit, we would need to add a small resistor in series after the battery.

Measuring Devices

There are several devices that allow various quantifiable properties of a circuit to be measured to a great degree of accuracy. An **ammeter** is a device placed in series with a circuit to measure the current through that location. Ideally, an ammeter has as little internal resistance as possible to prevent altering the current it is trying to measure. A **voltmeter** measures the voltage or potential difference between two locations in a circuit. It has two leads that are connected in parallel with the circuit and consists of a very high resistance and an ammeter in series. This allows only a very small amount of current to be diverted through the voltmeter, but enough to determine the voltage by Ohm's Law. A **galvanometer** is the primary working component of an ammeter. It operates based on the idea that a wire in a magnetic field will experience a force proportional to the amount of current it is carrying. It converts the observed current into a dial reading. A **potentiometer** is a variable resistor, often controlled by a knob, that allows an operator to control the amount of voltage or current provided to a given circuit. They are commonly used in volume-control knobs. Potentiometers can also be called voltage dividers. Their use in circuit measurement is for finding voltages by comparing them to known voltages. A **multimeter** is a device that combines the functions of all the above devices into one. In addition to voltage, current, resistance and capacitance, they can typically measure inductance, frequency, and other quantities.

Resistance in Series Circuits

A **series circuit** is a loop through which charge can flow along only one path. Resistance of resistors (labeled R_n) lined up in series is additive, so $R_{total} = R_1 + R_2 + R_3 + \cdots$ for all resistors in that series. Current (I) is consistent in all locations throughout a closed series circuit, so $I_{battery} = I_{R_1} = I_{R_2} = I_{R_3} = \cdots$, regardless of the number of elements in the series. Charge at the positive terminal of the battery experiences a **voltage drop** (ΔV), or loss of potential energy, as it passes through each resistor, such that its voltage will be zero at the negative terminal of the battery. Therefore, $\Delta V_{battery} = \Delta V_1 + \Delta V_2 + \Delta V_3 + \cdots$, where each ΔV_n represents the voltage drop across each resistor in series.

Problem Solving with Series Circuits

Using the labeled diagram of a series circuit, solve the following problems:

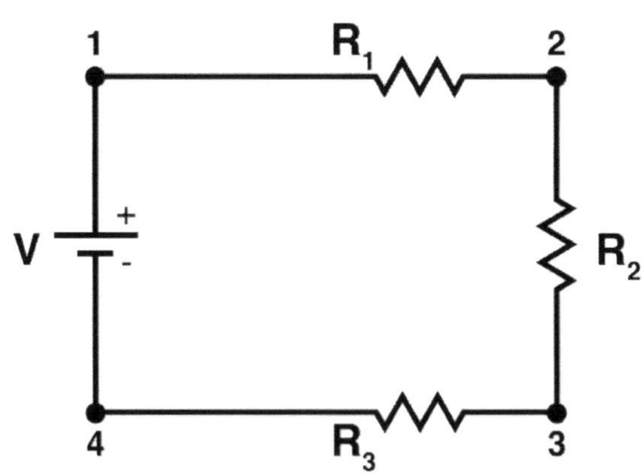

V = Voltage source (battery)

R = Resistor

Example 1: If each resistor is 3 Ω and the battery is 9 V, what is the current at each of the indicated corners?

Step 1:	Step 2:	Step 3:
Given: $R_1 = R_2 = R_3 = 3\ \Omega$ Equation: $R_{total} = R_1 + R_2 + R_3$ Solve: $\mathrm{R_{total}} = 3\ \Omega + 3\ \Omega + 3\ \Omega = 9\ \Omega$	Given: $V_{battery} = 9\text{ V}$ Equation: $I = \frac{V}{R}$ Solve: $I_{battery} = \frac{9\text{ V}}{9\ \Omega} = 1\text{ A}$	Because current is the same throughout the circuit, current at each corner is the same: $I_{total} = I_1 = I_2 = I_3 = I_4 = 1\ A$

Example 2: If the current at point 3 is 4 Amps, and each resistor is 1 Ω, what is the battery voltage?

Step 1:	Step 2:	Step 3:
Given: $I_3 = 4\text{ A}$ The circuit is in series so current is the same throughout: $I_{total} = 4\text{ A}$	Given: $R_1 = R_2 = R_3 = 1\ \Omega$ Equation: $R_{total} = R_1 + R_2 + R_3$ Solve: $R_{total} = 1\ \Omega + 1\ \Omega + 1\ \Omega = 3\ \Omega$	Equation: $V_{total} = I_{total}(R_{total})$ Solve: $V_{total} = (4\text{ A})(3\ \Omega) = 12\text{ V}$

Resistance in Parallel Circuits

Parallel circuits provide multiple pathways for current to follow, which adjusts the way that current, voltage, and resistance interact when compared to series circuits. Because current (I) can follow multiple pathways, it is divided among those pathways at each branch, so $I_{total} = I_1 + I_2 + I_3 + \cdots$, where 1, 2, and 3 represent each unique branch. In this example, there are 3.

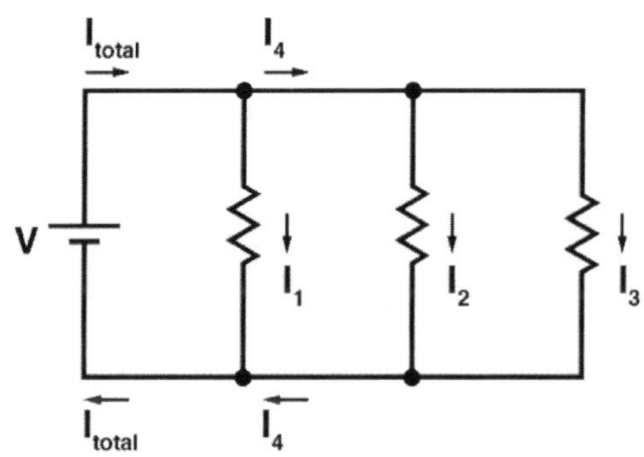

Equivalent resistance (R_{eq}) is the amount of resistance in a parallel circuit, represented as if there was only one resistor in series. All of the resistors in parallel can be simplified using the following equation:

$$\frac{1}{R_{eq}} = \frac{1}{R_1} + \frac{1}{R_2} + \frac{1}{R_3}$$

Because a charge will only pass through one resistor in the parallel circuit and not all three, the voltage drop across each resistor will be the same as that of the battery. Therefore, voltage drops for parallel circuits follow this rule:

$$\Delta V_{battery} = \Delta V_1 = \Delta V_2 = \Delta V_3 = \cdots$$

Note: If multiple resistors exist on a branch of a parallel circuit, they are in series and should be added together ($R_{total} = R_1 + R_2 + R_3 + \cdots$) before dealing with them as part of a parallel circuit.

Problem Solving with Parallel Circuits

Using the labeled diagram of a parallel circuit, solve the following problems:

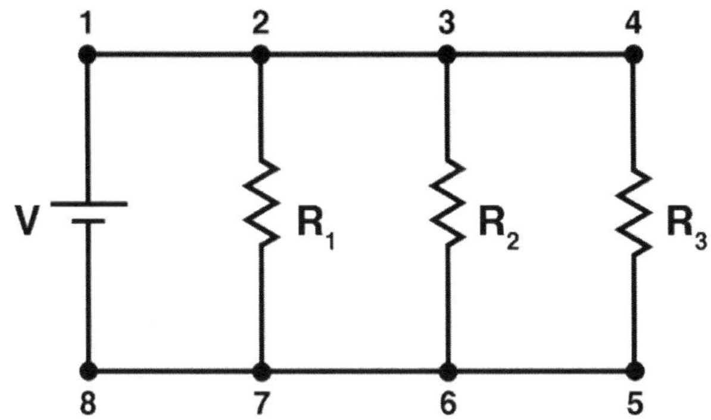

Example 1: If each resistor is 3 Ω and the battery is 9 V, what is the current at each of the indicated points (1-8) and each resistor?

Step 1:
Given: $R_1 = R_2 = R_3 = 3\ \Omega$
Equation: $\frac{1}{R_{eq}} = \frac{1}{R_1} + \frac{1}{R_2} + \frac{1}{R_3}$
Solve: $\frac{1}{R_{eq}} = \frac{1}{3\ \Omega} + \frac{1}{3\ \Omega} + \frac{1}{3\ \Omega}$

$$\frac{1}{R_{eq}} = \frac{3}{3\ \Omega}$$

$$R_{eq} = 1\ \Omega$$

Step 2:
Given: $V_{batt} = 9\text{ V}$
Equation: $I_{total} = \frac{V_{batt}}{R_{eq}}$
Solve: $I_{total} = \frac{9\text{ V}}{1\ \Omega} = 9\text{ A}$

Step 3:
Equation: $\Delta V_n = I_{R_n}(R_n)$
Solve: $I_{R_1} = \frac{9\text{ V}}{3\ \Omega} = 3\ A$
Current is the same for each branch in this example because $R_1 = R_2 = R_3 = 3\ \Omega$

Using this information and the additive properties of current in parallel circuits, the current through the following points and resistors is:

$$I_1 = I_2 = I_7 = I_8 = I_{total} = 9\text{ A}$$
$$I_3 = I_6 = 6\text{ A}$$
$$I_4 = I_5 = 3\text{ A}$$
$$I_{R_1} = I_{R_2} = I_{R_3} = 3\text{ A}$$

Example 2: If the current at point 4 is 4 Amps, and $R_1 = 3\ \Omega$; $R_2 = 2\ \Omega$; $R_3 = 6\ \Omega$, what is the total current?

Step 1:
Given: $R_3 = 6\ \Omega$; $I_4 = I_{R_3} = 4\ A$
Equation: $\Delta V_3 = I_{R_3}(R_3)$
Solve: $\Delta V_3 = (4\text{ A})(6\ \Omega) = 24\text{ V}$

Step 2:
Given: $R_1 = 3\ \Omega$; $R_2 = 2\ \Omega$
Equation: $I_n = \frac{V}{R_n}$
Solve: $I_1 = \frac{24\text{ V}}{3\ \Omega} = 8\text{ A}$

$$I_2 = \frac{24\text{ V}}{2\ \Omega} = 12\text{ A}$$

Step 3:
Equation: $I_{total} = I_1 + I_2 + I_3$
Solve: $I_{total} = 8\text{ A} + 12\text{ A} + 4\text{ A}$

$$I_{total} = 24\text{ A}$$

Capacitors and Inductors in Circuits

Capacitors have combination rules opposite to those of resistors. **Capacitors in series** have an equivalent value of:

$$C_{eq} = \left(\frac{1}{C_1} + \frac{1}{C_2} + \cdots + \frac{1}{C_n}\right)^{-1}$$

Capacitors in parallel have equivalence of:

$$C_{eq} = C_1 + C_2 + \cdots + C_n$$

Inductors follow the same combination rules as resistors. **Inductors in series** have an equivalent value of:

$$L_{eq} = L_1 + L_2 + \cdots + L_n$$

Inductors in parallel have equivalence of

$$L_{eq} = \left(\frac{1}{L_1} + \frac{1}{L_2} + \cdots + \frac{1}{L_n}\right)^{-1}$$

RC Circuits

An RC circuit consists of a battery wired in series with a **resistor** and a **capacitor**. Since a capacitor in steady state allows no current flow, it makes no sense to analyze a steady-state RC circuit. Instead, we will look at an RC circuit that has only just been connected, with the capacitor uncharged. The battery supplies voltage V_B to the circuit, and since the capacitor's voltage is initially zero, the voltage across the resistor is initially V_B, giving an initial current of $I = \frac{V_B}{R}$. As current flows, the charge on the capacitor increases, which in turn creates an opposing voltage that **lowers the voltage drop** across the resistor. Combining Ohm's Law with the KVL gives the voltage relation as $V_B = IR + \frac{Q}{C}$, where Q is the charge on the capacitor. Since the current is simply the transfer rate of the charge, this becomes a differential equation. Solving for charge and current yields the expressions $Q(t) = CV_B\left(1 - e^{-t/RC}\right)$ and $I(t) = \left(\frac{V_B}{R}\right)e^{-t/RC}$. The factor RC in the exponent is referred to as the circuit's time constant. It is the amount of time required for the capacitor to charge up to 63.2% capacity.

If the battery is removed from the circuit after the capacitor is charged and the circuit is reconnected with just the resistor and capacitor, the capacitor will begin to drain at the same rate that it was charged. The current magnitude will follow the same equation as before, though it will be in the opposite direction. The new expression for the charge will be $Q(t) = CV_B e^{-t/RC}$.

Power in AC Circuits

Unlike DC circuits, the power provided by an AC voltage source is not constant over time. Generally, an AC source will provide voltage in a sinusoidal pattern, $V(t) = V_{max}\sin(\omega t)$. Similarly, the current will be given by $I(t) = I_{max}\sin(\omega t)$. From our known equations for power, this yields a power of $P(t) = RI_{max}{}^2\sin^2(\omega t)$. However, if we wish to find the average power or the amount of energy transmission after a given period of time, we need to find some way to average voltage and current. The root-mean-square (rms) method, as the name suggests, takes the square root of the time average of the squared value. For sinusoidal functions such as the voltage and current here, the rms value is the maximum value divided by the square root of 2. For voltage and current, $V_{rms} = \frac{V_{max}}{\sqrt{2}}$, and $I_{rms} = \frac{I_{max}}{\sqrt{2}}$. In this way, the average power can be found as $P_{avg} = V_{rms} I_{rms}$, which can also be stated $P_{avg} = \frac{V_{max} I_{max}}{2}$. A DC source with supplied voltage V_B will provide the same power over time as an AC source if $V_B = V_{rms}$.

Properties of Magnets

Magnets and Magnetism

A **magnet** is any object or material, such as iron, steel, or magnetite (lodestone), that can affect another substance within its **field of force** that has like characteristics. Magnets can either attract or repel other substances. Magnets have two **poles**: north and south. Like poles repel and opposite poles (pairs of north and south) attract. The magnetic field is a set of invisible lines representing the paths of attraction and repulsion.

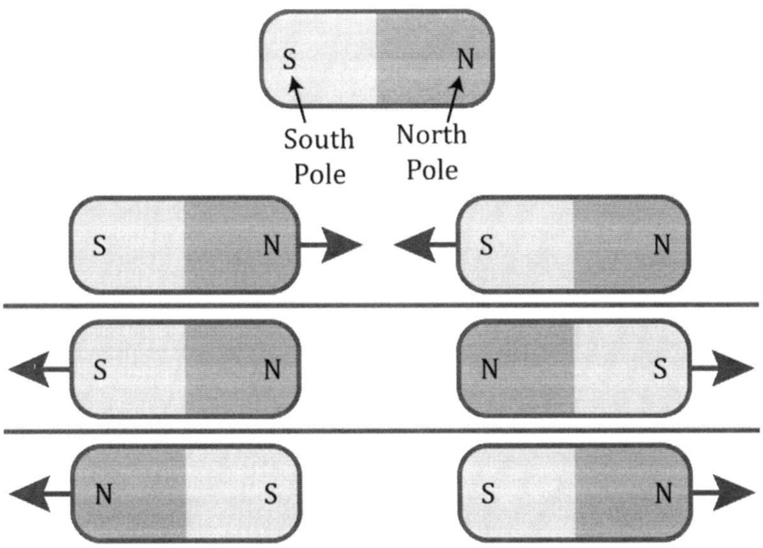

Magnetism can occur naturally, or ferromagnetic materials can be magnetized. Certain matter that is magnetized can retain its magnetic properties indefinitely and become a permanent magnet. Other matter can lose its magnetic properties. For example, an iron nail can be temporarily magnetized by stroking it repeatedly in the same direction using one pole of another magnet. Once magnetized, it can attract or repel other magnetically inclined materials, such as paper clips. Dropping the nail repeatedly will cause it to lose its magnetic properties.

Review Video: Magnets
Visit mometrix.com/academy and enter code: 570803

Magnetic Fields and Atomic Structure

Motion of a charge produces a **magnetic field**. Within an atom, the negatively-charged electrons moving around the nucleus each generate a magnetic field. In most materials, these fields all perfectly oppose and cancel each other, but in certain elements (e.g., iron, cobalt, nickel) the fields are not completely canceled, which makes each atom a tiny magnet. The strength and direction of a magnetic field is known as the magnetic moment.

Pairs of electrons moving in opposite directions cancel each other out, creating a **net magnetic field** of zero. Materials that have an unpaired electron are magnetic. Those with a weak attractive force are referred to as **paramagnetic materials**, while **ferromagnetic materials** have a strong attractive force. A **diamagnetic material** has electrons that are paired, and therefore does not typically have a magnetic moment. There are, however, some diamagnetic materials that have a weak magnetic field.

A magnetic field can be formed not only by a magnetic material, but also by electric current flowing through a wire. When a coiled wire is attached to the two ends of a battery, for example, an **electromagnet** can be formed by inserting a ferromagnetic material such as an iron bar within the coil. When electric current flows through the wire, the bar becomes a magnet. If there is no current, the magnetism is lost. A **magnetic domain** occurs when the magnetic fields of atoms are grouped and aligned. These groups form what can be thought of as miniature magnets within a material. This is what happens when an object like an iron nail is temporarily magnetized. Prior to magnetization, the organization of atoms and their various polarities are somewhat random with respect to where the north and south poles are pointing. After magnetization, a significant percentage of the poles are lined up in one direction, which is what causes the magnetic force exerted by the material.

Waves and Optics

Types of Waves and Their Characteristics

Transverse and Longitudinal Waves

Transverse waves have oscillations that are **perpendicular** to the direction of motion. A light wave is an example of a transverse wave. A group of light waves traveling in the same direction will be oscillating in several different planes. Light waves are said to be polarized when they are filtered such that only waves oscillating in a particular plane are allowed to pass, with the remainder being absorbed by the filter. If two such polarizing filters are employed successively and aligned to allow different planes of oscillation, they will block all light waves.

Longitudinal waves are waves that oscillate in the **same direction** as their primary motion. Their motion is restricted to a single axis, so they may not be polarized. A sound wave is an example of a longitudinal wave.

Velocity, Amplitude, Wavelength, and Frequency

- The **velocity of a wave**, v, is the rate at which it travels in a given medium. It is defined in the same way that velocity of physical objects is defined, a change in position divided by a change in time. A single wave may have a different velocity for every medium in which it travels. Some types of waves, such as light waves, do not require a medium.
- **Amplitude**, A, is one measure of a wave's strength. It is half the verticle distance between the highest and lowest points on the wave, the crest and trough, respectively. The vertical midpoint, halfway between the crest and trough, is sometimes called an equilibrium point, or a node.
- The **wavelength**, λ, is the horizontal distance between successive crests or troughs, or the distance between the first and third of three successive nodes.
- **Frequency**, f, is the number of crests or troughs that pass a particular point in a given period of time. It is the inverse of the period, the time required for the wave to cycle from one crest or trough to the next. Frequency is generally measured in hertz, or cycles per second.

Velocity, wavelength, and frequency are not independent quantities. They are related by the expression $v = \lambda f$. Note that amplitude, however, is independent from these quantities.

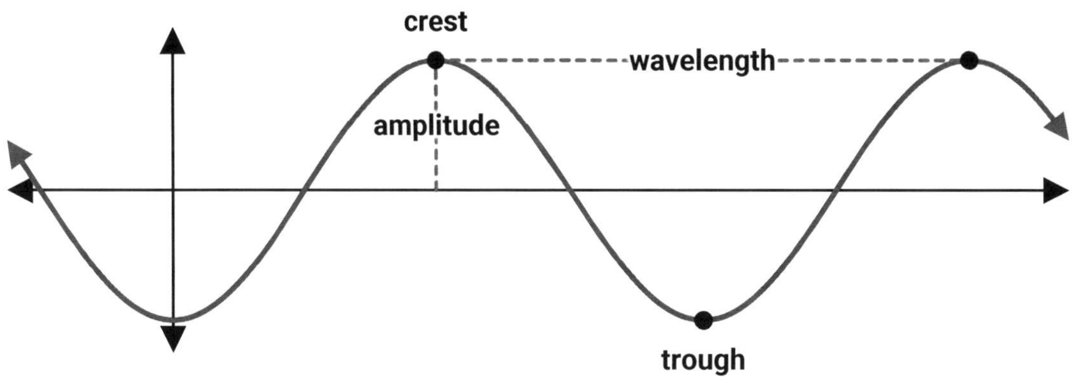

Intensity

The **intensity** I of a wave is equivalent to the flux through a given area over a period of time. It may also be defined as the energy density of a wave times its velocity. Intensity has units of watts per square meter. This can be seen in light waves as well. The intensity of light decreases as the distance from the light source increases. The inverse square law states that the intensity is inversely proportional to the square of the distance from the source. It is also directly proportional to the power P of the light source. This is shown mathematically by the expression $I = \frac{CP}{r^2}$, where C is the proportionality constant. This may be better understood by imagining the light waves emanating from a source as an expanding sphere. As their distance r from the source increases, the area over which they must divide themselves increases at a rate of $4\pi r^2$.

Standing Waves

A **standing wave** is the result of **interference** between two waves of the same frequency moving in opposite directions. These waves, although in constant motion, have certain points on the path where the amplitude is zero referred to as **nodes**. One example of a standing wave is a plucked guitar string. Since the string is attached at both ends, the fixed ends will be nodes. The primary tone will be that of the fundamental, or first harmonic, shown in the first figure below. It has a wavelength of twice the length of the string, L. The other three pictures below are those of the second through fourth harmonics. The nth harmonic has wavelength and frequency of $\lambda_n = \frac{2L}{n}$ and $f_n = \frac{nv}{2L}$, where v is wave velocity.

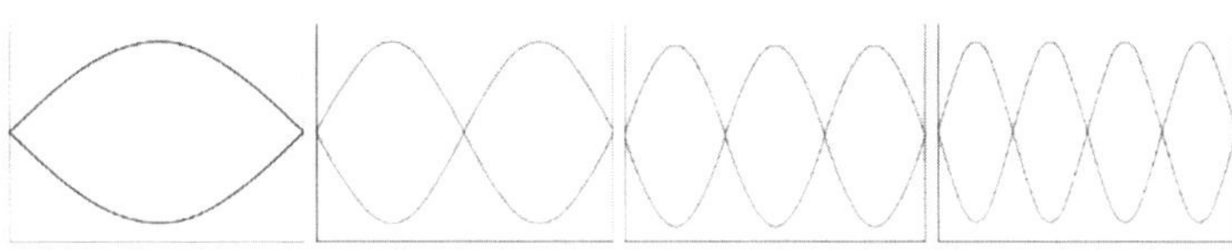

This same phenomenon occurs inside the tubes of wind instruments, though it is much more difficult to visualize. With a tube, however, there will be one or two open ends. Rather than a node, each open end will coincide with an **antinode**: that is, a crest or trough. For waves in a tube with two open ends, the wavelength and frequency calculations are the same as those for the plucked string. For the case with one open end, only the odd harmonics will be seen. The frequency of the nth harmonic becomes $f_n = \frac{nv}{4L}$, where n is odd.

Reflection, Refraction, Interference, and Diffraction of Waves

Reflection, Transmission, and Absorption

When light waves make contact with matter, they are either reflected, transmitted, or absorbed. If the light is **reflected** from the surface of the matter, the **angle** at which it hits the surface will be the same as the angle at which it leaves. If the ray of light is perpendicular to the surface, it will be reflected back in the direction from which it came.

When light is **transmitted** from one medium to another, its direction may be **altered** upon entering the new medium. This is known as **refraction**. The degree to which the light is refracted depends on the index of refraction, n, for each medium.

Light that is neither reflected nor transmitted will be **absorbed** by the surface and **stored as heat** energy. Because there are no ideal surfaces, most light and matter interaction will be a combination of two or even all three of these. Another result of imperfect surfaces is **scattering**, which occurs when waves are reflected in multiple directions. Rayleigh scattering is the specific case of a light wave being scattered by tiny particles that single out particular wavelengths. Dust particles in the atmosphere scatter primarily the blue wavelength of sunlight to give our sky a predominantly blue hue.

> **Review Video: Reflection, Transmission, and Absorption of Light**
> Visit mometrix.com/academy and enter code: 109410

Snell's Law

When light is transmitted from one medium to another, its direction may be altered upon entering the new medium. This is known as **refraction**. The degree to which the light is refracted depends on the index of refraction, n, for each medium. The **index of refraction** is a ratio of the speed of light in a vacuum to the speed of light in the medium in question, $n = \frac{c}{v_m}$. Since light can never travel faster than it does in a vacuum, the index of refraction is always greater than one. Snell's law gives the equation for determining the angle of refraction: $n_1 \sin(\theta_1) = n_2 \sin(\theta_2)$, where n is the index of refraction for each medium, and θ is the angle the light makes with the normal vector on each side of the interface between the two media.

We will examine a special case by trying to determine the angle of refraction for light traveling from a medium with $n_1 = 3$ to another medium with $n_2 = 1.5$. The light makes an angle $\theta_1 = 35°$ with the normal. Using Snell's law, we find that $\sin(\theta_2) = 1.15$. Since this is not mathematically possible, we conclude that the light cannot be refracted. This case is known as total internal reflection. When light travels from a more dense medium to a less dense medium, there is a minimum angle of incidence, beyond which all light will be reflected. This critical angle is $\theta_1 = \sin^{-1}\left(\frac{n_2}{n_1}\right)$. Fiber-optic cables make use of this phenomenon to ensure that the signal is fully reflected internally when it veers into the outer walls of the fiber.

Resonance and Natural Frequency

Every physical object has one or more **natural frequencies**, or frequencies at which it will naturally vibrate. The natural frequency is based on the object's dimensions, density, orientation, and other factors. If the object is acted on by a periodic force, it will vibrate at its natural frequency, regardless of the forcing frequency. If the excitation force is operating at the object's natural frequency, the object will experience **resonance**, in which the object receives all of the energy exerted by the excitation force. The amplitude of the vibration will increase rapidly and without bound until either the excitation force changes frequency or the natural frequency of the object is altered.

Diffraction and Dispersion

Diffraction occurs when a wave encounters a physical object. It includes phenomena such as bending, diverging, and other aperture effects. When light emerges from a single small slit, a rippling effect may be observed. The results of Young's double-slit experiment are due to diffraction as the light waves from these slits diverge. Similarly, light emerging from a circular aperture will project concentric light and dark rings due to diffraction. Diffraction grating is an arrangement of material whose reflective properties are intentionally varied at equally spaced intervals. Due to the arrangement, incident light is reflected in specific directions, known as diffraction orders, based on its wavelength.

Dispersion occurs when light consisting of multiple wavelengths enters a medium whose propagation behavior depends on the wavelength of transmitted light. This is what is observed when light passes through a prism, splitting it into its component colors.

Review Video: Diffraction of Light Waves
Visit mometrix.com/academy and enter code: 785494

Young's Double-Slit Experiment

Thomas Young's **double-slit experiment** visually demonstrated the interference between two sets of light waves. It consisted of shining light through two thin, closely spaced parallel slits and onto a screen. The interference between light waves from the two slits caused a pattern of alternately light and dark bands to appear on the screen, due to constructive and destructive interference, respectively. The dimensions of the experimental setup can be used to determine the wavelength of the light being projected onto the screen. This is given by the equation $\lambda = y\frac{d}{x}$, where y is the distance between the centers of two light bands, d is the distance between the slits, and x is the distance from the slits to the screen. Thin-film interference is caused when incident light is reflected both by a partially reflective thin layer on a surface and by the surface itself. This interference may be constructive or destructive.

Wave Superposition and Interference

The principle of **linear superposition** states that two or more waves occupying the same space create an effect equal to the sum of their individual amplitudes at that location. This is known as interference. If the resultant amplitude is larger than either individual amplitude, it is constructive interference. Similarly, if the interference reduces the effect, it is considered destructive.

Some special cases of interference are standing waves and beats, in which two waves having the same and nearly the same frequency, respectively, interfere with one another. Another concept related to interference is phase. If two waves with the same frequency are in phase, then they have perfectly constructive interference. The nodes in each wave will line up, as will the respective crests and troughs. If those same two waves are 180 degrees out of phase, they will experience perfectly destructive interference. The nodes will still line up, but each crest will be aligned with a trough, and vice versa. From this it can be seen that constructive interference results in a larger wave amplitude than destructive interference. If two identical waves are 180 degrees out of phase, the resultant wave will have zero amplitude. This effect is the design impetus for some noise-cancellation technology.

DOPPLER EFFECT

One common phenomenon of wave motion is the **Doppler effect**. It occurs when there is a **disparity** between the emitted frequency and the observed frequency of a wave. It is the caused by **relative motion** between the **wave source** and the **observer**. If the source and observer are both moving toward one another, the observed frequency is determined by the following equation: $f_o = f_e \frac{(v_w + v_o)}{(v_w - v_s)}$, where v_w is the speed of the wave. If the source or the observer is moving in the opposite direction, its sign must be reversed. The Doppler effect can occur with any wave (light, water, pressure, etc.), but it is most commonly observed when sound waves change pitch due to an observer's change in position relative to a loud train horn or emergency vehicle siren. The effect is also employed in the operation of speed-detecting radar guns. Microwaves are emitted at a known frequency and, after being reflected by the target, return at a different frequency, giving the object's speed.

SOUND WAVES

The **pitch of a sound** as it reaches one's ear is based on the frequency of the sound waves. A high-pitched sound has a higher frequency than a low-pitched sound. Like all waves, sound waves transmit energy. The rate at which this energy is transmitted is the sonic power. Loudness, or intensity of sound, is the sonic power received per unit area.

When a pair of sound waves with slightly different frequencies interfere with one another causing a periodic variation in sound intensity or a **beat**. The frequency of the variation, called the **beat frequency**, is equal to the difference between frequencies of the two sound waves. The phenomenon is used when tuning two instruments to one another. As the two pitches get closer, the beat frequency will become smaller and smaller until it disappears entirely, indicating that the instruments are in tune.

Review Video: Sound
Visit mometrix.com/academy and enter code: 562378

ELECTROMAGNETIC WAVES AND ELECTROMAGNETIC SPECTRUM

ELECTROMAGNETIC SPECTRUM

The **electromagnetic spectrum** is the range of all wavelengths and frequencies of known electromagnetic waves. Visible light occupies only a small portion of the electromagnetic spectrum. Some of the common classifications of electromagnetic waves are listed in the table below with their approximate frequency ranges.

Classification	Freq. (Hz)
Gamma Rays	$\sim 10^{19}$
X-Rays	$\sim 10^{17} - 10^{18}$
Ultraviolet	$\sim 10^{15} - 10^{16}$
Visible Light	$\sim 10^{14}$
Infra-red	$\sim 10^{11} - 10^{14}$
Microwaves	$\sim 10^{10} - 10^{11}$
Radio/TV	$\sim 10^{6} - 10^{9}$

Electromagnetic waves travel at the speed of light, $c = 3 \times 10^8$ m/s. To find the wavelength of any electromagnetic wave, simply divide c by the frequency. Visible light occupies a range of wavelengths from approximately 380 nm (violet) to 740 nm (red). The full spectrum of color can be found between these two wavelengths.

> **Review Video: Electromagnetic Spectrum**
> Visit mometrix.com/academy and enter code: 771761
>
> **Review Video: Light**
> Visit mometrix.com/academy and enter code: 900556

Thermodynamics

HEAT TRANSFER

Heat transfer is the flow of thermal energy, which is measured by temperature. Heat will flow from warmer objects to cooler objects until an **equilibrium** is reached in which both objects are at the same temperature. Because the particles of warmer objects possess a higher kinetic energy than the particles of cooler objects, the particles of the warmer objects are vibrating more quickly and collide more often, transferring energy to the cooler objects in which the particles have less kinetic energy and are moving more slowly. Heat may be transferred by conduction, convection, or radiation. In **conduction**, heat is transferred by direct contact between two objects. In **convection**, heat is transferred by moving currents. In **radiation**, heat is transferred by electromagnetic waves.

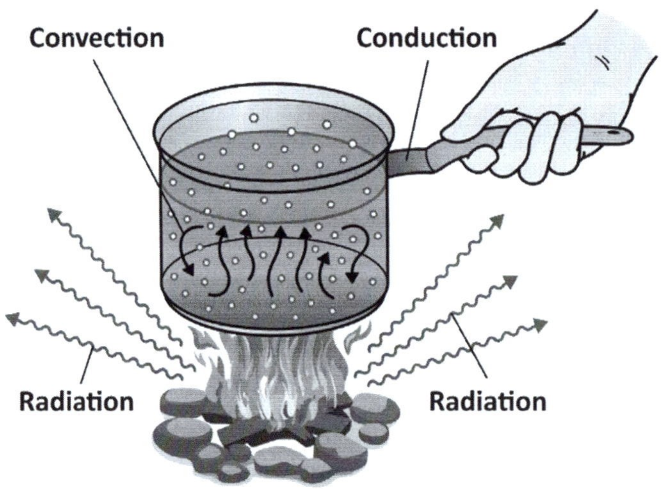

> **Review Video: Heat Transfer at the Molecular Level**
> Visit mometrix.com/academy and enter code: 451646

CONVECTION

Heat always flows from a region of higher temperature to a region of lower temperature. If two regions are at the same temperature, there is a thermal equilibrium between them and there will be no net heat transfer between them. Convection is a mode of heat transfer in which a surface in contact with a fluid experiences a heat flow. The heat rate for convection is given as $q = hA\Delta T$, where h is the convection coefficient, and q is the heat transferred per unit of time. The convection coefficient is dependent on a number of factors, including the configuration of the surface and the nature and velocity of the fluid. For complicated configurations, it often has to be determined experimentally.

Convection may be classified as either free or forced. In free convection, when a surface transfers heat to the surrounding air, the heated air becomes less dense and rises, allowing cooler air to descend and come into contact with the surface. Free convection may also be called natural convection. Forced convection in this example would involve forcibly cycling the air: for instance, with a fan. While this does generally require an additional input of work, the convection coefficient is always greater for forced convection.

Conduction

Conduction is a form of heat transfer that requires contact. Since heat is a measure of kinetic energy, most commonly vibration, at the atomic level, it may be transferred from one location to another or one object to another by contact. The rate at which heat is transferred is proportional to the material's thermal conductivity k, cross-sectional area A, and temperature gradient $\frac{\Delta T}{\Delta x}$:

$$q = kA\left(\frac{\Delta T}{\Delta x}\right)$$

If two ends of a rod are each held at a constant temperature, the heat transfer through the rod will be given as $q = kA\left(\frac{T_H - T_L}{d}\right)$, where d is the length of the rod. The heat will flow from the hot end to the cold end. The thermal conductivity is generally given in units of $\frac{\text{W}}{\text{m K}}$. Metals are some of the best conductors, many having a thermal conductivity around 400 $\frac{\text{W}}{\text{m K}}$. The thermal conductivity of wood is very small, generally less than 0.5 $\frac{\text{W}}{\text{m K}}$. Diamond is extremely thermally conductive and may have a conductivity of over 2,000 $\frac{\text{W}}{\text{m K}}$. Although fluids also have thermal conductivity, they will tend to transfer heat primarily through convection.

Radiation

Radiation heat transfer occurs via electromagnetic radiation between two bodies. Unlike conduction and convection, radiation requires no medium in which to take place. Indeed, the heat we receive from the sun is entirely radiation since it must pass through a vacuum to reach us. Every body at a temperature above absolute zero emits heat radiation at a rate of $q = e\sigma AT^4$, where e is the surface emissivity and σ is the Stefan-Boltzmann constant. The net radiation heat-transfer rate for a body is given by $q = e\sigma A(T^4 - T_0^4)$, where T_0 is the temperature of the surroundings. Emissivity, which has a value between 0 and 1, is a measure of how well a surface absorbs and emits radiation. Dark-colored surfaces tend to have high emissivity, while shiny or reflective surfaces have low emissivity. In the radiation heat-rate equation, it is important to remember to use absolute temperature units, since the temperature value is being raised to a power.

Types of Energy

Chemical, Electrical, Electromagnetic, Nuclear, and Thermal Energy

Different types of energy may be associated with systems:

- **Chemical energy** is the energy that is stored in chemical bonds and intermolecular forces.
- **Electrical energy** is the energy associated with the movement of electrons or ions through a material.
- **Electromagnetic energy** is the energy of electromagnetic waves of several frequencies including radio waves, microwaves, infrared light, visible light, ultraviolet light, x-rays, and gamma rays.
- **Nuclear energy** is the binding energy that is stored within an atom's nucleus.
- **Thermal energy** is the total internal kinetic energy of a system due to the random motions of the particles.

Phase Transitions

States of Matter

The four states of matter are solid, liquid, gas, and plasma. **Solids** have a definite shape and a definite volume. Because solid particles are held in fairly rigid positions, solids are the least compressible of the four states of matter. **Liquids** have definite volumes but no definite shapes. Because their particles are free to slip and slide over each other, liquids take the shape of their containers, but they still remain fairly incompressible by natural means. **Gases** have no definite shape or volume. Because gas particles are free to move, they move away from each other to fill their containers. Gases are compressible. **Plasmas** are high-temperature, ionized gases that exist only under very high temperatures at which electrons are stripped away from their atoms.

Review Video: States of Matter
Visit mometrix.com/academy and enter code: 742449

Review Video: Properties of Liquids
Visit mometrix.com/academy and enter code: 802024

Review Video: States of Matter [Advanced]
Visit mometrix.com/academy and enter code: 298130

The following table shows similarities and differences between solids, liquids, and gases:

	Solid	Liquid	Gas
Shape	Fixed shape	No fixed shape (assumes shape of container)	No fixed shape (assumes shape of container)
Volume	Fixed	Fixed	Changes to assume volume of container
Fluidity	Does not flow easily	Flows easily	Flows easily
Compressibility	Hard to compress	Hard to compress	Compresses

Six Different Types of Phase Change

A substance that is undergoing a change from a solid to a liquid is said to be melting. If this change occurs in the opposite direction, from liquid to solid, this change is called freezing. A liquid which is being converted to a gas is undergoing vaporization. The reverse of this process is known as condensation. Direct transitions from gas to solid and solid to gas are much less common in everyday life, but they can occur given the proper conditions. Solid to gas conversion is known as sublimation, while the reverse is called deposition.

Review Video: Chemical and Physical Properties of Matter
Visit mometrix.com/academy and enter code: 717349

Phase Diagram and Critical Point

A **phase diagram** is a graph or chart of pressure versus temperature that represents the solid, liquid, and gaseous phases of a substance and the transitions between these phases. Typically, **pressure** is located on the vertical axis, and temperature is located along the horizontal axis. The curves drawn on the graph represent points at which different phases are in an equilibrium state. These curves indicate at which pressure and temperature the phase changes of sublimation, melting, and boiling occur. Specifically, the curve between the liquid and gas phases indicates the pressures and temperatures at which the liquid and gas phases are in equilibrium. The curve between the solid and liquid phases indicates the temperatures and pressures at which the solid and liquid phases are in equilibrium. The open spaces on the graph represent the distinct phases solid, liquid, and gas. The point at which the solid-liquid, solid-gas, and liquid-gas phase boundaries intersect is called the triple point. At the triple point, the solid, liquid, and gas phases all exist in equilibrium. The critical point, by contrast, is the endpoint of the liquid-gas coexistence curve, where the liquid and gas phases become indistinguishable and form a supercritical fluid.

Lettered Regions of a Phase Diagram

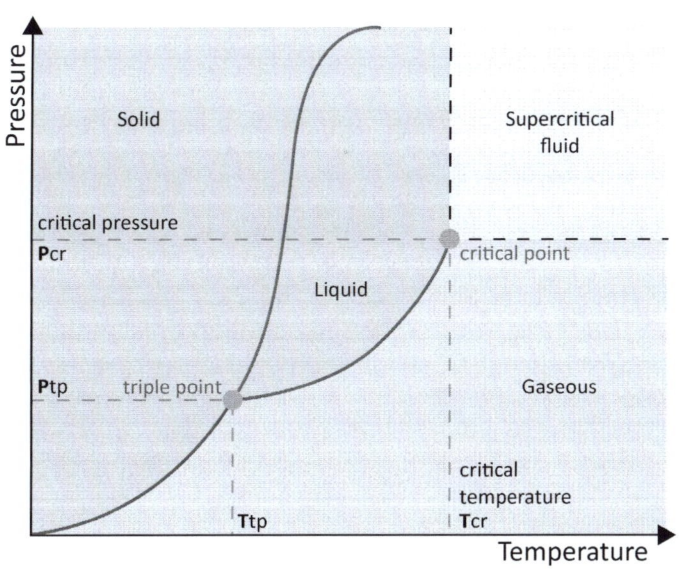

A—**Solid phase**: This is a region of high pressure and low temperature where the substance always exists as a solid.

B—**Liquid phase**: This is a region of pressure and temperature where the substance is in the liquid phase.

C—**Gas phase**: This is a region of pressure and temperature where the substance is in the gaseous phase.

D—**Sublimation point**: The portion of the curve that contains point D shows all the combinations of pressure and temperature at which the solid phase is in equilibrium with the gaseous phase.

E—**Triple point**: The point at which the solid, liquid, and gaseous phases are all in equilibrium.

F—**Boiling point**: The line that contains point F indicates all the combinations of pressure and temperature at which the liquid phase and gas phase are in equilibrium.

LAWS OF THERMODYNAMICS

FIRST LAW

The **first law of thermodynamics** states that energy cannot be **created** or **destroyed**, but only **converted** from one form to another. It is generally applied as $Q = \Delta U + W$, where Q is the net heat energy added to a system, ΔU is the change in internal energy of the system, and W is the work done by the system. For any input of heat energy to a system, that energy must be either converted to internal energy through a temperature increase or expended in doing work. For a system that gives off heat, either the temperature of the system must decrease or work must be done on the system by its surroundings. By convention, work done by the system is positive while work done on the system is negative.

For instance, suppose a gas is compressed by a piston while the gas temperature remains constant. If we consider the gas to be the system, the work is negative, since the work is being performed on the gas. Since the temperature remains constant, $\Delta U = 0$. Thus, Q must be a negative quantity, indicating that heat is lost by the gas. Conversely, if the gas does positive work on the piston while remaining at a constant temperature, the gas must be receiving heat input from the surroundings.

SECOND LAW

The **second law of thermodynamics** is primarily a statement of the natural tendency of all things toward disorder rather than order. It deals with a quantity called **entropy**, which is an inverse measure of the remaining useful energy in a system. If we take a system of a pot of hot water and an ice cube, the system entropy initially has a value of s_1. After the ice cube melts in the water and the system reaches an equilibrium temperature, the system has larger entropy value s_2, which is the maximum entropy for the system. The system cannot return to its initial state without work put into the system to refreeze the ice cube and reheat the water. If this is done and the system returns to a state with entropy s_1, then the entropy of the surroundings must at the same time increase by more than $s_2 - s_1$, since the net entropy from any process is always greater than zero. Reversible processes are those that may be accomplished in reverse without requiring additional work input. These processes do not exist in the real world, but can be useful for approximating some situations. All real processes are irreversible, meaning they require additional work input to accomplish in reverse. Another important concept is that of spontaneity, the ability of a process to occur without instigation. An ice cube located in an environment at a temperature above the freezing point will spontaneously melt. Although some processes can decrease system entropy at a cost to the entropy of the surroundings, all spontaneous processes involve an increase in the total entropy of the universe.

THIRD AND ZEROTH LAWS

The **third law of thermodynamics** regards the behavior of systems as they **approach absolute zero temperature**. Actually reaching a state of absolute zero is impossible. According to this law, all activity disappears as molecules slow to a standstill near absolute zero, and the system achieves a perfect crystal structure while the system entropy approaches its minimum value. For most systems, this would in fact be a value of zero entropy. Note that this does not violate the second law since causing a system to approach absolute zero would require an immense increase in the entropy of the surroundings, resulting in a positive net entropy. This law is used to determine the value of a material's standard entropy, which is its entropy at the standard temperature of 25 °C.

The **zeroth law of thermodynamics** deals with thermal equilibrium between two systems. It states that if two systems are both in thermal equilibrium with a third system, then they are in thermal equilibrium with each other. This may seem intuitive, but it is an important basis for the other thermodynamic laws.

Review Video: Laws of Thermodynamics
Visit mometrix.com/academy and enter code: 253607

Entropy

Entropy (S) is the amount of **disorder** or **randomness of a system**. According to the second law of thermodynamics, systems tend toward a state of greater entropy. The second law of thermodynamics can also be stated as $\Delta S > 0$. Processes with positive changes in entropy tend to be spontaneous. For example, melting is a process with a positive ΔS. When a solid changes into a liquid state, the substance becomes more disordered; therefore, entropy increases. Entropy also will increase in a reaction in which the number of moles of gases increases due to the amount of disorder increasing. Entropy increases when a solute dissolves into a solvent due to the increase in the number of particles. Entropy increases when a system is heated due to the particles moving faster and the amount of disorder increasing.

Spontaneous / Reversible Processes

Some chemical processes are **spontaneous**. According to the second law of thermodynamics, systems or processes always **tend to a state of greater entropy** or lower potential energy. Some exothermic chemical systems are spontaneous because they can increase their stability by reaching a lower potential energy. If processes or reactions have products at a lower potential energy, these processes tend to be spontaneous. Spontaneous reactions have only one direction as given by the second law of thermodynamics. Spontaneous processes go in the direction of greater entropy and lower potential energy. To be reversible, a reaction or process has to be able to go back and forth between two states. A spontaneous process is irreversible.

Concept of Change in Enthalpy

All chemical processes involve either the release or the absorption of heat. Enthalpy is this heat energy. **Enthalpy** is a state function that is equivalent to the amount of heat a system exchanges with its surroundings. For **exothermic processes**, which release heat, the change in enthalpy (ΔH) is negative because the final enthalpy is less than the initial enthalpy. For **endothermic processes**, which absorb heat, the change in enthalpy (ΔH) is positive because the final enthalpy is greater than the initial enthalpy.

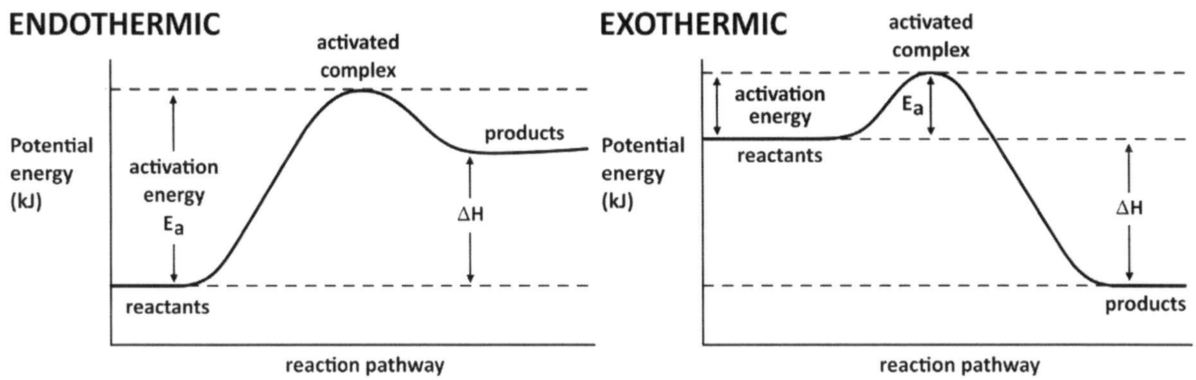

Review Video: Enthalpy
Visit mometrix.com/academy and enter code: 233315

GIBBS ENERGY

Gibbs energy (G), also known as Gibbs free energy, is the energy of the system that is available to do work. Gibbs energy determines the **spontaneity** of chemical and physical processes. Some processes are spontaneous because $\Delta H < 0$ or because $\Delta S > 0$. If one of the conditions is favorable but the other condition is not favorable, Gibbs energy can be used to determine if a process is spontaneous. Gibbs energy is given by $G = H - TS$. For processes that occur at constant temperature, $\Delta G = \Delta H - T\Delta S$. If ΔG is equal to zero, then the reaction is at equilibrium and neither the forward nor the reverse reaction is spontaneous. If ΔG is less than zero, then the forward reaction is spontaneous. If ΔG is greater than zero, then the reverse reaction is spontaneous.

Modern Physics and Additional Topics

MODERN PHYSICS AND ADDITIONAL TOPICS

WAVE-PARTICLE DUALITY AND HEISENBERG UNCERTAINTY PRINCIPLE

Wave-particle duality is the insight of quantum mechanics that states that energy will behave with the characteristics of both a **particle** and a **wave**. For most of the history of physics, it was believed that light was composed of electromagnetic waves and electrons were tiny particles of matter. However, experiments with light have created situations in which light will behave as if it were a particle (called a *photon*), and other experiments have suggested that photons will often behave as if they were waves. Essentially, quantum mechanics was created to resolve this conundrum. The result has been a series of theories, including the de Broglie hypothesis, that try to unify these seemingly contradictory attributes of matter.

One important measurement issue that arises from this dual nature is the **Heisenberg uncertainty principle**. This principle states that the position and linear momentum cannot be accurately measured beyond a certain level. Specifically, the minimum uncertainty in measuring the position, x, and linear momentum, p, in a given dimension is dictated by the relation $(\Delta x)(\Delta p) \geq \frac{h}{4\pi}$, where h is Planck's constant.

Photoelectric Effect

The **photoelectric effect** is the emission of electrons by substances when light falls on their surfaces. One of the main inspirations for the development of quantum theory was the inability of the standard theory of electromagnetic radiation to fully explain the photoelectric effect. Einstein declared that the incident light is composed of discrete particles of energy, known as **quanta**. The quanta of energy in light are known as **photons**. The energy of each photon is proportional to its frequency according to the equation $E = hf$, where E is energy, h is Planck's constant, and f is the frequency. When light is incident on a portion of an electric circuit, a current may be induced in the circuit. One property associated with this effect is stopping potential. This value is dependent on both the surface metal and the frequency of the incident light. Light of a given frequency will induce a current only if it does not have to overcome more potential in the circuit than the stopping potential. The stopping potential, V_0, is calculated by the equation $eV_0 = hf - \varphi$, where e is the elementary charge and φ is the work function of the metal. If $hf - \varphi$ is calculated in electron volts, V_0 is simply the equivalent number of volts.

De Broglie's Hypothesis

The de Broglie hypothesis is the assertion that all matter has a **wave-like nature**. According to the hypothesis, it is not just subatomic particles that exhibit wave properties; all objects do. This insight of de Broglie was confirmed by experiments that fired electrons at a very high speed at a crystalline nickel target. The diffraction of the electrons upon impacting the target was consistent with the diffraction exhibited by waves when passing through a slit with a width approximately the same as the wavelength of the wave. From these experiments, he produced two relations for an electron's frequency, f, and wavelength, λ, similar to those for photons: $f = \frac{E}{h}$ and $\lambda = \frac{h}{p}$, where E is the electron's energy, p is its linear momentum, and h is Planck's constant.

Michelson-Morley Experiment

The Michelson-Morley experiment proved that there is no substance like **ether** in outer space. It involved the use of a Michelson interferometer, a device that measures length to a great degree of precision by means of interference fringes. Basically, an interferometer sends two beams of light out, splits them at right angles to one another, and then brings them back to a central location with a mirror. Any very minor shift in the position of the beams will be seen as a shift in the interference fringes. Michelson and Morley wanted to use this device to determine the characteristics of the "luminiferous aether" wind that blew through outer space and affected the transmission of light, but instead they ended up disproving the existence of the ether altogether. They were also able to conclude from this experiment that the measured velocity of light is independent of the observer's reference-frame velocity.

Einstein's Theory of Relativity

Relativity is composed of special relativity and general relativity. **Special relativity** relates that those observers in inertial reference frames, in uniform motion relative to each other, cannot perform experiments to find out which is stationary. This is the principle of relativity, which says that regardless of an observer's velocity or position in the universe, all physical laws will appear constant. It was in this context that Einstein found that the speed of light in a vacuum had to be the same for all the observers despite their motion or the motion of the light source. **General relativity** is a geometrical theory that reasons that the presence of mass and energy will curve space-time, a model that combines mass and energy to form the space-time continuum, and that the curvature will affect the path of free particles. This includes the path of light. It uses differential geometry and the generalized quantity of tensors to describe gravitation without using the force of gravity. The theory postulates that all observers should be equivalent, not only those that move with uniform speed.

Lorentz Transformations and Equations

Because of the phenomena associated with Einstein's theory of relativity, measurements taken from **reference frames** traveling at high velocities may noticeably differ from those taken in a **stationary reference frame**. These differences in observation may be reconciled using Lorentz transformations. In the equations that follow, all quantities with a subscript zero represent those quantities as measured in a stationary frame. The primary conversion factor in these equations is the Lorentz factor (γ):

$$\gamma = \frac{1}{\sqrt{1 - \frac{v^2}{c^2}}}$$

The equations for length contraction and time dilation both use this factor. $L = \frac{L_0}{\gamma}$, where L is the observed length of an object in the direction of the frame's velocity. When observed from a high-velocity frame, objects will appear shorter. Also, $\Delta t = \Delta t_0 \gamma$, where Δt is elapsed time in a stationary frame as observed from a high-velocity frame. This means that from the high-velocity frame, time will seem to pass more quickly in the stationary frame.

One further equation relating high-velocity and stationary-frame measurements is velocity addition. For those velocities encountered in everyday life, an observer traveling at velocity, v, who measures an object's velocity as u', traveling in the same direction, will reasonably assume that the object's velocity in a stationary frame is $u = v + u'$. For velocities significant relative to the speed of light, c, the equation becomes $u = \frac{(v+u')}{(1+vu'/c^2)}$.

Simultaneous Events

Let us imagine a situation in which one **stationary observer** records two events that happen at the same time. If another observer moving at a **constant velocity** also records these two events, it is unlikely that the moving observer will record these two events as having happened simultaneously. In other words, two observers who are in relative motion will not generally agree as to whether two events are simultaneous. Neither observer is objectively right or wrong. We may therefore conclude that simultaneity is not an absolute concept but a relative one. It depends on the state of motion of the observer. Of course, since in most cases the speed of the observers will be a great deal less than the speed of light, this lack of simultaneity will be too small to notice.

Nuclear Binding Energy

The **nuclear binding energy** of an atom is the energy that would be required to **disassemble** the nucleus into its constituent nucleons. They are held together by a strong nuclear force in the nucleus. Nuclear binding energy may be calculated by determining the difference in mass between the nucleus and the sum of the masses of its constituent particles. This mass, m, is converted to energy by the equation $E = mc^2$, where c is the speed of light in a vacuum.

Nuclei may be transformed by a **rearrangement of nucleons**. These nuclear transformations may occur by many different means, including radioactive decay, nuclear fusion, and nuclear fission. In nuclear fusion, two light nuclei merge into a single nucleus that is heavier. In nuclear fission, a single large nucleus divides into two or more smaller nuclei. In either case, if the mass of the nuclei before transformation is greater than the mass after transformation, then it is an exothermic process. Conversely, if the mass is greater after transformation, the process is endothermic. Nickel and iron have the most stable nuclei of any elements, having the largest binding energies.

BLACKBODY RADIATION

A **black body** is an ideal black substance that will absorb all radiation and reflect none of the radiation energy that falls on it. Powdered carbon is the closest real approximation of a black body. Because a black body is a perfect absorber of radiation, it is also a perfect emitter of radiation. The distribution of radiant energy in a black body according to wavelength will depend on the absolute temperature of the body: the higher the temperature, the lower the wavelength at which energy is distributed as a maximum. Blackbody radiation was used by Max Planck to develop the quantum theory of mechanics in 1901.

ELEMENTARY PARTICLES

The two basic types of **elementary particles** are bosons, which have integer spin, and fermions, which have half-integer spin. There are a few different types of bosons, but the type most commonly encountered are photons, which make up the full spectrum of light.

There are only two types of fermions: leptons and quarks. Both leptons and quarks have antiparticles as well, with opposite charge.

- **Leptons** may be one of three different flavors: muon, tauon, or electron. Each of these is accompanied by a small electrically neutral particle called a neutrino, also differentiated by the same three flavors. Each lepton has a charge of -1, while its antiparticle has a charge of $+1$. The electron's antiparticle is the positron.
- **Quarks** are most commonly encountered as the constituent particles of nucleons. There are six different flavors of quark; the two most common are *up*, having a charge of $+\frac{2}{3}$, and *down*, having a charge of $-\frac{1}{3}$. Neutrons consist of one up quark and two down quarks, while protons have two up quarks and one down quark.

Chapter Quiz

Ready to see how well you retained what you just read? Scan the QR code to go directly to the chapter quiz interface for this study guide. If you're using a computer, simply visit the online resources page at **mometrix.com/resources719/texesmathpse** and click the Chapter Quizzes link.

Mometrix

TEST PREPARATION

TExES

Mathematics/Physical Science/Engineering 6-12 (274) Secrets Study Guide

art 3 of 3

Dear Future Exam Success Story

First of all, **THANK YOU** for purchasing Mometrix study materials!

Second, congratulations! You are one of the few determined test-takers who are committed to doing whatever it takes to excel on your exam. **You have come to the right place.** We developed these study materials with one goal in mind: to deliver you the information you need in a format that's concise and easy to use.

In addition to optimizing your guide for the content of the test, we've outlined our recommended steps for breaking down the preparation process into small, attainable goals so you can make sure you stay on track.

We've also analyzed the entire test-taking process, identifying the most common pitfalls and showing how you can overcome them and be ready for any curveball the test throws you.

Standardized testing is one of the biggest obstacles on your road to success, which only increases the importance of doing well in the high-pressure, high-stakes environment of test day. Your results on this test could have a significant impact on your future, and this guide provides the information and practical advice to help you achieve your full potential on test day.

Your success is our success

We would love to hear from you! If you would like to share the story of your exam success or if you have any questions or comments in regard to our products, please contact us at **800-673-8175** or **support@mometrix.com**.

Thanks again for your business and we wish you continued success!

Sincerely,
The Mometrix Test Preparation Team

Need more help? Check out our flashcards at:
http://mometrixflashcards.com/TExES

TABLE OF CONTENTS

Chemistry

Structure of Matter

HISTORICAL MODELS OF THE ATOM

ATOMIC MODELS AND THEORIES

There have been many theories regarding the **structure** of atoms and their particles. Part of the challenge in developing an understanding of matter is that atoms and their particles are too small to be seen. It is believed that the first conceptualization of the atom was developed by **Democritus** in 400 B.C. Some of the more notable models are the solid sphere or billiard ball model postulated by **John Dalton**, the plum pudding or raisin bun model by **J.J. Thomson**, the planetary or nuclear model by **Ernest Rutherford**, the Bohr or orbit model by **Niels Bohr**, and the electron cloud or quantum mechanical model by **Louis de Broglie** and **Erwin Schrödinger**. Rutherford directed the alpha scattering experiment that discounted the plum pudding model. The shortcoming of the Bohr model was the belief that electrons orbited in fixed rather than changing elliptical orbits.

Review Video: Atomic Models
Visit mometrix.com/academy and enter code: 434851

Review Video: John Dalton
Visit mometrix.com/academy and enter code: 565627

THOMSON "PLUM PUDDING" MODEL

J.J. Thomson, the discoverer of the electron, suggested that the arrangement of protons and electrons within an atom could be approximated by dried fruit in a **plum pudding**. Thomson, whose discovery of the electron preceded that of the proton or neutron, hypothesized that an atom's electrons, the dried plums, were **positioned uniformly** inside the atom within a cloud of positive charge, the pudding. This model was later disproved.

RUTHERFORD SCATTERING

Ernest Rutherford concluded from the work of Geiger and Marsden that the majority of the atom's mass was concentrated in a minute, positively charged region, the **nucleus**, which was surrounded by **electrons**. When a positive alpha particle approached close enough to the nucleus, it was strongly repelled, enough so that it had the ability to rebound at high angles. The small nucleus size explained the small number of alpha particles that were repelled in this fashion. The scattering led to development of the **planetary model of the atom**, which was further developed by Niels Bohr into what is now known as the Bohr model.

BOHR MODEL

Niels Bohr postulated that the electrons orbiting the nucleus must occupy **discrete orbits**. These discrete orbits also corresponded to discrete levels of energy and angular momentum. Consequently, the only way that electrons could move between orbits was by making nearly instantaneous jumps between them. These jumps, known as **quantum leaps**, are associated with the absorption or emission of a quantum of energy, known as a **photon**. If the electron is jumping to a higher energy state, a photon must be absorbed. Similarly, if the electron is dropping to a lower energy state, a photon must be emitted.

> **Review Video: Structure of Atoms**
> Visit mometrix.com/academy and enter code: 905932

Atomic and Subatomic Structure

Basic Organization of Matter

An **element** is the most basic type of matter. It has unique properties and cannot be broken down into other elements. The smallest unit of an element is the **atom**. Most elements are found somewhere in nature in single-atom form, but a few elements only exist naturally in pairs. These are called diatomic elements, and some of the most common of these are hydrogen, nitrogen, and oxygen. A chemical combination of two or more types of elements is called a compound. **Compounds** often have properties that are very different from those of their constituent elements. The smallest independent unit of an element or compound of two or more atoms is known as a **molecule**. Elements and compounds are represented by chemical symbols, one or two letters, most often the first in the element name. More than one atom of the same element in a compound is represented with a subscript number designating how many atoms of that element are present. Water, for instance, contains two hydrogens and one oxygen. Thus, the chemical formula is H_2O. Methane contains one carbon and four hydrogens, so its formula is CH_4.

> **Review Video: Molecules**
> Visit mometrix.com/academy and enter code: 349910

Protons, Neutrons, and Electrons

The three major subatomic particles are the proton, neutron, and electron. The **proton**, which is located in the nucleus, has a relative charge of +1. The **neutron**, which is located in the nucleus, has a relative charge of 0. The **electron**, which is located outside the nucleus, has a relative charge of −1. The proton and neutron, which are essentially the same mass, are much more massive than the electron and make up the mass of the atom. The electron's mass is insignificant compared to the mass of the proton and neutron.

Orbits and Orbitals

An orbit is a definite path, but an orbital is a region in space. The Bohr model described electrons as orbiting or following a definite path in space around the nucleus of an atom. But, according to **Heisenberg's uncertainty principle**, it is impossible to determine the location and the momentum of an electron simultaneously. Therefore, it is impossible to draw a definite path or orbit of an electron. An **orbital**, as described by the quantum-mechanical model or the electron-cloud model, is a region in space that is drawn in such a way as to indicate the probability of finding an electron at a specific location. The distance an orbital is located from the nucleus corresponds to the principal quantum number. The orbital shape corresponds to the subshell or azimuthal quantum number. The orbital orientation corresponds to the magnetic quantum number.

Quantum Numbers

The **principal quantum number** (n) describes an electron's shell or energy level and actually describes the size of the orbital. Electrons farther from the nucleus are at higher energy levels. The **subshell** or azimuthal quantum number (l) describes the electron's sublevel or subshell $(s, p, d,$ or $f)$ and specifies the shape of the orbital. Typical shapes include spherical, dumbbell, and clover leaf. The **magnetic quantum number** (m_l) describes the orientation of the orbital in space. The spin or magnetic moment quantum number (m_s) describes the direction of the spin of the electron in the orbital.

Atomic Number and Mass Number

The **atomic number** of an element is the number of protons in the nucleus of an atom of that element. This is the number that identifies the type of an atom. For example, all oxygen atoms have eight protons, and all carbon atoms have six protons. Each element is identified by its specific atomic number.

The **mass number** is the number of protons and neutrons in the nucleus of an atom. Although the atomic number is the same for all atoms of a specific element, the mass number can vary due to the varying numbers of neutrons in various isotopes of the atom.

Isotopes

Isotopes are atoms of the same element that vary in their number of neutrons. Isotopes of the same element have the same number of protons and thus the same atomic number. Because isotopes vary in the number of neutrons, they are identified by their mass numbers. For example, two naturally occurring carbon isotopes are carbon-12 and carbon-13, which have mass numbers 12 and 13, respectively. The symbols ${}^{12}_{6}C$ and ${}^{13}_{6}C$ also represent the carbon isotopes. The general form of the symbol is ${}^{M}_{A}X$, where X is the element symbol, M is the mass number, and A is the atomic number.

Average Atomic Mass

The **average atomic mass** is the weighted average of the masses of all the naturally occurring isotopes of an atom in comparison to the carbon-12 isotope. The unit for average atomic mass is the atomic mass unit (u). Atomic masses of isotopes are measured using a mass spectrometer by bombarding a gaseous sample of the isotope and measuring its relative deflections. Atomic masses can be calculated if the percent abundances and the atomic masses of the naturally occurring isotopes are known.

Cathode Ray Tube (CRT)

Electrons were discovered by Joseph John Thomson through scientific work with cathode ray tubes (CRTs). **Cathode rays** had been studied for many years, but it was Thomson who showed that cathode rays were **negatively charged particles**. Although Thomson could not determine an electron's charge or mass, he was able to determine the ratio of the charge to the mass. Thomson discovered that this ratio was constant regardless of the gas in the CRT. He was able to show that the cathode rays were actually streams of negatively charged particles by deflecting them with a positively charged plate.

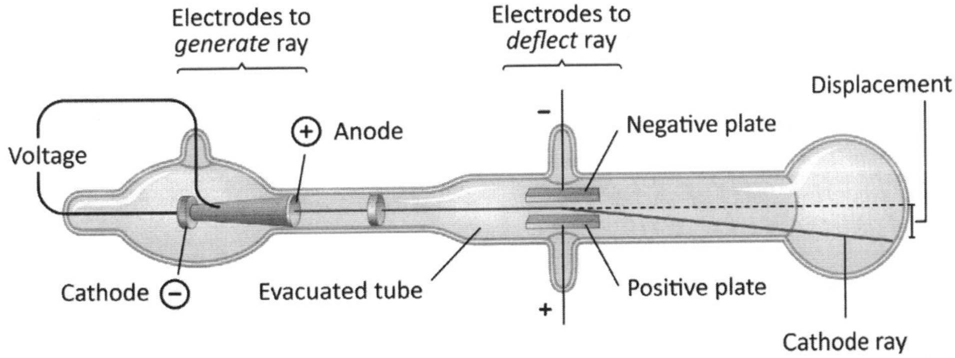

Gold Foil Experiment

After Thomson determined the ratio of the charge to the mass of an electron from studying cathode rays, he proposed the plum pudding model, in which he compared electrons to the raisins embedded in plum pudding. This model of the atom was disproved by the gold foil experiment. The gold foil experiment led to the discovery of the nucleus of an atom. Scientists at Rutherford's laboratory bombarded a thin gold foil with high-speed helium ions. Much to their surprise, some of the ions were reflected by the foil. The scientists concluded that the atom has a **hard central core**, which we now know to be the **nucleus**.

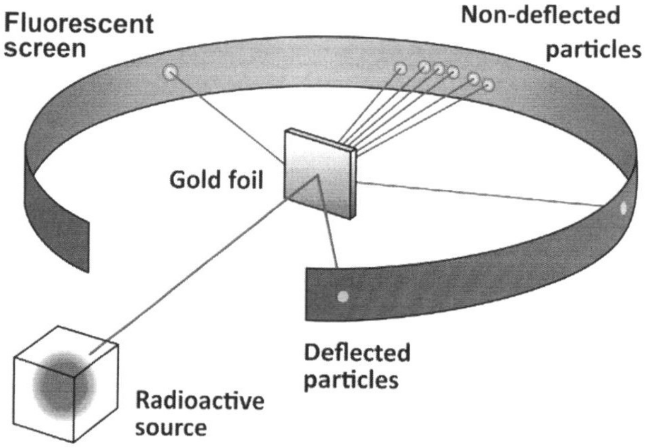

Problems that Rutherford's Model Had with Spectral Lines

Rutherford's model allowed for the electrons of an atom to be in an **infinite number of orbits** based on Newton's laws of motion. Rutherford believed that electrons could orbit the nucleus at any distance from the nucleus and that electrons could change velocity and direction at any moment. But, according to Rutherford's model, the electrons would lose energy and spiral into the nucleus. Unfortunately, if this was in fact true, then every atom would be **unstable**. Rutherford's model also does not correspond to the spectral lines emitted from gases at low pressure. The **spectral lines** are discrete bands of light at specific energy levels. These spectral lines indicate that electrons must be at specific distances from the nucleus. If electrons could be located at any distance from the nucleus, then these gases should emit continuous spectra instead of spectral lines.

Pure Substances and Mixtures

Pure Substances

Pure substances are substances that cannot be further broken down into simpler components or pieces and still retain their characteristics. Pure substances are categorized as either **elements** or **compounds**. Elements consist of only one type of atom may be monatomic, diatomic, or polyatomic. For example, helium (He) and copper (Cu) are monatomic elements, and hydrogen (H_2) and oxygen (O_2) are diatomic elements. Phosphorus (P_4) and sulfur (S_8) are polyatomic elements. Compounds consist of molecules of more than one type of atom. For example, pure water (H_2O) is made up of molecules consisting of two atoms of hydrogen bonded to one atom of oxygen, and glucose ($C_6H_{12}O_6$) is made up of molecules of six carbon atoms and twelve hydrogen atoms bonded together with six oxygen atoms.

Mixtures

Mixtures can be classified as either homogeneous or heterogeneous. The molecules of a **homogeneous mixture** are distributed uniformly throughout the mixture, whereas the molecules of a **heterogeneous mixture** are not. Air is an example of a homogeneous mixture, and a pile of sand and rock is an example of a heterogeneous mixture. Solutions are homogeneous mixtures consisting of a **solute** (the substance that is dissolved) and a **solvent** (the substance doing the dissolving).

Suspensions

Suspensions are heterogeneous mixtures in which the particle size of the substance **suspended** is too large to be kept in suspension by Brownian motion. Once left undisturbed, suspensions will settle out to form layers. An example of a suspension is sand stirred into water. Left undisturbed, the sand will fall out of suspension and the water will form a layer on top of the sand.

Mixtures with Compounds

Mixtures are similar to compounds in that they are produced when two or more substances are combined. However, there are some key differences as well. Compounds require a chemical combination of the constituent particles, while mixtures are simply the interspersion of particles. Unlike compounds, mixtures may be **separated** without a chemical change. A mixture retains the chemical properties of its constitutent particles, while a compound acquires a new set of properties. Given compounds can exist only in specific ratios, while mixtures may be any ratio of the involved substances.

Chemical and Physical Properties and Changes

Chemical and Physical Properties

Matter has both physical and chemical properties. **Physical properties** can be seen or observed without changing the identity or composition of matter. For example, the mass, volume, and density of a substance can be determined without permanently changing the sample. Other physical properties include color, boiling point, freezing point, solubility, odor, hardness, electrical conductivity, thermal conductivity, ductility, and malleability.

Chemical properties cannot be measured without changing the identity or composition of matter. Chemical properties describe how a substance reacts or changes to form a new substance. Examples of chemical properties include flammability, corrosivity, oxidation states, enthalpy of formation, and reactivity with other chemicals.

Intensive and Extensive Properties

Physical properties are categorized as either intensive or extensive. **Intensive properties** *do not* depend on the amount of matter or quantity of the sample. This means that intensive properties will not change if the sample size is increased or decreased. Intensive properties include color, hardness, melting point, boiling point, density, ductility, malleability, specific heat, temperature, concentration, and magnetization.

Extensive properties *do* depend on the amount of matter or quantity of the sample. Therefore, extensive properties do change if the sample size is increased or decreased. If the sample size is increased, the property increases. If the sample size is decreased, the property decreases. Extensive properties include volume, mass, weight, energy, entropy, number of moles, and electrical charge.

Atomic Properties of Neutral Atoms, Anions, and Cations

Neutral atoms have the same number of protons as electrons. **Cations** are positively-charged ions that are formed when atoms lose electrons. For example, the alkali metals sodium and potassium form the cations Na^+ and K^+, and the alkaline earth metals magnesium and calcium form the cations Mg^{2+} and Ca^{2+}. These elements easily lose electrons because the resulting ion is left with a full valence shell.

Anions are negatively-charged ions that are formed when atoms gain electrons. For example, the halogens fluorine and chlorine form the anions F^- and Cl^-. These elements easily gain electrons because the resulting ion has a full valence shell.

Chemical and Physical Changes

Physical changes do not produce new substances. The atoms or molecules may be rearranged, but no new substances are formed. **Phase changes**—changes of state such as melting, freezing, and sublimation—are physical changes. For example, physical changes include the melting of ice, the boiling of water, sugar dissolving into water, and the crushing of a piece of chalk into a fine powder.

Chemical changes involve a **chemical reaction** and do produce new substances. When iron rusts, iron oxide is formed, indicating a chemical change. Other examples of chemical changes include baking a cake, burning wood, digesting food, and mixing an acid and a base.

Energy in Chemistry

Conservation of Energy and Matter

Law of Conservation of Energy

The **law of conservation of energy** states that in a closed system, energy cannot be created or destroyed but only changed from one form to another. This is also known as the first law of thermodynamics. Another way to state this is that the **total energy in an isolated system is constant**. Energy comes in many forms that may be transformed from one kind to another, but in a closed system, the total amount of energy is conserved or remains constant. For example, potential energy can be converted to kinetic energy, thermal energy, radiant energy, or mechanical energy. In an isolated chemical reaction, there can be no energy created or destroyed. The energy simply changes forms.

Law of Conservation of Mass

The **law of conservation of mass** is also known as the **law of conservation of matter**. This law states that for a chemical reaction in a closed system, the total mass of the products must equal the total mass of the reactants. This could also be stated that in a closed system, mass never changes. A consequence of this law is that matter is never created or destroyed during a typical chemical reaction. The atoms of the reactants are only rearranged to form the products. The number and type of each specific atom involved in the reactants is identical to the number and type of atoms in the products. This is the key principle used when balancing chemical equations. In a balanced chemical equation, the number of moles of each element on the reactant side equals the number of moles of each element on the product side.

Review Video: Balancing Chemical Equations
Visit mometrix.com/academy and enter code: 341228

Conversion of Energy Within Chemical Systems

Chemical energy is the energy stored in molecules in the bonds between the atoms of those molecules and the energy associated with the intermolecular forces. This stored **potential energy** may be converted into **kinetic energy** and then into heat. During a chemical reaction, atoms may be rearranged and chemical bonds may be formed or broken accompanied by a corresponding absorption or release of energy, usually in the form of heat. According to the first law of thermodynamics, during these energy conversions, the **total amount of energy must be conserved**.

Basics of Radioactivity

Radioactivity

Radioisotopes: Also known as radionuclides or radioactive isotopes, radioisotopes are atoms that have an unstable nucleus. This is a nucleus that has excess energy and the potential to undergo radioactive decay, which most often results in the emission of alpha, beta, or gamma radiation. Many radionuclides occur naturally but others have only been produced artificially.

Radioactive decay: This occurs when an unstable atomic nucleus spontaneously loses energy by emitting ionizing particles and radiation. Decay is a form of energy transfer, as the energy lost by the nucleus is given to the particles or radiation emitted. It also results in products that are different from the initial atoms. Before decay there is one type of atom, called the **parent nuclide**. After decay there are one or more different products, called the **daughter nuclide(s)**.

Radioactivity: This refers to particles or energy that are emitted from nuclei as a result of nuclear instability.

Review Video: Radioactivity
Visit mometrix.com/academy and enter code: 537142

Radiation is the term for energy emitted or transmitted as waves or particles. Radiation is classified as either ionizing (able to detach an electron from an atom) or non-ionizing. Nuclear weapons, nuclear reactors, and radioactive substances are all examples of things that involve ionizing radiation. Acoustic radiation and electromagnetic radiation (with wavelength greater than 125 nm) are types of non-ionizing radiation.

Radioactive half-life is the time it takes for half of the radioactive nuclei in a sample to undergo radioactive decay. Radioactive decay rates are usually expressed in terms of half-lives. The different types of radioactivity lead to different decay paths, which transmute the nuclei into other chemical elements. **Decay products** (or daughter nuclides) make radioactive dating possible. **Decay chains** are a series of decays that result in different products. For example, uranium-238 is often found in granite. Its decay chain includes 14 daughter products. It eventually becomes a stable isotope of lead, which is why lead is often found with deposits of uranium ore. Its first half-life is equivalent to the approximate age of the earth, about 4.5 billion years. One of its products is radon, a radioactive gas.

Isotopes that have not been observed to decay are **stable**, or non-radioactive, isotopes. It is not known whether some stable isotopes may have such long decay times that observing decay is not possible. Currently, 80 elements have one or more stable isotopes. There are 256 known stable isotopes in total. Carbon, for example, has three isotopes. Two (carbon-12 and carbon-13) are stable and one (carbon-14) is radioactive.

Ionizing radiation comes in three types: alpha (α), beta (β), and gamma (γ). Alpha particles are positive, beta particles are negative, and gamma rays are neutral. **Alpha particles** are larger than beta particles and can cause severe damage if a source of alpha particles is ingested. Because of their large mass, however, they can be easily stopped. Even paper can protect against this type of radiation. **Beta particles** can be beta-minus or beta-plus. Beta-minus particles contain an energetic electron, while beta-plus particles are emitted by positrons. Beta particles can be stopped with a thin sheet of metal. **Gamma rays** are a type of high energy electromagnetic radiation. Gamma radiation is one of the ways a decaying nucleus emits excess energy after it has emitted either alpha or beta radiation. Gamma rays can cause serious damage when absorbed by living tissue, and it takes a lot of shielding (typically lead) to stop them. Alpha, beta, and gamma radiation can also have positive applications.

Nuclear fission and nuclear fusion are similar in that they occur in the nucleus of an atom, can release great amounts of energy, and result in the formation of different elements (nuclear transmutation). They are different in that **nuclear fission** is the splitting of a nucleus into smaller particles, and **nuclear fusion** is the joining of nuclei to form a heavier nucleus. It requires immense pressures and temperatures, but when fusion occurs, energy can either be absorbed or released, depending on the resultant nucleus. Fusion occurs naturally in stars, and is thought to be the process responsible for the generation of all naturally occurring elements (stellar nucleosynthesis).

Radioactive waste is a waste product that is considered dangerous because of either low levels or high levels of radioactivity. Radioactive waste could include discarded clothing that was used as protection against radiation, or decay products of substances used to create electricity through nuclear fission. Small amounts of radioactive material can be ingested as a method of tracing how the body distributes certain elements. Other radioactive materials are used as light sources because they glow when heated. Uncontrolled radiation or even small amounts of radioactive material can cause sickness and cancer in humans. **Gamma wave radiation** is fast-moving radiation that can cause cancer and damage genetic information by crashing into DNA molecules or other cells. Low-level radiation also occurs naturally. When related to everyday occurrences, radiation is measured in millirems per hour (mrem/hr). Humans can be exposed to radiation from stone used to build houses, cosmic rays from space, x-rays and other medical devices, and nuclear energy products.

Periodic Table Layout

PERIODIC TABLE LAYOUT

GROUPS AND PERIODS IN THE PERIODIC TABLE

A **group** is a vertical column of the periodic table. Elements in the same group have the same number of **valence electrons**. For the representative elements, the number of valence electrons is equal to the group number. Because of their equal valence electrons, elements in the same groups have similar physical and chemical properties. A **period** is a horizontal row of the periodic table. Atomic number increases from left to right across a row. The period of an element corresponds to the **highest energy level** of the electrons in the atoms of that element. The energy level increases from top to bottom down a group.

Period ↓ / Group →	1	2	3	4	5	6	7	8	9	10	11	12	13	14	15	16	17	18
1	1 H																	2 He
2	3 Li	4 Be											5 B	6 C	7 N	8 O	9 F	10 Ne
3	11 Na	12 Mg											13 Al	14 Si	15 P	16 S	17 Cl	18 Ar
4	19 K	20 Ca	21 Sc	22 Ti	23 V	24 Cr	25 Mn	26 Fe	27 Co	28 Ni	29 Cu	30 Zn	31 Ga	32 Ge	33 As	34 Se	35 Br	36 Kr
5	37 Rb	38 Sr	39 Y	40 Zr	41 Nb	42 Mo	43 Tc	44 Ru	45 Rh	46 Pd	47 Ag	48 Cd	49 In	50 Sn	51 Sb	52 Te	53 I	54 Xe
6	55 Cs	56 Ba	*	72 Hf	73 Ta	74 W	75 Re	76 Os	77 Ir	78 Pt	79 Au	80 Hg	81 Tl	82 Pb	83 Bi	84 Po	85 At	86 Rn
7	87 Fr	88 Ra	**	104 Rf	105 Db	106 Sg	107 Bh	108 Hs	109 Mt	110 Ds	111 Rg	112 Cn	113 Uut	114 Fl	115 Uup	116 Lv	117 Uus	118 Uuo
*			57 La	58 Ce	59 Pr	60 Nd	61 Pm	62 Sm	63 Eu	64 Gd	65 Tb	66 Dy	67 Ho	68 Er	69 Tm	70 Yb	71 Lu	
**			89 Ac	90 Th	91 Pa	92 U	93 Np	94 Pu	95 Am	96 Cm	97 Bk	98 Cf	99 Es	100 Fm	101 Md	102 No	103 Lr	

Review Video: Periodic Table
Visit mometrix.com/academy and enter code: 154828

ATOMIC NUMBER AND ATOMIC MASS IN THE PERIODIC TABLE

The elements in the periodic table are arranged in order of **increasing atomic number**, first left to right and then top to bottom across the periodic table. The **atomic number** represents the number of protons in the atoms of that element. Because of the increasing numbers of protons, the atomic mass typically also increases from left to right across a period and from top to bottom down a row. The **atomic mass** is a weighted average of all the naturally occurring isotopes of an element.

ATOMIC SYMBOLS

The **atomic symbol** for many elements is simply the first letter of the element name. For example, the atomic symbol for hydrogen is H, and the atomic symbol for carbon is C. The atomic symbol of other elements is the first two letters of the element name. For example, the atomic symbol for helium is He, and the atomic symbol for cobalt is Co. The atomic symbols of several elements are derived from Latin. For example, the atomic symbol for copper (Cu) is derived from *cuprum,* and the atomic symbol for iron (Fe) is derived from *ferrum.* The atomic symbol for tungsten (W) is derived from the German word *wolfram*.

Arrangement of Metals, Nonmetals, and Metalloids in the Periodic Table

The **metals** are located on the left side and center of the periodic table, and the **nonmetals** are located on the right side. The **metalloids** or **semimetals** form a zigzag line between the metals and nonmetals as shown below. Metals include the alkali metals, such as lithium, sodium, and potassium, and the alkaline earth metals, such as beryllium, magnesium, and calcium. Metals also include the transition metals, such as iron, copper, and nickel, and the inner transition metals, such as thorium, uranium, and plutonium. Nonmetals include the chalcogens, such as oxygen and sulfur; the halogens, such as fluorine and chlorine; and the noble gases, such as helium and argon. Carbon, nitrogen, and phosphorus are also nonmetals. Metalloids or semimetals include boron, silicon, germanium, antimony, and polonium.

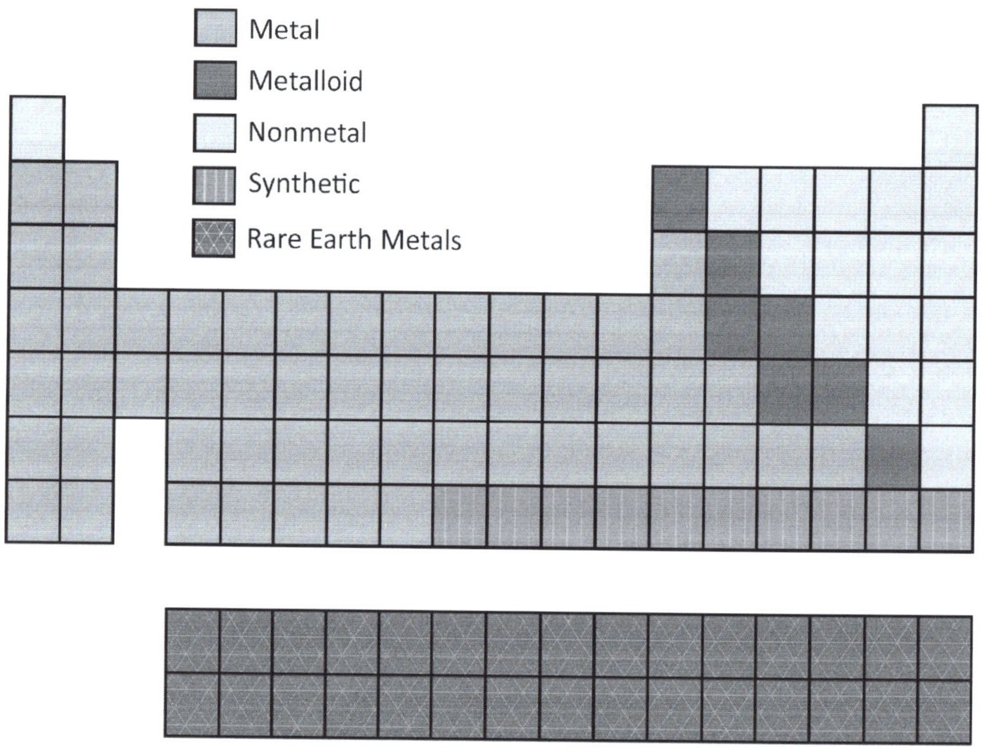

Arrangement of Transition Elements

The **transition elements** belong to one of two categories—transition metals or inner transition metals. The **transition metals** are located in the middle of the periodic table, and the inner transition metals are typically set off as two rows by themselves at the bottom of the periodic table. The transition metals correspond to the "*d* block" for orbital filling, and the inner transition metals correspond to the "*f* block" for orbital filling. Examples of transition metals include iron, copper, nickel, and zinc. The **inner transition metals** consist of the lanthanide or rare-earth series, which corresponds to the first row, and the actinide series, which corresponds to the second row of the inner transition metals. The **lanthanide series** includes lanthanum, cerium, and praseodymium. The **actinide series** includes actinium, uranium, and plutonium.

Bonds

Bond Types

Bonds

Chemical bonds are the attractive forces that bind atoms together into molecules. Atoms form chemical bonds in an attempt to satisfy the octet rule. These bond types include covalent bonds, ionic bonds, and metallic bonds. **Covalent bonds** are formed from the sharing of electron pairs between two atoms in a molecule. **Ionic bonds** are formed from the transferring of electrons between one atom and another, which results in the formations of cations and anions. **Metallic bonding** results from the sharing of delocalized electrons among all of the atoms in a molecule.

Ionic Bonding

Ionic bonding results from the transfer of electrons between atoms. A **cation** or positive ion is formed when an atom loses one or more electrons. An **anion** or negative ion is formed when an atom gains one or more electrons. An ionic bond results from the electrostatic attraction between a cation and an anion. One example of a compound formed by ionic bonds is sodium chloride or NaCl. Sodium (Na) is an alkali metal and tends to form Na^+ ions. Chlorine (Cl) is a halogen and tends to form Cl^- ions. The Na^+ ion and the Cl^- ion are attracted to each other. This electrostatic attraction between these oppositely charged ions is what results in the ionic bond between them.

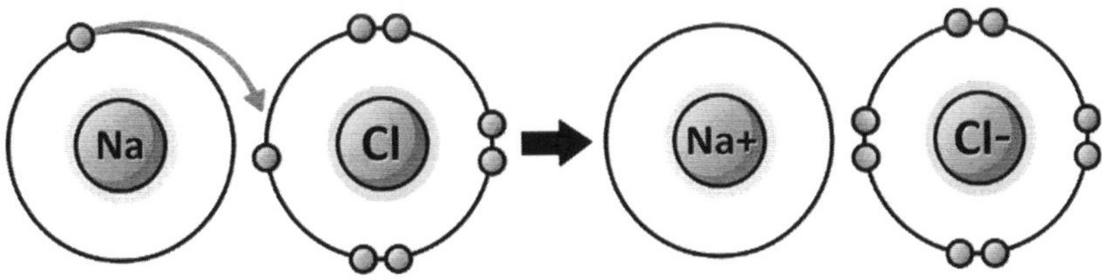

Review Video: Ionic Bonds
Visit mometrix.com/academy and enter code: 116546

Covalent Bonding

Covalent bonding results from the sharing of electrons between atoms. Atoms seek to fill their valence shell and will share electrons with another atom in order to have a full octet (except hydrogen and helium, which only hold two electrons in their valence shells). **Molecular compounds** have covalent bonds. **Organic compounds** such as proteins, carbohydrates, lipids, and nucleic acids are molecular compounds formed by covalent bonds. Methane (CH_4) is a molecular compound in which one carbon atom is covalently bonded to four hydrogen atoms as shown below.

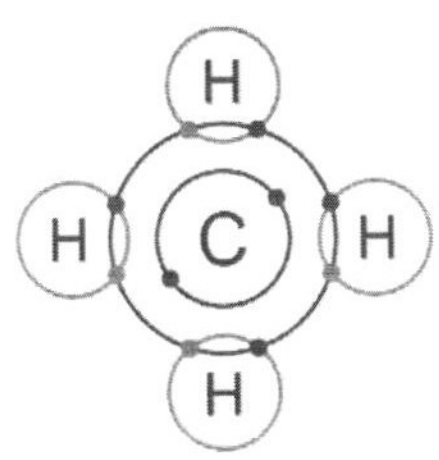

Polar Covalent Bonds, Nonpolar Covalent Bonds, and Hybridization

Polar covalent bonds result when electrons are shared unequally between atoms. **Nonpolar covalent bonds** result when electrons are shared equally between atoms. The unequal sharing of electrons is due to the differences in the electronegativities of the two atoms sharing the electrons. Partial charges develop due to this unequal sharing of electrons. The greater the difference in electronegativities between the two atoms, the stronger the dipole is. For example, the covalent bonds formed between the carbon atom and the two oxygen atoms in carbon dioxide are polar covalent bonds because the electronegativities of carbon and oxygen differ slightly. If the electronegativities are equal, then the covalent bonds are nonpolar. For example, the covalent double bond between two oxygen atoms is nonpolar because the oxygen atoms have the same electronegativities.

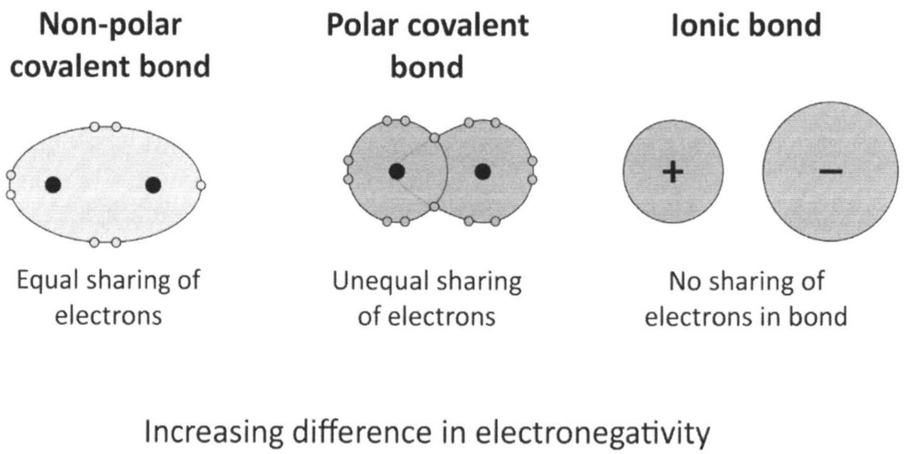

Review Video: Nonpolar Covalent Bonds
Visit mometrix.com/academy and enter code: 986465

Review Video: Covalent Bonds
Visit mometrix.com/academy and enter code: 482899

METALLIC BONDING

Metallic bonding is a type of bonding between metals. Metallic bonds are similar to covalent bonds in that they are a type of sharing of electrons between atoms. However, in covalent bonding, the electrons are shared with only one other atom. In metallic bonding, the electrons are shared with all the surrounding atoms. These electrons are referred to as delocalized electrons. Metallic bonding is responsible for many of the characteristics in metals including conductivity, malleability, and ductility. An example of metallic bonding is the metallic bond between the copper atoms in a piece of copper wire.

Review Video: Metallic Bonds
Visit mometrix.com/academy and enter code: 230855

Chemical Reactions

Reaction Types

Types of Reactions

One way to organize chemical reactions is to sort them into two categories: **oxidation/reduction reactions** (also called redox reactions) and **metathesis reactions** (which include acid/base reactions). Oxidation/reduction reactions can involve the transfer of one or more electrons, or they can occur as a result of the transfer of oxygen, hydrogen, or halogen atoms. The species that loses electrons (or increases its oxidation state) is oxidized and is referred to as the reducing agent. The species that gains electrons (or decreases its oxidation state) is reduced and is referred to as the oxidizing agent. **Single substitution reactions** are types of oxidation/reduction reactions. In a single substitution reaction, electrons are transferred from one chemical species to another. The transfer of electrons results in changes in the nature and charge of the species.

Review Video: Understanding Chemical Reactions
Visit mometrix.com/academy and enter code: 579876

Review Video: The Process of a Reaction
Visit mometrix.com/academy and enter code: 808039

Substitution Reactions

Single substitution, **displacement**, or **replacement reactions** are when one reactant is displaced by another to form the final product ($A + BC \rightarrow AB + C$). Single substitution reactions can be cationic or anionic. When a piece of copper (Cu) is placed into a solution of silver nitrate ($AgNO_3$), the solution turns blue. The copper appears to be replaced with a silvery white material. The equation is $2AgNO_3 + Cu \rightarrow Cu(NO_3)_2 + 2Ag$. When this reaction takes place, the copper dissolves and the silver in the silver nitrate solution precipitates (becomes a solid), resulting in copper nitrate and silver. Copper and silver have switched places in the nitrate.

Double substitution reactions, also called **double displacement**, **double replacement**, **metathesis**, or **ion exchange reactions**, are those where ions or bonds are exchanged by two compounds to form different compounds ($AC + BD \rightarrow AD + BC$). An example of this is that silver nitrate and sodium chloride form two different products (silver chloride and sodium nitrate) when they react. The formula for this reaction is $AgNO_3 + NaCl \rightarrow AgCl + NaNO_3$.

Review Video: Single-Replacement Reactions
Visit mometrix.com/academy and enter code: 442975

Combination and Decomposition Reactions

Combination, or **synthesis**, **reactions**: In a combination reaction, two or more reactants combine to form a single product ($A + B \rightarrow AB$). These reactions are also called synthesis or **addition reactions**. An example is burning hydrogen in air to produce water. The equation is $2H_2(g) + O_2(g) \rightarrow 2H_2O(l)$. Another example is when water and sulfur trioxide react to form sulfuric acid. The equation is $H_2O + SO_3 \rightarrow H_2SO_4$.

Decomposition (or desynthesis, decombination, or deconstruction) reactions: In a decomposition reaction, a reactant is broken down into two or more products ($AB \rightarrow A + B$). These reactions are also called analysis reactions. **Thermal decomposition** is caused by heat. **Electrolytic**

decomposition is due to electricity. An example of this type of reaction is the decomposition of water into hydrogen and oxygen gas. The equation is $2H_2O \rightarrow 2H_2 + O_2$.

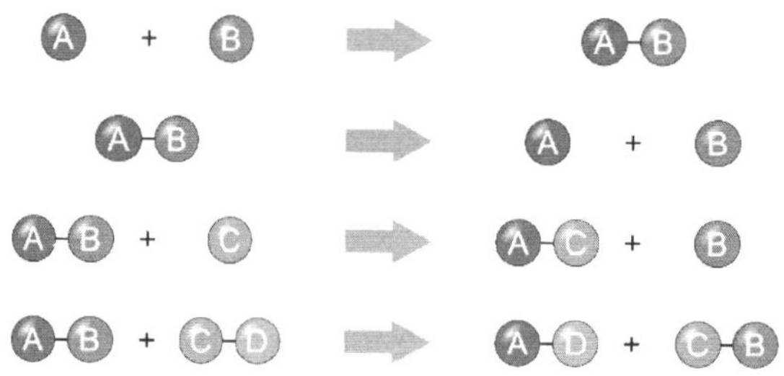

Acid/Base Reactions

In **acid/base reactions**, an **acid** is a compound that can donate a proton, while a **base** is a compound that can accept a proton. In these types of reactions, the acid and base react to form a salt and water. When the proton is donated, the base becomes water and the remaining ions form a salt. One method of determining whether a reaction is an oxidation/reduction or a metathesis reaction is that the oxidation number of atoms does not change during a metathesis reaction.

Isomerization and Neutralization Reactions

Isomerization, or **rearrangement**, is the process changing a compound to an isomer. Within a compound, bonds are reformed. The reactant and product have the same molecular formula, but different structural formulas and different properties ($A \rightarrow A'$). For example, butane (C_4H_{10}) is a hydrocarbon consisting of four carbon atoms in a straight chain. Heating it to 100 °C or higher in the presence of a catalyst forms isobutane (methylpropane), which has a branched-chain structure. Boiling and freezing points are greatly different for butane and isobutane.

A **neutralization**, **acid-base**, or **proton transfer reaction** occurs when one compound acquires H^+ from another. These types of reactions are also usually double displacement reactions. The acid has an H^+ that is transferred to the base and the acid and base are neutralized in the form of a salt that, depending on the salt's solubility, may precipitate from the solution.

Chemical Kinetics

Chemical kinetics is the study of the **rates** of **chemical reactions** and the various factors that affect these rates. The rate of a reaction is the change in concentration of the reactants or products per unit of time. Another way to state this is that chemical kinetics is the study of the rate of change of the concentrations of the reactants and products and the factors that affect that rate of change. The study of catalysts is part of chemical kinetics. Catalysts are substances that speed up the rate of reactions without being consumed. Examples of reactions that occur at different rates include the explosion of trinitrotoluene (TNT), which occurs at a very fast rate, compared to the burning of a log, which occurs at a much slower rate.

Give the Rate Law for this General Reaction: $aA + bB + cC \rightarrow$ Products. Define Each Letter.

The rate of a chemical reaction can be defined as the following:

$$\text{rate} = \frac{\text{change in concentration}}{\text{change in time}}$$

This is usually represented by a rate law. The rate law for the general reaction $aA + bB + cC \rightarrow$ Products is given by rate $= k[A]^x[B]^y[C]^z$, where k is the rate constant; [A], [B], and [C] represent the concentrations of the reactants; and x, y, and z represent the reaction orders. The exponents x, y, and z must be experimentally determined. They do not necessarily equal the coefficients from the balanced chemical equation.

Activation Energy

Activation energy is the minimum amount of energy that must be possessed by reactant atoms or molecules in order to react. This is due to the fact that it takes a certain amount of energy to break bonds or form bonds between atoms. Reactants lacking the activation energy required will not be able to perform the necessary breaking or forming of bonds regardless of how often they collide. Catalysts lower the activation energy of a reaction and therefore increase the rate of reaction.

Reaction Mechanism

Often, when studying specific reactions, only the net reactions are given. Realistically, reactions take place in a series of steps or elementary reactions as shown in the reaction mechanism. **Reaction mechanisms** show how a reaction proceeds in a **series of steps**. Some steps are slow, and some are fast. Each step has its own reaction mechanism. The slowest step in the reaction mechanism coincides with the step with the greatest activation energy. This step is known as the rate-determining step.

Catalyst

A **catalyst** is a chemical that **accelerates** or speeds up a chemical reaction without being consumed or used up in the reaction. Although catalysts are not consumed or permanently changed during the process of the reaction, catalysts do participate in the elementary reaction of the reaction mechanisms. Catalysts lower the **activation energy** meaning more of the reactant molecules will have sufficient energy to react.

Review Video: Catalysts
Visit mometrix.com/academy and enter code: 288189

Factors That Affect Reaction Rate

Factors that affect reaction rate include concentration, surface area, and temperature. Increasing the **concentration** of the reactants increases the number of collisions between those reactants and therefore increases the reaction rate. Increasing the **surface area of contact** between the reactants also increases the number of collisions and therefore increases the reaction rate. Finally, increasing the **temperature** of the reactants increases the number of collisions but more significantly also increases the kinetic energy of the reactants, which in turn increases the fraction of molecules meeting the activation energy requirement. With more molecules at the activation energy, more of the reactants are capable of completing the reaction.

Acids and Bases

Overview of Acids and Bases

Differences Between Acids and Bases

There are several differences between acids and bases. While it is never a good idea to taste chemicals directly or feel chemicals without gloves, it has been done in the past and we now know that acidic solutions tend to taste sour, whereas basic solutions tend to taste bitter. Dilute bases tend to feel slippery, whereas dilute acids feel like water. Active metals such as magnesium and zinc react with acids to produce hydrogen gas, but active metals usually do not react with bases. Acids and bases form electrolytes in aqueous solutions and conduct electricity. Acids turn blue litmus red, but bases turn red litmus blue. Acidic solutions have a pH of less than 7, whereas basic solutions have a pH of greater than 7.

Review Video: Properties of Acids and Bases
Visit mometrix.com/academy and enter code: 645283

Arrhenius Acid and Base

Arrhenius acids are substances that produce hydrogen ions (H^+) when dissolved in water to form aqueous solutions. Arrhenius bases are substances that produce hydroxide ions (OH^-) when dissolved in water to form aqueous solutions. The **Arrhenius concept** is limited to acids and bases in aqueous solutions and cannot be applied to other solids, liquids, and gases. Examples of Arrhenius acids include hydrochloric acid (HCl) and sulfuric acid (H_2SO_4). Examples of Arrhenius bases include sodium hydroxide (NaOH) and magnesium hydroxide ($Mg(OH)_2$).

Brønsted–Lowry Acid and Base

The Brønsted–Lowry concept is based on the donation or the acceptance of a proton. According to the **Brønsted–Lowry concept**, an acid is a substance that donates one or more protons to another substance and a base is a substance that accepts a proton from another substance. The Brønsted–Lowry concept can be applied to substances other than aqueous solutions. This concept is much broader than the Arrhenius concept, which can only be applied to aqueous solutions. The Brønsted–Lowry concept states that a substance cannot act like an acid (donate its proton) unless another substance is available to act as a base (accept the donated proton). In this concept, water may act as either an acid or a base. Hydrochloric acid (HCl) is an example of a Brønsted–Lowry acid. Ammonia (NH_3) is an example of a Brønsted–Lowry base.

Lewis Acid and Base

A **Lewis acid** is any substance that can accept a pair of nonbonding electrons. A **Lewis base** is any substance that can donate a pair of nonbonding electrons. According to the **Lewis theory**, all cations such as Mg^{2+} and Cu^{2+} are Lewis acids. Trigonal planar molecules, which are exceptions to the octet rule such as BF_3, are Lewis acids. Molecules such as CO_2 that have multiple bonds between two atoms that differ in electronegativities are Lewis acids, also. According to the Lewis theory, all anions such as OH^- are Lewis bases. Other examples of Lewis bases include trigonal pyramidal molecules such as ammonia and nonmetal oxides such as carbon monoxide, CO. Some compounds, such as water, can act as either Lewis acids or bases depending on the context.

Neutralization Reaction

Neutralization is a reaction of an acid and a base that yields a salt and water. The general form of the reaction is:

$$\text{acid} + \text{base} \rightarrow \text{salt} + \text{water}$$

The salt is formed from the cation of the base and the anion of the acid. The water is formed from the cation of the acid and the anion of the base.

An example is the neutralization reaction of hydrochloric acid and sodium hydroxide to form sodium chloride and water:

$$HCl(aq) + NaOH(aq) \rightarrow NaCl(s) + H_2O(l)$$

Equivalence Point

The **equivalence point** is by definition the point in a titration at which the analyte is neutralized. When the acid–base indicator starts to change color, the equivalence point has been reached. At this point, equivalent amounts of acids and bases have reacted. Also, at this point the concentration of cations of hydrogen is equal to the concentration of hydroxide anions. On an acid–base titration curve, the slope of the curve increases dramatically at the equivalence point. For strong acids and bases, the equivalence point occurs at a pH of 7. The figures below show the equivalence points for a strong acid titrated with a strong base (a) and a strong base titrated with a strong acid (b).

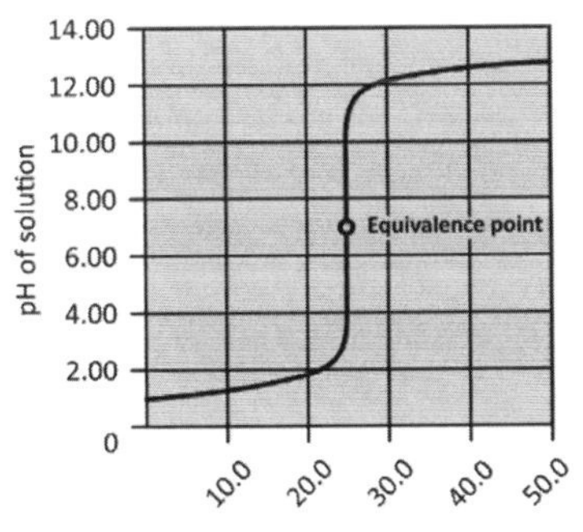

(a) Strong acid titrated with strong base

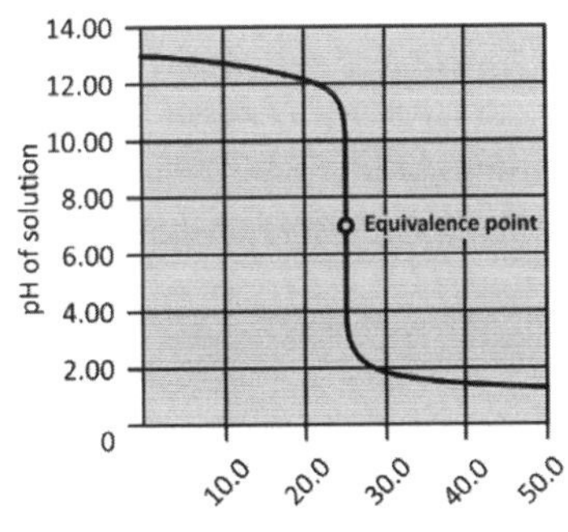

(b) Strong base titrated with strong acid

Review Video: Titration
Visit mometrix.com/academy and enter code: 550131

Solutions

Terminology for Solutions and Solubility

Dilute and Concentrated

The terms *dilute* and *concentrated* have opposite meanings. In a **solution**, the **solute** is dissolved in the **solvent**. The more solute that is dissolved, the more **concentrated** is the solution. The less solute that is dissolved, the less concentrated and the more **dilute** is the solution. The terms are often associated with the preparation of a stock solution for a laboratory experiment. Stock solutions are typically acquired in a higly concentrated form. Typically, diluted forms of the solutions are used which must be prepared from the concentrated stock solutions. The desired dilutions are achieved by combining a specific amount of a solvent with a specific amount of stock solution.

Saturated, Unsaturated, and Supersaturated

Solutions can be categorized based on their saturation. In a **saturated** solution, the solute is added to the solvent until no more solute is able to dissolve. The undissolved solute will settle down to the bottom of the beaker. A solution is considered **unsaturated** as long as more solute is able to go into solution under ordinary conditions. The solubility of solids in liquids typically increases as temperature increases. If the temperature of a solution is increased as the solute is being added, more solute than is normally possible may go into solution, forming a **supersaturated** solution.

Mixture, Solution, and Colloid

A **mixture** is made of two or more substances that are combined in various proportions. The exact proportion of the constituents is the defining characteristic of any mixture. There are two types of mixtures: homogeneous and heterogeneous. **Homogeneous** means that the mixture's composition and properties are uniform throughout. Conversely, **heterogeneous** means that the mixture's composition and properties are not uniform throughout.

A **solution** is a homogeneous mixture of substances that cannot be separated by filtration or centrifugation. Solutions are made by dissolving one or more solutes into a solvent. For example, in an aqueous glucose solution, glucose is the solute and water is the solvent. If there is more than one liquid present in the solution, then the most prevalent liquid is considered the solvent. The exact mechanism of dissolving varies depending on the mixture, but the result is always individual solute ions or molecules surrounded by solvent molecules. The proportion of solute to solvent for a particular solution is its **concentration**.

A **colloid** is a heterogeneous mixture in which small particles (<1 micrometer) are suspended, but not dissolved, in a liquid. As such, they can be separated by centrifugation. A commonplace example of a colloid is milk.

Review Video: Solutions
Visit mometrix.com/academy and enter code: 995937

Chapter Quiz

Ready to see how well you retained what you just read? Scan the QR code to go directly to the chapter quiz interface for this study guide. If you're using a computer, simply visit the online resources page at **mometrix.com/resources719/texesmathpse** and click the Chapter Quizzes link.

Scientific Learning

Developing Scientific Understanding

Scientific understanding involves not merely the knowledge of scientific theories and equations, but a comprehension of how science is done, how we come to know these theories (and how confident we are in them), and how the different domains of science fit together. Students are unlikely to develop a good scientific understanding merely by being presented with isolated facts. Rather, research suggests that a scientific understanding is best fostered by **inquiry** and by **problem-based learning** approaches, which help students develop their own critical thinking and reasoning skills. In these methods, students are not just provided with facts and theories to memorize but are led to "discover" principles on their own, through experimentation and analogy. The instructor must still provide guidance in the process; if students are completely left to their own devices they may be confused or arrive at incorrect conclusions that may do more harm than good. Furthermore, assessments used in the classroom should promote **higher-order learning**, focusing not just on repetition of facts but on reasoning and evaluation of claims. It is critical that students understand that science is a process and a way of knowing, not a collection of facts.

Prior Knowledge

Students vary in their prior knowledge and capabilities, and science instruction is not a one-size-fits-all process. Sometimes prior knowledge helps student, in that they already have some knowledge about the subject in question, but sometimes prior knowledge may seem to conflict with the new information being taught—a dilemma sometimes called the "**paradox of continuity**." Learning therefore can require a **conceptual change**, in a way that allows the students to reformulate their understanding to fit new information.

Students' experience and developmental characteristics can also affect their science learning. Some students learn more effectively through different **learning styles**, or modalities: some learn best from what they see (**visual learners**), others from what they hear (**auditory learners**), still others from handling objects (**tactile learners**), and others from active participation (**kinesthetic learners**). **Abstract thinking** develops during adolescence and may develop more rapidly in some students than others; students who have not fully developed this capability may benefit from more structured teaching methods. Adolescents tend to be at a stage in their social development in which they learn well in cooperative group activities.

Planning Activities

Instructors should be aware of and sensitive to students' different preferred styles of learning and prepare lessons that engage all these styles. The instructor should also try to tie lessons to students' individual interests in order to promote active engagement. A **positive learning environment** is one that adapts to students' individual needs and that often involves students working cooperatively.

In science in particular it's important for instructors not to exclude women and minorities, since they have been excluded so much in the past that it's easy to do so unconsciously. The instructor should make an effort to mention scientists of different ethnicities and genders and make it clear that women and minorities can be and are capable scientists.

Students currently learning English have their own needs that must be addressed. The instructor can help English learners, for instance, by speaking slowly and clearly, by writing down and providing definitions of key terms, by using visual aids and graphic organizers (which also may help visual learners who are not English language learners), and by giving access to translating devices if necessary. English learners can also benefit from working in groups with capable English speakers who can help explain instructions and procedures they don't understand.

Motivation and Engagement

Regardless of how clearly and accurately an instructor explains the topic, the students may not learn if they're unengaged and not paying attention. Therefore, it's important for the teacher to engage the students' interest and keep their attention. One of the advantages of inquiry-based learning is that it actively involves the students and keeps them more engaged by relating the topic to their interests and goals and finding ways to tie the topics in to the students' own experiences, prior knowledge, and daily lives. This requires the teacher to get to know the students and their interests, but this has other benefits as well: the students are also more engaged when there is a good relationship between the teachers and students.

Students also tend to be more engaged by collaborative group activities than by working on their own. Adolescents are at a stage in their social development in which they are increasingly driven to form social attachments with their peers. They are comfortable working in groups and benefit from collaborative learning environments.

Texts Used in the Classroom

Science instruction often involves the students acquiring information from textbooks and handouts, but not all students may be able to effectively use these texts without guidance. Most textbooks have various features designed to make it easier to locate information: an **index**, a **table of contents**, and often a **glossary** and/or a list of important variables and formulas. An instructor can explain how to use these features at the beginning of the year and perhaps even assign an activity that involves making use of them.

It may also be helpful to teach **active reading** techniques. One such technique is **pre-reading**—skimming and reading the headings before reading the text in depth, making predictions and building background knowledge. The instructor can also encourage active reading techniques through providing graphic organizers or techniques like **SQ3R**—a method that involves the student first Surveying the chapter, then formulating Questions about each section, then Reading the section, Reciting the main ideas (putting them in their own words), and Reviewing the material.

In the modern classroom, textbooks aren't the only kind of text that students can take advantage of. An effective teacher can also show students how to find information online, through web searches and reference sites.

Total School Program

While the science teachers plan the curriculum for their classes, they must also be aware of the **total school program**—the overall objectives for the students' learning in all subjects. The science teacher must be aware of school-wide objectives, and make sure that they are being adequately met in his or her class. The science instructor may also have a role in *setting* those objectives, in conjunction with other teachers and administrators; the science instructor in this case should work cooperatively with the rest of the team and ensure that any issues unique or important to the science classroom are properly addressed and incorporated into the objectives.

The science teacher must also be mindful of the statewide objectives. State standards lay out the curriculum requirements for the course and specify topics that must be covered. Students must master these topics to be ready not only for standardized exams, but to ensure that no gaps in understanding exist prior to advancing to the next grade-level.

Supportive Learning Environment

Creating a learning environment that supports student inquiries involves both setting certain procedures and expectations in the class and providing resources that lend themselves to inquiry-based learning. To encourage inquiry-based learning, the instructor should encourage students to ask questions, but try to guide them toward finding answers for themselves rather than giving direct answers to their questions. The instructor should pose questions that require higher-order thinking rather than rote recall or yes or no answers and include a time for reflection in each lesson. Lessons in inquiry-based classrooms are centered around projects and experiments rather than lectures—in fact, one increasingly popular technique is to "**flip the classroom**," having the students read the lesson or watch video lectures you provide as their homework and freeing up class time for discussion and analysis.

An inquiry-centered classroom environment should put a priority on student collaboration. The instructor should give the students assignments that involve their working together as much as practical. It is helpful to have some online resources that facilitate collaboration and sharing of information, such as a class website, and perhaps a class blog and wiki. Many online resources allow students to share documents and work on them together.

Participation in Scientific Investigation

Scientific investigations are an important part of science teaching, and it is vital that all students are given the opportunity to participate. Ideally, there will be enough space and equipment for the students to work in small groups on an experiment, but in practice this may not be possible. In this case, one solution is to have rotating stations in the classroom, where for one day or for part of the period one group works on one experiment, while another group works on a different activity that uses different equipment; as they rotate through the different stations, all the students will have the opportunity to do every activity, just not in the same order.

Another important part of making it possible for all students to participate in scientific investigations is to ensure that they all have the means to understand and carry out the instructions. Going over the procedure in a lecture may not be enough; it may be better to have a written handout and/or a screencast that the students can watch and refer back to as needed. Students with special needs must also be accommodated; for instance, English language learners can be given definitions of key terms.

Active Learning, Inquiry, and Reflection

Active learning and inquiry-based learning are two related pedagogical techniques that have been shown by research to be effective in teaching science. **Active learning** refers to teaching by making the student an active participant in the learning process. A class in which the instructor lectures, the students take notes, and the students later demonstrate their learning of the topic by taking a written exam is *not* engaged in active learning, and is not likely to be as effective. Active learning can include experiments that the students perform, interactive online simulations of processes that they can't physically experience in the classroom, and having the students create presentations and projects rather than have exams and worksheets as the main assessments.

Inquiry-based learning is a form of teaching by asking questions, having discussions, and helping students do their own research rather than just presenting them with lists of facts and formulas to be learned. Inquiry-based learning is effective not only because it involves the students directly, but because allowing them to formulate their own questions engages their curiosity and critical thinking. **Reflection** is also an important part of inquiry-based learning, having students think back on what they learned and how they learned it.

Modeling Scientific Thought

Modeling, in a pedagogical context, refers to *showing* the students what they should do, rather than telling them. This doesn't mean just demonstrating an activity at the front of the classroom while the students watch passively; effective modeling also involves the students as active participants. The important thing is that the teacher sets an example of the principles he or she wants to convey.

To model scientific attitudes, therefore, means to demonstrate and embody those attitudes. To instill curiosity and skepticism in students, the teacher should display those attributes. If the teacher doesn't know the answer to a question, the teacher should not be afraid to say "I don't know"—but should follow that by trying to find the answer, by looking it up online or by performing an experiment. When discussing a topic and coming up with questions about it, the instructor should come up with questions as well—ideally questions the instructor honestly doesn't know the answer to. On the other hand, the instructor should not be too quick to accept answers—not, for instance, immediately latching onto the first answer found online, but looking for multiple sources of information and analyzing their credibility.

Inquiry-Based Scientific Investigation

An **inquiry-based scientific investigation** is one that follows the **scientific method**. While the scientific method is often formalized in different ways, there are some essential aspects. The investigator formulates a specific **question** that the investigation will answer. Usually this question is based on an **observation** that the investigation is intended to explain. The investigator then does some background **research**, reviewing previously published information on the subject in question. For a professional scientist, this will usually involve reading articles in scientific journals; in a classroom setting, a web search may suffice. The investigator may formulate a **hypothesis**—a proposed possible answer to the question.

The investigator decides how to **gather evidence** to find an answer to the question and prove or disprove the hypothesis, designing an **experiment** that will test the hypothesis, and selecting the proper tools to carry it out. The investigator makes **predictions** as to what will happen in the experiment if the hypothesis is true or if it is not. The investigator then carries out the experiment, gathers data, and analyzes the results, drawing **conclusions** based on the data.

There remain other important steps: **communication** of the results to others, defending the results, and possibly formulating further questions.

Formulating Scientific Questions

Formulating scientific questions is an important part of an inquiry-based investigation; an investigation starts with a specific question, and then an experiment is designed to answer that question. The question usually is based on an observation: the student observes a phenomenon and then formulates a question about what was observed. The question should be as concrete, objective, quantitative, and measurable as possible. "Why did this object move?" is a vague and abstract question that cannot be easily answered. "Did this object move because of this force?" is more concrete. "What is the relationship between this force and the motion of this object?" is a good quantitative question that can potentially be answered by experiment.

To help the student to formulate a question, the instructor can first guide students through an observation, encouraging the students to think of anything about the observation they're curious about or that they don't understand. The instructor can then help the students come up with questions addressing the subject of their curiosity, and then gradually guide the students into making the questions more specific and measurable.

Hypotheses

The **hypothesis** is an educated guess as to the answer to the central question of a scientific investigation. It is an important part of the investigation because it helps guide the inquiry and suggest specific lines of investigation that can prove or disprove the hypothesis: the experiment at the heart of the investigation should be designed such that it will have different results depending on whether or not the hypothesis is correct.

It is important that the hypothesis is an *educated* guess; the student may not know the answer to the question, but there should be some basis for choosing the hypothesis—by extrapolation from known cases, or by analogy with similar scenarios. If the student has trouble coming up with a hypothesis, the instructor might prompt the student to think of similar situations the student understands better, or to research such situations that have been investigated before, and then to consider what those situations imply about the present question. Even a very loose analogy can be enough to make a hypothesis—for the purposes of the investigation, it doesn't matter that the student chooses a hypothesis that turns out to be *right*, only that it relates to the question.

Scientific Results

There are many methods that can be used to analyze and evaluate scientific results. Often **graphs** help investigators and readers visualize data better. If one variable is plotted against another and the points seem to form a straight line, that is evidence that a linear relationship may exist between these variables; if they form a parabola, they may have a quadratic relationship; and so on. In more advanced classes, **statistical methods** may be useful, from methods as simple as taking the **mean** of multiple measurements and comparing the means of sets of data rather than the individual points, to methods as complex as calculating **standard deviations** and **correlation coefficients**. All of these methods help show the relationships between quantities and can help to evaluate possible explanations of a result.

Error analysis is another important part of evaluating results. Students should have an idea of what possible sources of error exist in the experiment, and whether they are **random** or **systematic**. Random error can be identified by taking repeated measurements and seeing how close they are; identifying systematic error involves a more thoughtful consideration of what could lead results to be off in one direction or the other.

Higher-Level Thinking Skills

Students should be encouraged to engage in not just rote memorization and learning of procedures, but in higher-order thinking as well that involves putting together what they've learned in constructive ways. The most commonly used model of different levels of thinking in education is **Bloom's taxonomy**, which divides cognitive processes into six categories or levels. The lowest level, **Remember**, involves simple recall of data. The next, **Understand**, requires students to be able to explain or discuss concepts in their own words. Then come **Apply**, using the concepts in practice; **Analyze**, drawing connections and comparisons between ideas; **Evaluate**, judging and justifying ideas; and **Create**, synthesizing something new from the concepts.

It's easy to design activities that utilize the lower levels of Bloom's Taxonomy. Engaging the higher orders of thinking is more difficult, but it is important for developing a more thorough understanding of a topic. Some verbs commonly associated with each level of Bloom's Taxonomy give clues as to how to promote them. "Create", for example, is associated with the verbs "construct," "plan," and "design" (among others)—certainly designing an experiment to answer a specific question fits here. "Evaluate" is associated with "appraise," "argue," and "justify"—students could be asked to assess a scientific claim and argue for or against it.

Systematic Observations and Measurements

In a scientific investigation, observations are not haphazard; there are certain systematic principles that must be followed for useful observations. As far as possible, the observations should be **quantitative**; there should be some measured value recorded, and not simply a qualitative observation such as "it is longer". Measurements should be taken by a consistent method and recorded with proper units—and with an estimate of their **uncertainty**. A measurement taken with a meter stick with markings every millimeter, for instance, has an uncertainty of ±0.5 mm.

It is also important when making observations to vary only one quantity at a time. If you want to measure how a plant's growth is affected by temperature and by amount of light, it isn't useful to change both factors for each measurement—that would make it impossible to see how much of the effect was produced by each change. Rather, it is better to do at least one set of measurements in which the temperature is held constant and the amount of light is changed, and another where the reverse is true, so that the effects of each factor can be isolated. In many cases, an **experimental control** is also desirable.

Students' Prior Knowledge

Prior knowledge refers to the knowledge the student has about the subject matter before it's covered in class. This may come from previous classes, from books and television, from peers or parents, from experience, or from other sources. It's useful to know what prior knowledge students possess before the lesson begins, and there are a number of ways of finding out. One way is through **formative assessments**, assessments that are designed not to test what the student has learned but to test what the students already know in order to guide lesson planning. Another popular way of testing prior knowledge is a **K-W-L chart**, in which students write down what they *know* about the topic, what they *want* to know, and, after the lesson, what they *learned*.

The instructor can use the students' prior knowledge as a starting point for the lesson; having the students share what they already know can help introduce the topic. Prior knowledge may also guide the instructor's approach to the topic, since it may carry some assumptions or preconceptions that will affect the way the student might react to different presentations. In some cases, prior knowledge may even lead to misconceptions that must be overcome.

Performance in Inquiry-Based Investigations

The stereotypical classroom assessment may be a multiple-choice quiz, but this is not generally the most effective way of assessing student learning in an inquiry-based classroom. There may be a place for written exams as summative assessments, but more effective assessment methods will engage students' higher-order thinking processes and may involve collaboration and active participation.

For example, in a science class, a lab report can be a useful assessment; after performing an experiment, students may be asked to turn in a written account of the procedure and results. Along similar lines, a laboratory journal that students keep during an experiment can also be used for assessment, or a field journal for longer-term projects. The instructor may require students to compile all their work in a portfolio, to be turned in at the end of the semester or at shorter intervals; this can serve as a summative assessment in lieu of or in addition to a traditional exam. To assess the student's participation in a classroom activity as objectively as possible, rather than make a subjective judgment call the instructor can use checklists or a detailed rubric prepared ahead of time.

Assessment and Instruction

An **assessment** is an activity designed to measure students' knowledge, learning, or abilities, such as an exam. Assessments are not limited to testing how much the student has learned after a lesson; there are also formative assessments used before or during a lesson to test the student's prior knowledge and how well they are learning the topic.

There are important relationships between assessment and instruction, and the two must be designed together. Formative assessments guide instruction, since the instructor should take into account students' prior knowledge in planning a lesson, and if a formative assessment shows that students are not learning what the instructor expects, the instructor should use that information to try a different pedagogical approach. As for summative assessments, they should be designed to match the learning objectives; the instructor should make sure that the summative assessment is designed to test that the students have met the specific instructional goals of the lessons.

Ongoing Assessment

Ongoing assessment is vital in science instruction for several reasons. For one thing, formative assessments are important so that the instructor can be informed of the students' prior knowledge and plan the lesson accordingly. If the instructor learns from a formative assessment that the students lack some prior knowledge necessary to the lesson, then the instructor will have to be sure to cover that first; if the instructor learns that the students have a significant misconception about the topic, then the instructor may have to plan for a conceptual change. During the lesson, further formative assessments can monitor students' learning and inform the instructor whether the students are absorbing the information and methodologies that the instructor intends them to absorb, or whether the pace of the lesson should be changed or different pedagogical methods adopted.

Ongoing assessments can also benefit the students by reinforcing the subject matter. The assessments give the students another opportunity to put what they have learned to use, and may help them better retain it. They also give the students an idea of how well they are learning, and what topics they might need to review or about which they should ask more questions.

Types of Assessments

Assessments are divided into two main categories: **summative assessments** that measure how well students have learned the subject matter at the end of a unit, and **formative assessments** that are used before or during a lesson to test the student's prior knowledge and how well they are learning the topic. Both these types of assessment are important, and both can be carried out in a number of ways. Assessments can also be **formal**—data-driven, standardized assessments the results of which can be compared against preset benchmarks—or **informal**—less structured assessments based around performance and content. An effective science classroom utilizes a variety of different assessment methods.

For example, a **performance assessment** is an assessment that requires the student to demonstrate skills by completing a task, rather than by selecting a pre-set answer or filling in a blank. A **self-assessment** is an activity in which the student assesses his or her own work, perhaps using a rubric provided by the instructor; these are often not graded and serve to inform the student of his or her own learning. A **peer assessment** is an activity in which the student's work is assessed not by the instructor, but by a fellow student.

Review Video: Formative and Summative Assessments
Visit mometrix.com/academy and enter code: 804991

Combatting Misconceptions

One of the reasons it's important to gauge students' prior knowledge of a topic is because some of that prior knowledge may be incorrect or misleading, and the student may have misconceptions about the topic that must be overcome. Simply telling the students that their prior beliefs were incorrect is unlikely to be effective, and it may in fact be counterproductive, leading to their misconceptions being reinforced instead of removed. Rather, a better goal is to bring about a **conceptual change**, a gradual revision and rearrangement of prior knowledge to accommodate new ideas, in which the student is an active participant.

There are several research-based methods of bringing about conceptual change. One method is to promote **cognitive conflict**: presenting data or demonstrations that contradict the students' prior conceptions, and guiding the students into finding a resolution to the conflict. Another is the use of **refutational texts** that discuss and refute various views on the topic. Other methods include **collaborative argumentation**, in which students are encouraged to discuss, defend, and evaluate their positions; and **persuasive pedagogy**, applying methods of persuasion such as response shaping and reinforcing.

Reliability and Validity

Two measurements of the soundness of an assessment are reliability and validity. An assessment is **reliable** if it yields consistent results; students' scores on the assessment should not depend on external circumstances and should be similar for different questions that test the same skill. An assessment is **valid** if it measures what it is meant to measure. These two qualities can vary independently; it is possible for an exam to have a high reliability but a low validity, or vice versa.

The reliability of an assessment can be affected by many factors. Longer tests tend to be more reliable; tests with a short time limit so that many students cannot complete all the questions, or must rush to do so, tend to be less reliable. Reliability is also affected by difficulty; a test is most reliable when the questions are not so easy that almost every student answers the questions correctly, but not so hard that almost none do. It requires finding a suitable middle ground of difficulty. An assessment will tend to be more valid if it is designed to cover all the material that it is supposed to cover, but only that material. It will be less valid if it has hidden biases against certain categories of student.

Assessment as a Learning Experience

Though an obvious purpose of assessments is to allow the instructor to assign students a grade in the class, the assessments themselves can provide learning experiences. For one thing, as the students see what questions on the assessment they are unable to answer, or do not answer correctly, this helps them see what topics they have not fully learned and may need to further review. On the other hand, the questions that the students got right will help build their confidence and perhaps help them better remember in the future what they learned about those topics. Assessments also give students further practice with the methods and concepts they are testing, which may further work to reinforce them. They may also help students to learn new problem-solving strategies; as students go over the assessment after the fact and discuss how they were supposed to solve a particular problem, the answer might give them information about a strategy they were previously unaware of or underutilizing.

Equitable Use of Assessments

One important consideration that must be kept in mind in designing assessments is that they must be **equitable**—they must not be biased toward or against any part of the student population. Every student must have an adequate opportunity to demonstrate his or her skills and knowledge. There are many biases that may carelessly enter into assessments: cultural biases, language biases, biases against students with special needs.

There are a number of steps that instructors can take to ensure that assessments are equitable. Questions should not rely on "common knowledge" that may not be common to students of different cultures. Students with special needs must be provided with adequate accommodations. English language learners should be given definitions or paraphrases of difficult words and sentences. Other steps that can be taken toward making assessments more equitable include clearly laying out learning outcomes and grading rubrics, using many different methods of assessment that allow students to show their accomplishments in different ways, and ensuring that the subject matter covered in assessments is closely matched to what the instructor teaches in class.

Sharing Criteria and Results

It's important to share the evaluation criteria of assessments with students so that the students will know what to expect from the assessments and prepare accordingly, and so that during the assessment they will know where to best focus their time and attention. If the students have no idea how an assessment will be graded, then the assessment is not fair or equitable; students will not know what aspects of the assessment they should focus on the most and doing well on the assessment may be largely a matter of luck. Sharing the rubric for the assessment ahead of time makes the instructor's expectations clear and ensures that the students know what specifically they will be tested on and can prepare accordingly.

It is also important to share the results of assessments with the students. If the students know the results of their assessments, they can gauge their own progress and learning, and decide where they need to focus in the future and what topics they may need to revisit. Knowing their assessment results may also help students evaluate their study strategies and judge whether or not they are working and how or if they might need to be revised.

Scientific Inquiry Skills for Elementary Students

The six abilities that **grades K-4 students** should acquire are as follows:

- They should be able to ask questions about objects, organisms, and events in the environment.
- They should be able to devise a simple investigation to answer a question.
- They should be able to use tools such as magnifying glasses, rulers, and balances to gather data and make observations.
- They should be able to use the gathered data and observations to provide an explanation.
- They should be able to talk about, draw pictures, or use another method to communicate the results of an investigation and what they learned.
- With respect to the nature of scientific inquiry and scientists, students should understand that investigations involve formulating questions and answers, using different methods of discovering and disclosing answers, using basic tools, observing, sharing answers, and looking at and understanding others' work.

Scientific Inquiry Skills for Middle Grade Students

The five abilities that **grades 5–8 students** should acquire are as follows:

- They should be able to reformulate and clarify questions until they can be answered through scientific investigation.
- They should be able to create and carry out a scientific investigation, interpret the data to provide explanations, and use further data to revise explanations.
- They should be able to identify the tools necessary to gather and analyze data. They should be able to use computer hardware and software to store, organize, and gather data.
- They should be able to provide descriptions and explanations, create models, and make predictions based on the body of knowledge they possess.
- They should be able to explain cause and effect relationships using explanations and data from experiments.

Scientific Inquiry Skills for Older Students

The six abilities that **grades 9–12 students** should acquire are as follows:

- They should be able to identify questions and concepts that guide scientific investigation. In other words, they should be able to create a hypothesis and an appropriate experiment to test that hypothesis.
- They should be able to design and conduct a scientific investigation from start to finish. This includes being able to guide the inquiry by choosing the proper technologies and methods, determining variables, selecting an appropriate method for presenting data, and conducting peer review.
- They should be able to use technology and mathematics in investigations.
- They should be able to formulate and revise scientific explanations and models.
- They should be able to recognize and analyze alternative explanations. In other words, they should be able to devise other possibilities based on the current body of knowledge.
- They should be able to communicate and defend a scientific argument in both written and oral form.

Chapter Quiz

Ready to see how well you retained what you just read? Scan the QR code to go directly to the chapter quiz interface for this study guide. If you're using a computer, simply visit the online resources page at **mometrix.com/resources719/texesmathpse** and click the Chapter Quizzes link.

The Engineering Method

Design Process and Applications

Research and Conceptualization

The **research phase** is the first phase of the engineering design process. It involves **locating and examining** information on a specific engineering issue or problem. It may require studying literature and documents on the topic and identifying existing solutions, costs, and market needs. Reverse engineering of similar market products is also a potential avenue of research. Common sources of research information include trade journals, governmental documents, local libraries, the Internet, and interviews with subject matter experts.

The **conceptualization phase** is the second phase of the engineering design process. It involves **identifying potential solutions** for the problem using various techniques of ideation. One popular ideation technique is **brainstorming**, which involves rapidly thinking of a large number of solutions. Another technique is **trigger word**. One person says a word associated with the problem. Hopefully, this word evokes additional words and phrases that can be used to create solutions. Another technique is a **morphological chart**, which includes design characteristics of the problems. Engineers then propose solutions for each characteristic.

Feasibility Assessment and Design Requirements

The **feasibility assessment phase** is the third phase of the engineering design process. It **determines whether or not the proposed solution is possible** by asking two main questions: Is the project based on an achievable idea? Is the project within the cost constraints of the organizations? These questions are best answered by an experienced engineer with good judgment. He or she is arguably the most important component of this phase. If the project is feasible, it is sent through the design phase. The **design requirements phase** is the fourth phase of the engineering design process. It **establishes the software and hardware parameters and testability**, maintainability, and other key project requirements. It is carried out concurrently with the feasibility phase.

Preliminary Design and Detailed Design

The **Preliminary design phase**, also known as **embodiment design**, is the fifth phase of the engineering design process. It **defines** the overall system design—including schematics, layouts, and diagrams—in a very general way. The design will change as the project proceeds, but these early diagrams will provide guidance in the early stages. Preliminary design phases lead to the detailed design phase.

Detailed design phase is the sixth phase of the engineering design process. It **provides very specific and detailed specifications** (solid models and drawings) on the project. Common specifications include external markings, design life, packaging requirements, operating parameters, test requirements, external dimensions, materials requirements, reliability requirements, external surface treatments, maintenance and testability information, and operating and non-operating environmental stimuli. CAD, or computer-aided design, programs are very helpful during this phase. They increase design efficiency through optimization, which decreases part volume while simultaneously maintaining quality. CAD programs can also perform the finite element method, which calculates stress and displacement. The engineer then determines whether or not these stresses and displacements conform to project parameters.

Production Planning and Tool Design and Production Design

The **Production planning and tool design phase** is the seventh phase of the engineering design process. It **establishes a plan** for mass producing the product and identifies the manufacturing tools that should be used. It is during this phase that a working prototype is built and tested for standard compliance. Common tasks include material selection, production process selection, sequence of operation determination, and tool selection.

The **Production phase** is the eighth phases of the engineering design process. It involves **manufacturing** the product and conducting periodic tests of machinery.

Integrated Systems and Systems Thinking

Integrated systems consist of numerous systems working in conjunction. Technology often consists of smaller systems combined together to form larger systems. In this way, systems are the base components of technology. Consider, for example, an automobile. It consists of numerous electronic and mechanical parts. These parts work together to create the subsystems (steering, lighting, combustion, propulsion, etc.) of which the automobile is comprised.

Systems thinking involves viewing a system as a collection of interconnected parts or processes, and then analyzing the cause and effect relationships between those parts or processes. Systems thinking is necessary when creating new products to ensure that they always perform as intended.

Technology Systems and Feedback

A system consists of interrelated components that work together in order to bring about a certain outcome or achieve a specific goal. Systems exist in many different forms (e.g., technological, environmental, social). Some systems were created through natural processes while other systems are manmade. As a core concept of technology, systems include the following topics:

- A **technology system** is a man-made system. It combines materials, devices, energy, structures, and information as a means of solving problems or creating products.
- **Feedback** occurs when output produced by a particular event or behavior influences a recurrence of the same event or behavior in the future. There are two primary types of feedback: positive feedback, which increases the occurrence of the event or behavior that produced the output, and negative feedback, which decreases the occurrence of the event or behavior that produced the output. Systems often incorporate feedback components that allow for the system to be changed or refined.

Resources

Resources are required to carry out technological activities. The key resources in technology include the following:

- **Tools and machines** – devices and instruments intended to extend or improve human capabilities. Tools can be handheld or motor-driven, and often perform functions such as cutting, chopping, digging, etc. Machines are structures of moving and unmoving parts that perform work. They function by changing the application of energy. Simple machines include wheels, pulleys, screws, and wedges.
- **Processes** – systematic sequences of actions through which humans create, design, invent, produce, control, maintain, and use products and systems. They are the methods through which resources are turned into products.
- **Materials** – include natural resources such as wood and tone; synthetic resources such as plastics, alloys, and concrete; and mixed resources such as leather, plywood, and paper.

- **People** – include the manpower and labor that goes into performing some task or function related to technology. People are arguably the most important resource.
- **Capital** – is necessary to create products and maintain technological systems. This resource includes money and all other financial instruments.
- **Energy** – the ability to perform work. Technological systems input energy, and though application, convert it into a specific function or product.
- **Time** – must be allocated for the performance of any activity. Because time is limited and is required by all technological activities, it must be used as effectively and efficiently as possible.
- **Information** – includes any data that has been gleaned through reading, listening, observing, researching, or consulting any number of sources. Such data need not be factual, although facts are a type of information. When being used by technological systems, information should be arranged and presented in a rational and useful way.

In many cases, engineers must choose between resources. This decision will be made by analyzing tradeoffs, or the advantages and disadvantages of using one resource relative to another resource. Tradeoffs may include the cost, availability, desirability, and waste associated with a particular resource.

Requirements

Requirements are the criteria and constraints that determine the final design and development of a system or project. They are created by examining the system in terms of concept-generation, marketing, production, use, disposability, and fiscal issues. **Criteria** include the parameters of the system design. They encompass the elements and features that define the system and determine the manner in which it should operate. A common criterion is the level of efficiency at which the system should function. **Constraints** are the limits on system design. They often reflect restrictions on funding, human capabilities, space, material, time, and the environment. Constraints tend to be relative and must be balanced against each other based on the constraint's importance in the system design. Engineers must work within the criteria and constraints of the system design.

Quality Control

Quality control makes certain that products meet design requirements and customers receive functional products. It involves setting parameters for the system or product, then making certain the system or product operates within those parameters. Quality control is an ongoing process in which the materials that enter the system, system operation, and system output are constantly evaluated against an acceptable range. Nonconformances are then identified and corrected. The parameters used by quality control are often based on tolerances and specifications created from engineering standards and marketing research, which collects and examines customer reactions, both good and bad, that influence future designs and iterations of the project.

Processes

A **process** is usually a routine set of procedures through which materials are input and then converted into something more useful, such as a product, a service, or even a different process. In technology and engineering, a process is focused on completing a certain project, and is often described as a set of transformations that occur between input and output. These transformations are defined by their parameters and constraints. New processes are often the result of new technologies, which are the fruits of human creation and innovation. New processes lead to new products and systems that solve problems and enhance human capabilities. We create new technologies to make our lives easier and to increase our happiness and comfort.

Optimization and Tradeoffs

Optimization is a process through which designers and engineers attempt to make a product or system as efficient and functional as possible. Optimization **improves** the overall system by bettering the performance of specific characteristics. Mathematical models are an important component of optimization. They help engineer to test and predict possible variations in system design.

A **tradeoff** occurs when one characteristic is lost in exchange for another characteristic with a different set of strengths and weaknesses. When optimizing a product, engineers are often forced to make tradeoffs, and must do so with full understanding of the consequences. For instance, in order to achieve a relatively light product weight, an engineer may be forced to use weaker materials.

ISO 9000

ISO 9000 is a set of rigorous international quality standards that are applicable to numerous types of organizations. Maintained by the International Organization for Standardization, ISO 9000 is designed to help companies improve the quality of their products, processes, and services in a systematic and continuous manner. Companies can receive an ISO 9000 certification by meeting certain requirements, including the following:

- Proper **record keeping** system
- Constant **evaluation** of manufacturing processes to ensure the creation of quality products
- **Examination** of outgoing products for defects and taking appropriate corrective action when required
- Method for **continuous improvement**
- Regular **reviews** of processes and quality systems to ensure efficiency

Although an ISO 9000 certification does not guarantee a certain level of quality within end products and services, it does guarantee that certain quality and business processes are being practiced.

Quality Control Procedures with Engineering and Technology Situations

Quality engineers are responsible for managing, controlling, and addressing product quality. Quality engineers make use of statistical process control tools such as control charts, which identify statistical variations within a process. SPC (Statistical Process Control) tools help determine the specific metrics that should be monitored and the method by which they should be sampled. By following the control limits set by these tools, employees can identify nonconforming products and correct or remove them before they pass on to the next production step or the customer. Defects in the production process should be corrected as early as possible; consequently, the quality engineer will work closely with suppliers to ensure conformance and contain potential problems. Additionally, quality engineers are engaged in continuous improvement (such as Six Sigma and lean manufacturing) which seeks to reduce statistical variation and the number of nonconforming products.

Ergonomics and ADA Compliance

Ergonomics is used to create equipment and devices designed in such a way as to place the least amount of stress possible on the human body and its mental faculties. During the design process, ergonomists must **identify any stressors** (e.g., excessive force, unnatural postures, frequent repetition) that occur while using the equipment or device. If these stressors do not conform to ergonomic guidelines, they must be documented and their statistical variation quantified. Based on these findings, the ergonomist must determine whether there is any correlation between the nonconformances and injuries recorded while using the product and make recommendations to the product engineers.

ADA, or the Americans with Disabilities Act, creates and publishes construction standards intended to help provide disabled persons with better access to buildings. Since March 2012, all new construction must comply with ADA standards.

Research and Development

Research and development, or **R&D**, is a systematic and creative process undertaken with the intent of improving knowledge, culture, and society, and developing new applications. R&D is often focused specifically on scientific and technological endeavors, and it is carried out by both private industry and government. Most companies will not survive unless they consistently innovate and develop new technologies; consequently, companies with strong R&D departments tend to outperform those without consistent R&D departments. Pharmaceutical companies, on average, spend more on R&D than other companies. They devote much of this funding to researching mechanisms, identifying chemical compounds, proving a concept, fulfilling safety requirements, and discovering delivery methods. In some cases, different companies may form an R&D alliance, in which each party agrees to share their findings and new technology with the other parties. Businesses may form R&D alliances if they lack consistent R&D departments.

Troubleshooting Technology Systems

Troubleshooting procedures focus on solving problems that derive from issues other than a user's unfamiliarity with the technology system (as opposed to standard procedures, which focus on familiarizing the user with the system). Such problems include component failures, unforeseen product limitations, and incompatibility. The process of troubleshooting consists of two primary phases:

- **Diagnosis phase** – The user must identify and describe the issues he is experiencing, such as unusually slow performance or failure to complete tasks. These issues are symptoms of underlying problems. The user diagnoses the problem by matching the symptoms to symptoms listed in the troubleshooting procedures.
- **Resolution phase** – After identifying the problems, the user follows a solution path. There may be multiple possible solution paths available to the user, and these paths may vary in complexity.

Diagnosis and resolution are not always separate and distinct processes. Further diagnoses may be required during the resolution phase.

Manufacturability, Construction Costs and Consumer Feedback

Manufacturability determines the ease with which a product can be manufactured. Engineers seek to design for manufacturability—that is, when designing a product, engineers always ensure that there is feasible way in which the product can be produced. Otherwise, the product may fail at the manufacturing stage.

Construction costs are estimated by cost engineers, who use scientific principles and techniques. Construction costs encompass a wide array of problems, including business planning and management, project management, planning and scheduling, profitability analysis, cost estimation, and cost control.

Consumer feedback can be gathered by interviews, surveys, focus groups, meetings, and many other data gathering tools. Based on feedback from these tools, engineers can recommend and incorporate design revisions that will increase the usability of new products.

Experimentation and Invention

New technological innovations often lead to new business models and customer experiences that cannot be tested via conventional market research methods. Consequently, **experimentation** may be the only means of creating a product that will be useful to consumers and, therefore, successful on the market. Experimentation is far less predictable than established business models, but it is often necessary to develop new and useful technologies, processes, services, etc.

Invention is the process by which new technologies are developed. New inventions can build off of existing technologies or they can be revolutionary, representing a radical breakthrough. Every new technology is the product of invention. The concept of invention is the basis for patent law. By applying for a patent, the inventor of a new technology can exclude others from using, selling, or importing the technology for the duration of the patent.

Models and Modeling

Models are important to the design process because they help engineers and designers better visualize and understand the final product before it goes into production. There are different types of models. **Physical models**, for example, are physical, three-dimensional copies. They can be smaller than the products they represent (these are often used to test a specific design feature without incurring the expense of a full-sized prototype) or they can be larger (these are often used to provide a better view of smaller components that otherwise may be difficult to see). A **scale model** is a special type of physical model. Regardless of its size relative to the final project, a scale model is always exactly proportional. **Prototypes** are scale models that are usually the same size as the products they represent, and they are meant to be functional copies of the design. Certain graphics software programs are capable of modeling objects in 3D. Computer modeling may be less expensive than creating a physical model while giving engineers the same benefit of visualization.

Engineering Drawings

Engineering drawings are a specific type of technical representation based on the technical drawing discipline. They include and define all the requirements and critical information of a particular product, such as:

- **Geometry** – includes the shapes of the object and its appearance from various angles.
- **Dimensions** – include the size of the object expressed in standard units, such as inches, centimeters, feet, meters, etc.
- **Materials** – include the components of the product.
- **Finish** – identifies the required surface quality of the product. In most cases, products contained within industrial machines require lower surface quality than consumer products.

Based solely on the drawings, a manufacturer should be able to create the product or component in question. Engineering drawings generally follow certain standardized conventions, such as GD&T, which mandate the use of certain layouts, nomenclatures, interpretations, typefaces, line styles, sizes, etc.

Flowcharts

Flowcharts illustrate the steps within a various algorithm or process. They **offer solutions** to a particular problem, and help document particularly complex processes. Flowcharts consist of various types of shapes: boxes, which contain activities; diamonds, which contain decisions the user must make; and, arrows, which represent the flow of control. Additionally, flowcharts illustrate the following types of activities: start and end, processing steps, inputs and outputs, conditionals, decisions, junctions, and connectors.

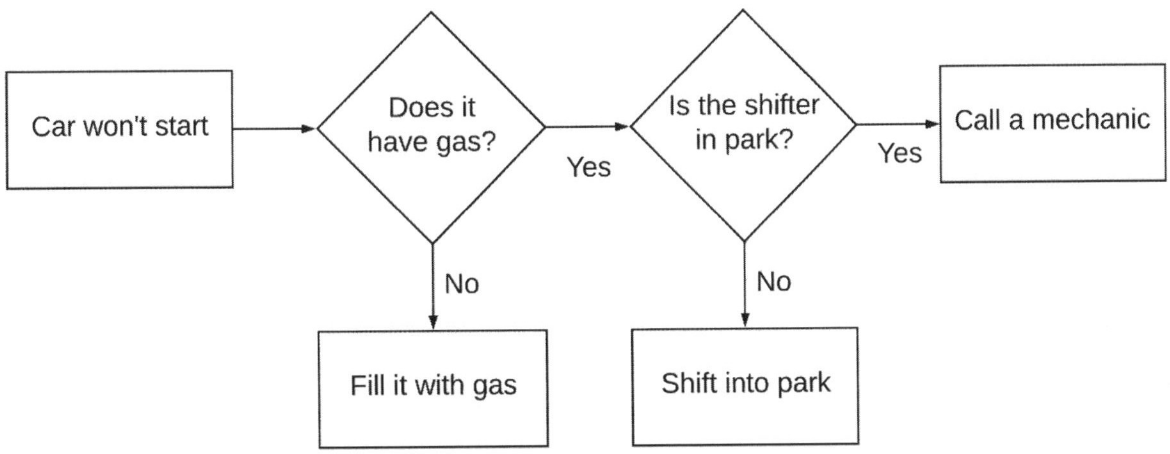

Spreadsheets, Graphs, and Time Charts

A **spreadsheet** is a digital simulation of a paper accounting worksheet. There are a number of software applications capable of generating spreadsheets. It contains multiple cells with each cell containing alphanumeric text, numeric data, or a formula that defines how information within the cell will be calculated.

	A	B	C
1	100	200	150
2	50	300	250
3			

In Excel, when the formula "=SUM(A1:A2)" is entered into cell A3 of this example, it should display a value of 150.

A **graph** is a visual representation that conveys complex information or concepts in quickly and easily understandable ways. Examples include bar charts, pie charts, column charts, organizational charts, and flowcharts.

Time charts serve as means of planning functions and activities.

Safety and Regulations

SDS

An **SDS**, or **Safety Data Sheet** (formerly MSDS), explains the properties of a specific substance, and provides a means of cataloging substances according to their effects and risks. It is an integral component of **workplace safety** as it provides information necessary to the safe handling and storage of the substance. SDS information has sixteen sections: Identification, Hazard identification,

Composition/information on ingredients, First-aid measures, Fire-fighting measures, Accidental release measures, Handling and storage, Exposure controls/ personal protection, Physical and chemical properties, Stability and reactivity, Toxicological information, Ecological information, Disposal considerations, Transport information, Regulatory information, and Other information. The SDS should be present wherever chemicals are being used or kept. SDS sheets are not necessarily intended for general consumers; rather, they are meant for those who work with chemicals in an occupational setting.

STANDARD PROCEDURES

Standard procedures when working around materials and equipment related to technology include the following:

- Do not bring pets or nonessential personnel.
- Do not consume food or drink.
- Familiarize yourself with the proper operation of all equipment and materials by consulting user guides.
- Wear shoes, shirts, and all other appropriate attire.
- Tie back long hair and remove loose clothing (ties, scarves, dangling jewelry, etc.) so that they do not contact equipment or materials.
- Refrain from dropping equipment.
- Observe appropriate precautions when working around electrical equipment.
- Ensure that all equipment and instrumentation is calibrated correctly.
- Ensure that that power is off before making circuit connections.
- Power untested circuits with adjustable power sources at their lowest levels.
- Be professional in your conduct.

EMERGENCY FIRE PROCEDURES

The following procedures should be undertaken in the event of fire:

- Sound the fire alarm if you will be unable to extinguish the fire on your own or a serious emergency has occurred, such as the release of toxic gas.
- Use a nearby fire extinguisher to extinguish the fire. If possible, extinguish the fire using CO2 units rather than dry chemical units. CO2 units often pose less risk to equipment.
- Carry a fire extinguisher with you when going to an area in which a fire might be present.
- When a person's clothing is on fire, roll them on the floor or wrap them in a coat or blanket.
- Immediately leave a building in which a fire alarm has been sounded.

ELECTROCUTION

Electrocution refers to severe injury or death caused by direct exposure to an electric current. The following procedures should be undertaken in the event that someone is being electrocuted:

- Never touch someone who is being electrocuted.
- Turn off the power supply if possible. This can be done at the work bench or at a breaker panel.
- If the power cannot be turned off, use a piece of non-conducting material (such as lumber) to separate the person from the energized conductor.
- Ensure that the person is breathing and check for pulse. Administer CPR if necessary; only qualified individuals should administer CPR.
- Seek medical assistance.

Whenever equipment is damaged, report it to the appropriate personnel for repair. Damaged equipment can be very hazardous. A blown fuse or circuit breaker indicates a faulty circuit; therefore, identify and correct the faulty circuit before resetting the breaker or replacing the fuse.

OSHA

OSHA, or **Occupational Safety and Health Administration**, is a federal regulatory agency that enforces workplace safety and health standards to prevent work-related injuries, illnesses, and fatalities. OSHA applies to most workplaces and requires the following workplace safeguards:

- **Guards** must be placed on all moving parts where contact is possible.
- **Permissible exposure limits**, or **PEL**, prevent chemical or dust concentrations from exceeding certain limits.
- **Personal protective equipment**, or **PPE**, require use of respirators, gloves, coveralls, goggles, face shields, and/or other protective equipment when working in certain industrial environments.
- **Lockout/tagout** requires that energy sources be secured in an off condition when maintenance or repairs are being performed.
- **Confined space** requires air sampling and use of a buddy system while working in enclosed areas, such as tanks, pits, manholes, etc.
- **Hazard communication** requires that workers are informed of workplace chemical hazards.
- **Process safety management** lessens risk of large industrial accidents.
- **Blood borne pathogens**, or **BBP**, protections prevent workers from being exposed to blood borne pathogens, such as HIV.
- **Excavations and trenches** must follow certain procedures and use certain safety equipment if they are more than five feet down.
- **Asbestos exposure** limit occupational exposure to asbestos.

Review Video: Intro to OSHA
Visit mometrix.com/academy and enter code: 913559

Career and Technical Education Course Approval and Re-Approval Process

According to the Carl D. Perkins Career and Technical Education Improvement Act of 2006, **career and technical education (CTE)** programs in all states must emulate the New York CTE program. In Washington, the CTE program has the following goals:

- Maintain rigorous academic standards.
- Provide the skills necessary to fill any deficiencies or gaps in Washington's economy.
- Ensure that all state education reform requirements are aligned.
- Create and design good career and technical education programs by building and facilitating relationships with local CTE advisory councils.

The approval/re-approval process for CTE courses can be performed online. Approval request deadlines vary by state or region. Approval and re-approval for specific courses follow a schedule that can be found at the same site.

Safety and Health Standards

The **Safety Guide for Career and Technical Education** contains the most recent instructions and checklists for vocational education curricula. This lengthy document is published by OSPI, and can be found online. It contains a comprehensive list of safety practices and requirements that students and teachers should observe in CTE courses. These practices and requirements include the following:

- Proper floor cleanliness and maintenance
- Proper maintenance, storage, and handling of power tools, shop machinery, and equipment
- Required shop equipment
- Safety rules and standards displayed in plain sight
- Proper material handling and storage
- Storage, labeling, and handling of electrical devices and equipment
- Disposal of hazardous waste
- Non-asbestos fire blankets
- Proper safety equipment, such as eyewear and face shields
- Eye wash stations
- Proper ventilation
- Safety Signs
- Ambient noise level limits

Career and Technical Education Curriculum Advisory Committee

The career and technical education (CTE) advisory committee is responsible for **determining and recommending a curriculum** that will best prepare students for passing state assessments and earning a Certificate of Academic Achievement, or CAA. The specific duties of the CTE advisory committee include the following:

- Establishing criteria, processes, and tools that state and district boards will use to identify and evaluate appropriate CTE equivalency courses. These courses should gain equivalent academic credit in the core subject areas of math, science, social studies, English, health/fitness, and art.
- Using these criteria, processes, and tools to determine if existing CTE courses fulfill the equivalency requirements.

Tech Prep Articulation

Tech Prep is a high school program that provides students with technical training, applied academics, and assistance in finding workplace internship and guidance. Tech Prep offers a number of advantages to high school students:

- Provides **college credit**, ultimately saving both time and money. Tech Prep enables high school graduates to bypass entry level courses and enroll in higher level classes. The manner in which college credit and standing are awarded is based on an articulation agreement between the high school and the college program. In most cases, this agreement awards college credit using tests, certification by a high school teacher, or college course completion.
- Prepares high school students for the **rigors of college courses**.
- Prepares high school students for a **career in technical professions**, such as engineering, science, health care, computers, etc. Upon leaving college, Tech Prep students often receive better wages and benefits than students who did not take Tech Prep courses.

Membership in Professional Career and Technical Organizations

There are many different **professional career and technical organizations**. When deciding which organization to join, the best choice will vary depending on the specific CTE field and personal preference. However, most organizations offer similar benefits, such as the following:

- **Networking and professional development** opportunities through expos, seminars, and webinars. Members have the opportunity to meet and speak with CTE educators, business partners, institutional representatives, and policy makers.
- Helpful **classroom tools**, best practices, and analysis.
- **Partnerships** with and access to industry experts.
- A **news periodical** that keeps members up-to-date on the newest developments in the field.
- **Awards programs** that offer national recognition.
- **Online courses** that may improve career advancement prospects.
- **Job banks**.
- **Connection** to other education worldwide.

Primary Business Management Functions

Business management usually includes the following functions:

- **Planning** involves creating plans for action based on forecasts over certain periods of time, such as weeks, months, and years.
- **Organizing** requires the optimization of resource usage so that plans will be successful and can be carried out in the most efficient ways possible.
- **Staffing** recruits and assigns personnel to the appropriate jobs. This function involves job analysis.
- **Directing** identifies the specific tasks necessary for plan completion and gets workers to carry them out.
- **Monitoring** checks the progress of the project team against the plan, and it determines whether it is on schedule.
- **Motivating** is fundamental and a very important aspect of business management. Workers must be motivated to carry out their specific tasks and contribute to other functions.

Work Schedule

A **work schedule** breaks a project down into its most basic work activities. These activities are known as terminal elements and cannot be further divided into smaller tasks. The work schedule will include estimates for the resources, cost, and duration of each activity, and then arrange them by their dependencies and order of completion. To create a work schedule, the project manager must have a **work breakdown structure**, which includes an effort estimate and the resource availability for each task. There is software that can perform much of the work necessary to create a work schedule; however, even when using these applications, the manager must have an understanding of certain key concepts and tools, such as dependencies, resource allocation, earned value, critical paths, and Gantt charts. A **Gantt chart** is a bar chart that shows each terminal element, its duration, and other summary information.

Workflow Tracking

A **workflow** is an abstraction of work that is performed by a single person or group of people. It depicts a sequence of steps that, upon completion, produces a certain outcome or product. Any workflow must have input, such as information or materials. This input then undergoes a change or transformation in accordance with certain rules. Finally, a workflow will produce an output, which consists of new information or a new product. When monitoring workflow, management may track a document as it passes through each step within the sequence. Workflow plays an important role in issue tracking, the purpose of which is identifying and resolving customer problems. A problem is input into the customer call support center (via a customer complaint), tracked as it passes through all the steps, and is then resolved.

Safety Assessments

A **safety assessment** is a method of quantifying and understanding the hazards and risks associated with certain products and materials, such as hazardous chemicals. Safety assessments incorporate multiple scientific disciplines, and they typically involve professional risk assessors hired by the company. Chemical companies, consumer product companies, government agencies, insurance agencies, consulting firms, medical device manufacturers, and many others make use of risk assessors. Most safety or risk assessments involve three steps:

- Identify the hazard (i.e. the consequences of exposure).
- Perform a dose-response analysis to determine the dosage necessary to produce a certain response.
- Perform exposure quantification in order to determine the dosage that the population is likely to receive.

The information gained during safety assessments should be incorporated into demonstrations, training, tests, and record keeping.

Project Planning and Management

Planning a Communication Project

A basic communication model involves several main components:

- A **sender**
- A **receiver**
- A **medium**
- **Contextual factors**
- The message
- Positive or negative **feedback**

Other factors may include **noise** (i.e., elements that interfere with message delivery) and **acknowledgement** (i.e., the receiver confirms with the sender that the message was received).

Each of these elements will need to be planned. For a large project, this may include:

- Deciding on the **scope** of the project and defining **goals**.
- Selecting the best **medium** for the project.
- Determining how many **personnel** will be required to perform the setup and actual project.
- Projecting the **cost** of staffing and equipment.
- Setting a **timeline** for completion of the project.

Producing a Communication Project

Producing the project may involve:

- **Set-up** – planning and procuring the medium (such as telephone systems or an email distribution software)
- **Hiring** and **training** staff – preparing them to communicate, such as following a telephone script and transcribing answers
- Collecting **data** – this may involve entering data into a software program or spreadsheet for analysis
- **Analyzing** and **reporting** the data – documenting the results of the project and what they mean, including recommendations for action

Managing a Communication Project

The manager of a communication project ensures that staff are prepared to **communicate** properly and effectively. Staff must have a full understanding of the communication model and the purpose of the project. The manager keeps the project on track, revising the **timeline** if necessary as changes are made. The manager also communicates with **stakeholders** and other involved parties as well as with staff to keep everyone on the same page. The manager helps to compile the collected data into the final **report** and delivers it to the stakeholders.

Planning a Manufacturing Project

There are several steps to planning a manufacturing project:

- First, clearly define the **goal** of the project. Determine why a new product should be manufactured, who is the target audience, and how to go about producing and marketing it.
- Study the **market**. Check competitors for pricing and market saturation. Take polls and interviews to gauge interest in a new product.
- Run a detailed **cost analysis**. This can include cost of machinery, building, personnel, materials, and advertising. The finished product must sell enough units at a high enough profit to offset these costs and return a profit.
- Create a **timeline**. Calculate how long it will take to design, test, and produce the new product. Plan advertising accordingly so the market is prepared for launch.
- Get **personnel** in place. A manufacturing project will need suppliers, distributors, designers, and advertisers, as well as the actual production team.

Producing a Manufacturing Project

Once the planning stage is complete, the actual production can start.

- The first step is to finalize **design**. This will go through stages of testing to make sure it will function appropriately and has the necessary features.
- A **prototype** can then be created. It will be put through rigorous testing to find weaknesses, and a test market may receive prototypes to try out and give feedback.
- Once all the errors are corrected, full production can begin. Contracts should be in place for **suppliers** to bring raw materials. These are processed and then manufactured into the product. Then **distributors** transport them to be purchased.

Managing a Manufacturing Project

Managing a manufacturing project means handling numerous variables. For a project to run smoothly, needed resources must be available. The manager must be in contact with **suppliers**, ensuring that materials are purchased and delivered regularly to keep up with demand. The manager must also oversee **design** and **production** teams, making sure they are on the same page and that any changes or problems have been communicated. Production must be on pace to meet demand, so the manager should **track progress and demand** and make adjustments as needed (such as hiring more staff or purchasing more machinery). Management of a manufacturing project also includes overseeing **marketing**. This includes advertisements, research, and testing. To keep a product relevant, it may be necessary to make changes or figure out how to make it more cost-effectively. The market constantly evolves, so this requires continual oversight.

Planning a Construction Project

When planning a construction project, there are several things that must first be assessed:

- The **location** should be studied. This includes testing soil, checking for geographic dangers such as flood zones, and researching zoning and other local laws.
- The **cost of production** should be projected, along with a **timeline** for completing the project. Cost includes materials, machinery, and personnel, along with other costs such as offsetting the environmental impact.
- The manager should define **roles and responsibilities** and create a schedule with these roles.
- A **quality control and assurance plan** should be developed for ensuring that both work and materials are sufficient for the project's purpose.
- A **communication plan** should also be in place to make sure each team is following the plan and implementing any changes that are made.

Producing a Construction Project

Producing a construction project includes:

- Acquiring all needed **materials** from suppliers. This may include lumber, gravel, metal, concrete, and many other materials, depending on what is being constructed: a building, a road, etc.
- Preparing the **site**. The site may need to be graded or otherwise prepped before construction can start.
- **Building** the project. This may involve many steps. For instance, in a house, this includes laying a foundation, putting up the framework, installing electrical and plumbing, finishing and painting walls, roofing, etc.
- Performing a **quality check** before handing off to the owner.
- **Cleaning** the site of all machinery, excess materials, tools, and trash.

Managing a Construction Project

When the project is ready to begin, the manager should do a final review of all **plans** and any related **documents** with stakeholders to ensure that no final changes need to be made. Then the manager can ensure that everyone on the production side has a thorough understanding of roles and what the project entails. The manager should also check with **suppliers** and make sure all materials will be delivered on time and in correct quantities. Throughout the project, the manager oversees progress, checking it against the timeline, and keeps **communication** open between the construction team, suppliers, stakeholders, and other involved parties. The manager also keeps in contact with **city or county personnel**, updating them on progress and ensuring that everything is done legally. As changes or delays occur, the manager revises the plan and communicates to all parties. Finally, when the project is completed, the manager officially hands it off to the owner.

PLANNING AN ENERGY, POWER, AND TRANSPORTATION PROJECT

An energy, power, and transportation project requires extensive planning. These projects often involve local, state, and/or federal government contracts, so this may involve numerous tests and precautions to ensure that each part of the project remains in **compliance**. The manager should project the total **cost** of the project, including research and planning, materials, manpower, and tools such as machinery.

PRODUCING AN ENERGY, POWER, AND TRANSPORTATION PROJECT

An energy, power, and transportation project requires several steps:

- All necessary **materials** should be collected from suppliers. This may occur in stages if some supplies will not be needed until later in the project, since some projects can take place over months.
- **Site prep** should be performed, whether this means preparing the ground for building a road or bridge, or to erect wind turbines.
- Following the plan, the project should be **implemented** with frequent reports to stakeholders and government officials.
- The project should undergo **quality checks** and **performance tests** to ensure that it is working properly.

MANAGING AN ENERGY, POWER, AND TRANSPORTATION PROJECT

The manager of an energy, power, and transportation project has the responsibility to **communicate** clearly and frequently between all parties. This often includes government officials as well as stakeholders, suppliers, and the actual production team. The manager should oversee **quality checks** at each stage of production, ensuring that regulations are followed and communicating any necessary changes that are made to the plan.

PLANNING A BIO-RELATED TECHNOLOGY PROJECT

Bio-related technology includes a variety of projects, such as genetically modifying foods or developing renewable fuel sources. This type of project spends much time in the development stage, researching and testing. When planning a bio-related technology project, one must go through several steps:

- Outlining a clear **plan** that describes the goals for the project and how they will be achieved. Many different ideas may be tested and discarded in pursuit of one that will work, so it is vital to have a clear vision for the final product.
- Deciding on the needed **materials** for the project. This may include a lab equipped with various tools and materials to study and test products during development.
- Finding qualified **personnel** to work on the project and **stakeholders** to support the project. The project will need personnel with backgrounds that qualify them to research and develop the specific product. It will also need to be funded and directed by **stakeholders** who see potential in the idea.

PRODUCING A BIO-RELATED TECHNOLOGY PROJECT

Once the planning stage is complete and financial backing is established, the bio-related technology project can begin. Stages of production include:

- **Research and development** – even with a clear idea of what the product should entail, it will need significant research into both the science behind the ideas and other research on the subject.

- **Design** – after research, it is time to begin working on design, creating a blueprint for the prototype. This may go through several iterations and tests before the prototype can be created.
- **Prototype** – a prototype can be created for more testing. Weaknesses and errors are noted so they can be corrected in the next prototype.
- **Working model** – once the prototype has been shown to work as expected, a working model can be shared with stakeholders. It will undergo more testing before obtaining final approval for distribution.

Managing a Bio-Related Technology Project

Managing a bio-related technology project involves careful oversight. These projects often include handling of hazardous materials so the manager must ensure that safety protocols are followed and appropriate protective equipment is available. The manager communicates between stakeholders and the research and development team. There are often numerous changes, both to the project and the timeline, that must be clearly communicated. The manager must also ensure that all governmental regulations are followed.

Planning a Computer Applications Project

A computer applications project usually involves developing new software. Planning this type of project includes:

- **Researching** the existing software options to see what is available and what is lacking, as well as what features are important to consumers.
- Setting a **goal** for what the project will accomplish and who will use it.
- Making a **timeline** and projecting what **materials and equipment** will be needed.
- Finding the necessary **personnel** (such as coders) to help develop the product.

Producing a Computer Applications Project

Producing a computer applications project involves a significant amount of **research and development**. There will be many stages of **programming**, **testing**, and **debugging** until the software works properly:

- After research, programmers can begin to **code** for the project. This is called **implementation**.
- At various points during coding, the software will be **tested** for bugs and changes will be made as necessary.
- **Documentation** is made throughout, keeping careful records of development and bugs.
- Final tests will be run after the software is completed, before it can be **launched** or **deployed**.
- Even after distribution, **maintenance** must be done to keep it working and fix any bugs that occur.

Managing a Computer Applications Project

The manager of a computer applications project oversees the development, from market research through production and post-production. The manager **communicates** between different teams and the stakeholders, and works to keep the project on **schedule**. This may include helping to find solutions to programming issues that arise as well as marketing issues. The manager should either remain on the team to head up maintenance issues or hand off the project to another manager for long-term maintenance.

Drafting

Tools and Materials for Sketching and Technical Drawing

It is important to be prepared both to make hand sketches and to make computer drawings. Typically one first creates a simple sketch to visualize something (top view, front view, side views, and 3D isometric view). Then the technical drawing can more easily be created.

Some tools and materials that are used for sketching include:

- **Paper** (it is handy to keep a sketchpad, but sheets of plain paper or graph paper will work as well)
- **Mechanical pencil** and **eraser**
- **Technical pens** (these are available in a variety of widths)
- **Ruler**
- **Compass**
- **Drawing board** (many people sketch without this, but it is useful for securing paper and ruler; preventing slipping, smudging, or tearing; and it includes small holes for the compass)

For technical drawings, computer-aided design (CAD) programs are used. This offers greater accuracy and ability to visualize a design, as well as ease in changing details without creating a whole new drawing.

Producing and Interpreting Drawings

There are a variety of types of technical drawings, as different types are needed for different situations. It is important to be able to understand and create these various types. Some of the common types include:

- **Multiview drawing** (this uses orthogonal projection to show a design from different 2D perspectives)
- **Sectional view** (this "cuts" into the image to show an interior part of the design)
- **Pictorial representation** (a 3D image of the design)
- **Detail drawing** (a small part of the overall design that is drawn separately in a larger scale to show detail)
- **Assembly drawing** (an image that shows all the design components in their final, connected form to show how the finished product will look)

Working Drawings, Presentation Drawings, and Models

Drawings and models are created for a variety of needs, such as residential, community, and business, and can differ according to their purpose. A **working drawing**, sometimes called a blueprint, has necessary information for construction such as dimensions and needed materials. **Presentation drawings** are made for the client rather than the contractor and are meant to show general design, such as a house floor plan. A **model** is a 3D representation of a design that can give an overall view of a structure as well as allowing a viewer to zoom in for detail. Models are especially helpful in large commercial structures with many components.

Scales and Dimensioning in Technical Drawings

Drawings are created to a specific **scale**. This can vary, depending on the size of the building and of the drawing. It is important to be able to both accurately calculate and notate the desired scale and to be able to interpret the listed scale on a drawing so that materials can be ordered and assembled accurately. Scales are written with the drawing measurement followed by the actual measurement. For example:

- A 1:10 scale means that the actual building is ten times the size of the drawing, or the measurements on the drawing are 1/10 of the actual measurements.
- A 1:48 scale means that the actual building is 48 times the size of the drawing. This scale is common for architectural drawings: one foot of a building is pictured as ¼ inch on a drawing.

For hand drawing, engineering scales can be used: similar to rulers but often triangular or beveled rather than flat.

Another component of technical drawings is **dimensioning**. Certain measurements are included directly on the drawings, such as lengths, widths, and angles on a blueprint.

Software for Technical Drawing

While hand drawing is still used, particularly for early sketches, there are many available types of **software** that can be used for drawing. These are often called **CAD (computer-aided design) programs**. These range from simple 2D capabilities that give a basic outline to complex 3D software that outlines every tiny component of a building. Most CAD programs include a **library** of symbols to specify various electrical, HVAC, and other components of a building. Walls can quickly be built and shifted by typing dimensions and angles rather than dragging a mouse to draw. **Scales** can be preset. One can navigate from one **view** to another, as in working on a 2D view of a single room, then switching to view a 3D model of the entire building.

Tools in Manufacturing

Manufacturing Tools and Equipment

Manufacturing uses many different tools to create and finish items. Some of these include:

- **Micrometer** – this is a tool for measuring small components with great precision.
- **Milling machine** – this removes excess material from an item with a rotary cutting tool, smoothing the surface.
- **Lathe** – this is used for shaping materials such as wood or metal. It rotates and can be used for drilling, cutting, and sanding, among other operations.
- **Jig** – a jig holds a tool in position for precise work.
- **Fixture** – this is similar to a jig but secures a workpiece instead of a tool.
- **Saw** – several different types of saws can be used in manufacturing, from heavy duty circular saw to a jigsaw or miter saw for fine work.
- **Drill** – a drill press or other drilling tool can be used to cut holes in manufactured products.
- **Welding machine** – this is frequently needed in manufacturing to join metal parts together.
- **Computer numerical control (CNC) machines** – this is an automated method for manufacturing. The CNC machine is programmed with coded instructions and controls the manufacturing machines to go through the entire manufacturing process.

Use of Manufacturing Tools and Equipment

To properly use manufacturing tools and equipment, it is important to understand how to work with them. For example, a micrometer is a very precise tool but is useless if one does not know how to read it. A component is placed against one side of the micrometer and a screw is tightened until it just touches the other side of the component. Then the value can be read. For many of the machines, materials must be securely fastened and safety equipment used. For automated equipment, the user must know how to program the machine so that it successfully runs the other machines.

Maintenance of Manufacturing Tools and Equipment

Tools and equipment should undergo routine inspection and maintenance. Parts can become loose, blades can become dull, and dust and debris can collect in crevices. All of these can lead to manufacturing mistakes or operator harm. Tools and equipment should be regularly **cleaned** and **stored** properly. Power tools should be tested from time to time to make sure they are working properly. Any loose parts should be tightened and dull blades sharpened as needed. Danger items like frayed cords should be replaced.

Safety Protocols for Manufacturing Tools and Equipment

Many manufacturing tools involve sharp blades or heavy, moving parts. Additionally, many tools sand off tiny pieces of wood or metal that can become airborne. Welding creates dangerous sparks. It is vital to be properly prepared for working with these tools. This may involve wearing eye and hearing protection, non-slip (and possibly steel-toed) shoes, and keeping hair secured so it cannot be caught in a machine. For welding, a full protective face shield may be required. Operators should be trained on how to use the machines and what safety precautions to take. A safety inspector may visit from time to time to ensure that all operators are following safety protocols.

Finishing, Hardening, Annealing, Normalizing and Tempering

- **Finishing** involves changing or coating the surface of a material in order to protect or beautify it. For instance, wooden decks are often coated with sealant as a protection from the elements.
- **Hardening** increases the hardness of a metal by heating and then rapidly cooling it. This increases internal stresses and, thereby, increases the metal's strength (resistance to deformation) while making it more brittle and reducing its toughness.
- **Annealing** softens a metal by heating and then slowly cooling it. This lessens internal stresses and, thereby, decreases the metal's brittleness and increases its toughness, malleability, and ductility (its ability to be shaped, stamped and worked on further).
- **Tempering** is a heat treatment that increases the metal's toughness, decreases its hardness and cracking, and makes it more malleable and ductile.
- **Normalizing** is a heat treatment that returns the metal to its near-equilibrium state. It strikes a balance between strength and hardness.

Casting, Forming, Separating, Conditioning and Assembling

- **Casting** involves pouring a molten or liquid material (such as metal, concrete, plaster, or clay) into a mold, and then letting it solidify into the shape determined by the mold. Casting is useful for forming complex shapes.
- **Forming** involves shaping a material using a die and external force. For instance, a person can shape a piece of clay by forming it around a metal cylinder.
- **Separating** involves removing excess material from an object in order to create size and shape. For instance, scissors can cut into a piece of fabric and, thereby, alter its size and shape.
- **Conditioning** involves applying heat, pressure or chemical reactions in order to change the properties of a material. For instance, pottery is baked as means of hardening it.
- **Assembling** involves fastening, bonding, or otherwise joining two pieces together, either permanently or temporarily. For instance, pieces of a plastic model are often glued together.

Computer-Aided Manufacturing and Robotics

Computer-aided manufacturing, or **CAM**, relies on computer software to **augment the manufacturing process** in some way. Its goal is increasing the efficiency, accuracy, consistency, and speed with which products are created. CAM software may guide the tools and machinery that create the products, or it may help coordinate management, planning, and other plant operations. CAM can control every step in the production process, from the processing of raw materials to their conversion into consumable products.

Robotics is an aspect of computer-aided manufacturing. Robots are capable of **automating certain manufacturing tasks** and are most prevalent with the automobile manufacturing industry. The most common manufacturing application for robots is materials handling, which involves moving materials and components with the factory. The second most common application is spot welding. More recently, robots have started performing lighter tasks, such as parts installation, packaging (e.g., foods and electronics), and service jobs (e.g., automatic tellers and checkouts).

Manufacturing Materials

Wood

Wood is used heavily within the manufacturing industry, which uses a variety of natural wood and engineered wood products such as plywood. Plywood is also formed from sheets of timber glued together. It possesses strong resistance to breaking, shrinkage, warping, and cracking. Plywood can be made from softwood, such as pine and fir, or hardwood such as birch. Softwood plywood is used prominently in furniture and house construction, including walls, floors, roofs, fences, and wind bracing panels. Hardwood plywood is very strong and resistant, and is used for the most demanding construction applications, such as heavily-trafficked floors, scaffolding, concrete formwork system panels, etc. Wood products are often less expensive and better for the environment than other materials, such as steel or concrete.

Masonry Materials

Masonry materials include bricks, concrete blocks, stone, marble, travertine, limestone, glass, stucco, tile, and granite. In masonry, these materials are stacked and bound together into structures. The binding material is known as mortar. Masonry construction has very high compressive strength (the ability to support weight vertically), but lacks in tensile strength (the ability to withstand twisting and stretching). It is resistant to heat, fire, and projectile impact, but is susceptible to weather wear and requires a strong foundation to support its weight. Masonry uses the following tools:

- **Masonry trowel** is used to level, shape, and spread mortar or concrete.
- **Joint filler** is a compressible material, such as rubber, that is used to fill and keep dry the joints between structural members.
- **Hawk** holds the mortar or joint compound as it is being applied.
- **Bricklayers hammer** is used during bricklaying.
- **Bull float** is used to smooth the surface of concrete.

Plastics

Plastics are synthetic polymers created from **petroleum and natural gas**. There are two basic types of plastics: **thermoplastics**, which can be remolded numerous times, and **thermosetting plastics**, which undergo irreversible curing. Numerous everyday products are created from plastics, such as grocery bags, storage bags, bottles, jars, food packaging, milk jugs, flooring, window frames, film, polyester fibers, textiles, pipes, gutters, show curtains, lights, straws, household appliances, furniture, siding, dishware, utensils, tooth brushes, automobile components, and many more. Plastics are fairly inexpensive and easily produced; however, they pose several environmental concerns. They emit pollutants such as greenhouse gases and accumulate in landfills and ocean gyres. Because they are created from a nonrenewable resource (petroleum), their cost will rise as the resource is depleted, and the cost of other petroleum-based products, such as gasoline, will also rise.

Metal Alloys

Metal alloys have many different manufacturing applications, ranging from construction to surgical equipment. One of the most commonly used metals is steel, which is produced by alloying iron with carbon (though other materials may be used as well). The tensile strength, hardness, and ductility of steel depend on the amount of carbon within it. Increased levels of carbon increase the alloys hardness while decreasing its ductility (i.e., the alloy is less resistant to twisting and warping). Long steel is used in the creation of high-strength wire, bridges, and building structures. Flat carbon steel is used in major appliances as well as automobiles and boats. Stainless steel is used in mechanical equipment, surgical equipment, and cutting tools. Other common manufacturing metals include aluminum alloys, which feature prominently in the aerospace, shipbuilding, cycling, and automotive industries.

Composites

A **composite** consists of multiple materials that differ widely in their properties and characteristics. Composites can be naturally-occurring, such as wood, or manmade, such as engineered wood, fiberglass, and concrete. Fiberglass combines plastic and thin fibers of glass, which provide structural reinforcement. It is lightweight while possessing good tension and compression strength. Fiberglass is used prominently in the manufacturing of storage tanks, pipes, houses, cars, and boats. Concrete is used in a variety of construction applications, but poses several environmental concerns. For instance, paved roadways are one of the major causes of the urban heat island effect, in which a city tends to be hotter than its surrounding area. Concrete surfaces also lead to increased surface runoff, which causes erosion. Additionally, the manufacture of concrete releases carbon dioxide, a greenhouse gas.

Manufacturing Processes and Quality Control

Manufacturing Processes

Manufacturing of materials is a multi-step process involving many different techniques and machines. Some of these include:

- **Separating** – when raw materials are mined, they must be separated into their chemical components so they can be used. There are multiple separation processes, depending on what is being separated (e.g., liquids or solids).
- **Casting** – a substance is heated and poured as a liquid into a mold, where it solidifies in the desired size and shape.
- **Molding** – molding is similar to casting but can include not only pouring liquid in a mold, but also soft solids that can be shaped.
- **Forming** – this is a method typically applied to metals to shape them. There are many different ways of forming, such as extruding and forging.
- **Conditioning** – this involves removing defects from metal with a variety of methods (chemical, thermal, or mechanical).

- **Assembling** – the materials are put together so that they can be used in construction.
- **Finishing** – this is one of the final stages in preparing materials and may involve polishing, painting, or dyeing a product.
- **Inspection** – before a product can be sold, it undergoes a quality check.

Automated Systems

Increasingly, manufacturing uses a multitude of automated systems, increasing efficiency and accuracy. Some of these include:

- **Robotics** – manufacturing can be improved in both productivity and precision by use of robots. They can be programmed to perform tasks at each stage of production and can work nonstop rather than in shifts like human workers. It can cut costs and simplify procedures.
- **Artificial intelligence** – this can be used to evaluate a manufacturing process, looking for ways to improve efficiency or cut costs in materials, as well as exploring new products and methods.
- **Computer-integrated manufacturing (CIM)** – this involves using computers for the entire manufacturing process. This improves efficiency and cuts down on errors.

Manufacturing Quality Control Procedures

It is important to check products before distribution to avoid defects or safety issues. There are several steps for quality control:

- First, it is necessary to **define** the product standards so quality can be tested. This includes methods of testing and the number of products from each batch that will be tested.
- Employees must be **trained** in these standards and a system of **reporting** must be established. Additionally, procedures must be established for what to do if defects are found.
- Tools like **statistical process control (SPC)** can track data to identify problem areas and propose solutions.

Construction

Careers

- **Civil engineering technicians** assist engineers, architects, and planners in planning, designing, locating, and constructing buildings. They estimate material costs and amounts, perform quality control inspections on materials, and conduct suitability tests on soil, concrete, and building materials.
- **Building inspectors** ensure that the structure complies with all applicable codes, such as building, plumbing, electrical, and mechanical codes.
- **Safety specialists** maintain safe environments within construction areas. They make sure that hazardous waste is disposed of properly, perform routine inspections on equipment and scaffolding, conduct safety education classes, consult with managers and engineers, and write safety reports.
- **Site managers** ensure that a building project does not exceed budget or the time schedule. They handle any delays or problems, and they maintain communication between parties. They are also involved in quality control.

- **Contractors** supervise the entire construction process including the construction of work spaces, homes, schools, and other buildings. They write contracts, make bids, estimate costs, perform scheduling, manage labor, and ensure safe storage of equipment and construction materials.

Types of Construction

- **Light construction** describes **light frame construction**, which is limited to floor and ceiling joists, rafters, and wood stud walls. Light construction is mostly residential; however, it can apply to smaller commercial buildings that do not exceed two stories.
- **Heavy construction** applies to any construction that uses cranes, excavators, and other **large machines**.
- **Civil construction** applies to the construction of **social infrastructure**, such as bridges, dams, irrigation projects, air field surfacing and grazing, sewer and water lines, highways, roadways, sidewalks, curbs, and railroads. In some definitions, heavy construction and civil construction are combined into a single category.
- **Industrial construction** applies to the construction of factories, manufacturing facilities, power plants, and processing plants. It requires extensive planning and teams of people with specialized skills in design and construction. Big industrial corporations carry out the majority of industrial construction projects.

Building Codes

Building codes are a set of **construction standards** that determine the manner in which structures are built and repaired. Building codes are established and enforced at the municipal level. They regulate building materials and workmanship quality, such as electrical wiring, sanitation facilities, fire and safety equipment, and similar building aspects. City officials conduct building inspections in order to ensure compliance. If compliance is met, the official will issue a certificate of occupancy, also known as an occupancy permit. This document explains the proper use of the building in sheltering people, animals, and property. For instance, in a single-family home, many building codes require an occupancy separation between the living space and the garage, in which flammable substances are kept. If a building has multiple uses (e.g., residential and commercial), building codes usually require that builders place fire barriers, such as fire doors and fire stops, between individual occupancies.

Federal Environmental Regulations

- The **Clean Air Act of 1970** regulates the **emission of six pollutants**—carbon monoxide, ozone, lead, sulfur dioxide, nitrogen dioxide, and particulate matter—according to the limits established by the national ambient air quality standards, or NAAQS.
- The Clean Air Act Amendment of 1990 regulates 189 additional toxic air pollutants.
- The **Clean Water Act**, or **CWA**, regulates the **quality and pollution content of all navigable waters** in the US, including lakes, rivers, streams, wetlands, ponds, territorial seas, and every other small or large body of water. Point source of water pollutions—such as construction sites, factories, and plants—must acquire a national pollution discharge eliminations system (NPDES) permit through their state regulatory agencies.
- The **Wilderness Act** established the **national wilderness preservation system** and forbids any road construction, settlement, mechanized transportation, or other forms of development within the boundaries of the system.

- The **Resource Conservation and Recovery Act**, or **RCRA**, regulates **industrial waste** and the manner in which it is generated, stored, treated, transported, and disposed of.
- The **Endangered Species Act**, or **ESA**, protects **threatened or endangered species** and their ecosystems on public and private land.

Permits

Permits empower their holders to **carry out certain development and construction activities**. Permits are usually granted by a **government agency**, such as the zoning board of appeals, which normally conduct a review of some sort before agreeing to the permit. There are many different types of permits. **Conditional-use permits**, also known as special-use permits, allow for land uses in zones where such land uses may be forbidden under existing ordinances but is generally considered for the common good. For instance, a planner may acquire a conditional-use permit in order to build residencies in an industrial zone. **Nonconforming use permits** are generally granted to structures that do not conform to current zoning ordinances because they were built before the ordinances were passed. **Variance permits** enable a landowner to use his property in a way that directly conflicts with zoning laws. A **right of way** is a granted by a private landowner. It empowers an agency or individual to use the landowner's property to build or maintain a road, pathway, or utility line.

Zoning

Zoning ordinances determine **the manner in which land can be used in a particular community**. They are designed to maintain public safety and promote public welfare. They are established and enforced by city governments via enabling acts. Zoning ordinances generally divide the community into multiple land-use districts and regulate district use, district size, the kinds of buildings that can be built, building height, setback distance (distance between the structure and streets and walkways), architecture, and density (land to structure ratio). Urban areas tend to be high-density. Low density ordinances increase the space between buildings, but they contribute to urban sprawl. Most zoning districts are classified as residential, industrial, commercial, or agricultural. Zoning ordinances normally contain general provisions, definitions, maps, zoning district delineation, and guidelines for enforcement and administration.

Zoning Methods

- **Euclidean zoning** divides a community into separate land use districts and then limits the kind of development which occurs within each district. Land use districts are designated according to the following uses: residential for single families, residential for multiple families, industrial, and commercial. A single district cannot mix land uses.
- **Euclidean II** zoning allows for mixed land uses within a single district.
- **Cumulative zoning** allows a single land use district to combine less intensive land uses, such as residential, with more intensive land uses, such as commercial. The only stipulation is that residences can only be mixed with light industrial uses (high-tech, warehouses, and other non-polluting industries). Heavy industrial uses must remain by themselves.
- **Exclusive**, or **non-cumulative, zoning** is the dominant contemporary zoning method. It forbids a land use district from incorporating any developments which do not conform to its designated use. Exclusive zoning allows for more excess room than cumulative zoning; consequently, existing businesses have more room for expansion.

- **Transect zoning** divides the development area into six zones. The first zone is the wilderness area. Each subsequent zone is progressively more urbanized. The sixth and final zone is the urban core. Transect-based ordinances encourage mixed land uses within districts, and regulate parking placement, street layout, building height, setback, façade, and design.
- **Overlay zoning** superimposes a new zone on top of an existing land use zone and imposes additional requirements and standards.
- **Floating zones** are **unmapped** zoning districts. They enable municipalities to promote certain land uses (apartments, research campuses, etc.) without actually reserving an area of land for such a use.
- **Cluster zoning** imposes **strict density standards** on development, but allows flexibility in setting lot size, setback distances, various characteristics related to individual house lots, street layout, utility sites, and building placement. In cluster zoning, developers can reserve a single high-density area for residences and leave large amounts of open space for uses such as agriculture, recreation, and preservation.

Rezoning, Upzoning, Downzoning, Variance and Extraterritorial Jurisdiction

- **Rezoning** is the act of changing the zoning classification of a land use district.
- **Upzoning** is a type of rezoning in which higher density developments are allowed within a land use district.
- **Downzoning** refers to two possible actions: reducing the intensity of development that is allowable within a specific land use district or increasing the intensity of development so that higher order development is allowed within a land use district. When intensity is reduced, minimum lot sizes are often increased.
- **Variances** allow land uses within particular district that are otherwise forbidden under existing zoning ordinances. Variances are not allowed unless an area of land is caused considerable hardship without the land use.
- **Extraterritorial jurisdiction**, or **ETJ**, is the power of a municipality to enforce zoning ordinances outside its jurisdiction. It is granted by the state.

Urban Analysis

An **urban analysis** helps determine the kind of development that best fits a certain site. It considers the context and characteristics of a location and identifies the urban design strategies and concepts which are best suited for the construction project. There are six types of urban analysis:

- **Community** – examines census and demographic information, previous planning information from past projects, and the wants and needs of the general public.
- **Continuity** – examines the developments patterns (e.g., buildings that are unique to the community) and changes that have occurred within the community throughout its history.
- **Character** – examines a community's urban form, topography, views, open space, population centers, architectural character, streetscape, and environmental issues.
- **Connections** – determines the accessibility of a community by examining its streets, rights-of-way, parking, traffic problems, transit service, and bicycle and pedestrian services.
- **Regulations and ownership** – reviews and reassesses based on more localized requirements for construction in a portion of a city, such as a neighborhood. Ownership may be a concern in certain areas, such as with features which are shared with neighbors or have unclear property definitions.
- **Economic and market setting** – examines the development within the scope of current economic and market trends.

Construction Financing

Private Sources

- **Private equity** comes from individuals and corporations.
- **Banks** provide loans for construction, such as mortgages. **Investment banks** offer equity financing.
- **Credit companies** offer equity financing.
- **Real estate investment trusts** are groups of developers, lenders and equity investors who pay out over 90 percent of their earnings so that they can avoid corporate income taxes.
- **Pension funds** provide both debt and equity financing.
- **Life insurance companies** provide both debt and equity financing.

Public Sources

- **Tax increment financing** is focused primarily on redevelopment and infrastructure, and it may assist developers as well.
- **Special service and assessment areas** are special tax districts in which new residents assume most of the financial burden.
- **Historic tax credits** are available for restoring certified historic structures.
- **Tax-exempt bonds** offer low-interest loans to industrial and low-income housing developers.
- **Home investment partnership program funds** are provided to municipalities, who give them to developers for the purposes of building affordable housing.

Land Use Regulation

- **Quota systems** place restrictions on the building permits that developers can acquire over a year. The restrictions include both the **number and type of permits**. Quota systems slow the future growth of communities and allow more time to assimilate existing growth. Quota systems are common in rapidly growing areas.
- **Moratorium** restricts or completely stops certain types of development until a more thorough plan can be developed and put in place. This plan must address the expansions of water, utilities, and other necessities.
- **Cost** is the property's value after improvements (i.e., buildings) have been added to it. Cost does not necessarily reflect the property's market value.
- **Cost-benefit analysis** is used to determine which proposed development will generate more value in the future. It compares the benefits and costs of each proposed development.

Urban Analysis

Economic and market setting analysis examines economic factors that may affect development. The factors include the current state and needs of the local real estate market; the existing market demand for certain land uses and land uses that need to be fulfilled (more office space, additional housing units, factories, etc.); available financing options (banks, tax credits, bonds, etc.); fiscal analysis of the community; and construction projects that are currently going on or have been recently approved.

Regulations and ownership examines zoning and land use regulations, design guidelines, and property ownership, including property boundaries, shapes, sizes and parcel distribution. Design guidelines include windows, doors, building types, signage, roof shapes, planting, and other construction elements. Design guidelines are often set by the community, and they can be determined by studying drawings and photographs.

Construction Site Management

Managing a construction site involves the following tasks:

- Supervising, coordinating, and scheduling every design and construction process throughout the project's lifetime, from its inception to the final phases. This includes meeting with owners, engineers, architects, and other important personnel.
- Determining the material, tools, and labor requirements of the project; finding the best way to acquire the necessary tools and materials and overseeing their delivery; and hiring and dismissing workers if necessary.
- Estimating all costs necessary to complete the project.
- Choosing, hiring, and overseeing carpenters, plumbers, electricians, metalworkers, roofers, and other specialty trade contractors.
- Ensuring the project stays on time and within budget.
- Overseeing site preparation, which involves clearing and excavating the land, building roads, landscaping, and installing sewage systems.
- Overseeing building construction, which involves laying foundation and building the structural framework, floors, walls, and roofs.
- Overseeing building system installation, such as fire suppression, electrical, HVAC, and plumbing systems.
- Acquiring all required building permits and licenses, ensuring compliance with building codes and any other regulations, and scheduling required inspections.
- Ensuring worker safety.

Construction Project Inspections

Before a building can receive an occupancy permit, it must receive the following inspections:

- **Public work inspections** ensure compliance with government regulations. Public works include sewer systems, bridges, dams, highways, streetsm, and other government contracts.
- **Building inspection** ensures compliance with applicable building codes. It occurs in stages throughout the construction process. Building inspectors examine the following: building plans; soil, including the position and depth of the footings; the foundation after it has been poured; fire suppression system, including sprinklers, alarms, smoke control, and exits; and the completed building.
- **Electrical inspections** ensure compliance with electrical codes and standards. The main panel, subpanels, junction boxes, and all wiring must be completed before an inspection can take place.
- **Elevator inspections** check all lifting and conveying devices.
- **Mechanical inspections** check all systems and equipment related to heating, air conditioning, ventilation, and refrigeration.
- **Plumbing inspections** examine the layout of the piping, venting, backflow protection, and fixture settings. They ensure safe drinking water and sanitary waste disposal.

Engineering Principles in Construction

Engineering Terms and Concepts

With several different branches of engineering, there are a multitude of terms used by engineers. Some common terms and concepts include:

- **Capacitance** – an object's ability to hold charge
- **Computer-aided design (CAD)** – using software to virtually create a design for a building or other object
- **Deflection** – a measure of the displacement caused by a load on some structural element
- **Density** – the mass per unit volume of a given substance
- **Elasticity** – an object's ability to resume its original shape and size after being stretched or squeezed
- **Faraday constant** – the amount of electric charge per mole of electrons
- **Friction** – the force that creates resistance when two surfaces slide against each other
- **International System of Units (SI)** – the universal system of measurement for length, mass, electric current, etc.
    - Length – meter
    - Mass – kilogram
    - Time – second
    - Amount of substance – mole
    - Thermodynamic temperature – kelvin
    - Electric current – ampere
    - Luminous intensity – candela
- **Resistivity** – a measure of how powerfully a material conducts (or resists) electrical current
- **Safety Data Sheet (SDS)** – sometimes called Material Safety Data Sheet (MSDS) or Product Safety Data Sheet (PSDS), these documents give occupational safety and health information for jobsite safety when using particular materials or substances.
- **Shear strength** – a substance's ability to resist shear stress, or force that attempts to cause the substance to separate either horizontally or vertically
- **Specific gravity** – the ratio of a substance's density to a given standard density (usually water or air)
- **Tensile strength** – the greatest amount of stress a substance can endure before breaking
- **Torque** – a force that twists to rotate

Engineering Principles in Construction

Construction is dependent on engineering principles in great detail, from the materials used to the way they are put together. For instance, a material's **shear strength** and **tensile strength** must be calculated and weighed against the amount of weight and stress that will be placed on it. Materials are also chosen based on **resistivity** and **tension** to ensure endurance and safety. Concepts of **wind load** and **fluid dynamics** must be applied to ensure that a building can withstand the elements. Angles of roofs are pitched according to engineering calculations to best work in the region (e.g., more steeply sloped in regions with heavy snowfall and flatter in warmer regions).

Structures

- An **arch** is a structure that supports weight atop an open space, such as the top of a window. It normally has a semicircular shape but can also have a flat or pointed shape. Arches remove tensile stress and support the entire load as compressive stress.

- A **cantilever** is a projecting structure that receives support at only one end and carries a load at the other end. Examples include diving boards and balconies.
- A **suspension** is a structure that consists of cables supporting a horizontal beam, such as a suspension bridge. The cables are hung from a long, very strong steel cable that is attached to support columns. The structure is supported by tension in the cables and compression in the columns.
- A **truss** is a triangular structure formed by straight beams. A **node** is formed where the ends of the beams connect. The node is also where tensile or compressive forces are absorbed. In a planar truss, the beams form a two-dimensional plan. In a space truss, the beams create a three-dimensional structure.

Tools Used in Construction

Construction Devices and Tools

Construction requires a vast array of equipment, ranging from a simple measuring tape to heavy machinery.

Measuring devices include:

- **Tape measures** – there are a variety of tape measures, from small tapes to check brief dimensions to long tapes that can measure hundreds of feet.
- **Speed squares** or **protractors** – these are used for making accurate angles, such as for roofs and corners.
- **Laser measures** – instead of a manual measuring tape, distance can be measured with a handheld laser device. This is especially useful for long distances, as several hundred feet can be accurately measured without moving.
- **Measuring wheels** – these roll along the ground to measure distance. They are useful for walking a site to check measurements. While some wheels are manual, some are digital and can be used to create a virtual map of an area, complete with dimensions and calculations.
- **Levels** – these are used to make sure construction is perfectly aligned. Levels check both level (horizontal) and plumb (vertical).

Hand tools include:

- **Hammers, screwdrivers, nails, screws, and bolts** – for joining wood and other materials.
- **Trowels and jointers** – for masonry work.
- **Saws** – several different types of saws may be helpful on construction sites, such as handsaws and hacksaws, depending on the material to be cut.
- **Wrenches** and **pliers** – wrenches can be used not only for turning bolts but also for gripping slick pipes and other objects to hold them steady, and pliers also hold objects in place as well as cutting or bending wire.
- **Chisels** and **files** – these tools can be used on a variety of materials, such as wood and metal, to remove imperfections or layers like paint and to smooth the surface.
- **Utility knives** – these are used for marking wood, scraping, or cutting.

Power tools include:

- **Saws** – there are a variety of power saws such as circular saws and jigsaws for heavy duty cutting.
- **Drills** – power drills are frequently used on the job for drilling holes, installing screws, and tightening nuts.
- **Nail guns** – these are much more efficient than a manual hammer for projects that require many nails.
- **Sander** – a power sander quickly removes layers of paint and varnish, smoothing the surface to prepare it to be finished.
- **Air compressors** – these are used for powering certain other tools such as nail guns and jackhammers.

Heavy equipment includes:

- **Backhoes** – these are primarily for digging or excavating, with a large bucket that scoops dirt and rocks.
- **Excavators** – these are also diggers. They are typically on tracks rather than wheels and can be used for demolition, mining, and drilling, along with digging trenches and holes.
- **Graders** – these are equipped with a wide, flat blade behind the front wheels that drags along the ground to smooth a site.
- **Bulldozers** – similar to graders, these have a large blade at the front, but it is for heavy moving rather than precision grading. Bulldozers are used for clearing rubble, rocks, and dirt off of a site.
- **Dump trucks** – backhoes and other machines empty dirt and rubble into dump trucks to be hauled offsite.
- **Skid steers** – a skid steer is one of the smallest machines you may see at a construction site. It is useful for tight quarters and small loads, and its lift arms can be equipped with various attachments for digging, moving, and transporting.

Use of Construction Tools and Equipment

Simply having the proper tools for construction is not sufficient without knowledge of how to use them. While many are straightforward, some require training. For **measuring devices**, it is vital to be precise. This is one reason that laser measuring devices are useful, particularly for long distances, since one end of a measuring tape may slip or the altitude may change. A laser device gives a precise, digital reading and can calculate area and volume. Some measuring tools are more challenging to use, such as a protractor or speed square. This can be used with the attached level to find the pitch of a roof. It can also be used to mark angles on a board by marking a vertical angle and then swinging it until the desired angle on the speed square touches the edge of the board.

Many tools have **overlapping functions** or **multiple options**. For instance, there are many types of hammers, depending on the use. The mallet may be steel or rubber, flat or rounded, and it may be circular, hexagonal, or square. They can be used not only for driving nails, but also shaping metal, dislodging parts, or separating boards. It is important to know which tool is ideal for each function.

Most heavy equipment requires **training** and often **certifications**. Each machine operates differently and an operator must know how to use the various functions, as well as being aware of its particular dangers and required maintenance.

MAINTENANCE OF CONSTRUCTION TOOLS AND EQUIPMENT

Like any equipment, construction tools must be treated properly. **Hand tools** should be stored neatly and in a building or secure container (such as a truck toolbox). While some tools can be stored loose in a toolbag or box, others such as laser measurers should be treated with more care to avoid harm. Most tools have metal parts that are subject to rust, so if they become wet they should be cleaned and dried. Tools with joints should be lubricated regularly. Tools with blades should be sharpened regularly. Extra batteries should be carried for tools that require them.

Power tools need additional care, storing them carefully to avoid damage to cords and motors. Tools should be fully cooled before puttting away. Some tools require regular calibration to maintain accuracy. Batteries should be replaced as needed.

Heavy equipment requires regular, continual maintenance. Machines should be cleaned at the end of the day to avoid buildup of dirt and debris. At the beginning of the day, before use, machines should receive a visual inspection. Regular tests should be performed to check operation. Oil changes, tire/track inspection, lubrication, and calibration are other routine preventive measures that should be taken.

SAFETY ISSUES

If tools and equipment are not properly maintained, they could become a safety hazard. A malfunctioning machine could cause serious harm. It is also important to follow safety precautions in using any tool. Even a simple hand tool can cause harm if used incorrectly, and of course large machines could cause serious harm if operated incorrectly or without proper safeguards. A company or jobsite should have specific safety protocols to follow, clearly posted on walls in a building or delivered to workers on a jobsite.

USING CONSTRUCTION TOOLS AND EQUIPMENT SAFELY

Construction sites typically have a safety officer who performs inspections and makes sure all on the site are following safety protocol:

- Everyone should be wearing proper **personal protective equipment (PPE)**, which may include hard hats, reflective vests, safety glasses, and steel-toed boots.
- **Fall protection equipment** should be in place (lanyards, lifelines, etc.) to keep workers from falling while working at heights or over holes. Guardrails or safety nets may also be set up.
- **Hazard communication** should be in place to warn workers about potential hazardous substances and proper handling of them with a Material Safety Data Sheet (MSDS).
- **Ladders** and **scaffolding** are some of the leading sites of construction accidents. Scaffolding should be inspected daily and should include safeguards such as guardrails. Tools should be secured before climbing, and they should never left on a scaffold. Fall arrest systems should be employed. When climbing a ladder, a worker should maintain three points of contact at all times (such as both feet and one hand). Ladders should be placed carefully (to avoid slipping) and tied off if needed. Tools should be carried in a tool bag rather than in hands.

Construction Materials

STEEL AND PLUMBING SYSTEM

Steel possesses better **compressive strength** and far more **tensile strength** than concrete; however, steel is also far **more expensive**. Steel is stronger and more resistant to rust than most other metals—though its strength depends heavily on the materials with which it has been alloyed.

Steel provides the support skeleton for most large buildings, such as skyscrapers. It also reinforces masonry walls and is used in railroad track construction. The steel industry is one of the leading producers of greenhouse gases.

The **plumbing system** within a building consists of **water supply lines**, which provide usable water, and **drain and vent lines**, which remove waste. Water supply pipes are created from nontoxic materials, such as plastic, brass, or copper. Drain pipes are usually created from plastic, steel, cast-iron, or lead. Lead is toxic and, therefore, cannot be used in water supply lines. Pipes are often joined using a welder, which creates a bond via molten material.

Wood and Concrete

Wood is a common building material. In construction, it is found in both its natural state and as an engineered product, such as glue laminated timber. Glue laminated timber consists of several layers of timber glued together into a single, large beam. It is stronger than most forms of solid timber, and is capable of serving as a support beam within a structure. Engineered wood requires smaller diameter trees, which can be farmed. This preserves natural forests.

Concrete is made from cement, cementitious materials, water, and chemicals. It is inexpensive compared to other building materials, and it is used in the construction of roads, parking lots, foundations, and block walls. Concrete can carry very heavy loads (high compressive strength), but has a very low resistance to stretching and twisting (low tensile strength); consequently, concrete structures are often reinforced with steel. Concrete is also very susceptible to thermal expansion, which causes it to shrink and crack as it ages.

Building, Maintaining, and Repairing Structures

Structural Determination

Urban development plans lay out the construction strategies for **high-density urban development**. Most construction incorporates the following elements: public spaces; restoration of old neighborhoods; compact design, which connects commercial and residential areas; good transit systems; walkways that encourage walking and bike riding; infill development rather than expansion; land use that improves the health and economic well-being of the poor; and affordable housing.

Suburban development plans lay out the construction strategies for **low-density, homogenous suburban areas**, which normally include single-family detached dwellings, office parks, retail centers, employment centers, and recreation areas. These plans facilitate automobile usage and allow for curving streets, lawns, garages, driveways, and parking lots

Capital facilities plans lay out the construction strategies for **roads, bridges and sewer lines** within a community over a 5 to 6 year period.

Parks and open space plans lay out the construction strategies for **park and open space systems**, such as play grounds, parks, athletic facilities, community gardens, and recreation parks.

Electrical Wiring System

Electrical wires usually consist of conductors that are twisted together and encased in insulating material. The voltage requirements determine the number of conductors that must be twisted together in a single wire. Two common conductors used in electrical systems are copper and aluminum. **Copper** is more expensive but poses fewer problems than aluminum. Copper is the most popular choice in residential structures. **Aluminum** is lighter, cheaper, and better suited to larger wires and circuits. In today's electrical systems, insulation is made from synthetic materials, such as thermoplastic and polymers that act and feel like rubber. The latter has an extremely high resistance to moisture, making it ideal for industrial and utility usage. According to most building codes, electrical systems must be fire-stopped, with sealing closing openings and joints, or fireproofed, which involves increasing the resistance of materials to fire. A building's electrical system includes junction boxes, through which electrical power can be rerouted.

Chapter Quiz

Ready to see how well you retained what you just read? Scan the QR code to go directly to the chapter quiz interface for this study guide. If you're using a computer, simply visit the online resources page at **mometrix.com/resources719/texesmathpse** and click the Chapter Quizzes link.

The Engineering Profession

History and Impact of Technology

Impact of Scientific and Technical Innovation

Scientific and technical innovation has played a major role in enhancing productivity, increasing society's wealth, and raising its standard of living. After a new innovation comes about, it must spread to other people and groups in order to be effective. This process is known as **diffusion**, and is illustrated using an **s-curve**, also known as a **diffusion curve**, which tracks an increase in revenue or productivity over time. An s-curve represents the product life of an innovation. During the early stages of product life, an innovation must establish its usefulness, and it experiences a very slow growth in terms of revenue and productivity. The middle stages of product life see rapid increases in growth, and the latter stages of product life involve gradual decline. Product improvements may extend the lifespan of an innovation, but it will inevitably fall off. Consequently, companies are always seeking new innovations to replace older ones.

Resource Management

Resource management seeks to allocate an organization's resources in the most efficient and economical ways possible—that is, the goal of resource management is the **optimization** of resource usage in a project. Resources include money, employees, inventory, production, and information technology, and they are allocated using a variety of processes and techniques. One such technique is **resource leveling**, which balances usage by eliminating inventory shortages and excesses. To avoid shortages and thereby reduce conflict, management should take care when scheduling multiple activities at the same time. If concurrent activities require more of one resource than is available or make use of the same person, they should be rescheduled. In many cases, management may be forced to delay an activity until the resource becomes available. If this activity is part of the critical path, the project may be delayed.

Stimulating Competitiveness and Creating New Goods and Services

Technological innovation provides a number of benefits to the marketplace. It can introduce new products, which are simply those with which customers have no prior experience. Technological innovation can also introduce an improved or more efficient means of production or commodity handling. In many cases, these new products or means of production will open up new markets and require the discovery of new sources of raw materials. This often stimulates the economy by creating additional competition and breaking up existing monopolies. Technological innovation is often the result of the pursuit of better quality, new market formation, new regulations, the need for replacement parts or services, decreased availability of materials, increased labor costs, or increased production costs, among other factors.

Major Scientific and Technological Innovations

The **automobile** was granted a patent in 1885. Karl Benz, who is widely regarded as the inventor of the gasoline-powered car, placed the first automobiles into production during the same year.

The **airplane** was developed in 1903 by Wilbur and Orville Wright. They used various principles of aerodynamics, such as drag and lift, to develop the first power and controlled flight.

The **integrated circuit** was developed in 1958 by Jack Kilby of Texas Instruments and Robert Noyce at Fairchild Semiconductor. It led to the development of the microchip by enabling semiconductor devices to perform the same functions as vacuum tubes. It revolutionized electronic equipment, leading to the development of personal computers, cellular phones, and various digital devices.

The **internet** came about with the first TCP/IP protocol, which was developed in 1983 by Robert E. Kahn and Vint Cerf.

Relationship Between Technology and Society and Culture

Technology and culture have a **synergistic relationship** which began with the simple tools developed during the dawn of man and continues today with modern technologies such as computers and other electronic devices. This relationship is **cyclical and codependent**, with each party exerting influence over the other. Funding for technological development comes from two primary sources in most modern cultures and societies: Private business and enterprise, or government programs. Once new technology is developed, it **influences** social attitudes and beliefs, which, in turn, influence the implementation of new technology. For instance, key values and beliefs that derive from this codependence between technology and culture are the notions that human productivity should work to achieve higher levels of efficiency and that technology drives social progress. According to these beliefs, humankind is improving as long as technology is improving.

Conservation and Sustainability

Conservation is the effort to reduce energy and material consumption by reducing usage and making more efficient use of existing resources. New technology can facilitate conservation in a variety of ways. Renewable energy sources (e.g., geothermal, hydroelectric energy, wind power), building techniques that take advantage of the local climate, and vehicles that consume less gas (such as hybrids) all help lower energy consumption. Real-time energy metering helps consumers to better understand the impact of their energy usage.

Sustainability determines the length of time over which an ecological system will endure. Sustainable systems are those that will remain healthy and productive for a long time. Technology is often a means of increasing energy efficiency and conserving natural resources so that the human environment can become more sustainable.

Biotechnology

Biotechnology is the technological application of biology. It uses living organisms and bioprocesses to create products or processes, and has numerous applications in the following fields:

- **Medicine** – includes drug production, gene therapy, gene testing, and pharmacogenomics (i.e. determining an individual's response to drugs based on inherited genetic traits).
- **Agriculture** – includes enhancing crop yield, increasing nutritional attributes of food, improving crop durability, producing new substances in crop plants, and reducing dependence on agrochemicals.
- **Biological engineering** – uses physics, chemistry, and mathematics to solve life science problems.
- **Bioremediation and biodegradation** – create organisms for purposes of removing environmental contamination.
- **Cloning** –two main types: reproductive, which brings a fully developed life into the world, and therapeutic, which involves using stem cells.
- **Human Genome Project** – seeks to discover all human genes and create a reference sequence for the human genome.

Biotechnology often makes use of mathematical biology, which models complex biological processes using various types of math: graph theory, calculus, probability theory, statistics, linear algebra, abstract algebra, combinatorics, algebraic geometry, topology, dynamical systems, differential equations, and coding theory.

Government Regulation and Facilitating Technological Development

Historically, the government has served a role not only in funding technological research but also in regulating its usage and side effects. One example of such regulation is the FDA, or Food and Drug administration. When selecting which types of research to fund, the government will choose those that offer the greatest benefit to mankind. However, the presence of different interest groups competing for resources can complicate the selection process. In reality, both the populace-at-large and special interests hold tremendous influence over governmental policy. The government also assumes a regulatory role in technological development, especially regarding the environment and the protection of ecological systems. The government is responsible for assigning liability to corporations whose products cause harm.

Material Disposals, and Environmental Emission Monitoring and Control

Materials disposal is carried out using a variety of technologies and techniques:

- **Incinerators** – subject solid waste to the process of combustion in order to convert it into residue and gas. This generates heat, gas, steam, and ash.
- **Landfills** – eliminate solid waste by burying it.
- **Recycling** – reprocesses discarded materials (e.g., aluminum cans, glass bottles, newspapers, cardboard boxes, paper) into their constituent materials and reuses them.
- **Sustainability methods** – include biological reprocessing (e.g., composting, anaerobic digestion) and energy recovery (which processes waste into fuel).

Environmental emission monitoring and control is performed by continuous emission monitoring systems, which use gas analyzers to test air samples for certain types of emissions (e.g., carbon dioxide, carbon monoxide, sulfur dioxide, mercury). Federal programs use these systems to ensure compliance with emission standards, such as the acid rain program and other EPA standards.

Medical and Agricultural Technology

Medical technology includes any device, procedure, pharmaceutical, or system whose purpose is improving health, preventing sickness, and diagnosing or treating disease. Medical technology covers a vast number of healthcare products, which often make use of mathematical principles and concepts. For instance, medical imaging machines (e.g., CAT, ultrasound) and pharmacology often make use of trigonometric functions for measurement problems. Mathematical tools such as dimensional analysis are often used to calculate the correct dosage for patients.

Agricultural technology encompasses a wide array of machinery, processes, and systems designed to enhance agricultural production. Agricultural technology also makes use of mathematical principles and concepts. For instance, dimensional analyses are often used to examine complex agricultural-social economic systems. Graph theory provides a means of modeling ecology, and quadratic equations are often used to solve economic problems related to agriculture.

PHYSICS

The following concepts and principles of physics have been essential to the development of new technologies:

- **Bernoulli's principle** states that, when the speed of an inviscid flow increases, the pressure (or potential energy) of the flow will decrease. Consequently, faster moving air creates slower static pressure and higher dynamic pressure. Carburetors and pitot tubes work on Bernoulli's principle.
- **Aerodynamics** includes four forces relevant to flight: thrust, lift, drag, and weight. Thrust is a reaction force explained by Newton's Second and Third Laws. When mass is accelerated in one direction, it will generate an equal force in the opposite direction. Jet engines, propeller blades, and rockets generate thrust by pushing air in the direction opposite to flight. Lift is a force that is generated perpendicular to the oncoming air flow (using Bernoulli's Principle). Airplane wings are designed to take advantage of lift (climbing, descending, banking). Drag is a force that is generated parallel to the oncoming air flow, and opposes the motion of an object. Weight is applied by gravity. In order to achieve flight, all forces must be balanced.

BIOLOGY

Biology includes several fields with an especially strong focus on developing new technologies. One such field is **biological engineering**, which attempts to emulate biological systems and, thereby, develop new products or enhance existing biological systems. Biological engineering is responsible for the creation of renewable bioenergy, biocompatible materials, medical devices, diagnostic equipment, and similar technologies. A second field is **molecular biology**. It helped create the therapies and techniques used in gene therapy, which treats diseases by inserting, altering, and removing genes within a person's cells and tissue. Using techniques developed in molecular biology, gene therapy is capable of replacing mutated genes or even modifying and correcting mutated cells. A third field is **pathology**, which uses laboratory equipment to diagnose disease. Another field is **biotechnology**, which uses living organisms and bioprocesses to create products or processes.

CHEMISTRY

An understanding of chemistry is necessary to convert raw materials (e.g., oil, air, water, minerals, metals) into usable and marketable materials such as solvents, soaps, pesticides, and cement. The chemical industry consists of numerous businesses that use chemical processes and reactions to create and refine products. Below is a partial list of such products:

- **Petrochemicals** include ethylene, propylene, benzene, and styrene.
- **Agrochemicals** include fertilizers, insecticides, and herbicides.
- **Polymers** include polyester, polyethylene, and Bakelite.
- **Fragrances/flavors** include vanillin and coumarin.
- **Inorganic industrial compounds** include ammonia, nitric acid, sodium hydroxide, and sulfuric acid.
- **Organic industrial compounds** include phenol, urea, and ethylene oxide.
- **Ceramics** include silica brick and frit.
- **Explosives** include ammonium nitrate, nitrocellulose, and nitroglycerin.
- **Oleochemicals** include lard and soybean oil.
- **Elastomers** includes polyisoprene, neoprene, and polyurethane.

Technology Education Goals, Instruction, and Assessment

Resources Available for Professional Development and Learning

- **Professional literature** - books and publications are examples of literature that can help a classroom teacher.
- **Colleagues** - a fellow member of a profession, staff, or academic faculty; an associate
- **Professional Associations** - an association of practitioners of a given profession, for example NEA, NSTA, etc.
- **Professional development activities** – sometimes put on by a local or state school board to teach educators the newest trends in education.

Code of Ethics

Ethical codes are specialized and specific rules of ethics. Such codes exist in most professions to **guide interactions** between specialists with advanced knowledge (e.g., doctors, lawyers, engineers) and the general public. They are often not part of any more general theory of ethics but accepted as pragmatic necessities. Ethical codes are distinct from moral codes that apply to the education and religion of a whole larger society. Not only are they more specialized, but they are more internally consistent, and they can typically be applied without a great deal of interpretation by an ordinary practitioner of the specialty.

Student Diversity

Cultural identities are strongly embraced by adolescents, but they also want to be recognized and treated as unique individuals. Teachers walk a fine line between respecting cultural differences and avoiding overly emphasizing them or disregarding them altogether. Responding to discriminatory comments immediately, using a wide variety of examples, quoting scholars from many cultures and identifying universal problems needing complex solutions can indirectly communicate appreciation of and respect for all cultures. Teachers must take care never to imply any kind of stereotype or make comments that might indicate a cultural bias. They must refrain from asking a student to respond as a member of a particular culture, class, or country. Teachers should learn as much as they can about every racial, ethnic and cultural group represented in their classroom. It is also important that teachers respect students' commitments and obligations away from school, their family responsibilities and job pressures.

Cultural Influences

Study after study has shown that a student's culture has a **direct impact on learning**. Since educational standards are based on white, middle class cultural identification, students who do not fall into that demographic face challenges every day. It's not that these students are incapable of learning; they simply judge that which is important and how they express that importance differently. Sometimes it is **difficult for them to understand and relate** to curriculum content, teaching methods, and social skills required because their culture does things differently, emphasizes different choices, and rewards different behavior. Adolescents identify with their culture; they become what they know. If teachers ignore cultural differences, it causes communication issues, inhibits learning, and increases the potential for behavior problems. As long as a child has no physical or mental health issues, he or she is capable of learning. He or she simply requires the information presented and examples used to be relevant to his or her life experiences; otherwise, it will not seem to make sense.

Social Environment

The **social environment** is the set of people and institutions with which one associates and communicates. It has both a **direct and indirect influence on behavior** by the individuals within the group. It is sometimes defined by specific characteristics such as race, gender, age, culture, or behavioral patterns. When defined by **behavioral patterns** it can lead to unproven assumptions about entire groups of people. In America's diverse society, it is essential that teachers recognize that **various social groups exist** within a classroom and thus determine the best strategies not only to facilitate the learning of "book" facts, but also to encourage understanding and acceptance between the groups. The learning theory called **social cognitivism** believes that people learn by observing others, whether they are aware of the process or not. Creating opportunities for students to interact with diverse social groups in a neutral, non-threatening situation can bring about positive interpersonal growth that could have long-term societal impact outside of the educational environment.

Cognitive Learning

Cognitive approaches to learning focus on emphasizing ways to enhance students' intrinsic nature to make sense of the world around them. Students do this by learning and organizing information, problem-solving and finally developing the concepts and language in order to convey what they see. It refers to the way that students process information. The style in which one learns is described as a **dimension of one's personality**. Attitudes, values, and social interactions are all dimensions of these influences. Once a teacher has an idea of the cognitive learning styles of his or her students, he or she can better gauge how to direct the information at them. The teacher may find that one class does much better with small group work, whereas another group works more effectively individually. There will always be a wide range of ability in any class, and getting to know the students' styles is always going to make teaching more effective.

Learning Styles

The different learning styles that affect how students learn and perform are:

- **Visual learners**: These students learn best by **seeing** written directions and benefit from having notes written down on a whiteboard or overhead. They are able to extract information from written text well and benefit from having main points summarized on the board during class discussions.
- **Oral learners**: These students perform better when information can be **heard**; for instance, they may prefer to read aloud or listen to someone else read aloud. Discussions can be helpful in order to hear the information once, and then repeat it to someone else.
- **Kinesthetic learners**: These students benefit from **hands-on** experiences and learn best from participating in the classroom, such as by conducting a science experiment.

Cultural Differences

The **cultural differences** that might affect behavior include eye contact, hand movements, silence, religious belief, and loss of face. It is important to know the differences that some students may have with eye contact; for example, in some cultures, looking down is seen as a sign of disrespect, whereas with some students that is the way to show respect and that they are paying attention. Some students may laugh or smile out of nervousness when under pressure, falsely leading teachers to assume that they are being rude or misbehaving. Silence is one that varies between genders and cultures. Girls tend to be quieter, and students who are silent when called upon could actually be waiting for more direction instead of showing that they are not paying attention. Religious beliefs come into effect when doing particular activities that certain religions would find inappropriate, therefore causing students to be reluctant to participate, not because they don't know what to do but because they feel that they cannot do the activity.

MAINSTREAMING

Traditional mainstreaming in public schools is defined as allowing students with physical disabilities to be placed in **certain regular education classes**. As practiced in the 1970s and early '80s, mainstreaming was an attempt to meet the LRE requirement by moving students from separate schools and classes into regular education classes for part or all of the school day. Often, students received most of their academic instruction in special classes and their time with nondisabled peers was spent in nonacademic activities such as lunch and recess, and in less rigid subjects such as physical education, art, and music. This seems to be an easy thing to do, but the fact is that in order for this to be effective and beneficial for all the students involved, there must be the correct support services in place. Otherwise, the classroom teacher may be spread too thin if he or she is expected to differentiate for the student with the disability on his or her own. Due to this, some schools will only mainstream children with mild to moderate disabilities, instead of all students with disabilities. If a school is fully committed to the idea of mainstreaming students with disabilities, it should be done with support in the regular classroom in order to make the transition run smoothly.

Review Video: Least Restrictive Environment
Visit mometrix.com/academy and enter code: 100354

EFFECTS OF MAINSTREAMING

Mainstreaming, when done correctly, can have **many positive effects** on social performance. If the students in the regular classroom are educated about the students with disabilities that could be entering their classrooms, then the rate of success tends to be much higher. If no transition work is done, then isolation can be the result, which is the exact opposite of the goal of mainstreaming. For academic performance, as long as the right support systems are in place in the regular classroom (such as a paraeducator and any necessary adaptations to the assigned work), then the academic performance of students with disabilities can only improve. Mainstreaming is meant to increase awareness and to welcome diversity, and when done properly, a classroom is a great place for this change to occur.

The traditional idea of **mainstreaming** allows students with disabilities to participate in **some regular classrooms** whereas **inclusion** allows these same students the ability to participate in **all regular classrooms and activities**. Generally, inclusion is thought of as the better option to better avoid the segregation that can sometime occur between students with disabilities and without. If they are mainstreamed, they are only mainstreamed in certain classes, whereas with inclusion, more possibilities are open to them, and depending on what is outlined in their **IEP**, they may have one-on-one support in the classrooms they are in. It also gives them the opportunity to participate in the same activities that all students participate in to the greatest extent possible, thus following the order that all students with disabilities be educated in the least restrictive environment possible.

INCLUSION

Inclusion is the meaningful participation of students with disabilities in general education classrooms. To practice inclusion successfully the school principal and staff must understand the history, terms, and legal requirements involved as well as have the necessary levels of support and commitment. The word *inclusion* is not a precise term, and it is often confused with similar concepts such as **least restrictive environment (LRE)** and mainstreaming. Educating children in the least restrictive environment has been mandated since the 1970s, when it was a major provision of the Education for All Handicapped Children Act. The law states that to the maximum extent appropriate, children with disabilities are educated with children who are nondisabled; and that special classes, separate schooling, or other removal of children from the regular educational environment occurs only if the nature or severity of the disability is such that education in regular classes with the use of supplemental aids and services cannot be achieved satisfactorily.

Pros and Cons of Inclusion

Inclusion is defined as the commitment to educate the child, to the highest possible effect, in a regular school and classroom. It outlines bringing the **support to the students in the classroom**, such as special supplies, or other teachers, rather than separating them in separate rooms or buildings altogether. People who support inclusion could argue that students with disabilities who are educated separately are being discriminated against and therefore it violates their rights. They also voice a need for reform in the special education programs, which they argue are costly for the often inadequate results that they produce, both academically and socially. However, some special educators and teachers have voiced their concerns that inclusion could result in insufficient services for students with disabilities. A regular classroom may not be the place for children with behavioral problems or anti-social disorders. There is also the concern that inclusion could replace special education altogether one day.

Motivation

Some ways in which teachers can motivate their students to learn are as follows:

- Ensure that students know what they are doing and how to know when they have achieved a goal in order for them to build their self-esteem and self-awareness.
- Do everything possible to satisfy the basic needs of the students, such as esteem, safety, and belongingness.
- Try to encourage students to take risks in order to grow by talking up the rewards.
- Direct learning experiences toward feelings of success, in order to direct students towards individual and group achievement.
- Encourage the development of self-confidence and self-direction in students who need help working on these qualities.
- Make learning relevant for the students by focusing on social interaction, usefulness, and activity.

Classroom Management

Classroom management is defined as the set of rules or activities that the teacher sets for his classroom that outline **effective and efficient instruction**. This can range from establishing attendance and homework routines to dealing with inappropriate behavior. Some would argue that classroom management cannot be taught and that it is something that can only be learned through experience. Nonetheless, it doesn't do anyone any good to have a new teacher in a classroom with no idea of good ways to instill order in the classroom. Being organized is the first way to start off with a good classroom management program, as is having an experienced teacher as a mentor. These are usually good ways for a new teacher to overcome his or her fears about classroom management as he or she will have someone to turn to for help.

Review Video: Classroom Management - Rhythms of Teaching
Visit mometrix.com/academy and enter code: 809399

Components of Classroom Management

In order to be successful, classroom management should consist of the following:

- **Positive classroom environment**: Developing a friendly rapport with students from the first day onwards so that students will feel eager to come to class is important. Criticism of work should be worded to begin with what the student has done well before some suggestions as to how to improve it, focusing on the positive aspects first.
- **Clear standards of behavior for students**: Rules should be enforced consistently so that there is no surprise as to what students should expect for misbehaving. Dealing with inappropriate behaviors should be done so with a calm and clear demeanor.
- **Student engagement**: Having students engaged in the task will help with classroom management as there should be less inappropriate behavior. Smooth transitions are also important so that there is no time in between activities for students to lose their concentration.

Tips for Classroom Management Success

Some tips for daily classroom management success are:

- Ensure that students know the routines.
- Always over-plan for lessons.
- Label materials clearly so that they do not need much further explanation.
- Make sure expectations are clearly set for your students.
- Discussions, debates, and consequences are more effective than nagging, lecturing, and threatening.
- Review rules for behavior and work periodically.
- Welcome students at the door.
- Make sure there is plenty of opportunity for student participation.
- Learn about the students' interests.
- Involve students who misbehave.
- Assign work ahead of time and give clear deadlines.
- Color code materials in order to help organization.
- Use eye contact.
- Use both verbal and non-verbal ways to correct behavior.
- Use humor daily.
- Give your students compliments when they deserve them.

Classroom Management Theory

The major developers in classroom management theories are:

- **B.F. Skinner**: He outlined behavior modification which originated from behavioral psychology. He thought that the best way to change students' behavior was to reward them for good behavior and either remove rewards or punish inappropriate behavior.
- **Carl Rogers**: Socioemotional climate was given importance by Rogers because he thought that having positive interpersonal relationship between students and teachers would foster a positive classroom.

- **Richard and Patricia Schmuck**: They derived group process from social psychology and group dynamics research and put the emphasis on the teacher establishing and maintaining an effectively controlled classroom with cooperation being the key skill needed in order to have groups work effectively together.
- **Lee and Marlene Canter**: They viewed classroom management as establishing and enforcing classroom rules as a way of controlling student behavior, mainly by discipline.

DAILY PROCEDURES, ROUTINES AND RULES

The most important thing to remember when dealing with students is that **consistency is vital**. If one student sees you deal with something in a certain way, the next student will expect the same treatment. If she is treated differently, then she will see your rules as flexible, or that they don't even matter. It is better to be tough at the beginning of the school year, and as many teachers will tell you (e.g., "Don't smile until after Christmas"), you are ultimately there in the classroom to be a teacher, not a friend to the students, and **remaining firm with your rules and routines** will earn their respect as well as maintain an orderly classroom. Empty threats can be especially damaging. It is best to clearly outline the consequences for misbehavior, or inability to produce class work or homework as soon as possible and then follow through.

CONSEQUENCES

When deciding on **rewards and consequences**, it is useful to make sure that they are **relevant to the students and the situation**. It makes sense to punish a student who does not complete his homework by having them complete the homework in a detention after school, or having the student complete it by a certain date, otherwise the parents would be notified. It would not be appropriate, for example, to have the student stand in the hallway when he or she could be in the class learning the material. When students see clear links between the consequences and their behavior, they will know their limits and be more inclined to behave appropriately or complete assignments on time.

POSITIVE GUIDANCE

When the differences between girls and boys were looked at in many gender studies, it was found that **boys tended to be more assertive and aggressive** while the **girls tended to be passive**. The way the teachers were dealing with the boys tended to be more verbal, thus reinforcing that calling out would get more attention than the more desirable behavior of the girls who would raise their hands and pay attention. Praising and giving compliments encourages students to focus and stay on task if they want to receive praise and attention. Ignoring misbehavior can be effective, as long as it doesn't get out of hand, as it ensures that the misbehaving students know that negative behavior will get a negative reaction, or no reaction at all. Focusing on the problems in a classroom can inadvertently be rewarding to those who misbehave and cause the negative behavior to manifest itself further.

CLASSROOM RULES

Starting off the school year with a clearly defined set of classroom rules will let your students know their limitations from the beginning. Many teachers have their **students participate in the creation of the rules**. Starting off by brainstorming ideas for rules may have you discover that student-created rules may be more strict that you would create yourself. Most students want to learn in a **safe environment** and feel better when there are **defined boundaries**. It is useful to **create consequences** after each repetition of the undesirable behavior; for example, after the first violation, the student's name goes on the board. After the second violation, the student stands in the hallway, and after the third violation there is a note home, detention, or whatever the relevant consequence may be.

The rules should be **positive by nature**. Some students tend to see rules that are worded negatively as a challenge and will attempt to break the rule, for example, "Raise your hand before speaking," is worded positively, whereas "Don't call out," is worded negatively. Each rule should also be worded as simply as possible, but it should be well-defined in a discussion before it is decided upon. For example, if "Be respectful to others" is one of your rules, make sure the students know what respecting someone looks like by providing examples. Keeping the list short is also important because students will be more likely to keep to the rules if there are just a few. Lastly, enforce the rules that are created. It does no good for the students to see a rule being broken by another student who does not receive the prescribed consequences.

Direct Instruction

Direct instruction is defined as the procedure that is **led by the teacher** and is **followed by the students**. Students are given **specific instructions** as to what they are supposed to do. The teacher will introduce the task, providing background information, give the students work to complete individually, and then provide immediate feedback. The two main forms are **lecturing and explaining**, but forms could also include a question-answer session or a class discussion. By having the teacher relaying all of the information to the students and then having the students practice the skills they have just learned, it can be easy to judge how well the students are progressing with the work.

Advantages

Direct instruction can have its advantages. If, for example, the material is simple and there is only one right answer, such as with rote facts, then direct instruction can be the quickest and easiest way to convey this material. The teacher has **control of the timing of the lesson** and can make sure that it moves at a pace that is accessible to everyone. Also, the teacher has control over what will be learned and how it will be taught, so he or she can make it relevant to the majority of the students and cater it to the needs of the students to some degree. It is also easier to measure if the curriculum is being taught using this model of instruction because the teacher will be able to progress along a certain line of thought while teaching.

Disadvantages

Some of the disadvantages of direct instruction is that it is **based on old theories of learning** that believe that simple tasks must be learned before complex ones, and that the emphasis is on learning that can be quantified. This type of instruction can also minimize the prior experiences and knowledge of the individual students as the students are taught as a whole, not as individuals. Sometimes, students can lose sight of the overall task as they are caught up in the series of tasks that can make learning seem irrelevant to them. If students are not given many opportunities to do the work themselves, they can have a **low retention level** of what they have learned. Finally, students who learn in styles other than verbally **may struggle to keep up with the lesson** because various learning strategies are not catered to.

Madeline Hunter Direct Instruction Model

- **Anticipatory Set**: This should involve the bait for students to show interest in the lesson and for the teacher to focus their attention.
- **Objectives**: The objectives should be clear so that the teacher knows what students will have achieved by the end of the lesson.
- **Teaching**: The teacher provides the information and then shows examples of the material.
- **Guided practice**: Students demonstrate what they have learned through an activity supervised by the teacher.

- **Checking for Understanding**: The teacher may ask students questions to check understanding in order to proceed to the next level of learning.
- **Independent practice**: Once students have mastered the skills, more practice can be done for reinforcement.
- **Closure**: The teacher gives the lesson a conclusion and gives the students a chance to make sense of what they have learned.

Assessment Station

An **assessment station** is a designated area, inside or outside of the classroom, used for the specific purpose of **evaluating students' progress performing a task**. Individuals or groups can be assigned to complete a task, use a piece of lab equipment, or work with some technological device. The purpose is to assess the knowledge acquired, processes used, skills displayed, and general attitude about the task, and if working in a group, how each student interacts with the other members of the team.

The assessment station should **function the same way every time** it is used. This builds consistency and reduces the time needed for explanations and demonstrations before and during future assessments. Instructions should be clear, concise, and specific and explain exactly how the area should be left for the next student. Activities performed in the assessment station should be simple, straightforward, and relate to the material being studied.

Using an Assessment Station

Because the assessment station is an interactive tool, the area needs to be **equipped with the appropriate equipment** necessary to complete the task. If the activity is an experiment, the area needs to be ventilated and appropriate safety precautions taken (e.g., having water available and a fire extinguisher at hand). The students need to understand how to operate the instruments in a safe manner and therefore instructions should be provided both in writing and verbally. Questions should be asked and answered before any activity is started. If it is a group activity, each student needs to contribute to the assigned task.

The work submitted by each student is **evaluated using a rating/grading scale or a checklist**. For example, if the task required the use of a microscope, the checklist should have points related to its use. If it was a group project, cooperation, helpfulness, and leadership skills should be noted.

Individual Assessments

Individual assessments focus on the **progress** each student made during a defined period of time (e.g., every six weeks, at the end of the semester) rather than in a team collaboration. A variety of activities such as written assignments, oral presentations, and class participation should be incorporated into the assessment in order to obtain a broader, more realistic view of the student's understanding of the material. The assessment process should be fully explained so that the student knows what is expected. He or she is evaluated using one or all of the following standards:

- **Self-referenced**: Based on the student's previous level of progress
- **Criterion-referenced**: A defined, school or district-wide standard
- **Norm-referenced**: Based on the progress of groups of students the same age or grade level

Using a combination of standards instead of relying on one method presents a clearer, more accurate picture of the student's growth.

Group Assessments

Group assessments focus on how students **cooperate and collaborate** in completing a project assigned to the group rather than to a single student. The same activities used in individual assessments are used, such as written assignments, oral presentations, and group participation, but they are used to evaluate social and interactive skills as well as the work produced. The students' willingness to accept being evaluated for a group project is based on if and how long they have been exposed to this type of cooperative collaboration and if they feel the grading system is applied fairly. If this project is the first time students in a competitive environment are expected to work together, there may be some misunderstandings and objections about what is expected, how it works, and how each student will be evaluated. It is critical that the teacher explains the evaluation process clearly, answers questions, addresses reservations, and closely monitors individual contributions as well as the progress of the project.

Advantages and Disadvantages of Assessments

Individual assessments are **easily understood** by students and parents and mesh with most school districts' systems. Because each student is **evaluated based on criteria established by state performance and/or content standards**, it is easy to measure the success of department curricula. Self-referenced standards provide feedback about the student's strengths and weaknesses. They can help **motivate** the student to work harder and take more responsibility for his learning. Students sometimes set personal goals and expectations. Individual assessments help them measure their success. These evaluations provide the teacher insight into any special help the student might need.

Individual assessment can create and encourage a **very competitive environment** in which some students are **unable to compete effectively**. It makes it **difficult to evaluate** students' ability to work with a team and judge their interaction with others, both of which are important to the educational experience. They can also be also very time consuming for the teacher to complete fairly and accurately.

There are three ways to evaluate a group project: **group grade only, individual grade only, or a combination of both**. The reason for group projects is to teach cooperation in a team environment. Giving everyone the same grade can foster some degree of esprit de corps. It also frees the teacher from having to decide who was responsible for what part of the project. A group grade, however, can cause resentment, especially if students are not used to working in a group and are used to earning grades based on a competitive scale. Students understand individual grades, but in a group project environment the competitive scale diminishes the spirit of cooperation because everyone is working for himself rather than for the good of the team. Giving a group grade and an individual grade addresses both issues. Basing eighty percent of the grade on cooperation and collaboration and twenty percent on individual production recognizes the importance of working for the group and the necessity of individual contributions.

Performance Contracts

A **performance contract** is a written agreement between an individual student or a group of students and a teacher about a specific activity. The assignment can be a research paper, an oral presentation with props, or some other project. The contract clearly states the goal, explains the activity, establishes a timeline, and describes who will do what and how it will be done. Sometimes the agreement also details the criteria to be used to evaluate the finished product. This tool helps students **learn to plan a project** by breaking it into manageable parts and shows them how to utilize their time more efficiently. Not only can the completed project be graded, but the performance contract itself can be evaluated. The teacher should assess the student's participation in setting up the contract, his or her willingness to compromise when necessary, and the student's general attitude about the concept and process.

Performance contracts can be a great learning experience for students by teaching them how to plan and prioritize, and it can encourage them to avoid procrastination. However, **some students may have trouble** understanding the concept, so it may be necessary to review the planning, organizing, and writing steps several times before they are able to grasp the idea. Using contracts can also help a struggling student in other areas of his life. These agreements can be developed to address attendance requirements and expected behavior standards or to plan weekly or monthly homework schedules.

If a teacher has never used performance contracts, he or she needs to understand that setting up the system and helping the students write their agreements is **very time consuming**, especially in the beginning. It can help, as a class project, to create a performance contract based on a completed project. This strategy sometimes reduces the learning curve for all the students.

In order for a performance contract to be a learning experience, the guidelines for writing one should be very general. The teacher can either give the student a written list of suggestions or, preferably, discuss them one-on-one. Some questions that might be used:

- What work items are you planning to include?
- Where you will find the necessary data: Personal reference books, the internet, the library? Do you have additional sources?
- How long will it take to outline a plan, research the topic, and finish the project?
- What criteria should be used to evaluate the finished product?

Questions that might be used to evaluate the completed contract:

- Is the contract realistic relative to required completion date?
- Are the contract questions appropriate to the project objectives?
- Were reliable and appropriate sources chosen?
- How comprehensive is the plan?
- Does the student understand his capabilities and recognize his limitations?

Example of a Performance Contract

Student's Name: ______________________
Teacher's Name: ______________________
Contract Dates: ______________________
Purpose of Contract: ______________________
I am planning a study of: ______________________
Reason for choosing this topic: ______________________
Main focus of the study: ______________________
Questions I want to answer (add as many lines as needed):
____
Sources I plan to use (check at least 5):
Books___; Interviews___; Experiments___; Magazines___; Encyclopedia___; Newspapers___; Museums___; Pictures, Films, Videos___; Other Sources/ My Research___
Explain: ______________________
The finished product will be in the form of: ______________________
The learning skills I will use: ______________________
The study will be completed by (different dates may be given for various segments):
____
The study will be reviewed by: ______________________
Evaluated by: ______________________
The evaluator will be looking for: ______________________
Student's Signature ______________________
Teacher's Signature ______________________

Portfolio

A **portfolio** is a collection of the student's work assembled over a period of time (e.g., six week grading period, one semester, the entire year). Various items can be included: contracts, copies of completed activities such as papers; presentations and pictures of props; performance assessments made by the student, his peers, and the teacher; copies of class work and homework; classroom tests; and state-mandated exams. A portfolio is a **powerful aide** in assessing the student's progress and an excellent format to present to parents so they can review their child's progress. The decision on what to include should be a collaboration between the student and the teacher. What will be included: examples of best work, worst work, typical work, or perhaps some of each? Will the student keep a copy as a reference point? Decisions need to be made and rules established as early as possible in the process so that progress is accurately and fairly recorded.

Considerations for Using Portfolios

Once decisions have been made about what will be included, it is important to begin with **baseline data for comparison** as the portfolio grows. Selected material can be placed in a folder or large envelope with the student's name on the front. Each addition needs to be dated with an explanation attached stating why the item was included and what features should be noted. Teachers who use portfolios will often create assignments with the intention of including it in the package. As the contents grow, it may become necessary due to space limitations to review the items and remove some daily work, quizzes, or tests. Once the portfolio is complete, the teacher needs to have a **method to evaluate the contents and review the student's progress** in areas such as creativity, critical thinking, originality, research skills, perseverance, responsibility, and communication effectiveness. A checklist can be useful.

Student Feedback Form

Use the following form when asking for student feedback on a group project:

Rating For Group Project

Student Name: ________________________________

Date of Project ____________ to ____________________

Circle the phrase that describes how you feel.

Choosing the members of your group:

I really like it. ***It's okay.*** ***I don't like it.***

Having the teacher choose group members:

I really like it. ***It's okay.*** ***I don't like it.***

The group deciding how you are going to complete the project?

I really like it. ***It's okay.*** ***I don't like it.***

Comments: ________________________________

____

____

____

Work Products, Response Groups

Work Products are completed assignments that are evaluated on the basis of the topic chosen as well as creativity, originality, organization, understanding of the subject matter, social and academic progress, and success in meeting and/or exceeding predetermined criteria along with any other items deemed important by the individual teacher. Work products can take many different forms, including but not limited to research papers, poems, fiction and non-fiction stories, bulletin boards, video and audio tapes, computer and laboratory demonstrations, dramatic performances, debates and oral presentations, paintings, drawings and sculptures, and musical compositions and performances.

Response Groups are discussions about a particular subject. Frequently, the students themselves start them spontaneously in response to a shared experience. They want to talk about the event because it affected all of them in some way. Teachers can gain insight into the students' critical thinking skills, information and observations shared, willingness to participate in the discussion, and behavior within the group.

Self and Peer-Assessment

Self-assessment allows the student to become involved in the evaluation process. The student takes more responsibility for the learning process because he or she is expected to reflect upon his or her attitude about and attention to assigned activities and the product produced. To be truly effective, the **student should be involved** in developing the evaluation criteria. It gives the student more control. Instead of the teacher having all of the power and being perceived as such, some power shifts to the student by allowing the student to help determine the rating scale used, to participate in evaluating the finished product, and to provide direct input into the grade which he or she receives.

During **peer-assessments**, students learn by listening to other students critique their work and make suggestions on ways to improve it. The student doing the evaluation must think analytically about their peer's work product; in doing so, it should help him become more critical about his own work. Teachers need to moderate these discussions and stress consistency, being descriptive and not judgmental, realistic, positive, and reflective.

Anecdotal Record

An **anecdotal record** is a written description of observed behavior. They are usually kept in an alphabetized book, binder, or folder and should be organized so it is easy to find notes concerning a particular student. There are computer programs available that make retrieving the data simple.

To be effective, **observations** need to be made frequently and **incidents** need to be described completely and objectively; the teacher's analysis should be used as a guide for appropriate responses. Both successful situations and unsuccessful attempts need to be recorded in order to present an accurate picture of the student's progress.

The evaluation context is:

- **Formative**: Recalling the incident may raise an alert that something that needs to be addressed.
- **Summative**: Since observations are made over a period of time, they are an effective way to track student attitude, behavior, knowledge acquired, cognitive skills learned, etc.
- **Diagnostic**: Consistent attention to performance may spotlight areas that need special attention.

Review Video: Formative and Summative Assessments
Visit mometrix.com/academy and enter code: 804991

Methods of Data Recording

There are three ways to record data about individual student performance. Each provides important information and lends itself to evaluating different aspects of student growth.

- **Anecdotal Records** are observations of day-to-day activities, such as how the student interacts in a group, his or her ability to complete a hands-on assignment, his or her demeanor while taking tests, and his or her development of particular cognitive skills. All of these offer opportunities for teacher comments.

- The criteria on **Observation Checklists** vary depending on what the teacher wants to evaluate. They can be used to measure the growth of knowledge, a change in attitude, or the understanding of new skills. Checklists can also be used to evaluate written assignments, oral presentations, class participation, completion of individual and/or group work, or any activity that requires assessment.
- **Rating Scales** are similar to observation checklists. The difference between the two is that checklists are used to determine the presence or absence of a skill, while rating scales measure the quality of the performance.

Observation Checklist

An **observation checklist** is a list of specific skills, behaviors, attitudes, and processes that are relevant to a student's development and contribute to his ability to successfully complete learning activities. To be effective, these checklists need to be used frequently and be collected over a period of time. One or two observations can be misleading and will not provide an accurate measurement to reach a fair evaluation. Before a using a checklist, a teacher must decide upon its purpose, how and when it will be used, and what the criteria will be. During the observation period, all occurrences of each item shown on the list need to be recorded. It is helpful for later evaluation if the teacher has a quick reference shorthand system to describe each appearance, such as "!" equals excellent, "@" equals adequate, "?" equals iffy, and "X" equals inappropriate. After the session, notes should be added to clarify or elaborate the shorthand ratings.

Sample Form for an Anecdotal Record

Anecdotal record for a group discussion

Subject Under Discussion: ______________________

Students' Names: ______________________

Date and Time Period of Observations: ______________________

Characteristics to be evaluated:

Balance between talking and listening: ______________________

Respect for others: ______________________

Actively participating in discussion: ______________________

Stating own opinion: ______________________

Acted as scribe: ______________________

Effectiveness: ______________________

Acted as reporter: ______________________

Effectiveness: ______________________

Acted as participant: ______________________

Effectiveness: ______________________

Acted as time-keeper: ______________________

Effectiveness: ______________________

NOTE: The form may be modified to fit the observer's particular requirements.

Developing an Observation Checklist

Developing an observation checklist takes time. It can be helpful to **write down** all the skills, behaviors, attitudes, and processes required to acquire mastery of the subject and that are appropriate for the particular age group. The language should be **simple and easy to understand** so that the checklists can be used during student and parent conferences. Items needed for the specific task or activity to be evaluated can be chosen from the master list. There should be no more than twelve items on a checklist; any more than twelve becomes difficult to track, especially when observing several students at the same time. Individual checklists can be developed for specific functions (e.g., participation in a class discussion, proficiency at using a microscope, the mechanics of preparing a term paper). Whatever the rating scale, it must be used consistently, applied fairly, and easy to use during the observation period.

Sample Observation Checklist

Observation Checklist

Subject Being Discussed: ____________________

Date: ____________________ Class: ____________________

Time Elapsed: ____________________

	Student Names		
Spoke Clearly			
Listened to Other Opinions			
Waited for turn			
Comment was Relevant			
Challenged a Comment			
Stated Reasons for Challenge			
Noticed a Discrepancy			
Stated a Relationship Between Ideas			
Offered a Conclusion			
Inclusive Behavior Shown			

NOTE: This can be modified according to teacher requirements.

Oral Presentations

Oral presentations offer a wealth of possibilities to evaluate student growth and development in several areas, including:

- Understanding of the subject
- Planning and organizing abilities
- Communication skills

This **flexible assessment tool** can be assigned to an individual student or as a group project. If given to a group, additional skills can be evaluated including response to other opinions, listening behaviors, active participation in discussions, and contributions to the work product. Teachers need to recognize that some students may have difficulty with or little or no experience conceptualizing, organizing, and delivering a presentation. To address these issues as well as any performance anxieties, it is necessary to establish a classroom atmosphere of acceptance so that students feel confident when giving a presentation. Allowing students some control over the choice of topic also helps alleviate some of the stress involved in standing up in front of the group.

Rating Scale

A **rating scale** is used to evaluate a student against a predetermined continuum. It is particularly useful for rating an oral presentation such as a speech, debate or stage performance, and for students to use as a self-assessment tool. To increase the scale's reliability, when developing the criteria to be evaluated, the activity needs to be broken into specific, manageable parts. Each criterion may need its own rating system and scale points need to be created.

- Will the evaluation be based upon the one to five number scale with five being the highest?
- Will the Very Good/Good/Average/Poor/Very Poor standard be used?
- Will another system be developed?

It is helpful for the teacher to decide at the beginning of the semester which units of study will be evaluated using this method and to develop the criteria and rating system ahead of time.

Written Assignments

Written assignments can take many forms, including essays, reports, term papers, short answers questions, journal and log entries, letters, articles, poetry, solutions to math puzzles, and research, to name a few. It is important that the teacher's expectations and the rating scale are explained with as much detail as possible, especially if students are unfamiliar with the process or are afraid of writing in general. The entire process should be **reviewed**: choosing a topic, planning, organizing, researching, outlining, writing a first draft, reviewing content, editing, writing a second draft, proofreading, asking someone to read the final draft, and meeting the deadline. Criteria need to be developed for each segment so that when the student and teacher meet for regular consultations during the process, there is a framework for discussion. If it is a group project, it is critical for the teacher to monitor the progress and make sure that every student is contributing to each phase of the process.

Classroom Activities

Students are expected to engage in and complete various activities as a normal part of daily classroom participation. Teachers not only rate work products but they can and should use these activities to gauge progress in other goals such as social development, communication skills, and cognitive growth.

- **Written Assignments**: The ability to plan, organize, and produce a coherent, well-written essay, report, or term paper is just as important as the content of the finished product.
- **Presentations**: Whether planned or spontaneous, oral presentations need to be organized, logical, and engage the attention of the audience.
- **Performance Assessment**: Evaluating a student's participation and performance is important for helping him develop social and communicational skills.
- **Homework**: Homework requires independent study, planning skills, and the ability to prioritize. The student is expected to remember to do the work and turn it in by the required deadline.

RATING SCALE FOR ORAL PRESENTATION

Rating Scale For An Oral Presentation

Student's Name: ____________________

Date & Class Period:

	5	4	3	2	1
Voice is well modulated.					
Presentation is well paced.					
Pauses and emphases are appropriate.					
Can be heard easily by everyone.					
Material is: Organized					
Logical					
Interesting					
Good preparation is evident.					
Information used is on topic.					
Language is appropriate.					
Creativity in preparation and presentation.					
Audience is involved.					

ORAL ASSESSMENTS

Oral assessments are used for two reasons: when written assessments are not feasible, and to evaluate a student's mastery of such topics as verbal language proficiency, debating skills, and the ability to think and respond quickly. These types of assessments can be stressful and some students may have trouble responding and become tongue-tied; therefore, it is important to conduct the session in **private or in an atmosphere of acceptance**. As an interactive form of communication, the teacher needs to avoid filling in the blanks and providing body language clues that might influence the student's response. It is also important to avoid accentuating gender, race, or cultural differences in the content or delivery of the questions and/or tasks. The examination period should be long enough and the tasks required general enough in order to ensure that the student's knowledge and proficiency can be adequately presented and evaluated.

PERFORMANCE ASSESSMENTS

Performance assessments are used to evaluate students' progress in specific tasks like demonstrating a skill, solving a complex problem with multiple parts, or participating in a general classroom discussion. The teacher is looking for what the student has learned and retained through what he or she does, and not merely what he or she says. Information gathered through performance assessments is easy to communicate to students and parents because it describes observable, verifiable actions and offers concrete discussion points to use during conferences. There are four steps to successfully integrate performance assessments into a balanced, comprehensive view of student progress:

- **Determine** What is to be observed and assessed.
- **Develop** the criteria to be used.

- **Decide** which recording method to use between anecdotal records, an observation checklist, or a rating scale.
- **Inform** the students that they are being evaluated, on what they are being evaluated, and the criteria being used.

Performance Test

A **performance test** is used to evaluate a particular skill that is one of the **primary objectives** of the class. Playing a musical instrument, using the backhand stroke in tennis, making a dress, doing a tune-up on a motor vehicle, and conducting a lab experiment are all skills that can be tested using this method. The teacher must ensure that the **same criteria** are used to evaluate each student and that every student has the same amount of time to demonstrate the skill. If it is an outdoor activity, climate conditions should be considered. Students need to be **informed ahead of time** about what they will be evaluated and when it will take place. In designing a performance task, teachers should be as specific as possible and consider the objective carefully. Students should be evaluated on both the **process and the results**. An observation checklist or rating scale is helpful in evaluating a performance test.

Quality Tests and Quizzes

Tests need to ask the right questions to **accurately measure** students' knowledge. There are several things to consider:

- Does each item represent an **important idea or concept**? If students understand the main objectives, their knowledge should be evident in their responses.
- Is each item an **appropriate measure** of the desired objective? Consider information presented and teaching strategies used.
- Are items presented in **easily comprehensible language** with **clearly defined tasks**? Students should not have to decode words or wonder what the item is asking them to do.
- Is the **difficulty** of the item appropriate? It should not be too difficult or too easy to complete.
- Is each item **independent and free from overlap**? Completing one item should not lead to completing additional items.
- Is the **subject matter covered** adequately?
- Is the test **free of gender, class, and racial bias**? Choose examples that are either familiar or unfamiliar to everyone.

Checklist for Written Assignment

Checklist for written assignment

Student Name: ______________________
Class: ______________________
Title of Paper: ______________________

	Yes	No	Comments
Understood objectives & requirements			
Met the timeline due dates			
Understood criteria for evaluation			
Actively participated in consultations			
Responded appropriately to suggestions			
Used reliable research sources			
Developed & followed a workable outline			
Used examples of prior knowledge			
Used good analytical & reasoning skills			
Developed good questions & answered them			
Worked in a methodical manner			
Used good grammar, sentence structure, spelling			

NOTE: This checklist may be modified to reflect teacher's particular requirements.

Homework

Homework should never be assigned as punishment or due to the teacher falling behind as a result of a poorly executed lesson plan or due to outside circumstances. It should be used if students are unable to complete a project during class, to gather information, to practice new skills, or to devise a solution to a complex problem based on a real life situation. Assigned tasks should be interesting and relevant to the students' daily experiences.

Guidelines for assigning homework:

- Provide clear, unambiguous, written instructions of what is expected and how the results will be evaluated.
- Answer questions and address concerns.
- Make sure the due date is reasonable.
- Consider other academic requirements students may have.
- Be sure resource material is adequate and readily available.

- Collect the assignment on the date specified, grade it, and return it promptly.
- Be consistent with assessment protocol and provide thoughtful, helpful comments.

Test Effectiveness

Teachers should have confidence that a test **accurately measures students' knowledge**: therefore, it is important to **monitor its effectiveness** each time it is used. Before the test is given, **all items should be reviewed** to ensure that they still meet the criteria established for understanding the material and if one item does not meet the criteria, either rework it or remove it. If most students, including the better ones, miss the same question, perhaps it is too difficult or is not worded properly. If the item is salvageable, rework it; if it is not, delete it. Asking for student feedback on one or two items is an effective way to determine if they are still appropriate or if they should be reworked or removed. Veteran teachers usually develop a "feel" for whether a test is an accurate reflection of what students know. If individual items or entire tests are reused, it is imperative to keep them in a secure place to minimize the possibility of cheating.

Role of Government in the School

One function of government is **education**, which is administered through the public-school system by the Federal Department of Education. The states have primary responsibility for the **maintenance and operation** of public schools. However, the Federal Government does maintain a heavy interest in education. The National Institute of Education was created to improve education in the United States.

Each state is required by its state constitution to provide a school system whereby children may receive an education, and state legislatures exercise power over schools in any manner consistent with the state's constitution. Many state legislatures delegate power over the school system to a state board of education.

Equal Education Opportunities Act of 1974

There is a strong concern for **equality in education**. Within states this leads to efforts to assure that each child receives an adequate education, no matter where he or she is situated. The **Equal Education Opportunities Act of 1974** provides that no state shall deny equal educational opportunity to an individual on the basis of race, color, sex, or national origin.

Review Video: Equality vs Equity
Visit mometrix.com/academy and enter code: 685648

Title 20- Equal Access

Title 20 states that denial of equal access is prohibited. More precisely:

Restriction of limited open forum on basis of religious, political, philosophical, or other speech content is prohibited. It shall be unlawful for any public secondary school which receives Federal financial assistance and which has a limited open forum to deny equal access or a fair opportunity to, or discriminate against, any students who wish to conduct a meeting within that limited open forum on the basis of the religious, political, philosophical, or other content of the speech at such meetings.

Confidentiality

Confidentiality provisions help protect families from embarrassing disclosures, discrimination against themselves or their children, differential treatment, and threats to family and job security.

Confidentiality provisions also may encourage students or families to take advantage of services designed to help them.

Many of the legal protections to confidentiality are constitutionally based on the fundamental right "to be let alone." Right-to-privacy protections also are reflected in federal and state statutes, statutory privileges, agency regulations, ethical standards, and professional practice standards.

FERPA

A 1974 federal law, the **Family Educational Rights and Privacy Act (FERPA)**, protects the **privacy interests of students** in elementary and secondary schools (and their parents) with regard to certain types of education records. FERPA requires that **prior consent be obtained** from the student (if 18 or older) or the student's parents before certain types of information can be released from school records. FERPA also gives parents and students **access to records**, along with the right to challenge the accuracy of those records and make necessary modifications. Changes to FERPA most recently were enacted as part of the Improving Schools Act of 1994, resulting in the issuance of final regulations of FERPA by the US Department of Education. These amendments help promote information sharing by educators.

Biotechnology in Business, Industry, and Society

Careers

The field of **biotechnology** is broad and lucrative. In addition, research continues to develop new areas for study, so the job supply is ever increasing. Perhaps the most basic job in biotechnology is the lab technician. **Lab techs** are employed by police departments, research facilities, and medical institutions. A **quality control analyst** is a special employee who continuously monitors lab performance to ensure that standards are being met. A **bioinformatician** uses computer science skills to convert the data gathered through research into actionable information. A **biomedical engineer** builds the equipment and develops the materials that make biotechnological research possible. Finally, a **validation technician** ensures that research adheres to the law and to the rules established by regulatory agencies and professional organizations. These professionals also work to improve productivity and efficiency within the lab.

Anthropometrics and Ergonomics

Anthropometrics is a systematic approach to **measuring the human body**. It originated after the Second World War, as designers began to notice that many machines and pieces of furniture were inappropriately configured for human bodies. It became clear that designing better-sized machines could improve productivity as well as comfort. At around the same time, the field of ergonomics was exploring how better design could reduce injury in the workplace. Ergonomically inclined designers used the data generated through anthropometrics to create equipment that was easier to use and less taxing on the body. An emphasis on ergonomics was enshrined in United States law by the Occupational Health and Safety Act, which established some requirements for workplace furniture and equipment.

Joint Replacements and Prosthetics

Advances in medical technology have made **joint and limb replacement surgery** an increasingly viable option for victims of pain or dysfunction. The most common joints to be replaced are the **knees and hips**. Typically, a hip replacement will entail replacing both the hip socket and the top of the femur; this leg bone will be cut off at the top so that the replacement bone and socket can be attached. An **artificial limb**, known as a **prosthesis**, must be precisely measured so that it will not throw off the balance of the body. Laser measurement techniques have made it possible to calculate the appropriate length for a prosthesis within thousandths of an inch. There are prosthetics available for every limb of the body, though the most common are arms and legs below the knee. There are now electronic prostheses that respond to nerve impulses and actually perform the movements of the limb they have replaced. For instance, there are amazing prosthetic arms capable of grasping and lifting objects in response to the myoelectric impulses transmitted by the muscles of the upper arm to which it is attached.

Artificial Organs

Biomedical research has produced **artificial replacements for virtually every organ** of the human body. There are electronic devices that stimulate certain parts of the brain, providing relief from depression and epilepsy. There are artificial ears that actually enable the recipient to hear. Artificial eyes are still improving, but already they have restored sight to many blind people. The most popular artificial organ is the replacement kidney. It functions like a dialysis unit, passing blood through a solution that extracts waste matter and restores electrolytes. Artificial bladders are unique in that they have been grown from living tissue in the laboratory. Artificial pancreases incorporate living tissue into a donor pancreas, which minimizes the risk of rejection by the recipient's body. **Stem cell research** has enabled doctors to grow replacement organs with cells from the recipient's own body. Perhaps the most difficult organ to replicate has been the heart. As of yet, there is not an artificial heart capable of sustaining life for more than a year and a half, though even this is quite a feat.

Common Devices for Monitoring Health

A **blood glucose meter** helps people with diabetes keep track of their blood sugar levels. These devices are portable and easy to use. The most common version uses a small tack to draw a tiny blood sample, though there are also devices that measure blood sugar in the urine. A **sphygmomanometer** measures blood pressure. Inexpensive versions of this device are now available for personal use. In addition, there are now **personal cholesterol monitors** that let people keep track of their levels of triglycerides, cholesterol (including HDL), glucose, and ketones. These devices are valuable for people with heart problems. **Digital thermometers** are ubiquitous and can provide a much more accurate measure of body temperature than **mercury thermometers**. Finally, there are a wide array of electronic asthma devices, including **nebulizers** (inhaler), **spirometers** (measures lung capacity), and **peak flow meters**.

Orthotics

Orthotics is the branch of medicine related to creating devices that improve physical performance and reduce pain. An **orthosis**, commonly called a **brace**, may control movement, limit the range of motion, provide support, or reduce the weight loaded on a certain part of the body. A common example of an orthosis is a back brace, which may be specially designed to treat a problem like lordosis or may simply diffuse the weight borne by the spine. The introduction of computer measurement has made it possible to create personalized braces quite inexpensively. Also, the development of extremely hard and durable plastics has enabled the production of lightweight, long-lasting braces. These devices have helped remediate pain and speed rehabilitation for millions of people.

Reproducing DNA in a Laboratory Through Polymerase Chain Reaction

Scientists have developed a technique, called **polymerase chain reaction**, for reproducing segments of DNA. Living cells are not required for this process. In a matter of hours, it is possible to create 100 billion molecules that are exactly the same as a given DNA molecule. This process can be used in DNA fingerprinting, molecular biology, and biomedical technology. The process is complex, but it basically entails separating the two strands of the DNA double helix, isolating a section of the

DNA to be replicated, and then using an enzyme to catalyze the formation of new bonds in that section. The result is that the amount of DNA in the specimen is doubled. Every time the process is repeated, the amount of DNA is doubled, so the total amount of DNA quickly gets very large.

DNA Technology in Criminal Science

The development of effective DNA identification procedures has revolutionized the branch of criminal science known as **forensics**. If doctors and law enforcement officers are able to recover some fresh tissue, blood, or semen after a violent crime, they can identify the perpetrator beyond a reasonable doubt. To begin with, laboratory technicians will use **antibodies** to identify the surface cells of the sample, which will indicate the particular type of tissue or fluid. Then, the DNA will be isolated and special enzymes will be applied to it. These enzymes cut the DNA into fragments. The fragments are different for every person, though identical twins will have the same fragmentation patterns. By analyzing the pattern of fragments, forensic scientists can make conclusive matches between samples taken from a crime scene and samples taken from suspects.

Improving Air Quality

Scientists have developed a number of ways to use **microorganisms** in the **improvement of air quality**. For instance, **biofiltering** is a technique in which microbes are placed on a support medium, like a sheet of plastic, and then bathed with aqueous nutrients. The microbes extract contaminants from a gas. In some instances, biofilters have removed 90 percent of the contamination. A similar method, **bioscrubbing**, entails the introduction of a microbe-filled liquid to the contaminated gas. This technique has also proved successful, though it can be difficult to enact on a small scale. Some labs have found it difficult to manage the pH of the resulting gas, while others have complained that the bioscrubber has an unpleasant smell. For these reasons, biotechnological efforts at air quality improvement have not been readily adopted by industry.

Resolving Oil Spills

There are several methods for cleaning up oil spills. One is **bioremediation**, in which microbes that "eat" oil are introduced in large quantities to the spill site. Another common approach for spills in water is to **burn the surface oil** carefully off. In some cases, oily water will be sucked up into a centrifuge, where it can be spun rapidly until the oil separates from the water. **Oil may be skimmed off the water surface**. Another approach is to **add dry hydrophobic solidifiers**, which mix with the oil and form a solid that can be more easily removed. Finally, scientists have developed **dispersant (or detergent) chemicals** that adhere to oil globules, neutralize them, and allow them to wash away naturally without damaging the environment.

Desalinization

When the salt content of soil becomes too high, a process known as **salinization**, it can prevent plant growth. Excessive salinization can effectively turn arable land into a desert. Areas that are frequently irrigated are susceptible to this problem, because even fresh water contains a tiny amount of salt. Irrigation washes away soluble nutrients and leaves behind a salt precipitate. This phenomenon suggests the need for a technique of soil **desalinization**. Converting salt water from the ocean into drinking water also requires desalinization. Thus, scientists have spent a great deal of time trying to develop an efficient means of removing salt from soil and water. The easiest way to remove salt from water is to heat the water within a glass or plastic enclosure, so that the salt adheres to the outside and can be scraped away. However, this typically requires a great deal of heating fuel.

Bioremediation

In **bioremediation**, microbes convert hazardous waste into other, less harmful materials. This process can be executed at the site of waste production or disposal. The most successful cases of bioremediation involve the use of microbes that already exist in the hazardous substance. For instance, many polychlorinated biphenyls and pesticides contain natural microbes that can be used in bioremediation. In addition, many laboratories are at work on genetically modified microbes that perform the same task. Some microbes are even capable of removing the toxins from heavy metals. Bioremediation is lauded by environmentalists and the general public, but it is unfortunately also very expensive, and therefore it is not used as often as it could be. Most companies determine that it is more cost-effective to bury their hazardous waste. Nevertheless, bioremediation has generated hope for future improvements in hazardous waste disposal.

Removal of Hazardous Waste

Scientists are constantly working on techniques for accelerating the **removal of hazardous waste** from the environment. One such technique is **biostimulation**, in which nitrogen-rich compounds are added to microbes in the hopes of speeding up natural bioremediation. Contaminated water sources have been improved rapidly by **infusions of methane**, which promote the growth of local bacteria that clean the water. Another method of improving bioremediation is to increase the accessibility, or bioavailability, of **insoluble toxins** to remediating plants and microbes. Scientists must be careful when increasing bioavailability, because a toxic substance that is more accessible to microbes is also more accessible to other organisms. It is important to combine these efforts with measures to prevent the toxins from entering the soil. The bioavailability of some hazardous wastes has been increased by heating, moistening, and treating with surfactants.

Wood Pellets and Methane Production

The invention and popularization of **wood pellets** have created a new way for people to obtain energy from the combustion of wood. Flammable wood is compressed into tiny pellets, which are burned in a special stove. These stoves are equipped with electronic sensors that automatically load more pellets when necessary to maintain a target temperature. These wood pellet stoves are extremely efficient and require very little care during their operation. Another source of energy from biogas is through the **production of methane**. When sewage undergoes anaerobic digestion, it produces a biogas that is mostly methane. The remaining components of the biogas can be used as fertilizer. Many rural and poor areas have developed systems for converting waste into fuel and fertilizer. In a typical setup, waste matter is placed in a well, where it is mixed with an equal amount of water and allowed to sit until the digestion process is complete. The methane can then be used for heating and cooking, while the fertilizer is great for agriculture.

Ethanol and Biodiesel

Ethanol is a popular alternative fuel created by fermenting starches or sugars, most commonly corn or sugar cane. The resulting alcohol is distilled so that it can be used to power vehicles. At present, the cost of producing ethanol makes it much more expensive than gasoline, so ethanol is typically mixed with regular gas to make "gasohol." In countries like Brazil, there is a thriving ethanol industry. Ethanol makes fuel burn cleaner. In the United States, it is especially popular in the Midwest, because it provides an outlet for excess corn. Another alternative fuel, **biodiesel**, is made from vegetable oil. In most cases, biodiesel consists of 20% natural oil and 80% regular diesel fuel. Many biodiesel manufacturers obtain their oil from the deep fryers of local restaurants. Like ethanol, biodiesel is better for the environment than regular gasoline. However, it is also costly to manufacture, and it only works in diesel engines.

Applications of Bioengineering to Medicine

One of the earliest examples of bioengineering in medicine is **amniocentesis**, a technique for identifying chromosomal abnormalities in fetuses. In recent years, DNA probes have made it possible to isolate individual sequences of DNA and thereby learn about mutations in the genes. This would enable doctors to identify problems with fetuses conceived through in vitro fertilization. Some of the most common medical products of bioengineering are based on recombinant DNA technology, which encourages the creation of specific proteins. The most popular recombinant DNA products are insulin (Humulin), interferons, and erythropoietins. **Interferons** fight specific diseases, while **erythropoietins** encourage the production of red blood cells. **Recombinant DNA** is most often produced in bacterial cells, though yeast and mammalian cells are also used for certain applications. Scientists are very optimistic about the possibility of creating recombinant DNA in egg whites. Similar technology has been used to create transgenic varieties of corn, potatoes, and tobacco.

Dialysis

Dialysis is a medical procedure for **failing kidneys**. When a person's kidneys stop working, a dangerous level of toxins can build up in the body. One way to resolve this is to process the blood outside of the body. In dialysis, the blood is taken out of the body and passed through a special machine that filters out the toxins. A dialysis machine has a selectively permeable membrane that functions like the nephrons at the end of tubules inside the kidneys. This membrane allows urea and salts to pass out of the blood, while glucose passes in the other direction and reenters the stream. The blood then leaves the machine and is fed back into the person's body. Dialysis is an effective technique, but it takes several hours and must be performed three times a week. For this reason, many people with failing kidneys prefer to receive a kidney transplant if possible.

Laser Surgery

In **laser surgery**, a concentrated beam of light severs tissue precisely and cleanly. Lasers may be used to perform the cuts normally made with a scalpel or to vaporize extremely moist flesh. Perhaps the most widely known form of laser surgery is the **LASIK eye procedure**, in which a laser cuts the cornea and corrects near- or far-sightedness. One advantage of laser surgery is that no physical contact is required, so there is very little risk of infection. Also, computer-guided lasers are able to make much more precise and even cuts than even the finest human hand. The scars from laser surgeries heal more quickly and with considerably less pain. Indeed, lasers have even been used at low intensity levels to encourage wound healing.

Pacemakers and Defibrillators

An **artificial pacemaker** is an electronic device that **provides the rhythmic electrical impulses** necessary for proper heart function. When a person's natural pacemaker is degraded or destroyed, doctors can implant a tiny electrode attached to a small generator to replicate its function. A temporary pacemaker may be affixed to the outside of the chest, while a permanent one may be attached to the heart itself. A somewhat similar device is the electronic defibrillator, which delivers a sharp electrical shock to the heart in the event of arrhythmia and cardiac arrest. A typical defibrillator consists of two pads attached by wires to a generator. The pads are placed on the chest and the generator sends a series of increasingly powerful charges to the heart, with the intention of restoring a normal natural rhythm.

Yeast

Yeast is a microscopic fungus that brewers and bakers have used for millennia in food production. Yeast, when deprived of oxygen, will ferment sugar and other substances. **Fermentation** creates adenosine triphosphate without requiring oxygen. When yeast ferments something, ethyl alcohol and carbon dioxide are produced. In the brewing process, the fermentation caused by yeast makes beer bubbly and intoxicating. In bread, the release of carbon dioxide causes the dough to expand during the baking process. The heat of baking evaporates the ethyl alcohol created by fermentation, which is why bread is not alcoholic. In both brewing and baking, yeast ferments because it is mixed with other substances such that it is no longer exposed to oxygen. Yeast will not ferment if it is simply placed on top of bread dough, however.

INDUSTRIAL USE OF BIOREAGENTS

A **bioreagent** is a chemical that is extracted from a living cell and used as a reagent during some production process. Bioreagents are currently used in the **production of pharmaceuticals, food, chemicals, and textiles**. For instance, pharmaceutical steroids are made from plant steroids using bioreagents. Other cellular enzymes are used in the production of high-fructose corn syrup, a popular sweetener in processed foods. To find the right bioreagent for a particular process, a company first has to find a cell that is already performing the desired task. Then, the company must examine the amino acid sequences of each enzyme in the cell until it can be determined which enzyme is responsible. Another method for finding the right bioreagent is to isolate the mRNA in a cell that is performing the desired process and see into which enzymes that mRNA translates. A final method is to assemble collections of inactive cells, add promising enzymes, and see which cells begin to behave in the desired manner.

HYDROPONICS

Hydroponics is a system for growing plants by placing their roots in an **inorganic salt solution** rather than soil. This technique was pioneered in the eighteenth century and was the first to suggest that plants could survive on sunlight and inorganic substances alone. It has since been refined so that plants can be grown with a precise admixture of nutrients. However, hydroponic cultivation is expensive and time-consuming, so it is not viable on a large scale. Some scientists believe that this technique will be especially useful if people ever need to grow plants in space. One spin-off of hydroponic technology has been hydroponic culturing, which identifies the relative importance of various nutrients. In a **hydroponic culture**, different mineral solutions are applied to the roots of plants: some plants receive a solution in which one mineral is missing, while the other plants receive the full range of minerals. The relative growth of the plants is then observed to indicate the importance of each mineral. For instance, if the leaves of a plant become discolored or are smaller than usual, it would indicate that the omitted mineral is essential to that plant's health.

GENETICALLY MODIFIED CROPS

Genetically modified (GM) crops contain foreign genes, known as transgenes, that give them special properties. Crops have been modified to be hardier, more productive, and even to contain certain pharmaceutical substances. At present, the most popular genetic modifications are for resistance to insects, pathogens, and herbicides. The vast majority of research on genetic modification has been on corn, soybeans, cotton, and other mass-produced plants. The development of recombinant DNA technology has exponentially increased the number of possible modifications. There is a great deal of resistance to GM crops, though it is mainly in developed nations where the need for reliable food sources is less desperate. In impoverished countries, there is great hope that genetic modification can create **more nutritious and durable foods**.

IMPACT OF GENETICALLY MODIFIED CROPS

Genetically modified crops promise to **improve productivity and nutrition**, but many people remain skeptical of their overall impact on the environment. For instance, crops that are modified to tolerate herbicides may eventually spur the development of "super weeds" that are impervious to any herbicide. However, in the short term these crops will reduce the use of herbicides that may be destructive to the environment. Crops that improve resistance to insects may increase agricultural yields and decrease the need for harmful insecticides, but at the same time they may encourage insects to mutate such that they become resistant to common insecticides. For example, many organic farmers rely on the soil bacterium Bt (*Bacillus thuringiensis*) as an insecticide; scientists fear that GM crops will render Bt useless. There are pros and cons with all GM crops. Those that are grown to be more nutritious may benefit poor people but may also lead to excessive influence for multinational corporations in poor countries. Extremely hardy GM crops may prove to be too durable, to the extent that they drive native species off land that could not be cultivated before.

Bioengineering of Livestock

Most people know about genetically modified plants, but few are aware of the similar efforts to develop "enhanced" livestock. One example of **bioengineered livestock** is the **transgenic salmon**, in which a growth hormone gene is spliced to a promoter, which encourages transcription of the growth hormone gene. The result is a fish that grows throughout the year and thus reaches a harvestable size much faster. Another example of bioengineered livestock is the **Enviropig**, which was created in the lab of a Canadian university. The Enviropig has a phytase gene that diminishes the amount of phosphorous in the pig's excrement, thereby reducing the environmental impact of pig farming. Biotechnology has also been used to identify popular and lucrative breeds, like the **Angus cow**. Bioengineering has often been controversial, as in the case of **bovine growth hormones**, which increase the growth and milk production of cows but also necessitate the use of more antibiotics on the farm. Many people are concerned that feeding more antibiotics to food animals will decrease the effectiveness of these drugs for people.

Aquaculture

Aquaculture is any cultivation of marine life in an artificial setting. Aquaculture may include fish, shellfish, and even aquatic plants. This practice has become extremely popular in the past few decades, as the market for certain species has increased while natural supplies have shrunk. Critics of aquaculture claim that it causes the rapid expansion of some populations, which puts stress on other parts of the marine ecosystem. Also, aquaculture is commonly practiced in estuaries and lagoons, which have more stagnant water and are therefore more likely to be polluted. There is a growing movement to promote aquaculture in curated environments several miles out at sea. This is called open-ocean aquaculture. Another potential improvement to aquaculture as it is currently practiced would be a greater focus on herbivorous species, which do not wreak such havoc on the ecosystem when they are encouraged to propagate.

Bio-Related Technology

Scientific Principles of Bio-related Technologies

Bio-related technologies include a variety of methods of producing items or providing services using properties of living things, in fields ranging from healthcare to agriculture to waste management. This can include using living cells or bacteria directly, such as genetically modified food, or simply using principles of living organisms to improve processes. There are several branches of biotechnology:

- **Medical biotechnology** focuses mainly on illness prevention and cures. Bacteria, plant and animal cells, and DNA are studied and information about their functions and makeup is used to create vaccines and drugs. For instance, plants may be genetically modified to produce needed antibodies for certain diseases. These plants can then be harvested to create antibiotics.
- **Environmental biotechnology** improves waste management and combats pollution. Studying how certain bacteria digest and break down certain objects can help researchers find new ways of safely disposing of waste without damaging the planet. Further, some bacteria can be used directly, either introducing them to a site or encouraging their growth if they already exist there.
- **Industrial biotechnology** uses microorganisms, or the principles seen in these microorganisms, to improve efficiency and production. These can be used to create renewable raw materials that decrease the need for traditional fuels and chemicals that can be harmful to the environment. Microorganisms can also be used to make replacements for plastic and other textiles, creating less waste.
- **Agricultural biotechnology** aims to develop new and more efficient methods of growing crops. Many of these efforts are devoted to genetically modifying food to create greater production and to make plants more resilient to weather conditions or pests. Similarly, agricultural biotechnology can be used in livestock to develop hardier, larger, or higher-producing animals by isolating the genetic markers for desirable traits and breeding animals that exhibit those markers.

Principles and Methods of Environmental Engineering

Environmental engineering focuses its efforts in several fields such as recycling, healthcare, and water management. Each of these fields (and many others) face environmental challenges such as waste disposal and pollution. Environmental engineers evaluate the impact of human development on the earth and seek ways to alleviate or reverse this impact. **Pollution** is a large area of impact, affecting the earth's air, water, and soil. Environmental engineers study how air is affected by transportation and manufacturing and propose solutions or precautions. They study how water is affected by water treatment, by waste disposal, and by diverting water sources for irrigation or residential use, and seek new methods that will be less harmful, such as developing bacteria to treat wastewater without chemicals that can harm the organisms that live in it.

When new human developments are proposed, such as roads or pipelines, environmental engineers project the expected impact to the ecosystem from these developments and recommend any needed **mitigation measures** to offset the impact. Environmental engineers also help to track pollutants, tracing them to find their source so it can be dealt with. They work with manufacturers and other businesses to help them reduce pollution. Environmental engineers must be knowledgeable in many areas such as chemistry, geology, geography, and biology, as well as knowing local, state, and national laws that apply to their field.

Renewable and Nonrenewable Resources

Significant strides have been made toward renewable energy in the past few decades. Several different biofuels are available to replace fossil fuels and other nonrenewable resources. These include plant-based fuels such as ethanol, as well as solar and wind power. However, some biotechnology focuses on converting nonrenewable resources such as coal into cleaner energy by filtering out the harmful elements. The challenge to many renewable resources is cost;

implementing new methods often has a significant startup cost along with ongoing costs for maintenance. As future developments are made, improved technology may bring these costs down and make biotechnological advances more practical for widespread use.

Tools, Equipment, and Materials for Bio-Related Technologies

Those who work in a biotechnological field will need specialized tools for their job. Since there are a variety of bio-related tech jobs, the needed tools can vary greatly.

An **environmental engineer** may use the following equipment and materials:

- Devices to monitor and test quality of water, air, and soil (these can include PH meters, ozone monitors, and nitrogen and carbon analyzers)
- Radiation detectors
- Tools and containers for taking soil and groundwater samples
- GPS equipment for land surveying
- Software programs for analyzing data
- Lab equipment such as autoclaves, centrifuges, gas/ion chromatographs, and multiple other instruments for evaluating samples

Chapter Quiz

Ready to see how well you retained what you just read? Scan the QR code to go directly to the chapter quiz interface for this study guide. If you're using a computer, simply visit the online resources page at **mometrix.com/resources719/texesmathpse** and click the Chapter Quizzes link.

TExES Practice Test

Want to take this practice test in an online interactive format?
Check out the online resources page, which includes interactive practice questions and much more: **mometrix.com/resources719/texesmathpse**

Mathematics

1. A circular bracelet contains 5 charms, A, B, C, D, and E, attached at specific points around the bracelet, with the clasp located between charms A and B. The bracelet is unclasped and stretched out into a straight line. On the resulting linear bracelet, charm C is between charms A and B, charm D is between charms A and C, and charm E is between charms C and D. Which of these statements is (are) necessarily true?

I. The distance between charms B and E is greater than the distance between charms A and D.
II. Charm E is between charms B and D.
III. The distance between charms D and E is less than the distance of bracelet between charms A and C.

a. I, II, and III
b. II and III
c. II only
d. None of these must be true.

2. The path of a ball thrown into the air is modeled by the first quadrant graph of the equation $h(t) = -18t^2 + 72t + 4$, where $h(t)$ is the height of the ball in feet and t is time in seconds after the ball is thrown. What is the average rate of change in the ball's height with respect to time over the interval $[0, 3]$?

a. 0 feet/second
b. 6 feet/second
c. 18 feet/second
d. 24 feet/second

3. Zeke drove from his house to a furniture store in Atlanta and then back home along the same route. It took Zeke three hours to drive to the store. By driving an average of 20 mph faster on his return trip, Zeke was able to save an hour of driving time. What was Zeke's average driving speed on his round trip?

a. 24 mph
b. 48 mph
c. 50 mph
d. 60 mph

4. Which of these statements is (are) true for deductive reasoning?

I. A general conclusion is drawn from specific instances.
II. If the premises are true and proper reasoning is applied, the conclusion must be true.

a. Statement I is true
b. Statement II is true
c. Both statements are true
d. Neither statement is true

5. Given that premises "all *a* are *b*," "all *b* are *d*," and "no *b* are *c*" are true and that premise "all *b* are *e*" is false, determine the validity and soundness of the following arguments:

Argument I: All *a* are *b*. No *b* are *c*. Therefore, no *a* are *c*.
Argument II: All *a* are *b*. All *b* are *d*. Therefore, all *d* are *a*.
Argument III: All *a* are *b*. All *b* are *e*. Therefore, all *a* are *e*.

a.

	Invalid	Valid	Sound
Argument I		X	X
Argument II	X		
Argument III		X	

b.

	Invalid	Valid	Sound
Argument I	X		
Argument II		X	X
Argument III	X		

c.

	Invalid	Valid	Sound
Argument I		X	X
Argument II		X	X
Argument III	X		

d.

	Invalid	Valid	Sound
Argument I		X	X
Argument II	X		
Argument III	X		

6. Given statements p and q, which of the following is the truth table for the statement:

$$q \leftrightarrow \neg(p \wedge q)$$

a.

p	q	$q \leftrightarrow \neg(p \wedge q)$
T	T	F
T	F	T
F	T	T
F	F	T

b.

p	q	$q \leftrightarrow \neg(p \wedge q)$
T	T	T
T	F	T
F	T	T
F	F	F

c.

p	q	$q \leftrightarrow \neg(p \wedge q)$
T	T	F
T	F	F
F	T	F
F	F	T

d.

p	q	$q \leftrightarrow \neg(p \wedge q)$
T	T	F
T	F	F
F	T	T
F	F	F

7. Which of these demonstrates the relationship between the sets of prime numbers, real numbers, natural numbers, complex numbers, rational numbers, and integers?

$\mathbb{P}$–Prime; $\mathbb{R}$–Real; $\mathbb{N}$–Natural; $\mathbb{C}$–Complex; $\mathbb{Q}$–Rational; $\mathbb{Z}$–Integer

a. $\mathbb{P} \subseteq \mathbb{Q} \subseteq \mathbb{R} \subseteq \mathbb{Z} \subseteq \mathbb{C} \subseteq \mathbb{N}$
b. $\mathbb{P} \subseteq \mathbb{N} \subseteq \mathbb{Z} \subseteq \mathbb{Q} \subseteq \mathbb{R} \subseteq \mathbb{C}$
c. $\mathbb{C} \subseteq \mathbb{R} \subseteq \mathbb{Q} \subseteq \mathbb{Z} \subseteq \mathbb{N} \subseteq \mathbb{P}$
d. None of these

8. To which of the following sets of numbers does –4 NOT belong?

a. The set of whole numbers
b. The set of rational numbers
c. The set of integers
d. The set of real numbers

9. Which of these forms a group?

a. The set of prime numbers under multiplication
b. The set of negative integers under subtraction
c. The set of counting numbers under addition
d. The set of complex numbers other than zero under multiplication

10. Which of these sets forms a group under multiplication?

a. $\{-i, 0, i\}$
b. $\{-1, 1, i, -i\}$
c. $\{i, 1\}$
d. $\{i, -i, 1\}$

11. The set $\{a, b, c, d\}$ forms a group under operation #. Which of these statements is (are) true about the group?

#	**a**	**b**	**c**	**d**
a	c	d	b	a
b	d	c	a	b
c	b	a	d	c
d	a	b	c	d

I. The identity element of the group is d.
II. The inverse of c is c.
III. The operation # is commutative.

a. I
b. III
c. I, III
d. I, II, III

12. Given that x is a prime number and the greatest common factor of x and y is greater than 1, compare the two quantities.

Quantity A	Quantity B
y	the least common multiple of x and y

a. Quantity A is greater.
b. Quantity B is greater.
c. The two quantities are the same.
d. The relationship cannot be determined from the given information.

13. The cost of admission to a theme park is shown below.

Under age 10	Ages 10-65	Over age 65
\$15	\$25	\$20

Yesterday, the theme park sold 810 tickets and earned \$14,500. There were twice as many children under 10 at the park as there were other visitors. If x, y, and z represent the number of \$15, \$25, and \$20 tickets sold, respectively, which of the following can be used to find how many of each sold?

a. $\begin{bmatrix} 1 & 1 & 1 \\ 15 & 25 & 20 \\ 1 & -2 & -2 \end{bmatrix} \begin{bmatrix} x \\ y \\ z \end{bmatrix} = \begin{bmatrix} 810 \\ 14{,}500 \\ 0 \end{bmatrix}$

b. $\begin{bmatrix} 1 & 1 & 1 \\ 15 & 25 & 20 \\ 1 & -2 & -2 \end{bmatrix} \begin{bmatrix} 810 \\ 14{,}500 \\ 0 \end{bmatrix} = \begin{bmatrix} x \\ y \\ z \end{bmatrix}$

c. $\begin{bmatrix} 1 & 15 & 1 \\ 1 & 25 & -2 \\ 1 & 20 & -2 \end{bmatrix} \begin{bmatrix} x \\ y \\ z \end{bmatrix} = \begin{bmatrix} 810 \\ 14{,}500 \\ 0 \end{bmatrix}$

d. $\begin{bmatrix} 1 & 15 & 1 \\ 1 & 25 & -2 \\ 1 & 20 & -2 \end{bmatrix} \begin{bmatrix} 810 \\ 14{,}500 \\ 0 \end{bmatrix} = \begin{bmatrix} x \\ y \\ z \end{bmatrix}$

14. Solve the system of equations.

$$\begin{cases} 2x - 4y + z = 10 \\ -3x + 2y - 4z = -7 \\ x + y - 3z = -1 \end{cases}$$

a. $(-1, -3, 0)$
b. $(-\frac{3}{4}, -\frac{21}{8}, -1)$
c. $(1, -2, 0)$
d. No solution

15. Solve $3x^3y^2 - 45x^2y = 15x^3y - 9x^2y^2$ for x and y.

a. $x = \{0, -3\}, y = \{0, 5\}$
b. $x = \{0\}, y = \{0\}$
c. $x = \{0, -3\}, y = \{0\}$
d. $x = \{0\}, y = \{0, 5\}$

16. If $2\log_4 y + \log_4 16 = 3$, what is $\log_y 256$?

a. 16
b. 8
c. 4
d. 2

17. Simplify: $\frac{(x^2y)(2xy^{-2})^3}{16x^5y^2} + \frac{3}{xy}$.

a. $\frac{3x+24y^6}{8xy^7}$
b. $\frac{x+6y^6}{2xy^7}$
c. $\frac{x+24y^5}{8xy^6}$
d. $\frac{x+6y^5}{2xy^6}$

18. Which of these statements is NOT necessarily true when $f(x) = \log_b x$ and $b > 1$?

a. The x-intercept of the graph of $f(x)$ is 1.
b. The graph of $f(x)$ passes through $(b, 1)$.
c. $f(x)$ is undefined when $x < 1$.
d. If $g(x) = b^x$, the graph of $f(x)$ is symmetric to the graph of $g(x)$ with respect to $y = x$.

19. A colony of Escherichia coli is inoculated from a Petri dish into a test tube containing 50 mL of nutrient broth. The test tube is placed in a 37 °C incubator and agitator. After one hour, the number of bacteria in the test tube is determined to be 8×10^6. Given that the doubling time of Escherichia coli is 20 minutes with agitation at 37 °C, approximately how many bacteria should the test tube contain after eight hours of growth?

a. 2.56×10^8
b. 2.05×10^9
c. 1.7×10^{14}
d. 1.7×10^{13}

20. Simplify $\sqrt{\frac{-28x^6}{27y^5}}$.

a. $\frac{2x^3i\sqrt{21y}}{9y^3}$
b. $\frac{2x^3i\sqrt{21y}}{27y^4}$
c. $\frac{-2x^3\sqrt{21y}}{9y^3}$
d. $\frac{12x^3yi\sqrt{7}}{27y^2}$

21. Solve the inequality: $|x+6| < 9$

a. $(-15,-3)$
b. $(-15,3)$
c. $(3,-3)$
d. $(6,-9)$

22. Which of these functions includes 1 as an element of the domain and 2 as an element of the range?

a. $y = \frac{1}{x-1} + 1$
b. $y = -\sqrt{x+2} - 1$
c. $y = |x+2| - 3$
d. $y = \begin{cases} x & x < -1 \\ -x-3 & x \geq -1 \end{cases}$

23. At today's visit to her doctor, Josephine was prescribed a liquid medication with instructions to take 25 cc's every four hours. She filled the prescription on her way to work, but when it came time to take the medicine, she realized that the pharmacist did not include a measuring cup. Josephine estimated that the plastic spoon in her desk drawer was about the same size as a teaspoon and decided to use it to measure the approximate dosage. She recalled that one cubic centimeter (cc) is equal to one milliliter (mL) but was not sure how many milliliters were in a teaspoon. So, she noted that a two-liter bottle of soda contains about the same amount as a half-gallon container of milk and applied her knowledge of the customary system of measurement to determine how many teaspoons of medicine to take. Which of these calculations might she have used to approximate her dosage?

a. $25 \times \frac{1}{1{,}000} \times \frac{2}{0.5} \times 16 \times 48$
b. $25 \times \frac{1}{100} \times \frac{0.5}{2} \times 16 \times 4 \times 12$
c. $\frac{1{,}000}{25} \times \frac{0.5}{2} \times 16 \times 4 \times 12$
d. $\frac{25}{1{,}000} \times \frac{1}{4} \times 16 \times 48$

24. To test the accuracy and precision of two scales, a student repeatedly measured the mass of a 10g standard and recorded these results.

	Trial 1	Trial 2	Trial 3	Trial 4
Scale 1	9.99 g	9.98 g	10.02g	10.01g
Scale 2	10.206 g	10.209 g	10.210 g	10.208 g

Which of these conclusions about the scales is true?

a. Scale 1 has an average percent error of 0.15%, and Scale 2 has an average percent error of 2.08%. Scale 1 is more accurate and precise than Scale 2.
b. Scale 1 has an average percent error of 0.15%, and Scale 2 has an average percent error of 2.08%. Scale 1 is more accurate than Scale 2; however, Scale 2 is more precise.
c. Scale 1 has an average percent error of 0%, and Scale 2 has an average percent error of 2.08%. Scale 1 is more accurate and precise than Scale 2.
d. Scale 1 has an average percent error of 0%, and Scale 2 has an average percent error of 2.08%. Scale 1 is more accurate than Scale 2; however, Scale 2 is more precise.

25. A developer decides to build a fence around a neighborhood park, which is positioned on a rectangular lot. Rather than fencing along the lot line, he fences x feet from each of the lot's boundaries. By fencing a rectangular space 141 yd^2 smaller than the lot, the developer saves \$432 in fencing materials, which cost \$12 per linear foot. How much does he spend?

a. \$160
b. \$456
c. \$3,168
d. The answer cannot be determined from the given information.

26. A rainbow pattern is designed from semicircles, as shown below.

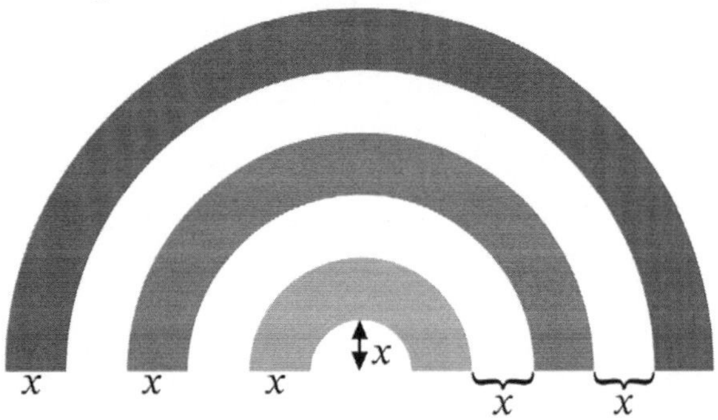

Which of the following gives the area A of the shaded region as a function of x?

a. $A = \frac{21\pi x^2}{2}$
b. $A = 21\pi x^2$
c. $A = 42\pi x^2$
d. $A = 82\pi x^2$

27. Which of the following expressions gives the area A of the triangle below as a function of sides a and b?

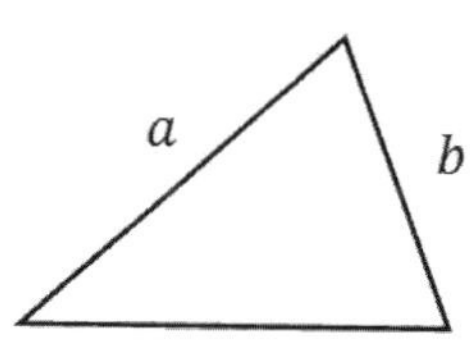

a. $\frac{2a^2-b^2}{4}$
b. $\frac{ab-a^2}{2}$
c. $\frac{b\sqrt{a^2-b^2}}{2}$
d. $\frac{b\sqrt{4a^2-b^2}}{4}$

Refer to the following for question 28:

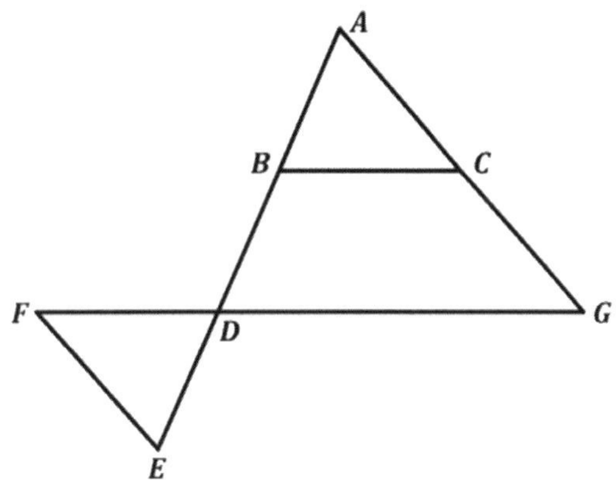

Statement	Reason
1. $\overline{BC} \parallel \overline{FG}$	Given
2.	
3. $\overline{FD} \cong \overline{BC}$	Given
4. $\overline{AB} \cong \overline{DE}$	Given
5. $\Delta ABC \cong \Delta EDF$	________
6. __________	
7. $\overline{FE} \parallel \overline{AG}$	

■

Given: $\overline{BC} \parallel \overline{FG}$; $\overline{FD} \cong \overline{BC}$; $\overline{AB} \cong \overline{DE}$

Prove: $\overline{FE} \parallel \overline{AG}$

28. Which of the following justifies step 5 in the proof?

a. AAS
b. SSS
c. ASA
d. SAS

29. Identify the cross-section polygon formed by a plane containing the given points on the cube.

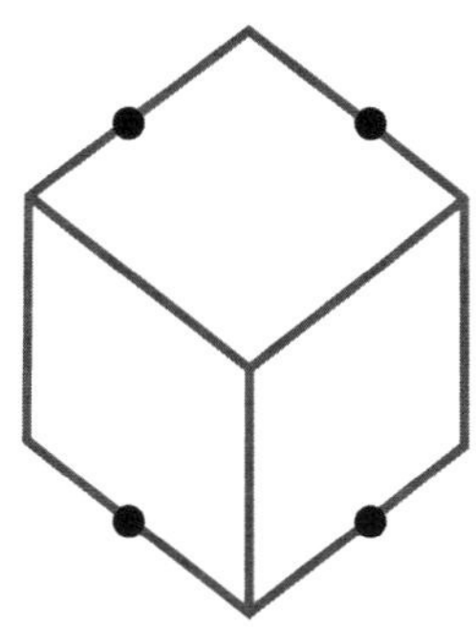

a. Rectangle
b. Trapezoid
c. Pentagon
d. Hexagon

30. Line segment $\overline{PQ}$ has endpoints (a, b) and (c, b). If $\overline{P'Q'}$ is the translation of $\overline{PQ}$ along a diagonal line such that P' is located at point (c, d), what is the area of quadrilateral $PP'Q'Q$?

a. $|a - c| \times |b - d|$
b. $|a - b| \times |c - d|$
c. $|a - d| \times |b - c|$
d. $(a - c)^2$

31. Solve $\sec^2\theta = 2\tan\theta$ for $0 < \theta \leq 2\pi$.

a. $\theta = \frac{\pi}{6}$ or $\frac{7\pi}{6}$
b. $\theta = \frac{\pi}{4}$ or $\frac{5\pi}{4}$
c. $\theta = \frac{3\pi}{4}$ or $\frac{7\pi}{4}$
d. There is no solution to the equation.

32. Evaluate: $\lim_{x\to\infty} \frac{x^2+2x-3}{2x^2+1}$

a. -3
b. 0
c. $\frac{1}{2}$
d. ∞

33. Approximate the area A under the curve by using left and right Riemann sums with $\Delta x = 1$.

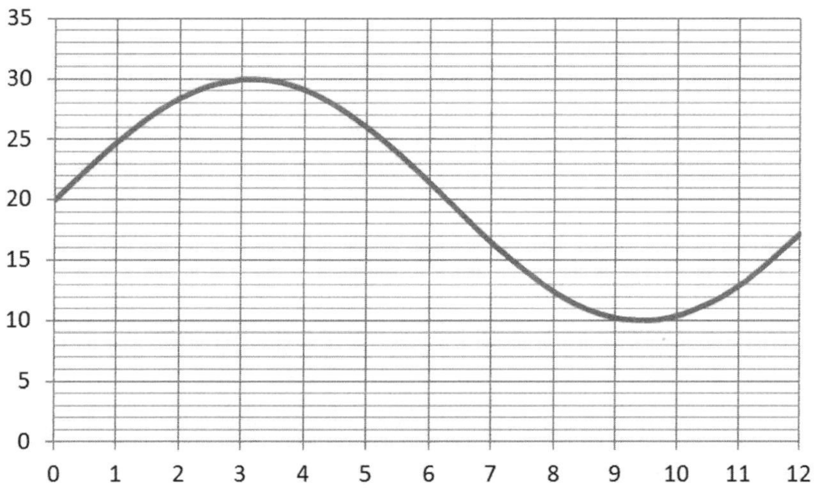

a. $209 < A < 211$
b. $230 < A < 235$
c. $238 < A < 241$
d. $246 < A < 250$

34. Find the area A of the finite region between the graphs of $y = -x + 2$ and $y = x^2 - 4$.

a. 18
b. $\frac{125}{6}$
c. $\frac{45}{2}$
d. 25

35. Which of these graphs is NOT representative of the data set shown below?

Stem	Leaf
3	6799
4	23889
5	011158
6	00123

Key
$2|123 = 21, 22, 23$

a. 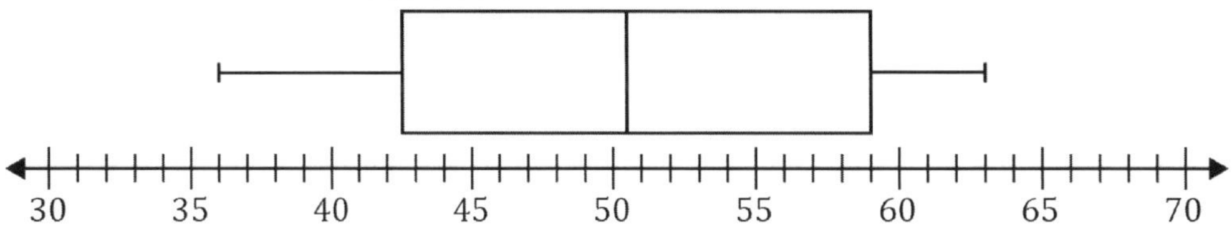

b. 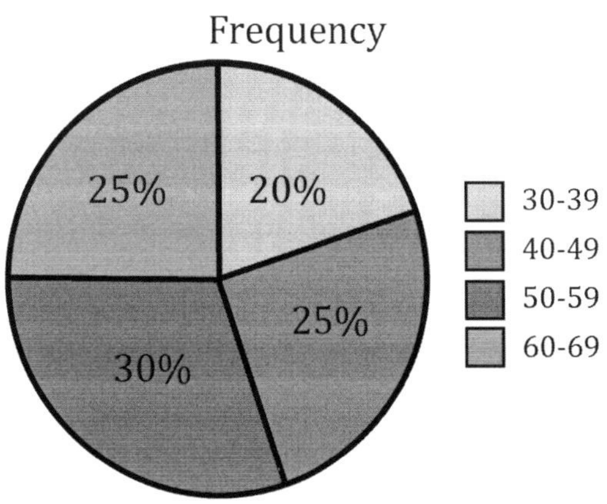

c. 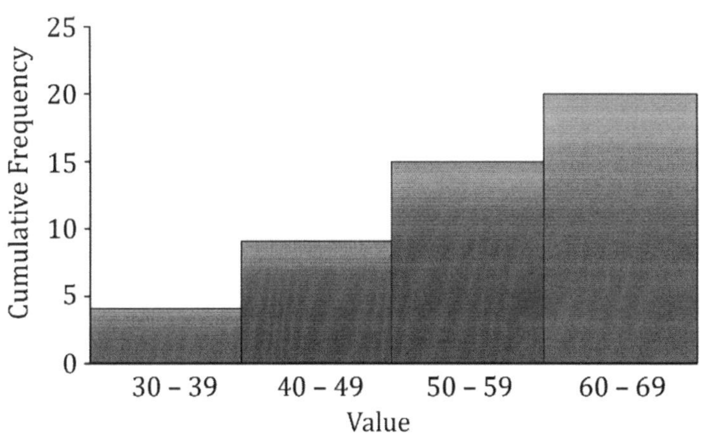

d. All of these graphs represent the data set.

36. Which of these tables properly displays the measures of central tendency that can be used for nominal, interval, and ordinal data?

a.

	Mean	Median	Mode
Nominal			x
Interval	x	x	x
Ordinal		x	x

b.

	Mean	Median	Mode
Nominal			x
Interval	x	x	x
Ordinal	x	x	x

c.

	Mean	Median	Mode
Nominal	x	x	x
Interval	x	x	x
Ordinal	x	x	x

d.

	Mean	Median	Mode
Nominal			x
Interval	x	x	
Ordinal	x	x	x

37. In order to analyze the real estate market for two different zip codes within the city, a realtor examined the most recent 100 home sales in each zip code. She considered a house which sold within the first month of its listing to have a market time of one month; likewise, she considered a house to have a market time of two months if it sold after having been on the market for more than one month but before the end of the second month. Using this definition of market time, she determined the frequency of sales by the number of months on the market. The results are displayed below. Which of the following is a true statement for these data?

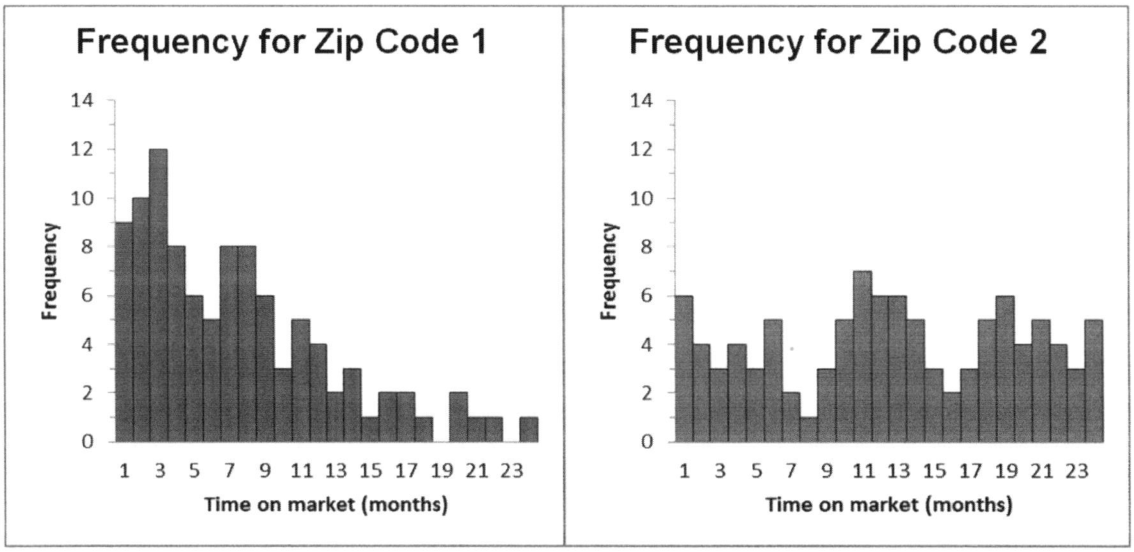

a. The median time a house spent on the market in Zip Code 1 is five months less than Zip Code 2.
b. On average, a house spent seven months longer on the market in Zip Code 2 than in Zip Code 1.
c. The mode time on the market is higher for Zip Code 1 than for Zip Code 2.
d. The median time on the market is less than the mean time on the market for Zip Code 1.

Refer to the following for questions 38–39:

Each day for 100 days, a student tossed a single misshapen coin three times in succession and recorded the number of times the coin landed on heads. The results of his experiment are shown below.

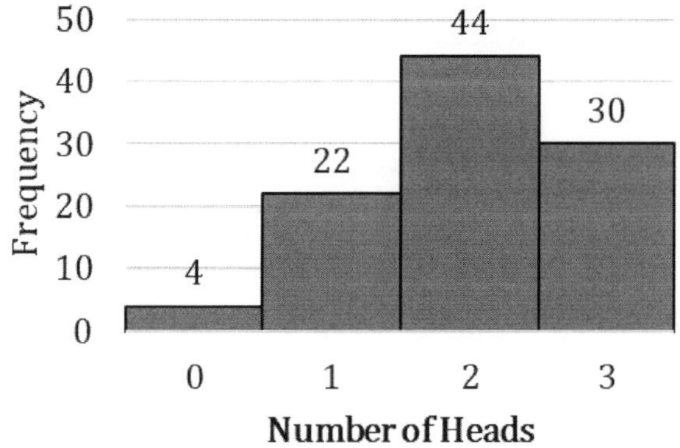

38. Given these experimental data, which of these approximates P(heads) for a single flip of this coin?

a. 0.22
b. 0.5
c. 0.66
d. 0.74

39. Which of these shows the graphs of the probability distributions from 10 flips of this misshapen coin and 10 flips of a fair coin?

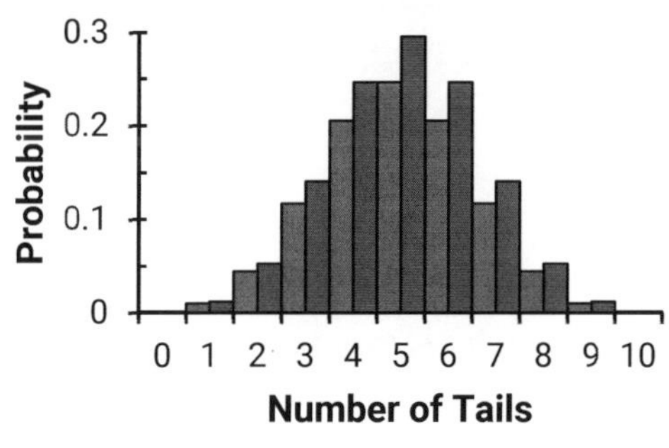

a.

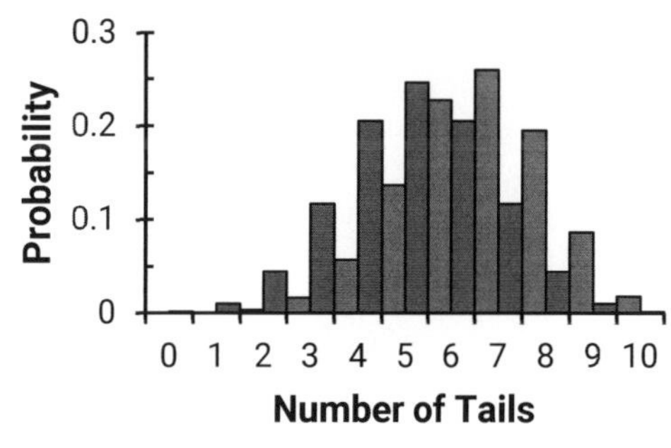

c.

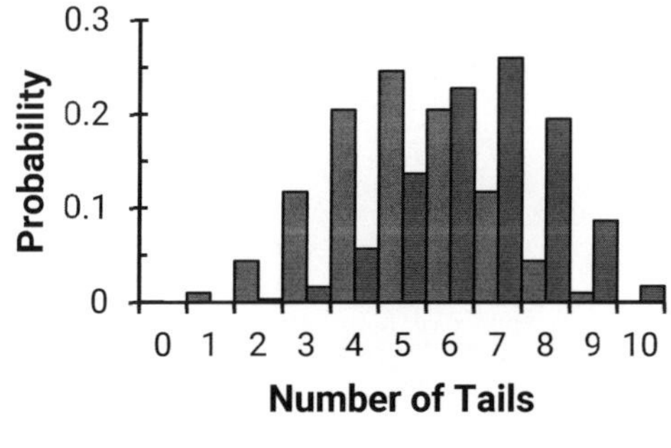

b.

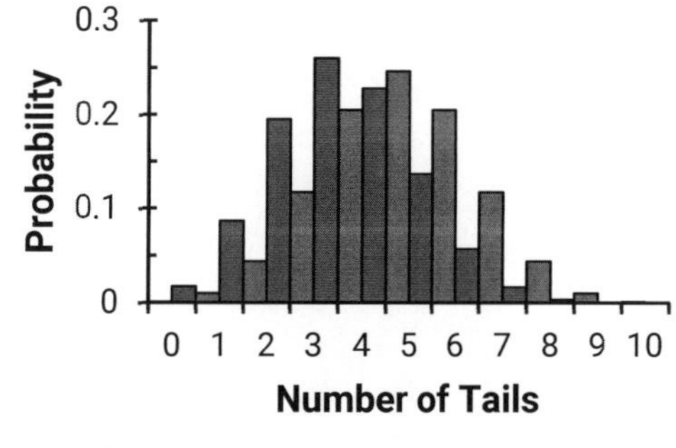

d.

40. Which of these does NOT simulate randomly selecting a student from a group of 11 students?

a. Assigning each student a unique card value of A, 2, 3, 4, 5, 6, 7, 8, 9, 10, or J, removing queens and kings from a standard deck of 52 cards, shuffling the remaining cards, and drawing a single card from the deck
b. Assigning each student a unique number 0–10 and using a computer to randomly generate a number within that range
c. Assigning each student a unique number from 2 to 12, rolling two dice, and finding the sum of the numbers on the dice
d. All of these can be used as a simulation of the event.

41. The intelligence quotients (IQs) of a randomly selected group of 300 people are normally distributed with a mean IQ of 100 and a standard deviation of 15. In a normal distribution, approximately 68% of values are within one standard deviation of the mean. About how many individuals from the selected group have IQs of at least 85?

a. 96
b. 200
c. 216
d. 252

42. How many different seven-digit telephone numbers can be created in which no digit repeats and in which zero cannot be the first digit?

a. 5,040
b. 35,280
c. 544,320
d. 3,265,920

43. A teacher wishes to divide her class of 20 students into 4 groups, each of which will have 3 boys and 2 girls. How many different ways are there to form a single group?

a. 248
b. 6,160
c. 73,920
d. 95,040

44. Consider three sets, A, B, and C. One is the set of even integers, one contains the factors of 12, and one contains the elements 1, 2, 4, and 9. If $A \cap B \subseteq B \cap C$, which of them must be set C?

a. The set of even integers
b. The set of factors of 12
c. The set $\{1, 2, 4, 9\}$
d. The answer cannot be determined from the given information.

45. A triangle has vertices $(0,0,0)$, $(0,0,4)$, and $(0,3,0)$ in the xyz-space. In cubic units, what is the difference in the volume of the solid formed by rotating the triangle about the z-axis and the solid formed by rotating the triangle about the y-axis?

a. 0
b. 4π
c. 5π
d. 25

Physics

1. A ball is released from a certain height along a frictionless track that does a loop-the-loop. The loop-the-loop part of the track is a perfect circle of radius R. At what height above the ground must the ball be released from in order to not fall off the track when it gets to the top of the loop-the-loop?

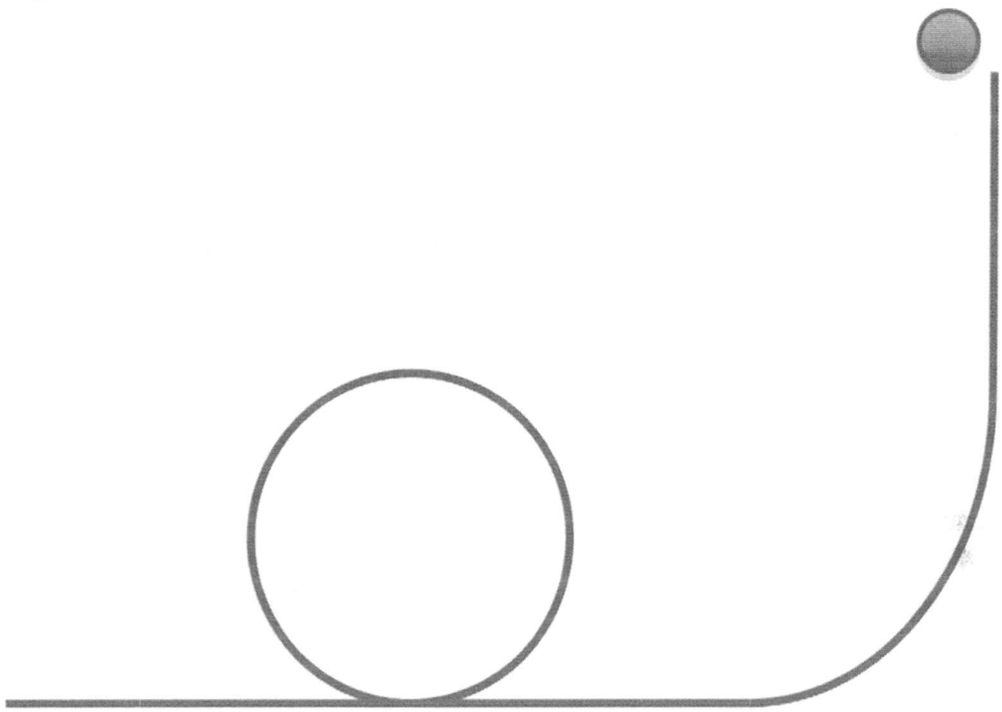

a. R
b. $2R$
c. $\frac{5R}{2}$
d. $3R$

2. Which of the following statements about energy is false?

a. Mechanical energy is always conserved in an isolated system.
b. Total energy is always conserved in an isolated system.
c. Energy is never created or destroyed.
d. Matter can be transformed into energy

3. A magnetic field is directed into this page and an electron is moving from left to right as indicated in the diagram below.

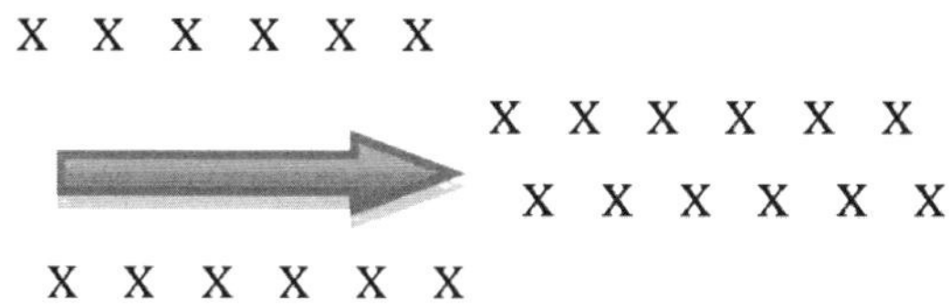

In which direction will the electron move when it enters the magnetic field?

a. It will curve upward.
b. It will curve downward.
c. It will curve in the direction of the magnetic field.
d. It will curve in the direction opposite the magnetic field.

4. A capacitor is connected in series to a battery and a resistor. After the capacitor is charged, the battery is disconnected and replaced by a battery with a greater electromotive force (emf), causing the capacitor to gain additional charge. After the capacitor has fully charged again, which of the following statements is true about the capacitance of the circuit?

a. It has increased.
b. It has decreased.
c. It has remained the same.
d. It has become zero.

5. A hydrogen atom makes a transition from the first excited state to the ground level. Which of the following statements is true?

a. A 10.2 eV photon is emitted.
b. A 13.6 eV photon is emitted.
c. A 1.9 eV photon is absorbed.
d. No photon is emitted.

6. A charge $+2q$ is placed at the origin of a coordinate system and a charge of $-q$ is placed at a distance d from the origin. How far from the origin must a third charge $+q$ be placed so that the net force on it is 0 newtons?

a. Less than $\frac{d}{2}$
b. Between $\frac{d}{2}$ and d
c. Between d and $2d$
d. Greater than $2d$

7. When light from a single source strikes two slits, alternating bright and dark lines appear on a screen on the far side. What is the best explanation for this phenomenon?

a. Doppler shift
b. Diffraction and interference
c. Chromatic aberration
d. Total internal reflection

8. Which type of aberration does NOT occur with concave spherical mirrors?

a. Astigmatism
b. Chromatic aberration
c. Spherical aberration
d. Distortion

9. A nucleus absorbs a neutron and undergoes a fission reaction. Which of the following statements explains why this happens?

a. The nucleus is more stable with the additional neutron.
b. The new nucleus is unstable.
c. Energy is released.
d. The binding energy per nucleon decreases.

10. Cobalt-63 can be produced in a laboratory and is unstable. When it decays, a neutron in its core will likely decay into a proton, changing Cobalt-63 into Nickel-63. Which of the following products will be emitted from this transition?

I. alpha particles
II. beta particle
III. gamma rays

a. I only
b. III only
c. II and III
d. I, II and III

11. A school nurse measures the height of every boy in a school with 1,000 pupils and determines that the average height is 1.64 meters with a standard deviation of 0.05 meter. Which of the following statements is true?

a. Sixty-eight percent of the students have heights between 1.59 meters and 1.69 meters.
b. There are as many students with heights above 1.64 meters as below 1.64 meters.
c. More students are 1.64 meters tall than any other height.
d. None of these statements may be made conclusively.

12. A 75-kg ice skater moving eastward at 5 m/s collides with a 100-kg skater moving northward at 4 m/s. Anticipating the collision, they hug each other and produce an inelastic collision. What is their final speed?

a. It cannot be determined from the information given.
b. 3.1 m/s
c. 4.1 m/s
d. 2.1 m/s

13. How much does it cost to operate a 5-kilowatt electric motor for 12 hours if electricity is 6 cents per kilowatt-hour?

a. $0.025
b. $3.60
c. $14.40
d. $360

14. The equation for the position of an object undergoing simple harmonic motion as a function of time is $A\sin[(5.0\text{ Hz})t]$. Assuming the wave's phase is measured in radians, what is the period of the motion?

a. $\sin[(5.0\text{ Hz})t]$
b. 2.5 seconds
c. 1.26 seconds
d. A

15. In musical instruments with two open ends, the first harmonic fits one-half wave inside the tube. The second harmonic fits 1 full wave in the tube. The third harmonic fits 1.5 full waves in the tube. Etc. An organ pipe, open at both ends, has a length of 1.2 meters. What is the frequency of the third harmonic? The speed of sound is 340 meters per second.

a. 142 Hz
b. 284 Hz
c. 425 Hz
d. 568 Hz

16. The speed of a travelling wave in a stretched string is given by $\sqrt{\frac{T}{\mu}}$, where T is the tension in the string and μ is the mass per unit length. A 2-meter-long stretched string with a mass of 0.010 kilograms is made to resonate with standing waves at 50 Hz. What tension in the string is needed to produce the fourth harmonic? (Note: the fourth harmonic fits 2 full waves into the length of the string).

a. 12. 5 newtons
b. 25 newtons
c. 50 newtons
d. 10,000 newtons

17. A hydraulic lift needs to raise a 3.5×10^3 newton truck. The input piston has a diameter of 2.0 cm, and the output piston has a diameter of 24 cm. What minimum force must be applied to the input piston?

a. 24 N
b. 292 N
c. 42,000 N
d. 504,000 N

18. A submarine sits underwater at a constant depth of 50 meters. Which of the following is true about the submarine's buoyant force?

a. It is 0 N.
b. It is greater than 0 N but less than the submarine's weight.
c. It is equal to the submarine's weight.
d. It is greater than the submarine's weight.

19. A force of 25.0 N pulls three blocks connected by a string on a frictionless surface. What is the tension in the rope between the 4.0-kg block and the 2.0-kg block?

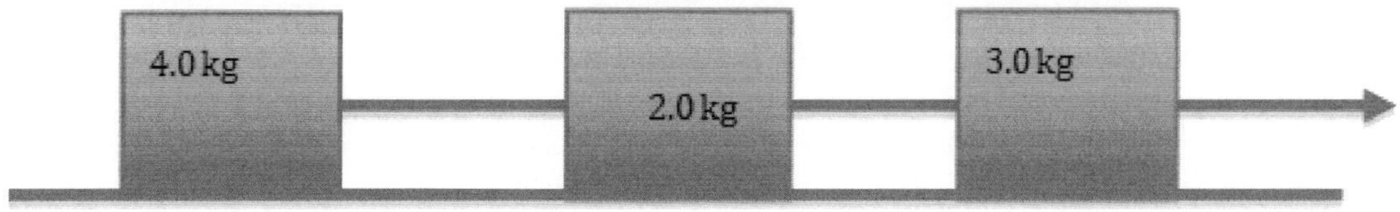

a. 0 N
b. 11.1 N
c. 16.7 N
d. 25 N

20. A piece of art with a mass of 200 kg is suspended from two nails so that the angle the hanging wires make is 40° with the horizontal. What is the tension in the hanging wires? (Note: $\sin 40° = 0.6428$ and $\cos 40° = 0.7660$).

a. 1,279 N
b. 1,525 N
c. 1,960 N
d. 3,049 N

21. Transverse traveling waves propagate through a taut string of length 20 meters at a speed of 4 m/s. Standing waves are set up in this string which is fixed at both ends. What is the smallest frequency possible for the standing waves?

a. 0.1 Hz
b. 0.05 Hz
c. 0.2 Hz
d. 0.4 Hz

22. The charged particle moving through a magnetic field will be subject to a force of $F = qvB \sin\theta$, where q is the charge, v is the particle's velocity, B is the magnetic field strength, and θ is the particle's angle between the magnetic field vector and the velocity vector. Charged particles from space enter the earth's atmosphere all the time. For example, the Aurora Borealis or Northern Lights are created by positive and negative charges passing through the Earth's magnetic field. Assume a proton with a speed of 8.0×10^6 meters per second enters a magnetic field at an angle of 45°, at a point where the magnetic field is 0.5 tesla. What is the magnetic force acting on the proton? Note: the proton has a charge of 1.6×10^{-19} coulombs.

a. 6.4×10^{-17} N
b. 4.5×10^{-17} N
c. 4.5×10^{-13} N
d. 5.5×10^{-17} N

23. What is the total resistance between points X and Y in the circuit diagram below?

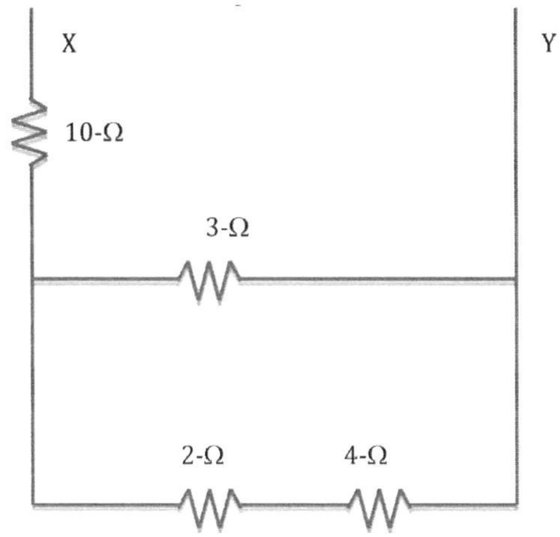

a. 0 Ω
b. 12 Ω
c. 19 Ω
d. 16 Ω

24. The center of a circular aquarium window with a radius of 1 meter is 14 meters below the surface. What is the force of the water at this depth pushing on this window? The density of water is 1,000 kg/m³.

a. 1.37×10^5 newtons
b. 1.08×10^5 newtons
c. 4.3×10^5 newtons
d. 0 newtons

25. An incompressible ideal fluid is flowing through a pipe 5.0 cm in radius at a speed of 6.0 m/s. The pipe narrows to 3.0 cm. What is the speed of flow in the narrower section?

a. 10 m/s
b. 3.6 m/s
c. 16.7 m/s
d. Can't be determined from the given information.

Chemistry

1. A gas at constant volume is cooled. Which statement about the gas must be true?

a. The kinetic energy of the gas molecules has decreased.
b. The gas has condensed to a liquid.
c. The weight of the gas has decreased.
d. The density of the gas has increased.

2. A weather balloon is filled with 1,000 mol of He gas at 25 °C and 101 kPa of pressure. What is the volume of the weather balloon?

a. 24,518 m^3
b. 24.5 m^3
c. 2 m^3
d. 245 m^3

3. Graham's law is best used to determine what relationship between two different materials?

a. Pressure and volume
b. Volume and temperature
c. Mass and diffusion rate
d. Diffusion rate and temperature

4. Which is the correct order of increasing attractive forces between particles?

a. Dipole – dipole < ionic < hydrogen bonding < London dispersion
b. Ionic < dipole – dipole < London dispersion < hydrogen bonding
c. Hydrogen bonding < London dispersion < ionic < dipole – dipole
d. London dispersion < dipole – dipole < hydrogen bonding < ionic

5. A 10 L cylinder contains 4 moles of oxygen, 3 moles of nitrogen and 7 moles of neon. The temperature of the cylinder is increased from 20 °C to 40 °C. Determine the partial pressure of neon in the cylinder as a percentage of the whole.

a. 50%
b. 70%
c. 90%
d. 40%

6. Which of the following statements generally describes the trend of electronegativity on the periodic table of elements?

a. Electronegativity increases going from left to right and from top to bottom
b. Electronegativity increases going from right to left and from bottom to top
c. Electronegativity increases going from left to right and from bottom to top
d. Electronegativity increases going from right to left and from top to bottom

7. 1 mole of water and 1 mole of argon are in a cylinder at 110 °C and 1 atm of pressure. The temperature of the cylinder is reduced to –5 °C. Which statement about the contents of the cylinder is most accurate?

a. The pressure in the cylinder is decreased, and the partial pressure of argon is less than that of water.
b. The pressure in the cylinder is about the same, and the partial pressure of water is less than that of argon.
c. The pressure in the cylinder is decreased, and the partial pressure of water is much less than that of argon.
d. The pressure in the cylinder is decreased, and the partial pressure of water is the same as argon.

8. A solid is heated until it melts. Which of the following is true about the solid melting?

a. ΔH is positive, and ΔS is positive.
b. ΔH is negative and ΔS is positive.
c. ΔH is positive and ΔS is negative.
d. ΔH is negative and ΔS is negative.

9. A liquid is heated from 50 °C to 80 °C. Which of the following statements is generally true about the solubility of solids and gases in the liquid?

a. The solubility of solids will increase, and the solubility of gases will decrease.
b. The solubility of solids will decrease, and the solubility of gases will increase.
c. The solubility of solids will increase, and the solubility of gases will increase.
d. The solubility of solids will decrease, and the solubility of gases will decrease.

10. 100 mL of a 0.1 M solution of NaOH is neutralized to pH 7 with H_2SO_4. How many grams of H_2SO_4 are required to achieve this neutralization?

a. 4.9 g
b. 0.98 g
c. 9.8 g
d. 0.49 g

11. Place the following in the correct order of increasing solubility in water.

a. Butanol $<$ ethanol $<$ octane $<$ NaCl
b. Ethanol $<$ NaCl $<$ octane $<$ butanol
c. NaCl $<$ octane $<$ butanol $<$ ethanol
d. Octane $<$ butanol $<$ ethanol $<$ NaCl

12. The isotope carbon-14 has a half-life of 5,730 years. If you started with 1 mg of carbon-14 today, about how much would be left in 20,000 years?

a. 0.06 mg
b. 0.07 mg
c. 0.11 mg
d. 0.09 mg

13. The best way to separate isotopes of the same element is to exploit:

a. Differences in chemical reactivity
b. Differences in reduction potential
c. Differences in toxicity
d. Differences in mass

14. Nuclear chain reactions, such as the kind that is exploited in nuclear power plants, are propagated by what subatomic particle(s)?

a. Protons
b. Neutrons
c. Electrons
d. Neutrons and protons

15. Which of the following statements about radioactive decay is true?

a. The sum of the mass of the daughter particles is less than that of the parent nucleus.
b. The sum of the mass of the daughter particles is greater than that of the parent nucleus.
c. The sum of the mass of the daughter particles is equal to that of the parent nucleus.
d. The sum of the mass of the daughter particles cannot be accurately measured.

16. Describe the correct outer shell electronic arrangement of phosphorous.

a. $4s^2 4p^3$
b. $3s^2 3p^3$
c. $2s^2 3p^3$
d. $2s^2 2p^3$

17. Hund's rule regarding electronic configuration states:

a. Electrons in the same orbital must have an opposite spin.
b. Electrons must fill lower energy orbitals before filling higher energy orbitals.
c. Electrons must populate empty orbitals of equal energy before filling occupied orbitals.
d. Electrons must have the same nuclear spin as the nucleus.

18. When a solid is heated and transforms directly into the gaseous phases, this process is called:

a. Sublimation
b. Fusion
c. Diffusion
d. Condensation

19. Determine a possible set of oxidation states for the elements in $KMnO_4$:

a. K^{1+}, Mn^{7+}, O^{8-}
b. K^{1-}, Mn^{7+}, O^{2-}
c. K^{1+}, Mn^{3+}, O^{4-}
d. K^{1+}, Mn^{7+}, O^{2-}

20. Which of the following are incorrect Lewis structures?

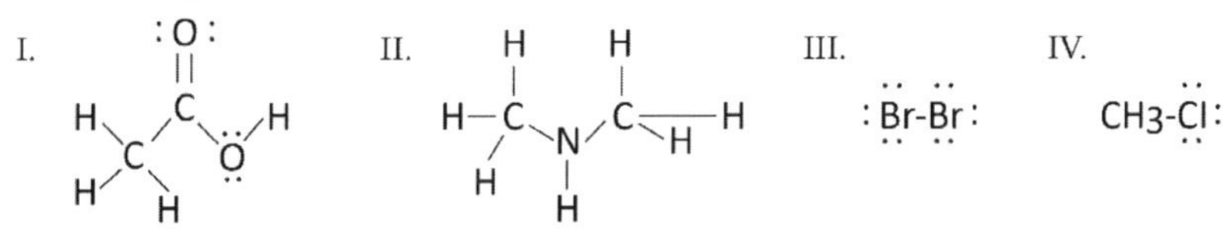

a. I and II
b. II and IV
c. I and III
d. III and IV

21. Balance the following reaction between sulfuric acid and aluminum hydroxide by filling in the correct stoichiometric values for each chemical.

$$\_\, H_2SO_4 + \_\, Al(OH)_3 \rightarrow \_\, Al_2(SO_4)_3 + \_\, H_2O$$

a. 3, 2, 1, 6
b. 2, 3, 1, 3
c. 3, 3, 2, 6
d. 1, 2, 1, 4

22. The overall reaction A → D can be described by the following equation:

$$A \xrightarrow{\text{fast}} B \xrightarrow{\text{slow}} C \xrightarrow{\text{fast}} D$$

What would be the rate law for the overall reaction of A to D?

a. $\text{Rate} = \frac{k[D]}{[A]}$
b. $\text{Rate} = k[B]$
c. $\text{Rate} = [B]$
d. $\text{Rate} = \frac{k[C]}{[B]}$

23. For the reaction $CO_2(g) + H_2(g) \rightleftharpoons CO(g) + H_2O(l)$, which of the following will occur if the pressure of the reaction is increased?

a. The reaction order will increase.
b. The forward reaction rate will decrease.
c. The reaction equilibrium will shift to the right.
d. The reaction will stop.

24. To make a good buffering system in the pH range of 5-9, which acid/base combinations would likely work the best?

a. $HCl/NaOH$
b. $HNO_3/NaNO_3$
c. $H_2SO_4/NaHSO_4$
d. NaH_2PO_4/Na_2HPO_4

25. Which of the following molecules is an alkene?

I. 

II. 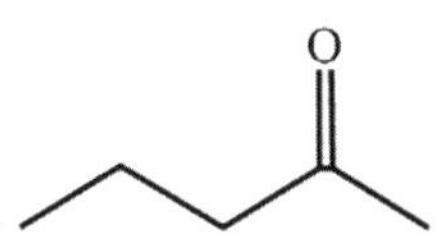

III. 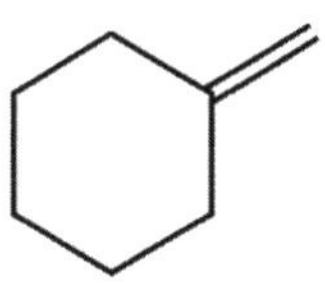

IV. 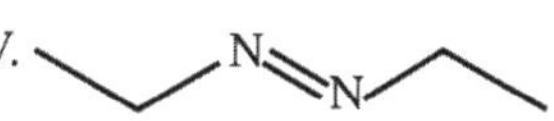

a. I
b. II
c. III
d. IV

Engineering

1. An engineer measures the total length of a screw to be 5.44 ± 0.03 cm. The length of the threaded part of the screw is 3.55 ± 0.04 cm. The length of the unthreaded part is therefore $5.44 \text{ cm} - 3.55 \text{ cm} = 1.89$ cm. What is the uncertainty in this value?

a. 0.01 cm
b. 0.026 cm
c. 0.035 cm

d. 0.05 cm

2. A uniform beam with a mass of 20 kg and a length of 4.0 m holds up a sign at its end with a mass of 50 kg. The beam is supported by a guyline attached to its end that makes an angle of 30° with the beam. (See the diagram.) Assuming the system is in equilibrium, what is the tension on the guyline?

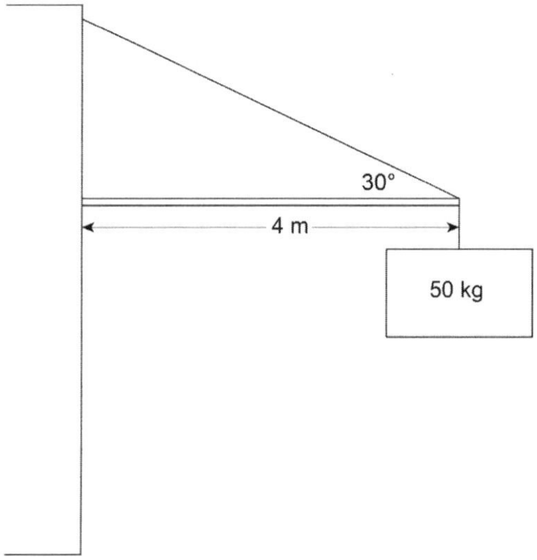

a. 680 N
b. 980 N
c. 1200 N
d. 1400 N

3. A geology lab experiment requires the rotation of groups of students through five lab stations to analyze rocks. The stations require the use of equipment including eye protection, hearing protection, thick gloves, microscopes, hammers, and loud rock cutting tools. Which of the following protective equipment requirements is most appropriate and feasible for the class.

a. Students should be able to perform the microscopy section in a separate classroom so they do not have to wear protective equipment.
b. Students should wear hearing and eye protection at all times during the lab experiment.
c. Students should wear all available protective equipment through all stations.
d. Students should only wear the protective equipment pertaining to their current station.

4. A student wishes to program a robot to move forward until it is within 10 inches of a target and then stop. Which of the following pieces of pseudocode best shows how to accomplish this task? (Assume that "start()" starts the robot moving, "stop()" stops it, "wait()" waits a short period of time, and "measure_distance()" returns the distance to the obstacle in inches.)

a.

```
start();
distance = measure_distance();
if (distance < 10.0)
   stop();
end if
```

b.

```
start();
distance = measure_distance();
while (distance < 10.0)
   stop();
   distance = measure_distance();
end while
```

c.

```
start();
distance = measure_distance();
while (distance > 10.0)
   wait();
end while
distance = measure_distance();
stop();
```

d.

```
start();
distance = measure_distance();
while (distance > 10.0)
   wait();
   distance = measure_distance();
end while
stop();
```

5. A company purchases a certain apparatus for $12000. If the apparatus has a useful life of 10 years and a salvage value of $4000, what is its annual depreciation expense, applying straight-line depreciation?

a. $800
b. $1200
c. $1455
d. $1600

6. Which of the following assignments would be most helpful for a high school engineering class to improve their understanding of the responsibilities and experience in the workplace?

a. An authentic practice job interview by business owners within the community
b. A brief, daily discussion of an ethics-focused scenario in the classroom
c. A portfolio including a sales call, a presentation, and written professional goals
d. A graded policy requiring students to dress professionally once a week

7. Which of the following is the best method for assessing a student's progress on a single design assignment over the course of a year?

a. Portfolio
b. Field-learning project
c. Capstone project
d. Research report and presentation

8. Which of the following accurately describes a difference between the manufacturing processes of casting and molding?

a. Casting applies to metals; molding applies to plastics
b. Casting is an additive process; molding is a subtractive process
c. Casting involves letting a liquid set; molding involves shaping a solid
d. Casting is done before other processes such as joining; molding is done afterward

9. The illustration below shows the closeup of the thimble and sleeve of a 0 to 1" micrometer being used to measure the diameter of a thin rod. What is the reading of this micrometer?

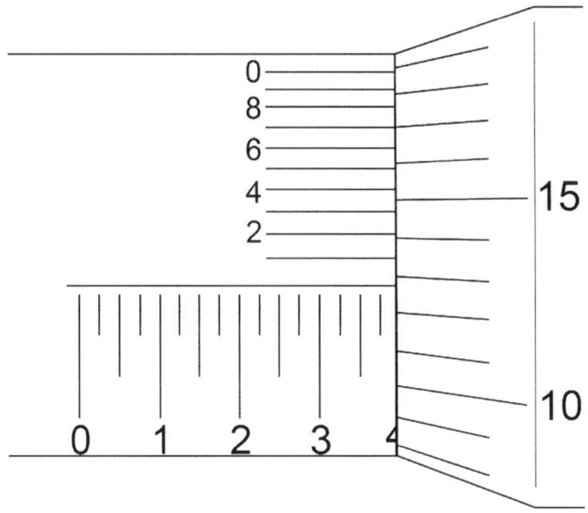

a. 0.3427"
b. 0.3877"
c. 0.4127"
d. 0.4197"

10. What does a galvanometer measure?

a. Capacitance
b. Current
c. Inductance
d. Voltage

11. Which of the following policies would be most helpful for keeping students safe in a field activity related to gathering specimens of pinecones on school grounds for a biology class?

a. Ensure all students have gloves and collection bags.
b. Establish a buddy system to keep students accounted for in the field.
c. Review possible related hazards to avoid before going into the field.
d. Refresh the students on behavior policies before going into the field.

12. A new ventilation hood is being installed in a chemistry lab that needs to meet certain airflow requirements, but must be quiet enough for the teacher to be exposed to the noise level for up to seven hours per day. The laboratory is 1,200 square feet. The Uniform Mechanical Code requires a minimum of one cubic foot per minute (cfm) for each square foot in an educational laboratory setting. Which of the following is the most ideal unit for this application?

OSHA Permissible Noise Exposures

Permissible Daily Exposure	Sound Level (dB)
1 hour	105
2 hours	100
3 hours	97
4 hours	95
6 hours	92
8 hours	90

a. Centrigrade Extractor 1500 cfm at 88dB
b. Velociking HEPA Ventilator1800 cfm at 93dB
c. Air Sentry 800 cfm at 50dB
d. Fescool Vent Hood 1100cfm at 80dB

13. The development of the automobile had a profound impact on global society, increasing people's mobility and opening up many new lifestyle opportunities. However, like most new developments, it had both advantages and disadvantages. Which of the following describes one negative consequence of the widespread use of automobiles?

a. New jobs were created to supply parts and materials for automobiles
b. Electrical systems became overtaxed, leading to widespread blackouts
c. Cities spread out over larger areas, causing environmental destruction and increased travel times
d. The invention of long-distance communication systems was delayed because the automobile rendered them unnecessary

14. In a computer-integrated engineering system, which of the following steps should come first?

a. Calculation of costs
b. Manufacturing
c. Purchasing materials
d. Quality control

15. The flow of water in a system varies periodically with time according to the following equation, where *t* is measured in minutes:

$$Q(t) = (2{,}000\ \text{m}^3/\text{min})|\sin(0.02t)|$$

What is the water's *average* rate of flow?

a. 608 m^3/min
b. 1,270 m^3/min
c. 2,000 m^3/min
d. 20,000 m^3/min

16. Which of the following materials is most reasonable for a project requiring the design of a two-foot-tall mechanical structure replicating an architectural design. The project needs to be designed at home and transported to class in its assembled form and will be tested for structural strength.

a. Extruded aluminum with connectors
b. Plastic straws
c. Wooden craft sticks
d. PVC pipe

17. Which of the following would be most useful to include in the professional portfolio of an electrical engineer?

a. A copy of the engineer's full college transcripts
b. A letter of recommendation from a former supervisor
c. The code listing to a computer program the engineer wrote
d. The design documents from an electrical device the engineer created

18. Which of the following accurately describes a consideration of the jigsaw approach to cooperative learning?

Jigsaw Approach to Cooperative Learning

Phase 1: Focus groups learn about individual target topics.

1	1	2	2	3	3	4	4
1	1	2	2	3	3	4	4

Phase 2: Task groups bring their knowledge together to accomplish a specific task or objective.

1	2	1	2	1	2	1	2
3	4	3	4	3	4	3	4

a. The jigsaw approach is used to have students learn deeply about one aspect of a topic.
b. The jigsaw approach relies heavily on the students for independent learning.
c. The jigsaw approach is not able to target specific learning objectives.
d. The jigsaw approach is primarily used for authentic, or real-world, learning experiences.

19. Which of the following is the best time and reason to implement a two-week unit where various trade and engineering professionals present on their specific fields?

a. Midway through the course to develop understanding of a variety of fields to understand upstream and downstream supply chains.
b. At the end of the course, so that students can see how the engineering concepts they have been learning can be applied.
c. At the end of the course, before an internship fair, so the students have information to help them find the best possible internship.
d. At the beginning of the course to provide students with a variety of career opportunities to consider before learning engineering concepts.

20. The designer of a factory must choose between two different kinds of generator. Generator 1 requires 200,000 Btu of heat energy to produce 20 kWh of electrical energy. Generator 2 uses 60,000 Btu of heat energy to produce 5 kWh of electrical energy. Which generator has a higher thermal efficiency?

a. Generator 1
b. Generator 2
c. The two generators have the same thermal efficiency.
d. Generator 1 has a higher thermal efficiency in the short run, but Generator 2 has a higher thermal efficiency in the long run.

21. A city's public light rail system has not been well maintained, and some of its tracks and interchanges are dangerously close to wearing out. Local engineers want the upkeep of the rail system to be improved, both out of concerns for public safety and so that they'll have more work opportunities. What is the most effective way to make sure that such policies are carried out?

a. Stage a train accident to bring attention to the problems with the service
b. Raise money from the public on online fundraising sites to pay for the maintenance of the rail system
c. Lobby local politicians to pass laws mandating that elements of the rail system be periodically inspected and repaired or replaced as necessary
d. Write a letter to the editor of a local newspaper expressing concerns about the condition of the rail system and pointing out specific areas that need to be addressed

22. A web-based application causes a student's computer to slow down greatly every time a student attempts to render a CAD design he has created. When reviewing the computer process utilization, the following metrics were recorded at the time the CAD designs were rendered.

Component	Utilization
CPU	50%
Memory	85%
SSD	1%
GPU	15%

Based on the available information, which of the following is likely the most strained component?

a. CPU
b. Memory
c. SSD
d. GPU

23. An engineer wants to keep track of information on hundreds of suppliers, including their addresses and other contact information and the specific parts they supply. What would be the most appropriate software tool for this task?

a. A database management system
b. An operating system
c. A spreadsheet
d. A word processor

24. The same Earth science test is administered each year with student performance statistics analyzed for the effectiveness of each test item. The chart below shows the distribution of answer choices chosen by students in a standard geography class compared to students in an advanced geography class and the average overall score of students who chose each answer choice.

Answer Choice	Standard Geography Students	Advanced Geography Students	Average Score of Students based on Answer Choice
a. *correct choice*	45%	63%	88%
b.	18%	4%	72%
c.	19%	8%	76%
d.	18%	25%	82%

Which of the following conclusions could be drawn from the data provided?

a. The answer choices are not statistically reliable, as the question does not perform consistently.
b. The question is not statistically valid, as it did not correlate with overall student performance.
c. The results demonstrate that the question fails to discriminate knowledge of geography from knowledge of Earth science.
d. The results demonstrate a relationship with concepts learned in geography and Earth science.

25. The image below shows a slide from an engineer's PowerPoint presentation.

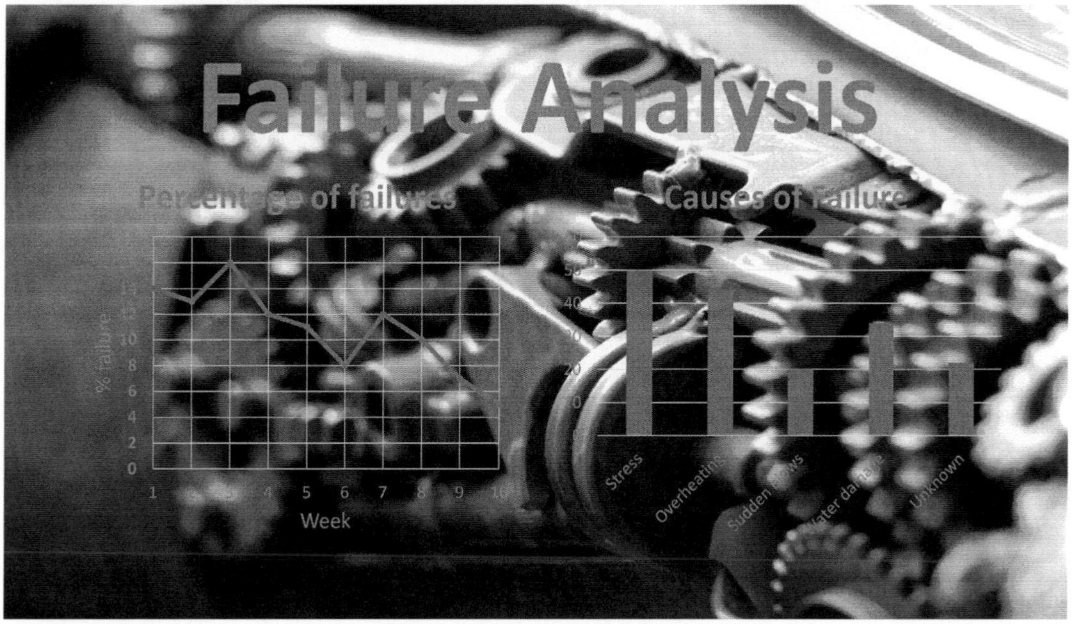

Which of the following choices best describes something that could be done to make the slide more effectively communicate the necessary information?

a. Add a detailed description of the graphs
b. Combine the two graphs into one
c. Replace the graphs with a text description of the data
d. Use a less distracting background

26. Which of the following is a good practice when engaging in written communication about an engineering matter?

a. Use long sentences to be sure to include all relevant details
b. Never repeat the same word more than once in a paragraph
c. Use different fonts to set apart different kinds of information
d. Define any technical terms that might be unfamiliar to readers

27. One of the most notable technological developments of the fifteenth century was the invention of the printing press. What was the most immediate historical impact of this event?

a. It facilitated the spread of information and mass communication.
b. It caused increased class divisions, cementing the power of the elites.
c. It led to the development of the steam engine and the Industrial Revolution.
d. It encouraged the development of trade unions, granting bargaining power to workers.

28. The line of code "`if (counter > 12) finished = true;`" is an example of which of the following?

a. Compiler directive
b. Conditional statement
c. Control loop
d. Declaration statement

Refer to the following for question 29:

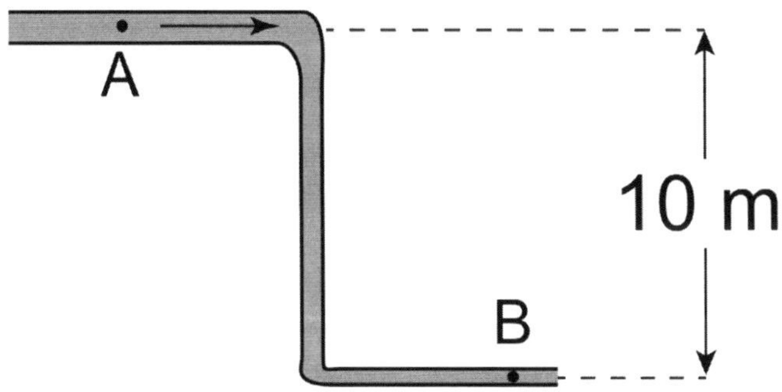

29. Water flows at a steady rate through a pipe as shown in the diagram. The rate of flow of the water is 10 m/s at point A, and 20 m/s at point B. Just after point B, the tube is open to the air, so the water at point B is at atmospheric pressure. What is the approximate pressure at point A? (Assume that the gravitational acceleration is 10 meters per second squared and that atmospheric pressure is 100,000 Pascals.)

a. 50,000 Pa
b. 100,000 Pa
c. 150,000 Pa
d. 200,000 Pa

30. A reservoir is filling at a rate of 1200 gallons per hour. What is this rate in milliliters per second? (Note that 1 gallon = 3.785 liters.)

a. 880 mL/s
b. 1140 mL/s
c. 1260 mL/s
d. 16350 mL/s

31. An engineering firm develops a new method of refining a certain material and wishes to protect its proprietary right to the process. What type of intellectual property protection would apply?

a. Copyright
b. Fair Use
c. Patent
d. Trademark

32. The manager of a team of engineers is asked to complete a project that lies within her particular field of expertise. However, the project is too involved for her to be able to complete it on time during regular work hours. What is the best course of action for her to take?

a. Complete the project herself, working extra hours if necessary to do so
b. Tell her team about the project and let them decide how they want to handle it
c. Oversee the project while assigning different parts of it to different team members according to their strengths
d. Assign the project to the team member with the least experience to help them grow, leading them through each step as they go

33. What kind of engineer would most likely be involved in designing a freeway interchange?

a. Civil engineer
b. Environmental engineer
c. Industrial engineer
d. Mechanical engineer

34. In the development cycle of a product, which of the following steps comes *last*?

a. Product design
b. Material selection
c. Analysis of customer needs
d. Manufacturing process design

35. As part of the quality assurance process for a new part, a mechanical engineering firm constructs a prototype and distributes it for feedback. The most common complaints from those testing the prototypes are summarized in the Pareto chart below.

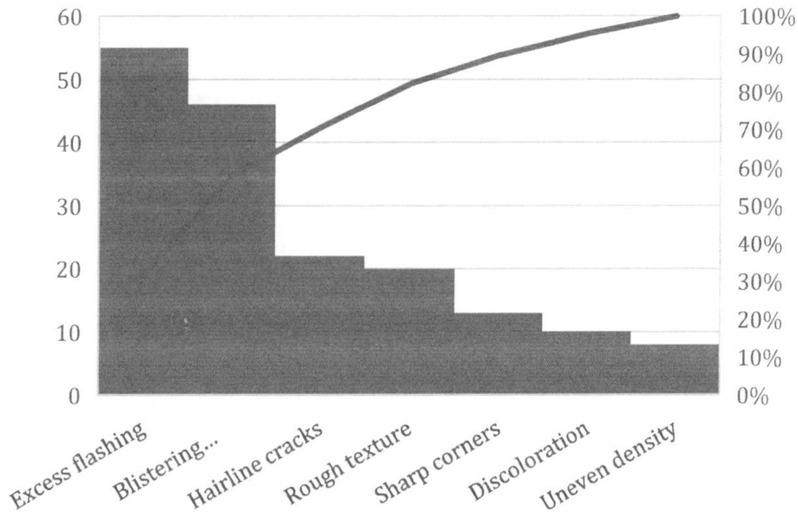

What is the minimum number of issues that must be corrected to address 80% of the complaints?

a. 2
b. 3
c. 4
d. 5

36. In every field of engineering, new technologies and techniques are continually being developed. How can an engineer best adapt to these changes in his or her field?

a. Learn how to use new technologies on the job as they happen to come up
b. Enroll in continuing education courses and seminars to learn about the new technologies
c. Request to be given assignments where the existing technologies can be used that the engineer is already familiar with
d. In general, a capable engineer will be quickly promoted to a supervisory position where he or she will not have to personally use these technologies, making it unnecessary to learn them.

37. An engineer designing an internal component to an industrial machine decides that the ideal material is a rare earth alloy that requires specialized equipment to manufacture. However, due to the criteria and constraints of the project, he is unable to use this alloy and must settle for another material that performs the necessary function, but does so less efficiently. What kind of constraint most likely led to this result?

a. A safety concern about noise pollution
b. A limitation on the cost of the component
c. A limitation on the maximum size of the component
d. An aesthetic concern regarding the appearance of the machine

38. A programmer wants to create a new database system using an iterative design process. After the programmer completes a working prototype of the database system, what is the next step in the process?

a. Use a code profiler to identify performance bottlenecks
b. Have users test the prototype and get their feedback on it
c. Add additional features to improve the program's capabilities
d. Produce at least two more, different prototypes to compare it with

39. A company finds that it needs a way to raise cargo containers to the top of a steep cliff. It hires a mechanical engineer to design a mechanism to perform this task. Which of the following pieces of information is it most important for the engineer to find out before beginning the design?

a. The color of the cargo containers
b. Where the cargo containers are coming from
c. The value of the contents of the cargo containers
d. The weight of the cargo containers (including their contents)

40. An engineer uses a layer-based CAD program to design a new three-plate injection mold. She wants to be able to work on the design of each plate without her view being obstructed by the others, while still being able to see how they fit together. What is the best way to accomplish this?

a. Put each plate in a different layer
b. Design each plate in a separate file
c. Draw each plate in a different color
d. Use the box select tool to select one plate at a time

Answer Key and Explanations

Mathematics

1. B: The problem does not give any information about the size of the bracelet or the spacing between any of the charms. Nevertheless, creating a simple illustration which shows the order of the charms will help when approaching this problem. For example, the circle below represents the bracelet, and the dotted line between A and B represents the clasp. On the right, the line shows the stretched-out bracelet and possible positions of charms C, D, and E based on the parameters.

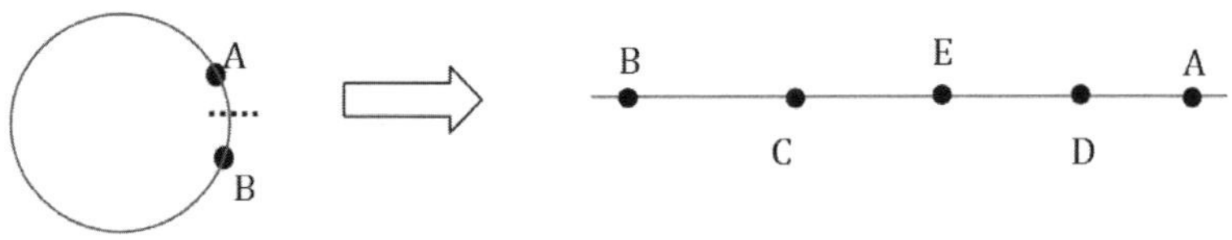

From the drawing above, it appears that statement I is true, but it is not necessarily so. The alternative drawing below also shows the charms ordered correctly, but the distance between B and E is now less than that between D and A.

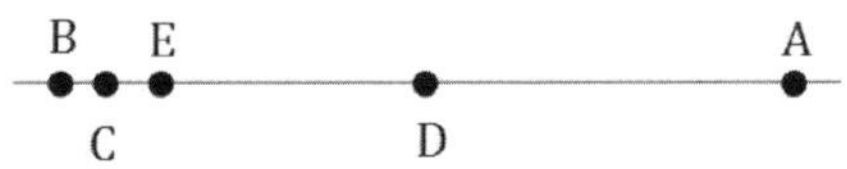

Statement II must be true: charm E must lie between B and D. Statement III must also be true: the distance between charms E and D must be less than that between C and A, which includes charms E and D in the space between them.

2. C: The height of the ball is a function of time, so the equation can be expressed as $h(t) = -18t^2 + 72t + 4$, and the average rate of change can be found by calculating $\frac{h(3)-h(0)}{3-0}$.

$$\frac{[-18(3)^2 + 72(3) + 4] - [-18(0)^2 + 64(0) + 4]}{3}$$
$$= \frac{(-162 + 216 + 4) - (0 + 0 + 4)}{3}$$
$$= \frac{54}{3}$$
$$= 18$$

The average rate of change in the ball's height is 18 feet/second.

3. B: Rate in miles per hour can be expressed as, mph $= \frac{\text{distance in miles}}{\text{time in hours}}$. So, Zeke's driving speed on the way to Atlanta and home from Atlanta in mph can be expressed as $\frac{d}{3}$ and $\frac{d}{2}$, respectively, where d is the distance between Zeke's house and his destination. Since Zeke drove 20 mph faster on his way home, (speed home) $-$ (speed to store) $= 20$. Substitute Zeke's speeds and solve for d.

$$\frac{d}{2} - \frac{d}{3} = 20$$

$$6\left(\frac{d}{2}-\frac{d}{3}=20\right)$$
$$3d-2d=120$$
$$d=120$$

Since the distance between Zeke's house and the store in Atlanta is 120 miles, Zeke drove a total distance of 240 miles in five hours. Therefore, his average speed was $\frac{240 \text{ miles}}{5 \text{ hours}} = 48$ mph.

4. B: Deductive reasoning moves from one or more general statements to a specific, while inductive reasoning makes a general conclusion based on a series of specific instances or observations. Whenever the premises used in deductive reasoning are true, the conclusion drawn is necessarily true. In inductive reasoning, it is possible for the premises to be true and the conclusion to be false since there may exist an exception to the general conclusion drawn from the observations made.

5. A: The first argument's reasoning is valid, and since its premises are true, the argument is also sound. The second argument's reasoning is invalid; that the premises are true is irrelevant. (For example, consider the true premises "all cats are mammals" and "all dogs are mammals;" it cannot be logically concluded that all dogs are cats.) The third argument's reasoning is valid, but since one of its premises is false, the argument is not sound.

6. D: The symbol $\wedge$ is the logical conjunction symbol. In order for statement $(p \wedge q)$ to be true, both statements p and q must be true. The $\neg$ symbol means "not," so if $(p \wedge q)$ is true, then $\neg(p \wedge q)$ is false, and if $(p \wedge q)$ is false, then $\neg(p \wedge q)$ is true. The statement $q \leftrightarrow \neg(p \wedge q)$ is true when the value of q is the same as the value of $\neg(p \wedge q)$.

p	q	$(p \wedge q)$	$\neg(p \wedge q)$	$q \leftrightarrow \neg(p \wedge q)$
T	T	T	F	F
T	F	F	T	F
F	T	F	T	T
F	F	F	T	F

7. B: The notation $\mathbb{P} \subseteq \mathbb{N} \subseteq \mathbb{Z} \subseteq \mathbb{Q} \subseteq \mathbb{R} \subseteq \mathbb{C}$ means that the set of prime numbers is a subset of the set natural numbers, which is a subset of the set of integers, which is a subset of the set of rational numbers, which is a subset of the set real numbers, which is a subset of the set of complex numbers. The set of prime numbers ($\mathbb{P}$) are natural numbers that have no factors other than 1 and itself. The set of natural numbers ($\mathbb{N}$) are all positive integers. The set of integers ($\mathbb{Z}$) are all positive and negative whole numbers, numbers without a fraction or decimal part to them. The set of rational numbers ($\mathbb{Q}$) are all numbers that can be expressed as the quotient of two integers. The set of real numbers ($\mathbb{R}$) are all numbers that can be expressed on a number line. The set of all complex numbers ($\mathbb{C}$) are all real and imaginary numbers.

8. A: The set of whole numbers, $\{0, 1, 2, 3, \ldots\}$, does not contain the number -4. Since -4 is an integer, it is also a rational number and a real number.

9. D: In order for a set to be a group under an operation, it must be closed and demonstrate associativity under the operation, there must exist an identity element, and for every element in the group, there must exist an inverse element in the group.

The set of prime numbers under multiplication is not closed. For example, $2 \times 3 = 6$, and 6 is not a member of the set of prime numbers. Similarly, the set of negative integers under subtraction is not closed since subtracting two negative integers can yield a positive integer. Though the set of counting numbers under addition is closed, it is not is associative, and there exists no identity element (the number zero in this case) in the group. The set of complex numbers other than zero under multiplication is closed and associative; the identity 1 is a member of the group, and for each element in the group, there is a multiplicative inverse (reciprocal), since zero is excluded.

10. B: In order for a set to be a group under operation $*$:

- The set must be closed under that operation. In other words, when the operation is performed on any two members of the set, the result must also be a member of that set.
- The set must demonstrate associativity under the operation: $a * (b * c) = (a * b) * c$.
- There must exist an identity element e in the group: $a * e = e * a = a$.
- For every element in the group, there must exist an inverse element in the group: $a * b = b * a = e$.

Choice A can be eliminated as the correct answer because the set $\{-i, 0, i\}$ does not contain the multiplicative identity 1. Though choices C and D contain the element 1, neither is closed: for example, since $i \times i = -1$, -1 must be an element of the group. Choice B is closed, contains the multiplicative identity 1, and the inverse of each element is included in the set as well. Of course, multiplication is an associative operation, so the set $\{-1, 1, i, -i\}$ forms a group under multiplication.

$\times$	-1	1	i	$-i$
-1	1	-1	$-i$	i
1	-1	1	i	$-i$
i	$-i$	i	-1	1
$-i$	i	$-i$	1	-1

11. D: The identity element is d since $d\#a = a\#d = a, d\#b = b\#d = b, d\#c = c\#d = c$, and $d\#d = d$. The inverse of element c is c since $c\#c = d$, the identity element. The operation # is commutative because $a\#b = b\#a, a\#c = c\#a$, etc. Rather than check that the operation is commutative for each pair of elements, note that elements in the table display symmetry about the diagonal elements; this indicates that the operation is indeed commutative.

#	a	b	c	d
a	c	d	b	a
b	d	c	a	b
c	b	a	d	c
d	a	b	c	d

12. C: If x is a prime number and the greatest common factor of x and y is greater than 1, the greatest common factor of x and y must be x. The least common multiple of two numbers is equal to the product of those numbers divided by their greatest common factor. So, the least common multiple of x and y is $\frac{xy}{x} = y$. Therefore, the two quantities are the same.

13. A: First, write three equations from the information given in the problem. Since the total number of tickets sold was 810, $x + y + z = 810$. The ticket sales generated \$14,500, so $15x + 25y + 20z = 14{,}500$. The number of children under ten was the same as twice the number of adults and seniors, so $x = 2(y + z)$, which can be rewritten as $x - 2y - 2z = 0$.

The coefficients of each equation are arranged in the rows of a 3×3 matrix, which, when multiplied by the 3×1 matrix arranging the variables x, y, and z, will give the 3×1 matrix which arranges the constants of the equations.

14. C: Multiply the second equation by 2 and combine it with the first equation to eliminate y.

$$\begin{array}{rrrrcr} & 2x & -4y & +1z & = & 10 \\ + & -6x & +4y & -8z & = & -14 \\ \hline & -4x & & -7z & = & -4 \end{array}$$

Multiply the third equation by -2 and combine it with the original second equation to eliminate y.

$$\begin{array}{rrrrcr} & -3x & +2y & -4z & = & -7 \\ + & -2x & -2y & +6z & = & 2 \\ \hline & -5x & & +2z & = & -5 \end{array}$$

Multiply the equation from step one by 5 and the equation from step two by -4 and combine to eliminate x.

$$\begin{array}{rrrcr} & -20x & -35z & = & -20 \\ + & 20x & -\ 8z & = & 20 \\ \hline & & -43z & = & 0 \\ & & z & = & 0 \end{array}$$

Substitute 0 for z in the equation from step 2 to find x.

$$\begin{aligned} -5x + 2(0) &= -5 \\ -5x &= -5 \\ x &= 1 \end{aligned}$$

Substitute 0 for z and 1 for x into the first original equation to find y.

$$\begin{aligned} 2(1) - 4y + (0) &= 10 \\ 2 - 4y &= 10 \\ -4y &= 8 \\ y &= -2 \end{aligned}$$

Therefore, the solution to the system of equations is $(1, -2, 0)$.

15. A: First, set the equation equal to zero, then factor it.

$$3x^3y^2 - 45x^2y = 15x^3y - 9x^2y^2$$
$$3x^3y^2 - 15x^3y + 9x^2y^2 - 45x^2y = 0$$
$$3x^2y(xy - 5x + 3y - 15) = 0$$
$$3x^2y[x(y-5) + 3(y-5)] = 0$$
$$3x^2y[(y-5)(x+3)] = 0$$

Use the zero product property to find the solutions.

$$3x^2y = 0 \qquad y - 5 = 0 \qquad x + 3 = 0$$
$$x = 0 \qquad y = 5 \qquad x = -3$$
$$y = 0$$

So, the solutions are $x = \{0, -3\}$ and $y = \{0,5\}$.

16. B: First, use the properties of logarithms to solve for y:

$2\log_4 y + \log_4 16 = 3$	Write out the original equation.
$\log_4 y^2 + \log_4 16 = 3$	Use the power rule for logarithms: $\log_b(x^a) = a \cdot \log_b x$.
$\log_4 16y^2 = 3$	Then, use the product rule for logarithms: $\log_b x + \log_b y = \log_b(xy)$.
$16y^2 = 4^3$	Next, convert the logarithm to an exponential expression.
$16y^2 = 64$	Simplify the right side.
$y^2 = 4$	Divide both sides by 16.
$y = 2$	Take the positive square root of both sides.

Finally, substitute 2 for y in the expression $\log_y 256$ and simplify: $\log_2 256 = 8$ since $2^8 = 256$.

17. B: First, apply the laws of exponents to simplify the expression on the left. Then, find a common denominator to add the fractions.

$\frac{(x^2y)(2xy^{-2})^3}{16x^5y^2} + \frac{3}{xy}$	
$\frac{(x^2y)(8x^3y^{-6})}{16x^5y^2} + \frac{3}{xy}$	Simplify the second term in the left numerator using the exponent rule $(x^m)^n = x^{m \cdot n}$.
$\frac{8x^5y^{-5}}{16x^5y^2} + \frac{3}{xy}$	Simplify the numerator of the left fraction using the exponent rule $x^m \cdot x^n = x^{m+n}$.
$\frac{1}{2y^7} + \frac{3}{xy}$	Simplify the left fraction using the exponent rule $\frac{x^m}{x^n} = x^{m-n}$.

$$\frac{1}{2y^7} \cdot \frac{x}{x} + \frac{3}{xy} \cdot \frac{2y^6}{2y^6}$$ Create common denominators between the two fractions.

$$\frac{x}{2xy^7} + \frac{6y^6}{2xy^7}$$ Simplify the multiplication.

$$\frac{x + 6y^6}{2xy^7}$$ Add the two numerators over the common denominator.

18. C: The x-intercept is the point at which $f(x) = 0$. When $0 = \log_b x$, $b^0 = x$; since $b^0 = 1$, the x-intercept of $f(x) = \log_b x$ is always 1. If $f(x) = \log_b x$ and $x = b$, then $f(x) = \log_b b$, which is, by definition, 1 ($b^1 = b$). If $g(x) = b^x$, then $f(x)$ and $g(x)$ are inverse functions and are therefore symmetric with respect to $y = x$. The statement choice C is not necessarily true since $x < 1$ includes numbers between 0 and 1. The function is undefined when $x < 0$, but not necessarily for $0 < x < 1$.

19. D: Bacterial growth is exponential. Let x be the number of times the population doubles, a be the number of bacteria in the colony originally transferred into the broth, and y be the number of bacteria in the broth after x doubling times. After 1 hour, the population would have doubled three times:

$$a(2)^x = y$$
$$a(2^3) = 8 \times 10^6$$
$$8a = 8 \times 10^6$$
$$a = 10^6$$

So, the number of bacteria originally transferred into the petri dish was 10^6. The equation for determining the number of bacteria is $y = (2^x) \times 10^6$. Since the bacteria double every twenty minutes, they go through three doubling times every hour. So, when the bacteria are allowed to grow for eight hours, they will have gone through $8 \times 3 = 24$ doubling times. When $x = 24$, $y = (2^{24}) \times 10^6 = 16{,}777{,}216 \times 10^6$, which is approximately 1.7×10^{13}.

20. A: Get as many terms as possible out from the radical and any radicals out from the denominator. First, identify perfect squares under the radical.

$$\sqrt{\frac{-28x^6}{27y^5}} = \sqrt{\frac{-4x^6 \times (7)}{9y^4 \times (3y)}} = \sqrt{\frac{-(2x^3)^2 \times (7)}{(3y^2)^2 \times (3y)}}$$

Then, pull out the perfect squares from under the radical.

$$\frac{2x^3 i\sqrt{7}}{3y^2\sqrt{3y}}$$

Finally, rationalize the denominator.

$$\frac{2x^3 i\sqrt{7}}{3y^2\sqrt{3y}} \times \frac{\sqrt{3y}}{\sqrt{3y}} = \frac{2x^3 i\sqrt{21y}}{9y^3}$$

Therefore, the simplified expression is $\frac{2x^3 i\sqrt{21y}}{9y^3}$.

21. B: The inequality is solved by writing a double inequality equivalent to the given inequality but without the absolute value bars.

$$-9 < x + 6 < 9$$

Solve the double inequality by subtracting 6 from all three parts.

$$-15 < x < 3$$

The solution set can be written using interval notation.

$$(-15,3)$$

22. C: We can look at each equation separately.

Choice A, $y = \frac{1}{x-1} + 1$, has a zero denominator at $x = 1$, so we can eliminate it immediately.

Choice B, $y = -\sqrt{x+2} - 1$, does include $x = 1$ in its domain: $y = -\sqrt{(1)+2} - 1 \approx -2.73$. But we can see that all y-values will be a negative number (or zero) minus 1, which means all y-values will be negative, so 2 is outside the range.

Choice C, $y = |x+2| - 3$, also includes $x = 1$ in its domain: $y = |(1)+2| - 3 = 0$. And we can see that $y = |(3)+2| - 3 = 2$, so 2 is in the range. So choice C meets both criteria.

Choice D also includes $x = 1$ in its domain: $y = -(1) - 3 = -4$. But by graphing this piecewise linear function, we can see that its range is $y < -1$, which excludes 2.

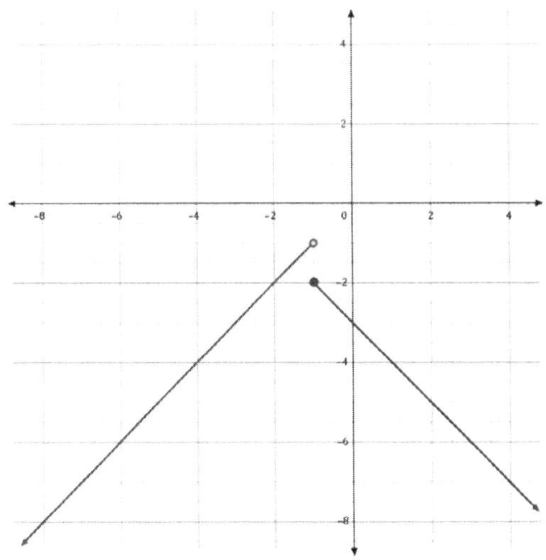

23. D: There are many ways Josephine may have applied her knowledge to determine how to approximately measure her medicine using her plastic spoon. The expression below shows how she converts from cubic centimeters to spoons.

$$25\text{ cc} \times \frac{1\text{ mL}}{1\text{ cc}} \times \frac{1\text{L}}{1{,}000\text{ mL}} \times \frac{0.5\text{ gal}}{2\text{ L}} \times \frac{16\text{ c}}{1\text{ gal}} \times \frac{48\text{ t}}{1\text{ c}} \times \frac{1\text{ spoonful}}{1\text{ t}}$$

$$\frac{25}{1{,}000} \times \frac{1}{4} \times 16 \times 48$$

The only choice which correctly uses dimensional analysis is choice D.

24. B: Percent error $= \frac{|\text{actual value} - \text{measured value}|}{\text{actual value}} \times 100\%$, and the average percent error is the sum of the percent errors for each trial divided by the number of trials.

	Percent Error Trial 1	Percent Error Trial 2	Percent Error Trial 3	Percent Error Trial 4	Average Percent Error
Scale 1	0.1%	0.2%	0.2%	0.1%	0.15%
Scale 2	2.06%	2.09%	2.10%	2.08%	2.08%

The percent error for Scale 1 is less than the percent error for Scale 2, so it is more accurate. The more precise scale is Scale 2 because its range of values, $10.210 \text{ g} - 10.206 \text{ g} = 0.004 \text{ g}$, is smaller than the Scale 2's range of values, $10.02 \text{ g} - 9.98 \text{ g} = 0.04 \text{ g}$.

25. C: If l and w represent the length and width of the enclosed area, its perimeter is equal to $2l + 2w$; since the fence is positioned x feet from the lot's edges on each side, the perimeter of the lot is $2(l + 2x) + 2(w + 2x)$. Since the amount of money saved by fencing the smaller area is \$432, and since the fencing material costs \$12 per linear foot, 36 fewer feet of material are used to fence around the playground than would have been used to fence around the lot. This can be expressed as the following equation.

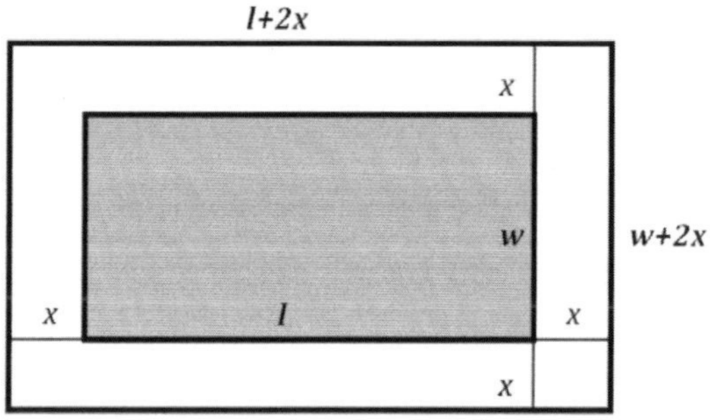

$$2(l + 2x) + 2(w + 2x) - (2l + 2w) = 36$$
$$2l + 4x + 2w + 4x - 2l - 2w = 36$$
$$8x = 36$$
$$x = 4.5 \text{ ft}$$

The difference in the area of the lot and the enclosed space is 141 yd^2, which is the same as 1,269 ft^2. So, $(l + 2x)(w + 2x) - lw = 1{,}269$. Substituting 4.5 for x, we get the following equation that we can solve for $l + w$.

$$(l + 9)(w + 9) - lw = 1{,}269$$
$$lw + 9l + 9w + 81 - lw = 1{,}269$$
$$9l + 9w = 1{,}188$$
$$9(l + w) = 1{,}188$$
$$l + w = 132 \text{ ft}$$

Therefore, the perimeter of the enclosed space, $2(l + w)$, is $2(132) = 264$ ft. The cost of 264 ft of fencing is $264 \times \$12 = \$3{,}168$.

26. A: The area of a circle is πr^2, so the area of a semicircle is $\frac{\pi r^2}{2}$. Illustrated below is a method that can be used to find the area of the shaded region.

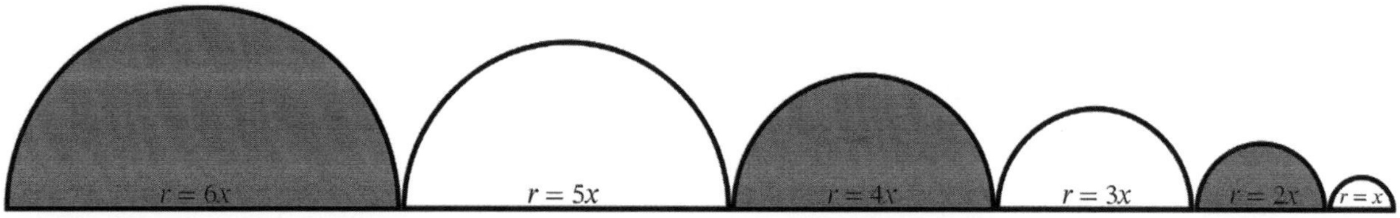

$$\begin{aligned} A &= \frac{\pi(6x)^2}{2} - \frac{\pi(5x)^2}{2} + \frac{\pi(4x)^2}{2} - \frac{\pi(3x)^2}{2} + \frac{\pi(2x)^2}{2} - \frac{\pi(x)^2}{2} \\ &= \frac{36\pi x^2}{2} - \frac{25\pi x^2}{2} + \frac{16\pi x^2}{2} - \frac{9\pi x^2}{2} + \frac{4\pi x^2}{2} - \frac{\pi x^2}{2} \\ &= \frac{(36 - 25 + 16 - 9 + 4 - 1)\pi x^2}{2} \\ &= \frac{21\pi x^2}{2} \end{aligned}$$

27. D: Let b represent the base of the triangle. The height h of the triangle is the altitude drawn from the vertex opposite of b to side b.

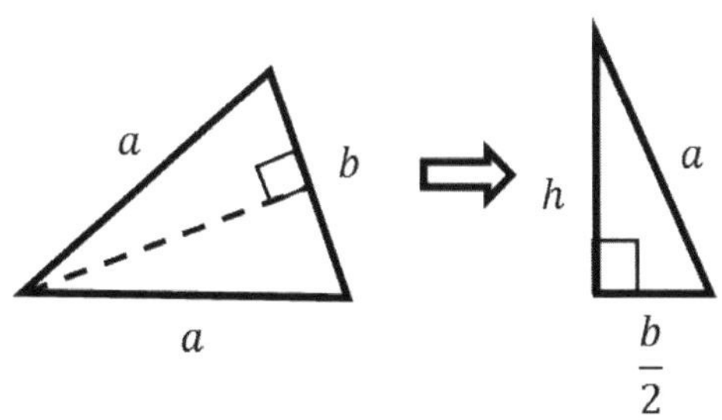

The height of the triangle can be found in terms of a and b by using the Pythagorean theorem.

$$h^2 + \left(\frac{b}{2}\right)^2 = a^2$$

$$h = \sqrt{a^2 - \frac{b^2}{4}}$$

$$h = \sqrt{\frac{4a^2 - b^2}{4}}$$

$$h = \frac{\sqrt{4a^2 - b^2}}{2}$$

The area of a triangle is $A = \frac{1}{2}bh$, so $A = \frac{1}{2}b\left(\frac{\sqrt{4a^2-b^2}}{2}\right) = \frac{b\sqrt{4a^2-b^2}}{4}$.

28. D: Since it is given that $\overline{FD} \cong \overline{BC}$ and $\overline{AB} \cong \overline{DE}$, step 2 needs to establish either that $\overline{AC} \cong \overline{EF}$ or that $\Delta ABC \cong \Delta FDE$ in order for step 5 to show that $\Delta ABC \cong \Delta EDF$. The statement $\overline{AC} \cong \overline{EF}$ cannot be shown directly from the given information. On the other hand, $\Delta ABC \cong \Delta FDE$ can be determined: when two parallel lines $\overline{BC} \parallel \overline{FG}$ are cut by a transversal ($\overline{AE}$), alternate exterior angles ($\Delta ABC, \Delta FDE$) are congruent. Therefore, $\Delta ABC \cong \Delta EDF$ by the side-angle-side (SAS) theorem.

29. D: The cross-section is a hexagon.

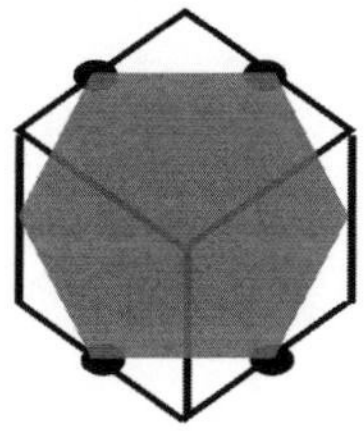

30. A: Since the y-coordinates of points P and Q are the same, line segment $\overline{PQ}$ is a horizontal line segment whose length is the difference in the x-coordinates a and c. Because the length of a line cannot be negative, and because it is unknown whether $a > c$ or $a < c$, $PQ = |a - c|$ or $|c - a|$. Since the x-coordinates of Q and P' are the same, line segment $\overline{P'Q}$ is a vertical line segment whose length is $|d - b|$ or $|b - d|$. The quadrilateral formed by the transformation of $\overline{PQ}$ to $\overline{P'Q'}$ is a parallelogram. If the base of the parallelogram is $\overline{PQ}$, then the height is $\overline{P'Q}$ since $\overline{PQ} \perp \overline{P'Q}$. For a parallelogram, $A = bh$, so $A = |a - c| \times |b - d|$.

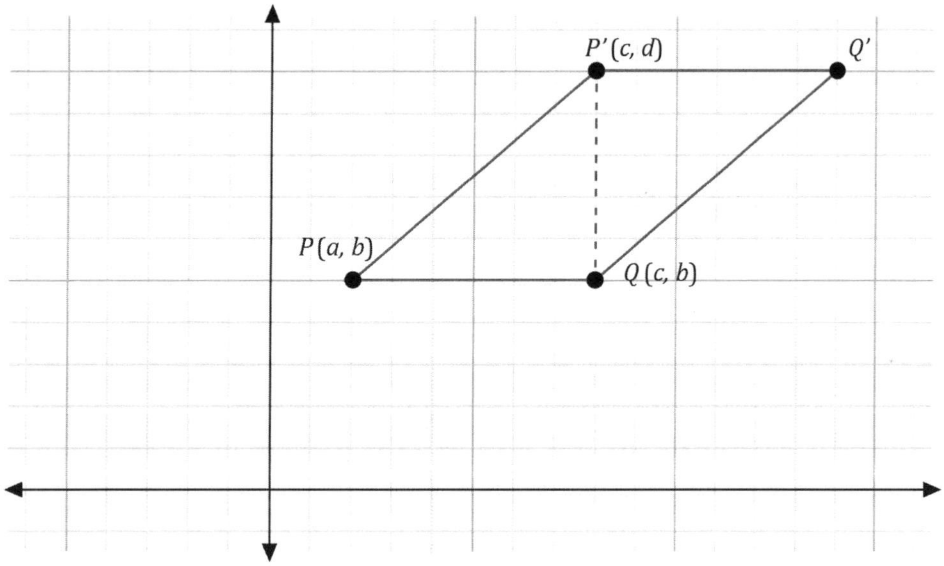

31. B: The trigonometric identity $\sec^2\theta = \tan^2\theta + 1$ can be used to rewrite the equation $\sec^2\theta = 2\tan\theta$ as $\tan^2\theta + 1 = 2\tan\theta$, which can then be rearranged into the form $\tan^2\theta - 2\tan\theta + 1 = 0$. Solve by factoring and using the zero-product property.

$$\begin{aligned} \tan^2\theta - 2\tan\theta + 1 &= 0 \\ (\tan\theta - 1)^2 &= 0 \\ \tan\theta - 1 &= 0 \\ \tan\theta &= 1 \end{aligned}$$

Since $\tan\theta = 1$ when $\sin\theta = \cos\theta$, for $0 < \theta \leq 2\pi$, $\theta = \frac{\pi}{4}$ or $\frac{5\pi}{4}$.

32. C: To evaluate a limit going to infinity, look at the degree of the numerator (call it N) and the degree of the denominator (call it D). If $N > D$, the limit is $\pm\infty$. If $N < D$, the limit is 0. If $N = D$, the limit equals the coefficient of the highest exponent's term in the numerator divided by the coefficient of the highest exponent's term in the denominator. Since $N = D = 2$ for this function, divide the coefficient of the x^2 term in the numerator (1) by the coefficient of the x^2 term in the denominator (2) to find the limit: $\frac{1}{2}$.

33. C: Using rectangles with a width of 1, we can find the left and right Riemann sums to approximate the area under the curve.

The left Riemann sum: $20 + 25 + 28 + 30 + 29 + 26 + 22 + 16 + 12 + 10 + 10 + 13 = 241$

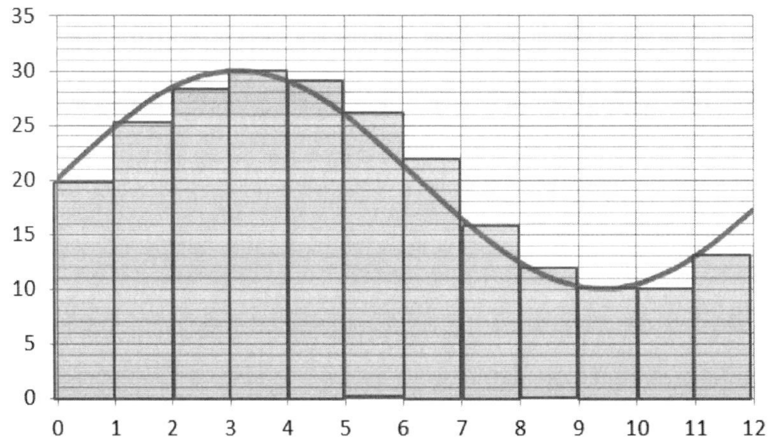

The right Riemann sum: $25 + 28 + 30 + 29 + 26 + 22 + 16 + 12 + 10 + 10 + 13 + 17 = 238$

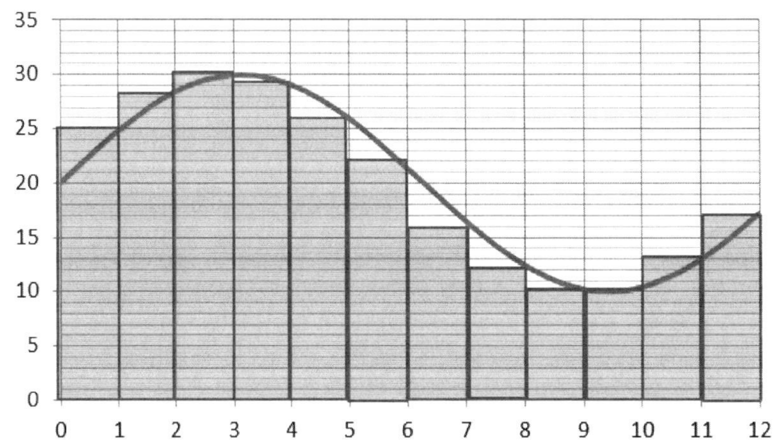

Thus, the bounds on A are: $238 < A < 241$.

34. B: Find the points of intersection of the two graphs:

$$x^2 - 4 = -x + 2$$
$$x^2 + x - 6 = 0$$
$$(x + 3)(x - 2) = 0$$
$$x = -3, x = 2$$

So, the area is between the graphs on $[-3,2]$. To determine which of the graphs is the upper or lower bound, pick a test point in the interval. Using $x = 0$ as the test point.

$$\begin{array}{cc} y = x^2 - 4 & y = -x + 2 \\ y = (0)^2 - 4 & y = -(0) + 2 \\ y = -4 & y = 2 \end{array}$$

The finite region is bound at the top by the line $y = -x + 2$ and at the bottom by $y = x^2 - 4$, and the height of the region at point x is defined by $[(-x + 2) - (x^2 - 4)]$, so the area of the region is:

$$\begin{aligned} A &= \int_{-3}^{2} [(-x + 2) - (x^2 - 4)]dx \\ &= \int_{-3}^{2} (-x^2 - x + 6\,)\,dx \\ &= \left[-\frac{1}{3}x^3 - \frac{1}{2}x^2 + 6x\right]_{-3}^{2} \\ &= \left[-\frac{1}{3}(2)^3 - \frac{1}{2}(2)^2 + 6(2)\right] - \left[-\frac{1}{3}(-3)^3 - \frac{1}{2}(-3)^2 + 6(-3)\right] \\ &= \left[-\frac{8}{3} - 2 + 12\right] - \left[9 - \frac{9}{2} - 18\right] \\ &= \frac{22}{3} - \left(-\frac{27}{2}\right) \\ &= \frac{125}{6} \end{aligned}$$

35. D: To draw a box-and-whisker plot from the data, find the median, quartiles, and upper and lower limits.

Stem	Leaves	Key
3	6 799	
4	2|3889	
5	0|11158|	2|123 = 21, 22, 23
6	0 0123	

The median is $\frac{50+51}{2} = 50.5$, the lower quartile is $\frac{42+43}{2} = 42.5$, and the upper quartile is $\frac{58+60}{2} = 59$. The box of the box-and-whisker plot goes through the quartiles, and a line through the box represents the median of the data. The whiskers extend from the box to the lower and upper limits, unless there are any outliers in the set. In this case, there are no outliers, so the box-and-whisker plot in choice A correctly represents the data set.

To draw a pie chart, find the percentage of data contained in each of the ranges shown. There are four out of twenty numbers between 30 and 39, inclusive, so the percentage shown in the pie chart for that range of data is $\frac{4}{20} \times 100\% = 20\%$; there are five values between 40 to 49, inclusive, so the percentage of data for that sector is $\frac{5}{20} \times 100\% = 25\%$; $\frac{6}{20} \times 100\% = 30\%$ of the data is within the range of 50–59, and $\frac{5}{20} \times 100\% = 25\%$ is within the range of 60–69. The pie chart shows the correct percentage of data in each category.

To draw a cumulative frequency histogram, find the cumulative frequency of the data.

Range	Frequency	Cumulative frequency
30–39	4	4
40–49	5	9
50–59	6	15
60–69	5	20

The histogram shows the correct cumulative frequencies. Therefore, all of the graphs represent the data set.

36. A: Nominal data are data that are collected which have no intrinsic quantity or order. For instance, a survey might ask the respondent to identify his or her gender. While it is possible to compare the relative frequency of each response (for example, "most of the respondents are women"), it is not possible to calculate the mean, which requires data to be numeric, or median, which requires data to be ordered. Interval data are both numeric and ordered, so mean and median can be determined, as can the mode, the interval within which there are the most data. Ordinal data has an inherent order, but there is not a set interval between two points. For example, a survey might ask the respondents whether they were very dissatisfied, dissatisfied, neutral, satisfied, or very satisfied with the customer service received. Since the data are not numeric, the mean cannot be calculated, but since ordering the data is possible, the median has context.

37. D: Since there are 100 homes' market times represented in each set, the median time a home spends on the market is between the 50th and 51st data point in each set. The 50th and 51st data points for Zip Code 1 are six months and seven months, respectively, so the median time a house in Zip Code 1 spends on the market is between six and seven months (6.5 months), which by the realtor's definition of market time is a seven-month market time. The 50th and 51st data points for Zip Code 2 are both thirteen months, so the median time a house in Zip Code 2 spends on the market is thirteen months. Therefore, there is a six-month difference between the median of Zip Code 1 and the median of Zip Code 2.

To find the mean market time for 100 houses, find the sum of the market times and divide by 100. If the frequency of a one-month market time is 9, the number 1 is added nine times (1×9), if the frequency of a two-month market time is 10, the number 2 is added ten times (2×10), and so on. So, to find the average market time, divide by 100 the sum of the products of each market time and its corresponding frequency. For Zip Code 1, the mean market time is 7.38 months, which, by the realtor's definition of market time, is an eight-month market time. For Zip Code 2, the mean market time is 12.74, which, by the realtor's definition of market time, is a thirteen-month market time. Therefore, the difference between the mean of Zip Code 1 and the mean of Zip Code 2 is 5 months.

The mode market time is the market time for which the frequency is the highest. For Zip Code 1, the mode market time is three months, and for Zip Code 2, the mode market time is eleven months. Therefore, the median time a house spends on the market in Zip Code 1 is less than the mean time a house spends on the market in Zip Code 1.

38. C: Since each coin toss is an independent event, the probability of the compound event of flipping the coin three times is equal to the product of the probabilities of the individual events. For example, $P(HHH) = P(H) \times P(H) \times P(H)$, $P(HHT) = P(H) \times P(H) \times P(T)$, etc. When a coin is flipped three times, all of the possible outcomes are HHH, HHT, HTH, HTT, THH, THT, TTH, and TTT. Using the data from the all heads and all tails results, calculate an experimental probability $P(H)$:

$$\begin{aligned} P(\text{three heads}) &= P(HHH) \\ &= P(H) \times P(H) \times P(H) \\ &= [P(H)]^3 \\ [P(H)]^3 &= \frac{30}{100} \\ [P(H)] &= \sqrt[3]{0.3} \approx 0.67 \end{aligned}$$

$$\begin{aligned} P(\text{no heads}) &= P(TTT) \\ &= P(T) \times P(T) \times P(T) \\ &= [P(T)]^3 \\ [P(T)]^3 &= \frac{4}{100} \\ [P(T)] &= \sqrt[3]{0.04} \approx 0.34 \\ P(H) &= 1 - P(T) \approx 0.66 \end{aligned}$$

Notice that these calculated values of $P(H)$ are approximately the same. Since 100 is a fairly large sample size for this kind of experiment, the approximation for $P(H)$ ought to be consistent for the compiled data set. Rather than calculating $P(H)$ using the data for one head and two heads, use the average calculated probability to confirm that the number of expected outcomes of one head and two head matches the number of actual outcomes.

$$\begin{aligned} P(\text{one head}) &= P(HTT) + P(THT) + P(TTH) \\ &= 3 \times P(H) \times P(T) \times P(T) \\ &= 3 \times P(H) \times [P(T)]^2 \end{aligned}$$

$$\begin{aligned} P(\text{two heads}) &= P(HHT) + P(HTH) + P(THH) \\ &= 3 \times P(H) \times P(H) \times P(T) \\ &= 3 \times [P(H)]^2 \times P(T) \end{aligned}$$

The number of expected outcomes of getting one head in three coin flips out of 100 trials $100\{3(0.665)[(1-0.665)^2]\} \approx 22$, and the expected outcome getting of two heads in three coin flips out of 100 trials three flips is $100\{3(0.665)^2(1-0.665)\} \approx 44$. Since 22 and 44 are, in fact, the data obtained, 0.665 is indeed a good approximation for $P(H)$ when the coin used in this experiment is tossed.

39. D: A fair coin has a symmetrical binomial distribution which peaks in its center. Since choice C shows a skewed distribution for the fair coin, it cannot be the correct answer. From the frequency histogram given for the misshapen coin, it is evident that the misshapen coin is more likely to land on heads. Therefore, it is more likely that 10 coin flips would result in fewer tails than 10 coin flips of a fair coin; consequently, the probability distribution for the misshapen coin would be higher than the fair coin's distribution toward the smaller number of tails. Choice A shows a probability distribution which peaks at a value of 5 and which is symmetrical with respect to the peak, which verifies that it cannot be correct. Furthermore, in choice A, the sum of the probabilities shown for each number of tails for the misshapen coin is not equal to 1. The distribution for the misshapen coin in choice B is skewed in the wrong direction, favoring tails instead of heads, and must therefore also be incorrect. Choice D shows the correct binomial distribution for the fair coin and the appropriate shift for the misshapen coin.

40. C: When rolling two dice, there is only one way to roll a sum of 2 (rolling a 1 on each die) and 12 (rolling 6 on each die). In contrast, there are two ways to obtain a sum of 3 (rolling a 2 and 1 or a 1 and 2) and 11 (rolling a 5 and 6 or a 6 and 5), three ways to obtain a sum of 4 (1 and 3; 2 and 2; 3 and 1) or 10 (4 and 6; 5 and 5; 6 and 4), and so on. Since the probability of obtaining each sum is inconsistent, this is not a random selection.

41. D: A score of 85 is one standard deviation below the mean. Since approximately 68% of the data is within one standard deviation of the mean, about 32% (100% − 68%) of the data is outside of one standard deviation within the mean. Normally distributed data is symmetric about the mean, which means that about 16% of the data lies below one standard deviation below the mean and about 16% of data lies above one standard deviation above the mean. Therefore, approximately 16% of individuals have IQs less than 85, while approximately 84% of the population has an IQ of at least 85. Since 84% of 300 is 252, about 252 people from the selected group have IQs of at least 85.

42. C: There are nine ways to assign the first digit since it can be any of the numbers 1-9. There are nine ways to assign the second digit since it can be any digit 0-9 except for the digit assigned in place 1. There are eight ways to assign the third number since there are ten digits, two of which have already been assigned. There are seven ways to assign the fourth number, six ways to assign the fifth, five ways to assign the sixth, and four ways to assign the seventh. Multiply to find the total number of combinations.

$$9 \times 9 \times 8 \times 7 \times 6 \times 5 \times 4 = 544{,}320.$$

Another way to approach the problem is to notice that the arrangement of nine digits in the last six places is a sequence without repetition, or a permutation. (Note: this may be called a partial permutation since all of the elements of the set need not be used.) The number of possible sequences of a fixed length r of elements taken from a given set of size n is permutation ${}_nP_r = \frac{n!}{(n-r)!}$. So, the number of ways to arrange the last six digits is ${}_9P_6 = \frac{9!}{(9-6)!} = \frac{9!}{3!} = 60{,}480$. Multiply this number by nine since there are nine possibilities for the first digit of the phone number: ${}_9P_6 \times 9 = 544{,}320$.

43. B: If each of the 4 groups in the class of 20 will contain 3 boys and 2 girls, there must be 12 boys and 8 girls in the class. The number of ways the teacher can select 3 boys from a group of 12 boys is:

$${}_{12}C_3 = \frac{12!}{3!\,(12-3)!} = \frac{12!}{3!\,9!} = \frac{12 \times 11 \times 10 \times 9!}{3!\,9!} = \frac{12 \times 11 \times 10}{3 \times 2 \times 1} = 220$$

The number of ways she can select 2 girls from a group of 8 girls is:

$${}_8C_2 = \frac{8!}{2!\,(8-2)!} = \frac{8!}{2!\,6!} = \frac{8 \times 7 \times 6!}{2!\,6!} = \frac{8 \times 7}{2 \times 1} = 28$$

Since each combination of boys can be paired with each combination of girls, the number of group combinations is $220 \times 28 = 6{,}160$.

44. B: The table below shows the intersections of each set with each of the other sets.

Set	{2,4,6,8,10,12, … }	{1,2,3,4,6,12}	{1,2,4,9}
{2,4,6,8,10,12, … }	{2,4,6,8,10,12, … }	{2,4,6,12}	{2,4}
{1,2,3,4,6,12}	{2,4,6,12}	{1,2,3,4,6,12}	{1,2,4}
{1,2,4,9}	{2,4}	{1,2,4}	{1,2,4,9}

Notice that {2,4} is a subset of {2,4,6,12} and {1,2,4}. So, the intersection of {1,2,4,9} and the even integers is a subset of the intersection of the even integers and the factors of twelve, and the intersection of the set of even integers and {1,2,4,9} is a subset of the intersection of {1,2,4,9} and the factors of twelve. So, while it is not possible to determine which set is A and which is B, set C must be the set of factors of twelve: {1,2,3,4,6,12}.

45. B: The triangle is a right triangle with legs 3 and 4 units long.

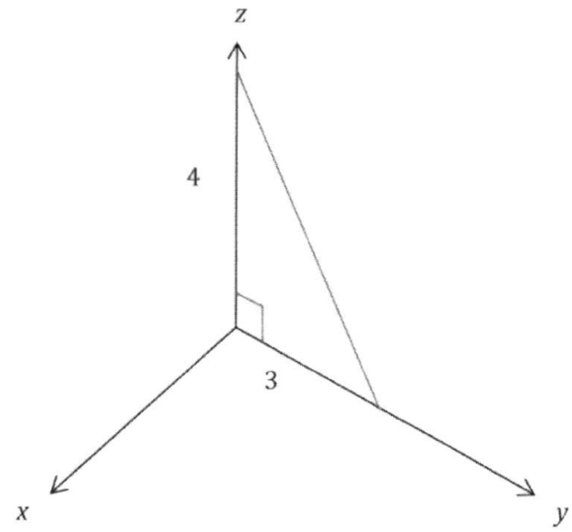

If the triangle is rotated about the z-axis, the solid formed is a cone with a height of 4 and a radius of 3. If the triangle is rotated about the y-axis, the solid formed is a cone with a height of 3 and a radius of 4.

$$V = \frac{1}{3}\pi r^2 h$$
$$V = \frac{1}{3}\pi(3^2)4 \quad V = \frac{1}{3}\pi(4^2)3$$
$$V = 12\pi \qquad V = 16\pi$$

The difference in the volumes of the two cones is $16\pi - 12\pi = 4\pi$ cubic units.

Physics

1. C: The initial gravitational potential energy of the ball is mgh, where h is the height above the ground. At the top of the loop, some of this energy will be converted into kinetic energy $\left(\frac{1}{2}mv_{top}{}^2\right)$. Since its height is $2R$ at the top of the loop, it will have a potential energy here of $mg(2R)$. Using the conservation of energy: $mgh = \frac{1}{2}mv_{top}{}^2 + mg(2R)$. Additionally, in order to maintain a circular path, the centripetal force must equal the gravitational force at the top of the loop: $\frac{(mv_{top}{}^2)}{R} = mg$, which can be rewritten as $v_{top}{}^2 = gR$. Putting this into the energy equation, you find $mgh = \frac{1}{2}m(gR) + mg(2R)$. Dividing m and g from both sides of this equation shows that $h = \frac{1}{2}R + 2R = \frac{5}{2}R$. Answers A, B and C represent choices that testers are likely to find if they do the math incorrectly.

2. A: The total energy of an isolated system is always conserved. However, the mechanical energy may not be, since some mechanical energy could be converted into radiation (light) or heat (through friction). According to Einstein's famous equation $\mathrm{E} = \mathrm{mc}^2$, where E is energy, m is mass, and c is the speed of light, energy can be converted into mass, and vice versa (like in nuclear reactions). This does not affect the conservation of energy law, however, since the mass is considered to have an energy equivalent. This equation does not tell anything about the mechanical energy of a particle; it just shows how much energy would be generated if the mass was converted directly into energy.

3. B: For a positively charged particle, you would use the right hand rule (RHR) to solve this. Since this is an electron, you can either use the left hand rule, or use the RHR and switch the direction of the inducted force. The RHR gives you the direction of a force exerted by a magnetic field on a magnetic field. Holding your right hand flat, the fingers point in the direction of the velocity of a positive charge, the palm points in the direction of the magnetic field, and the thumb points in the direction of the magnetic force. For a negative charge, the force is in the opposite direction, or downward in this case.

4. C: A capacitor connected to a battery with a small internal resistance will charge up very quickly because of the high current flow. Once the potential difference on the two plates becomes equal to the emf of the battery, the electrons will stop flowing from the positive plate to the negative plate and the capacitor will be fully charged up. Connecting the capacitor to a battery with a greater emf will cause the plates to acquire a greater charge. However, the charge is directly proportional to the voltage. The capacitance is the ratio of charge to voltage and depends only on the physical characteristics of the capacitor.

5. A: When electrons drop to the ground level, they emit energy. In the same way, they can absorb energy and jump from the ground state to an excited state, or from an excited state to a more excited state. To completely ionize a Hydrogen atom — for an electron to jump from the ground level and completely escape—takes 13.2 eV. However, it takes less energy to simply jump from the ground level to the first excited state. However, most of the energy needed to escape is used for that first jump. Answer C would be correct if the transition was from $n = 3$ to $n = 2$. Answer B would be correct if the hydrogen atom in the ground state was ionized by the absorption of a photon. Answer D would be correct if the hydrogen atom absorbed a photon and became more excited.

6. D: The third charge, which is positive, will be repelled by the charge of $+2q$ and attracted to the charge of $-q$. For this reason, the third charge can't be between the two other charges and have a net force of 0, since it would always jointly be pushed and pulled towards the negative charge. It must be past the more distant negative charge. If the charge were situated at a distance of $2d$ from the origin, which is distance d from the negative charge, it would have a repulsive force of $F = k(q)(2q)/(2d)^2$ and an attractive force of $F = k(q)(q)/(d)^2$, meaning the attractive force is still too small by half the repulsive force. Thus, the particle must be past the distance of $2d$, or (D). If you solve this distance quadratically, the particle is at $3.41d$.

7. B: The two slits cause the light beams to diffract, that is, spread out instead of traveling in a straight line. As a result, there are two light beams superimposed on one another. When the two light beams constructively interfere, there are bright lines, and when the two light beams destructively interfere, there are dark lines. A chromatic aberration has to do with blurring through a lens due to different colors of light. Doppler shift affects the wavelength of light from moving sources. Total internal reflection is 100% reflection of light at the boundary between certain materials.

8. B: This question is asking about a concave mirror, not a lens. Since light does not pass through a mirror—it only reflects off of it—the different colors of light all bend the same amount. If light was passing through a lens, the different colors would bend slightly different amounts, causing chromatic aberration. That's not the case here. Spherical aberration occurs because the focal point of the mirror changes slightly as you move away from the center (optical axis). Astigmatism occurs when incident rays are not parallel to the optical axis. A circular beam, striking a lens or mirror at an angle to the optical axis, will become a parabola. Distortion concerns magnification and occurs in both mirrors and lenses.

9. B: Fission occurs when the nucleus breaks up into two smaller nuclei. When certain nuclear isotopes absorb a neutron, they become unstable and split, starting the process of fission. The average binding energy per nucleon increases with a fission reaction, and the two new nuclei are more stable than the initial nucleus. The increase in binding energy comes from the changes in mass of the protons and neutrons (note: both protons and neutrons are nucleons). The release of energy is part of the fission reaction, but this does not explain why the fission reaction occurs.

10. C: Cobalt-63 has too many neutrons to be stable. By emitting a beta particle (aka an electron, one of the neutrons in the cobalt is converted to a proton, thereby maintaining the mass number but changing the atomic number from 27 (cobalt) to 28 (nickel). In addition, some energy is radiated away in the form of gamma radiation. Electron emission is usually associated with the emission of gamma rays because the daughter nucleus is not likely to be in a ground state. The daughter nucleus, in other words, is likely to be unstable and emit a gamma ray.

11. D: Because you do not know the exact distribution of heights, answer D is correct. The deviation of a measurement is the difference between the mean (average measurement) and the measurement. The standard deviation is the square root of the mean of the deviations squared. On average, about 68% of a sample will fall within one standard deviation. So if the standard deviation is 0.05 meters, ABOUT 68% of the students will stand between 1.64 ± 0.05 meters. But this is only true if you have a fairly normal distribution of values. Similarly, this does not mean that half of the students are necessarily taller or shorter than the average. Since it is an average, you could have a class with a 20-foot giant and seven 5-foot-tall students and have an average that is a fairly large 6.857 feet. Answer C refers to the Mode, which looks for the most popular value.

12. B: Because momentum is conserved in collisions, the combined initial momentums of the two skaters needs to equal the final momentum of the two skaters together.

$$p_1 = m_1 v_1 = 75 \text{ kg} \times 5 \text{ m/s} = 375 \text{ kg} \cdot \text{m/s}$$
$$p_2 = m_2 v_2 = 100 \text{ kg} \times 4 \frac{\text{m}}{\text{s}} = 400 \text{ kg} \cdot \text{m/s}$$

Remember, the first skater was moving eastward and the second skater was moving northward, which means that we need to find their combined momentum in the final direction they will be moving (northeast). This can be done by using the Pythagorean theorem.

$$p_i = \sqrt{375^2 + 400^2} \approx 548$$

Therefore, the initial momentum of the system is approximately 548 kg · m/s. This is equal to the final momentum of the system. Since the collision is inelastic, the two masses need to be added together before they are multiplied by the final velocity.

$$\begin{aligned} p_f &= (m_1 + m_2) v_f \\ 548 &= (75 + 100) v_f \\ 548 &= 175 v_f \\ v_f &\approx 3.1 \text{ m/s} \end{aligned}$$

Therefore, the final velocity, and speed since the velocity is positive, is approximately 3.1 m/s.

13. B: Power is the amount of work done divided by the time it took to do the work. A kilowatt-hour is a unit of work. A 5 Kw engine running for 12 hours produces $5 \times 12 = 60$ kilowatt-hours of work. At $0.06 per Kw-h, this is $60 \times 0.06 = \$3.60$. The other answers all arise from math mistakes.

14. C: The phase will cycle through 2π radians. Therefore, $(5.0 \text{ Hz})t = 2\pi$ and $t = \frac{2\pi}{5} =$ 1.26 seconds.

15. C: Three full waves fit into the pipe, according to the question description. The wavelength of the third harmonic in this pipe organ is $\frac{1.2 \text{ m}}{1.5 \text{ waves}} = 0.8$ m. Using the wave equation $(v = \lambda f)$, $\text{f} = \frac{340 \text{ m/s}}{0.8 \text{ m}} = 425$ Hz.

16. A: For standing waves, the string must be fixed at both ends. The wavelength at the fundamental frequency is 4 meters and the wavelength when the string resonates at the fourth harmonic is 1 meter. Using the wave equation $v = \lambda f$, the frequency at the fourth harmonic is $\frac{v}{1 \text{ m}} =$ 50 Hz. Hence the necessary speed is 50 m/s. Furthermore, the mass per unit length is $\frac{0.01 \text{ kg}}{2 \text{ meters}} =$ 0.005 kg/m. Thus, the tension is the string is $v^2 \times \mu = 50^2 \times 0.005 = 12.5$ newtons.

17. A: Pascal's law states that the pressure on the input piston is equal to the pressure on the output piston. (To move the truck, of course, the input piston moves a much greater distance than the output piston.) Since the pressure depends on the area of the pistons, and the area is πr^2, one needs only find the ratio of the two areas to find the necessary force. Since the diameter is twice the radius, one can simplify this step by taking the ratio of the square of the diameters. $\frac{2^2}{24^2} = 0.007$. Multiplying this by the weight of the car gets $0.007 \times 3{,}500 \text{ N} = 24$ N. It is also important to note that the point of a hydraulic lift is to reduce the force, not increase it.

18. C: If the sub stays at a constant depth, its buoyant force must be equal to its weight. If the buoyant force were larger, it would rise. If the buoyant force were lower, it would sink. All objects underwater experience a buoyant force, so it cannot be zero.

19. B: Using Newton's second law $F = ma$, the acceleration of all three blocks, which have a combined mass of 9 kg, is $a = \frac{25 \text{ N}}{9 \text{ kg}} = 2.78 \text{ m/s}^2$. The force pulling the rear block is $F = ma =$ $4 \text{ kg} \times 2.78 \text{ m/s}^2 = 11.1$ N. Another way of thinking of this is the tension represents $\frac{4}{9}$ of the total force, since the total mass is 9 kg and the rear block has a mass of 4 kg. This must equal the tension on the rope pulling on that block. Answer C is the tension of the string connecting the 3 kg and 2 kg masses. Answer D is the tension on the rope pulling all 3 masses.

20. B: The weight of the art is $200 \text{ kg} \times 9.8 \text{ m/s}^2 = 1{,}960$ N. This is the total force pulling DOWN on the wires. However, the tension acts along a 40° angle, and the vertical force is $T \sin\theta$. Additionally, there are two ends to the wire, which splits the tension, meaning the weight is spread across $2T \sin\theta$. So $2T \sin\theta = w$. Therefore, $T = \frac{1}{2} \times \frac{1{,}960 \text{ N}}{\sin(40°)} = 1{,}525$ N. Note: There's also a horizontal component to the tension forces, each expressed as $T \cos\theta$. The net force of the left and right tensions is zero. Answer A is calculated using the cos(40°) instead of sin(40°).

21. A: A standing wave remains stationary, and the fixed points at both ends are the wave's nodes. Nevertheless, a standing wave with nodes at both ends of the string can have several forms. It may have one anti-node (i.e., it will arc across), two anti-nodes (this looks like a sine wave), three anti-nodes (with 1.5 sine waves), etc. However, waves with just one anti-node will have the longest wavelength and thus the smallest frequency. For a wave with one anti-node, the string will have only one-half of a wave, so 20 m represents a half-wavelength, and the full wavelength is 40 m. Using the wave equation ($v = \lambda f$) gives the correct answer. $f = \frac{v}{\lambda} = \frac{4 \text{ m/s}}{40 \text{ m}} = 0.1 \text{ Hz}$.

22. C: The force $F = qvB \sin\theta = (1.6 \times 10^{-19} \text{ coulombs})(8.0 \times 10^6 \text{ m/s})(0.5 \text{ T}) \sin(45°) = 4.5 \times 10^{-13} \text{ N}$.

23. B: For resistors in series, the total resistance is the sum of their individual resistances. For resistors in parallel, the total resistance is given by $\frac{1}{R} = \frac{1}{R_1} + \frac{1}{R_2} + \cdots$. First, the bottom two resistors have a total resistance of $2\ \Omega + 4\ \Omega = 6\ \Omega$. Then add this in parallel with the 3 Ohm resistor. $\frac{1}{R} = \frac{1}{3} + \frac{1}{6} = \frac{1}{2}$. So $R = 2\ \Omega$ for the bottom three elements. To find the total resistance, add this in series to the top resistor, for a total $R = 10\ \Omega + 2\Omega = 12\Omega$.

24. C: The pressure of water at a depth h is given by ρgh where ρ is the density of water. Here $P = (1{,}000 \text{ kg/m}^3 \times 9.8 \text{ m/s}^2 \times 14 \text{ m}) = 1.37 \times 10^5 \text{ N/m}^2$. To find the force of the water on the window, multiply this pressure by the window's area. $F = \pi(1 \text{ m})^2 \times 1.37 \times 10^5 \text{ N/m}^2 = 4.3 \times 10^5 \text{ N}$.

25. C: In an ideal fluid, from the conservation of mass, ρvA is constant. Since the area (A) decreases by a factor $\frac{3^2}{5^2} = 0.36$, the speed increases by $\frac{5^2}{3^2}$. So $6 \text{ m/s} \times \frac{5^2}{3^2} = 16.7 \text{ m/s}$. Incompressible means the density (ρ) is a constant. An ideal fluid has no viscosity, there is no rotational flow, and the flow is the same throughout the liquid, so answer D is not correct.

Chemistry

1. A: The kinetic energy of the gas molecules is directly proportional to the temperature. If the temperature decreases, so does the molecular motion. A decrease in temperature will not necessarily mean a gas condenses to a liquid. Neither the mass nor the density is impacted, as no material was added or removed, and the volume remained the same.

2. B: The ideal gas law PV = nRT is rearranged to solve for V, and we get $\text{V} = \frac{\text{nRT}}{\text{P}}$. R is the gas constant, $\frac{0.08206 \text{ L atm}}{\text{mol K}}$, and the Celsius temperature must be converted to Kelvin, by adding 273 to 25 °C to obtain 298 K. The pressure must be converted to atmospheres, which 101 kPa is essentially 1 atm (0.9967 atm). Plugging the numbers into the equation, we get $\text{V} = 1{,}000 \text{ mol} \times \frac{\left(\frac{0.08206 \text{ L atm}}{\text{mol K}}\right)(298 \text{ K})}{1 \text{ atm}}$, which gives V = 24,453 L. A liter is a cubic decimeter (dm^3), and when converted, this gives $\text{V} = 24.5 \text{ m}^3$.

3. C: Graham's law of diffusion allows one to calculate the relative diffusion rate between two different gases based on their masses.

4. D: London dispersion forces are the weakest interparticle forces. These interactions occur in all molecules due to unequal electron density around the nucleus, which results in a momentary dipole. Dipole-dipole interactions are those between two polar molecules. The more positive portion of one molecule is attracted to the negative portion of a different molecule. Hydrogen bonding is a stronger type of dipole-dipole interaction which occurs between a hydrogen in one molecule and a nitrogen, oxygen or fluorine atom in another molecule. Hydrogen bonding only occurs between molecules containing H-F, H-O, or H-N bonds. Ionic bonds are the strongest interparticle forces. In ionic compounds, a positive ion is attracted to a negative ion. NaCl is entirely ionic with full charge separation, and the ions are tightly bound to each other in an organized crystalline network.

5. A: Since there are 7 moles of neon out of a total of 14 moles of gas in the cylinder, the partial pressure of neon will always be 50% of the total pressure, regardless of the temperature.

6. C: The most electronegative atoms are found near the top right of the periodic table. Fluorine has a high electronegativity, while Cesium, located near the bottom left of the table, has a low electronegativity.

7. C: As the temperature drops to –5 °C, the water vapor condenses to a liquid, and then to a solid. The partial pressure of a solid is much less than that of the corresponding gas. The argon is still a gas at –5 °C, so almost all the pressure in the cylinder is due to argon. Since the partial pressure of the water decreases as it turns to a solid, the totally pressure in the cylinder also decreases.

8. A: Heat is absorbed by the solid during melting; therefore, ΔH is positive. Going from a solid to a liquid greatly increases the freedom of the particles, which increases the entropy, so ΔS is also positive.

9. A: The higher the temperature of the liquid, the greater the solubility of the solid, while the higher the temperature, the lower the solubility of the gas.

10. D: 100 mL of a 0.1 M solution of NaOH contains 0.01 moles of NaOH. That means 0.01 moles of acid are required to completely neutralize the solution. The MW of sulfuric acid is 98, so 0.98 g of sulfuric acid is 0.01 mole. But since sulfuric acid has two equivalents of acid per mole, only 0.005 mole of the acid is required or 0.49 g.

11. D: Octane is a nonpolar hydrocarbon with little or no water solubility. Butanol is an alcohol with a small amount of solubility due to its polar —OH group. Ethanol is a smaller, more polar alcohol that is very soluble in water. NaCl is an ionic salt that is highly soluble in water.

12. D: This problem is best solved using the decay formula, $\text{remaining} = \text{initial}(0.5)^{\left(\frac{t}{t_{\text{half-life}}}\right)}$.

$$1\text{ mg}(0.5)^{\left(\frac{20{,}000}{5{,}730}\right)} \approx 0.09\text{ mg}$$

However, if a student is careful in their reasoning, this problem can be solved without the formula. Since after 3 half-lives $\frac{1}{8}$ would remain, after 4 half-lives $\frac{1}{16}$ would remain, and 3.5 is right in the middle, the amount remaining should be close to the average of the values:

$$\left(\frac{1}{8}+\frac{1}{16}\right) \div 2 = \frac{3}{32} = 0.09375$$

This makes 0.09 mg the best option for material remaining after 3.5 half-lives.

13. D: Isotopes of the same element must have the same chemical behavior, and (A), (B), and (C) all represent, in one form or another, chemical behavior. Isotopes differ in mass, and this can be used to separate them by some appropriate physical property.

14. B: In a nuclear chain reaction, free neutrons released from nuclear fission cause a nucleus to split and release more neutrons.

15. A: Radioactive decay converts mass into energy ($E = mc^2$). The mass of products is always less than that of the starting materials since some mass is now energy.

16. B: Phosphorus is in the third period, so the outermost levels must be 3*s*, 3*p*. Phosphorus is in Group 5A, which indicates that it has 5 valence electrons. To fill the 3*s* and 3*p*, 2 electrons first fill the *s* orbital, and then the remaining 3 electrons enter the *p* orbitals, making $3s^23p^3$.

17. C: Hund's rule states that electrons must populate empty orbitals of similar energy before pairing up. The Aufbau principle states that electrons must fill lower energy orbitals before filling higher energy orbitals. The Pauli Exclusion Principle states that no two electrons in the same atom can have the same four quantum numbers, and, therefore, two electrons in the same orbital will have opposite spins.

18. A: Sublimation is the process of a solid changing directly into a gas without entering the liquid phase. Fusion refers to melting a solid into a liquid. Diffusion is the process of a material dispersing throughout another. Condensation is generally a gas turning into a liquid.

19. D: Each oxygen has an oxidation state of –2. Potassium (K) only exists in compounds as +1. Therefore, for the molecule to have a neutral charge, the Mn must be in a +7 oxidation state.

$$4(-2) + 1 + 7 = 0$$

None of the other options would result in a neutral molecule.

20. B: The nitrogen is missing its lone pair of electrons, and should have two dots above it. A correct Lewis structure shows how the atoms are connected to each other as well as all of the valence electrons in the compound, so the abbreviated methyl group is also incorrect.

21. A: By comparing the products to the reactants, there must be at least two Al atoms in the starting material, and at least three sulfate groups. Therefore, a coefficient of 2 must be placed in front of $Al(OH)_3$ and a coefficient of 3 must be placed in front of H_2SO_4. To make the number of hydrogen and oxygen atoms equal on both sides of the equation, a coefficient of 6 must be placed in front of H_2O.

22. B: Since the conversion of B to C is the slow step, this is the only one that determines the reaction rate law. Therefore, the rate law will be based on B since it is the only reactant in producing C.

23. C: Because there are 2 moles of gas on the reactant side and 1 mole of gas on the product side, a pressure increase will increase the forward reaction rate force the reaction to go further to the right. This, in turn, lowers gas pressure to restore equilibrium. Reaction order is not affected by environment changes.

24. D: To make a buffer, a weak acid and its conjugate base or a weak base and its conjugate acid are commonly used. Buffers work by using the common-ion effect and result in little change in the pH when an acid or a base is added. HCl/NaOH is a strong acid/strong base combination and will not result in a buffer solution. Although the $HNO_3/NaNO_3$ and $H_2SO_4/NaHSO_4$ mixtures are conjugate acid/base pairs, both HNO_3 and H_2SO_4 are strong acids, not weak acids. Neither of these solutions would result in a buffer. Only the NaH_2PO_4/Na_2HPO_4 mixture would result in a buffer as it is a combination of a weak acid and its conjugate base.

25. C: The first is an alkyne, which contains a triple bond between carbon atoms. The second is a ketone and contains a carbon-oxygen double bond. The third is an alkene, which has a double bond between two carbon atoms. The fourth is an imide, which contains a double bond between two nitrogen atoms.

Engineering

1. D: Option D is correct because according to the rules of propagation of error, if you take the sum or difference of two values a and b with respective uncertainties δa and δb, then the uncertainty of the result Q is equal to $\delta Q = \sqrt{(\delta a)^2 + (\delta b)^2}$. In this case then, $\delta Q = \sqrt{(0.03\text{ cm})^2 + (0.04\text{ cm})^2} = 0.05\text{ cm}$.

Option A is incorrect because it simply takes the difference of the uncertainties. **Option B is incorrect** because it takes the square root of the difference of the squares, $\sqrt{(\delta a)^2 - (\delta b)^2}$. **Option C is incorrect** because it takes the average of the uncertainties of the two values. None of these is the proper method of propagating uncertainty.

2. C: Option C is correct because it correctly satisfies the equilibrium conditions. The most straightforward way of solving this problem is using the net moment around the point where the beam meets the wall. (Note that the wall exerts an unknown force on the beam at this point, but if we find the torque around this point we don't have to find this force.) There are three contributions to the moment: the weight of the sign, the weight of the beam itself (which, since the beam is uniform, we can consider to apply at its center), and the tension of the guyline. Each of these moments can be calculated as $\tau = F \cdot r \cdot \sin\theta$, where F is the force, r is the distance between the line of action of the force and the point around which we are calculating the torque, and θ is the angle the force makes with the line from that point to the point where the force is applied. (Note that for both the weight of the sign and the weight of the beam, $\theta = 90°$, so $\sin\theta = 1$.) The moment is positive if it would tend to cause the beam to rotate in a counter-clockwise direction, and negative if clockwise. For the system to be in equilibrium, the net moment must be zero. We therefore have:

$$\tau_{guyline} + \tau_{beam} + \tau_{sign} = 0$$

$$T(4.0\text{ m})(\sin 30°) - (m_{beam}g)(2.0\text{ m}) - (m_{sign}g)(4.0\text{ m}) = 0$$

$$T(4.0\text{ m})(0.5) - (20\text{ kg})(9.8\text{ m/s}^2)(2.0\text{ m}) - (50\text{ kg})(9.8\text{ m/s}^2)(4.0\text{ m}) = 0$$

$$T(2.0\text{ m}) - 390\text{ N m} - 1960\text{ N m} = 0$$

$$T(2.0\text{ m}) = 2350\text{ N m}$$

$$T \approx 1200\text{ N m}$$

Option A is incorrect because it is calculated using the cosine of the angle instead of the sine (or equivalently using the sine of the angle with the normal rather than the angle with the beam). **Option B is incorrect** because it ignores the weight of the beam itself, using only the weight of the sign and the tension in the guyline. **Option D is incorrect** because it is calculated by setting the sum of vertical forces to zero, but incorrectly ignores the (unknown) vertical force exerted on the beam by the wall.

3. B: Students should wear hearing and eye protection at all times in the classroom while the lab is taking place. This type of rule does not inhibit any other station as all of the required equipment can be used with eye and hearing protection. Other equipment, such as thick gloves, can hinder other portions of the lab and should not be used when unnecessary. In some cases, the use of safety equipment in the wrong application can be a safety hazard, such as gloves or long aprons with spinning or cutting equipment. It may be helpful to allow students to work in separate areas if the space and supervision is available, but it is more feasible to provide protective equipment within the same space when the lab work is a rotating station format.

4. D: Option D is correct because it will correctly have the robot stop when it comes within ten inches of the obstacle. Consider what the code does: It first starts the robot moving, then finds the distance to the obstacle. (All four options start with those steps.) If it is already within ten inches of the obstacle, the while loop is never entered, and it executes the stop() command. Otherwise, after a brief wait, the robot checks the distance again, and if it is still more than ten inches away from the obstacle, it repeats the check after a brief wait (resetting the variable appropriately). Once the check does show it to be within 10 inches of the obstacle, it will exit the loop, falling through to the next command, which will stop the robot.

Further improvements to the code are possible; it may be desirable, for example, to check at the beginning whether the robot is already within ten inches of the target, and if so to not start the robot in the first place. However, even if it may not be ideal, option D is clearly the best of the four options, and the only one that exhibits the described behavior.

Option A is incorrect because the robot will only check once whether it is within 10 inches of the obstacle; if it passes that first check, it will continue moving regardless of how close it may pass to the target thereafter. **Option B is incorrect** because if the robot starts out more than 10 inches from the target, the execution will immediately pass out of the while loop and no further checks will be carried out; as with option A, it will then continue moving regardless of its distance to the target in the future. (On the other hand, if it starts out less than 10 inches from the target, it will continue to measure the distance even though it's no longer moving.) **Option C is incorrect** because it fails to set the value of the measure variable within the while loop. It will continue to check whether its *initial* distance from the target is greater than 10 inches, and so, as with options A and B, if it starts out more than 10 inches from the target it will keep moving regardless of its distance to the target later.

5. A: Option A is correct because straight-line appreciation assumes that the value of an asset decreases by a constant amount, d_t, each year of its useful life until it reaches its salvage value. That amount d_t is its annual depreciation expense. Formulaically, if we call the asset's book value B, its salvage value S, and its useful life in years N, then we can write $S = B - Nd_t$. Solving for d_t gives us $d_t = \frac{B-S}{N}$. Using the given values, we have $d_t = \frac{\$12000-\$4000}{10} = \$800$.

Option B is incorrect because it simply divides the book value by the useful life, without taking into account the salvage value. **Option C is incorrect** because it is calculated using the Sum-of-Years-Digits depreciation method instead of straight-line depreciation; while this is in fact the correct value for the depreciation expense in the first year using the SOYD method, the problem specified that the straight-line method was to be used. **Option D is incorrect** because it adds the salvage value to the book value before dividing by the useful life instead of subtracting it.

6. C: Each of these assignments reflects workforce skills, but option C would best improve their understanding of the actual experience and responsibilities they can expect in the workplace. An interview would be useful for improving understanding of the pre-hire experience but not the workplace. Discussions about ethics concepts are helpful, but ethical decision-making does not comprise the full workplace experience. Dressing well for a job can be important; however, requiring students to dress professionally at school does not yield much varied experience for the student, and it may be difficult to implement or unreasonable to ask of students on a weekly basis.

7. C: A capstone project is a cumulative project that takes place over the course of time, guiding a student through different phases to complete a large objective, such as performing research or designing something. This is an excellent method for both instructing and assessing a student throughout a unit, acting as both a formative and summative assessment. A rubric is usually employed with capstone projects to ensure more objective grading. Students periodically submit their work, which is graded and given back for the next step. This is distinct from a portfolio, which is made up of several smaller works. A field-learning project is generally more open to direction from a field mentor, and may be made up of smaller experiences or larger experiences and isn't as reliable as an assessment method, despite its authenticity. A research report and presentation does not generally lend itself to a design assignment, as it is not directly related to creation of new content or innovation as much as it is related to a review of existing information.

8. A: Option A is correct because casting refers to the creation of metal objects by pouring molten metal into a mold, while molding involves a similar process using molten plastic.

Option B is incorrect because both casting and molding are neither additive nor subtractive. An additive process involves adding more material to an object, as with 3D printing. A subtractive process involves the removal of material; machining processes such as drilling and milling are subtractive. Neither of these describes casting or molding. **Option C is incorrect** because both casting and molding involve letting a liquid set in a form; the main difference is in the nature of that liquid. **Option D is incorrect** because neither casting nor molding is done after joining or similar processes. Casting may be followed by other manufacturing processes such as machining or joining; molding usually results in a finished product with no further steps necessary.

9. B: Option B is correct because it correctly interprets the meanings of the markings on the micrometer. Each of the main divisions on the sleeve of the micrometer represents 0.1"; each is divided into four subdivisions, so each subdivision represents 0.025". The reading on the sleeve comes from the last line not covered by the thimble. This is the third line after the 0.3" mark, which represents 0.3" + 3×0.025" = 0.375".

For further division, we look at the markings on the thimble. The thimble bears markings from 0 to 24, each representing 0.001". (Only half of them are, of course, visible on each side of the thimble.) We read the highest marking under the long line on the sleeve; in this case that is the second marking after 10, so this marking represents 0.012". Adding that to the reading from the sleeve, we get 0.375" + 0.012" = 0.387". To get the final digit, we look at which of the horizontal markings on the sleeve is best aligned with one of the lines on the thimble. In this case, that's the seventh marking up (the one between the lines marked 6 and 8), so the final digit is a 7. The full reading of the micrometer is 0.3877".

Option A is incorrect because it misinterprets the third line after the 0.3" as representing 0.03" rather than 0.075"—as if each of the four subdivisions represented only 0.01" instead of 0.025". **Option C is incorrect** because it uses the first line hidden by the sleeve (0.4") instead of the last line *not* hidden by it (0.375"). **Option D is incorrect** because it makes the same mistake as option C, and in addition reads the mark on the thimble lined up with the top horizontal line on the sleeve rather than the one lined up with the long central line.

10. B: Option B is correct because a galvanometer is an instrument that measures electric current. It differs from an ammeter in that the galvanometer shows both the direction and magnitude of the current (though its measurement of the current may be less precise).

Options A, C, and D are incorrect because they name other electrical properties that are not measured by a galvanometer.

11. C: The most reasonable and applicable policy for this type of activity is to review possible related hazards before going into the field. Depending on the location and duration of the activity, there could be weather-related risks, such as heat or cold, or wildlife-related. The environment may be home to animals and insects that students should be aware of; for instance, pinecones and pine straw frequently house spiders. Students are unlikely to need particular personal protective equipment, such as gloves and bags. A buddy system may not be necessary in a short field excursion. This should be considered, but not always employed if the group is small enough or the environment is not one that requires that type of safeguard. Behavior policies should be well-established, but does not always directly relate to safety in the field.

12. A: Since there is no available standard of permissible noise exposure for seven hours, we must rely on the standard for eight hours, which allows for 90dBA, so the unit chosen must have a sound level rating lower than 90dBA. Since the laboratory is 1,200 square feet, the unit must be able to cycle 1,200 cfm to provide proper ventilation. The only unit available that meets a minimum of 1,200 cfm and operates under 90 dBA is the Centrigrade Extractor. Depending on other machinery used simultaneously, teachers using the ventilation hood must take into account the cumulative sound level of multiple machines when teaching.

13. C: Option C is correct because the fact that cars allowed cheap long-distance travel made it more economical for urban areas to spread out widely into peripheral areas from which the automobile ensured the urban centers were still accessible—a phenomenon often called urban sprawl. The seeds of suburbanization had already been in place to some degree before automobiles were invented, but the automobile facilitated and accelerated the process. While this allowed people to live in low-density communities that many found pleasant, it had the unfortunate side effects of increasing travel times and traffic congestion and causing environmental damage.

Option A is incorrect because while it's true that the development of the automobile created new jobs, this could hardly be considered a *negative* consequence. This seems more appropriately counted as a *positive* consequence of the development of the automobile. **Option B is incorrect** because early cars did not run on electricity, and even today electrical cars are very much in the minority, and not a significant drain on the electrical grid. There is no reason that the widespread use of the automobile would have led to electrical systems becoming overtaxed. **Option D is incorrect** because long-distance communications had already been in place before the invention of the automobile, so it could not have delayed their invention: the telegraph was invented in the 1830s; the first automobile was not created until the 1880s. Besides, today long-distance communication systems such as telephones and the internet are still widely used; it doesn't seem that the automobile is doing anything to suppress them.

14. A: Option A is correct; of the given choices, calculation of costs should come first. A computer-integrated engineering process begins with the use of computer-aided design to develop the product; after this, a prototype is created. The calculation of costs for the manufacture of the actual product comes just after the creation of the prototype, perhaps concurrent with the determination of the hardware that will be necessary for the manufacture.

Option B is incorrect because the manufacturing clearly cannot take place before the purchase of the materials; the product cannot be manufactured without the materials it is to be manufactured from. **Option C is incorrect** because the purchase of materials does not take place until after the costs are calculated so the amount that must be spent is known. **Option D is incorrect** because quality control is one of the *last* steps in the process, just before the product distribution (assuming the product passes the quality control check) and the subsequent updating of financial records.

15. B: Option B is correct; to find the average value of a function over a given interval of time, we integrate that function over the interval and then divide by the length of the interval. To find the average value of a periodic function, we can find its average over an interval of one period. The period of the function $\sin x$ is 2π, but the period of $|\sin x|$ is just π. The period of $|\sin(0.02t)|$ is therefore $\pi/0.02 = 50\pi$. So we can use the following equation to find the average value of the function in m^3/min:

$$\begin{aligned} |Q| &= \frac{1}{50\pi}\int_0^{50\pi} 2{,}000|\sin(0.02t)|\,dt \\ &= \frac{40}{\pi}\int_0^{50\pi} |\sin(0.02t)|dt \end{aligned}$$

In the interval $0 \le t \le 50\pi$, $\sin(0.02t)$ is nonnegative, so we can dispense with the absolute value sign:

$$\begin{aligned} |Q| &= \frac{40}{\pi}\int_0^{50\pi} \sin(0.02t)\,dt \\ &= \frac{40}{\pi}\left[\frac{1}{0.02}(-\cos(0.02t))\right]_0^{50\pi} \\ &= \frac{2{,}000}{\pi}[-\cos(0.02t)]_0^{50\pi} \\ &= \frac{2{,}000}{\pi}((-\cos(\pi)) - (-\cos(0))) \\ &= \frac{2{,}000}{\pi}(-(-1) - (-1)) \\ &= \frac{2{,}000}{\pi}(2) \\ &= \frac{4{,}000}{\pi} \\ &= 1{,}270\ \text{m}^3/\text{min} \end{aligned}$$

Option A is incorrect because it uses the wrong interval; it is the average value of the function over the interval $[0, \pi]$, which is not the period of $Q(t)$. **Option C is incorrect** because it simply repeats the constant factor in the function but ignores the time-dependent part; this would give the correct answer if the time-dependent part of the function averaged to a value of 1, but here that's not the case. **Option D is incorrect** because it gives the value of the integral but does not divide by the length of the interval to find the average.

16. C: The best listed choice is wooden craft sticks as it is inexpensive for the school district to provide and does not require any special tools to assemble. Simple white glue or wood glue is effective and safe for home use. The final assembly should be reasonably durable for transportation.

Extruded aluminum is cost prohibitive for students or most school districts to provide for each student. This may be a worthy expectation for an in-class activity, but it is likely too large, too durable, and is not very flexible for small-scale modeling. Plastic straws are a good second-choice, but they are not as durable or cooperative with simple glues, which make them less safe and accessible as a building material. PVC is the most challenging to work with out of these materials and would require special tools to cut and would require many fittings, which could make this material less monetarily feasible. Furthermore, most PVC pipe is likely too large to be an effective small-scale modeling material.

17. D: Option D is correct because the main purpose of an engineer's professional portfolio is to demonstrate the engineer's knowledge, accomplishments, and capabilities to a prospective employer. Showing the design documents to a successful project is one way to do that. An engineer's portfolio should include materials like a resume or CV, a listing of any awards the engineer has received, and a brief personal statement about the engineer's goals and objectives—but direct evidence of the engineer's past accomplishments is also definitely useful to include. **Option A is incorrect** because employers are not likely to want to look over every college class an engineer took. Certainly employers want to know about a candidate's degrees, and perhaps the applicant's GPA (especially for recent graduates), and any academic honors the engineer received, but they don't need to see the full transcripts unless they request them. **Option B is incorrect** because while letters of recommendation may be helpful, they would generally be submitted separately and not included in the portfolio. **Option C is incorrect** because writing computer code is not a core part of the job description of an electrical engineer. A description of a computer program could be an appropriate part of the portfolio of a *computer* engineer, though even then a complete listing of the code could be unwieldy, and it might be better to just include a description of the program—or perhaps the program itself, for an electronic portfolio.

18. B: The jigsaw approach to cooperative learning refers to a two-phase instructional method in which the class is divided into small groups that are assigned distinctive topics to study and report on. These groups are responsible for educating themselves about their assigned topic and becoming the experts on that topic or perspective. The groups are then blended with members of other groups for discussion of the various ideas, making it an excellent method for independent investigation and efficient use of class time as the whole class benefits from the knowledge that each group attains. The jigsaw approach is effective with most subjects and can fit with conceptual or practical topics, as long as the topics can be subdivided into smaller ideas to be considered. Drawbacks of this method are that the impetus of learning is placed on the individual students and the groups, which means that the teacher needs to be diligent to include a specific and measurable learning objective and employ the use of a rubric to ensure that grading is fair and clear.

Jigsaw Approach to Cooperative Learning

Phase 1: Focus groups learn about individual target topics.

1	1	2	2	3	3	4	4
1	1	2	2	3	3	4	4

Phase 2: Task groups bring their knowledge together to accomplish a specific task or objective.

1	2	1	2	1	2	1	2
3	4	3	4	3	4	3	4

19. C: The purpose of a short grouping of brief presentations of a variety of career options is to help students understand what is available to them. Whereas seeing real-world applications of the concepts they have been learning in class would be extremely valuable, short presentations do not provide enough depth or hands-on experience to communicate that sort of information. Instead, internships or shadowing of a single professional would be more helpful. It is best to present information when the information is most useful to the students, so timing this unit before a career fair is very valuable as the students are more likely to be able to put the information into action.

20. A: Option A is correct because Generator 1 produces more electrical energy per unit of heat energy input. This is the definition of thermal efficiency—the higher the thermal efficiency, the less energy must be used to do the same amount of work, or in this case to generate the same amount of electricity.

A standard method for calculating the thermal efficiency of a generator is to first find the *heat rate*, the amount of input energy required to generate one kWh of electricity. Although other units are used elsewhere, in the US heat rate is usually measured in Btu/kWh, or British thermal units per kilowatt-hour. The heat rate of generator 1 is 20,000 Btu/20 kWh = 10,000 Btu/kWh. The heat rate of generator 2 is 60,000 Btu/5 kWh = 12,000 Btu/kWh.

We can then find the thermal efficiency by dividing 3,412 Btu/kWh by the heat rate—3,412 being the number of Btu in one kWh of electricity. This means the efficiency of Generator 1 is 3,412/10,000 $\approx$ 0.34, or 34%, and the efficiency of Generator 2 is 3,412/12,000 $\approx$ 0.28, or 28%. However, it's not actually necessary to perform this last step to answer the question; since the thermal efficiency is inversely proportional to the heat rate, we know without calculating the exact efficiencies that the generator with the lower heat rate must have the higher efficiency.

Options B and C are incorrect because they misstate which generator has the higher thermal efficiency. **Option D is incorrect** because the question says nothing of either the input energy or the output electricity of either generator changing with time. This means the efficiencies of the generators also don't change with time, so which generator is more efficient is not time dependent; there's no reason one should be more efficient in the "short term" and the other in the "long term".

21. C: Option C is correct because the maintenance of a public rail system is ultimately a political matter, and is best addressed through political channels. While many engineers may prefer to remain apolitical, the fact is that engineering, like other human pursuits, exists in a political context, as well as an economic, cultural, and environmental one. Engineers have lobbying organizations such as the American Society of Civil Engineers.

Option A is incorrect because staging a train accident would be not only difficult but dangerous, and may well be counterproductive. Rather than call attention to the real problems with the rail system, it could be seen as a wasteful publicity stunt. **Option B is incorrect** because public infrastructure is most appropriately paid for with public funds. It would be very unlikely that the engineers could raise enough money through online fundraising to pay for it, and even if they did they would still need the city's permission to carry out the repairs. **Option D is incorrect** because while a letter to the editor may help raise awareness of the issues with the rail system, it is not the most effective means of doing so. Rather than publish a general letter that may or may not be read by anyone in a position to do anything about the issues, it is likely to be more useful to directly address the officials who are in such a position.

22. B: The utilization percentages in the chart refer to what percentage of a component's capacity is being used for a task. Higher numbers, therefore, mean that the component is working harder than those with lower numbers. With the metrics recorded, the computer's memory seemed to be the most strained component. Memory, also known as Random Access Memory (RAM), refers to the amount of information a computer can process at one time. This computer's RAM was likely overtasked by the application in question or by other applications being used at the same time. CPU refers to the computer's main processing unit, and GPU is a computer's graphics-dedicated processing speed. The SSD refers to a solid-state drive that is used for storing information on a computer. Some computers have a similar component called a hard disk drive (HDD) that performs the same function.

23. A: Option A is correct because a database management system, such as Microsoft Access, OpenOffice Base, or MySQL, is designed to handle collections of related data in an efficient way and to allow for easy modification and retrieval of the data. This is exactly what is described as needed in this question.

Option B is incorrect because an operating system is the underlying software that interfaces most directly with the hardware and manages other programs, such as Microsoft Windows or Linux. Operating systems are not used to store data. **Option C is incorrect** because while spreadsheets *could* be used to store data sets, they become inefficient compared to databases when they have too many rows. Spreadsheets are best used in circumstances when detailed calculations are required, which does not seem to be the case here. **Option D is incorrect** because word processors are used to create documents, but are not a good way of storing data. Data records *could* be stored in a table in a word processor, but it would be slow and inefficient and wouldn't give as many options for easily modifying or rearranging the data.

24. D: The reported results show that students who chose the correct answer were more likely to score well overall, showing some measure of validity and reliability in the construction of this question. The results also demonstrated that students in the advanced geography class were more likely to eliminate (B) and (C), showing that students who have more knowledge in geography may have a better understanding of the concepts included in those answer choices. Although they did have an edge in eliminating answer choices, many students in the advanced geography class still chose incorrectly. This shows that the question likely did successfully discriminate between knowledge of geography and knowledge of Earth science.

25. D: Option D is correct; the text and graphs in the slide are difficult to read against the high-contrast background. While the choice of light blue for the text color might not be ideal, there probably isn't any color that would be easily legible against such a busy background. Plain black text on a blank white background can be boring, but this background goes much too far in the opposite direction. A splash of color or some simple shapes could be enough to give some interest to the slides without impeding legibility or drawing the reader's attention away from the content.

Option A is incorrect because individual slides should be kept simple; a detailed written description of the graphs is unnecessary. Presumably the presenter will explain verbally anything that needs to be explained on the graphs when the slide comes up. If it is considered desirable to have a written description of the graphs in the presentation, it may be better to have it on a separate slide rather than cluttering one slide with too much information. **Option B is incorrect** because these two graphs show complete different data, and cannot readily be combined. Sometimes combining two similar graphs may save space and make a slide easier to read, but in this case neither axis measures the same quantity on both graphs, and they're not even the same kind of graph—one is a line graph and one is a bar graph. There's no obvious way to combine these graphs that wouldn't be confusing. **Option C is incorrect** because in general it's easier to understand at a glance data presented graphically than data presented in text form. Replacing the graphs with text would probably make the slide *less* easy to comprehend.

26. D: Option D is correct because for effective communication to take place, your reader must know the meanings of the words you use. This doesn't mean you have to avoid technical jargon altogether; technical terms may help you be more precise and more succinct. But if there's a chance that the term may not be familiar to your reader, you should define it at first use.

You should consider your audience when deciding what words may need to be defined, and how much technical language you should use in the first place. If you're writing a report intended only for your peers who are highly knowledgeable in your field, you may expect that the relevant jargon is already a part of their vocabularies, and you may not need to provide definitions. On the other hand, for highly nontechnical readers completely unfamiliar with your field, technical terms may be confusing or offputting even if definitions are provided, and such language may be best avoided altogether if possible.

Option A is incorrect because long sentences do not necessarily make for better communication. In fact, short, concise sentences are usually easier to follow and understand—and there can be just as much information in several short sentences as in one long one. **Option B is incorrect** because the course of action it suggests is impractical. While too much repetition of an uncommon word can be distracting, *never* repeating a word within a paragraph is neither an easily achievable nor a desirable goal. If nothing else, short, common words like "the" and "of" are certainly likely to appear multiple times in a paragraph! **Option C is incorrect** because too many fonts in combination can be annoying and difficult to read. It's generally advisable to limit the text to no more than one or two font types within a single document, or at least within a single page.

27. A: Option A is correct because the printing press allowed books and other printed matter to be printed much more cheaply and in greater volume than before. This enabled efficient mass communication in a way that wasn't possible when each text had to be individually created. The easy availability of books and other printed matter led to an increase in literacy, and allowed information to be widely shared more easily than ever before.

Option B is incorrect because the printing press did not increase the power of the elites at the expense of the lower classes. If anything, it did the opposite; the democratization of information loosened the hold of rulers and religious leaders over their subjects by breaking their monopoly on important knowledge. **Option C is incorrect** because the Industrial Revolution and the widespread use of the steam engine did not occur until centuries after the development of the printing press. While it may be possible to draw a line from the development of the printing press to the Industrial Revolution, and an argument could be made that the Industrial Revolution would not have occurred without the printing press, it certainly wasn't an *immediate* consequence. **Option D is incorrect** for similar reasons; the first trade unions in the modern sense did not appear until the nineteenth century, so they can't be said to be an *immediate* consequence of the development of the printing press four centuries earlier.

28. B: Option B is correct because a conditional statement is a statement that evaluates an expression and uses the result of that evaluation to select which code block to execute next. In this case, the `if` statement evaluates the expression `counter > 12`. If this expression is true, the following statement is executed, setting the value of the variable `finished` to `true`. If the expression is *not* true, this following statement is *not* executed, and the program execution skips to the next statement after it.

The `if` statement is the most common conditional statement in most popular programming languages, though it can usually be combined with `else` statements designating blocks to be executed if the evaluated statement is false. Another conditional statement in C-based programming languages is the `switch` statement, which selects between several alternatives depending on the value of an expression.

Option A is incorrect because a compiler directive is not part of the program itself, but is as the name implies a direction to the compiler—directing it to include a certain external file, for instance, or to compile a given block of code only under certain conditions. In C-based languages, compiler directives usually start with the hash sign, #. The given line of code is clearly not a compiler directive. **Option C is incorrect** because a control loop is a code structure that executes a block of code repeatedly as long as—or until—a condition is met. Regardless of whether the expression evaluates as true, the given code will not run more than once. **Option D is incorrect** because a declaration statement defines an identifier, such as a function or variable. Some computer languages require the variable's type to be specified when it is declared; others have no such requirement and may take the first mention of a variable as a tacit declaration. In any case, the given line of code is clearly

29. C: Option C is correct because the flow of an incompressible fluid obeys Bernoulli's equation, which can be written as $\frac{1}{2}\rho v_A^2 + \rho g z_A + P_1 = \frac{1}{2}\rho v_B^2 + \rho g z_B + P_2$. In this case, point A is 10 m higher than point B, so we can set $z_A = 10$ m and $z_B = 0$ m. The density of water is 1000 kg/m^3. Putting these values in with the other given information, we have:

$$\frac{1}{2}(1000\text{ kg/m}^3)(10\text{ m/s})^2 + (1000\text{ kg/m}^3)(10\text{ m/s}^2)(10\text{ m}) + P_1$$
$$= \frac{1}{2}(1000\text{ kg/m}^3)(20\text{ m/s})^2 + 0 + 100{,}000\text{ Pa}$$

This reduces to

$$50{,}000\text{ Pa} + 100{,}000\text{ Pa} + P_1 = 200{,}000\text{ Pa} + 100{,}000\text{ Pa}$$
$$150{,}000\text{ Pa} + P_1 = 300{,}000\text{ Pa}$$
$$P_1 = 150{,}000\text{ Pa}$$

Options A, B, and D are incorrect because the values of the pressure are wrong.

30. C: Option C is correct because there are 60 seconds in a minute, 60 minutes in an hour, 1000 milliliters in a liter, and, as stated in the problem, 3.785 liters in a gallon. Dimensional analysis thus shows that 1200 gal/hr = 1260 mL/s:

$$1200\,\frac{\text{gallons}}{\text{hour}} \times \frac{3.785\text{ liters}}{1\text{ gallon}} \times \frac{1000\text{ milliliters}}{1\text{ liter}} \times \frac{1\text{ hour}}{60\text{ minutes}} \times \frac{1\text{ minute}}{60\text{ seconds}} = 1260\,\frac{\text{milliliters}}{\text{second}}$$

Note that the terms are arranged so that each unit, except for those we want in our final answer, appears both in the numerator of one term and in the denominator of another, and thus cancels. This is how we know whether a conversion factor goes on the top or the bottom of a fraction. We know to use $\frac{1\text{ hour}}{60\text{ minutes}}$ and not $\frac{60\text{ minutes}}{1\text{ hour}}$, for example, because hours appear in the denominator of the units of $1200\,\frac{\text{gallons}}{\text{hour}}$, and so we need to have hours in the numerator of another term to cancel them.

Option A is incorrect because it inverts the liters to gallons conversion factor, multiplying by $\frac{1\text{ gallon}}{3.785\text{ liters}}$ instead of $\frac{3.785\text{ liters}}{1\text{ gallon}}$. This means the units will not cancel correctly; the final answer will be in the awkward units of $(\text{mL}\cdot\text{gal}^2)/(\text{L}^2\cdot\text{s})$.

Option B is incorrect because it inverts *all* the conversion factors.

Option D is incorrect because it inverts all the conversion factors *except* the liters to gallons conversion factor.

31. C: Option C is correct because a patent is a kind of intellectual property protection that covers inventions, processes, and discoveries. When an individual or company wishes to protect their right to some new procedure or mechanism they developed, it is by filing a patent that they can accomplish this.

Option A is incorrect because a copyright protects some particular created work. Copyrights apply to books, music, and artworks, for example, but not to procedures or algorithms. **Option B is incorrect** because "fair use" is not a type of intellectual property protection, but rather a set of circumstances under which it may be allowable to use protected property. **Option D is incorrect** because a trademark protects a symbol, design, or phrase that is associated with a given product or company. Trademarks apply to titles and logos, but not to manufacturing processes.

32. C: Option C is correct because delegation is one of the essential skills of an engineering manager. A good manager knows how to delegate tasks to his or her team members, matching them to the team members' individual strengths and weaknesses. The manager can then oversee the project, keeping track of the "big picture" and giving guidance and answering questions as needed.

Option A is incorrect because even if the manager's supervisor approves of her working overtime, trying to do all the work herself is a recipe for burnout. Even if the project does lie within her specific field of expertise, she's better off getting her team members to help her. **Option B is incorrect** because while the manager should leave room for her team members to make some of their own decisions, she should still provide them with direction and advice. Stepping back and letting her team members make *all* the decisions would be failing to perform her job as a manager. **Option D is incorrect** because while it may be a good idea to give her team members growth opportunities, throwing them into situations they're unprepared for is not an effective way of achieving this. Furthermore, micromanaging an employee through each step is likely to be not only frustrating for the employee but a waste of the manager's time.

33. A: Option A is correct because civil engineers work on large-scale infrastructure, including bridges, roads, dams, and airports. Freeway interchanges are a part of transportation infrastructure, and fall within the purview of the civil engineer.

Option B is incorrect because environmental engineers address waste disposal, pollution control, and other issues related to the maintenance of the environment. Freeway interchanges would not be included in this area. **Option C is incorrect** because industrial engineers generally focus on developing and improving production processes, not on construction projects. **Option D is incorrect** because mechanical engineers build machines and devices such as generators and engines, but do not generally deal with large-scale infrastructure.

34. D: Option D is correct because the manufacturing process cannot be designed until the details are decided about what is being manufactured. All of the steps named in the other options must take place before this step can be carried out.

Option A is incorrect because product design must take place before the design of the manufacturing process. **Option B is incorrect** because the manufacturing process may depend on the material the product is made of, so this step too must precede the manufacturing process design. **Option C is incorrect** because the customer needs must inform the design of the product; this should be the *first* step, before all the steps named in the other options.

35. C: Option C is correct; a Pareto chart shows both the number of defects or complaints falling into each category as well as the cumulative percentage represented by all the categories up to a given number. To answer the question in this problem, we need to know how many complaints, combined, make up at least 80% of the total. For this, we look to the cumulative part of the graph. The first complaint accounts for about 30% of the total; the first two combined make up about 60%; and the first three combined make up around 70%. It is not until the fourth complaint that the cumulative percentage exceeds 80%.

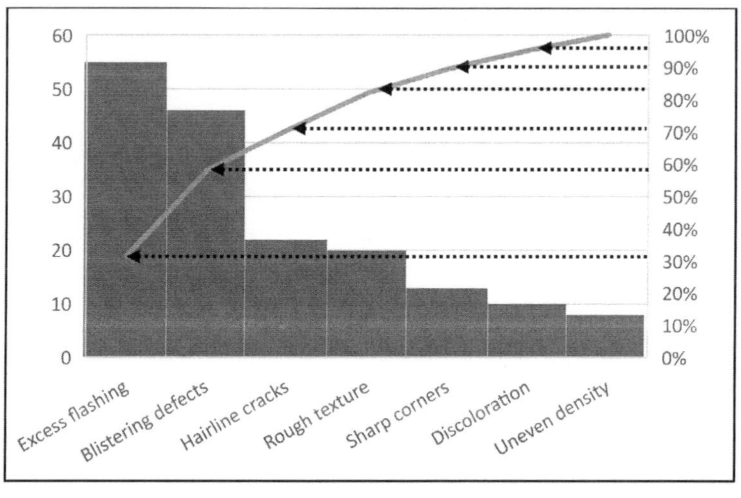

Options A and B are incorrect because, as noted above, the first two or three complaints combined do not make up 80% of the total. **Option D is incorrect** because we are asked for the *minimum* number of issues that must be corrected. Correcting the first five issues would account for about 90% of the complaints, which is indeed greater than 80%, but this is more than we need.

36. B: Option B is correct because many continuing education opportunities are available to engineers where they can learn about new developments in their field as well as refresh their knowledge of existing practices. Changes in the engineering profession due to new technologies make up one reason why continuing education is important to engineers. Continuing education can also add to job satisfaction and, of course, may be necessary for licensing renewals.

Option A is incorrect because while it may be possible to learn new technologies on the job, this is rarely the most efficient method, and may in some cases carry significant risks if those technologies are misused due to unfamiliarity. **Option C is incorrect** because as new techniques arise that improve on older methods, many of those older technologies may become obsolete, and there may not be assignments available where it still makes sense to use them. Besides, even if there is still a place for the use of the older technologies, an engineer who can use both the old *and* new technologies will have more opportunities. **Option D is incorrect** because not every engineer can count on quick promotion—and in any case a capable supervisor should still understand the techniques and technologies that the engineers under him or her are using, so becoming a supervisor does not remove the need to understand and adapt to new developments.

37. B: Option B is correct because engineering projects often have budgetary constraints limiting the amount of money that can be spent on them, and the fact that the alloy requires specialized equipment to manufacture implies that it may be expensive. Cost of materials is just one of many criteria and constraints that engineers must be aware of when solving a problem or designing a product, but it is the constraint that was most likely the deciding factor in this example.

Option A is incorrect because even if the machine that the engineer is designing does produce noise pollution, it seems unlikely that the specific metal that this one part is made of will affect that. Noise pollution and other health and safety hazards are common and important considerations in engineering designs, but this doesn't seem to be the most relevant criterion in this case. **Option C is incorrect** because while there may be a limitation on the maximum size of the part, there's no apparent reason that the size should depend on the metal the part is made of. **Option D is incorrect** because while an object's appearance may be a valid consideration, the part in question is specified to be an *internal* part of the machine, so it would presumably not be visible. (In addition, aesthetic concerns are most likely to be important for consumer products, while this part is said to be for an industrial machine.)

38. B: Option B is correct because the next step in the iterative design process, after creating a prototype, is to test that prototype and see what aspects users find confusing, inefficient, or otherwise suboptimal. Refinements are then made to the prototype to address these issues; the improved version is then tested, and the process repeats.

Option A is incorrect because it is not a step in the iterative design process. While it may sometimes be useful to employ a code profiler to find performance bottlenecks or other similar issues, this is something that can be done in the prototyping phase before the program is sent out to users. **Option C is incorrect** because it also is not a step in the iterative design process. Certainly it's possible to add more features to the program later, but this is a separate issue from iterative design. **Option D is incorrect** because the iterative design process deals with incrementally refining an existing design, not creating different versions at the outset.

39. D: Option D is correct because the weight of the cargo containers has a direct impact on the design of the mechanism to lift them up the cliff. Heavier cargo containers would require thicker cables, a sturdier frame for the mechanism, and so on. To solve a problem using engineering concepts, it must be clearly and precisely formulated, including any relevant quantitative constraints and considerations. The weight of the cargo containers is not the *only* thing the engineer should find out in order to properly formulate the problem—for instance, the height of the cliff is another important consideration—but of the given answer options, it is the one that it is most important for the engineer to know.

Options A, B, and C are incorrect because they have little or no bearing on the design of the mechanism. There's no clear reason why the color of the cargo containers should matter, nor where they are coming from. The value of the cargo might have some relevance in that the more valuable the cargo is, the greater the importance that it arrive undamaged at the top of the cliff, but this is a less vital consideration than the weight of the cargo; presumably the engineer plans to design the mechanism to be as reliable as possible anyway.

40. A: Option A is correct because layers are a feature of layer-based CAD programs that allows the user to isolate specific parts or collections of parts, which is what the engineer needs to do in this situation. If the plates are in different layers, then if the engineer wants to work on one plate without obstruction she can hide the layers containing the other plates. When she wants to see how the plates fit together, she can turn all the layers back on.

Option B is incorrect because while creating a separate file for each plate would certainly make it easy to work on them in isolation, without an assembly, there would be no simple way to see how they fit together. **Option C is incorrect** because it would not solve the problem of the plates obstructing each others' view; at best the different colors might make it easier for the engineer to ignore the plates she isn't working on, but it's not an ideal solution. **Option D is incorrect** because it does not address the problem. While the engineer will have to select the plate she wants to work on (using the box select tool or some other method), this does not solve the issue of her view being obstructed by the other plates.

How to Overcome Test Anxiety

Just the thought of taking a test is enough to make most people a little nervous. A test is an important event that can have a long-term impact on your future, so it's important to take it seriously and it's natural to feel anxious about performing well. But just because anxiety is normal, that doesn't mean that it's helpful in test taking, or that you should simply accept it as part of your life. Anxiety can have a variety of effects. These effects can be mild, like making you feel slightly nervous, or severe, like blocking your ability to focus or remember even a simple detail.

If you experience test anxiety—whether severe or mild—it's important to know how to beat it. To discover this, first you need to understand what causes test anxiety.

Causes of Test Anxiety

While we often think of anxiety as an uncontrollable emotional state, it can actually be caused by simple, practical things. One of the most common causes of test anxiety is that a person does not feel adequately prepared for their test. This feeling can be the result of many different issues such as poor study habits or lack of organization, but the most common culprit is time management. Starting to study too late, failing to organize your study time to cover all of the material, or being distracted while you study will mean that you're not well prepared for the test. This may lead to cramming the night before, which will cause you to be physically and mentally exhausted for the test. Poor time management also contributes to feelings of stress, fear, and hopelessness as you realize you are not well prepared but don't know what to do about it.

Other times, test anxiety is not related to your preparation for the test but comes from unresolved fear. This may be a past failure on a test, or poor performance on tests in general. It may come from comparing yourself to others who seem to be performing better or from the stress of living up to expectations. Anxiety may be driven by fears of the future—how failure on this test would affect your educational and career goals. These fears are often completely irrational, but they can still negatively impact your test performance.

Elements of Test Anxiety

As mentioned earlier, test anxiety is considered to be an emotional state, but it has physical and mental components as well. Sometimes you may not even realize that you are suffering from test anxiety until you notice the physical symptoms. These can include trembling hands, rapid heartbeat, sweating, nausea, and tense muscles. Extreme anxiety may lead to fainting or vomiting. Obviously, any of these symptoms can have a negative impact on testing. It is important to recognize them as soon as they begin to occur so that you can address the problem before it damages your performance.

The mental components of test anxiety include trouble focusing and inability to remember learned information. During a test, your mind is on high alert, which can help you recall information and stay focused for an extended period of time. However, anxiety interferes with your mind's natural processes, causing you to blank out, even on the questions you know well. The strain of testing during anxiety makes it difficult to stay focused, especially on a test that may take several hours. Extreme anxiety can take a huge mental toll, making it difficult not only to recall test information but even to understand the test questions or pull your thoughts together.

Effects of Test Anxiety

Test anxiety is like a disease—if left untreated, it will get progressively worse. Anxiety leads to poor performance, and this reinforces the feelings of fear and failure, which in turn lead to poor performances on subsequent tests. It can grow from a mild nervousness to a crippling condition. If allowed to progress, test anxiety can have a big impact on your schooling, and consequently on your future.

Test anxiety can spread to other parts of your life. Anxiety on tests can become anxiety in any stressful situation, and blanking on a test can turn into panicking in a job situation. But fortunately, you don't have to let anxiety rule your testing and determine your grades. There are a number of relatively simple steps you can take to move past anxiety and function normally on a test and in the rest of life.

Physical Steps for Beating Test Anxiety

While test anxiety is a serious problem, the good news is that it can be overcome. It doesn't have to control your ability to think and remember information. While it may take time, you can begin taking steps today to beat anxiety.

Just as your first hint that you may be struggling with anxiety comes from the physical symptoms, the first step to treating it is also physical. Rest is crucial for having a clear, strong mind. If you are tired, it is much easier to give in to anxiety. But if you establish good sleep habits, your body and mind will be ready to perform optimally, without the strain of exhaustion. Additionally, sleeping well helps you to retain information better, so you're more likely to recall the answers when you see the test questions.

Getting good sleep means more than going to bed on time. It's important to allow your brain time to relax. Take study breaks from time to time so it doesn't get overworked, and don't study right before bed. Take time to rest your mind before trying to rest your body, or you may find it difficult to fall asleep.

Along with sleep, other aspects of physical health are important in preparing for a test. Good nutrition is vital for good brain function. Sugary foods and drinks may give a burst of energy but this burst is followed by a crash, both physically and emotionally. Instead, fuel your body with protein and vitamin-rich foods.

Also, drink plenty of water. Dehydration can lead to headaches and exhaustion, especially if your brain is already under stress from the rigors of the test. Particularly if your test is a long one, drink water during the breaks. And if possible, take an energy-boosting snack to eat between sections.

Along with sleep and diet, a third important part of physical health is exercise. Maintaining a steady workout schedule is helpful, but even taking 5-minute study breaks to walk can help get your blood pumping faster and clear your head. Exercise also releases endorphins, which contribute to a positive feeling and can help combat test anxiety.

When you nurture your physical health, you are also contributing to your mental health. If your body is healthy, your mind is much more likely to be healthy as well. So take time to rest, nourish your body with healthy food and water, and get moving as much as possible. Taking these physical steps will make you stronger and more able to take the mental steps necessary to overcome test anxiety.

Mental Steps for Beating Test Anxiety

Working on the mental side of test anxiety can be more challenging, but as with the physical side, there are clear steps you can take to overcome it. As mentioned earlier, test anxiety often stems from lack of preparation, so the obvious solution is to prepare for the test. Effective studying may be the most important weapon you have for beating test anxiety, but you can and should employ several other mental tools to combat fear.

First, boost your confidence by reminding yourself of past success—tests or projects that you aced. If you're putting as much effort into preparing for this test as you did for those, there's no reason you should expect to fail here. Work hard to prepare; then trust your preparation.

Second, surround yourself with encouraging people. It can be helpful to find a study group, but be sure that the people you're around will encourage a positive attitude. If you spend time with others who are anxious or cynical, this will only contribute to your own anxiety. Look for others who are motivated to study hard from a desire to succeed, not from a fear of failure.

Third, reward yourself. A test is physically and mentally tiring, even without anxiety, and it can be helpful to have something to look forward to. Plan an activity following the test, regardless of the outcome, such as going to a movie or getting ice cream.

When you are taking the test, if you find yourself beginning to feel anxious, remind yourself that you know the material. Visualize successfully completing the test. Then take a few deep, relaxing breaths and return to it. Work through the questions carefully but with confidence, knowing that you are capable of succeeding.

Developing a healthy mental approach to test taking will also aid in other areas of life. Test anxiety affects more than just the actual test—it can be damaging to your mental health and even contribute to depression. It's important to beat test anxiety before it becomes a problem for more than testing.

Study Strategy

Being prepared for the test is necessary to combat anxiety, but what does being prepared look like? You may study for hours on end and still not feel prepared. What you need is a strategy for test prep. The next few pages outline our recommended steps to help you plan out and conquer the challenge of preparation.

Step 1: Scope Out the Test

Learn everything you can about the format (multiple choice, essay, etc.) and what will be on the test. Gather any study materials, course outlines, or sample exams that may be available. Not only will this help you to prepare, but knowing what to expect can help to alleviate test anxiety.

Step 2: Map Out the Material

Look through the textbook or study guide and make note of how many chapters or sections it has. Then divide these over the time you have. For example, if a book has 15 chapters and you have five days to study, you need to cover three chapters each day. Even better, if you have the time, leave an extra day at the end for overall review after you have gone through the material in depth.

If time is limited, you may need to prioritize the material. Look through it and make note of which sections you think you already have a good grasp on, and which need review. While you are studying, skim quickly through the familiar sections and take more time on the challenging parts.

Write out your plan so you don't get lost as you go. Having a written plan also helps you feel more in control of the study, so anxiety is less likely to arise from feeling overwhelmed at the amount to cover.

Step 3: Gather Your Tools

Decide what study method works best for you. Do you prefer to highlight in the book as you study and then go back over the highlighted portions? Or do you type out notes of the important information? Or is it helpful to make flashcards that you can carry with you? Assemble the pens, index cards, highlighters, post-it notes, and any other materials you may need so you won't be distracted by getting up to find things while you study.

If you're having a hard time retaining the information or organizing your notes, experiment with different methods. For example, try color-coding by subject with colored pens, highlighters, or post-it notes. If you learn better by hearing, try recording yourself reading your notes so you can listen while in the car, working out, or simply sitting at your desk. Ask a friend to quiz you from your flashcards, or try teaching someone the material to solidify it in your mind.

Step 4: Create Your Environment

It's important to avoid distractions while you study. This includes both the obvious distractions like visitors and the subtle distractions like an uncomfortable chair (or a too-comfortable couch that makes you want to fall asleep). Set up the best study environment possible: good lighting and a comfortable work area. If background music helps you focus, you may want to turn it on, but otherwise keep the room quiet. If you are using a computer to take notes, be sure you don't have any other windows open, especially applications like social media, games, or anything else that could distract you. Silence your phone and turn off notifications. Be sure to keep water close by so you stay hydrated while you study (but avoid unhealthy drinks and snacks).

Also, take into account the best time of day to study. Are you freshest first thing in the morning? Try to set aside some time then to work through the material. Is your mind clearer in the afternoon or evening? Schedule your study session then. Another method is to study at the same time of day that you will take the test, so that your brain gets used to working on the material at that time and will be ready to focus at test time.

Step 5: Study!

Once you have done all the study preparation, it's time to settle into the actual studying. Sit down, take a few moments to settle your mind so you can focus, and begin to follow your study plan. Don't give in to distractions or let yourself procrastinate. This is your time to prepare so you'll be ready to fearlessly approach the test. Make the most of the time and stay focused.

Of course, you don't want to burn out. If you study too long you may find that you're not retaining the information very well. Take regular study breaks. For example, taking five minutes out of every hour to walk briskly, breathing deeply and swinging your arms, can help your mind stay fresh.

As you get to the end of each chapter or section, it's a good idea to do a quick review. Remind yourself of what you learned and work on any difficult parts. When you feel that you've mastered the material, move on to the next part. At the end of your study session, briefly skim through your notes again.

But while review is helpful, cramming last minute is NOT. If at all possible, work ahead so that you won't need to fit all your study into the last day. Cramming overloads your brain with more information than it can process and retain, and your tired mind may struggle to recall even previously learned information when it is overwhelmed with last-minute study. Also, the urgent nature of cramming and the stress placed on your brain contribute to anxiety. You'll be more likely to go to the test feeling unprepared and having trouble thinking clearly.

So don't cram, and don't stay up late before the test, even just to review your notes at a leisurely pace. Your brain needs rest more than it needs to go over the information again. In fact, plan to finish your studies by noon or early afternoon the day before the test. Give your brain the rest of the day to relax or focus on other things, and get a good night's sleep. Then you will be fresh for the test and better able to recall what you've studied.

Step 6: Take a Practice Test

Many courses offer sample tests, either online or in the study materials. This is an excellent resource to check whether you have mastered the material, as well as to prepare for the test format and environment.

Check the test format ahead of time: the number of questions, the type (multiple choice, free response, etc.), and the time limit. Then create a plan for working through them. For example, if you have 30 minutes to take a 60-question test, your limit is 30 seconds per question. Spend less time on the questions you know well so that you can take more time on the difficult ones.

If you have time to take several practice tests, take the first one open book, with no time limit. Work through the questions at your own pace and make sure you fully understand them. Gradually work up to taking a test under test conditions: sit at a desk with all study materials put away and set a timer. Pace yourself to make sure you finish the test with time to spare and go back to check your answers if you have time.

After each test, check your answers. On the questions you missed, be sure you understand why you missed them. Did you misread the question (tests can use tricky wording)? Did you forget the information? Or was it something you hadn't learned? Go back and study any shaky areas that the practice tests reveal.

Taking these tests not only helps with your grade, but also aids in combating test anxiety. If you're already used to the test conditions, you're less likely to worry about it, and working through tests until you're scoring well gives you a confidence boost. Go through the practice tests until you feel comfortable, and then you can go into the test knowing that you're ready for it.

Test Tips

On test day, you should be confident, knowing that you've prepared well and are ready to answer the questions. But aside from preparation, there are several test day strategies you can employ to maximize your performance.

First, as stated before, get a good night's sleep the night before the test (and for several nights before that, if possible). Go into the test with a fresh, alert mind rather than staying up late to study.

Try not to change too much about your normal routine on the day of the test. It's important to eat a nutritious breakfast, but if you normally don't eat breakfast at all, consider eating just a protein bar. If you're a coffee drinker, go ahead and have your normal coffee. Just make sure you time it so that the caffeine doesn't wear off right in the middle of your test. Avoid sugary beverages, and drink enough water to stay hydrated but not so much that you need a restroom break 10 minutes into the test. If your test isn't first thing in the morning, consider going for a walk or doing a light workout before the test to get your blood flowing.

Allow yourself enough time to get ready, and leave for the test with plenty of time to spare so you won't have the anxiety of scrambling to arrive in time. Another reason to be early is to select a good seat. It's helpful to sit away from doors and windows, which can be distracting. Find a good seat, get out your supplies, and settle your mind before the test begins.

When the test begins, start by going over the instructions carefully, even if you already know what to expect. Make sure you avoid any careless mistakes by following the directions.

Then begin working through the questions, pacing yourself as you've practiced. If you're not sure on an answer, don't spend too much time on it, and don't let it shake your confidence. Either skip it and come back later, or eliminate as many wrong answers as possible and guess among the remaining ones. Don't dwell on these questions as you continue—put them out of your mind and focus on what lies ahead.

Be sure to read all of the answer choices, even if you're sure the first one is the right answer. Sometimes you'll find a better one if you keep reading. But don't second-guess yourself if you do immediately know the answer. Your gut instinct is usually right. Don't let test anxiety rob you of the information you know.

If you have time at the end of the test (and if the test format allows), go back and review your answers. Be cautious about changing any, since your first instinct tends to be correct, but make sure you didn't misread any of the questions or accidentally mark the wrong answer choice. Look over any you skipped and make an educated guess.

At the end, leave the test feeling confident. You've done your best, so don't waste time worrying about your performance or wishing you could change anything. Instead, celebrate the successful completion of this test. And finally, use this test to learn how to deal with anxiety even better next time.

Review Video: Test Anxiety
Visit mometrix.com/academy and enter code: 100340

Important Qualification

Not all anxiety is created equal. If your test anxiety is causing major issues in your life beyond the classroom or testing center, or if you are experiencing troubling physical symptoms related to your anxiety, it may be a sign of a serious physiological or psychological condition. If this sounds like your situation, we strongly encourage you to seek professional help.

Online Resources

Due to our efforts to try to keep this book to a manageable length, we've created a link that will give you access to all of your online resources:

mometrix.com/resources719/texesmathpse

It's Your Moment, Let's Celebrate It!

Share your story @mometrixtestpreparation